HTML Master Reference

HTML Master Reference

Heather Williamson

IDG Books Worldwide, Inc.

An International Data Group Company

Foster City, CA ■ Chicago, IL ■ Indianapolis, IN ■ New York, NY

HTML Master Reference

Published by
An International Data Group Company
919 E. Hillsdale Blvd., Suite 400
Foster City, CA 94404
www.idgbooks.com (IDG Books Worldwide Web site)

Cover photo © Tony Stone Images / Chicago Inc.

ISBN: 0-7645-3256-1

Printed in the United States of America

10 9 8 7 6 5 4 3 2

1P/RR/QT/ZZ/FC

Distributed in the United States by IDG Books Worldwide, Inc.

Distributed by Macmillan Canada for Canada; by Transworld Publishers Limited in the United Kingdom; by IDG Norge Books for Norway; by IDG Sweden Books for Sweden; by Woodslane Pty. Ltd. for Australia; by Woodslane (NZ) Ltd. for New Zealand; by Addison Wesley Longman Singapore Pte Ltd. for Singapore, Malaysia, Thailand, and Indonesia; by Norma Comunicaciones S.A. for Colombia; by Intersoft for South Africa; by International Thomson Publishing for Germany, Austria and Switzerland; by Distribuidora Cuspide for Argentina; by Livraria Cultura for Brazil; by Ediciencia S.A. for Ecuador; by Ediciones ZETA S.C.R. Ltda. for Peru; by WS Computer Publishing Corporation, Inc., for the Philippines; by Contemporanea de Ediciones for Venezuela; by Express Computer Distributors for the Caribbean and West Indies; by Micronesia Media Distributor, Inc. for Micronesia; by Grupo Editorial Norma S.A. for Guatemala; by Chips Computadoras S.A. de C.V. for Mexico; by Editorial Norma de Panama S.A. for Panama; by Wouters Import for Belgium; by American Bookshops for Finland. Authorized Sales Agent: Anthony Rudkin Associates for the Middle East and North Africa.

For general information on IDG Books Worldwide's books in the U.S., please call our Consumer Customer Service department at 800-762-2974. For reseller information, including discounts and premium sales, please call our Reseller Customer Service department at 800-434-3422.

For information on where to purchase IDG Books Worldwide's books outside the U.S., please contact our International Sales department at 317-596-5530 or fax 317-596-5692.

For consumer information on foreign language translations, please contact our Customer Service department at 800-434-3422, fax 317-596-5692, or e-mail rights@idgbooks.com.

For information on licensing foreign or domestic rights, please phone +1-650-655-3109.

For sales inquiries and special prices for bulk quantities, please contact our Sales department at 650-655-3200 or write to the address above.

For information on using IDG Books Worldwide's books in the classroom or for ordering examination copies, please contact our Educational Sales department at 800-434-2086 or fax 317-596-5499.

For press review copies, author interviews, or other publicity information, please contact our Public Relations department at 650-655-3000 or fax 650-655-3299.

For authorization to photocopy items for corporate, personal, or educational use, please contact Copyright Clearance Center, 222 Rosewood Drive, Danvers, MA 01923, or fax 978-750-4470.

Library of Congress Cataloging-in-Publication Data

Williamson, Heather.
      HTML master reference / Heather Williamson.
           p.   cm.
      Includes index.
      ISBN 0-7645-3256-1 (hardbound : alk. paper)
      1. HTML (Hypertext document markup language)
      I. Title
QA76.76.H94W59   1999
005.7'2 — dc21   98-52121
                                                               CIP

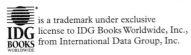

is a trademark under exclusive license to IDG Books Worldwide, Inc., from International Data Group, Inc.

ABOUT IDG BOOKS WORLDWIDE

Welcome to the world of IDG Books Worldwide.

IDG Books Worldwide, Inc., is a subsidiary of International Data Group, the world's largest publisher of computer-related information and the leading global provider of information services on information technology. IDG was founded more than 30 years ago by Patrick J. McGovern and now employs more than 9,000 people worldwide. IDG publishes more than 290 computer publications in over 75 countries. More than 90 million people read one or more IDG publications each month.

Launched in 1990, IDG Books Worldwide is today the #1 publisher of best-selling computer books in the United States. We are proud to have received eight awards from the Computer Press Association in recognition of editorial excellence and three from Computer Currents' First Annual Readers' Choice Awards. Our best-selling *...For Dummies*® series has more than 50 million copies in print with translations in 31 languages. IDG Books Worldwide, through a joint venture with IDG's Hi-Tech Beijing, became the first U.S. publisher to publish a computer book in the People's Republic of China. In record time, IDG Books Worldwide has become the first choice for millions of readers around the world who want to learn how to better manage their businesses.

Our mission is simple: Every one of our books is designed to bring extra value and skill-building instructions to the reader. Our books are written by experts who understand and care about our readers. The knowledge base of our editorial staff comes from years of experience in publishing, education, and journalism — experience we use to produce books to carry us into the new millennium. In short, we care about books, so we attract the best people. We devote special attention to details such as audience, interior design, use of icons, and illustrations. And because we use an efficient process of authoring, editing, and desktop publishing our books electronically, we can spend more time ensuring superior content and less time on the technicalities of making books.

You can count on our commitment to deliver high-quality books at competitive prices on topics you want to read about. At IDG Books Worldwide, we continue in the IDG tradition of delivering quality for more than 30 years. You'll find no better book on a subject than one from IDG Books Worldwide.

John Kilcullen
John Kilcullen
Chairman and CEO
IDG Books Worldwide, Inc.

Steven Berkowitz
Steven Berkowitz
President and Publisher
IDG Books Worldwide, Inc.

IDG is the world's leading IT media, research and exposition company. Founded, in 1964, IDG had 1997 revenues of $2.05 billion and has more than 9,000 employees worldwide. IDG offers the widest range of media options that reach IT buyers in 75 countries representing 95% of worldwide IT spending. IDG's diverse product and services portfolio spans six key areas including print publishing, online publishing, expositions and conferences, market research, education and training, and global marketing services. More than 90 million people read one or more of IDG's 290 magazines and newspapers, including IDG's leading global brands — Computerworld, PC World, Network World, Macworld and the Channel World family of publications. IDG Books Worldwide is one of the fastest-growing computer book publishers in the world, with more than 700 titles in 36 languages. The "...For Dummies®" series alone has more than 50 million copies in print. IDG offers online users the largest network of technology-specific Web sites around the world through IDG.net (http://www.idg.net), which comprises more than 225 targeted Web sites in 55 countries worldwide. International Data Corporation (IDC) is the world's largest provider of information technology data, analysis and consulting, with research centers in over 41 countries and more than 400 research analysts worldwide. IDG World Expo is a leading producer of more than 168 globally branded conferences and expositions in 35 countries including E3 (Electronic Entertainment Expo), Macworld Expo, ComNet, Windows World Expo, ICE (Internet Commerce Expo), Agenda, DEMO, and Spotlight. IDG's training subsidiary, ExecuTrain, is the world's largest computer training company, with more than 230 locations worldwide and 785 training courses. IDG Marketing Services helps industry-leading IT companies build international brand recognition by developing global integrated marketing programs via IDG's print, online and exposition products worldwide. Further information about the company can be found at www.idg.com.   10/8/98

Credits

Acquisitions Editor
Greg Croy

Development Editor
Barbra Guerra

Technical Editor
Ken Cox

Copy Editors
Barry Childs-Helton
Victoria Nuttall
Amanda Kaufmann

Project Coordinator
Tom Debolski

Book Designer
Kurt Krames

Graphics and Production Specialist
Christopher Pimentel

Quality Control Specialists
Mick Arellano
Mark Schumann

Proofing & Indexing
York Production Services

Cover Design
Sestina Quarequio

Cover Photo
Tony Stone Images/Chicago Inc.

About the Author

Heather Williamson is both the manager and owner of Cat's Back Consulting in the Wallowa Valley of Oregon. She specializes in technical writing and training for all ranges of computer users and topics, including the Internet, fax technology, data communications, operating systems, and Microsoft Office applications. She has served as editor, author, and contributor to a variety of computer books covering diverse topics.

In her free time, between writing and raising her family, Heather raises American Quarter Horses, barrel-races in local rodeo circuits, spoils her cocker spaniel, and gets shot while robbing a bank every Wednesday during the summer (she is in an Old West reenactment group).

For those who helped to make me smile,
For those who walked that extra mile,
For those who cared when I was blue,
I fondly dedicate this book to you.
— H.W.

Preface

Every book is written for a reason—this one for many reasons. It has become the reference book I was looking for when I started developing Web sites—although it is much larger than I ever envisioned and covers topics that hadn't come into the public eye back then. It also offers one solution to the frustrating experience of scouring the Web (or a dozen books) for that one little command I used last week but have since forgotten. Of course, this book was also written to prove to myself that it could be done, done well, and done quickly.

What Will I Learn?

I want to clarify a point for everyone: This book was never designed as a tutorial. It is a reference book. Compare it your *Encyclopedia Britannica* that takes up that entire shelf in your office, or maybe your well-thumbed Webster's dictionary. Even so, the *HTML Master Reference* does give you the opportunity to learn a lot. It's like a self-directed study course for those who already "have a clue."

This book will help anyone who wants to develop Web sites; take your basic (or advanced) knowledge and get started. Almost every page is linked to almost every other through a vast web of Cross-References and Element lists. If your mind is like mine, you can't remember all the attributes for every HTML element, especially if you add the Cascading Style Sheet attributes, the Channel Definition Format elements and attributes, and the Open Software Description specifications, especially with your normal *life* getting in the way. This reference book discusses hundreds of elements, attributes, properties, methods, and collections. It also offers discussions of the latest Web standards, some important ISO standards, characters, scripting languages, and a large variety of concepts that are useful for understanding many of the occurrences on the Web.

Many examples given in the book are available on the accompanying CD-ROM; others are code segments to add to documents and play with on your own. No set of examples can give you exhaustive instructions for doing everything possible with the objects and attributes discussed in this book, but the collection assembled here can give you a pretty good start.

How Do I Find the Information I Want?

HTML Master Reference is organized alphabetically. You can look up any term by its spelling, just as with a dictionary. If you find that a term is not quite what you were looking for, try one of the items noted in the Cross-Reference. Each term listed in the book is in alphabetical order; each letter's section is identified with corresponding page markers. You can flip immediately to the appropriate letter without having to thumb through the entire book.

The appendixes at the back of the book describe the color codes adopted with HTML 4.0, the features Microsoft has added for Internet Explorer, the attributes of each HTML element, and a chart of the Unicode characters you can use on HTML pages.

The CD-ROM accompanying the book provides a variety of software products that may help you use and understand the contents of the book, and the Internet in general. All examples that appear on the CD-ROM as well as in the book are marked so you can find them easily.

Formatting and Conventions

We have tried to make the information in this book as accessible (and as easy to understand) as possible. As with most computer programming or development books, we use a `monospace font` for all programming code and term names. This allows you to immediately identify terms used in the text and sets apart the code and instructions found between close-knit paragraphs. **Bold** text identifies values for the attributes, parameters, or properties of the elements being discussed.

A variety of icons should help you identify several useful features of this book, whether you're skimming or reading:

CROSS-REFERENCE
Following each command's description, you can find a list of associated terms (or terms with similar functions) that could be useful in your page development.

NOTE
Notes provide you with tidbits of information I have gleaned while writing this book. Some of them point out differences between what is available for Internet Explorer and Netscape browsers; others point out information to keep in mind as you develop your pages.

TIP
Tips are techniques and ideas that work well when you use these commands in some special situations.

JAVASCRIPT

Special scripting icons introduce properties of JavaScript that mirror those of HTML and/or the attributes of Cascading Style Sheets.

 ON THE CD-ROM

This icon appears next to examples included on the CD-ROM; a short note identifies the file to look for.

Feedback, Anyone?

As with all books, no matter how hard the people involved may work, questions arise. You will find some information on the IDG Books Worldwide Web site:

```
http://www.idgbooks.com
```

If you can't find your answer at the Web site (or if you have a specific note for me), you can reach me at

```
okohke@hotmail.com
```

If you would like to let IDG Books Worldwide know what you think of this book, you can register comments at

```
http://my2cents.idgbooks.com
```

When you register, you are entered into a monthly drawing for books or other prizes. (Good luck!)

Acknowledgments

What book could ever make it this far without a great team of editors and production folks to keep it running? Well, this book had the best. Barb, Greg, Ken, Barry, Vicky, Amanda, Lenora, and Tom got to read my e-mails and cry over the state of the manuscript with me. Then there's the supporting cast of graphic artists, indexers, binders, papermakers — maybe a few elves or dwarves thrown in for good measure — without whose efforts you still wouldn't be holding this book. The entire crew at IDG Books Worldwide should be given a round of applause for their wonderful work (and maybe a big bonus...hint, hint...).

I also want to thank David and Sherry at Studio B, not only for taking me under their wing and introducing me to Greg and IDG Books Worldwide, but also for being there when I had a question or needed to hear a cheerful voice.

And last, but definitely not least, I want to thank my daughter Ann for letting Mommy work so much, and all my friends (yes, that *is* you!) who did their best to keep me from going insane while I was keeping up with the deadlines.

Contents

<!— —>

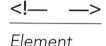

Element

HTML

Start Tag: Required
End Tag: Forbidden

This notation represents an HTML comment. Comments are used to provide instructions within an HTML document for the programmer and anyone performing follow-up maintenance. They are not interpreted by the user agent viewing the document. Comments are often used in the following situations:

- To note specific cells within a table.
- To add comments to specific sections of code found on an HTML document, or to hide that code from browsers that don't fully support it.
- To note changes that were made to a previous version of the document.
- To note the author and editing date of the document.

Comments can occupy a single line or multiple lines, as shown in the following example.

```
<!—This is a comment —>
<!—Comments can have multiple lines.
    If they do, they will appear like this. —>
```

Any text found between the comment markers is not visible to a site visitor.

 TIP

You shouldn't place more than two dashes in line together within a comment. In some older browsers, your comment may be truncated if you do so, and any portion of your comment past the multiple dashes will be visible to your visitors.

Examples

Comments used in a table allow the document's author a way to track their current location within the table.

1

```
<HTML>
<BODY>
   <TABLE>
      <TR>
      <TD> <!—R1:C1—> </TD>
      <TD> <!—R1:C2—> </TD>
      <TD> <!—R1:C3—> </TD>
      </TR>
      <TR>
      <TD> <!—R2:C1—> </TD>
      <TD> <!—R2:C2—> </TD>
      <TD> <!—R2:C3—> </TD>
      </TR>
   </TABLE>
</BODY>
</HTML>
```

Comments serve to set aside specific sections of code. This use makes it easier for HTML programmers and developers to edit the code.

```
<HTML>
<BODY>
   <!— Start of code for Customer List —>
   <UL>
      <LI> Cat's Back Consulting
      <LI> Toucan Alley Graphics
      <LI> Alligator Music Galore
   </UL>
</BODY>
</HTML>
```

<!DOCTYPE>

Element

HTML

Start Tag: Required
End Tag: Forbidden

Use the !DOCTYPE tag to specify the type of document your user agent (or Web browser) is viewing. This element's specific parts allow your Web browser to identify the elements used in your document.

```
<!DOCTYPE HTML PUBLIC "-//W3C//DTD HTML 4.0//EN"
"http://www.w3.org/TR/REC-html/strict.dtd">
```

The `!DOCTYPE` statement just given can be broken into the following parts:

- `HTML` — Document Class Name
- `PUBLIC` — Public or System designation
- `"-//W3C//DTD HTML 4.0//EN"` — Public Identifier
- `"http://www.w3.org/TR/REC-html/strict.dtd"` — Filename

Document Class Name

The *document class name* specifies the type of document markup language used in the current document. Some valid parameters for this include the following:

```
HTML
SGML
XML
```

PUBLIC or SYSTEM

This parameter defines whether the DTD being used is a system dependent definition, or not. When developing publicly accessible Web pages, the `PUBLIC` keyword should be used. If you specify `SYSTEM`, then the next attribute specified is the filename of the DTD being referenced. If you are using the `PUBLIC` parameter, the next information will be the Public Identifier string.

PUBLIC Identifier

This string, surrounded by quotation marks, is intended to be meaningful to all systems that read it. The Identifier is made up of multiple parts all delineated by double forward slashes. The first part is the "owner identifier." If the official "owner" has not been registered, this field will contain a hyphen. In this case, the second part would contain the name of the organization that developed the DTD. If the owner has been identified the second part would contain the "text identifier." This section specifies the public text class, such as DTD or ENTITIES, followed by the public text description, such as HTML or Latin 1. The third part contains a code representing the language being used in the document, for example EN for English or FR for French. If you wish to specify a specific display version of the DTD, it can be placed as a fourth or fifth part of your public identifier. The following examples show you some combinations that may appear in your public identifier string.

```
"-//W3C//DTD HTML 4.0//EN"
"ISO 12083:1994//DTD Math//EN"
"-//IETF//ENTITIES Latin 1//FR"
"-//W3C//DTD HTML//EN//4.0"
```

Filename

A filename must be specified for either a PUBLIC or a SYSTEM declaration. In a Public declaration you much include the full URL of the document being referenced as shown in the following example.

```
"http://www.w3.org/TR/REC-html/strict.dtd">
```

Although many browsers process your HTML documents without this tag, the !DOCTYPE element is used to declare the document type definition used in the document. Without this tag, your documents will not meet proper HTML 4.0 specification. There is a document type definition (DTD) specification for each version, and implementation of HTML. Three specifications are provided within the HTML 4.0 specification.

Strict

The HTML 4.0 Strict DTD includes all the HTML elements and attributes that have not been marked to be removed. This specification does not include documents that use frames. The !DOCTYPE specification for these documents is

```
<!DOCTYPE HTML PUBLIC "-//W3C//DTD HTML 4.0//EN"
"http://www.w3.org/TR/REC-html40/strict.dtd">
```

Transitional

The HTML 4.0 Transitional DTD includes all the elements and attributes specified in the Strict DTD, plus the deprecated elements and attributes that affect the visual presentation of your document. For documents that use this DTD, use this document type declaration:

```
<!DOCTYPE HTML PUBLIC "-//W3C//DTD HTML 4.0 Transitional//EN"
"http://www.w3.org/TR/REC-html40/loose.dtd">
```

Frameset

If you are using Frames on your pages, you will need to use the HTML 4.0 Frameset DTD. This DTD adds the ability to use frames to all the elements available with the transitional DTD. The following document type definition will allow you to access this DTD:

```
<!DOCTYPE HTML PUBLIC "-//W3C//DTD HTML 4.0 Frameset//EN"
"http://www.w3.org/TR/REC-html40/frameset.dtd">
```

CROSS-REFERENCE
See **DTD**.

symbols &
numbers

!Important

Declaration

CSS

Designers of Cascading Style Sheets can add implied importance to various specified styles by using the !Important declaration. The default result, when working with both author and user style sheets, is for the author style sheet to override the users. By declaring a property !Important you will add more force to the specification, making it harder to be overwritten by a viewer's software. This declaration will override any normal ruling specified in a reader's user agent software. An important declaration in the viewer's software will override a normal declaration in the documents. If a user's style has been declared !Important it will override an !Important declaration in the author's document. By declaring a property !Important, you are declaring all of that property's sub-properties important also.

Example

When using the following code in your style sheet, every piece of text tagged <H1> will be displayed maroon in a Verdana font even if the reader has specified that all text be black and Times New Roman, unless that user has a style sheet with the same rule marked !important. On systems that don't have the Verdana font, Helvetica will be used.

```
H1 { color: maroon !important;
        font-family: Verdana, Helvetica !important;
        font-style: bold}
```

 CROSS-REFERENCE
See **Cascading Style Sheets**.

:active

Pseudo-Class

CSS

The :active Anchor pseudo-class is applied only when the link is being selected by the user. This pseudo-element allows you to control the color of your anchors while they are active.

```
A:active {color: lime}
```

CROSS-REFERENCE
See **:hover**, **:link**, and **:visited**.

:after

Pseudo-Element

CSS

The :after pseudo-element is used to insert the information specified in the content parameter after every instance of the tag, or tags, that it has been applied to.

Attributes
content

This tag specified the specific text or file to be placed after the associated tag's contents.

Example
This code places a small blue ball behind every paragraph tag.

ON THE CD-ROM
Look for **after.htm** on the accompanying CD-ROM.

```
<HTML>
   <HEAD>
      <TITLE> Insert Before </TITLE>
      <STYLE type="text/css">
         P:after {content:"blueball.gif"}
      </STYLE>
   </HEAD>
   <BODY>
      <p> This is line 1.</p>
      <p> This is line 2.</p>
   </BODY>
</HTML>
```

This code should create the following text appearance.
This is line 1.
This is line 2.

NOTE
This feature is not supported in Internet Explorer 4 or Netscape Communicator 4 as of this writing.

CROSS-REFERENCE
See **:before**.

:before

Pseudo-Element

CSS

The :before pseudo-element is used to insert the information specified in the content parameter before every instance of the tag, or tags, that it has been applied to.

Attributes
content

This tag specified the specific text or file to be placed before the associated tag's contents.

Example
This code places a small blue ball in front of every line break tag.

ON THE CD-ROM
Look for **before.htm** on the accompanying CD-ROM.

```
<HTML>
   <HEAD>
      <TITLE> Insert Before </TITLE>
      <STYLE type="text/css">
         BR:before {content:"blueball.gif"}
      </STYLE>
   </HEAD>
   <BODY>
      This is line 1.<BR>
      This is line 2.<BR>
   </BODY>
</HTML>
```

This code should create the following text appearance.

This is line 1.
This is line 2.

CROSS-REFERENCE
See **:before**.

:first

Pseudo-Class

CSS

This pseudo-class is only applied to the @page rule. Using this pseudo-class, you can apply information directly to the page layout of the first printed page of your document. You can specify the following properties for your :first pseudo-class.

Attributes

margin

```
@page:first { margin=10cm}
```

This property sets the margin for each side of the first page of your document to the same distance.

margin-bottom

```
@page:first { margin-bottom=1in}
```

This property sets only the bottom margin of the first page of your document to the value specified.

margin-left

```
@page:first { margin-left=7cm}
```

This property sets only the left margin of the first page of your document to the value specified.

margin-right

```
@page:first { margin-right=10cm}
```

This property sets only the right margin of the first page of your document to the value specified.

margin-top

```
@page:first { margin-top=5cm}
```

This property sets only the top margin of the first page of your document to the value specified.

Example

The following example prints a page with a 3-inch vertical margin and a 2-inch horizontal margin.

ON THE CD-ROM

Look for **firstpage.htm** on the accompanying CD-ROM.

```
<HTML>
  <HEAD>
    <TITLE> Insert Before </TITLE>
    <STYLE type="text/css">
      @page:first {margin-top= 3in !important;
                   margin-bottom= 3in !important;
                   margin-left= 2in !important;
                   margin-right= 2in !important }
    </STYLE>
  </HEAD>
  <BODY>
    <p>This is a test. This is only a test. If this were a
    real emergency, this message would have been followed by
    an official announcement.
    <p> This was a test of the American Broadcasting system.
  </BODY>
</HTML>
```

NOTE

This feature is not supported in Internet Explorer 4 or Netscape Communicator 4.

CROSS-REFERENCE

See **:first-letter**, **:first-line**, **margin**, and **@page**.

:first-letter

Pseudo-Element

CSS

This element is used to create graphical effects — such as drop caps and initial caps. These elements can be either inline or floating, depending upon the status of the "float" attribute of :first-letter.

The specification identifies which characters, such as quotation marks, are a part of the first letter. Parenthesis and ellipses are generally ignored if they occur in the position of a first letter, because they are not considered general characters. Some languages have specific rules that control how special letter combinations are dealt with. Languages that have special two-letter sound combinations are treated as a single character, and both are contained within the :first-letter pseudo-element.

Attributes

The following properties can be applied to the :first-letter pseudo-elements:

background

```
background-attachment: scroll | fixed | inherit
background-color: <color-name> | <color-RGB> | transparent |
inherit
background-image: <uri> | none | inherit
background-position: [[<percentage> | <length>]{1,2} | [top |
center | bottom] | [ left | center | right]] | inherit
background-repeat: repeat | repeat-x | repeat-y | no-repeat |
inherit
```

Using these properties you can set the color, image, repetition and position of any items that occur in the background behind the letter.

border

```
border-bottom-width: thin | medium | thick | <length> |
inherit
border-left-width: thin | medium | thick | <length> | inherit
border-right-width: thin | medium | thick | <length> | inherit
border-top-width: thin | medium | thick | <length> | inherit
border-width: [thin | medium | thick | <length>]{1,4} |
inherit
```

The document author can use these properties to set the border color, thickness, and style of the "box" containing your drop cap.

clear

```
clear: none | left | right | both | inherit
```

The clear property controls the sides of an element that can't have a floating element next to it.

color

```
color: <color-name> | <color-RGB> | inherit
```

You can set the color on both the character itself and the background over which it's placed.

float

```
float: left | right | none | inherit
```

When the float property of an element is applied to block level elements, you can control where an element will appear in relation to the box surrounding the element.

font

```
font-family : family-name | generic-family | inherit
font-size: integer | +(1 to 9) | -(1 to 9)
font-style: normal | italic | oblique | inherit
font-variant: normal | small-caps | inherit
font-weight: normal | bold | bolder | lighter | 100 | 200 |
300 | 400 | 500 | 600 | 700 | 800 | 900 | inherit
```

This set of properties allows you to control the way the character will look, including among others family, style, variant, weight, and size.

line-height

```
line-height: normal | <number> | <length> | <percentage> |
inherit
```

This property controls the height of each line in your block of text.

margin

```
margin: : [<length> | <percentage>] {1,4} | inherit
margin-bottom: [<length> | <percentage>] | inherit
margin-left: [<length> | <percentage>] | inherit
margin-right: [<length> | <percentage>] | inherit
margin-top: [<length> | <percentage>] | inherit
```

You can control the amount of external space surrounding the "box" containing your first character using these properties.

padding

```
padding: : [<length> | <percentage>] {1,4} | inherit
padding-bottom: [<length> | <percentage>] | inherit
padding-left: [<length> | <percentage>] | inherit
padding-right: [<length> | <percentage>] | inherit
padding-top: [<length> | <percentage>] | inherit
```

The padding properties set the amount of space that is taken up by the content contained within a "box".

text-decoration

```
text-decoration: none | [underline || overline || line-through
|| blink] | inherit
```

This property allows you to set an underline, overline, strike, or blink for the first letter of your text.

text-transform

```
text-transform: capitalize | uppercase | lowercase | none |
inherit
```

This property controls the capitalization of your character.

vertical-align (only if float **is** none**)**

```
vertical-align: baseline | sub | super | top | text-top |
middle | bottom | text-bottom | <percentage> | <length> |
inherit
```

If you do not have the float property activated, you can control where on the line your drop cap will appear. It can be set to the baseline, the middle, the top, or it can be aligned as a superscript or a subscript.

Example

The following example will make a dropcap initial letter span two lines:

 ON THE CD-ROM

Look for **dropcap.htm** on the accompanying CD-ROM.

```
<HTML>
    <HEAD>
        <TITLE>Dropcap initial letter</TITLE>
        <STYLE type="text/css">
            P { font-size: 12pt; line-height: 12pt }
            P:first-letter { font-size: 200%;
                    font-style: italic;
                    font-weight: bold;
                    float: left }
            SPAN { text-transform: uppercase }
        </STYLE>
    </HEAD>
<BODY>
    <P><SPAN>Peter Piper</SPAN> <BR>
picked a peck of <BR>
pickled peppers.</P>
</BODY>
</HTML>
```

This example should appear as follows:

PETER PIPER
picked a peck of
pickled peppers.

NOTE
This feature is not supported in Internet Explorer 4 or Netscape Communicator 4.

CROSS-REFERENCE
See **:first**, **:first-line**, and **dropcaps**.

:first-line

Pseudo-Element

CSS

This pseudo-element applies special style properties to the first line of a block-level element. It cannot be used with any other style of element. This pseudo-element is similar to inline elements, but has some specific restrictions.

Attributes

The only properties that can be applied to the `:first-line` element are as follows:

background

```
background-attachment: scroll | fixed | inherit
background-color: <color-name> | <color-RGB> | transparent |
inherit
background-image: <uri> | none | inherit
background-position: [[<percentage> | <length>]{1,2} | [top |
center | bottom] | [ left | center | right]] | inherit
background-repeat: repeat | repeat-x | repeat-y | no-repeat |
inherit
```

Using these properties you can set the color, image, repetition and position of any items that occur in the background behind the letter.

clear

```
clear: none | left | right | both | inherit
```

The `clear` property controls the sides of an element that can't have a floating element next to it.

color

```
color: <color-name> | <color-RGB> | inherit
```

You can set the color on both the character itself and the background over which it's placed.

font

```
font-family : family-name | generic-family | inherit
font-size: integer | +(1 to 9) | -(1 to 9)
font-style: normal | italic | oblique | inherit
font-variant: normal | small-caps | inherit
font-weight: normal | bold | bolder | lighter | 100 | 200 |
300 | 400 | 500 | 600 | 700 | 800 | 900 | inherit
```

This set of properties allows you to control the way the character will look, including among others family, style, variant, weight, and size.

letter-spacing

```
letter-spacing: normal | <length> | auto | inherit
```

This property controls the amount of space that is allowed between the individual characters making up the words on a document. Depending upon the value of this property, the space between characters may be set at a static distance or it may be manipulated by the user agent.

text-decoration

```
text-decoration: none | [underline || overline || line-through
|| blink] | inherit
```

This property allows you to set an underline, overline, strike, or blink for the first line of your text.

text-transform

```
text-transform: capitalize | uppercase | lowercase | none |
inherit
```

This property controls the capitalization of your character.

vertical-align (only if float **is** none**)**

```
vertical-align: baseline | sub | super | top | text-top |
middle | bottom | text-bottom | <percentage> | <length> |
inherit
```

If you do not have the float property activated, you can control the vertical alignment of the text. It can be set to the baseline, the middle, the top, or it can be aligned as a superscript or a subscript.

word-spacing

```
word-spacing: normal | <length> | inherit
```

This property controls the amount of space that is allowed between the words of text on a document. Depending upon the value of this property the space between words is either set at a static distance, or it is allowed to be manipulated by the user agent.

Example

The following code forces the first line of the following text to appear in Aqua and all small caps.

ON THE CD-ROM

Look for **firstline.htm** on the accompanying CD-ROM.

```
<HTML>
   <HEAD>
      <TITLE>Special First Line</TITLE>
      <STYLE type="text/css">
          P { font-size: 12pt; line-height: 12pt }
          P:first-line {font-color= aqua;
                        font-variant= small-caps}
          SPAN { text-transform: uppercase }
      </STYLE>
   </HEAD>
<BODY>
   <P:first-line>
   <SPAN>This is the time when all good men </SPAN>
         must come to the aid of their country. The
         quick brown fox jumped over the lazy dog.
         Peter Piper picked a peck of pickled peppers.</p>

</BODY>
</HTML>
```

This code results in text that should appear similar to the following:

THIS IS THE TIME WHEN ALL GOOD MEN must come to the aid of their country. The quick brown fox jumped over the lazy dog. Peter Piper picked a peck of pickled peppers.

NOTE

This feature is not supported in Internet Explorer 4 or Netscape Communicator 4.

CROSS-REFERENCE

See **:first**, and **:first-letter**.

:hover

Pseudo- Class

CSS

This Anchor pseudo-class is applied to all links that currently have the mouse hovering over then. A link with the `:hover` class applied will automatically become the color specified when the mouse is dragged over them.

```
A:hover {color: red}
```

 CROSS-REFERENCE
See **:active**, **:link**, and **:visited**.

:left

Pseudo-Class

CSS

This pseudo-class is only applied to the `@page` rule. Using this pseudo-class you can apply information directly to the page layout of the left-hand printed page of your document. You can specify the following properties for your `:left` pseudo-class.

Attributes
margin

```
@page:left { margin=10cm}
```

This property sets the margin for each left-hand page of your document to the same distance.

margin-bottom

```
@page:left { margin-bottom=1in}
```

This property sets only the bottom margin of the left-hand page of your document to the value specified.

margin-left

```
@page:left { margin-left=7cm}
```

This property sets only the left margin of the left-hand page of your document to the value specified.

margin-right

```
@page:left { margin-right=10cm}
```

This property sets only the right margin of the left-hand page of your document to the value specified.

margin-top

```
@page:left { margin-top=5cm}
```

This property sets only the top margin of the left-hand page of your document to the value specified.

Example

The following example prints a page with a 12-centimeter vertical margin and a 6-centimeter horizontal margin.

```
<HTML>
   <HEAD>
      <TITLE> Insert Before </TITLE>
      <STYLE type="text/css">
         @page:left {margin-top= 12cm !important;
                 margin-bottom= 12cm !important;
                 margin-left= 6cm !important;
                 margin-right= 6cm !important }
      </STYLE>
   </HEAD>
   <BODY>
      <p>This is a test. This is only a test. If this were a
real emergency, this message would have been followed by an
official announcement.
      <p> This was a test of the American Broadcasting system.
   </BODY>
</HTML>
```

NOTE
This feature is not supported in Internet Explorer 4 or Netscape Communicator 4.

CROSS-REFERENCE
See **:right**.

:link

Pseudo- Class

CSS

This Anchor pseudo-class is applied to all links that have not been selected. A link with the :link class applied will automatically be displayed with the color specified.

```
A:link {color: blue}
```

 CROSS-REFERENCE
See **:active**, **:hover**, and **:visited**.

:right

Pseudo-Class

CSS

This pseudo-class is only applied to the @page rule. Using this pseudo-class you can apply information directly to the page layout of the right-hand printed pages of your document. You can specify the following properties for your :right pseudo-class.

Attributes
margin

```
@page:right { margin=10cm}
```

This property sets the margin for each side of the right-hand pages of your document to the same distance.

margin-bottom

```
@page:right { margin-bottom=1in}
```

This property sets only the bottom margin of the right-hand pages of your document to the value specified.

margin-left

```
@page:right { margin-left=7cm}
```

This property sets only the left margin of the right-hand pages of your document to the value specified.

margin-right

```
@page:right { margin-right=10cm}
```

This property sets only the right margin of the right-hand pages of your document to the value specified.

margin-top

```
@page:right { margin-top=5cm}
```

This property sets only the top margin of the right-hand pages of your document to the value specified.

Example

The following example prints a page with a 10-centimeter vertical margin and a 10-centimeter horizontal margin.

ON THE CD-ROM

Look for **rightpage.htm** on the accompanying CD-ROM.

```
<HTML>
    <HEAD>
        <TITLE> Insert Before </TITLE>
        <STYLE type="text/css">
            @page:right {margin-top= 10cm !important;
                    margin-bottom= 10cm !important;
                    margin-left= 10cm !important;
                    margin-right= 10cm !important }
        </STYLE>
    </HEAD>
    <BODY>
        <p>This is a test. This is only a test. If this were a
        real emergency, this message would have been followed by
        an official announcement.
        <p> This was a test of the American Broadcasting system.
    </BODY>
</HTML>
```

NOTE

This feature is not supported in Internet Explorer 4 or Netscape Communicator 4.

CROSS-REFERENCE

See **:left**.

:visited

Pseudo-Classes

CSS

This Anchor pseudo-class is applied to all links that have been selected. A link with the :visited class applied will automatically change to the color specified after they have been visited.

```
A:visited {color: fuschia}
```

CROSS-REFERENCE
See **:active**, **:hover**, and **:links**.

@-rules

Concept

CSS

An @rule is one of the two types of statements that are allowed within CSS style sheets. These rules all begin with the @ character and are used to specify a particular action to take in regards to a specific situation. These rules are available with Cascading Style Sheets.

@font-face

```
@font-face { descriptor: value }
```

This rule allows you to designate specific font families to appear in your document. If your font can't be found on the computer running the user agent, it can be downloaded from a source specified in the font description.

@import

```
@import <uri> || <media type>
```

This rule allows you to specify a style sheet for your HTML document. The style sheet must have a .css extension, and be readable by the user agent that the viewer is using. You can use the @import rule to limit the type of stylesheets that you are importing. Using this rule you can specify whether the style sheet you are importing is for a print, TV, screen, or other media type. You can only have one @import rule in any document.

@media

```
@media <mediatype>{descriptors....}
```

This rule defines the type of media that is affected by the set of elements and classes defined in the code block following this rule designator. You can have as many @media rules in a document, as you have media types to specify.

@page

```
@page{[:<page selector>] {descriptors...}
```

This rule, only available with user agents that support the CSS2 specification, controls how your printed page will appear. Any of the elements specified in the block following this designator will not be shown on the screen. Using this rule, you can identify individual page margins for your left-hand, right-hand, and first printed page.

@font-face

Rule

CSS

CSS2 allows you to use the `@font-face` rule to control how a viewer's user agent selects the fonts to be displayed on a Web page that has fonts that have been specified by the document author. With this system, you can have an identical match of the font, an intelligent match of the font, synthesis, or download the font that is required for the page.

If the fonts are matched, the user agent viewing the document will have access to a local system font with the same family name. The fonts may not necessarily match in appearance if the font that the client is using came from a source other than the server. Once the match is made, the user agent loads the document and displays it in the font it found.

In the case of an intelligent match, the user agent will display a font that is accessible on its system and closest in appearance to the font that was requested. This will not be an exact match, but it should be very close. The font is matched according to the kind of font it is, whether it uses serifs or not, its weight, and the height of its capital letters, in addition to other font characteristics.

If your user agent must synthesize a font, it will create a font that will not only closely resemble the font that was designated, but it will also match the metrics of that font. When a font is synthesized, it will generally be a closer duplicate than a font found during a matching exercise. Synthesis requires more accurate substitution and position information in order for all the specific characteristics of the font to be preserved.

If the @font-face command is used to provide the user agent with download access to the specified fonts, the font can simply be retrieved over the Web. The process involved is the same as downloading an image or sound to be displayed with the current document. Users that download fonts will experience similar delays as downloading images will cause.

The last alternative for managing fonts is progressive rendering. This is a combination of downloading and matching that allows you to create a temporary font so your document's content can be read while the originally designated font downloads. After the real font has been downloaded, it will replace the substitution font in subsequent documents. In order to avoid having a document rendered twice, your font description must contain the metric information that describes the font. The more complete a font's metric information, the less likely that document will need to be re-rendered once the download is complete.

The Cascading Style Sheets 2 specification allows the document creator to specify which of these methods, if any, are used when a designated font is not available on the reading system. The @font-face command allows a document author to provide a font-description, created out of a series of font-descriptors, to be used to define specific pieces of information about the fonts to be used on the page. Each font-descriptor allows you to characterize a specific piece of information about the font being used. This description can include the URI which defines the location of the font on the Web, the font family name, and font size. Any piece of information that can be described about a font can be set using the font descriptors within the @font-face rule.

You can classify a font-descriptor as one of three types:

- Those that provide a link between the style sheet usage of the font and its description
- Those that provide a URL for the location of the font or its pertinent information
- Those that provide character information for the font

All font-descriptions that are specified through the @font-face rule use the following format:

```
@font-face { descriptor: value;
        descriptor: value;
        descriptor: value;
        [ ... ]
        descriptor: value}
```

where all the descriptor: value sets provide a description of the font being used.

The @font-face rules apply only to the fonts specified within the document. If you are using multiple fonts in your document, you will need multiple @font-face specifications.

Example

The following example shows you how this rule affects your document's appearance when multiple fonts are specified.

```
<HTML>
<HEAD>
    <TITLE>Font test</TITLE>
    <STYLE TYPE="text/css" MEDIA="screen, print">
        @font-face { font-family: "Comic Sans";
        src: url(http://site/fonts/comicsans)}
        @font-face { font-family: "Jester";
                font-weight: bold;
                font-style: italic}
        H1 {font-family: "Comic Sans"}
        H2 {font-family: "Jester", serif}
    </STYLE>
</HEAD>
<BODY>
    <H1> Comic Sans is a cool font.</H1>
    <H2> But Jester has more pizzazz.</H2>
</BODY>
</HTML>
```

 NOTE

Neither Netscape 4.5, Internet Explorer 4, nor Internet Explorer 5 preview correctly match the fonts identified with this rule.

As a user agent parses this chunk of code, it will attempt to find a set of rules that specify how each heading should be rendered. In this example the STYLE element, which is used to specify the style sheet, sets all H1 elements to the Comic Sans font family, at the same time it sets all H2 elements to the Jester font. A user agent that supports CSS1 will search for the Comic Sans and Jester font families; if it can't find them, then it will use its default text font for the Comic family, and the specified fallback serif font for the Jester family. If you are using a CSS1 implementation the @font-face rule's font-descriptors will be ignored. Because this rule conforms to the forward-compatible parsing requirements of CSS, your user agent will be able to safely skip over this command without encountering an error.

User agents that support CSS2 will examine the @font-face rules in an attempt to match a font description to the Comic Sans and Jester fonts. In the above example, it will find a partial description of the Jester font, but it will find an URI from which it can download the Comic Sans font. The user agent will use supplied URI to download Comic Sans. If Comic Sans were found on the client system, the user agent would have used it, instead of downloading the font. In the case of Jester, the user agent will use one of the matching rules, or the synthesis rule to create a similar font from the descriptors provided. If the user agent could not find a matching @font-face rule for the font family specified it will attempt to match the fonts using the rules specified in CSS1.

CSS2 allows any font-descriptor that is not recognized, or useful to the user agent, to be skipped. This provides a built in means for increasing the descriptors in an effort to improve the font substitution, matching, or synthesis rules being used.

The following descriptors are currently available with CSS2:

Font-family	Font-size	Font-weight	Font-variant
Font-style	Font-face	Font-set	Src

CROSS-REFERENCE
See **Discriptor**, **@import**, **@media**, and **:@rule**.

@Import

Rule

CSS

The @Import rule allows you to import a specific external style sheet into your HTML document. These style sheets use a .css extension, and must be readable by the user agent that the viewer is using. You can use the @import rule to limit the type of style sheets that you are importing. Using this rule you can specify whether the style sheet you are importing is for a print, tv, screen, or other media type.

When you use the @import rule you are essentially embedding a style sheet import command within an @media rule. This prevents your user agent from retrieving resources for media types that are unsupported. The following examples show how the @import command can be used. You can only have one @import rule in any document.

If no media type has been specified, the @import rule is considered unconditional, and will be used for all media types.

Examples
The following code imports the specified Cascading Style Sheet file to be used only in print media.

```
<HEAD>
  <STYLE TYPE="text/css">
      @import url (printmedia.css) print;
  </STYLE>
</HEAD>
```

The following code imports the specified Cascading Style Sheet file will be imported and used for both of the TV and screen media types. With this designation, the style sheet will be used when information is being displayed upon your PC or terminal screen.

```
<HEAD>
    <STYLE TYPE="text/css">
        @import url (continuous.css) tv, screen;
    </STYLE>
</HEAD>
```

The following code imports the specified Aural Cascading Style Sheet file to be used on systems that actively support speech synthesizers.

```
<HEAD>
    <STYLE TYPE="text/css">
        @import url (voices.css) aural;
    </STYLE>
</HEAD>
```

@media

Rule

CSS

Many types of media are used to impart information to readers, and each media type is best presented in a specific fashion. Cascading Style Sheets allow you to specify a particular presentation style for each identified media type. For example, text is easier to read on the screen if it uses a sans serif font, while text on paper is generally easiest to read if it is written in a serif font. The property that controls this feature is font-family, and can be used for both print and screen media. You will often require a larger font on screen than you will on paper. The property, which controls this feature, is font-size.

Example

In order to define a specific style sheet for each of the media, use multiple @media rules as shown in the following example.

```
<HEAD>
    <STYLE TYPE="text/css">
        @media print {
            BODY { font-size: 11pt;
                   font-family: Times New Roman }
            H1 { font-family: Comic Sans}
```

```
          H2 { font-family: Comic Sans;
             font-style: italic }
      }
      @media screen {
          BODY { font-size: 12pt;
             font-family: Arial }
         H1 { font-family: Comic Sans}
          H2 { font-family: Comic Sans;
                 font-style: italic }
      }
    @media screen, print {
          BODY { line-height: 1.2 }
      }
    </STYLE>
  </HEAD>
```

The first two information blocks provide information specific to an individual media type, in this case print and screen. The third information block provides style sheet instructions for both of these media types. To designate style sheet instructions for multiple media types in the same command, list them following the @media rule designator with commas between them.

Some properties are only available with specific media. One example of this is the "cue-after" property that is available only with aural style sheets. CSS2 does not specify a definitive list of media types, although it does provide a list of current values for the @media rule. These values are not case sensitive.

Values
All

This value designates that the following style sheet is suitable for all devices.

Aural

This value designates that the following style sheet is to be used with speech synthesizers.

CROSS-REFERENCE
See **Aural Style Sheets**.

Braille

This value designates that the following style sheet is to be used with Braille tactile feedback devices.

Embossed

This value designates that the following style sheet is to be used with paged Braille printers.

Handheld

This value designates that the following style sheet is to be used with handheld devices such as Windows CE palmtops, monochromatic monitors, and Palm Pilots.

Print

This value designates that the following style sheet is to be used with all printed material, opaque material, and for documents which are viewed on-screen in print preview mode.

CROSS-REFERENCE
See **Paged Media**.

Projection

This value designates that the following style sheet is to be used with projected presentations. The presentation can be either on a projector or have been printed to transparencies.

CROSS-REFERENCE
See **Paged Media**.

Screen

This value designates that the following style sheet is to be used primarily for color computer screens.

CROSS-REFERENCE
See **Continuous Media**.

TTY

This value designates that the following style sheet is to be used for teletypes and terminals that use a fixed-pitch character grid. Document developers should avoid using pixel units with the TTY media type.

TV

This value designates that the following style sheet is to be used with color television-type devices using a low resolution with a limited ability to scroll.

@page

Rule

CSS

The @page rule allows you to designate specific constraints to apply to the page box. Document creators can specify the dimensions, layout, orientation, and margins of the pages. The page box is a rectangular area, roughly the size of a printed page, which contains the page area and the margin block. The page area which contains all the material to be displayed on a page, and the edges of this box provide a particular container for the layout of the page that occurs between page breaks. The margin block designates the white space that must be maintained around the printed material.

In CSS2 neither the border nor padding properties apply to the page box, they may in the future. The properties available with the @page rule are for controlling the dimensions of your page box.

The typical page box looks like the one shown in Figure Symbols/Numbers-1.

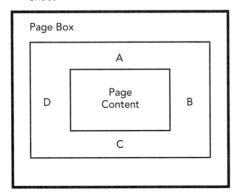

Figure Symbols/Numbers-1 A: margin-to;
B: margin-right;
C: margin-bottom;
D: margin-left

The @page rule applies to every page of a document, although you can use one of the page pseudo-class properties such as :first, :left, and :right to specify which page some specific margins are going to be used with.

As you increase the size of vertical margins on your pages, content will be moved onto the page. This is referred to as *margin collapsing*. Because the @page command is unaware of the content of your page, and is therefore unaware of the fonts used on it, it can't understand em and ex unit measurements. All other forms of measurement are acceptable, including percentages. If you use percentages on your margins, they will be a percentage of the size of the total page box. Page boxes allow you to use negative values for your margins, which can place content outside of the area normally acceptable for use by your user agent or printer. In most of these cases your information is simply cut. The use of absolute positioning on your document objects can also allow information to be placed outside of the page box.

Attributes

:first

```
@page:first
```

Using this pseudo-class you can apply information directly to the page layout of the first printed page of your document.

:left

```
@page:left
```

Using this pseudo-class you can apply information directly to the page layout of the left-hand printed page of your document.

:right

```
@page:right
```

Using this attribute you can apply information directly to the page layout of the right-hand printed pages of your document.

margin

```
@page { margin=10cm}
```

This attribute sets the margin for each side of the right-hand pages of your document to the same distance.

margin-bottom

```
@page { margin-bottom=1in}
```

This attribute sets only the bottom margin of the right-hand pages of your document to the value specified.

margin-left

```
@page { margin-left=7cm}
```

This attribute sets only the left margin of the right-hand pages of your document to the value specified.

Mmargin-right

```
@page { margin-right=10cm}
```

This attribute sets only the right margin of the right-hand pages of your document to the value specified.

margin-top

```
@page { margin-top=5cm}
```

This attribute sets only the top margin of the right-hand pages of your document to the value specified.

mark

```
@page { mark=cross}
```

This attribute creates light marks on the outside of the page box that tells a printer where the page should be cut, or it can be used to create registration marks for aligning sheets.

size

```
@page { size=landscape}
```

This attribute allows you to specify the size and the dimensions of the page box.

Example

In this example the page box is being controlled through a variety of settings. The margin of the first page is set to different dimensions from the left and right pages. The pages are being turned so they should print in landscape mode and show cropping marks.

```
<HTML>
  <HEAD>
    <TITLE> Insert Before </TITLE>
    <STYLE type="text/css">
      @page { size= landscape;
        marks= crop}
      @page:right { margin-top= 10cm !important;
        margin-bottom= 10cm !important;
        margin-left= 10cm !important;
        margin-right= 10cm !important }
      @page:left  { margin-top= 12cm !important;
        margin-bottom= 12cm !important;
        margin-left= 6cm !important;
        margin-right= 6cm !important }
      @page:first { margin-top= 3in !important;
        margin-bottom= 3in !important;
        margin-left= 2in !important;
```

```
          margin-right= 2in !important }
      </STYLE>
    </HEAD>

    <BODY>
      <p>This is a test. This is only a test. If this were a
      real emergency, this message would have been followed by
      an official announcement.
      <p> This was a test of the American Broadcasting system.
    </BODY>
  </HTML>
```

%attrs

DTD parameter

This parameter has been defined in the !ENTITY section of the DTD for HTML. The HTML DTD uses a series of parameters to define its entries. The parameter entry definition defines a specific type of macro that is referenced elsewhere in the DTD. Generally these macros will only appear in the DTD, and not in the HTML document. This particular parameter provides for a series of attributes to be used with each HTML element. This parameter is strictly a convenience, since most specific elements have already been defined for the specific element types.

CROSS-REFERENCE
See **Attributes**.

%block

DTD parameter

The HTML DTD uses a series of parameters to define its entries. The parameter entry definition defines a specific type of macro that is referenced elsewhere in the DTD. Generally these macros will only appear in the DTD, and not in the HTML document. The %block parameter is used to define block-level elements that are used in HTML.

CROSS-REFERENCE
See **block elements**.

%character

DTD parameter

When a specific attribute of an element requires a single character from the document character set, the attribute is specified in the DTD with the %Character parameter.

CROSS-REFERENCE
See the **Character Tables** in the **Appendix C**.

%charset

DTD parameter

This parameter is used in the HTML DTD to refer to the character encoding used to convert a sequence of bytes into a series of characters. This conversion occurs when Web servers send HTML documents to the user agents as a string of bytes. The user agent takes these bytes and interprets them as characters before displaying them on the screen. The conversion of characters can be simple or complicated, but the values expressed in the %charset parameter has to be in the format of a string. The names of the characters being encoded are not case sensitive.

CROSS-REFERENCE
See the **Character Tables** in the **Appendix C**.

%color

DTD parameter

This parameter allows you to pass on information about the color of an element to the user agent. The value of %color can either be one of the color names specified in the Color Tables appendix, or the color's hexadecimal number. If a name is used, it will not be case sensitive.

CROSS-REFERENCE
See the **Color Tables** in **Appendix B**.

%contentType

DTD parameter

This DTD parameter holds the name of a specific type of linked media source. %ContentType is not case sensitive. There are a few content types that are available to be used including:

- text/html
- text/tcl
- text/javascript
- text/vbscript
- image/png
- image/gif
- video/mpeg
- audio/basic

There are many more MIME types that have been registered and are usable with this DTD parameter. You can read about them in the section covering MIME types. The "text/css" type is not registered yet, but it should be used for importing or linking to a CSS style sheet.

CROSS-REFERENCE
See **MIME Types**.

%dateTime

DTD parameter

This parameter used in the HTML DTD, allows you to use many different representations of dates and times within your HTML documents. The current default format for a date/time string is

```
YYYY-MM-DDThh:mm:ssTZD
```

where

```
YYYY = four-digit year
MM = two-digit month (01=January, etc.)
DD = two-digit day of month (01 through 31)
hh = two digits of hour (00 through 23) (am/pm NOT allowed)
mm = two digits of minute (00 through 59)
```

```
ss = two digits of second (00 through 59)
TZD = time zone designator
```

which displays 9:30 PM PST on January 16, 1999, in the following manner:

```
1999-01-16/21:30:00PST
```

All time zones are indicated as a local time that is a specific number of hours and minutes ahead or behind the UTC (an acronym for the French words meaning *Coordinated Universal Time*).

 CROSS-REFERENCE
See **<StartDate>** and **<EndDate>**.

%frametarget

DTD parameter

This DTD parameter provides a means of identifying the reserved frame target names. Other than the following list of reserved names, frame target names, which are passed using the %FrameTarget parameter identified in the DTD, must begin with an alphabetic character (a-zA-Z). User agents should ignore all target names that do not conform to this standard.

_blank

The user agent loads the designated document in a new, unnamed window.

_parent

The user agent loads the document into the immediate FRAMESET parent of the current frame. This value is equivalent to _self if the current frame has no parent.

_self

The user agent loads the document into the frame that the element was called from.

_top

The user agent will load the document into the full, original window thereby deleting all other frames. This value is equivalent to _self if the current frame has no parent.

 CROSS-REFERENCE
See **<FRAME>**, **<FRAMESET>** and **<IFRAME>**.

%inline

DTD parameter

The HTML DTD uses a series of parameters to define its entries. The parameter entry definition defines a specific type of macro that is referenced elsewhere in the DTD. Generally these macros will only appear in the DTD, and not in the HTML document. The `%inline` parameter is used to define inline-level elements that are used in HTML.

CROSS-REFERENCE
See **inline elements**.

%LanguageCode

DTD parameter

This parameter holds the values of attributes that specify a specific language code to be used in a document or for a particular block. This parameter is not case specific, although there is a list of values that are legal to use.

CROSS-REFERENCE
See **lang**.

%length

DTD parameter

The `%length` parameter can contain either a `%pixel` or a percentage of the horizontal or vertical space that is available.

CROSS-REFERENCE
See **<length>**, and **<percentage>**.

%LinkTypes

DTD parameter

The `%LinkTypes` parameter contains one of the recognized link types that are shown in the following list. This value is not case sensitive. Each link may be interpreted differently by the user agent, search engine, or other device that may be accessing the link.

Values

Alternate

An `alternate` link designates a substitute version of the document in which the link occurs. If it is used with a `lang` attribute it implies a translated version of the document is available. If it is used with a `media` attribute, it implies that there is a version designed specifically for that medium.

Appendix

This link points to a document that serves as an appendix for an organized collection of documents.

Bookmark

This link is a bookmark that serves as an entry point into another document.

Chapter

This link points to a document that works as an individual chapter within an organized collection of documents.

Contents

This link refers to a document that is currently serving as a table of contents. User agents may, at their discretion, support the term TOC.

Copyright

This link refers to the copyright statement for the document.

Glossary

This link refers to a document that is providing a list of terms that are applicable to the current document.

Help

This link points to a document that serves as a source of more information for the current series of documents.

Index

This link refers to a document that is currently serving as an Index.

Next

This link refers to the next document in a sequence of documents. User agents can employ this link to pre-load a document and reduce its perceived load time.

Prev

This link refers to the previous document in a sequence of documents. User agents may, at their discretion, support the term Previous.

Section

This link points to a document that works as an individual section within an organized collection of documents.

Start

When search engines are looking at a site, this link will inform the engine which document, in a collection of documents, is the starting point.

Stylesheet

This designates an external style sheet is to be used. If you wish the user to be able to select the style sheet, use this parameter in conjunction with the `alternate` link type.

Subsection

This link points to a document that serves as a subsection within an organized collection of documents.

If document authors wish to create their own link types, they should use a `HEAD` element `profile` to cite the conventions with which they are defining the link type.

CROSS-REFERENCE
See **<HEAD>**, **Profile**, **<LINK>**, and **<A>**.

%MediaDesc

DTD parameter

The `%MediaDesc` parameter is used to pass information dealing with the following media types to your user agent.

Values
All

Used for all devices.

Aural

Used for speech synthesizers.

Braille

Used for Braille tactile feedback devices.

Embossed

Used for paged Braille printers.

Handheld

Used for handheld devices such as Windows CE palmtops, monochromatic monitors, and Palm Pilots.

Print

Used for all printed material, opaque material, and for documents that are viewed on-screen in print preview mode.

Projection

Used for projected presentations.

Screen

Used for color computer screens.

TTY

Used for teletypes and terminals that use a fixed-pitch character grid. Document developers should avoid using pixel units with the TTY media type.

TV

Used for television-type devices using a low resolution and having limited scrolling capability.

 **CROSS-REFERENCE**
See **@media**.

%MultiLength

DTD parameter

This parameter is just one of three ways to describe a length. The %MultiLength parameter may be either relative, or a true %Length. Relative lengths use the form "i★" where i is any integer. If a user agent has multiple elements competing for the same space on a document or the screen, they will first allot all the pixel and percentage lengths, then divide the remaining space among any relative lengths defined. When the remaining space is divided, it will be allocated proportionally, based on the integer preceding the asterisk.

For example, assume you had 100 pixels of space available after a user agent allots pixel and percentage space. If the remaining relative values which are competing for the space are 1*, 3*, and 4*, the 1* will be allotted 12.5 pixels, the 3* will be allotted 37.5 pixels, and the 4* will be allotted 50 pixels.

```
1+3+4 = 8
100 px / 8=12.5 px
12.5 X 1  = 12.5 px
12.5 X 3 = 37.5 px
12.5 X 4  = 50 px
```

CROSS-REFERENCE
See **Absolute Reference**, **<length>**, **<number>**, and **Absolute Value**.

%Pixels

DTD parameter

This integer value is used in the HTML DTD to represent the number of pixels of the paper or screen on which the particular element takes up. This value does not look at the case of the character.

CROSS-REFERENCE
See **pixel**.

%Script

DTD parameter

This DTD parameter is used to identify the contents of the SCRIPT element and its attributes. Your user agent will not process the information contained within this parameter, but will instead pass the values on to a script engine. As some scripting languages are case sensitive, the information in the %script parameter may need to appear in a specific case. If your %script parameter contains information about the SCRIPT element, it cannot contain character references, although if it is referring to an attribute of the SCRIPT element, character references are allowed.

CROSS-REFERENCE
See **Scripts**, **JavaScript**, **ECMAScript**, and **VBScript**.

%StyleSheet

DTD parameter

Style sheet data is passed to the user agent using the `%stylesheet` parameter. This parameter can contain the contents of the `STYLE` element of any of the style attributes that are available. Any information passed to the user agent using this parameter will not be interpreted as part of the HTML markup, but will use it to define a specific set of instructions for displaying the HTML markup. If the `%stylesheet` parameter contains information on the `STYLE` element, it can't contain any character-based data, although when it is passing information for an attribute of the `STYLE` element character data is acceptable. If you are using a style sheet language that is case sensitive, the contents of the `%stylesheet` parameter will be treated as such.

 CROSS-REFERENCE
See **Cascading Style Sheets**, and **Style Sheets**.

%Text

DTD parameter

This parameter is used to pass information to the user agent that should appear in a human readable format. The HTML DTD specifies that this parameter should pass character based string information that the user agent will then use to correctly organize the document's contents and layout.

 CROSS-REFERENCE
See **CDATA**.

%URI

DTD parameter

This DTD parameter identifies the URI's that are used within an HTML document. In most cases `URI` are case sensitive, although there are some instances where case doesn't matter, but the document author should treat all URI's as if case was always important.

 **CROSS-REFERENCE**
See **URI**, and **URL**.

2D Layouts

Concept

This term is applied to the ability to create HTML-based documents that can show multiple items being placed within the same space to create the image of multiple dimensions on your documents.

2 _ D Borders

Concept

CSS

This term is loosely applied to the roughly 3D-looking borders surrounding tables and the cells within tables. The so-called 2D borders allow you to set individual attributes for the ridge, groove, inset, and outset that make up the borders of the individual cells.

<A>

Element

HTML

Start Tag: Required
End Tag: Required

Use this element to insert an Anchor into a document. An anchor provides either absolute or relative links to other documents, internal links to specific sections of the current document, or links to another computer through e-mail, newsgroups, FTP, or gopher servers. Most user agents display links in a way that makes them obvious to the document readers. Some of the ways that they do this are through underlining information, reversing the background of the links, changing their text color, or changing a font style.

NOTE

You cannot have nested links or anchors defined by the A element. This means you can't load documents into multiple frames from a single link unless you trigger the second loading mechanism through a JavaScript.

Attributes

accesskey

```
accesskey="character"
```

You can assign an access key to an element. This key enables you to put the focus on an element quickly. In the case of a form element, the user is immediately able to input information. In the case of a link, the link is activated and followed.

charset

```
charset=charset
```

This attribute specifies the character encoding of the resource identified by the link.

class

```
class="cdata-list"
```

This attribute assigns a class name to an element. User agents use classes to group specific types of information for later use.

coords

```
coords=x1,y1,x2,y2        /** shape=rect , x1y1 = top left pt,
    x2y2 = lower right pt **/
coords=x1,y1,rad          /** shape=circle , x1y1 = center pt,
    rad = circle radius **/
coords=x1,y1,x2,y2,... xn yn    /** shape=poly , x1y1 = 1st
    corner pt, x2y2 = 2nd corner pt, xnyn= final corner pt **/
```

This attribute provides the point coordinates that enable the map to be drawn over the image. You can use any combination of shapes and coordinates on a map. Although hot spots are not required to be adjacent, it is acceptable if they are. If two hot spots overlap, the area designated to use that space first in the list of coordinates is used as the active destination.

href

```
href="url"
```

This attribute specifies the location of the document or resource to which this link refers.

hreflang

```
hreflang=langcode
```

This attribute specifies the language used by the document or resource identified by the href attribute.

id

```
id="name"
```

This attribute assigns a name to an element. See the name attribute of this element to see the valid formats for the name.

name

```
name=cdata
```

This attribute gives the element a name, which serves an identifier when it is used as a destination for other links. When you are defining a name for an anchor, you must observe the following rules:

- Anchor names must be unique. You cannot have Anchor names that differ only in case appearing within the same document.
- Comparisons between fragment identifiers and anchor names are case-sensitive and must match.

Because both the `id` and `name` attributes use the same name space, you can't use one to define a "titlepage" anchor and the other to define a "Titlepage" anchor. When deciding whether to use the `id` or the `name` attributes to set the name for your anchor, you need to consider a few things. On one hand, the `id` attribute can invoke a style sheet or work with a script process, although it might not be supported in all older user agents. On the other hand, the `name` attribute enables you to create more distinctive names for your object. When considering which attribute to use, you need to take into account what the object will be used for and who will be viewing it.

onblur

```
onblur=script
```

This attribute becomes active when an on-screen element loses the focus either through the actions of a mouse or another pointing device or through tabbed navigation.

onclick

```
onclick=script
```

This attribute takes effect when a user clicks the button on a pointing device while the pointer is over an on-screen element.

ondblclick

```
ondblclick=script
```

This attribute takes effect when a user double-clicks the button on a pointing device while the pointer is over an on-screen element.

onfocus

```
onfocus=script
```

This attribute takes effect when an on-screen element receives focus either from a mouse or another pointing device or through tabbed navigation.

onkeydown

```
onkeydown=script
```

This attribute takes effect when a user presses a key while the pointer is over an on-screen element.

onkeypress

`onkeypress=`*`script`*

This attribute takes effect when a user either presses or releases a key while the pointer is over an on-screen element.

onkeyup

`onkeyup=`*`script`*

This attribute takes effect when a user releases a key while the pointer is over an on-screen element.

onmousedown

`onmousedown=`*`script`*

This attribute takes effect when a user presses the button on a pointing device while the pointer is over an on-screen element.

onmousemove

`onmousemove=`*`script`*

This attribute becomes active when a user moves the mouse while the pointer is over an on-screen element.

onmouseout

`onmouseout=`*`script`*

This attribute becomes active when a user moves the mouse pointer away from an on-screen element.

onmouseover

`onmouseover=`*`script`*

This attribute becomes active when a user moves the mouse pointer over an on-screen element.

onmouseup

`onmouseup=`*`script`*

This attribute takes effect when a user releases the button on a pointing device while the pointer is over an on-screen element.

rel

`rel=`*`linktype`*

This attribute describes the relationship between the current document and the document specified by the `href` attribute. The value of this attribute is a space-separated list of *linktypes*.

rev

> `rev=linktype`

This attribute describes the reverse link from the document specified in the `href` attribute to the current document. The value of this attribute is a space-separated list of *linktypes*.

shape

> `shape= default | circle | rect | poly`

This attribute describes the shape of one area on an image map. The **default** setting specifies the entire image. A **circle** needs to have its center point and radius specified. A **rect**angle uses two points, one describing the upper left corner and the other describing the lower right corner. A **poly**gon needs the corner points of all the edges of the shape specified.

style

> `style=style descriptors`

This attribute applies specific style-sheet information to one particular element.

tabindex

> `tabindex=number`

This attribute provides the position of the current element within the overall tabbing order of the document.

target

> `target=frame-target`

This attribute specifies the destination frame of the link's reference document.

title

> `title=text`

This attribute provides annotation information to the element.

type

> `type=content-type`

This attribute specifies the MIME type of the document being linked to.

Example

The following example uses a variety of A links to jump internally within a document, send e-mail, open an FTP site, link to another HTML document on the same server, and link to an HTML document on a remote server.

ON THE CD-ROM

Look for **a.htm** on the accompanying CD-ROM.

```
<HTML>
<HEAD>
<TITLE>Dectiod - Uses Links</TITLE>
</HEAD>

<BODY bgcolor="#FFFFFF" background="cartbkg.jpg">
<p align="center"><img src="cartoon.jpg" width="400" height="210">
</P>
<H1 align="center"><font face="Verdana, Arial, Helvetica, sans-
serif" color="#FF3300">DECTOID
  <BR>
  - The Scourge of the Universe -</FONT></H1>
<TABLE border="1" width="75%" align="center">
  <TR>
    <TD colspan="2">
      <DIV align="center">
      <FONT size="+1" face="Verdana, Arial, Helvetica, sans-serif"
      color="#CC3300"> WATCH OUT!</font>
      <font size="+1" face="Verdana, Arial, Helvetica, sans-
      serif">
        Dectoid is after YOU. <BR>
        If you haven't deduced the despoiling destruction that
        Dectoid delivers on the desolate Universe, hold onto your
        derriere, you're about to be devastated.<BR>
        <BR>
        <a href="#contactinfo">Contact us for more
        information.</a>
        </font>
         </div>
    </TD>
  </TR>
  <TR>
    <TD width="49%" valign="top">
      <P><font size="+2" face="Verdana, Arial, Helvetica, sans-
      serif">
       The Story:</FONT></P>
      <P><FONT face="Verdana, Arial, Helvetica, sans-serif"
      size="+1">Decature is the creation of <a
      href="drdec.html">Dr. Decmented.</a> He was once a great
      geneticist working for the Decathlon Federal Government. One
      day, a huge explosion shook his laboratory while he was
```

a
b
c

working with the genetic material of a Giant Red Octopus,
and a blow-up Happy Face doll. The explosion merged their
materials, and the evil creature known as Dectoid was born.
</FONT></P>
<P><FONT face="Verdana, Arial, Helvetica, sans-serif"
size="+1">
The world has never been the same . . . and never will be
again.</FONT></P>
</TD>
<TD width="51%" valign="top">
<P><FONT size="+2" face="Verdana, Arial, Helvetica, sans-
serif">Other Links:</FONT></P>
<UL>
  <LI><FONT size="+1" face="Verdana, Arial, Helvetica, sans-
  serif">
    <A href="http://cyclone.cs.clemson.edu/%7Eshughes/
    scooby/villains.html">
    Scooby Doo Villains</A></FONT></LI>
  <LI><FONT size="+1" face="Verdana, Arial, Helvetica, sans-
  serif">
    <A href="http://www.paramount.com/virtuosity/index.
    html">
    Virtuosity</A></FONT></LI>
  <LI><FONT size="+1" face="Verdana, Arial, Helvetica, sans-
  serif">
    <A href="http://www.calweb.com/%7Efrawgboy/index.
    htm"> Star Wars
    </A></FONT></LI>
  <LI><FONT size="+1" face="Verdana, Arial, Helvetica, sans-
  serif">
    <A href="http://www.foxkids.com/thexmen.htm">X-MEN
    </A></FONT></LI>
  <LI><FONT size="+1" face="Verdana, Arial, Helvetica, sans-
  serif">
    <A href="http://www.foxkids.com/spidrman.htm"> Spider-
    Man
    </A></FONT></LI>
  <LI><FONT size="+1" face="Verdana, Arial, Helvetica, sans-
  serif">
    <A href="http://www.netside.com/%7Echl3/toon96ls.
    html">
    Hulk
    </A></FONT></LI>

```
          <LI><FONT size="+1" face="Verdana, Arial, Helvetica, sans-
          serif">
               <A href="http://www.batman-superman.com/superman/
               cmp/index.html">
               Superman
               </A></FONT></LI>
          <LI><FONT face="Verdana, Arial, Helvetica, sans-serif"
          size="+1">
               <A href="http://www.batmantas.com/">
               Batman
             </A></FONT></LI>
          <LI><FONT size="+1" face="Verdana, Arial, Helvetica, sans-
          serif">
               <A href="http://www.foxkids.com/nthome.htm"> Teenage
               Mutant Ninja Turtles
               </A></FONT></LI>
       </UL>
     </TD>
   </TR>
</TABLE>
<P align="center">
<FONT size="+2" color="#CC3300">DECATURE Creation Staff
<A name="contactinfo"></A></FONT><BR>
  101010 Decaway Ave.<BR>
  Dectune, DE 00011</P>
<P align="center">(555) 111 - 2222<BRr>
  email:
<A href="mailto:dectoid@decature.com"> dectoid@decature.com</A>
</P>
</BODY>
</HTML>
```

CROSS-REFERENCE
See **Anchor**, **<LINK>**, **<AREA>**, and **<MAP>**.

<ABBR>

Element

HTML

Start Tag: Required
End Tag: Required

This element displays abbreviations within your HTML document. You should surround abbreviations such as CGI, WWW, HTML, SCUBA, SGML, and MathML with ABBR tags. Although you are not required to use the ABBR element, you should if you plan to adjust abbreviations using style sheets.

Attributes

class

```
class="cdata-list"
```

This attribute assigns a class name to an element. User agents use classes to group specific types of information for later use.

id

```
id="name"
```

This attribute assigns a name to an element.

lang

```
lang="language code"
```

This attribute specifies the language that renders an element and its values.

onclick

```
onclick=script
```

This attribute takes effect when a user clicks the button on a pointing device while the pointer is over an on-screen element.

ondblclick

```
ondblclick=script
```

This attribute takes effect when a user double-clicks the button on a pointing device while the pointer is over an on-screen element.

onkeydown

> onkeydown=*script*

This attribute takes effect when a user presses a key while the pointer is over an on-screen element.

onkeypress

> onkeypress=*script*

This attribute takes effect when a user either presses or releases a key while the pointer is over an on-screen element.

onkeyup

> onkeyup=*script*

This attribute takes effect when a user releases a key while the pointer is over an on-screen element.

onmousedown

> onmousedown=*script*

This attribute takes effect when a user presses the button on a pointing device while the pointer is over an on-screen element.

onmousemove

> onmousemove=*script*

This attribute becomes active when a user moves the mouse while the pointer is over an on-screen element.

onmouseout

> onmouseout=*script*

This attribute becomes active when a user moves the mouse pointer away from an on-screen element.

onmouseover

> onmouseover=*script*

This attribute becomes active when a user moves the mouse pointer over an on-screen element.

onmouseup

> onmouseup=*script*

This attribute takes effect when a user releases the button on a pointing device while the pointer is over an on-screen element.

style

```
style=style descriptors
```

This attribute applies specific style-sheet information to one particular element.

title

```
title=text
```

This attribute provides annotation information to the element to which it is applied.

Example

ON THE CD-ROM

Look for **abbr.htm** on the accompanying CD-ROM.

```
<HTML>
<HEAD>
   <TITLE> Military Directions - Can you understand
them?</TITLE>
</HEAD>
<BODY>
   <IMG src="millogo.jpg" alt = "Jabberwakki Base Logo">
   <H1> Jabberwakki Base -  Wonderland, LC </H1>
<P>
   <STRONG> Need directions to the Golf Course…</STRONG>
   <P>To find the <ABBR>CBPO</ABBR> you need to go down
McKinley about 1 Click at The <ABBR>401 SGS</ABBR> turn Left
and go three blocks. Turn Right at the <ABBR>MAC</ABBR>
terminal and Go down past the <ABBR>BX</ABBR> and take the
next left. Go two blocks north on Jackson and you will see the
<ABBR>542 CES</ABBR> on the left and the <ABBR>403 POL
</ABBR>on the right go to the next street turn right and you
will find the <ABBR>5092 CBPO</ABBR> there.
</BODY>
</HTML>
```

CROSS-REFERENCE

See **<EM>**, **<STRONG>**, **<CITE>**, **<DFN>**, **<CODE>**, **<SAMP>**, **<KBD>**, **<VAR>**, and **<ACRONYM>**.

Absolute Length

Concept

CSS

Absolute lengths do not change to accommodate the user agent or rendering style of a user agent. Use them only when you know the physical properties of the output medium. You create absolute lengths with the following units: in (inches), cm (centimeters), mm (millimeters), pt (points), and pc (picas).

Example

The following code examples show you a variety of ways to use absolute lengths.

```
P { margin: 0.5in } /* inches, 1in = 2.54cm */
H1 { line-height: 3cm } /* centimeters */
DIV { word-spacing: 4mm } /* millimeters */
B { font-size: 12pt } /* points, 1pt = 1/72 in */
ADDRESS { font-size: 1pc } /* picas, 1pc = 12pt */
```

 CROSS-REFERENCE
See **length property** and **Absolute Value**.

Absolute Positioning

Concept

An *absolutely positioned* element is placed in reference to a containing block. Because of the type of position it holds, the element establishes a new containing block for descendent boxes. The contents of absolutely positioned elements do not flow around other boxes, so they may obscure the contents of other boxes displayed on the document. Absolutely positioned elements have no impact on the flow of their following siblings, so elements that follow the absolutely positioned one act as if it were not there. If you position an element using absolute positioning, the elements that follow it are positioned with respect to the previous floating box.

In *fixed positioning* (a variant of absolute positioning), the user agent establishes fixedly positioned containing boxes. If you are viewing a document composed of continuous media, the fixed box will not move when you scroll the document. If the fixed box is located on paged media, it always appears at the end of each page. This enables you to place a footer or header on a document or a signature at the end of a series of one-page letters.

a
b
c

Example

You can use fixed and absolute positioning to create a frame-like layout similar to the screen shown in Figure A-1. Use the code following the image to create this screen layout in HTML.

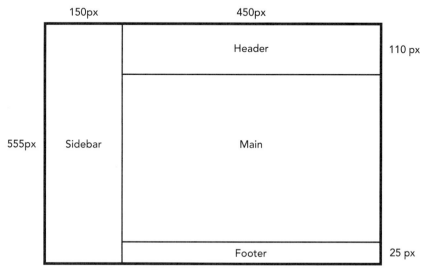

Figure A-1 A frame-like layout

ON THE CD-ROM

Look for **absolutepos.htm** on the accompanying CD-ROM.

```
<HTML>
<HEAD>
<TITLE>Absolute and Fixed Positioning</TITLE>
</HEAD>
<BODY bgcolor="#FFFFFF">
<DIV id="sidebar" style="position:absolute; left:0px; top:0px;
width:150px; height:555px; z-index:1">
  <P><IMG src="boot.gif" width="150" height="55"></P>
  <P><IMG src="bootbut1.gif" width="150" height="100"></P>
  <P><IMG src="bootbut3.gif" width="150" height="100"></P>
  <P><IMG src="bootbut2.gif" width="150" height="100"></P>
  <P><FONT color="#006600">Check these links out!</font></P>
  <P><IMG src="boot2.gif" width="150" height="55"></P>
</DIV>
<DIV id="heading" style="position:absolute; left:150px;
top:0px; width:450px; height:110px; z-index:2">
<CENTER>
```

```
<IMG src="tracks.gif" width="400" height="100">
</CENTER>
</DIV>
<DIV id="footer" style="position:absolute; left:150px;
top:528px; width:450px; height:25px; z-index:4">
  <DIV align="center"><font color="#006600">In a silly mood I
made this site.
     - Heather</FONT></DIV>
</DIV>
<DIV id="mainscreen" style="position:absolute; left:150px;
top:110px; width:450px; height:420px; z-index:3">
  <P align="center">Cock-a-doodle-do,<BR>
    My dame has lost her shoe.< BR >
    My Master's lost his fiddling stick<BR>
    And knows not what to do.</P>
  <P align="center">Cock-a-doodle-do,<BR>
    What is my dame to do?< BR >
    Till master finds his fiddling stick,<BR>
    She'll dance without her shoe.</P>
  <P align="center">Cock-a-doodle-do,<br>
    My dame has found her shoe,<br>
    And master's found his fiddling stick.<br>
    Sing doodle-doodle-doo!</P>
  <P align="center">Cock-a-doodle-do,<br>
    My dame will dance with you,<br>
    While master fiddles his fiddling stick<br>
    For dame and doodle-doo.</P>
  <P align="center">- Mother Goose - </P>
  </DIV>
</BODY>
</HTML>
```

Absolute Value

Concept

Absolute values are used to define explicit parameters for document objects. These values can be set by using scripts that work on the attributes that can be applied to the objects being configured.

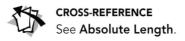

CROSS-REFERENCE
See **Absolute Length**.

Absolute Size

Concept

CROSS-REFERENCE
See **Absolute Length**.

<ABSTRACT>

Element

CDF and OSD

Start Tag: Required (OSD & CDF)
End Tag: Required (OSD & CDF)

For all practical purposes, the ABSTRACT element in both OSD and CDF disperses information about the channel or software being discussed, like an abstract at the beginning of a document. Because there are no character restrictions on the size of the ABSTRACT, you can use it to describe fully the purpose and contents of both software and pushed channels.

Example (OSD)

This example uses the ABSTRACT tag to describe a company's requirements concerning the use of a program installed on its desktop machines.

```
<SOFTPKG>
   <ABSTRACT>
   Total Recollection, a day timer and contact manager from
Recog Software, Inc. This software should be in use by all
members of the sales and marketing force. It can also be used
by any other staff after receiving permission from the Network
Administrator.
   </ABSTRACT>
</SOFTPKG>
```

Example (CDF)

This example uses the ABSTRACT tag to describe the channel contents pushed onto the viewers' machines.

```
<CHANNEL>
   <ABSTRACT>
```

```
    This site keeps you up to date and informed on all the
latest changes and developments associated with Recog
Software's latest software products. Through this channel you
can access our online store or read the latest product reviews
from the top magazines in the computer industry.
    </ABSTRACT>
</CHANNEL>
```

Elements (OSD)

This is a child element of

SOFTPKG

Elements (CDF)

This is a child element of

CHANNEL

Access Keys

Concept

 **CROSS-REFERENCE**
See **accesskey**.

Accessibility

Concept

A wide variety of changes have been implemented in HTML 4.0 to accommodate the vast diversity of user levels and needs. These improvements include the following:

- IMG elements now **require** an alt attribute to make the object fully HTML 4.0 compliant, although the image will render with or without the attribute.
- Distinctions have been made between the document structure and its presentation, making it easier to control appearances for specific media types.

- Better and more advanced forms that enable users to use access keys, group form controls, group `SELECT` options, and use active labels are now available.
- The `title` and `lang` attributes are supported for all elements.
- A wider range of supported media types such as TTY, TV, Braille, and speech synthesizers are included.
- The `ABBR` and `ACRONYM` elements have been added.
- Improved client-side image maps using the `MAP` element can incorporate both text and image links.
- More descriptive definitions for laying out tables have been added, including captions, column groups, and methods for nonvisual rendering.
- Long descriptions are now available for tables, images, and frames, to name a few.
- You can now use the `OBJECT` element to mark up a text description of included objects.

CROSS-REFERENCE
See **accesskey**, **alt**, **longdesc**, **noframes**, **noscript**, and **style sheets**.

accesskey

Attribute

HTML

An *access key* is a single keystroke assigned by a document author that enables a document reader to activate a link or immediately to select a form input field. These keys are similar in use to the underlined characters found on menu items in most Windows-compliant software products. When you press Alt+F in a Windows product, you most often open the File menu. When you press **Alt+F** in an HTML document that has defined access keys, you automatically activate the element assigned the F key.

The syntax for the `accesskey` attribute is

```
accesskey="character"
```

Values
"character"

This can be any alphanumeric character found within the document character set, which typically consists of the letters A–Z and a–z and the numerals 0–9.

Example

The following lines of code apply an access key to a link for easy maneuverability.

```
<P>
<A accesskey="H" rel="contents"
href="mailto:htmlref@catsback.com">
HTML Master Reference Contact Info</A>
```

Elements

A	AREA	BUTTON	INPUT
LABEL	LEGEND	TEXTAREA	

<ACRONYM>

Element

HTML

Start Tag: Required
End Tag: Required

This element displays acronyms within your HTML documents. You should surround words such as *SCUBA* with `<ACRONYM>` tags. Although this is not necessary for most documents, users of style sheets who wish acronyms to have a specific appearance must use these tags.

Attributes

class

```
class="cdata-list"
```

This attribute assigns a class name to an element. User agents use classes to group specific types of information for later use.

id

```
id="name"
```

This attribute assigns a name to an element.

lang

```
lang="language code"
```

This attribute specifies the language that renders an element and its values.

onclick

```
onclick=script
```

This attribute takes effect when a user clicks the button on a pointing device while the pointer is over an on-screen element.

ondblclick

```
ondblclick=script
```

This attribute takes effect when a user double-clicks the button on a pointing device while the pointer is over an on-screen element.

onkeydown

```
onkeydown=script
```

This attribute takes effect when a user presses a key while the pointer is over an on-screen element.

onkeypress

```
onkeypress=script
```

This attribute takes effect when a user either presses or releases a key while the pointer is over an on-screen element.

onkeyup

```
onkeyup=script
```

This attribute takes effect when a user releases a key while the pointer is over an on-screen element.

onmousedown

```
onmousedown=script
```

This attribute takes effect when a user presses the button on a pointing device while the pointer is over an on-screen element.

onmousemove

```
onmousemove=script
```

This attribute becomes active when a user moves the mouse while the pointer is over an on-screen element.

onmouseout

```
onmouseout=script
```

This attribute becomes active when a user moves the mouse pointer away from an on-screen element.

onmouseover

```
onmouseover=script
```

This attribute becomes active when a user moves the mouse pointer over an on-screen element.

onmouseup

```
onmouseup=script
```

This attribute takes effect when a user releases the button on a pointing device while the pointer is over an on-screen element.

style

```
style=style descriptors
```

This attribute applies specific style-sheet information to one particular element.

title

```
title=text
```

This attribute provides annotation information to the element it is applied to.

Example

ON THE CD-ROM

Look for **acronym.htm** on the accompanying CD-ROM.

```
<HTML>
<HEAD>
<TITLE>SCUBA - and Acronyms</TITLE>
<style type="text/css">
<!—
acronym {  font-family: Arial, Helvetica, sans-serif;
           font style: italic;
           line-height: 2em;
           text-decoration: underline;
           letter-spacing: 1em;
           color: #660066}
—>
</STYLE>
</HEAD>
<BODY bgcolor="#FFFFFF">
<TABLE border="1" width="75%">
  <TR>
    <TD width="32%">
```

```
      <IMG src="scuba.gif" width="200" height="600">
    </TD>
    <TD width="68%" valign="top">
      <H1 align="center">
      <FONT color="#0033CC">Death Valley SCUBA Club</FONT>
      </H1>
      <P align="center"><FONT color="#660099" size="+1">
      Come explore the vast  unknown caverns of water<BR>
        under the world's hottest valley.</FONT ></P>
      <HR>
      <P align="left">We have three <ACRONYM>SCUBA</ACRONYM>
Masters who lead every exploration into the caves, and you must
have a currently valid  dive certificate before you can book a
tour. All of our equipment is inspected daily for wear and
mechanical malfunctions. You are also welcome to bring
your own equipment, with proof of insurance of course.</P>
      <P align="left">Each <ACRONYM>SCUBA</ACRONYM> Master
carries an underwater
<ACRONYM>radio</ACRONYM> just in case someone encounters a
problem. Every trip has a backup team available for rescue
operations, and our local county Sheriff's Rescue Squad are all
certified divers with many hours spent in our caverns.</P>
      <HR>
      <P align="left">If you would be interested in one of our
trips, please contact
us at:</P>
      <P align="center">Death Valley SCUBA Club<BR>
        1813 Underwater Rd<BR>
        Death Valley, CA 99906</P>
      <P align="center">-or-</P>
      <P align="center"><A href="mailto:scubadeath@deathvalley.
net">scubadeath@deathvalley. net</A></P>
    </TD>
  </TR>
  </TABLE>
</BODY>
</HTML>
```

CROSS-REFERENCE
See **<EM>**, **<STRONG>**, **<CITE>**, **<DFN>**, **<CODE>**, **<SAMP>**, **<KBD>**,
<VAR>, and **<ABBR>**.

action

Attribute

HTML

This attribute identifies the address to deliver the form data to. You can use the address of another HTTP site or a program, or you can submit the form data to an e-mail address through a `mailto:` URI.

Values
"uri"

This is the address to which all of the form data is delivered. It must be either a valid HTTP processing engine or a valid mailto: e-mail address. When entering the URI, you should be aware of the case sensitivity of most URIs.

Example
The following code submits form information to an e-mail recipient.

```
<FORM action="mailto:htmlref@catsback.com" method="post">
   Name: <INPUT type="text" name="fname"><BR>
   Question: <INPUT type="text" name="question"><BR>
   Email Addy: <INPUT type="text" name="email"><BR>
   <INPUT type="submit" name="submit">
</FORM>
```

Elements

FORM

Active

Pseudo-Class

CROSS-REFERENCE
See **:active**.

Active Channel

Concept

Microsoft has implemented support for Channels with its Internet Explorer 4.0 Web browser. A Channel is a Web site specifically designed to deliver information across the Internet to an individual's computer and then to update that information automatically on a regularly scheduled basis. Channel readers can receive fresh content daily. An Active Channel works by collecting a list of "subscribed" users and then using "push" technology to distribute its updated information.

 CROSS-REFERENCE
See **Active Desktop**, **CDF**, and **Push**.

Active Desktop

Concept

The Active Desktop is only available in Internet Explorer browsers, Version 4.0 and higher. It serves to integrate the Web browser software into the remainder of the Windows operating system. This provides Windows users with a completely Web-integrated operating system that flows over into many of their other activities. The Active Desktop is composed of two distinct layers. The first is a transparent layer that contains the existing desktop shortcuts. If you turn off Active Desktop in your Windows 95 Display Properties, this is the layer that is left. The second layer is an opaque background HTML layer that can display any HTML-based item, such as ActiveX components, Java scripts, and links to HTML documents on the Internet or a company's intranet.

This background HTML layer is 100-percent customizable by users, corporations, or Internet Content Providers (ICPs). Because of its customizable nature, you can use the Active Desktop as a launching base for programs, documents, and files and as an information resource for individuals who thrive on keeping up-to-date with the latest feats of the "movers and shakers."

Installing Internet Explorer 4.0 affects the functioning of many of your desktop programs. For example, the My Computer icon enables you to view in both the standard Explorer mode and the WebView mode. The WebView mode emulates the Active Desktop in a fashion by providing HTML-style links to each file and program found within your current system.

On the Active Desktop's HTML layer, the HTML-based entities can be any size, shape, or color and can display any type of HTML content, including images, dynamic characters, scripts, ActiveX components, and channels. Because of their flexibility, users of Windows 95 can create automatically updated Web pages from their desktops.

CROSS-REFERENCE
See **Active Channel** and **CDF**.

activeElement

Property

DHTML

This read-only document object command identifies the element that currently has the focus on the HTML document.

Its syntax is

```
object.activeElement
```

Objects

document

CROSS-REFERENCE
See **:active** and **activekey**.

ActiveX

Concept

ActiveX, also referred to as COM by Microsoft followers, is a concept that Microsoft originated to manipulate third-generation OLE controls across the Internet or other high-latency networks. ActiveX enables document creators to integrate controls acting on Web-based information directly into the browser software. Three types of ActiveX controls are commonly used on the Internet—those that run miniature programs on HTML pages, those that play special content through your Web browser, and those that Web developers use when creating advanced documents.

CROSS-REFERENCE
See **CDF** and **Active (Content)**.

add

Method

DHTML

This document object method adds an element to a specified collection, but first you must create the element by using the `createElement` method.

The syntax for this command is

```
object.add(element [, index])
```

NOTE

If you wish to add an additional `AREA` element, you must do this after the document has been fully loaded. Any attempt to do this "inline" will cause a runtime error.

Parameters

element

This is the name of the element to add.

index

This value is optional, although it specifies the position of the new element within the collection. The default position in which to place these elements is at the end of the collection.

Collections

areas   options

CROSS-REFERENCE

See **remove**.

addImport

Method

DHTML

Use this scripting method to add a style sheet to the `imports` collection or to return an integer identifying the position of an imported style sheet. But first you must create the style sheet by using the `createElement` method.

The syntax for this command is

```
integer = stylesheet.addImport(url [, index])
```

Parameters
url

This contains a string that specifies the location of the style sheet's source file.

index

This parameter is optional, although it is a zero-based integer that specifies the position of the style sheet in the collection. The default position in which to place a style sheet is at the end of the collection.

CROSS-REFERENCE
See **<STYLE>**, **style sheets**, and **Cascading Style Sheets**.

addReadRequest

Method

DHTML

This document scripting command adds an entry to the read-request queue. The read-request queue is a list of questions about the readers of your page that you, the document author, wish to have answered. It can only be used with the userProfile object.

The syntax for the command is

```
navigator.userProfile.addReadRequest(attributeName
[, isRequired], success)
```

Parameters
attributeName

This identifies the vCard name to alter. If this name is not accepted, the request is ignored, and nothing is added to the queue.

isRequired

This parameter is optional. Internet Explorer ignores it.

success

This parameter returns either a TRUE or FALSE value. If the request has been added to the queue successfully, TRUE is the result. If the result is FALSE, it could mean that either the attribute name was not recognized or the attribute had already appeared in the queue.

CROSS-REFERENCE
See **profile**.

<ADDRESS>

Element

HTML

Start Tag: Required
End Tag: Required

This element shows contact information for either an entire document or a section of the document. You can use it to identify an individual to contact about problems concerning a form, a frame, or a specific segment of images. Although most browsers do not do anything specific with the ADDRESS elements other than change the general appearance of the text they contain, other user agents may use them to parse data or import information into a database.

Attributes
class

```
class="cdata-list"
```

This attribute assigns a class name to an element. User agents use classes to group specific types of information for later use.

id

```
id="name"
```

This attribute assigns a name to an element.

lang

```
lang="language code"
```

This attribute specifies the language that renders an element and its values.

onclick

```
onclick=script
```

This attribute takes effect when a user clicks the button on a pointing device while the pointer is over an on-screen element.

ondblclick

> ondblclick=*script*

This attribute takes effect when a user double-clicks the button on a pointing device while the pointer is over an on-screen element.

onkeydown

> onkeydown=*script*

This attribute takes effect when a user presses a key while the pointer is over an on-screen element.

onkeypress

> onkeypress=*script*

This attribute takes effect when a user either presses or releases a key while the pointer is over an on-screen element.

onkeyup

> onkeyup=*script*

This attribute takes effect when a user releases a key while the pointer is over an on-screen element.

onmousedown

> onmousedown=*script*

This attribute takes effect when a user presses the button on a pointing device while the pointer is over an on-screen element.

onmousemove

> onmousemove=*script*

This attribute becomes active when a user moves the mouse while the pointer is over an on-screen element.

onmouseout

> onmouseout=*script*

This attribute becomes active when a user moves the mouse pointer away from an on-screen element.

onmouseover

> onmouseover=*script*

This attribute becomes active when a user moves the mouse pointer over an on-screen element.

a
b
c

onmouseup

```
onmouseup=script
```

This attribute takes effect when a user releases the button on a pointing device while the pointer is over an on-screen element.

Example

The following example code uses the ADDRESS element to set apart the mailing addresses listed in a short address book that uses positioned SPAN elements.

ON THE CD-ROM

Look for **address.htm** on the accompanying CD-ROM.

```
<HTML>
<HEAD>
<TITLE>My Address Book</TITLE>
</HEAD>

<BODY bgcolor="#FFFFFF">
<SPAN id="Layer1" style="position:absolute; left:82px;
top:62px; width:219px; height:243px; z-index:1">
<IMG src="addylabel.gif" width="200" height="200"></span>
<DIV id="Layer2" style="position:absolute; left:305px;
top:61px; width:213px; height:239px; z-index:2">
  <ADDRESS>
  <P><FONT face="Verdana, Arial, Helvetica, sans-serif"
color="#006633">If you would like to <BR>
    read my personal <BR>
    address book, you will need to contact me <BR>
    at:</FONT></P>
  <P><FONT face="Verdana, Arial, Helvetica, sans-serif"
color="#006633">Heather Williamson<BR>
    htmlref@catsback.com</FONT></P>
  <P><FONT face="Verdana, Arial, Helvetica, sans-serif"
color="#006633">Last Updated:<BR>
    Oct. 15, 1998</FONT></P></ADDRESS>
</DIV>
<IMG src="book.gif" width="533" height="394">
</BODY>
</HTML>
```

> **CROSS-REFERENCE**
> See **<EM>**, **<STRONG>**, **<CITE>**, **<DFN>**, **<CODE>**, **<SAMP>**, **<KBD>**, **<VAR>**, **<ACRONYM>**, and **<ABBR>**.

addRule

Method

DHTML

This document object scripting method creates new style rules for `styleSheet` objects. It can also return the index value of that rule in the `Rules` collection, but this value is reserved, so you shouldn't use it. You can add rules to disabled style sheets if you wish, although they do not apply to the document until the style sheet is enabled.

The syntax of this command is

```
integer = object.addRule(selector, style [, index])
```

Parameters
selector

This string lists the types of HTML elements for which the rule is being added.

style

This style sheet command, such as "font-family: Arial," is assigned as part of the rule.

index

This optional integer-based parameter specifies where to add the new style rule in the `Rules` collection. By default, a rule is added to the end of the collection.

Example
The following new rule searches for text displayed in bold font style within `DIV` and `P` elements, and then changes the text to green.

```
var add_rule;
add_rule = styleSheets[6].addRule("DIV P B", "color:green",
0);
```

Objects

styleSheet

> **CROSS-REFERENCE**
> See **Style Sheet**, **Collections**, and **<STYLE>**.

alert

Method

DHTML

This scripting method displays an Alert dialog box with a message and an OK button.

The syntax of this command is

```
object.alert([message])
```

Parameters

message

This optional parameter provides you with the string message to display in your dialog box.

Objects

window

CROSS-REFERENCE
See **status**, **write**, **writeln**, and **error**.

align

Attribute

HTML

The `align` attribute is used differently depending upon the element that it is used with. In general, it controls the horizontal and vertical alignment of text and objects within the bounds of a containing block or the document page.

Values: <CAPTION>

bottom

This value forces the caption to appear at the bottom of the table.

left

This value directs the caption to appear to the left edge of the table.

right

This value directs the caption to appear to the right edge of the table.

top

This value forces the caption to appear at the top of the table.

Values: <APPLET>, <FRAME>, <IMG>, <INPUT>, <OBJECT>

bottom

When you reference an object, this value aligns that object with the bottom of the current text line.

middle

When you reference an object, this value aligns that object with the middle of the current text line.

top

When you reference an object, this value aligns that object with the top of the current text line.

Values: <LEGEND>

bottom

This value aligns text to the bottom of the form `fieldset`.

left

This value aligns text to the left of the form `fieldset`.

right

This value aligns text to the right of the form `fieldset`.

top

This value aligns text to the top of the form `fieldset`.

Values: <TABLE>, <HR>

center

In the case of a table or horizontal rule, this value centers the element in the document.

left

In the case of a table or horizontal rule, this value left-justifies the element with the document.

right

In the case of a table or horizontal rule, this value right-justifies the element with the document.

Values: <DIV>, <H1–H6>, <P>

center

This value centers the line of text between the document margins.

Justify

This value justifies the line of text to both the left and right document margins.

left

This value makes the line of text left-justified with the document margins.

right

This value makes the line of text right-justified with the document margins.

Values: <COL>, <COLGROUP>, <TBODY>, <TD>, <TFOOT>, <TH>, <THEAD>, <TR>

center

This value centers both the text and data within a cell or column.

char

This value aligns the contents of the cell against a specific character, such as a period or comma.

justify

This value justifies the text and data to both the left and right cell margins.

left

This value left-justifies both the data and text within the table cell.

right

This value right-justifies both the line of text and the data within the cell.

Example

The following example code uses the `align` attribute to control the placement of text within a table. The table displays financial data for a small company.

ON THE CD-ROM

Look for **align.htm** on the accompanying CD-ROM.

```
<HTML>
<HEAD>
<TITLE>Aligning a Table</TITLE>
</HEAD>
```

```
<BODY BGCOLOR="#ffffff">
<H2><FONT FACE="Arial">Expected Cash Flow/Budget:</FONT></H2>
<TABLE WIDTH="75%" BORDER="1">
  <TR>
<TD> </TD>
<TD><B><FONT FACE="Times New Roman">Income:</FONT></B></TD>
<TD><B><FONT FACE="Times New Roman">Expense:</FONT></B></TD>
</TR>
<TR>
<TD><B><FONT FACE="Times New Roman">Operating Costs -
</FONT></B></TD>
<TD> </TD>
<TD> </TD>
</TR>
<TR>
<TD><FONT FACE="Times New Roman">Network Storage (after 7
months - $29.00/month)</FONT></TD>
<TD> </TD>
    <TD align="right"><FONT FACE="Times New Roman">
348.00</FONT></TD>
</TR>
<TR>
<TD><FONT FACE="Times New Roman">Internic Registration (after
2 years)</FONT></TD>
<TD> </TD>
    <TD align="right"><FONT FACE="Times New Roman">
50.00</FONT></TD>
</TR>
<TR>
<TD><FONT FACE="Times New Roman">Business Cards</FONT></TD>
<TD> </TD>
    <TD align="right"><FONT FACE="Times New Roman">
30.00</FONT></TD>
</TR>
<TR>
<TD><FONT FACE="Times New Roman">Business
Letterhead</FONT></TD>
<TD> </TD>
    <TD align="right"><FONT FACE="Times New Roman">
50.00</FONT></TD>
</TR>
<TR>
<TD> </TD>
<TD> </TD>
<TD> </TD>
```

```
</TR>
<TR>
<TD><B><FONT FACE="Times New Roman">Office Supplies</FONT>
</B></TD>
<TD> </TD>
<TD> </TD>
</TR>
<TR>
<TD><FONT FACE="Times New Roman">Printer Cartridges - Existing
HP Printer</FONT></TD>
<TD> </TD>
    <TD align="right"><FONT FACE="Times New Roman">
240.00</FONT></TD>
</TR>
<TR>
<TD><FONT FACE="Times New Roman">Bubble-Jet Print
Paper</FONT></TD>
<TD> </TD>
    <TD align="right"><FONT FACE="Times New Roman">
120.00</FONT></TD>
</TR>
<TR>
<TD><FONT FACE="Times New Roman">Printer Cartridges - Travel
Printer</FONT></TD>
<TD> </TD>
    <TD align="right"><FONT FACE="Times New Roman">
120.00</FONT></TD>
</TR>
<TR>
<TD><FONT FACE="Times New Roman">Miscellaneous Supplies
(Pencils, Notebooks, staples, Pens, Envelopes, File folders,
etc)</FONT></TD>
<TD> </TD>
    <TD align="right"><FONT FACE="Times New Roman">
90.00</FONT></TD>
</TR>
<TR>
<TD> </TD>
<TD> </TD>
<TD> </TD>
</TR>
<TR>
<TD><B><FONT FACE="Times New Roman">Facilities - operating out
of home office</FONT></B></TD>
<TD> </TD>
```

```
<TD> </TD>
</TR>
<TR>
<TD><FONT FACE="Times New Roman">Rent </FONT></TD>
<TD> </TD>
    <TD align="right"><FONT FACE="Times New Roman">
0.00</FONT></TD>
</TR>
<TR>
<TD><FONT FACE="Times New
Roman">Gas/Electricity/Oil</FONT></TD>
<TD> </TD>
    <TD align="right"><FONT FACE="Times New Roman">
0.00</FONT></TD>
</TR>
<TR>
<TD> </TD>
<TD> </TD>
<TD> </TD>
</TR>
<TR>
    <TD><B>Equipment</B> -</TD>
<TD> </TD>
<TD> </TD>
</TR>
<TR>
<TD><FONT FACE="Times New Roman">Equipment Maintenance
(maintenance plan)</FONT></TD>
<TD> </TD>
    <TD align="right"><FONT FACE="Times New Roman">
99.00</FONT></TD>
</TR>
<TR>
<TD><FONT FACE="Times New Roman">Equipment Purchase (other
than listed above)</FONT></TD>
<TD> </TD>
<TD> </TD>
</TR>
<TR>
<TD> </TD>
<TD> </TD>
<TD> </TD>
</TR>
<TR>
```

```
<TD><B><FONT FACE="Times New Roman">Estimated Accounts
Receivable</FONT></B></TD>
<TD> </TD>
<TD> </TD>
</TR>
<TR>
<TD><FONT FACE="Times New Roman">With Estimated 10 accounts (3
accounts are already in the process of signing up with
us.)</FONT></TD>
    <TD align="right"><FONT FACE="Times New Roman">
3000.00</FONT></TD>
<TD> </TD>
</TR>
<TR>
<TD><FONT FACE="Times New Roman">With Estimated Logo/Graphics
Work</FONT></TD>
    <TD align="right"><FONT FACE="Times New Roman">
450.00</FONT></TD>
<TD> </TD>
</TR>
<TR>
<TD> </TD>
<TD> </TD>
<TD> </TD>
</TR>
<TR>
<TD><B><FONT FACE="Times New Roman">Totals:</FONT></B></TD>
    <TD align="right"><B><FONT FACE="Times New Roman">
$3450.00</FONT></B></TD>
    <TD align="right"><B><FONT FACE="Times New
Roman">$1147.00</FONT></B></TD>
</TR>
</TABLE>
</BODY>
</HTML>
```

Elements

APPLET	CAPTION	COL	COLGROUP
DIV	FRAME	H1–H6	HR
IMG	INPUT	LEGEND	OBJECT
P	TABLE	TBODY	TD
TFOOT	TH	THEAD	TR

CROSS-REFERENCE
See **Alignment**.

Alignment

Concept

Many techniques are employed to control how objects line up on a document. Most of them are based on one of two types of alignment:

- **Baseline alignment**—This type of alignment is mostly used on fonts or objects that are being aligned with a font. The baseline of the font is the bottom edge of standard characters such as *a, e,* and *o* that have neither a tail nor a hat. This line serves as a means of aligning the top, bottom, or middle of an object or line of text.

- **Margin alignment**—This type of alignment is mainly used for objects that are going to be aligned in reference to the outside margins of a page.

Figure A-2 shows you a comparison between these two types of alignment.

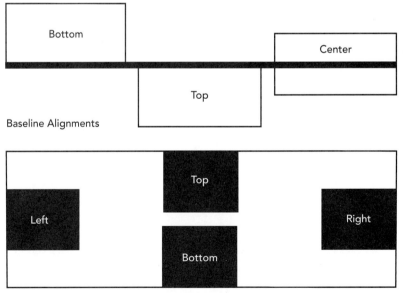

Figure A-2 This chart shows the two typical ways of aligning items using HTML: against a baseline or against a containment box margin.

In HTML documents, as in all other documents, you must have the ability to line up the objects and text that you place on a page. In the past, HTML was very limited. Other than using tables, you had very little control over the objects on your pages.

CROSS-REFERENCE
See **align**.

alink

Attribute

HTML

This attribute sets the color for an active link. Although this attribute has been deprecated in favor of the `:active` pseudo-class, it is still safe to use with all current browsers. It may be removed from use at a later date.

The syntax for `alink` is

```
alink=color
```

Values
color

The color can be either a valid HTML color name or a Hex value representing the RGB value of the color.

Example
In the following example code, the `alink` attribute turns all links in a document green when they are active.

```
<HTML>
<HEAD>
<TITLE> Use alink to change link colors </TITLE>
<BODY alink="green">
<H1> My Favorite Web Sites </H1>
    <A href="http://www.catsback.com/sbothum"> Shirly Bothum -
World Class Artist in Bronze </A>
    <A href="http://www.bluemountain.com"> Blue Mountain
Greeting Cards </A>
    <A href="http://www.homearts.com">HomeArts - Horoscopes
</A>
    <A href="http://www.cnn.com">CNN</A>
 </BODY>
</HTML>
```

Elements

BODY

CROSS-REFERENCE
See **color, Appendix A, alinkColor, :active, :hover,** and **:visited**.

alinkColor

Property

DHTML

This readable and writable script statement sets the color for an active link. The syntax of this command is

```
object.alinkColor[ = color]
```

Values

color

The color can be either a valid HTML color name or a hex value representing the RGB value of the color.

Objects

document

CROSS-REFERENCE
See **linkColor, vlinkColor, color, Appendix A, alinkColor, :active, :hover,** and **:visited**.

all

Collection

DHTML

This document object statement returns an object's reference to the collection of elements contained by the object. This collection includes one element object for each valid HTML tag set. It includes the HTML, HEAD, TITLE, and BODY elements regardless of whether they are included in the document. If the document contains invalid tags, the all collection contains a separate entry for each start and end tag of the invalid pair. The HTML source code orders all tags contained in the collection.

The syntax of this command is

```
object.all(index)
```

Parameters

index

> This optional parameter is the integer or string used to specify the index value of the element you are attempting to retrieve. Because all indices are zero-based, the first element, such as HTML, is identified as 0. A string value for the index is only valid if the element has been given a specific name through either the name or the id attributes.

Methods

> item   tags

Objects

applets	anchors	areas	cells
children	documents	elements	embeds
event	filters	forms	frames
images	links	options	rows
scripts			

Elements

A	ACRONYM	ADDRESS	APPLET
AREA	B	BASE	BASEFONT
BGSOUND	BIG	BLOCKQUOTE	BODY
BR	BUTTON	CAPTION	CENTER
CITE	CODE	COL	COLGROUP
COMMENT	DD	DEL	DFN
DIR	DIV	DL	DT
EM	EMBED	FIELDSET	FONT
FORM	FRAME	FRAMESET	H1–H6
HEAD	HR	HTML	IFRAME
IMG	INPUT	INS	KBD
LABEL	LEGEND	LI	LINK
LISTING	MAP	MARQUEE	MENU
OBJECT	OL	P	PLAINTEXT

PRE	S	SAMP	SCRIPT
SELECT	SMALL	SPAN	STRIKE
STRONG	STYLE	SUB	SUP
TABLE	TBODY	TD	TEXTAREA
TFOOT	TH	THEAD	TITLE
TR	TT	U	UL
VAR	XMP		

CROSS-REFERENCE
See **collections** and **elements**.

All

Media Group

CSS

Cascading Style Sheets, level 2, has defined the following media groups, which are referred to with `all`:

- Visual/Aural/Tactile
- Continuous/Paged
- Grid/Bitmap
- Interactive/Static

Each media group describes a specific type of medium. Many media types are identified as part of these groups. Most of the media types fall into multiple categories. For example, Visual media can be either Continuous, like a computer screen, or Paged, like a newspaper. The identified media types include aural, Braille, embossed, handheld, print, projection, screen, TTY, and TV.

CROSS-REFERENCE
See **Media Groups** and **Media Types**.

alt

Attribute

HTML

This attribute provides textual information for those elements such as APPLET, AREA, IMG, and INPUT that are not always displayed by user agents. When one of these objects is not displayed, the alt attribute's text content is displayed in its place. This lets the document reader know what was supposed to be in the document at that position, to prevent loss of any important information that those elements contained. The text also works in the place of an IMG or AREA element to serve as a link to other documents.

NOTE

Users who have no graphic displays, use agents with graphics turned off, or use browsers that don't support forms, can still view the pages fully by specifying alternate text. The same holds true for users who are visually impaired or those who use speech synthesizers.

When you are developing a page using alt text, you will not want to specify text for images used as formatting or as placeholders. All the text you place in an alt string should provide meaning for the page, not frustrate your readers with statements such as "silly link" that add no meaning to the document's contents.

NOTE

This attribute is required for both the IMG and AREA tags. It is optional for the APPLET and INPUT elements.

Values

text

This text string is displayed whenever the main element is not displayable for any reason.

Example

The following example creates an image map using AREA tags. All of the elements in this map are using the alt attribute.

ON THE CD-ROM

Look for **alt.htm** on the accompanying CD-ROM.

```
<HTML>
<HEAD>
```

```
<TITLE>Using the Alt Tag in an Image Map</TITLE>
</HEAD>

<BODY bgcolor="#FFFFFF">
<IMG src="bookstack.gif" width="450" height="365"
usemap="#bookstackmap" alt="Image Map linking to Web
Programming Related Sites">
<MAP name="bookstackmap">
  <AREA shape="poly"
coords="39,252,38,301,246,361,431,324,431,279,242,312,38,255"
href="xml.html" alt="Open XML Reference">
  < AREA shape="poly"
coords="250,249,406,224,402,278,238,308,7,241,8,180,254,249"
href="css.html" alt="Open CSS Reference">
  < AREA shape="poly"
coords="26,134,24,182,250,247,413,220,419,170,250,187,27,135"
href="dom.html" alt="Open DOM Reference">
  < AREA shape="poly"
coords="22,103,23,103,57,104,59,111,256,156,393,144,391,174,25
3,191,13,132,15,103,58,104" href="MathML.html" alt="Open
MathML Reference">
  < AREA shape="poly"
coords="69,42,60,109,255,157,416,142,429,77,266,83,66,42"
href="html.html" alt="Open HTML Reference">
  < AREA shape="poly"
coords="64,9,60,40,269,82,441,73,441,39,226,5,64,11"
href="java.html" alt="Open Java Reference">
</MAP>
</BODY>
</HTML>
```

Elements

APPLET   AREA IMG   INPUT

CROSS-REFERENCE
See **longdesc**.

Alternate Text

Concept

CROSS-REFERENCE
See **alt** and **longdesc**.

altHTML

Property

DHTML

This document object property executes an alternate script if the element fails to load properly. Because this property can be both read and set, you can change as well as retrieve its current value.

The syntax of this command is

```
object.altHTML
```

Elements

APPLET   OBJECT

altKey

Property

DHTML

Use this property to discover the current state of the ALT key on the keyboard. If the value of this property is TRUE, the key is currently pressed.

The syntax for this command is

```
object.altKey
```

Objects

event

Ancestor

Concept

When a user agent converts a document from its document language, the agent creates a document tree in which every element except one has exactly one parent element. The only exception to this is the root HTML element, which has no parents. A parent element is an ancestor to all of its child elements and their children. To make this simpler to understand, let's look at it graphically.

For example, if you were to evaluate the following HTML document

```
<HTML>
<TITLE>Example Document structure</TITLE>
<BODY>
    <H1>Document Trees</H1>
    <P>Here are some of my favorite one liners.
    <UL>
        <LI> Eagles may soar, but weasels don't get sucked into
jet engines.
        <LI> Early bird gets the worm, but the second mouse gets
the cheese.
        <LI> I intend to live forever - so far, so good.
        <LI>The only substitute for good manners is fast
reflexes.
        <LI>When everything's coming your way, you're in the
wrong lane.
        <LI>Ambition is a poor excuse for not having enough
sense to be lazy.
        <LI>If I worked as much as others, I would do as little
as they.
        <LI>Everyone has a photographic memory. Some don't have
film.
    </UL>
</BODY>
</HTML>
```

it would result in the document tree shown in Figure A-3.

NOTE

If a HEAD or BODY element is not a part of the document, it is inferred during the parsing of the document. This forces these elements to become part of the document tree and ancestors of other elements.

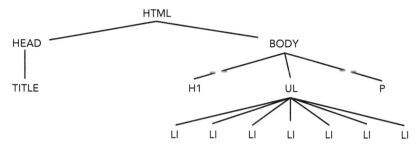

Figure A-3 Each element creates a node on this inverted tree, making it easy to see the relationships between each element contained within a document.

In Figure A-3, HTML is the root element with no parents and no ancestors. The HEAD element is inferred. Both the HEAD and BODY elements are children of HTML. This makes HTML both the parent and ancestor of these two elements. An element is an ancestor of another element if it is either the parent of that element or the parent of some other element that is an ancestor of the element. The HEAD element is the parent of TITLE, and HTML is the ancestor of TITLE.

On the second side of this document table, BODY is the child of HTML and the parent of H1, UL, and P. H1, UL, and P are siblings because they share the same parent. This makes BODY, UL, and HTML all ancestors of the LI elements, while H1 and P are not "related."

CROSS-REFERENCE
See **child**, **sibling**, **parent**, and **progenitor**.

Anchor

Concept

An anchor sets the boundaries on text or images used as links to other documents on the Web, intranet, or any other hypertext system. The first anchor is on the source document that contains the actual hypertext link. The destination anchor is on the document that is being linked to. Together these two anchors work to control the direction of the link between the resources. In some cases, the originating and destination anchors may be on the same document. In this case, the destination anchor can also be referred to as a target or a bookmark. Most user agents provide a mechanism for returning to an originating link after visiting a destination link, even when the documents being viewed do not track this type of information.

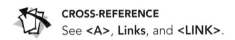

CROSS-REFERENCE
See **<A>**, **Links**, and **<LINK>**.

Anchor Pseudo-Classes

Concept

Anchor pseudo-classes are special pseudo-classes specifically designed to work with links and anchors. These classes were originally designed to give Cascading Style Sheets a means of affecting information that did not have any specific element defining it. Pseudo-classes are designed to look specifically at groups of events, such as all the left-hand pages of a document or all the links that have been visited. This makes these classes independent of the document tree created by user agents when the original HTML document is parsed.

:active

```
A:active {color: aqua}
```

The `:active` Anchor pseudo-class is applied only when the link is being selected by the user.

:hover

```
A:hover {color: red}
```

This Anchor pseudo-class is applied to all links that currently have the mouse pointer hovering over them.

:link

```
A:link {color: purple}
```

This Anchor pseudo-class is applied to all links that have not been selected.

:visited

```
A:visited {color: fuchsia}
```

This Anchor pseudo-class is applied to all links that have been viewed.

CROSS-REFERENCE
See **:active**, **:hover**, **:link**, **:visited**, and **pseudo-elements**.

anchors

Collection

DHTML

This object collection retrieves a list of all A elements with a `name=` and/or `id=` attribute. The compiled collection arranges all the elements in which they are read from the HTML source document.

The syntax of this command is

```
object.anchors(index)
```

Parameters

index

This optional integer or string index value identifies the element to be retrieved. Because all indexes are zero-based, the first Anchor on this document is indexed at 0.

NOTE

String indexes are only valid when the string is a name or identifier that has been used for at least one element in the document. Because this collection is indexed first by name and then by identifier, duplicate names are returned in a collection of their own. The names in this subcollection must then be referred to by their index positions in the subcollection. This makes assigning a separate name identifier to each anchor preferable.

Example

The following segment of code displays the `name` of the third element in an alert window.

```
<HTML>
<HEAD>
<TITLE>Anchors and names, and indexes</TITLE>
<BODY alink="green" >
<H1> My Favorite Web Sites </H1>
    <A name="a"> Shirly Bothum - World Class Artist in Bronze </A>
    <A name="b"> Blue Mountain Greeting Cards </A>
    <A name="c">HomeArts - Horoscopes </A>
    <A name="d">CNN</A>
<script>
window.alert(document.anchors(2).name);
</script>
</BODY>
</HTML>
```

Methods

items   tags

Objects

document

CROSS-REFERENCE
See **<A>**, **anchors**, **Links**, and **<LINK>**.

angle

Value

CSS

Angle values, displayed as `angle` in the attribute definitions, are used with aural style sheets. The format of this value consists of a signed character followed by a `number` and the unit identifier. The default value of the sign is positive. The only three legal angle unit identifiers are

- **deg**   degrees
- **grad** gradient
- **rad**   radians

NOTE
The user agent automatically normalizes the angle value, so a value of –30 degrees is equivalent to **330deg**.

CROSS-REFERENCE
See **length**, **number**, and **percentage**.

appCodeName

Property

DHTML

This scripting property retrieves the code name of the browser that is viewing the current document in a string format.

The syntax of this command is

```
object.appCodeName
```

Objects

navigator

CROSS-REFERENCE
See **appMinorVersion, appName, appVersion, browserLanguage, connection-Speed, cookieEnabled, cpuClass, onLine, platform, systemLanguage, userAgent, userLanguage,** and **userProfile.**

<APPLET>

Element

HTML

Start Tag: Required
End Tag: Required

This tag enables you to insert the code that calls a Java applet into your HTML document. This element has been deprecated in favor of the <OBJECT> element, although it is still supported for those browsers that otherwise could not use Java applets.

Attributes
align

```
align=bottom | middle | top
```

This attribute controls the visual alignment of the applet within its bounding box. A value of **top** aligns the objects against the box's top border, and a value of **bottom** places the object against the box's bottom. A value of **middle** vertically centers the object within the box.

alt

```
alt=text
```

This attribute provides you with alternate text to display when a user agent cannot show the applet.

archive

archive=*uri-list*

This attribute identifies the list of URIs or the resources that contain the classes and resources that need to be preloaded by the user agent. Each URI is separated by a comma.

class

class="*cdata-list*"

This attribute assigns a class name to an element. User agents use classes to group specific types of information for later use.

code

code=*cdata*

This attribute identifies the name of the class file containing the applet's compiled subclasses and the class file itself. You must use either a code or an object attribute in all APPLET specifications.

codebase

codebase=*URI*

This attribute specifies the base URI for the specified applet. When an applet is not specified, this attribute defaults to the same URI that is used for the containing document. You can only refer to the current directory and its subdirectories in this attribute. Any other values are invalid.

height

height=*length*

This attribute specifies the height of the applet's display area.

hspace

hspace=*length*

This attribute specifies the amount of white space to insert to the left and right of the applet box.

id

id="*name*"

This attribute assigns a name to an element. See the name attribute of this element to see the valid formats for the name.

name

name=*cdata*

This attribute gives the <APPLET> element a name that is used as an identifier when the <APPLET> element is used as a reference for other applets.

object=*cdata*

The value of this attribute identifies the resource containing a serialized representation of an applet's state. This, in plain English, is simply a way of identifying the current activity of an applet in a numerical format. This information is interpreted relative to the value of the applet's codebase attribute. The user agent uses the class name in this serialized data to retrieve the implementation from the class file or archive.

NOTE

Authors should use this feature with extreme caution. An applet should be stopped before it is serialized.

Document authors must provide either a code or an object attribute. If both of these attributes are supplied, they must provide the same class name, or else an error is created.

style

style=*style descriptors*

This attribute applies specific style-sheet information to one particular element.

title

title=*text*

This attribute provides annotation information to the element it is applied to.

vspace

vspace=length

This attribute specifies the amount of white space to insert above and below the applet box.

width

width=length

This attribute specifies the width of the applet's display area.

Example

The following code shows how to run a Java applet found on the JDK 1.1 CD-ROM. This class animates an image wishing everyone a Merry Christmas.

ON THE CD-ROM
Look for **applet.htm** on the accompanying CD-ROM.

```
<HTML>
<HEAD>
    <TITLE> Example using a Java Applet</TITLE>
</HEAD>
<BODY>
    <P> The following image is animated by a Java Class to add
motion and attraction to your document.
    <applet codebase="java" code=Animator.class width=460
height=160>
    <param name=imagesource value="java/images">
    <param name=backgroundcolor value="0xc0c0c0">
    <param name=endimage value=12>
    <param name=soundsource value="java/audio">
    <param name=soundtrack value=spacemusic.au>
    <param name=sounds
value="1.au|2.au|3.au|4.au|5.au|6.au|7.au|8.au|9.au|0.au">
    <param name=pause value=200>
    </applet>

</BODY>
</HTML>
```

CROSS-REFERENCE
See **<OBJECT>**.

applets

Collection

DHTML

This collection retrieves a list of all APPLET objects in the document.
The syntax of this command is

```
object.applets(index)
```

Parameters
index

This optional integer or string-index value identifies the element to be retrieved.
Because all indexes are zero-based, the first applet on this document is indexed at 0.

NOTE

String indexes are only valid when the string is a name or identifier that has been used for at least one element in the document. Because this collection is indexed first by name and then by identifier, duplicate names are returned in a collection of their own. The names in this subcollection must then be referred to by their index positions in the subcollection. This makes assigning a separate name identifier to each applet preferable.

Methods

> item   tags

Objects

> document

CROSS-REFERENCE
See **<APPLET>** and **<OBJECT>**.

Application Program Interface

Concept

The *Application Program Interface (API)* is the juncture between the operating system and the applications. This includes the methods that are employed by the application software when communicating with the operating system and the services that the operating system provides to the applications. Some of these services include the instructions for drawing windows, opening menus, and displaying message boxes. The operating system also controls the display colors of your applications for the most part.

An API can also provide an interface between high-level programming languages and other utilities and services. When serving this function, the main job of the API is to translate the calls and parameter lists from one format to another.

CROSS-REFERENCE
See **user agent**.

appMinorVersion

Property

DHTML

This script property only retrieves the user agent's minor version value. If used with Internet Explorer 4.01, it returns 1; with service pack additions, it returns the service pack number, such as `SR1`; and with Internet Explorer 5.0, it returns 0.

The syntax of this command is

```
stringVar=object.appMinorVersion
```

Objects

navigator

CROSS-REFERENCE
See **appCodename**, **appName**, **appVersion**, **browserLanguage**, **connection-Speed**, **cookieEnabled**, **cpuClass**, **onLine**, **platform**, **systemLanguage**, **userAgent**, **userLanguage**, and **userProfile**.

appName

Property

DHTML

This attribute retrieves the name of the user agent, most often a Web browser that is looking at the current document.

The syntax of this command is

```
stringVar=object.appName
```

Objects

navigator

CROSS-REFERENCE
See **appCodeName**, **appMinorVersion**, **appVersion**, **browserLanguage**, **connection-Speed**, **cookieEnabled**, **cpuClass**, **onLine**, **platform**, **systemLanguage**, **userAgent**, **userLanguage**, and **userProfile**.

appVersion

Property

DHTML

This property returns a string that shows the full version number of the browser or user agent being used.

The syntax of this command is

```
stringVar=object.appVersion
```

Objects

navigator

CROSS-REFERENCE

See **appCodeName**, **appMinorVersion**, **appName**, **browserLanguage**, **connectionSpeed**, **cookieEnabled**, **cpuClass**, **onLine**, **platform**, **system-Language**, **userAgent**, **userLanguage**, and **userProfile**.

archive

Attribute

HTML

This attribute works with both the `APPLET` and the `OBJECT` elements. When used with either element, it specifies a space-separated list of URIs. When used with the `APPLET` element, these URIs are for Java classes and other resources that need to be preloaded. When used with the `OBJECT` element, it contains a list of resources that are relevant to the object, which may include the resources specified by the `classid` and `data` attributes. You can use the archives listed for the `OBJECT` element to reduce the load time for your object.

The syntax for the archive attribute is

```
archive=uri-list
```

Values

uri-list

This is a space-separated list of URIs, both relative and absolute, that point to various resources on the Internet or local system that are to be used by the `OBJECT` or `APPLET` in question.

Elements

APPLET   OBJECT

 CROSS-REFERENCE
See **URI**, **href**, **codebase**, **src**, **object**, and **name**.

<AREA>

Element

HTML

Start Tag: Required
End Tag: Forbidden

The AREA tag draws the dimensions of a hot link on an image map that has been designated using the MAP element. AREA works very similarly to the A element, with a few exceptions to the attributes that are available for use. Both of these elements create areas on a map that direct the user agent to load another HTML document, image, sound file, or other Web-based program or file.

The main difference between the A and the AREA elements is with the alt attribute. The alt attribute is required for AREA and is used to designate alternate text that is displayed when a user agent is incapable of displaying images. AREA also is not required to have a target URL specified when it has the nohref attribute applied. The A element must always have a URL supplied.

Attributes
accesskey

```
accesskey="character"
```

You can assign an access key to an element. This key enables you to put the focus on an element quickly. In the case of a form element, the user is immediately able to input information. In the case of a link, the link is activated and followed.

alt

```
alt=text
```

This attribute provides you with alternate text to display when a user agent cannot show the image. This attribute is required for HTML 4.0 compliance.

class

```
class="cdata-list"
```

This attribute assigns a class name to an element. User agents use classes to group specific types of information and use them later.

coords

```
coords=x1,y1,x2,y2        /** shape=rect , x1y1 = top left pt,
x2y2 = lower right pt **/
coords=x1,y1,rad          /** shape=circle , x1y1 = center pt,
rad = circle radius **/
coords=x1,y1,x2,y2,... xn yn    /** shape=poly , x1y1 = 1st
corner pt, x2y2 = 2nd corner pt, xnyn= final corner pt **/
```

This attribute provides the point coordinates that allow the map to be drawn over the image. You can use any combination of shapes and coordinates on a map. The regions designated as hot spots on the map are not required to touch other hot spots, although they can. If two hot spots overlap, the area designated to use that space first in the list of coordinates is used as the active destination.

dir

```
dir = LTR | RTL | [CS | CI | CN | CA | CT]
```

This attribute defines the direction of the text flow in a document so a user agent can correctly display it to the reader.

href

```
href="url"
```

This attribute specifies the location of the document or resource to which this link refers.

id

```
id="name"
```

This attribute assigns a name to an element.

lang

```
lang="language code"
```

This attribute specifies the language that renders an element and its values.

name

```
name=cdata
```

This attribute gives the MAP a name that is used as an identifier when you automate your map data or outline your map areas.

nohref

Use this attribute when there is no URL to specify as a target for this link.

onblur

onblur=*script*

This attribute becomes active when an on-screen element loses the focus either through the actions of a mouse or another pointing device or through tabbed navigation.

onclick

onclick=*script*

This attribute takes effect when a user clicks the button on a pointing device while the pointer is over an on-screen element.

ondblclick

ondblclick=*script*

This attribute takes effect when a user double-clicks the button on a pointing device while the pointer is over an on-screen element.

onfocus

onfocus=*script*

This attribute takes effect when an on-screen element receives focus either from a mouse or another pointing device or through tabbed navigation.

onkeydown

onkeydown=*script*

This attribute takes effect when a user presses a key while the pointer is over an on-screen element.

onkeypress

onkeypress=*script*

This attribute takes effect when a user either presses or releases a key while the pointer is over an on-screen element.

onkeyup

onkeyup=*script*

This attribute takes effect when a user releases a key while the pointer is over an on-screen element.

onmousedown

```
onmousedown=script
```

This attribute takes effect when a user presses the button on a pointing device while the pointer is over an on-screen element.

onmousemove

```
onmousemove=script
```

This attribute becomes active when a user moves the mouse while the pointer is over an on-screen element.

onmouseout

```
onmouseout=script
```

This attribute becomes active when a user moves the mouse pointer away from an on-screen element.

onmouseover

```
onmouseover=script
```

This attribute becomes active when a user moves the mouse pointer over an on-screen element.

onmouseup

```
onmouseup=script
```

This attribute takes effect when a user releases the button on a pointing device while the pointer is over an on-screen element.

shape

```
shape= default | circle | rect | poly |
```

This attribute describes the shape taken up by the area on the map. The **default** setting specifies the entire image. A **circle** needs to have its center point and radius specified. A **rect**angle uses two points, one describing the upper left corner and the other describing the lower right corner. A **poly**gon needs the corner points of all the edges of the shape specified.

style

```
style=style descriptors
```

This attribute applies specific style-sheet information to one particular element.

tabindex

```
tabindex=number
```

This attribute provides the position of the current element within the overall tabbing order of the document.

target

```
target=frame-target
```

This attribute specifies the destination frame of the link's reference document.

title

```
title=text
```

This attribute provides annotation information to the element.

Example

The following example code creates a menu from which you can select a variety of services. The animation does not change the effectiveness of the image map.

 ON THE CD-ROM

Look for **area.htm** on the accompanying CD-ROM.

```
<HTML>
<HEAD>
<TITLE>Animated GIF Image map</TITLE>
</HEAD>
<BODY>
  <P>
  <MAP name="animap">
   <AREA href="email.html" shape="poly"
coords="40,40,146,146,0,146,40,40">
   <AREA href="fax.html" shape="poly"
coords="40,40,146,146,146,0,40,40">
   <AREA href="faq.html" shape="poly"
coords="146,0,146,146,256,40,146,0">
   <AREA href="online.html" shape="poly"
coords="256,40,146,146,299,146,256,40">
   <AREA href="news.html" shape="poly"
coords="299,146,146,146,260,260,299,146">
   <ARFA href="dbase.html" shape="poly"
coords="260,260,146,146,146,299,260,260">
   <AREA href="write.html" shape="poly"
coords="146,299,146,146,40,260,146,299">
```

```
    <AREA href="call.html" shape="poly"
coords="40,260,146,146,0,146,40,260">
    </MAP>
    <IMG src="tswheelani.gif" type="image/gif"
usemap="#animap">
</BODY>
</HTML>
```

CROSS-REFERENCE
See **areas**, **\<MAP\>**, **\<IMG\>**, **\<OBJECT\>**, and **\<A\>**.

areas

Collection

DHTML

This collection retrieves a list of the AREA elements defined for a specified MAP element.

The syntax for this command is

```
object.areas(index)
```

Parameters

index

This optional integer or string-index value identifies the element to be retrieved. Because all indexes are zero-based, the first area on this document is indexed at 0.

NOTE
String indexes are only valid when the string is a name or identifier that has been used for at least one element in the document. Because this collection is indexed first by name and then by identifier, duplicate names are returned in a collection of their own. The names in this subcollection must then be referred to by their index positions in the subcollection. This makes assigning a separate name identifier to each area preferable.

Methods

add   item   remove   tags

Objects

map

CROSS-REFERENCE
See <AREA>, <MAP>, <IMG>, <OBJECT>, and <A>.

ascent

Descriptor

CSS

This descriptor defines the maximum unaccented height for a font. This height is used in conjunction with other font characteristics when a font family is being matched using intelligent font matching.

CROSS-REFERENCE
See @font-face.

ASCII Characters

Concept

The American Standard Code for Information Interchange (ASCII) is a 7-bit binary code that is used as the standard code in PC and PC-compatible machines such as printers. This makes the transfer of text-based files a snap. The code represents each alphanumeric character, punctuation mark, and control code as a number from 0 to 127. An additional 128 characters have been added to the original 128 to create a complete character set containing 256 characters. This second set of 128 usually contains characters used in foreign languages, such as the Greek characters, math or graphics symbols, and other special characters. The second set of 128 is not standard and will be different based upon the type of computer that you are using.

assign

Method

DHTML

This scripting method loads the document specified by the URL if the document exists.

The syntax for this command is

`object.assign(url)`

Parameters
url

This string specifies the URL of the document to load.

Objects

location

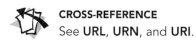

CROSS-REFERENCE
See **URL**, **URN**, and **URI**.

At-Rules

Concept

CSS

CROSS-REFERENCE
See **@-rules**.

Attribute

Concept

Attributes are associated with various elements to provide more control over the display or implementation of the element. All attributes are assigned to an element and appear with their associated value before the closing angle bracket (>) of the element's start tag. Although elements may have multiple attributes, the attributes can be applied in any order. All attributes are required to be set to a value, unless they are Boolean, and that value should be displayed surrounded by either double or single quotation marks. You can include single quotation marks within a value that is delimited by double quotation marks and vice versa if you wish. If a value is applied to an attribute without the use of quotation marks, that value can only contain the characters of the alphabet (a–z), the numerals 0–9, hyphens, and periods.

NOTE
An attribute's names and values are generally case-insensitive.

Attribute Defaults

Concept

XML

An XML attribute declaration provides the user agent and its programmers with information on the attributes that are acceptable with specific elements. It specifies whether the attribute's presence is required and, if not, how a processor should deal with its absence.

The syntax for an attribute declaration is

```
DefaultDecl ::= attValue ['#REQUIRED' | '#IMPLIED' | '#FIXED']
```

NOTE

When a default value is identified, the XML processor behaves as though the attribute were present with the declared default value whether it is there or not. If the attribute is present and set to a value other than the default, that value is used. If the attribute is also set to #FIXED in the declaration, the default value overrides the document settings.

Values

attValue

The value implied by this variable sets the default value of this attribute.

#IMPLIED

This identifies no default value for the attribute.

#REQUIRED

This implies that the attribute must always be specified for all of the elements listed in the declaration.

#FIXED

This setting forces the attribute always to use the default value specified with the attValue variable.

Example

In the following partial attribute list, declarations for the A and AREA elements show how the IMPLIED, REQUIRED, and AttValue settings can be applied.

```
<!ATTLIST A
charset    %Charset;                       #IMPLIED
type       %ContentType;    #IMPLIED
name       CDATA                           #IMPLIED
```

```
href        %URI;                           #IMPLIED
shape       %Shape;                         rect
>
<!ATTLIST AREA
shape       %Shape;                         rect
coords      %Coords;                        #IMPLIED
href        %URI;                           #IMPLIED
alt         %Text;                          #REQUIRED
>
```

CROSS-REFERENCE
See **Attribute-List**, **Attribute Types**, **Attribute**, and **<!DOCUMENT>**.

Attribute-List

Declaration

XML

Attributes are associated with various elements to provide more control over the display or implementation of the elements. All attributes are assigned to an element and appear with their associated value before the closing angle bracket (>) of the element's start tag. Although elements may have multiple attributes, the attributes can be applied in any order. All attributes must be set to a value, and that value must be displayed surrounded by either double or single quotation marks. Use an Attribute-list declaration to define valid attributes. This declaration enables you to

- Define the set of attributes valid for a given element type
- Establish type constraints for attributes
- Provide default attribute values

CROSS-REFERENCE
See **Attribute Types**, **Attribute**, and **<!DOCUMENT>**.

Attribute Types

Concept

XML

There are three kinds of XML attributes: enumerated types, string types, and tokenized types. The following definitions explain the difference between each type of attribute.

EnumeratedType

Enumerated attributes can hold one item from a list of values provided in the document type declaration. There are two kinds of enumerated types: Notation and Enumeration. In the case of a Notation-type enumerated type, the value is constrained to the list provided with that attribute. In the Enumeration type, you select from a list of tokens valid for that specific type of entry. For example, the shape attribute used with the A and AREA tags is constrained to a list of **rect | circle | poly.** This is a notation-type attribute. An enumeration, such as lang, is able to select from a larger list of acceptable values provided for the entire DTD.

StringType

```
StringType ::= 'CDATA'
```

String attributes can hold any type of string literal.

TokenizedType

```
TokenizedType ::= 'ID' | 'IDREF' | 'IDREFS' | 'ENTITY' |
'ENTITIES' | 'NMTOKEN' | 'NMTOKENS'
```

Tokenized types have varying lexical and semantic constraints.

CROSS-REFERENCE
See **Attribute-List**, **Attribute**, and **DTD**.

Attr(x)

Function

CSS

Document authors use this function to read the value of an attribute *x* used in a declaration. The value is returned in string format. The Cascading Style

Sheets processor does not parse this string. If the specified attribute *x* does not exist, an empty string is returned.

Example
The following example code forces the `alt` text used with the `IMG` element to be displayed before the image is. If a user agent is not capable of displaying the images, then the `alt` text is still visible.

```
IMG:before { content: attr(alt) }
```

 CROSS-REFERENCE
See **function** and **content**.

Aural

Media Group

CSS

Cascading Style Sheets, level 2, has defined the following media groups:

- Visual/Aural/Tactile
- Continuous/Paged
- Grid/Bitmap
- Interactive/Static

Each media group describes a specific type of media. A variety of media types are identified as part of these groups. Most of the media types fall into multiple categories. For example, Visual media can be either Continuous, like a computer screen, or Paged, like a newspaper. The identified media types include aural, Braille, embossed, handheld, print, projection, screen, TTY, and TV.

`Aural` media can only be rendered using a speech synthesizer or another device that reads off the document content. The radio is strictly an `aural` media type.

 CROSS-REFERENCE
See **Aural Style Sheets**, **Media Ggroups**, and **Media Types**.

Aural Style Sheets

Concept

CSS

With the constant growth of impaired communities' use of the Web, the World Wide Web Consortium (W3C) decided that a style sheet should be devoted to the blind and print-impaired communities. When you attempt to render a printed document aurally, you combine speech-synthesis technology with a variety of audio icons. Often, in order to synthesize the text, you have to convert the document to a straight text file and then feed that text through a screen reader. This type of rendering results in a less-informative document because the structure of the document is not retained. The W3C intends that this collection of Aural style sheet properties will enable both aural and visual rendering of a document to maintain a document's full meaning.

 NOTE

In addition to the most obvious uses of aural style sheets for the visually disabled, they can also be used for in-car readings of information, assisting illiterate users, industrial or corporate documentation systems, home entertainment, and more.

Attributes
azimuth

```
azimuth=<angle> | [[ left-side | far-left | left | center-left
| center | center-right | right | far-right | right-side ] ||
behind ] | leftwards | rightwards | inherit
```

This attribute defines the angle of approach that a speaker's voice sounds from. This attribute is used with elevation to provide a range of voices to a multipart document.

cue

```
cue=[ <'cue-before'> || <'cue-after'> ] | inherit
```

Use this attribute as shorthand for setting both the cue-before and cue-after attributes. When two values are supplied, the first applies to cue-before and the second applies to cue-after. When only one value is given, it applies to both properties.

cue-after

```
cue-after'=<uri> | none | inherit
```

This attribute specifies the sound that plays after a speaker utters an element's contents.

a
b
c

cue-before

```
cue-before=<uri> | none | inherit
```

This attribute specifies the sound that plays before a speaker utters an element's contents.

elevation

```
elevation=<angle> | below | level | above | higher | lower |
inherit
```

This attribute controls the height from which the sound of the speaker's voice appears to be coming at you.

pause

```
pause=[ [<time> | <percentage>]{1,2} ] | inherit
```

Use this attribute as shorthand for setting both the `pause-before` and `pause-after` attributes. When two values are supplied, the first applies to `pause-before` and the second applies to `pause-after`. When only one value is given, it applies to both properties.

pause-after

```
pause-after=<time> | <percentage> | inherit
```

This attribute specifies the length of time that a pause is in effect after a speaker utters an element's contents.

pause-before

```
pause-before=<time> | <percentage> | inherit
```

This attribute specifies the length of time that a pause is in effect before a speaker utters an element's contents.

pitch

```
pitch=<frequency> | x-low | low | medium | high | x-high |
inherit
```

This attribute controls the average pitch and speaking range of the voice.

pitch-range

```
pitch-range=<number> | inherit
```

This attribute specifies the acceptable variations in the speaker's average pitch.

play-during

```
play-during=<uri> | mix? repeat? | auto | none | inherit
```

Similar to `cue-before` and `cue-after`, this attribute specifies a sound to play in the background while an element's content is spoken.

richness

```
richness=<number> | inherit
```

This attribute controls the richness of the speaking voice.

speak

```
speak= normal | none | spell-out | inherit
```

This attribute specifies whether text is rendered aurally and, if so, how.

speak-numeral

```
speak-numeral=digits | continuous | none | inherit
```

This attribute controls how numerals are spoken.

speak-punctuation

```
speak-punctuation-code | none | inherit
```

This attribute controls how punctuation is spoken.

speech-rate

```
speech-rate=<number> | x-slow | slow | medium | fast | x-fast
| faster | slower | inherit
```

This attribute specifies the speaking rate of the speech synthesizer.

stress

```
stress-<number> | inherit
```

This attribute specifies the level of assertiveness or emphasis (stress) in the speaking voice. When using this attribute with languages such as English, which use stresses on sentence position, you can select primary, secondary, or tertiary stress points. The points control the style of inflection applied to these areas of the sentence.

voice-family

```
voice-family=[[<specific-voice> | <generic-voice> ],]*
[<specific-voice> | <generic-voice> ] | inherit
```

This comma-separated, prioritized list of voice family names controls the voices used when reading the text of the document.

volume

```
volume=<number> | <percentage> | silent | x-soft | soft |
medium | loud | x-loud | inherit
```

This attribute controls the median volume of the waveform. In other words, it adjusts the dynamic range over which a voice inflects during a speech-synthesized readout of a document.

Example

The following code shows an aural style sheet that identifies specific ways to speak information found in common HTML elements.

ON THE CD-ROM

Look for **aural.htm** on the accompanying CD-ROM.

```
/* Aural Style Sheets
 * Use with all HTML Documents
 */
H1, H2, H3, H4, H5, H6 {
        voice-family: paul;
        stress: 20;
        richness: 90;
        cue-before: url("ping.au")
    }

H1 { pause: 20ms;
     cue-before: url("pop.au");
     cue-after: url("pop.au");
     azimuth: 30deg;
     elevation: above }

H2 { pause: 30ms 40ms } /* pause-before: 30ms; pause-after:
40ms */

H3 { pause-after: 10ms } /* pause-before: ?; pause-after: 10ms
*/

A {cue-before: url("bell.aiff"); cue-after: url("dong.wav") }

BLOCKQUOTE.sad { play-during: url("violins.aiff") }
BLOCKQUOTE Q { play-during: url("harp.wav") mix }

SPAN.quiet { play-during: none }

TD.a { azimuth: far-right } /* 60deg */
```

```
#12 { azimuth: behind far-right } /* 120deg */

P.comment { azimuth: behind } /* 180deg */
P.part.romeo { voice-family: romeo, male }
P.part.juliet { voice-family: juliet, female }
P.heidi { azimuth: center-left }
P.peter { azimuth: right }
P.goat { volume: x-soft }

TR.a { elevation: 60deg }
TR.b { elevation: 30deg }
TR.c { elevation: level }
```

CROSS-REFERENCE
See **Aural (Media Group)**, **style sheets**, and **Cascading Style Sheets**.

Author

Concept

The individual who creates and most often maintains a document is considered the document *author*. When document readers are viewing a document, they will often wish to comment on or question the document's contents. To do this, they need the contact information on the author. This information can be provided in two ways: either through the use of a META element, which is invisible to the document reader except through the document's source text, or through the ADDRESS element that is visible to the document reader. The method the author chooses to employ is strictly a personal or corporate decision.

Authoring Tool

Concept

An authoring tool is any device, generally computer software, that allows you to design, develop, and implement programs and documents. A variety of authoring tools are included on this book's CD-ROM. For more information on these specific tools, read their introductions in Appendix F.

CROSS-REFERENCE
See **Appendix F**.

Automatic Counters

Concept

CROSS-REFERENCE
See **Counters**.

Automatic Numbering

Concept

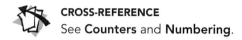

CROSS-REFERENCE
See **Counters** and **Numbering**.

availHeight

Property

DHTML

This scripting property retrieves the height of the working area of the user agent's screen in pixels, excluding the toolbar.

The syntax of this command is

```
object.availHeight
```

Objects

screen

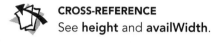

CROSS-REFERENCE
See **height** and **availWidth**.

availWidth

Property

DHTML

This object property retrieves the width of the working area of the user agent's screen in pixels, excluding the toolbar.

The syntax of this command is

`object.availWidth`

Objects

screen

CROSS-REFERENCE
See **width** and **availHeight**.

axis

Attribute

HTML

This attribute enables document authors to organize information in tables by creating categories that form an axis in the table. Some user agents provide the user a mechanism to query for the data from the identified categories. After the information is queried, the user agent can display it in any fashion that is apt. For example, if you were reading a table containing information on sales figures for a large software development company, you might wish to see the composite income figures from each department.

NOTE
No directives exist to require user agents to support the information provided with the `axis` attribute. No recommendations have been made directing how user agents present `axis` information to users or how this information may be queried by the user.

Values
cdata

The value of this attribute is a comma-separated list of category names.

Example

Because users may want to collect information from more than one cell in a table, the standard header information provided at the cell level may not be adequate. Consider Table A-1, which charts an individual's travel expenses for a series of trips.

Table A-1 Travel Expenses

Dates	Mileage	City	Meals	Hours
Sept. 1	324	Portland	$32	6
Sept. 7	400	San Francisco	$38	8
Sept. 14	320	Los Angeles	$45	8

When you look at this table, you might want to find out your total food costs or how many hours you spent driving altogether or how many miles you traveled. For a user agent to collect the data from this table to answer user queries such as these, the agent must have a way of identifying the individual cells that need to be involved in the computation.

ON THE CD-ROM

Look for **axis.htm** on the accompanying CD-ROM.

```
<HTML>
<HEAD>
    <TITLE>Table Axis Attributes</TITLE>
</HEAD>
<BODY bgcolor="#FFFFFF">
<TABLE border="1" width="75%">
  <TR>
    <TD>Date</TD>
    <TD>Mileage</TD>
    <TD>City</TD>
    <TD>Meals</TD>
    <TD>Hours</TD>
  </TR>
  <TR>
    <TD axis="date">Sept 1</TD>
    < TD axis="miles">324</TD>
    < TD axis="city">Portland</TD>
    < TD axis="meals">$32</TD>
    < TD axis="hours">6</TD>
  </TR>
```

```
<TR>
  < TD axis="date">Sept 7</TD>
  < TD axis="miles">400</TD>
  < TD axis="city">San Francisco</TD>
  < TD axis="meals">$38</TD>
  < TD axis="hours">8</TD>
</TR>
<TR>
  < TD axis="date">Sept 14</TD>
  < TD axis="miles">320</TD>
  < TD axis="city">Los Angeles</TD>
  < TD axis="meals">$45</TD>
  < TD axis="hours">8</TD>
</TR>
</TABLE>
</BODY>
</HTML>
```

Elements

TD   TH

azimuth

Attribute

CSS

This Aural Style Sheet attribute controls the horizontal spatial relationship of the audio presentation. This enables you to add depth to your range of speaking voices so they do not all appear to be coming at you from a stationary location. When you are listening to audio through stereo speakers, you create a lateral sound stage. The azimuth attribute can be used with this type of stereo system to create angles to the sound you hear. When you add a total surround-sound system (using either a binaural headphone or a five-speaker home theater setup), the azimuth becomes even more noticeable and creates a true three-dimensional sound arena.

The syntax of this attribute is

```
azimuth=<angle> | [[ left-side | far-left | left | center-left
| center | center-right | right | far-right | right-side ] ||
behind ] | leftwards | rightwards | inherit
```

Values
angle

This value describes the position of the voice in degrees. The allowable range is −360deg to 360deg. The values **0deg** and **360deg** position the voice directly in front of you, while **180deg** positions it directly behind. A value of −30 degrees would be **330deg**, 30 degrees to the left of your position.

center

This setting is the same as **0deg** (or, if used with behind, **180deg**).

center-left

Same as **340deg**. If used with behind, **200deg**.

center-right

Same as **20deg**. If used with behind, **160deg**.

far-left

Same as **300deg**. If used with behind, **240deg**.

far-right

Same as **60deg**. If used with behind, **120deg**.

left

Same as **320deg**. If used with behind, **220deg**.

left-side

Same as **270deg**. If used with behind, **270deg**.

leftwards

This setting moves the sound an additional 20 degrees to the left, relative to the current angle. This might be most easily understood as turning the sound counter-clockwise. So even if the sound is already behind the listener, it will continue to move "left" around the circle.

right

Same as **40deg**. If used with behind, **140deg**.

right-side

Same as **90deg**. If used with behind, **90deg**.

a
b
c

rightwards

This setting moves the sound an additional 20 degrees to the right, relative to the current angle.

Examples

```
H1 { azimuth: 30deg }
TD.a { azimuth: far-right }              /* 60deg */
TH { azimuth: behind far-right }  /* 120deg */
P { azimuth: behind }                   /* 180deg */
```

Elements

This attribute is applied to all elements.

CROSS-REFERENCE
See **Aural Style Sheets** and **Aural (Media Group)**.

<B>

Element

HTML

Start Tag: Required
End Tag: Required

Use this HTML element to create the appearance of bolded text on the document. You must use the end tag to turn off the bolding.

Attributes

class

```
class="cdata-list"
```

Use this attribute to assign a class name to an element. User agents employ classes to group specific types of information for later use.

id

```
id="name"
```

Use this attribute to assign a name to an element.

lang

```
lang="language code"
```

This attribute specifies the language in which an element and its values should be rendered.

onclick

```
onclick=script
```

This attribute, or event, is triggered when a user clicks the button on a pointing device with the pointer over an element.

ondblclick

> ondblclick=*script*

This attribute takes effect when a user double-clicks the button on a pointing device with the pointer over an element.

onkeydown

> onkeydown=*script*

This attribute takes effect when a user presses a key and the pointer is over an element.

onkeypress

> onkeypress=*script*

This attribute takes effect when a user presses and releases a key with the pointer over an element.

onkeyup

> onkeyup=*script*

This attribute takes effect when a user releases a key with the pointer over an element.

onmousedown

> onmousedown=*script*

This attribute takes effect when a user presses the button on a pointing device while the pointer is over an element.

onmousemove

> onmousemove=*script*

This attribute is activated when the mouse pointer is moved while it is over an element.

onmouseout

> onmouseout=*script*

This attribute is activated when the mouse pointer is moved away from an element.

onmouseover

> onmouseover=*script*

This attribute is activated when the mouse pointer is moved over an element.

onmouseup

```
onmouseup=script
```

This attribute takes effect when the button on a pointing device is released while the pointer is over an element.

style

```
style=style descriptors
```

This attribute applies specific style-sheet information to one particular element.

title

```
title=text
```

This attribute provides annotation information to the element to which it is applied.

Example

The following sample code shows a series of bolded words in the midst of a cooking recipe.

ON THE CD-ROM

Look for **b.htm** on the accompanying CD-ROM.

```
<HTML>
<HEAD>
<TITLE> Cooking with Boldness</TITLE>
</HEAD>
<BODY>
    <H1> Cooking with Cleo</H1>
    <H2> Cleo's Fabulous Dish Pan Cookies </H2>
    <P> <IMG src="chocchip.gif" alt="Dish Pan Cookies"><BR>
    First collect the following ingredients:
    <UL>
        <LI> 2 Cups <B> Sugar</B>
        <LI> 2 Cups <B>Brown Sugar</B>
        <LI> 1Cup <B>Butter</B>
        <LI> 2 tsp. <B> Vanilla</B><BR>
        _____

        <LI> 2 Cups <B>Oats</B>
        <LI> 4 Cups <B>Flour</B>
        <LI> 4 <B>Eggs</B>
        <LI> 1 lb. <B>Chocolate Chips</B>
        <LI> 2 Cups <B>Coconut</B>
        <LI> 2 Cups <B>Corn Flakes</B>
        <LI> 1.5 Cups <B>Nuts</B>
        <LI> 1 Cup <B>Raisins</B>
```

```
        <LI> 2 Tsp. <B>Salt</B>
</UL>
    <P>Now follow all the remaining directions to mix and bake
your cookies:
    <UL>
        <LI>Mix the brown sugar, sugar, butter, and vanilla.</LI>
        <LI>Mix the remaining ingredients thoroughly.</LI>
        <LI>Bake 9 - 10 minutes at 350 degrees.
    </UL>
    <H2> Don't Over Bake!!!</H2>
</BODY>
</HTML>
```

CROSS-REFERENCE
See **<STRONG>** and **<BIG>**.

back

Method

DHTML

Use this document method to move the browser back within the browser list. This command works the same as the `history.go(-1)`. If you attempt to go back past the original document in the History list, you won't create an error, but you will remain on the last valid document in the list.

The syntax of this command is

```
object.back()
```

Objects

history

CROSS-REFERENCE
See **forward**, **go**, and **User Agent**.

background

Attribute

CSS

This attribute is used as shorthand to define the values of the individual background properties listed. When using this property, the user agent first sets every background property to its default. After accomplishing that, the user agent sets the individual properties that need to be adjusted to the explicit value expressed in the attribute's statement.

The syntax of this command is

```
background: background-attachment || background-color ||
background-image || background-position || background-repeat |
inherit
```

Values

background-attachment

The value specified here controls the manner in which the background attachment is displayed. The background attachment is generally an image that has been applied to the HTML "page." Valid values for this option are **scroll, fixed,** and **inherit.**

background-color

This value controls the default background color—which is shown if no image is specified—for the selected element or document part. Valid values for this option are *color,* **transparent,** and **inherit.**

background-image

This value controls the background image used with the element. If the image is unavailable, the value of `background-color` is used in its place. The possible values for this attribute are *uri,* **none,** and **inherit.**

background-position

This option controls the position of the background image in reference to your element. Valid values for this option are *percentage, length,* **top, center, bottom, left, right,** and **inherit.**

background-repeat

This option controls the repeat pattern and tiling of images used in the background. Valid values for this option are **repeat, repeat-x, repeat-y, no-repeat,** and **inherit.**

Example

In the following code, the `background` attribute is applied to both the main `BODY` of the document and some individual element blocks such as `H1` and `BLOCKQUOTE`.

ON THE CD-ROM

Look for **background.htm** on the accompanying CD-ROM.

```
<HTML>
<HEAD>
    <TITLE> Adjusting your Backgrounds</TITLE>
    <STYLE type="text/css">
    <!-
        BODY { background: url("bground.gif") white fixed top
left no-repeat }
        H1 { background: red center repeat-x}
        BLOCKQUOTE { background: green 75% center }
    ->
    </STYLE>
</HEAD>
<BODY>
    <H1> American Broadcasting System</H1>
    <BLOCKQUOTE>
    This is a test. This is only a test. This is a test of the
American Broadcasting system. If this were not a test, this
message would be followed by a service announcement for your
immediate area.
    </BLOCKQUOTE>
</BODY>
</HTML>
```

Elements

This attribute can be applied to all HTML elements.

CROSS-REFERENCE

See **background-attachment**, **background-color**, **background-position**, **background-repeat**, and **background-image**.

background-attachment

Attribute

CSS

This attribute controls the scrolling of the background image (provided the image is already specified). You can fix the image in relation to the viewport or enable it to change as the document is read.

The syntax of this attribute is

```
background-attachment: scroll | fixed | inherit
```

Values

scroll

This is the attribute's default value. It lets the background image scroll along with the document text.

fixed

This value prohibits the background from scrolling with the remainder of the text.

inherit

This value forces the current element to use whatever setting the parent element has.

Example

The following example code creates a horizontal band across the top of the page. This band is stationary when the remainder of the document is scrolled.

```
<STYLE type="text/css">
<!--
    BODY {background-attachment: fixed;
          background-color: red;
          background-image: url("bgrounda.gif");
          background-position: top;
          background-repeat: repeat-x;}
-->
</STYLE>
```

Elements

This attribute applies to all HTML elements.

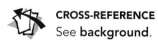

CROSS-REFERENCE
See **background**.

background-color

Attribute

CSS

This attribute sets the default background color when no background image is specified or when the background image is unable to load.

The syntax of this command is

```
background: color-name | #RGB-value
```

Values

color-name

This is one of the valid color names identified in Appendix A.

#RGB-value

This is the RGB three- or six-digit hex value representing a color on the color chart.

Example

The following lines of code show you how to use both the RGB values for a color and the color name.

```
<STYLE type="text/css">
<!-
    BODY { background: url("bground.gif") #FFFFFF fixed top
    left no-repeat }
    H1 { background-color: red }
    BLOCKQUOTE { background-color: #0C0  }
->
    </STYLE>
```

Elements

This attribute applies to all HTML elements.

CROSS-REFERENCE
See **background** and **color**.

background-image

Attribute

CSS

Use this attribute to specify an image to display in the background of the document or element to which it is applied. You can use the other background attributes to control how the image is displayed on the page. When you are using the `background-image` element, it is generally a good plan to include a setting for your document's background color in case the image cannot be displayed.

The syntax for this command is

```
background-image: url("uri")
```

Values

uri

This is either a relative or an absolute reference to the image's URL that is displayed in the background of the current document or element.

Elements

This attribute applies to all HTML elements.

CROSS-REFERENCE

See **background**, **background-color**, **background-position**, and **background-repeat**.

background-position

Attribute

CSS

Use this attribute to control the initial horizontal and vertical positions of the image on the document page.

The syntax for this command is

```
background-position: [ [percentage | length ]{1,2} | [ [top |
center | bottom] || [left | center | right] ] ] | inherit
```

Values

percentage

This value controls the position of the background image by organizing the image properties against the percentage of the padding box created by the element. For example, if you use the values 15% and 85%, the user agent displays the point 15% in from the left edge and 85% down from the top of the image into the same coordinates within the padding box.

length

This value specifies the amount of space below and to the right of the top-left corner of the padding area in which the image should be located.

top left and left top

These values produce the same effect as using the percentages 0% and 0%.

top, top center, and center top

These values produce the same effect as using the percentages 0% and 50%.

right top and top right

These values produce the same effect as using the percentages 100% and 0%.

left, left center, and center left

These values produce the same effect as using the percentages 0% and 50%.

center and center center

These values produce the same effect as using the percentages 50% and 50%.

right, right center, and center right

These values produce the same effect as using the percentages 100% and 50%.

bottom left and left bottom

These values produce the same effect as using the percentages 0% and 100%.

bottom, bottom center, and center bottom

These values produce the same effect as using the percentages 100% and 50%.

bottom right and right bottom

These values produce the same effect as using the percentages 100% and 100%.

Elements
This attribute applies to all HTML box elements.

CROSS-REFERENCE
See **background**.

backgroundPositionX

Property

DHTML

Use this property to retrieve the current horizontal position of the Cascading Style Sheets background image.
The syntax of this command is

```
object.backgroundPositionX [= backgroundPositionX]
```

CROSS-REFERENCE
See **background-position** and **backgroundPositionY**.

backgroundPositionY

Property

DHTML

Use this property to retrieve the current vertical position of the Cascading Style Sheets background image.
The syntax of this command is

```
object.backgroundPositionY [= backgroundPositionY]
```

CROSS-REFERENCE
See **background-position** and **backgroundPositionX**.

background-repeat

Attribute

CSS

This attribute is used to control how a background image is repeated to cover the complete background of a document.

The syntax is

```
background-repeat: repeat | repeat-x | repeat-y | no-repeat
```

Values

repeat

This value instructs the user agent to repeat the image both horizontally and vertically. This is the default value of this attribute.

repeat-x

This value instructs the user agent to repeat the image only horizontally.

repeat-y

This value instructs the user agent to repeat images only vertically.

no-repeat

When this value is used, the image is not repeated on the document. The original image is placed according to the positioning instructions included in the `background-positioning` attribute. Any space on the visual screen outside the image is displayed in the color specified by the `background-color` attribute.

Elements

This attribute applies to all HTML elements.

CROSS-REFERENCE
See **background**.

Backslash (\) Escapes

Concept

CSS

The Cascading Style Sheets specification uses the backslash (\) character to indicate one of three types of character escape sequences.

- When found inside a string, a backslash followed by a new line is ignored since the string is deemed to contain neither the backslash nor the new line.
- When found inside quotation marks, the backslash removes any special meaning applied to Cascading Style Sheets characters. One of the most common uses for this is to remove the special meaning of the double-quote character. The string to do so is "\"".
- This character enables document authors to refer to individual characters that they can't otherwise put into a document. Using up to six hexadecimal characters that represent the ISO10646 character with that identification number does this. That character can be identified two ways: either by using a space character as in "\26 D" or by providing the exact six-digit hex character "\000026D."

CROSS-REFERENCE
See **Unicode**.

balance

Property

DHTML

This document object property is used to return the balance value of the background sound being played. This value is used to determine how the volume has been divided between the right and left speakers.

The syntax of this command is

```
VolumeVar=object.balance
```

Elements

BGSOUND

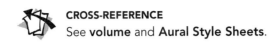

CROSS-REFERENCE
See **volume** and **Aural Style Sheets**.

<BASE>

Element

HTML

Start Tag: Required
End Tag: Forbidden

This HTML tag is used to specify the base URL of the document. It can only be used within the HEAD tags.

Attributes
href

```
href=url
```

This attribute contains the URL of the main document so that relative URLs contained within the document can be referenced correctly.

target

```
target= window_name | _blank | _parent | _self | _top
```

This attribute sends the contents of the linked URL to the specified target frame. If the target does not exist, the link is loaded into a new window. If **_blank** is the value of the target, the link is loaded into a new window without a title. If **_parent** is identified, the link is loaded into the parent document of the current one. If **_self** is selected, the link is loaded into the current window or frame. A value of **_top** loads the link into the full body of the current window.

Example
The following code example uses the BASE element to ensure that all relative links in the document are correctly interpreted.

ON THE CD-ROM
Look for **base.htm** on the accompanying CD-ROM.

```
<HTML>
<HEAD>
   <TITLE> Aligning Links with BASE</TITLE>
   <BASE target="_top" href="http://catsback.com">
</HEAD>
<BODY>
```

```
        <A href="aboutus.htm"> About Cat's Back Consulting</A>
        <A href="http://nfqhajournal.com">Our Client the NFQHA</A>
    </BODY>
    </HTML>
```

CROSS-REFERENCE
See **<BASEFONT>**, **URI**, and **URL**.

<BASEFONT>

Element

HTML

Start Tag: Required
End Tag: Forbidden

This attribute is used to identify the characteristics displayed by the basic font used for the standard text on an HTML document. This element should be placed in the HEAD block of your document. This element has been deprecated in favor of the use of style sheets.

Attributes

class

```
class="cdata-list"
```

Use this attribute to assign a class name to an element. User agents employ classes to group specific types of information for later use.

color

The color can be either a valid HTML color name or a hex value representing the RGB value of the color.

dir

```
dir = LTR | RTL | [CS | CI | CN | CA | CT]
```

This attribute defines the direction of the text flow in a document so that a user agent can correctly display it to the reader.

face

```
face=font-name
```

This attribute controls the type of font used to display the text

id

```
id="name"
```

Use this attribute to assign a name to an element.

lang

```
lang="language code"
```

This attribute specifies the language in which an element and its values should be rendered.

size

```
size=number
```

This is the size of the font. The valid range of numbers is one to seven.

style

```
style=style descriptors
```

This attribute applies specific style-sheet information to one particular element.

title

```
title=text
```

This attribute provides annotation information to the element to which it is applied.

Example

The following code sets the base size and dimensions of the fonts used on this HTML document.

ON THE CD-ROM

Look for **basefont.htm** on the accompanying CD-ROM.

```
<HEAD>
<BASEFONT color="purple" face="Verdana" size="12pt"">
</HEAD>
```

CROSS-REFERENCE

See **\<FONT>**, **font-family**, and **@font-face**.

baseline

Descriptor

CSS

This Cascading Style Sheets descriptor is used to describe the lower baseline of a font. A baseline is the line on which all characters of the alphabet rest when typed or written. The baseline of the phrase "The cat ate the rat" is easy to find. It lies directly below the bottom of each character. The baseline of the phrase "The cat ate the pigeon" is along the bottom edge of the majority of the characters. The tails of letters like *p*, *g*, *q*, and *y* fall below the baseline. The default value is 0. If you apply a *number* value to this descriptor other than the default, use the `units-per-em` descriptor to define it properly.

 CROSS-REFERENCE
See **centerline**, **mathline**, and **topline**.

<BDO>

Element

HTML

Start Tag: Required
End Tag: Required

This element is used in conjunction with the `dir` attribute to manage direction changes of embedded text. The bidirectional algorithm, built into most user agents, generally controls these direction changes, but sometimes this results in incorrect rendering. The `BDO` element enables document authors to turn off the algorithm for specific selections of text.

This element is provided for use in scenarios where the document author needs absolute control over sequence order. The `dir` attribute is required for this element.

You can also use special Unicode characters to override the bidirectional algorithm:

- Left to Right Override = 202D.
- Right to Left Override = 202E.
- Pop Directional Formatting = 202C. This character ends either of the other Unicode bidirectional overrides.

NOTE
Conflicts can arise if the `dir` attribute is used simultaneously on inline elements and on corresponding formatting characters.

Attributes

lang

```
lang="language code"
```

This attribute specifies the language in which an element and its values should be rendered.

dir

```
dir = LTR | RTL | [CS | CI | CN | CA | CT]
```

This attribute defines the direction of the text flow in a document so that a user agent can correctly display it to the reader.

Example

The following example code shows you how to use the BDO element to override the normal bidirectional algorithm. Consider the following text:

```
Peter Piper Picked a Peck of Pickle
Peppers that were covered with
&gamma;-radiation
```

This can be coded in either of the two following ways.

ON THE CD-ROM
Look for **bdo.htm** on the accompanying CD-ROM.

```
<HTML>
<HEAD>
   <TITLE> Take a look at Bi-directional text</TITLE>
</HEAD>
<BODY>
  <PRE>
  Peter Piper Picked a Peck of Pickle
  Peppers that were covered
  with &gamma;-radiation
  </PRE>

  <P>
  <BDO dir="RTL">
  Peter Piper Picked a Peck of Pickle <BR>
  Peppers that were covered <BR>
  with &gamma;-radiation<BR>
  </BDO>
```

```
</BODY>
</HTML>
```

 **CROSS-REFERENCE**
See **dir**.

behavior

Attribute

HTML

This attribute is used to control the behavior of the MARQUEE displayed on Internet Explorer-based HTML pages. Because MARQUEE is an Internet Explorer-only element, this attribute will not work with Netscape browsers.

The syntax of this attribute is

```
behavior alternate | scroll | slide
```

Values
alternate

This value causes the contents of the <MARQUEE> to slide left-to-right and then right-to-left, never leaving the bounds of its containment box.

scroll

This value causes the contents to scroll across the <MARQUEE> containment box in the direction specified by the direction attribute. The text will scroll to the end of the box, disappear, and begin again at the originating side.

slide

This value causes the contents to scroll across the <MARQUEE> containment box in the direction specified by the direction attribute. The text will scroll to the end of the box and stop.

Example
The following example code uses the behavior attribute of the MARQUEE element to show you the different effects of all its available values.

 ON THE CD-ROM
Look for **behaviour.htm** on the accompanying CD-ROM.

```
<MARQUEE behavior="slide"direction="left"> This is a test.
This is only a test.</MARQUEE>
<MARQUEE behavior="scroll" direction="right"> This is a test.
This is only a test.</MARQUEE>
<MARQUEE behavior="alternate"> This is a test. This is only a
test.</MARQUEE>
```

Elements

MARQUEE

bgcolor

Attribute

HTML

This attribute is used in a variety of elements to set the background color of the object. This attribute is available only for elements that have a visual containment block such as a document or the cells of a table.

```
bgcolor= colorname | #RGBcolor
```

Values

colorname

This is one of the valid color names specified by the HTML 4.0 standard or, if viewed with Internet Explorer 4.0, one of Microsoft's identified color names.

#RGBcolor

This is either a three- or six-digit hexadecimal number that represents the Red-Green-Blue (RGB) value of the color.

Example

The following example document uses the bgcolor attribute to set the color for the document background and individual parts of the table.

ON THE CD-ROM

Look for **bgcolor.htm** on the accompanying CD-ROM.

```
<html>
<head>
<title>A Look At Color</title>
</head>
```

a

b

c

```
<body bgcolor="#FFFF99" text="#000000" link="#FF0000"
vlink="#00FF00" alink="#FFCC00">
<p>Lets look at all the places color can be added to table
cells:</p>
<table border="1" width="75%">
  <tr>
    <td bgcolor="Red">Red</td>
    <td bgcolor="white">White</td>
    <td bgcolor="Green">Green</td>
  </tr>
  <tr>
    <td bgcolor="#0000FF">Blue</td>
    <td bgcolor="#9900CC">Purple</td>
    <td bgcolor="#FFCC00">Orange</td>
  </tr>
  <tr>
    <td bgcolor="#FFFF00">Yellow</td>
    <td bgcolor="#FF00FF">Pink</td>
    <td bgcolor="#00FFFF">Light Blue</td>
  </tr>
</table>
<p>And here is how it can be added to tables and individual
rows:</p>
<table border="1" width="75%" bgcolor="#FFCC00">
  <tr>
    <td>Cat</td>
    <td>Duck</td>
    <td>Cow</td>
  </tr>
  <tr bgcolor="#66FF00">
    <td>Dog</td>
    <td>Goose</td>
    <td>Goat</td>
  </tr>
  <tr>
    <td>Rabbit</td>
    <td>Swan</td>
    <td>Sheep</td>
  </tr>
</table>
<p>  </p>
</body>
</html>
```

Elements

BODY   TABLE   TD   TH
TR

CROSS-REFERENCE
See **color** and **background**.

bgProperties

Property

DHTML

This document object property is used to set or retrieve the background properties for a background image. It can tell you whether the image is fixed or scrolls with the document.

The syntax of this property is

```
object.bgProperties[=bgProperties]
```

Elements

BODY

CROSS-REFERENCE
See **background** and **bgcolor**.

<BGSOUND>

Element

HTML — Internet Explorer Only

Start Tag: Required
End Tag: Optional

This tag is used to create background sounds for Internet Explorer users. Netscape does not support it. You can place this element within the HEAD if you wish to.

Attributes
balance

```
balance=n
```

Use this attribute to determine how the available volume level is divided between the speakers. The valid range for this attribute is –10,000 to 10,000, with zero being the balance point between the right and left speakers.

class

```
class="cdata-list"
```

Use this attribute to assign a class name to an element. User agents employ classes to group specific types of information for later use.

id

```
id="name"
```

Use this attribute to assign a name to an element. This value must begin with an alphabetic character and should be unique within the document.

lang

```
lang="language code"
```

This attribute specifies the language in which an element and its values should be rendered.

loop

```
loop=n
```

This attribute controls the number of times the sound should repeat itself.

src

```
src=url
```

This attribute is used to specify the URL of the sound being played.

title

```
title=text
```

Use this to provide information about the song, music, or sound effect being played. In the case of songs or music, you can specify the title of the piece in this attribute. For a sound effect, you can add a short description of the effect here.

volume

```
volume=n
```

This attribute is used to control the volume on the page. You can use it to send a loud sound, such as a trumpet blare, to get a viewer's attention or to play soft background music while a viewer reads a large stretch of text. This setting can be any number between –10,000 and 0, with zero being full-wave output (based on the computer's current speaker-volume settings).

Example

This example uses the BGSOUND Internet Explorer element to play sound and shows the alternate EMBED method that can be used to play the sound in any browser, including Netscape- and NCSA-based user agents.

 ON THE CD-ROM
Look for **bgsound.htm** on the accompanying CD-ROM.

```
<HTML>
<HEAD>
   <TITLE>Listening to sound flow around</TITLE>
   <BGSOUND balance="0" loop="1" src="titanic.wav" volume="-2500">
</HEAD>
<BODY>
<H1>Listen to lots o' Music</H1>
   <P> In a romantic mood? Love those old silent movies? Well
   close your eyes and enjoy, cause this is what love sounds like.
   <TABLE width="45" border="0" cellspacing="0" cellpadding="0"
   align="CENTER" valign="BOTTOM" bgcolor="Gray">
      <EMBED src="titanic.wav" autostart="true" height="0"
      width="0" loop="true">
      </EMBED>
   </TABLE>
</BODY>
</HTML>
```

 **CROSS-REFERENCE**
See **<EMBED>**.

Bidirectional Text

 **CROSS-REFERENCE**
See **<BDO>**.

<BIG>

Element

HTML

Start Tag: Required
End Tag: Required

This tag is used to enlarge the size of your text without explicitly changing the font size.

Attributes

class

```
class="cdata-list"
```

Use this attribute to assign a class name to an element. User agents employ classes to group specific types of information for later use.

id

```
id="name"
```

Use this attribute to assign a name to an element.

lang

```
lang="language code"
```

This attribute specifies the language in which an element and its values should be rendered.

onclick

```
onclick=script
```

This attribute takes effect when a user clicks the button on a pointing device with the pointer over an element.

ondblclick

```
ondblclick=script
```

This attribute takes effect when a user double-clicks the button on a pointing device with the pointer over an element.

onkeydown

`onkeydown=script`

This attribute takes effect when a user presses a key and the pointer is over an element.

onkeypress

`onkeypress=script`

This attribute takes effect when a user presses and releases a key with the pointer over an element.

onkeyup

`onkeyup=script`

This attribute takes effect when a user releases a key with the pointer over an element.

onmousedown

`onmousedown=script`

This attribute takes effect when a user presses the button on a pointing device while the pointer is over an element.

onmousemove

`onmousemove=script`

This attribute is activated when the mouse pointer is moved while it is over an element.

onmouseout

`onmouseout=script`

This attribute is activated when the mouse pointer is moved away from an element.

onmouseover

`onmouseover=script`

This attribute is activated when the mouse pointer is moved over an element.

onmouseup

`onmouseup=script`

This attribute takes effect when the button on a pointing device is released while the pointer is over an element.

style

```
style=style descriptors
```

This attribute applies specific style-sheet information to one particular element.

title

```
title=text
```

This attribute provides annotation information to the element to which it is applied.

Example

The following example code uses the `BIG` element to provide emphasis to specific words in a sales paragraph.

ON THE CD-ROM

Look for **big.htm** on the accompanying CD-ROM.

```
<HTML>
<HEAD>
    <TITLE>Various forms of Emphasis being Used    </TITLE>
</HEAD>
<BODY bgcolor="#FFFFFF">
    <H1><FONT color="#FF9933">Looking for Computer
    Help</font></H1>
    <BIG>HTML, VB, DHTML, JAVA, ODBC, OLE, XMP,
    MathML</BIG>,<BR>
    Not up to speed on the latest technological innovations?
    <P align="left"><b>We are. </b>
    <P>Whether it's <BIG>Web</BIG> pages, <BIG>brochures</BIG>,
    <BIG>business cards</BIG>, or <BIG>databases</BIG>, Cat's
    Back <BR>
    Consulting can get your company up and running in the
    technological age.
    <P>Give us a call.
    <H3><FONT color="#FF9933">Cat's Back Consulting</FONT></H3>
    555-CATS or <FONT color="#FF9933">www.catsback.com</FONT>
    on the Internet.<BR>
    We're the answer to your information needs.
</BODY>
</HTML>
```

CROSS-REFERENCE

See **<B>**, **<EM>**, and **<STRONG>**.

Bitmap

Media Group

CSS

Cascading Style Sheets, level 2, has defined the following media groups:

- Visual/Aural/Tactile
- Continuous/Paged
- Grid/Bitmap
- Interactive/Static

Each media group is used to describe a specific type of medium. Many media types are identified as part of these groups. The bitmap media group is used to identify specific types of media that use a series of dots to create an image or text. Bitmap media include television screens, computer monitors, newspaper print, and projection machines. Bitmap media use a series of colored dots to create the images that we see. Take, for example, your computer screen. The computer screen is composed of thousands of individual pixels (dots) that are individually colored to create the images that you see on your screen. As you click buttons and type documents, those pixels are updated to reflect the changes made to the interface.

CROSS-REFERENCE
See **Media Groups** and **Media Types**.

\<BLINK>

Element

HTML — Netscape Browsers Only

Start Tag: Required
End Tag: Required

This element, created by Netscape, is used to create blinking text on your HTML document.

NOTE
Blinking text is very difficult to read; use it sparingly.

Attributes

class

```
class="cdata-list"
```

Use this attribute to assign a class name to an element. User agents employ classes to group specific types of information for later use.

id

```
id="name"
```

Use this attribute to assign a name to an element.

language

```
lang="language code"
```

This attribute specifies the language in which an element and its values should be rendered.

style

```
style=style descriptors
```

This attribute applies specific style-sheet information to one particular element.

Example

The following example code uses the BLINK element to highlight special advertising information on a series of ads.

ON THE CD-ROM

Look for **blink.htm** on the accompanying CD-ROM.

```
<html>
<head>
<title>Bargains for the House</title>
</head>

<body bgcolor="#FFFFFF">
<h1 align="center"><font color="#FF3300">On Sale!</font></h1>
  <table border="0" width="75%" align="center">
  <tr>
     <td colspan="3" align="left">
     <p>Look at these great Bargains:</p>
  </td>
  </tr>
  <tr>
```

```
        <td align="left"> </td>
        <td colspan="2">
          <ul>
            <li>PII 333 MMX system, 64MB RAM, 4 gig HD, w/
            monitor</li>
            <li>P300 MMX system, 64MB RAM, 6 gig HD, w/
            monitor</li>
            <li>P200 system, 32MB RAM, 8 gig HD, w/ monitor and
            printer
          </ul>
        </td>
      </tr>
    </table>
    <blink>
    <p align="center"><font size="+3">Now till
    Saturday!</font></p>
    </blink>
    <p align="center">For more information call: 555-6666</p>
    <hr>
    <p align="center"><blink> </blink></p>
    <blink>
    <h1 align="center"><font color="#FF9999">Wanted!!!!</font>
    </h1>
    </blink>
    <p align="center">
      Need a small black and white bunny for child's<br>
      Easter present. Bunny should be young and<br>
      used to children. Either upright or flopped ears<br>
      are acceptable. Please call: 555-1111.</p>
    <hr>
    <p align="center"> </p>
  </body>
</html>
```

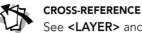

CROSS-REFERENCE

See **\<LAYER>** and **User Agents**.

Block

Concept

CSS

A *block*, in the Cascading Style Sheets language, is a group of related attributes that has been enclosed in curly braces and applied to a single element. Each block starts with a left curly brace ({) and ends with a right curly brace (}). Between these braces, any characters may appear, including parentheses, brackets, and additional braces, with the exception that these types of bounding characters must occur in pairs. Other characters that must also appear in pairs within a block include single and double quotation marks. All information found between the start and end braces of a block will be parsed as a string identifier.

Example

The following block example shows you how to stack multiple blocks within a single style-sheet definition. This is a valid Cascading Style Sheets example.

```
<style type="text/css">
<!-
acronym {  font-family: Arial, Helvetica, sans-serif;
                font-style: italic;
                line-height: 2em;
                text-decoration: underline;
                letter-spacing: 1em;
                color: #660066}
img        {  left: 5cm}
@page:first {  margin-top= 3in !important;
                margin-bottom= 3in !important;
                margin-left= 2in !important;
                margin-right= 2in !important }
->
</STYLE>
```

CROSS-REFERENCE
See **Block-Level Element**.

Block-Level Element

Concept

CSS

Block-level elements are those elements that are visually formatted in a block, such as a paragraph or table. These types of elements create containment blocks based upon the value of the Cascading Style Sheets `display` property. This means that they take up a complete rectangular area of your document when they are displayed on your HTML page. When the `display` property is set to **block, list-item, compact, run-in,** and **table,** the element takes on the characteristics of a block-level element.

When you are coding a document using HTML, a block-level element can only contain information in block boxes. This means that any text or images found within these blocks are placed in a box even if they would not normally be block-level elements. The user agent places text that is not contained in any other fashion in an anonymous box strictly for display purposes if another block element is also contained within the parent block. The following example code and Figure B-1 display this effect.

```
<DIV>
    Learning the best way to throw a curve ball…
    <PRE>
    1. Pick up the phone.
    2. Dial the NY Yankees pitcher.
    3. Beg him to throw the ball for you.
    </PRE>
</DIV>
```

Elements

BODY	BLOCKQUOTE	BUTTON	CAPTION
CENTER	COL	COLGROUP	DIV
FIELDSET	FORM	FRAME	FRAMESET
H1–H6	HEAD	HR	IFRAME
INPUT	LABEL	LAYER	LEGEND
LI	MAP	MARQUEE	OBJECT
OL	P	PRE	Q
SCRIPT	SELECT	SPAN	TABLE
TD	TEXTAREA	TFOOT	TH
THEAD	TR	UL	

DIV

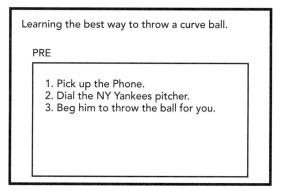

Learning the best way to throw a curve ball.

PRE

1. Pick up the Phone.
2. Dial the NY Yankees pitcher.
3. Beg him to throw the ball for you.

Figure B-1 The DIV element is a block element that contains the block created by the PRE element.

CROSS-REFERENCE
See **Containing Block**, **Inline Element**, and **Block**.

<BLOCKQUOTE>

Element

HTML

This element is used to identify large blocks of quoted text. The text found between BLOCKQUOTE tags is indented slightly on the page; the user agent decides how far to indent. Although the Q element automatically places quotation marks around the text that it marks, the BLOCKQUOTE element does not do so. The lack of quotation marks allows this element to be used, incorrectly, to indent text. If you wish quotation marks to appear around your quoted text, do so with a style sheet.

Attributes
cite

    cite="*url*"

This attribute is used to identify the URL of the original material that has been quoted in this document.

class

    class="*cdata-list*"

Use this attribute to assign a class name to an element. User agents employ classes to group specific types of information for later use.

id

```
id="name"
```

Use this attribute to assign a name to an element.

lang

```
lang="language code"
```

This attribute specifies the language in which an element and its values should be rendered.

onclick

```
onclick=script
```

This attribute takes effect when a user clicks the button on a pointing device with the pointer over an element.

ondblclick

```
ondblclick=script
```

This attribute takes effect when a user double-clicks the button on a pointing device with the pointer over an element.

onkeydown

```
onkeydown=script
```

This attribute takes effect when a user presses a key and the pointer is over an element.

onkeypress

```
onkeypress=script
```

This attribute takes effect when a user presses and releases a key with the pointer over an element.

onkeyup

```
onkeyup=script
```

This attribute takes effect when a user releases a key with the pointer over an element.

onmousedown

```
onmousedown=script
```

This attribute takes effect when a user presses the button on a pointing device while the pointer is over an element.

onmousemove

```
onmousemove=script
```

This attribute is activated when the mouse pointer is moved while it is over an element.

onmouseout

```
onmouseout=script
```

This attribute is activated when the mouse pointer is moved away from an element.

onmouseover

```
onmouseover=script
```

This attribute is activated when the mouse pointer is moved over an element.

onmouseup

```
onmouseup=script
```

This attribute takes effect when the button on a pointing device is released while the pointer is over an element.

style

```
style=style descriptors
```

This attribute applies specific style-sheet information to one particular element.

title

```
title=text
```

This attribute provides annotation information to the element to which it is applied.

Example

The following example code uses BLOCKQUOTE to set aside some quotations on your document.

ON THE CD-ROM

Look for **blockquote.htm** on the accompanying CD-ROM.

```
<HTML>
<HEAD>
  <TITLE>BlockQuotes Anywhere</TITLE>
</HEAD>

<BODY>
  <H1>Some of my Favorite Quotes</H1>
  <BLOCKQUOTE cite="http://rbhatnagar.ececs.uc.edu:8080/
  vivekananda/quotes/quotes_intro" title="Swami Vivekananda
  Quotes">
  BE FREE ; hope for nothing from any one. I am sure if you
  look back upon your lives, you will find that you were
  always vainly trying to get help from others which never
  came. All the help that has come was from within
  YOURSELVES.
  </BLOCKQUOTE>
  <BLOCKQUOTE cite="http://rbhatnagar.ececs.uc.edu:8080/
  vivekananda/quotes/quotes_intro" title="Swami Vivekananda
  Quotes">
  Whatever you THINK, that you WILL BE. If you think
  yourselves weak, weak you will be; if you think yourselves
  strong, strong you will be.
  </BLOCKQUOTE>
  <BLOCKQUOTE     cite="http://rbhatnagar.ececs.uc.edu:8080/
  vivekananda/quotes/quotes_intro" title="Swami Vivekananda
  Quotes">
  The remedy for weakness is not brooding over weakness, but
  thinking of strength. Teach men of the STRENGTH that is
  already WITHIN them.
  </BLOCKQUOTE>
</BODY>
</HTML>
```

CROSS-REFERENCE
See **Block**, **Block-Level Element**, and **<Q>**.

blur

Method

DHTML

This document object method causes the `onblur` HTML attribute to fire. The syntax of this command is

```
object.blur()
```

Example

The following code uses the `onblur` event to trigger an alert box as if the mouse had moved within the boundaries of the image.

```
<BODY>
<SCRIPT language="JavaScript">
<!—
img1.blur()
—>
</SCRIPT>

  <IMG id="img1" src="blueball.gif" onblur="alert("This image
  was blurred.")"
</BODY>
```

Elements

A	APPLET	AREA	BODY
BUTTON	CAPTION	DIV	EMBED
FIELDSET	FRAME	FRAMESET	HR
IFRAME	IMG	INPUT	MARQUEE
OBJECT	SELECT	SPAN	TABLE
TD	TEXTAREA	TR	

Objects

window

<BODY>

Element

HTML

Start Tag: Optional
End Tag: Optional

You can use this element to mark the beginning and end of the body of an HTML document. The body of the document stores all of its contents, which can be presented by the user agent in a variety of ways. Visual user agents display the images, text, colors, and graphics on the page as if it were a canvas being painted. Audio agents generally speak the textual contents of a document. Because style sheets are not being used to control presentations, all the presentational attributes of BODY have been deprecated.

Attributes

alink

```
alink=color
```

Although deprecated, this attribute is used to set the color of the text that marks the hyperlinks currently selected by the user.

background

```
background=uri
```

This attribute contains the URI of the image that is displayed as the background wallpaper of the document in visual browsers.

bgcolor

```
bgcolor=color
```

This attribute is used to set the default background color of the document if an image is not specified.

class

```
class="cdata-list"
```

Use this attribute to assign a class name to an element. User agents employ classes to group specific types of information for later use.

id

> id="*name*"

Use this attribute to assign a name to an element.

lang

> lang="*language code*"

This attribute specifies the language in which an element and its values should be rendered.

link

> link=*color*

Although deprecated, this attribute is used to set the color of the text marking hyperlinks that have not been visited and are not currently selected.

onclick

> onclick=*script*

This attribute takes effect when a user clicks the button on a pointing device with the pointer over an element.

ondblclick

> ondblclick=*script*

This attribute takes effect when a user double-clicks the button on a pointing device with the pointer over an element.

onkeydown

> onkeydown=*script*

This attribute takes effect when a user presses a key and the pointer is over an element.

onkeypress

> onkeypress=*script*

This attribute takes effect when a user presses and releases a key with the pointer over an element.

onkeyup

> onkeyup=*script*

This attribute takes effect when a user releases a key with the pointer over an element.

onload

```
onload=script
```

This attribute is triggered when a document is first loaded into the user agent.

onmousedown

```
onmousedown=script
```

This attribute takes effect when a user presses the button on a pointing device while the pointer is over an element.

onmousemove

```
onmousemove=script
```

This attribute is activated when the mouse pointer is moved while it is over an element.

onmouseout

```
onmouseout=script
```

This attribute is activated when the mouse pointer is moved away from an element.

onmouseover

```
onmouseover=script
```

This attribute is activated when the mouse pointer is moved over an element.

onmouseup

```
onmouseup=script
```

This attribute takes effect when the button on a pointing device is released while the pointer is over an element.

onunload

```
onunload=script
```

This attribute is triggered when a document is removed from the document or frame within which it was displayed.

style

```
style=style descriptors
```

This attribute applies specific style-sheet information to one particular element.

text

```
text=color
```

Visual browsers use this attribute to set the foreground color of the text on the document. This attribute has also been deprecated.

title

```
title=text
```

This attribute provides annotation information to the element to which it is applied.

vlink

```
vlink=color
```

Although deprecated, this attribute is used to set the color of the text marking hyperlinks that have been visited and are not currently selected.

Example

Here is an example of the basic HTML document.

ON THE CD-ROM

Look for **body.htm** on the accompanying CD-ROM.

```
<HTML>
<HEAD>
    <TITLE> The Document Body Electric</TITLE>
</HEAD>
<BODY text="red" link="black" vlink="lime" alink="fuschia"
bgcolor="ivory">
This is the body of the document electric.
</BODY>
</HTML>
```

CROSS-REFERENCE

See **<HEAD>** and **<HTML>**.

Boolean

Concept

Some attributes have only two values (`true` and `false` or `on` and `off`, for example). These values are considered Boolean states, and as with everything else, the user agent can control how these attributes are dealt with inside your HTML document. This means that you may need to write your Boolean attributes as

```
<OPTION selected>
```

instead of the more traditional

```
<OPTION selected="selected">
```

Boolean values are also used in MathML statements when identifying some identifiers and operators.

CROSS-REFERENCE
See **<mi>** and **<mo>**.

Border

Attribute

CSS

This attribute is used to control the outline of each block-level element that can have a border applied to it. This attribute is a shorthand attribute that is used to set the width, color, and style for all four borders of a containing box. Unlike the shorthand attributes for margins and padding, the border attribute can only set options for the box as a whole, not for its individual edges.

The syntax of border is

```
border=border-width | border-style | border-color | inherit
```

NOTE
Neither Internet Explorer 4.0 nor Netscape Navigator 4.0 supports this attribute.

JAVASCRIPT
```
object.style.border [ = width | style | color ]
```

This sets the width, style, and color of the border of the specified object.

Values
border-width

The value in this location is one of the valid properties for the border-width attribute, including **medium, thin, thick,** or *length.*

border-style

The value in this location is one of the valid properties for the border-style attribute, including **none, dotted, dashed, outset, inset, groove, ridge, solid,** and **double.**

border-color

The value in this location is one of the valid properties for the `border-color` attribute, which include a valid HTML color name or the three- or six-hex-digit RGB representation of a color. You can also set this attribute to **transparent.** If this attribute is not supplied, the text color is used automatically.

Example

The following segment of code shows how you can use the border property in a style sheet to set the borders for each type of element:

```
<STYLE type="text/css">
<!-
    H1    {  border: thin dashed red }
    H6    {  border: inset }
->
</STYLE>
```

Elements

BLOCKQUOTE	BODY	BUTTON	CAPTION
CENTER	DD	DIR	DIV
DL	DT	EMBED	FIELDSET
FORM	H1–H6	HR	IFRAME
IMG	INPUT	ISINDEX	LI
LISTING	MARQUEE	MENU	OBJECT
OL	P	PLAINTEXT	PRE
SPAN	TABLE	TD	TEXTAREA
TH	TR	UL	XMP

NOTE
Both the SPAN and the DIV elements must have the `position` or the `width` attribute applied before the border will be displayed.

CROSS-REFERENCE
See **border-width, border-style,** and **border-color.**

border

Attribute

HTML

This attribute is used with many HTML elements to specify the width in pixels of any border surrounding an object on an HTML page. The `border` attribute works differently depending upon the element that you are working with. When used on an image or an object, the `border` attribute doesn't work with any other attribute. When used on a table, the `border` attribute works in conjunction with the `frame` and `rules` attributes to create a variety of effects.

When used on a table, `border="0"` negates the use of the `frame` attribute, essentially making it `frame="void"`. The `border="0"` command also assumes that there are no rules to be displayed unless otherwise specified, essentially setting `rules="none"`.

The syntax of this command is

```
border=number
```

JAVASCRIPT

```
object.border [ = space]
```

This sets the width of the border on an object.

Attributes
number

This number is the width, in pixels, of the lines composing the border.

Examples
The following statements, whose results are shown in Figures B-2 and B-3, create the same table format:

ON THE CD-ROM

Look for **border.htm** for all of these examples on the accompanying CD-ROM.

```
<TABLE border="5">
<TABLE border="5" frame="border" rules="all">
```

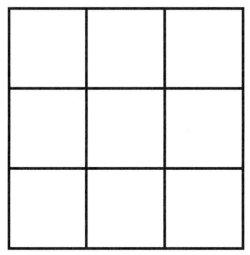

Figure B-2 A table displaying a 5-point border with both the outside
frame and the lines that make up the columns and rows

```
<TABLE border>
<TABLE frame="border" rules="all">
```

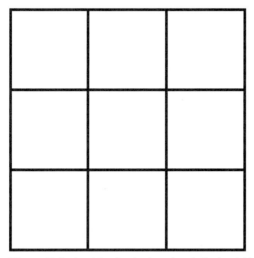

Figure B-3 A table displaying the default width frame for a user agent
that displays both the outside frame and the lines that make
up the columns and rows

As you can see from the preceding examples, all values of border imply `frame="border"` and, unless otherwise specified, `rules="all"`. If you wish to create a different-looking table, you need to set your `frame` and `rules` attributes to different values. The following two examples, whose results are displayed in Figures B-4 and B-5, show how you can change the borders on a table to create a specific effect.

```
<TABLE border="2" frame="vsides" rules="cols">
```

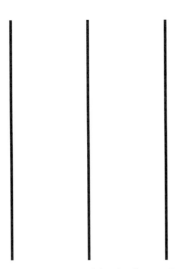

Figure B-4 A table displaying 2-point vertical
lines and no horizontal borders

```
<TABLE border="2" frame="hsides" rules="rows">
```

Elements
This attribute is used with the following HTML elements:

FRAMESET   IMG   OBJECT   TABLE

CROSS-REFERENCE
See **Border, border-bottom, border-left, border-right, border-top, border-style, border-color,** and **border-width**.

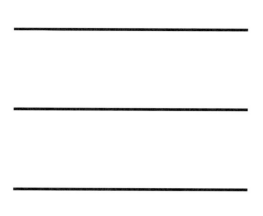

Figure B-5 A table displaying 2-point horizontal borders and no vertical lines

border-bottom

Attribute

CSS

This attribute is used to set the values for the `border-bottom-width`, `border-bottom-style`, and `border-bottom-color` attributes.

The syntax of this command is

```
border-bottom: border-bottom-width | border-bottom-style |
border-bottom-color
```

 JAVASCRIPT

```
object.style.borderBottom [ = width | style | color ]
```

This sets the width, style, and color of the bottom border of the specified object.

Values
border-bottom-width

The value in this location is one of the valid properties for the `border-bottom-width` attribute, including **medium**, **thin**, **thick**, or *length.*

border-bottom-style

The value in this location is one of the valid properties for the `border-bottom-style` attribute, including **none, dotted, dashed, outset, inset, groove, ridge, solid,** and **double.**

border-bottom-color

The value in this location is one of the valid properties for the `border-bottom-color` attribute, which include a valid HTML color name or the three- or six-hex-digit RGB representation of a color.

Example

The following example shows a variety of ways to use the border attributes, including `border-bottom`.

 ON THE CD-ROM

Look for **borderbottom.htm** on the accompanying CD-ROM.

```
<html>
<head>
<title>Border Properties</title>
<style type="text/css">
<!-
h1 {  border-color: #FFCCCC black black;
      border-style: inset;
      border-bottom-width: thick}
h2 {  border-style: groove}
h3 {  border-top-width: medium;
      border-right-width: thin;
      border-bottom-width: thick;
      border-left-width: thin}
h4 {  border-color: #FF33CC #FFCCFF}
h5 {  border-bottom: thick #FFFF00 }
->
</style>
</head>

<body bgcolor="#FFFFFF">
   <h1>Candy Canes for the Masses </h1>
   <h2>Christmas Cheer Comes to Drysville</h2>
   <h3>Henableed ground gets Stepped On</h3>
   <h4>He Wished a Horse and Rode</h4>
   <h5>Wyatt OK'd Tombstone's Renovation Projects</h5>
</body>
</html>
```

Elements

BLOCKQUOTE	BODY	BUTTON	CAPTION
CENTER	DD	DIR	DIV
DL	DT	EMBED	FIELDSET
FORM	H1–H6	HR	IFRAME
IMG	INPUT	ISINDEX	LI
LISTING	MARQUEE	MENU	OBJECT
OL	P	PLAINTEXT	PRE
SPAN	TABLE	TD	TEXTAREA
TH	TR	UL	XMP

NOTE

Both the SPAN and the DIV elements must have the position or the width attribute applied before the border will be displayed.

CROSS-REFERENCE

See **length**, **border-right**, **border-left**, **border-top**, **border-color**, **border-width**, and **border-style**.

border-bottom-color

Attribute

CSS

This attribute is used to set the color of the element's bottom border. Each edge of the border can be displayed in a different color using the individual border-x-color attributes.

The syntax for this command is

```
border-bottom-color: colorname | #RGB
```

JAVASCRIPT

```
object.style.borderBottomColor [ = color ]
```

This sets the color of the bottom border of the specified object.

Values

color

> The value can be either a valid HTML color name or the three- or six-hex-digit RGB representation of a color.

Example

The following code shows how the `border-bottom-color` can be used to change the bottom edge of a box without affecting the remaining edges.

```
<STYLE type="text/css">
<!—
   blockquote  { border-width: 2;
                 border-bottom-color: #FFCCFF }
   p           { border-width: 2;
                 border-bottom-color: red }
—>
</STYLE>
<BODY>
<P>This is the time that all good men must come to the aid of
their country.
<BLOCKQUOTE>
This is the time that all good men must come to the aid of
their country.
</BLOCKQUOTE>
</BODY>
```

NOTE

This attribute does not work properly in Internet Explorer 4.0 or Netscape 4.0.

Elements

BLOCKQUOTE	BODY	BUTTON	CAPTION
CENTER	DD	DIR	DIV
DL	DT	EMBED	FIELDSET
FORM	H1–H6	HR	IFRAME
IMG	INPUT	ISINDEX	LI
LISTING	MARQUEE	MENU	OBJECT
OL	P	PLAINTEXT	PRE
SPAN	TABLE	TD	TEXTAREA
TH	TR	UL	XMP

NOTE
Both the SPAN and the DIV elements must have the position or the width attribute applied before the border will be displayed.

CROSS-REFERENCE
See **border-bottom** and **border-color**.

border-bottom-style

Attribute

CSS

This attribute is used to control the style of the border being displayed for the bottom edge of the box.

The syntax for this attribute is

```
border-bottom-style: none | hidden | dotted | dashed | solid |
double | groove | ridge | inset | outset  | inherit
```

JAVASCRIPT

```
object.style.borderBottomStyle [ = style ]
```

This sets the style of the bottom border of the specified object.

Values
dashed

The border is composed of a series of dashes.

dotted

The border is composed of a series of dots.

double

The border is composed of two solid lines, with the clear space between the lines being equal to the value of the border-width attribute.

groove

The border looks as if it were engraved into the page.

hidden

There is no border shown for this element, but the width of the border is reserved.

inset

The border is displayed in a way that makes the entire box look pressed into the document.

none

There is no border shown for this box. This value forces the `border-width` value to be zero.

outset

The border is displayed in a way that makes the entire box look extended out of the document.

ridge

The border looks as if it were coming out of the page.

solid

The border is composed of a single line.

Example

The following example code uses a style sheet to set the border styles for all `BLOCKQUOTE` elements in the current document.

```
<STYLE type="text/css">
<!—
   blockquote { border-top-style: ridge;
          border-left-style: double;
          border-right-style: double;
          border-bottom-style: ridge;  }
—>
</STYLE>
```

Elements

This attribute is applied to all elements.

CROSS-REFERENCE

See **border**, **border-top-style**, **border-style**, **border-left-style**, and **border-right-style**.

border-bottom-width

Attribute

CSS

This attribute is used to set the width of the bottom border of a box. It can be used with the remaining `border-x-width` attributes to control the size of each individual border of the containing box of a block element.

The syntax of this attribute is

```
border-bottom-width: medium | thin | thick | length
```

JAVASCRIPT

```
object.style.borderBottomWidth [ = width]
```

This sets the width of the bottom border of the specified object.

Values

medium

This displays a medium-thick line, which is roughly 1 point thick on most user agent displays. **Medium** is the default value.

thin

This value displays a width less-than-medium, on most user agents.

thick

This value displays a width greater than medium, generally 1 to 2 points thick, although it is set by the user agent.

length

This is a floating-point number with either an absolute or a relative unit designator following it.

Example

The following example shows a variety of widths that can be used for borders on specified property boxes.

```
H1 { border-bottom-width: 5pt;}
img { border-bottom-width: thick;}
blockquote { border-bottom-width: thin; }
```

Elements

BLOCKQUOTE	BODY	BUTTON	CAPTION
CENTER	DD	DIR	DIV
DL	DT	EMBED	FIELDSET
FORM	H1–H6	HR	IFRAME
IMG	INPUT	ISINDEX	LI
LISTING	MARQUEE	MENU	OBJECT
OL	P	PLAINTEXT	PRE
SPAN	TABLE	TD	TEXTAREA
TH	TR	UL	XMP

NOTE
Both the SPAN and the DIV elements must have the position or the width attribute applied before the border will be displayed.

CROSS-REFERENCE
See **length**, **border-right-width**, **border-left-width**, **border-top-width**, **border-width**, **border-color**, and **border-style**.

border-collapse

Attribute

CSS

This attribute is used to force the border of HTML tables to join into a single line or to be separated as they arc by default.

The syntax for this attribute is

```
border-collapse: separate | collapse
```

Values

separate

This value forces the table borders to be detached as they are in standard HTML.

collapse

This setting forces the borders to collapse into a single line at the border joints.

Elements

TABLE

Objects

style

CROSS-REFERENCE
See **border**.

border-color

Attribute

CSS

This attribute is used to set the color of the left, right, top, and bottom borders of a box. Up to four values can be entered with this attribute. If one value is entered, it is used for all four edges of the containing box. If two values are entered, the first is used for the top and bottom edges of the box, and the second is used for the left and right edges of the box. If three values are entered, they are applied to the top, left and right, and bottom edges respectively. When all four values are supplied, they are applied to the top, right, bottom, and left edges respectively.

The syntax of this attribute is

```
border-color: [colorname | #RGB] {1,4}
```

Values

colorname

This is a string value representing one of the identified color names.

#RGB

This is the three- or six-digit hexadecimal number that represents the Red-Green-Blue value of the selected color.

Example

The following code shows how you can change the color of a block element's border in a style sheet.

```html
<html>
<head>
<title>Border Properties</title>
<style type="text/css">
<!—
h1 {  border-color: #FFCCCC black black;
      border-style: inset;
      border-bottom-width: thick}
h2 {  border-style: groove}
h3 {  border-top-width: medium;
      border-right-width: thin;
      border-bottom-width: thick;
      border-left-width: thin}
h4 {  border-color: #FF33CC #FFCCFF}
h5 {  border-bottom: thick #FFFF00 }
—>
</style>
</head>

<body bgcolor="#FFFFFF">
    <h1>Candy Canes for the Masses </h1>
    <h2>Christmas Cheer Comes to Drysville</h2>
    <h3>Henableed ground gets Stepped On</h3>
    <h4>He Wished a Horse and Rode</h4>
    <h5>Wyatt OK'd Tombstone's Renovation Projects</h5>
</body>
</html>
```

Elements

BLOCKQUOTE	BODY	BUTTON	CAPTION
CENTER	DD	DIR	DIV
DL	DT	EMBED	FIELDSET
FORM	H1–H6	HR	IFRAME
IMG	INPUT	ISINDEX	LI
LISTING	MARQUEE	MENU	OBJECT
OL	P	PLAINTEXT	PRE
SPAN	TABLE	TD	TEXTAREA
TH	TR	UL	XMP

NOTE

Both the SPAN and the DIV elements must have the position or the width attribute applied before the border will be displayed.

CROSS-REFERENCE

See **color**, **border-bottom-color**, **border-left-color**, **border-right-color**, **border-top-color**, **borderColorDark**, and **borderColorLight**.

borderColorDark

Property

DHTML

This object property sets or retrieves the "dark" color used for drawing the border. It is the opposite of the borderColorLight attribute and must be used with a valid border attribute setting.

The syntax of this command is

```
object.borderColorDark [=colorname | #RGB]
```

Parameters

colorname

This is a string value representing one of the identified color names.

#RGB

This is the three- or six-digit hexadecimal number that represents the Red-Green-Blue value of the selected color.

Elements

TABLE   TD   TH   TR

CROSS-REFERENCE

See **border**, **border-color**, and **borderColorLight**.

borderColorLight

Property

DHTML

This scripting property sets or retrieves the "light" color used for drawing the border. It is the opposite of the `borderColorDark` attribute and must be used with a valid `border` attribute setting.

The syntax of this command is

```
object.borderColorLight [=colorname | #RGB]
```

Parameters

colorname

This is a string value representing one of the identified color names.

#RGB

This is the three- or six-digit hexadecimal number that represents the Red-Green-Blue value of the selected color.

Elements

TABLE   TD   TH   TR

CROSS-REFERENCE
See **border**, **border-color**, and **borderColorDark**.

border-left

Attribute

CSS

This attribute is used to set the values for the `border-left-width`, `border-left-style`, and `border-left-color` attributes.

The syntax of this command is

```
border-left: border-left-width | border-left-style | border-left-color
```

JAVASCRIPT
```
object.style.borderLeft [ = width | style |color ]
```
This sets the width, style, and color of the left border of the specified object.

Values
border-left-width

The value in this location is one of the valid properties for the `border-left-width` attribute, including **medium**, **thin**, **thick**, or *length*.

border-left-style

The value in this location is one of the valid properties for the `border-left-style` attribute, including **none**, **dotted**, **dashed**, **outset**, **inset**, **groove**, **raised**, **solid**, and **double**.

border-left-color

The value in this location is one of the valid properties for the `border-left-color` attribute, which include a valid HTML color name or the three- or six-hex-digit RGB representation of a color.

Example

The following segment of code uses the `border-left` attribute to set a variety of border configurations for various elements.

```
<style type="text/css">
<!-
h3 {  border-width: dotted purple}
q   {  border-bottom: thick raised green;
         border-left: thick raised green}
p   {  border-width: 3pt dashed red;}
->
</style>
```

NOTE

Internet Explorer does not support all of these attributes.

Elements

BLOCKQUOTE	BODY	BUTTON	CAPTION
CENTER	DD	DIR	DIV
DL	DT	EMBED	FIELDSET
FORM	H1–H6	HR	IFRAME
IMG	INPUT	ISINDEX	LI
LISTING	MARQUEE	MENU	OBJECT
OL	P	PLAINTEXT	PRE
SPAN	TABLE	TD	TEXTAREA
TH	TR	UL	XMP

NOTE
Both the SPAN and the DIV elements must have the position or the width attribute applied before the border will be displayed.

CROSS-REFERENCE
See **length**, **border-right**, **border-bottom**, **border-top**, **border-color**, **border-width**, and **border-style**.

border-left-color

Attribute

CSS

This attribute is used to set the color of the element's left border. Each edge of the border can be displayed in a different color using that edge's respective color attribute.

The syntax for this command is

```
border-left-color: colorname | #RGB
```

JAVASCRIPT
```
object.style.borderLeftColor [ = color ]
```

This sets the color of the left border of the specified object.

Values
color

The value can be either a valid HTML color name or the three- or six-hex-digit RGB representation of a color.

Example
The following code shows how the border-left-color can be used to change the left edge of a box without affecting the remaining edges.

```
<STYLE type="text/css">
<!-
    q      { border-left-color: #FFCCFF }
    p      { border-left-color: red }
->
</STYLE>
```

Elements

BLOCKQUOTE	BODY	BUTTON	CAPTION
CENTER	DD	DIR	DIV
DL	DT	EMBED	FIELDSET
FORM	H1–H6	HR	IFRAME
IMG	INPUT	ISINDEX	LI
LISTING	MARQUEE	MENU	OBJECT
OL	P	PLAINTEXT	PRE
SPAN	TABLE	TD	TEXTAREA
TH	TR	UL	XMP

NOTE
Both the SPAN and the DIV elements must have the position or the width attribute.

CROSS-REFERENCE
See **border-left** and **border-color**.

border-left-style

Attribute

CSS

This attribute is used to control the style of the border that is displayed for the leftmost edge of the box.

The syntax for this attribute is

```
border-left-style: none | hidden | dotted | dashed | solid |
double | groove | ridge | inset | outset  | inherit
```

JAVASCRIPT
```
object.style.borderLeftStyle [ = style ]
```

This sets the style of the left border of the specified object.

Values
dashed

The border is composed of a series of dashes.

dotted

The border is composed of a series of dots.

double

The border is composed of two solid lines, with the clear space between the lines being equal to the value of the border-width attribute.

groove

The border looks as if it were engraved into the page.

hidden

There is no border shown for this element, but the width of the border is reserved.

inset

The border is displayed in a way that makes the entire box look pressed into the document.

none

There is no border shown for this box. This value forces the border-width value to be zero.

outset

The border is displayed in a way that makes the entire box look extended out of the document.

ridge

The border looks as if it were coming out of the page.

solid

The border is composed of a single line.

Example

The following example code uses a style sheet to set the border styles for all BLOCKQUOTE elements in the current document.

```
<STYLE type="text/css">
<!-
   blockquote { border-top-style: dotted;
            border-left-style: groove;
            border-right-style: groove;
            border-bottom-style: dotted;  }
->
</STYLE>
```

Elements
This attribute is applied to all elements.

CROSS-REFERENCE
See **border**, **border-top-style**, **border-style**, **border-bottom-style**, and **border-right-style**.

border-left-width

Attribute

CSS

This attribute is used to set the width of the left border of a box. It can be used with the remaining `border-x-width` attributes to control the size of each individual border of the containing box of a block element.

The syntax of this attribute is

```
border-left-width: medium | thin | thick | length
```

JAVASCRIPT
```
object.style.borderLeftWidth [ = width ]
```

This sets the width of the left border of the specified object.

Values

medium

This displays a medium-thick line, which is roughly 1 point thick on most user agent displays. **Medium** is the default value.

thin

This value displays a width less-than-medium, on most user agents.

thick

This value displays a width greater than medium, generally 1 to 2 points thick, although it is set by the user agent.

length

This is a floating-point number with either an absolute or a relative unit designator following it.

Example

The following example shows a variety of widths that can be used for borders on specified property boxes.

```
H1 {  border-left-width: 5pt;}
img { border-left-width: thick;}
blockquote { border-left-width: thin; }
```

Elements

BLOCKQUOTE	BODY	BUTTON	CAPTION
CENTER	DD	DIR	DIV
DL	DT	EMBED	FIELDSET
FORM	H1–H6	HR	IFRAME
IMG	INPUT	ISINDEX	LI
LISTING	MARQUEE	MENU	OBJECT
OL	P	PLAINTEXT	PRE
SPAN	TABLE	TD	TEXTAREA
TH	TR	UL	XMP

NOTE
Both the SPAN and the DIV elements must have the position or the width attribute applied before the border will be displayed.

CROSS-REFERENCE
See **length, border-bottom-width, border-right-width, border-top-width, border-width, border-color,** and **border-style.**

border-right

Attribute

CSS

This attribute is used to set the values for the border-right-width, border-right-style, and border-right-color attributes.

The syntax of this command is

```
border-right: border-right-width | border-right-style |
border-right-color
```

JAVASCRIPT

```
object.style.borderRight [ = width | style |color ]
```

This sets the width, style, and color of the right border of the specified object.

Values

border-right-width

The value in this location is one of the valid properties for the `border-right-width` attribute, including **medium, thin, thick,** or *length.*

border-right-style

The value in this location is one of the valid properties for the `border-right-style` attribute, including **none, dotted, dashed, outset, inset, groove, raised, solid,** and **double.**

border-right-color

The value in this location is one of the valid properties for the `border-right-color` attribute, which include a valid HTML color name or the three- or six-hex-digit RGB representation of a color.

Example

The following segment of code uses the `border-right` attribute to set a variety of border configurations for various elements.

```
<style type="text/css">
<!-
h3 {  border-right: dotted purple}
q   {  border-left: thick raised green;
        border-right: thick raised green}
p   {  border-right: 3pt dashed #FFCCCC;}
->
</style>
```

Elements

BLOCKQUOTE	BODY	BUTTON	CAPTION
CENTER	DD	DIR	DIV
DL	DT	EMBED	FIELDSET
FORM	H1–H6	HR	IFRAME
IMG	INPUT	ISINDEX	LI
LISTING	MARQUEE	MENU	OBJECT
OL	P	PLAINTEXT	PRE
SPAN	TABLE	TD	TEXTAREA
TH	TR	UL	XMP

NOTE
Both the SPAN and the DIV elements must have the position or the width attribute applied before the border will be displayed.

CROSS-REFERENCE
See **length**, **border-bottom**, **border-left**, **border-top**, **border-color**, **border-width**, and **border-style**.

border-right-color

Attribute

CSS

This attribute is used to set the color of the element's right border. Each edge of the border can be displayed in a different color using that edge's respective color attribute.

The syntax for this command is

```
border-right-color: colorname | #RGB
```

JAVASCRIPT
```
object.style.borderRightColor [ = color ]
```

This sets the color of the right border of the specified object.

Values
color

The value can be either a valid HTML color name or the three- or six-hex-digit RGB representation of a color.

Example
The following code shows how the border-right-color can be used to change the right edge of a box without affecting the remaining edges.

```
<STYLE type="text/css">
<!--
    q       { border-right-color: #FF00FF }
    p       { border-right-color: aqua }
-->
</STYLE>
```

Elements

BLOCKQUOTE	BODY	BUTTON	CAPTION
CENTER	DD	DIR	DIV
DL	DT	EMBED	FIELDSET
FORM	H1–H6	HR	IFRAME
IMG	INPUT	ISINDEX	LI
LISTING	MARQUEE	MENU	OBJECT
OL	P	PLAINTEXT	PRE
SPAN	TABLE	TD	TEXTAREA
TH	TR	UL	XMP

NOTE

Both the `SPAN` and the `DIV` elements must have the `position` or the `width` attribute applied before the border will be displayed.

CROSS-REFERENCE

See **border-right** and **border-color**.

border-right-style

Attribute

CSS

This attribute is used to control the style of the border being displayed for the rightmost edge of the box.

The syntax for this attribute is

```
border-right-style: none | hidden | dotted | dashed | solid |
double | groove | ridge | inset | outset | inherit
```

JAVASCRIPT

```
object.style.borderRightStyle [ = color ]
```

This sets the style of the right border of the specified object.

Values

dashed

The border is composed of a series of dashes.

dotted

The border is composed of a series of dots.

double

The border is composed of two solid lines, with the clear space between the lines being equal to the value of the `border-width` attribute.

groove

The border looks as if it were engraved into the page.

hidden

There is no border shown for this element, but the width of the border is reserved.

inset

The border is displayed in a way that makes the entire box look pressed into the document.

none

There is no border shown for this box. This value forces the `border-width` value to be zero.

outset

The border is displayed in a way that makes the entire box look extended out of the document.

ridge

The border looks as if it were coming out of the page.

solid

The border is composed of a single line.

Example

The following example code uses a style sheet to set the border styles for all `BLOCKQUOTE` elements in the current document.

```
<STYLE type="text/css">
<!--
   blockquote { border-top-style: solid;
           border-left-style: groove;
           border-right-style: double;
           border-bottom-style: dashed;  }
-->
</STYLE>
```

Elements
This attribute is applied to all elements.

CROSS-REFERENCE
See **border**, **border-top-style**, **border-style**, **border-bottom-style**, and **border-left-style**.

border-right-width

Attribute

CSS

This attribute is used to set the width of the right border of a box. It can be used with the remaining `border-x-width` attributes to control the size of each individual border of the containing box of a block element.

The syntax of this attribute is

```
border-right-width: medium | thin | thick | length
```

JAVASCRIPT
```
object.style.borderRightWidth [ = width ]
```

This sets the width of the right border of the specified object.

Values
medium

This displays a medium-thick line, which is roughly 1 point thick on most user agent displays. **Medium** is the default value.

thin

This value displays a width less-than-medium, on most user agents.

thick

This value displays a width greater than medium, generally 1 to 2 points thick, although it is set by the user agent.

length

This is a floating-point number with either an absolute or a relative unit designator following it.

Example
The following example shows a variety of widths that can be used for borders on specified property boxes.

```
H1 {  border-right-width: 5pt;}
img { border-right-width: thick;}
blockquote { border-right-width: thin; }
```

Elements

BLOCKQUOTE	BODY	BUTTON	CAPTION
CENTER	DD	DIR	DIV
DL	DT	EMBED	FIELDSET
FORM	H1–H6	HR	IFRAME
IMG	INPUT	ISINDEX	LI
LISTING	MARQUEE	MENU	OBJECT
OL	P	PLAINTEXT	PRE
SPAN	TABLE	TD	TEXTAREA
TH	TR	UL	XMP

NOTE
Both the SPAN and the DIV elements must have the position or the width attribute applied before the border will be displayed.

CROSS-REFERENCE
See **length**, **border-bottom-width**, **border-left-width**, **border-top-width**, **border-width**, **border-color**, and **border-style**.

border-style

Attribute

CSS

This attribute is used to control the style of the border that is displayed for the entire box. It can have between one and four listed values representing each side of the box.

The syntax for this attribute is

```
border-style:< none | hidden | dotted | dashed | solid |
double | groove | ridge | inset | outset > {1,4}| inherit
```

JAVASCRIPT

        `object.style.borderStyle [ = style]`

This sets the style of the border of the specified object.

Values

dashed

The border is composed of a series of dashes.

dotted

The border is composed of a series of dots.

double

The border is composed of a two solid lines, with the clear space between the lines being equal to the value of the `border-width` attribute.

groove

The border looks like as if it were engraved into the page.

hidden

There is no border shown for this element, but the width of the border is reserved.

inset

The border is displayed in a way that makes the entire box look pressed into the document.

none

There is no border shown for this box. This value forces the `border-width` value to be zero.

outset

The border is displayed in a way that makes the entire box look extended out of the document.

ridge

The border looks as if it were coming out of the page.

solid

The border is composed of a single line.

Example

The following example code uses a style sheet to set the border styles for a variety of elements in the current document.

```
<STYLE type="text/css">
<!—
    blockquote  { border-style: solid; }
    p  { border-style: outset; }
    table  { border-style: inset; }
    h1        { border-style: dashed;  }
—>
</STYLE>
```

Elements

This attribute is applied to all elements.

CROSS-REFERENCE

See **border, border-top-style, border-bottom-style, border-left-style,** and **border-right-style**.

border-top

Attribute

CSS

This attribute is used to set the values for the `border-top-width`, `border-top-style`, and `border-top-color` attributes.

The syntax of this command is

```
border-top: border-top-width | border-top-style | border-top-
color
```

JAVASCRIPT

```
object.style.borderTop [ = color | width | style ]
```

This sets the style, width, and color of the top border of the specified object.

Values

border-top-width

The value in this location is one of the valid properties for the `border-top-width` attribute, including **medium, thin, thick,** or *length.*

border-top-style

The value in this location is one of the valid properties for the `border-top-style` attribute, including **none, dotted, dashed, outset, inset, groove, raised, solid,** and **double.**

border-top-color

The value in this location is one of the valid properties for the `border-top-color` attribute; these properties include a valid HTML color name or the three- or six-hex-digit RGB representation of a color.

Example

The following segment of code uses the `border-top` attribute to set a variety of border configurations for various elements.

```
<style type="text/css">
<!--
h3 {  border-top: dotted blue}
q   {  border-bottom: thick raised green;
         border-top: thick raised #00FF00}
p   {  border-top: 3pt dashed red;}
-->
</style>
```

Elements

BLOCKQUOTE	BODY	BUTTON	CAPTION
CENTER	DD	DIR	DIV
DL	DT	EMBED	FIELDSET
FORM	H1–H6	HR	IFRAME
IMG	INPUT	ISINDEX	LI
LISTING	MARQUEE	MENU	OBJECT
OL	P	PLAINTEXT	PRE
SPAN	TABLE	TD	TEXTAREA
TH	TR	UL	XMP

NOTE

Both the `SPAN` and the `DIV` elements must have the `position` or the `width` attribute applied before the border will be displayed.

CROSS-REFERENCE

See **length, border-right, border-left, border-bottom, border-color, border-width,** and **border-style.**

border-top-color

Attribute

CSS

This attribute is used to set the color of the element's top border. Each edge of the border can be displayed in a different color using that edge's respective color attribute.

The syntax for this command is

```
border-top-color: colorname | #RGB
```

 JAVASCRIPT

```
object.style.borderTopColor [ = color ]
```

This sets the color of the top border of the specified object.

Values
color

The value can be either a valid HTML color name or the three- or six-hex-digit RGB representation of a color.

Example
The following code shows how the border-top-color can be used to change the top edge of a box without affecting the remaining edges.

```
<STYLE type="text/css">
<!—
    q      { border-top-color: #008800 }
    p      { border-top-color: fuchsia }
—>
</STYLE>
```

Elements

BLOCKQUOTE	BODY	BUTTON	CAPTION
CENTER	DD	DIR	DIV
DL	DT	EMBED	FIELDSET
FORM	H1–H6	HR	IFRAME
IMG	INPUT	ISINDEX	LI
LISTING	MARQUEE	MENU	OBJECT
OL	P	PLAINTEXT	PRE
SPAN	TABLE	TD	TEXTAREA
TH	TR	UL	XMP

NOTE

Both the SPAN and the DIV elements must have the position or the width attribute applied before the border will be displayed.

CROSS-REFERENCE

See **border-top** and **border-color**.

border-top-style

Attribute

CSS

This attribute is used to control the style of the border that is displayed for the topmost edge of the box.

The syntax for this attribute is

```
border-top-style: none | hidden | dotted | dashed | solid |
double | groove | ridge | inset | outset  | inherit
```

JAVASCRIPT

```
object.style.borderTopStyle [ = style]
```

This sets the style of the top border of the specified object.

Values

dashed

The border is composed of a series of dashes.

dotted

The border is composed of a series of dots.

double

The border is composed of a two solid lines, with the clear space between the lines being equal to the value of the border-width attribute.

groove

The border looks as if it were engraved into the page.

hidden

There is no border shown for this element, but the width of the border is reserved.

inset

> The border is displayed in a way that makes the entire box look pressed into the document.

none

> There is no border shown for this box. This value forces the `border-width` value to be zero.

outset

> The border is displayed in a way that makes the entire box look extended out of the document.

ridge

> The border looks as if it were coming out of the page.

solid

> The border is composed of a single line.

Example

The following example code uses a style sheet to set the border styles for all `BLOCKQUOTE` elements in the current document.

```
<STYLE type="text/css">
<!-
    blockquote { border-top-style: solid;
                 border-left-style: groove;
                 border-right-style: double;
                 border-bottom-style: dashed;  }
->
</STYLE>
```

Elements

This attribute is applied to all elements.

CROSS-REFERENCE

See **border, border-style, border-left-style, border-bottom-style,** and **border-right-style.**

border-top-width

Attribute

a
b
c

CSS

This attribute is used to set the width of the top border of a box. It can be used with the remaining `border-x-width` attributes to control the size of each individual border of the containing box of a block element.

The syntax of this attribute is

```
border-top-width: medium | thin | thick | length
```

 JAVASCRIPT

```
object.style.borderTopWidth [ = Width]
```

This sets the width of the top border of the specified object.

Values

medium

This displays a medium-thick line, which is roughly 1 point thick on most user agent displays. Medium is the default value.

thin

This value displays a width less-than-medium, most user agents.

thick

This value displays a width greater than medium, generally 1 to 2 points thick, although it is set by the user agent.

length

This is a floating-point number with either an absolute or a relative unit designator following it.

Example

The following example shows a variety of widths that can be used for borders on specified property boxes.

```
H1  { border-top-width: 1pt; }
img { border-top-width: thick; }
blockquote {border-top-width: thin; }
```

Elements

BLOCKQUOTE	BODY	BUTTON	CAPTION
CENTER	DD	DIR	DIV
DL	DT	EMBED	FIELDSET
FORM	H1–H6	HR	IFRAME
IMG	INPUT	ISINDEX	LI
LISTING	MARQUEE	MENU	OBJECT
OL	P	PLAINTEXT	PRE
SPAN	TABLE	TD	TEXTAREA
TH	TR	UL	XMP

 NOTE
Both the SPAN and the DIV elements must have the position or the width attribute applied before the border will be displayed.

 CROSS-REFERENCE
See **length**, **border-right-width**, **border-left-width**, **border-bottom-width**, **border-width**, **border-color**, and **border-style**.

border-width

Attribute

CSS

This attribute is used to set the width of the left, right, top, and bottom borders of a box. Up to four values can be entered with this attribute. If one value is entered, it is used for all four edges of the containing box. If two values are entered, the first is used for the top and bottom edges of the box, and the second is used for the left and right edges of the box. If three values are entered, they are applied to the top, left and right, and bottom edges respectively. When all four values are supplied, they are applied to the top, right, bottom, and left edges respectively.

The syntax of this attribute is

```
border-width: [medium | thin | thick | length] {1,4}
```

JAVASCRIPT

```
object.style.borderWidth [ = width]
```

This sets the width of the border of the specified object.

Values
medium

This displays a medium-thick line, which is roughly 1 point thick on most user agent displays. **Medium** is the default value.

thin

This value displays a width less-than-medium, most user agents.

thick

This value displays a width greater than medium, generally 1 to 2 points thick, although it is set by the user agent.

length

This is a floating-point number with either an absolute or a relative unit designator following it.

Examples

The following examples show a variety of widths that can be used for borders on specified property boxes. The following groups of examples are equal statements.

This group uses three values to set dimensions for all four sides of the box.

```
H1 { border-width:  1pt thin 3pt }
H1 {border-top-width: 1pt;
   border-right-width t: thin;
  border-left-width: thin;
    border-bottom-width: 3pt  }
```

This second group uses a single setting to control the margins of the entire document.

```
img { border-width: thick }
img { border-top-width: thick;
      border-right-width: thick;
      border-left-width: thick;
      border-bottom-width: thick }
```

This third group has two values that are used to set the top and bottom and the left and right margins separately for a particular block element.

```
blockquote { border-width: thin thick }
blockquote {border-top-width: thin;
            border-right-width: thick;
            border-left-width: thick;
            border-bottom-width: thin }
```

Elements

BLOCKQUOTE	BODY	BUTTON	CAPTION
CENTER	DD	DIR	DIV
DL	DT	EMBED	FIELDSET
FORM	H1–H6	HR	IFRAME
IMG	INPUT	ISINDEX	LI
LISTING	MARQUEE	MENU	OBJECT
OL	P	PLAINTEXT	PRE
SPAN	TABLE	TD	TEXTAREA
TH	TR	UL	XMP

NOTE
Both the SPAN and the DIV elements must have the position or the width attribute applied before the border will be displayed.

CROSS-REFERENCE
See **length**, **border-right-width**, **border-left-width**, **border-top-width**, **border-bottom-width**, **border-color**, and **border-style**.

bottom

Attribute

CSS

The bottom Cascading Style Sheets attribute specifies the distance between the bottom edge of the object box and the bottom edge of the containing block.

```
bottom=length | percentage | auto | inherit
```

Box • 203

Values
length

This is the amount of the offset in pixels. This value is any whole signed or unsigned integer.

percentage

This is the percentage of offset from the edge of the reference side of the containing block. The percentage is based on the visible area of the page in your user agent.

auto

This is the default setting. It automatically calculates the offset based upon the width and height of the object box.

inherit

The value for this distance is inherited from the parent elements.

Elements
This attribute is available for all HTML elements.

CROSS-REFERENCE
See **@page**, **margin**, **padding**, **left**, **top**, **right**, and **containing block**.

Box

Concept

CSS

When you are using HTML to define a page and its contents, think in terms of objects with borders and dimensions. Each HTML object or element creates a containment box for the contents of that element's tags. Theses boxes stack together and wrap around each other so that the contents of each element are aligned in an orderly fashion based upon the rules of the user agent and the attributes included with the elements. Take a look at Figure B-6 and its associated code.

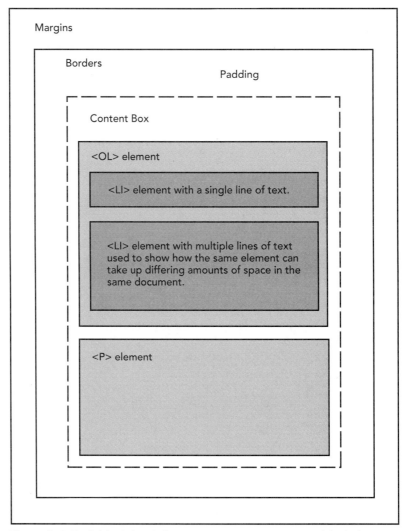

Figure B-6 Each block-level element creates a containment block that controls the arrangement of the elements on the HTML document.

All HTML documents are laid out in a series of containment boxes that organize the placement and flow of each element. This structure permits text to be placed before images are fully loaded and assists in the creation of the documents when you use WYSIWYG authoring tools.

```
<BODY>
   <UL>
      <LI> This is a single line text statement.<LI>
      <LI> This is a multi-line text statement that
            is being used to display how the containment
            boxes created by the same type of element
            can be of varying size.</LI>
   </UL>
   <P> This is just a normal paragraph</P>.
</BODY>
```

You can see that each element in Figure B-6 has its own box surrounding it. For the BODY element, the margin provides an invisible border, which provides the original level of direction for the placement of the remaining elements. Your elements are then surrounded by a layer of padding that adds white space to your documents and further restricts the organization of the documents' content. Each element's containment box, such as the UL and P boxes, is also surrounded by padding that helps it be laid out amidst the space allocated to the content box. Some element boxes, such as the UL, have other element boxes within them. This stacking or cascading effect creates a mappable system wherein style sheets can be used to control both levels and types of elements. This adds extra control to your documents and enables the document-creation system to grow and change as needed.

CROSS-REFERENCE
See **margin, padding, containment block,** and **Block-Level Element.**

Element

HTML

Start Tag: Required
End Tag: Forbidden

This element is used to insert a break into a line of streaming text. Unlike the P element, which automatically inserts both vertical space and the horizontal break, the BR element functions like a forced soft carriage return in a word processor.

Attributes

class

```
class="cdata-list"
```

Use this attribute to assign a class name to an element. User agents employ classes to group specific types of information for later use.

clear

```
clear= none | left | right | all
```

This attribute controls how the <BR> element interacts with images and other objects that appear within the document.

id

```
id="name"
```

Use this attribute to assign a name to an element.

style

```
style=style descriptors
```

This attribute applies specific style-sheet information to one particular element.

title

```
title=text
```

This attribute provides annotation information to the element to which it is applied.

Example

The following code uses the BR element to provide a soft carriage return within the variety of paragraphs of text.

```
<H5>Web Developer/Graphic Designer</H5>
    <I>March 1997 - Present</I> - Cat's Back Consulting, <BR>
    <UL TYPE="CIRCLE">
      <LI>Design, develop, and create HTML pages for a variety
      of clients. Implement Java, CGI, and MSQL solutions to
      meet their information dispersal needs.<BR>
        <A HREF=" http://www.catsback.com/"> Cat's Back
        Consulting</A><BR>
        <A HREF=" http://www.catsback.com/outbackranch/">
        Outback Ranch
      Outfitters</A><BR>
        <A HREF="http://www.catsback.com/sbothum/"> Shirly
        Bothum - Bronze Artist</A><BR>
        <A HREF=" http://www.proaxis.com/~ofc/">
```

```
Oregon Fishing Club</A><BR>
<LI>Design personalized images, graphics, and logos to
meet customer's visual requirements for both Web sites,
brochures, business cards, and other marketing materials.
</UL>
```

CROSS-REFERENCE
See **<P>** and **<HR>**.

browserLanguage

Property

DHTML

As a document object property attribute, browserLanguage identifies the language being used by the user agent viewing the current document. It can only set, not retrieve, this value.

The syntax of this command is

```
langvar = navigator.browserLanguage
```

Values

langvar

This variable contains one of the valid language codes listed with the lang attribute. The default value of this property is en-us.

Objects

Navigator

CROSS-REFERENCE
See **lang** and **User Agent**.

<BUTTON>

Element

HTML

This element creates a push button that can be used to start scripts that do anything from loading a new document to changing the location of text on your screen. The BUTTON element creates buttons that function just like those created with the INPUT element. Because BUTTON element buttons are not tied to form functions, however, you can create much richer results with them.

Attributes

accesskey

```
accesskey="character"
```

You can assign an access key to an element. This key enables you to put the focus on an element, including a button, quickly. In the case of a form element, the user is immediately able to input information. In the case of a link, the link is activated and followed.

disabled

```
disabled
```

This is a Boolean attribute that, when set, disables the button, preventing any user input.

name

```
name=cdata
```

Use this attribute to assign a control name to the element.

onblur

```
onblur=script
```

This attribute is activated when an element loses the focus either through the actions of a mouse or another pointing device or through tabbing navigation.

onfocus

```
onfocus=script
```

This attribute takes effect when an element receives focus from either a mouse or another pointing device or through tabbed navigation.

onclick

```
onclick=script
```

This attribute takes effect when a user clicks the button on a pointing device with the pointer over an element.

ondblclick

```
ondblclick=script
```

This attribute takes effect when a user double-clicks the button on a pointing device with the pointer over an element.

onkeydown

```
onkeydown=script
```

This attribute takes effect when a user presses a key and the pointer is over an element.

onkeypress

```
onkeypress=script
```

This attribute takes effect when a user presses and releases a key with the pointer over an element.

onkeyup

```
onkeyup=script
```

This attribute takes effect when a user releases a key with the pointer over an element.

onmousedown

```
onmousedown=script
```

This attribute takes effect when a user presses the button on a pointing device while the pointer is over an element.

onmousemove

```
onmousemove=script
```

This attribute is activated when the mouse pointer is moved while it is over an element.

onmouseout

```
onmouseout=script
```

This attribute is activated when the mouse pointer is moved away from an element.

onmouseover

```
onmouseover=script
```

This attribute is activated when the mouse pointer is moved over an element.

onmouseup

```
onmouseup=script
```

This attribute takes effect when the button on a pointing device is released while the pointer is over an element.

tabindex

```
tabindex=number
```

This attribute provides the position of the current element within the overall tabbing order of the document.

type

```
type = submit | button | reset
```

This attribute controls the type of button that this element creates. If the value of this attribute is **submit** (which is the default), you create a standard submission-type button that can, for example, submit a form or mail a letter. The value of **button** creates a standard push button whose event attributes trigger the running of an associated script. A **reset** button simply resets all the variables and content positions back to their original values.

NOTE

It is always a good idea to include a reset button on your HTML pages so that your document viewers have an easy way to revert to the document's original state in case of trouble.

value

```
value=cdata
```

This attribute is used to set the initial value of the button.

Example

The following example code displays a short online resume using the BUTTON command to load various DIV blocks into the visible area of the user agent's screen.

ON THE CD-ROM

Look for **button.htm** on the accompanying CD-ROM.

```
<HTML>
<HEAD>
   <TITLE> Heather's - Resume </TITLE>
</HEAD>
<STYLE TYPE="text/css">
  <!—
    #layer1 {position:absolute; top: 160px; left:40px; height:
    350; width:650px; overflow: auto;}
    #layer3 {position:absolute; top: 125px; left:35px; height:
    25; width:650px; overflow: auto;}
    #layer4 {position:absolute; top: 185px; left:40px; height:
    350; width:650px; overflow: auto; visibility: hidden;}
```

```
    ->
</STYLE>
<SCRIPT LANGUAGE="JavaScript">
        <!-
        var bName = navigator.appName;
        var bVer = parseInt(navigator.appVersion);
        var NS4 = (bName == "Netscape" && bVer >= 4);
        var IE4 = (bName == "Microsoft Internet Explorer" &&
        bVer >= 4);
        // ->
</SCRIPT>
<SCRIPT LANGUAGE="JavaScript">
   <!-
    function ProExp() {
        ResumeStuff.innerHTML = saveResume;
    }
    function Education() {
    ResumeStuff.innerHTML = saveEdu;
    }
    function CompStuff() {
    ResumeStuff.innerHTML = saveComp;
    }
    function Activities() {
    ResumeStuff.innerHTML = saveActs;
}
function doOver() {
    ResumeStuff.innerHTML = saveResume;
}
//->
</SCRIPT>
<BODY bgcolor=ffffff>
<p>
<IMG SRC="resume.gif"><br>
<center>
<BUTTON onClick="doOver()"><B>RESET</B></BUTTON>
</center>
<Span id="layer1">
<DIV id="ResumeStuff">
<font size=-1>
<H5>Web Developer/Graphic Designer</H5>
    <I>March 1997 - Present</I> - Cat's Back Consulting, <BR>
<UL TYPE="CIRCLE">
```

```
<LI>Design, develop, and create HTML pages for a variety of
clients. Implement Java, CGI, and MSQL solutions to meet their
information dispersal needs. <BR>
<A HREF="http://www.catsback.com/">
http://www.catsback.com/</A> <BR>
<A HREF="http://www.catsback.com/outbackranch/">
http://www.catsback.com/outbackranch/</A> <BR>
<A href= "http://www.catsback.com/sbothum/">
http://www.catsback.com/sbothum/</A> <BR>
<A HREF="http://www.proaxis.com/~ofc/">
http://www.proaxis.com/~ofc/</A> <BR>
<LI>Design personalized images, graphics, and logos to meet
customer's visual requirements for both Web sites, brochures,
business cards, and other marketing materials.
</UL>
<p>
<H5>Freelance Author /Editor </H5>
    <I>June 1995 - Present </I>- Variety of National
    Publishers<BR>
    <ul TYPE="CIRCLE">
      <li>Write and/or edit nationally published documentation
      discussing a variety of topics ranging from on-line
      service providers, such as CompuServe and America
      Online, to installing and using a variety of Internet
      software. Book titles include HTML Master Reference and
      Internet Explorer 6-in-1.
      <li>Develop material for weekly updates to a Netscape
      Resource Center. This material includes product reviews,
      user interviews, product introductions, feature
      introductions and explanations, and common questions
      with answers.
      </ul>
    </font></DIV>
  </span>
<span id="layer3">
  <BUTTON onClick="ProExp()">Professional Experience</BUTTON>
  <BUTTON onClick="CompStuff()">Computer Skills</BUTTON>
  <BUTTON onClick="Education()">Academics</BUTTON>
</span>
<span id="layer4">
  <DIV id="EduStuff">
<font size=-1>
<B>Education:</B>        A college in Middle America<BR>
```

```
<B>Degree:</B> BA in Mathematics and Computer Information
Science<BR>
<B>w/ Emphasis:</B>
<table border=0 cellpadding=3>
<tr>
<td width=150><font size=-1>Technical Writing</font></td>
<td width =150><font size=-1>Human/Computer
Interaction</font></td>
</tr>
<tr>
<td><font size=-1>Database Applications</font></td>
<td><font size=-1>Systems Analysis and Design</font></td>
</tr>
<tr>
<td><font size=-1>CASE Tools</font></tr>
<td><font size=-1>Advanced Mathematics</font></td>
</tr>
</table>
</font>
</DIV>
<DIV id="PuterStuff">
<H5>Programming Languages:</H5>
<font size=-1>
<table border=0 cellpadding=3>
<tr>
<td width = 120><font size=-1>Visual Basic</font></td>
<td width = 120><font size=-1>HTML 4.0</font></td>
<td width = 120><font size=-1>PASCAL</font></td>
<td width = 120><font size=-1>SQL</font></td>
</tr>
<tr>
<td><font size=-1>JavaScript</font></td>
<td><font size=-1>COBOL</font></td>
<td><font size=-1>ASPECT</font></td>
<td><font size=-1>HyperTalk7</font></td>
</tr>
</table>
<H5>Software Used:</H5>
<table border=0 cellpadding=3>
<tr>
<td width = 120><font size=-1>MS Word</font></td>
<td width = 120><font size=-1>Adobe Photoshop</font></td>
<td width = 120><font size=-1>MS PowerPoint</font></td>
<td width = 120><font size=-1>Adobe PageMaker</font></td>
```

a
b
c

```
</tr>
<tr>
<td width = 120><font size=-1>MS FrontPage97</font></td>
<td width = 120><font size=-1>MAcromedia Dreamweaver</font></td>
<td width = 120><font size=-1>NetObjects ScriptBuilder</font>
</td>
<td width = 120><font size=-1>Adobe Illustrator</font></td>
</tr>
<tr>
<td width = 120><font size=-1>MS Exchange</font></td>
<td width = 120><font size=-1>Lotus Notes</font></td>
<td width = 120><font size=-1>HotDog Pro</font></td>
<td width = 120><font size=-1>Acrobat</font></td>
</tr>
</table>
<H5>Operating Systems:</H5>
<table border=0 cellpadding=3>
<tr>
<td width = 120><font size=-1>Windows 95</font></td>
<td width = 120><font size=-1>Windows NT</font></td>
<td width = 120><font size=-1>Windows 3.x / WFWG</font></td>
<td width = 120><font size=-1>OS/2 WARP</font></td>
</tr>
</table>
</font>
</DIV>
</span>
<SCRIPT LANGUAGE="JavaScript1.1">
<!--
    var saveResume = "";
    var saveEdu= "";
    var saveComp="";
    var saveActs="";
if (IE4) { saveResume = ResumeStuff.innerHTML };
if (IE4) { saveEdu = EduStuff.innerHTML };
if (IE4) { saveComp = PuterStuff.innerHTML };
if (IE4) { saveActs = ActStuff.innerHTML };
if (!IE4) {NewWindow=window.open("resumens.html")};
//-->
</SCRIPT>
</BODY>
</HTML>
```

CROSS-REFERENCE
See **<LAYER>**, **<SPAN>**, **positioning**, and **buttons**.

Buttons

Concept

Buttons are used within HTML to control forms and to activate scripted elements. These scripts can be used to alter text, activate animations, submit form information, accept an agreement, or do just about anything else that your imagination can devise. You can use either the BUTTON element or the INPUT element to create a button in HTML. Although both of these elements create buttons, you have more options for rendering and activating information with the BUTTON element. The INPUT element has been traditionally used with form content, although it is by no means restricted to such a use. When using the BUTTON element, you can use images or content other than a standard button face if you wish. You can force the button to appear to press when you click it with your mouse. These things are not possible with the INPUT element.

CROSS-REFERENCE
See **<BUTTON>** and **<INPUT>**.

cancelBubble

Property

DHTML

This property is used in scripts to control whether the current event should bubble up the hierarchy of event handlers. It can also be used to determine whether bubbling is enabled for that event. Using this event to cancel bubbling for an event does not affect any subsequent events.

The syntax for this property is

```
object.cancelBubble [=boolean]
```

Parameters
boolean

This value can be either true or false. If it is **true**, bubbling for this event is canceled, which prevents the next event handler in the hierarchy from receiving the event. If the value is **false**, bubbling is enabled.

Elements

This property can affect any element that supports event handlers such as `onclick`, `onblur`, `ondblclick`, and so on.

Objects

event

CROSS-REFERENCE
See **event**.

Canvas

Concept

Canvas is a term that—for all media types—describes the space used for formatting and structuring the objects' contents. The size of a canvas is inherently infinite, although the area used for drawing the objects being formatted is generally finite. The dimensions of the formatted area are most often established by the user agent in relation to the media being targeted. Document authors generally conform to the implied dimensions of the user agent. For example, if the dimensions of a computer screen are 640 × 480 pixels, the user agent sets a minimum width and an initial width based upon this size. When the document is designed, the author often takes into consideration this screen dimension. The user agent displays a page within the height and width offered to it through the size of the viewport, whether that size is 6' × 4' or 640 × 480 pixels. If the document has been designed for a wider screen than the viewport, the document is wrapped and reformatted to fit the narrower screen. If the document is narrower than the screen, it is aligned within the screen according to the formatting instructions.

If the media used is aural, the canvas consists of the three-dimensional physical space that creates surrounding sound and a temporal space that enables the author to control the order of multiple sounds. Properties affecting the canvas, as defined by Cascading Style Sheets, enable the user to control the quality of the synthesized speech.

CROSS-REFERENCE
See **media groups**, **media types**, **user agent**, **Style Sheets**, and **Aural Style Sheets**.

cap-height

Descriptor

CSS

This descriptor is used to define the height of uppercase characters for a font. If the value is undefined, user agents do not use this descriptor when matching fonts. If this descriptor is used, the `units-per-em` descriptor must also be used.

```
cap-height=number
```

CROSS-REFERENCE
See **baseline**, **Characters**, **glyphs**, and **height**.

<CAPTION>

Element

HTML

Start Tag: Required
End Tag: Required

This element is used to identify a caption for a table located in an HTML document. When this element is used, it should be used to describe the nature of the table. You can only use this element directly after the TABLE start tag. You cannot have multiple captions for a single table. The caption should be wrapped to the same width as the TABLE and should not be cropped by the user agent.

Visual user agents make the information in a table and its caption readily available for sighted people. For individuals who use nonvisual user agents, captions are rarely adequate in providing a summary of the purpose and structure of the table. As a document author, you should therefore make the effort to provide additional information in the caption and in the summary attribute of the TABLE element.

Attributes
align

```
align=top | bottom | left | right
```

This attribute enables the document author to specify the position of the attribute with respect to the table it is representing. If the value of the attribute is **top** or **bottom**, the contents of the caption are located above or below the table, respectively. A value of **left** places the caption to the table's left, and a value of **right** places the caption to the table's right.

class

```
class="cdata-list"
```

This attribute is used to assign a class name to an element. User agents employ classes to group specific types of information for later use.

dir

```
dir = LTR | RTL | [CS | CI | CN | CA | CT]
```

This attribute defines the direction of the text flow in a document so that a user agent can correctly display it to the reader. This attribute can also be used to specify information about the case of the characters.

id

    `id="`*name*`"`

This attribute is used to assign a name to an element.

lang

    `lang="`*language code*`"`

This attribute specifies the language in which an element and its values should be rendered.

onclick

    `onclick=`*script*

This attribute takes effect when a user clicks the button on a pointing device with the pointer over an element.

ondblclick

    `ondblclick=`*script*

This attribute takes effect when a user double-clicks the button on a pointing device with the pointer over an element.

onkeydown

    `onkeydown=`*script*

This attribute takes effect when a user presses a key and the pointer is over an element.

onkeypress

    `onkeypress=`*script*

This attribute takes effect when a key is either pressed and released while the pointer is over an element.

onkeyup

    `onkeyup=`*script*

This attribute takes effect when a user releases a key with the pointer over an element.

onmousedown

    `onmousedown=`*script*

This attribute takes effect when a user presses the button on a pointing device while the pointer is over an element.

onmousemove

```
onmousemove=script
```

This attribute is activated when the mouse pointer is moved while it is over an element.

onmouseout

```
onmouseout=script
```

This attribute is activated when the mouse pointer is moved away from an element.

onmouseover

```
onmouseover=script
```

This attribute is activated when the mouse pointer is moved over an element.

onmouseup

```
onmouseup=script
```

This attribute takes effect when the button on a pointing device is released while the pointer is over an element.

style

```
style=style descriptors
```

This attribute applies specific style-sheet information to one particular element.

title

```
title=text
```

This attribute provides annotation information to the element.

Example

The following example code creates a three-by-four table showing the quarterly income and expenses for a small consulting company.

ON THE CD-ROM

Look for **caption.htm** on the accompanying CD-ROM.

```
<html>
<head>
<title>Table Captions</title>
</head>
```

```
<body bgcolor="#FFFFFF">
<h1>Cat's Back Consulting</h1>
<h2>Income and Expenses for 1998</h2>
<table border="1" width="75%" summary="The quarterly income
and expense comparison for CBC leaves us with a total profit
of $1150 in 1998.">
  <caption> The quarterly income and expense comparison for
  CBC shows a varying, but profitable, year for CBC. With a
  yearly income of $4400 and expenses of $3250, an overall
  profitable year was achieved.</caption>
  <tr>
    <td bgcolor="#FFFF99"> </td>
    <td bgcolor="#FFCCFF">Q1</td>
    <td bgcolor="#FFCCFF">Q2</td>
    <td bgcolor="#FFCCFF">Q3</td>
    <td bgcolor="#FFCCFF">Q4</td>
  </tr>
  <tr>
    <td bgcolor="#FFFF99">Income</td>
    <td bgcolor="#CCFFFF">1200</td>
    <td bgcolor="#CCFFFF">1000</td>
    <td bgcolor="#CCFFFF">1000</td>
    <td bgcolor="#CCFFFF">1200</td>
  </tr>
  <tr>
    <td bgcolor="#FFFF99">Expense</td>
    <td bgcolor="#CCFFFF">700</td>
    <td bgcolor="#CCFFFF">750</td>
    <td bgcolor="#CCFFFF">900</td>
    <td bgcolor="#CCFFFF">900</td>
  </tr>
  <tr>
    <td bgcolor="#66FF99">Profit</td>
    <td bgcolor="#66CCCC">500</td>
    <td bgcolor="#66CCCC">250</td>
    <td bgcolor="#66CCCC">100</td>
    <td bgcolor="#66CCCC">300</td>
  </tr>
</table>
<p> </p>
</body>
</html>
```

CROSS-REFERENCE
See **caption**, **caption-side**, **<TABLE>**, and **summary**.

caption

Property

DHTML

This property is used in scriptlets to retrieve the CAPTION associated with the selected TABLE. It cannot be used to set the wording of the CAPTION, but it can be used to change its appearance.

The syntax for this command is

```
Null | [oCaption=] object.caption
```

Values
Null

If set to Null, then no caption exists for this table. This is the default value.

oCaption

This is the object that is used to represent the table's caption.

Example
The following example code changes the font-family used to display the caption to Verdana from the default set in the document.

```
<SCRIPT language="JavaScript">
   {
   document.all.Table1.caption.style.fontfamily="Verdana";
   }
</SCRIPT>
```

Objects
table

 CROSS-REFERENCE
See **caption-side**, **style**, **<TABLE>**, and **<CAPTION>**.

caption-side

Attribute

CSS

This property is used to specify the position of the caption box with respect to the table. When a caption is placed above or below a table, it is formatted as if it were a block element either before or after the table. The width of the caption is formatted based upon the width of the table it is describing. There are two exceptions to this rule: (1) caption-side boxes inherit many properties from the table, and (2) they are not considered to be a block for the purpose of compact or run-in elements that precede the table.

Captions that are located to the left or right side of a table need to have their widths specified. This forces the width of the caption to be within your idea of an acceptable range. If you specify **auto** for left- and right-side widths, you could end up with a single character column, which is impossible for viewers to read.

The syntax of this property is

```
caption-side= top | bottom | left | right | inherit
```

Values

top

This value places the caption box above the table.

bottom

This value places the caption box below the table.

left

This value places the caption box to the left of the table.

right

This value places the caption box to the right of the table.

Examples

The following code shows you how to place the caption along the top of the table, forcing it to use the same margins as the table and selecting the font for the caption's text.

```
<STYLE type="text/css">
<!—
CAPTION  { caption-side: top;
          width: auto;
```

```
              font-family: Verdana, cursive; }
      ->
    </STYLE>
```

The following code aligns the caption to the left of the table. The table has been centered, and the box containing both the table and the caption has been shifted toward the left margin the same amount as the width of the caption box.

```
<STYLE type="text/css">
  <!-
  BODY      { margin-left: 12em; }
  TABLE     { margin-left: auto;
              margin-right: auto; }
  CAPTION   { caption-side: left;
              width: 12em;
              margin-left: -12em;
              text-align: left; }

  ->
</STYLE>
```

Elements
    CAPTION

CROSS-REFERENCE
See **<CAPTION>**, **<TABLE>**, **margins**, and **caption**.

Cartesian Positioning Points

Concept

The Cartesian space is represented by a two-axis grid that identifies both axes of two-dimensional space. Positions on the vertical and horizontal axes are identified through the use of an ordered pair. An ordered pair, specified by (x,y), contains one number representing the x position and another representing the y position on the grid. The x and y axes meet at the point identified as $(0,0)$. This means that you travel 0 units across the horizontal x axis and 0 units up the vertical y axis. This is the center of the grid. A point specified as $(4,8)$ places your position 4 units to the right and 8 units above the center of the grid (see Figure C-1).

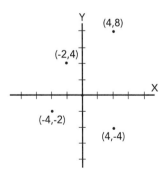

Figure C-1 Each position on the grid representing Cartesian space is identified by an ordered pair using the form of the points highlighted here.

CROSS-REFERENCE
See **z-index**, **x**, and **y**.

Cascade

Concept

CSS

Style sheets used in a document can come from one of three sources: the document author, the user, or the user agent.

- **The Document Author.** When the author writes the document, he or she specifies particular style sheets to use when displaying the document. In the case of HTML documents, style sheets can be included within the heading of the document or linked externally.

- **The User.** Some user agents enable the user to specify a style sheet to use when displaying documents.

- **The User Agent.** For a user agent to conform to Cascading Style Sheets specifications, it must apply a default style sheet to a document before any other style sheets. This default style sheet should present the elements of the document in a way that satisfies the mainstream presentation expectations for the document language. Some of the settings used in the user agent's style sheet might be configurable by the user. Most of the time, the user-configurable options are limited to font color, font face, background color, link colors, and default language.

As style sheets from these three sources are implemented, areas of the style sheets overlap. The Cascading Style Sheets cascade determines how they interact with each other by assigning a weight to each style rule. When several rules apply to a single element, the rule with the greatest weight is implemented, taking precedence over all other rules.

The cascade generally gives rules in an author's style sheet a greater weight than rules in a user's style sheet, although this precedence is reversed when `!Important` rules are used in the user's style sheet. However, all user and author rules have more weight than a user agent's style-sheet rules.

Along those same lines, imported style sheets are also worked into the cascade and weighted according to their order of importation. Local style sheets override rules in imported style sheets. Imported style sheets can import new style sheets. Each successive style sheet to be imported receives a lighter weight, so it is less likely to be implemented than the preceding style sheets.

CROSS-REFERENCE

See **!Important**, **Cascading Order**, **Cascading Style Sheets**, and **User Agent**.

Cascading Order

Concept

CSS

User agents employ a specified sorting order when identifying the specific value for an element and its attributes. This order has specific rules, which have been identified by the Cascading Style Sheets, level 2, specification and are listed below:

1. Find all the style-sheet rules that are to be applied to the specific element and property for the identified media type.

2. Sort the declarations by weight and origin. For a normal declaration, the author style sheet overrides a user style sheet, which in turn overrides the user agent's default style sheet. For elements using the "`!Important`" declaration, a user style sheet overrides an author style sheet, which in turn overrides the default user-agent style sheet. Any element in any style sheet with an "`!Important`" declaration overrides any normal declaration on a higher-ranking style sheet. Imported style sheets are deemed to have the same origin as the style sheet that imported them; if the user agent's default style sheet imports an additional style sheet, the imported style sheet is treated as coming from the user agent.

3. Sort the items by the level of specificity associated with a selector. This means that the more specific a style sheet is in its specifications, the more weight is applied to that particular element

on the style sheet. For example, in the font-family Cascading Style Sheets attribute, specifying a generic name is less specific than specifying a font-family name and would therefore have a lighter weight. Pseudo-elements and pseudo-classes are sorted in the same manner as normal elements and classes, and they are treated with no more weight than a normal element or class.

4. The final sort includes sorting by order. If two rules have the same origin, weight, and specificity, the rule that was specified last is used. In this case, rules in imported style sheets are considered to occur before any rules in the style sheet itself.

This strategy of weighing elements and their attributes enables authors to have greater control over the display of their information than the user does, unless, of course, the "!Important" declaration is used.

 CROSS-REFERENCE
See **!Important**, **Cascade**, **Cascading Style Sheets**, and **User Agent**.

Cascading Style Sheets

Language

Cascading Style Sheets (CSS) is a style-sheet language designed to enable document authors and users to control the presentation of a document. CSS separates the presentation elements of a document from the content of that document so that Web authoring and site maintenance are made easier and the jobs of HTML and XML developers more efficient. As a document or application developer, you can even tailor the design of your document for visual display applications, aural devices, printed pages, Braille devices, TTY machines, or the television, to name a few. You can control the position of your content and the layout of your tables, and you have more control over the fonts used to display your documents. Cascading Style Sheets, level 2 (CSS2), the current version of CSS that is available, has built on the previous version so that compatibility between previously conforming user agents and documents designed for them is still available with the next generation of user agents.

The CSS1 and CSS2 specifications are based on a set of design principles that have come from both the software development world and the world of graphic design and layout. This set of principles includes the following features:

- **Forward and backward compatibility.** All user agents, not just CSS2-compatible ones, are able to display the content of these enhanced documents. All CSS2 user agents are able to display CSS1-enhanced documents.

- **Complementary structure.** Style sheets are designed to complement the structure of the documents so that an author can change a style sheet with little to no change in the markup file. This makes the author's job more efficient and enables the author to update an entire suite of documents quickly in a single pass.

- **Independence from all.** Style sheets are not specific to a single vendor, platform, or device. This enables documents to work in all venues, although you can specify a style sheet for a particular device.

- **Easy maintenance.** External style sheets, linked to a document, enable HTML and XML developers to update an entire site's presentation with little or no markup changes in the documents themselves.

- **Simplicity.** All style sheets are easily read and written by humans. They are simple text files that can be read in any text editor and are identified as style sheets by their `.css` extension. Generally, there is only one way to achieve a specific effect, and most Cascading Style Sheets attributes function independently of each other. Because `.css` files affect the presentation of the information, you can often use a style-sheet specification, rather than an image or audio file, and save space on your network by downloading the information.

- **Rich variety of scripts.** Along with providing document authors a way to render information on the Web in a more dynamic fashion, CSS2 provides a means for scripting languages such as JavaScript to interface with the style specifications, either retrieving or setting their values.

- **Accessibility.** Document authors using Cascading Style Sheets are able to delve into a variety of features that make the Web more accessible for individuals with disabilities. You can eliminate the invisible GIF trick from your repertoire and quit making text images to force a font to appear in the color and style of your choosing. Your readers can create their own style sheet to override the author's style sheets, giving them the power to ensure that the documents they read are legible for them. With the enhanced list of media groups, users of Braille, embossed, and TTY media devices can have information tailored specifically to the equipment that they use. Individuals using speech synthesizers or other aural devices can control the voice and audio output used when reading a document.

In addition to this set of principles, Cascading Style Sheets has broken its individual style-sheet rules into two main parts: a *selector* and a *declaration* (see Figure C-2). The selector identifies the HTML or XML element, such as BODY or TABLE, to which the rule is being applied. The declaration has two parts, the *attribute name* and the *value*. The attribute name identifies the aspect of the selector that you wish to change (for example, the `color` or `width` of an HR element). The value of the attribute identifies the specific instructions for the display of the element (for example, if the attribute is `color`, a possible value would be **red,** forcing the HR element to be displayed in red).

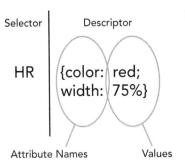

Selector   Descriptor

HR   {color: red; width: 75%}

Attribute Names   Values

Figure C-2 Each CSS rule consists of a selector and a two-part declaration that identifies the aspect of the element to be changed.

Within an HTML 4.0 document, you can specify a style sheet in one of two ways: either within the HTML markup document using the `STYLE` element, or in an external style sheet using the `LINK` element.

The syntax for using the `STYLE` element is

```
<STYLE type="text/css">
  H1     { color: blue;
           line-height: 2em;
           font-weight: bold }
</STYLE>
```

If a document author is working on multiple pages of a similar design, an external style sheet would best serve him or her. External style sheets also give developers more flexibility over their work, enabling them to alter the presentation of a scries of documents without modifying the source document. The `LINK` command can be used to link to an external style sheet in the following fashion:

```
<LINK href="extstyle.css" rel="stylesheet" type="text/css"
```

This element identifies the type of resource being linked to with the `rel` attribute, the location of the style sheet through the `href` attribute, and the type of style sheet being linked with the `type` attribute. Table C-1 lists the CSS attributes; Table C-2 lists the CSS descriptors.

Table C-1 CSS Attributes

Attribute Name	Syntax	Default Value
azimuth	*angle* | ⌈left-side | far-left | left | center-left | center | center-right | right | far-right | right-side⌉ | behind | leftwards | rightwards | inherit	center
background	[background-color || background-image || background-repeat || background-attachment || background-position] | inherit	
background-attachment	Scroll | fixed | inherit	scroll
background-color	*color* | transparent | inherit	transparent
background-image	*uri* | none| inherit	none
background-position	[*percentage* | *length*] | [top | center | bottom] || [left | center | right] | inherit	0% 0%
background-repeat	Repeat | repeat-x | repeat-y | no-repeat | inherit	repeat
border	[border-width || border-style || *color*] | inherit	
border-bottom	[border-bottom-width || border-style || *color*] | inherit	
border-bottom-color	*color* | inherit	*color*
border-bottom-style	*border-style* | inherit	none
border-bottom-width	*border-width* | inherit	medium
border- collapse	Collapse | separate | inherit	separate
border-color	*color* | transparent | inherit	*color*
border-left	[border-left-width || border-style || *color*] | inherit	
border-left-color	*color* | inherit	*color*
border-left-style	*border-style* | inherit	none
border-left-width	*border-width* | inherit	medium
border-right	[border-right-width || border-style || *color*] | inherit	
border-right-color	*color* | inherit	*color*
border-right-style	*border-style* | inherit	none
border-right-width	*border-width* | inherit	medium
border-style	:< none | hidden | dotted | dashed | solid | double | grooved | ridge | inset | outset > {1,4}| inherit	none
border-top	[border-top-width || border-style || *color*] | inherit	

Continued

Table C-1 *Continued*

Attribute Name	Syntax	Default Value
border-top-color	*color* | inherit	*color*
border-top-style	*border-style* | inherit	none
border-top-width	*border-width* | inherit	medium
border-width	Medium | thin | thick | *length*] {1,4}	medium
bottom	*length* | *percentage* | auto | inherit	auto
caption-side	Top | bottom | left | right | inherit	top
cell-spacing	none | *length* | inherit	none
clear	none | left | right | both | inherit	none
clip	*shape* | auto | inherit	auto
color	*color* | inherit	*user agent*
column-span	*integer* | inherit	1
content	[*string* | *uri* | *counter* | attr(x) | open-quote | close-quote | no-open-quote | no-close-quote] + | inherit	empty string
counter-increment	[*identifier integer*] | none | inherit	none
counter-reset	[*identifier integer*] | none | inherit	none
cue	cue-before | cue-after | inherit	
cue-after	*uri* | none | inherit	none
cue-before	*uri* | none | inherit	none
cursor	[[auto | crosshair | default | pointer | move | e-resize | ne-resize | nw-resize | n-resize | se-resize | sw-resize | s-resize | e-resize | w-resize | text | wait | help] || *uri*] | inherit	auto
direction	Ltr | rtl | inherit	ltr
display	Inline | block | list-item | none | run-in | compact | marker | table | inline-table | table-row-group | table-column-group | table-header-group | table-footer-group | table-row | table-cell | table-caption | inherit	inline
elevation	*angle* | below | level | above | below | higher | lower | inherit	level
empty-cells	Show | hide | inherit	

Attribute Name	Syntax	Default Value
float	Left | right | none | inherit	none
font	[[font-style || font-variant || font-weight] font-size [/line height] font family] | caption | icon | menu | messagebox | smallcaption | statusbar | inherit–	
font-family	*family-name* || *generic-family* list	*user agent*
font-size	*absolute-size* | *relative-size* | *length* | *percentage* | inherit	medium
font-size-adjust	*number* | none | inherit	none
font-stretch	Normal |wider | narrower | ultra-condensed | extra-condensed | condensed | semi-condensed | semi-expanded | expanded | extra-expanded | ultra-expanded]	
font-style	Normal | italic | oblique | inherit	normal
font-variant	Normal | small-caps | inherit	normal
font-weight	Normal | bold | bolder | lighter | 100 | 200 | 300 | 400 | 500 | 600 | 700 | 800 | 900 | inherit	normal
height	*length* | *percentage* | auto | inherit	auto
left	*length* | *percentage* | auto | inherit	auto
letter-spacing	Normal | *length* | *percentage* | inherit	normal
line-height	Normal | *number* | *length* | *percentage* | inherit	normal
list-style	[list-style-type || list-style-position || list-style-image] | inherit	
list-style-image	*uri* | none | inherit	none
list-style-position	Inside | outside | inherit	outside
list-style-type	disc | circle | square | decimal | decimal-leading-zero | lower-roman | upper-roman | lower-alpha | upper-alpha | lower-greek | lower-latin | upper-latin | hebrew | armenian | georgian | cjk-ideographic | hiragana | katakana | hiragana-iroha | katakana-iroha | none | inherit	disc
margin	*margin-width* {1,4} | inherit	
margin-bottom	*margin-width* | inherit	0

Continued

Table C-1 *Continued*

Attribute Name	Syntax	Default Value
margin-left	*margin-width* | inherit	0
margin-right	*margin-width* | inherit	0
margin-top	*margin-width* | inherit	0
marker-offset	*length* | auto | inherit	auto
marks	[crop || cross] | none | inherit	none
max-height	*length* | *percentage* | none | inherit	100%
max-width	*length* | *percentage* | none | inherit	100%
min-height	*length* | *percentage* | inherit	0
min-width	*length* | *percentage* | inherit	*user agent*
orphans	*length* | inherit	2
outline	[outline-color || outline-style || outline-width] | inherit	
outline-color	*color* | invert | inherit	invert
outline-style	*border-style* | inherit	none
outline-width	*border-width* | inherit	medium
overflow	Visible | hidden | scroll | auto | inherit	visible
padding	*padding-width* {1,4} | inherit	
padding-bottom	*padding-width* | inherit	0
padding-left	*padding-width* | inherit	0
padding-right	*padding-width* | inherit	0
padding-top	*padding-width* | inherit	0
page	*identifier* | auto	auto
page-break-after	auto | always | avoid | left | right | inherit	auto
page-break-before	auto | always | avoid | left | right | inherit	auto
page-break-inside	Avoid | auto | inherit	auto
pause	[[*time* | *percentage*]{1,2}] | inherit	*user agent*
pause-after	[*time* | *percentage*]| inherit	*user agent*
pause-before	[*time* | *percentage*]| inherit	*user agent*
pitch	*frequency* | x-low | low | medium | high | x-high | inherit	medium
pitch-range	*number* | inherit	50
play-during	*uri* | mix? repeat? | auto | none | inherit	normal
position	Static | relative | absolute | fixed | inherit	normal
quotes	[*string string*]+ | none | inherit	*user agent*

Attribute Name	Syntax	Default Value
richness	*number* | inherit	50
right	*length* | *percentage* | auto | inherit	auto
size	*length* {1,2} | auto | portrait | landscape | inherit	auto
speak	Normal | none | spell-out | inherit	normal
speak-header	once | always | inherit	once
speak-numeral	Digits | continuous | inherit	continuous
speak-punctuation	code | none | inherit	none
speech-rate	*number* | x-slow | slow | medium | fast | x-fast | faster | slower | inherit	50 medium
stress	*number* | inherit	
table-layout	auto | fixed | inherit	auto
text-align	Left | right | center | justify | *string* | inherit	*user agent*
text-decoration	none | [underline || overline || line-through || blink] | inherit	none
text-indent	*length* | *percentage* | inherit	0
text-shadow	none | [*color* || *length*] | inherit	none
text-transform	Capitalize | uppercase | lowercase | none | inherit	none
top	*length* | *percentage* | auto | inherit	auto
unicode-bidi	Normal | embed | bidi-override | inherit	
vertical-align	Baseline | sub | super | top | text-top | middle | bottom | text-bottom | *percentage* | *length* | inherit	baseline
visibility	Inherit | visible | collapse | hidden	inherit
voice-family	[*specific-voice* || *generic-voice* list] | inherit	*user agent*
volume	*number* | *percentage* | silent | x-soft | soft | medium | loud | x-loud | inherit	medium
white-space	Normal | pre | nowrap | inherit	normal
widows	*integer* | inherit	2
width	*length* | *percentage* | auto | inherit	auto
word-spacing	Normal | *length* | inherit	normal
z-index	auto | *integer* | inherit	auto

Table C-2 CSS Descriptors

Attribute Name	Values	Default
ascent	*number*	
baseline	*number*	0
bbox	*number*, *number*, *number*, *number*	
cap-height	*number*	
centerline	*number*	
definition-src	*uri*	
descent	*number*	
font-family	[*family-name* | *generic-family*] list	user agent
font-size	all | [*length*]	all
font-stretch	all | [normal | ultra-condensed | extra-condensed | condensed | semi-condensed | semi-expanded | expanded | extra-expanded | ultra-expanded]	normal
font-style	[normal | italic | oblique] list	normal
font-variant	[normal | small-caps] list	normal
font-weight	all | [normal | bold | 100 | 200 | 300 | 400 | 500 | 600 | 700 | 800 | 900]	normal
mathline	*number*	
panose-1	[*number*] {10}	0000000000
slope	*number*	0
src	[*uri* [format-list] [font-face -name]]	
stemh	*number*	
stemv	*number*	
topline	*number*	
unicode-range	*urange+*	U+0-7FFFFFFF
units-per-em	*number*	
widths	[*urange*]? [*number*] comma defined list	
x-height	*number*	

Example

The following example shows an external style sheet that could be used with an HTML 4.0 document.

```
/*
 * Style sheet for use with Catawompus Bold Arts pages
```

```
*/
BODY {
    padding: 12px;
    line height: 2om
}

H1 {
    font-size: 2em;
    color: blue;
    clear: left;
    text-align: center;
}

H2 {
    font-size: 1.5em;
    margin: .83em 0
}

H3 {
    font-size: 1.25em;
    margin: 1em 0
}
H4 {
    font-size: 1em;
    margin: 1.2em 0
}

H5 {
    font-size: ..75em;
    line-height: 1.17em;
     margin: 1.67em 0
}

H6 {
    font-size: .67em;
    margin: 2em 0
}

H1, H2, H3, H4,
H5, H6, B,
STRONG {
    font-weight: bolder
}
```

b
c
d

```
I, CITE, EM,
VAR, ADDRESS {
   font-style: italic
}

PRE, TT, CODE,
KBD, SAMP {
   font-family: monospace
}

BIG {
   font-size: 2em
}

SMALL, SUB, SUP {
   font-size: .75em
}

S, STRIKE, DEL {
   text-decoration: line-through
}

HR {
   border: 1px inset
}

OL {
   list-style-type: lower-greek
}

H1, H2, H3,
H4, H5, H6 {
   page-break-after: avoid;
   page-break-inside: avoid
}

BLOCKQUOTE,
PRE {
   page-break-inside: avoid
}
```

CROSS-REFERENCE
See **<LINK>**, **<STYLE>**, **Style Sheet**, **HTML**, **XML**, and **User Agent**.

Case Sensitivity

Concept

CSS, HTML, and XML

In most cases, the terms associated with Cascading Style Sheets and HTML elements and attributes are case-insensitive. In some cases, specifically the `id` and `name` HTML attributes, case sensitivity is important. In both of these attributes, the individual item that you are naming, and often referencing, in a script must be completely identifiable. Some script collections treat items with varying case as separate individuals, whereas other collections treat them as an individual subcollection.

 NOTE
URLs and XML commands may be case-sensitive.

 CROSS-REFERENCE
See **characters** and **CDATA**.

CDATA

Concept

HTML, XML, and CSS

Text within a document consists of mixed character data and markup. Markup is composed of start tags, end tags, empty-element tags, entity references, character references, comments, CDATA section delimiters, document type declarations, and processing instructions. Any text that is not part of a document's markup is considered the character data of the document. When found in the contents of an element, character data is any string of characters not including the start-delimiter of markup text. In the value of an attribute, character data is any string of characters not including the `CDATA`-section-close delimiters, `"]]>"`.

User agents should interpret `CDATA` attribute values by replacing all character entities with standard characters, replacing each carriage return or tab with a space, and ignoring all line feed characters. They should also ignore leading and trailing white space around the `CDATA` values, for example, `"    blue    "` would be interpreted as `"blue"` with regard for the extra space.

In some cases, HTML 4.0 attributes using CDATA values have further restrictions on their set of legal values, which might not be identified in the DTD. The elements STYLE and SCRIPT are two of these. The content of each of these commands has a set of rules that directs how an author must enter the information for it to be readable and correctly interpreted by the user agent.

CROSS-REFERENCE
See **Characters** and **Character Encoding**.

cellIndex

Property

DHTML

This DOM property is used to retrieve the index value of a specific cell in the cells collection of a specified row. These index values are in the order of the cell's appearance in the HTML source document. If a cell expands multiple rows, the only cell that appears within the cells collection is the one on the first row.

The syntax of this command is

```
[ Index = ] object.cellIndex
```

Values
Index

This is an integer-based index value that specifies the object's position in a collection.

Elements
TD

CROSS-REFERENCE
See **cellspacing**, **cells**, and **cellpadding**.

cellpadding

Attribute

HTML

When a document author is designing a table, he or she often needs to force a specific amount of space between the cell's border and its contents. The cellpadding attribute does just this. When you increase your cell padding, you may need to increase the width of your TABLE to avoid unnecessary wrapping of your text.

The syntax of this attribute is

```
cellpadding=length | percentage
```

JAVASCRIPT

```
table.cellPadding [ = integer ]
```

This JavaScript property is used to set or retrieve the value of the cellpadding HTML attribute.

Values
length

This specifies the number of pixels that are reserved between the contents of the table cell and all four margins.

percentage

This specifies a percentage to be set aside for the top and bottom and for the left and right margins. The percentage is measured against the height of the cell to find the top and bottom padding measurement and against the width for the left and right padding measurement.

Elements
TABLE

CROSS-REFERENCE
See **cells**, **cellspacing**, **<TABLE>**, and **cellIndex**.

cells

Collection

DHTML

This document object collection is used to retrieve a collection of TH and TD cells in the row of a table. If a cell spans multiple rows, only the first cell appears in the collection.

This command can be used in either of the following ways:

```
[CellColl = ] object.cells
[ Object = ] object.cells(vIndex [, iSubIndex] )
```

Parameters
CellColl

This variable refers to the array of elements contained by the object.

Object

This variable refers to an individual item in the array.

vIndex

This parameter is required and contains the number or string identifying the element or collection to retrieve. When a number is specified, the method returns the element in the zero-based collection at the identified position. When a string identifier is used and multiple elements with the same name or id attributes match the string, this method returns a collection of those matched elements.

iSubIndex

This optional parameter is used to identify the position of the element being retrieved when vIndex is a string. ISubIndex becomes the index of the specific item in the collection of matching elements identified by the vIndex string contents.

Example

The following JavaScript code uses the rows and cells collections on a TABLE object to insert a number into each cell of the table.

```
<HTML>
<SCRIPT LANGUAGE="JavaScript">
function cellContents() {
    var count=0;
    for (i=0; i < document.all.oGrid.rows.length; i++) {
        for (j=0; j < document.all.oGrid.rows(i).cells.length;
j++) {
            document.all.oGrid.rows(i).cells(j).innerText =
count;
            count++;
        }
    }
}
</SCRIPT>

<BODY onload="cellContents()">
<TABLE id=oGrid border=1 bgcolor=red>
<TR>
    <TH> </TH>
    <TH> </TH>
```

```
      <TH> </TH>
      <TH> </TH>
   </TR>
   <TR>
      <TD> </TD>
      <TD> </TD>
      <TD> </TD>
      <TD> </TD>
   </TR>
   <TR>
      <TD> </TD>
      <TD> </TD>
      <TD> </TD>
      <TD> </TD>
   </TR>
   <TR>
      <TD> </TD>
      <TD> </TD>
      <TD> </TD>
      <TD> </TD>
   </TR>
   </TABLE>
   </BODY>
   </HTML>
```

Elements
> TR

CROSS-REFERENCE
See **<TD>**, **<TH>**, **cellpadding**, **cellspacing**, and **cells**.

cellspacing

Attribute

HTML

When a document author is designing a table, he or she often needs to force a specific amount of space between the edge of the table and its cells and between the cells themselves. When you increase your cellspacing, you may need to increase the width of your TABLE to avoid unnecessary wrapping of your text.

The syntax of this attribute is

```
cellspacing=length | percentage
```

JAVASCRIPT
```
table.cellSpacing [ = integer ]
```

This JavaScript property is used to set or retrieve the value of the `cellspacing` HTML attribute.

Values
length

    This specifies the number of pixels that are reserved between the individual cells of the table and around the interior edge of the table border.

percentage

    This is a percentage of the width of an individual cell that is set aside as padding.

Elements
TABLE

CROSS-REFERENCE
See **cells**, **cellpadding**, **<TABLE>**, and **cellIndex**.

<CENTER>

Element

HTML

    Start Tag: Required
    End Tag: Required

    Although this element has been deprecated in favor of the `DIV align=cen-ter` combination, it is still valid for all user agents. This element centers all of the objects, whether text or graphics, found between its tags in relation to the size of the window or screen being used to display the HTML document.

Attributes
class

```
class="cdata-list"
```

    This attribute is used to assign a class name to an element. User agents employ classes to group specific types of information for later use.

dir

```
dir = LTR | RTL | [CS | CI | CN | CA | CT]
```

This attribute defines the direction of the text flow in a document so that a user agent can correctly display it to the reader. This attribute can also be used to specify information about the case of the characters.

id

```
id="name"
```

This attribute is used to assign a name to an element.

lang

```
lang="language code"
```

This attribute specifies the language in which an element and its values should be rendered.

onclick

```
onclick=script
```

This attribute takes effect when a user clicks the button on a pointing device with the pointer over an element.

ondblclick

```
ondblclick=script
```

This attribute takes effect when a user double-clicks the button on a pointing device with the pointer over an element.

onkeydown

```
onkeydown=script
```

This attribute takes effect when a user presses a key and the pointer is over an element.

onkeypress

```
onkeypress=script
```

This attribute takes effect when a key is either pressed and released while the pointer is over an element.

onkeyup

```
onkeyup=script
```

This attribute takes effect when a user releases a key with the pointer over an element.

onmousedown

> onmousedown=*script*

This attribute takes effect when a user presses the button on a pointing device while the pointer is over an element.

onmousemove

> onmousemove=*script*

This attribute is activated when the mouse pointer is moved while it is over an element.

onmouseout

> onmouseout=*script*

This attribute is activated when the mouse pointer is moved away from an element.

onmouseover

> onmouseover=*script*

This attribute is activated when the mouse pointer is moved over an element.

onmouseup

> onmouseup=*script*

This attribute takes effect when the button on a pointing device is released while the pointer is over an element.

style

> style=*style descriptors*

This attribute applies specific style-sheet information to one particular element.

title

> title=*text*

This attribute provides annotation information to the element.

Example

The following example document uses both the CENTER and the DIV elements to align a series of elements, including the contents of a table and a few paragraphs.

ON THE CD-ROM

Look for **center.htm** on the accompanying CD-ROM.

```
<html>
<head>
   <title> A Centering Test </title>
</head>
<body background="blocks.jpg" bgcolor="White">
   <div align="left">
      This first paragraph of text is left justified.<br>
      This first paragraph of text is left justified.<br>
      This first paragraph of text is left justified.<br>
      This first paragraph of text is left justified.<br>
   </div>
   <center>
   <p>
      This second paragraph of text is centered using CENTER.<br>
      This second paragraph of text is centered using CENTER.<br>
      This second paragraph of text is centered using CENTER.<br>
      This second paragraph of text is centered using CENTER.<br>
   </p>
   </center>
   <div align="right">
      This third paragraph of text is right justified.<br>
      This third paragraph of text is right justified.<br>
      This third paragraph of text is right justified.<br>
      This third paragraph of text is right justified.<br>
   </div>
   <div align="center">
      This fourth paragraph of text is centered using DIV.<br>
      This fourth paragraph of text is centered using DIV.<br>
      This fourth paragraph of text is centered using DIV.<br>
      This fourth paragraph of text is centered using DIV.<br>
   </div>
</body>
</html>
```

CROSS-REFERENCE

See **<DIV>** and **align**.

centerline

Descriptor

CSS

This descriptor identifies the baseline for a font. When the value is undefined, the user agent applies heuristics to determine the baseline of the font. Generally, this point is the midpoint of the ascent and decent values. If this descriptor is specified, the `units-per-em` descriptor must also be used.

The syntax for this descriptor is

```
centerline: number
```

 CROSS-REFERENCE
See **baseline**, **topline**, and **bottomline**.

CERN

Concept

From the beginning of the Internet until today, CERN (European Laboratory for Particle Physics) has played a very large role in the development of the World Wide Web. Many of the protocols we use today on the Web were originally developed and implemented at CERN before being adopted in many other parts of Europe, including the ITU and the ISO in Geneva.

At the start of the Internet, the TCP/IP protocols—as they were then called—were being used by CERN. When the Web was prototyped in 1990–91, it took only three years before it was fully accepted; but those three years were spent developing standards for computer systems, programming, networks, and computer hardware. The mentality of the computer manufacturers and users changed so that it became necessary for users' systems to be able to communicate freely with one another. The price reductions occurring around that time, which still continue today, only encouraged the growth of the Internet and the Web by making computer systems available to a wider range of socioeconomic groups than ever before.

In the 1970s, there were almost no truly networked systems. CERNET was the closest thing to a network system being used during the mid-'70s, and it only supported 100 other systems, with a limited remote access login to its central mainframe and a form of a LAN bridge to connect to some of the first Ethernet systems in CERN's repertoire. Although CERN resembled ARPANET architecturally, it used proprietary protocols that doomed its effectiveness from the beginning.

b
c
d

When the 1980s began, CERN was working on the second phase of the STELLA Satellite Communication Project when one of the satellite channels was used to connect to remote segments of CERNET, a segment between CERN and Pisa, and a Cambridge Ring network running between CERN and the Rutherford Laboratory. Although this network was based on the ARPA IP model, this experiment implemented the protocol independently of other systems and used a STELLA-specific higher level protocol on top of it rather than TCP.

Around 1983, Ethernet joined the scene at CERN, along with a true implementation of TCP/IP, and for the first time, a Data Communications Group was organized at CERN. This group, then under David Lord, worked on unifying the whole of the networking systems across CERN. When they were trying to build the backbone infrastructure for the network, they were also stressing ISO standards, which contributed to the push for standards across their networking systems.

Around 1984, things started to change both at CERN and around the world. When TCP/IP was fully introduced to CERN and was being used on non-UNIX systems, it was decided that TCP/IP could help solve the problem of truly heterogeneous connectivity between systems. TCP/IP wasn't used outside the internal CERN sites, however, until 1989. Throughout the time between 1984 and 1989, more networks that used the TCP/IP protocol were being created, including the incorporation of the protocol on IBM VM/CMS mainframes, the University of Wisconsin's WISCNET, and VMS systems.

Through the steady progression and development of TCP/IP based networks, the European side of the USENET was switched to an IP network around 1988, matching what was occurring in the United States. When the news and mail had been directed to run over a TCP/IP network, using SMTP, all the other Internet utilities such as Telnet and FTP became available over the Atlantic. It was time for CERN to join the Internet in earnest.

By 1990, CERN had become the largest Internet site in Europe. This dramatically affected the acceptance and spread of Internet techniques and standards around the world. Today, CERN promotes the development of Internet technology and training in developing countries, assists speakers at Internet gatherings, and works with the world authorities on Internet traffic and routing questions. All of this is only natural, since many of the people CERN supports have aided the development of the Internet that we see today.

All of this development led to the visionary idea of Tim Berners-Lee for the World Wide Web. In CERN's Internet facility, Tim developed the software portability techniques and the protocols to share information throughout the world.

CROSS-REFERENCE
See **HTTP** and **User Agent**.

CGI

Language

The Common Gateway Interface (CGI) is the interface used between a server and the server-side gateway programs. This specification identifies how information is to be sent to the gateway program and how it must be returned by the gateway. The main systems for performing this are

- From Server to Gateway — Data can be sent to the gateway as environment variables or as data read from standard input by the gateway program itself. The gateway reads all the data sent by the client and any extra environment variables that describe the current server status.

- From Gateway to Client — When returning information to the client program, which is generally a user's Web browser, the gateway writes the data to its standard output. When the client receives the data, it is processed to ensure that the headers are correct and that the information transaction occurred properly.

CROSS-REFERENCE
See **Perl**, **ECMAscript**, **JavaScript**, **Jscript**, and **VBScript**.

<CHANNEL>

Element

CSD

The CHANNEL element is used to identify the location, name, and delivery schedule of the channel. It is the primary element used to identify a channel to be distributed to Channel Definition Format-compatible systems.

Attributes
href

This attribute is used to specify the location of the next updated version of this channel.

isclonable

This attribute is used to specify whether a channel can be copied or moved within the channel changer hierarchy.

Example

The following example code identifies a channel document to be accessed by a CDF-compatible software package.

```
<CHANNEL href="http://mychannels.com/mychannel.cdf"
isclonable=yes>
    <INTROURL value="http://mychannels.com/setup.htm" />
    <LASTMOD value="1999.01.01T12:10-0300" />
    <TITLE value="My Favorite Hobbies Channel" />
    <ABSTRACT value="The latest information in sports hobby
gear." />
    <AUTHOR value="Webner Masterson" />
</CHANNEL
```

CROSS-REFERENCE
See **<ITEM>**.

Channel Definition Format

Concept

The Channel Definition Format (CDF) is a specification proposed by Microsoft to the World Wide Web Consortium (W3C) in early 1997. This specification provides a Web developer, or content provider, with the ability to make frequently updated pieces of information available, automatically, to readers using any Web server. The only hitch is that the receiving program must be compatible with the Channel Definition Format before it can receive your information correctly.

The Channel Definition Format is an application developed from the eXtensible Markup Language (XML). Because XML is still evolving, Channel Definition Format will continue to evolve.

Elements

Channel

This is the primary element that defines the channel. Table C-3 lists Channel's subelements and attributes.

Table C-3 Subelements and Attributes of Channel

Element Name	Description
LastMod	Last date page was modified
Title	Title of channel
Abstract	Short description of site
Author	Channel author
Publisher	Channel publisher
Copyright	Channel copyright information
PublicationDate	Channel publication date
Logo	Channel logo
Keywords	Comma-delimited keywords for the channel
Category	Category to which the Web site belongs
Ratings	A rating service's rating of the channel
Schedule	Schedule for updating channel
UserSchedule	User-specified channel
Channel	A subchannel of the current channel
Item	Identification of an article
IntroURI	URI for a Web page introducing the channel
Authorization	Certification for downloadable executables
MinStorage	Minimum storage required
Tracking	Profile identifying how user tracking is performed

Item

This element is used to identify a channel item or a piece of information that is available from that channel. Table C-4 lists Item's subelements and attributes.

Table C-4 Subelements and Attributes of Item

Element Name	Description
LastMod	Last date page was modified
Title	Title of channel
Abstract	Short description of site
Author	Channel author
Publisher	Channel publisher
Copyright	Channel copyright information
PublicationDate	Channel publication date
Logo	Channel logo
Keywords	Comma-delimited keywords for the channel

Element Name	Description
Keywords	Comma-delimited keywords for the channel
Category	Category to which the Web site belongs
Ratings	A rating service's rating of the channel
Schedule	Schedule for updating channel
UserSchedule	User-specified channel
Usage	Specification about how the item should be used

UserSchedule

This references the client-specified information retrieval schedule.

Schedule

This identifies the general information dispersal schedule used by the channel. Table C-5 lists Schedule's subelements and attributes.

Table C-5 Subelements and Attributes of Schedule

Element Name	Description
StartDate	Day to start distributing the channel
EndDate	Day to stop distributing the channel
IntervalTime	Interval to repeat schedule on
EarliestTime	Earliest time during that interval that the schedule starts
LatestTime	Latest time during the interval that the schedule starts

Logo

This element identifies an image that is used to represent the channel or one of its items.

Tracking

This element is used to define the user tracking parameters of a channel. Table C-6 lists Tracking's subelements and attributes.

Table C-6 Subelements and Attributes of Tracking

Element Name	Description
PostURL	URL to post tracking results to

CategoryDef

This element defines the name of a category in which the channel can be categorized. Table C-7 lists CategoryDef's subelements and attributes.

Table C-7 Subelements and Attributes of CategoryDef

Element Name	Description
CategoryName	Name of the category
Description	Text description of the category
CategoryDef	Identification of any subcategories

Example

The following code defines a sample channel and its delivery schedule.

```
<CHANNEL href="http://mychannels.com/mychannel.cdf"
isclonable=yes>
    <INTROURL value="http://mychannels.com/setup.htm" />
    <LASTMOD value="1999.01.01T12:10-0300" />
    <TITLE value="My Favorite Hobbies Channel" />
    <ABSTRACT value="The latest information in sports hobby
gear." />
    <AUTHOR value="Webner Masterson" />
    <SCHEDULE>
        <ENDDATE value="1999.12.31T23:59:5999" />
        <INTERVALTIME day=2 />
        <EARLIESTTIME hour=12 />
        <LATESTTIME hour=20 />
    </SCHEDULE>
    <LOGO href="http://mychannels.com/chanlogo.gif" type=
"regular" />
    <ITEM href="http://mychannels.com/articles/item1.html">
        <LASTMOD value="1999.01.15T12:10-0300" />
<TITLE value="Tying a Ragtail Whimper Fly" />
        <ABSTRACT value="Learn fly tying from an old pro." />
    </ITEM>
</CHANNEL>
```

CROSS-REFERENCE
See **HTML** and **XML**.

Channels

Concept

CROSS-REFERENCE
See **Channel Definition Format**.

char

Attribute

HTML

This attribute enables you to specify a particular character to serve as an alignment point within a table and its subdivisions. Common characters to use for alignment points include periods, commas, spaces, and hyphens.

The syntax for this attribute is

```
char = "character"
```

NOTE
User agents are not required to support this attribute to be HTML 4.0-compatible.

Values
"character"

This can be any alphanumeric character found within the document character set, which typically includes the letters A–Z and a–z and the numerals 0–9. The default is a period (.) in English and a comma (,) in French documents.

Elements

COL	COLGROUP	TBODY	TD
TFOOT	TH	THEAD	TR

CROSS-REFERENCE
See **charoff**.

Character Encoding

Concept

Character encoding is the simple correlation between the character that our eyes see on paper or a screen and the character's representation in a standard chart of glyphs.

When an XML application is encoded, it must use either UTF-8 or UTF-16 encoding. If the UTF-16 encoding scheme is used, then a Byte Order Mark must also be used at the beginning of the document. This encoding signature is used to differentiate between UTF-8 and UTF-16 encoded documents.

CROSS-REFERENCE
See **UTF-8**, **UTF-16**, **Characters**, and **CDATA**.

Characters

Concept

A character is, at its most basic, a glyph, or visual representation of a meaning. The range of characters allowed within a document is controlled by ISO 10646. A text string is simply a sequence of characters that can be used to represent content or markup within a document. ASCII characters such as the tab, carriage return, and line feed, in addition to the standard graphic characters (ASCII 1-128), are considered legal for use with HTML and XML documents. Use of any other characters is discouraged.

CROSS-REFERENCE
See **glyph**, **Character Encoding**, and **CDATA**.

charoff

Attribute

HTML

This attribute is used to offset the first occurrence of the alignment character specified by the `char` attribute. If a line does not actually contain the specified alignment character, the whole line should be shifted to end at the alignment position. When this attribute is used to set the offset of an alignment character, the direction of that offset is determined by the current text direction, as set by the `dir` attribute. In left-to-right flowing text, the offset is from the left margin, and in right-to-left flowing text, the offset is from the right.

The syntax of this attribute is

```
charoff = length
```

Values
length

This is the amount of the offset in pixels. This value is any whole signed or unsigned integer.

NOTE

User agents are not required to support this attribute to be considered HTML 4.0-compatible.

Elements

COL	COLGROUP	TBODY	TD
TFOOT	TH	THEAD	TR

CROSS-REFERENCE

See **char**.

charset

Attribute

HTML

This HTML attribute is used to identify the character set that is used by the resource pointed to in the link or in the script.

The syntax for this attribute is

```
charset=charsetname
```

JAVASCRIPT
```
object.charset [ = sCharSet ]
```

This script property can be used to set and retrieve the name of the character encoding set that is in use by a particular object.

Values

charsetname

This string value identifies the name of the character set that the resource identified in the link or script should use.

Elements

A   LINK   SCRIPT

 CROSS-REFERENCE
See **lang**.

Checkboxes

Concept

Checkboxes are a type of on/off toggle switch within a form. Checkboxes are generally used when you are providing readers with a list of possibilities and wish them to choose as many of the options as are valid. A checkbox is considered "on" when its selected attribute is set, and this attribute is used when the form is submitted to identify the values to be applied to a specific property. In HTML, the INPUT element is used to create checkbox controls within a FORM object.

 CROSS-REFERENCE
See **<FORM>**, **<INPUT>**, **radio button**, **menus**, **text input**, **buttons**, **file select**, **hidden controls**, and **object controls**.

checked

Attribute

HTML

This Boolean attribute is used to specify whether a FORM object's INPUT element—when it is either a radio button or a checkbox—is selected. This attribute must be used in conjunction with a type='radio' or a type='checkbox' INPUT attribute.

This command can be used in either of the following situations.

```
<INPUT type="radio" checked... >
<INPUT type="checkbox" checked... >
```

JAVASCRIPT

```
input.checked [ = bChecked ]
```

This object property is used to select a radio button or a checkbox or to identify whether the given checkbox or radio button is selected.

Example
The following example code enables you to open a Web site automatically when you select a specific checkbox.

```
<HEAD>
<SCRIPT>
function itsChecked()
{
    if (goWebSite.checked == true)
    {
        alert("We are off to a new Web Site!");
        window.open("http://www.idgbooks.com");
    }
}
</SCRIPT>
</HEAD>
<BODY>
Check here if you wish to go see another Web Site:
<INPUT ID=goWebSite TYPE=checkbox onclick=itsChecked()>
</BODY>
```

CROSS-REFERENCE
See **Checkboxes** and **Radio Buttons**.

Child Element

Concept

A child element is any element that occurs within the block boundaries of another element. Although a child may have only one parent element, it can have multiple ancestors, and parent elements can have multiple children. Take the following HTML code as an example:

```
<DIV align=center>
Turn Car into Pot in Three Steps!!!
    <UL>
        <LI>Car
```

```
        <LI>Cat
        <LI>Cot
        <LI> Pot
    </UL>
  </DIV>
```

In this example, the LI elements are children of the UL element, and DIV is their ancestor. UL is a child of DIV.

 CROSS-REFERENCE
See **Ancestor** and **Parent Element**.

children

Collection

DHTML

This document collection is used to identify the direct descendants of an object.

Either one of the following statements enables you to use this collection:

```
[ChildColl = ] object.children
[ oObject = ] object.children(vIndex [, iSubIndex])
```

Parameters
ChildColl

This variable refers to the array of elements contained by the object.

oObject

This variable refers to an individual item in the array.

vIndex

This parameter is required and contains the number or string identifying the element or collection to retrieve. When a number is specified, the method returns the element in the zero-based collection at the identified position. When a string identifier is used and multiple elements with the same name or id attributes match the string, this method returns a collection of those matched elements.

iSubIndex

This optional parameter is used to identify the position of the element being retrieved when vIndex is a string. ISubIndex becomes the index of the specific item in the collection of matching elements identified by the vIndex string contents.

Elements

A	ACRONYM	ADDRESS	APPLET
AREA	B	BASE	BASEFONT
BGSOUND	BIG	BLOCKQUOTE	BODY
BR	BUTTON	CAPTION	CENTER
CITE	CODE	COL	COLGROUP
COMMENT	DD	DEL	DFN
DIR	DIV	DL	DT
EM	EMBED	FIELDSET	FONT
FORM	FRAME	FRAMESET	HEAD
H1–H6	HR	HTML	I
IFRAME	IMG	INPUT	INS
KBD	LABEL	LEGEND	LI
LINK	LISTING	MAP	MARQUEE
MENU	OBJECT	OL	OPTION
P	PLAINTEXT	PRE	Q
S	SAMP	SCRIPT	SELECT
SMALL	SPAN	STRIKE	STRONG
STYLE	SUB	SUP	TABLE
TBODY	TD	TEXTAREA	TFOOT
THEAD	TITLE	TR	TT
U	UL	VAR	XMP

Objects

document   nextid

CROSS-REFERENCE
See **Child Element** and **all**.

<CITE>

Element

HTML

Start Tag: Required
End Tag: Required

This element is used to identify information that provides a reference or citation to another source of information. This element is generally displayed in italicized characters.

Attributes

class

```
class="cdata-list"
```

This attribute is used to assign a class name to an element. User agents employ classes to group specific types of information for later use.

dir

```
dir = LTR | RTL | [CS | CI | CN | CA | CT]
```

This attribute defines the direction of the text flow in a document so that a user agent can correctly display it to the reader. This attribute can also be used to specify information about the case of the characters.

id

```
id="name"
```

This attribute is used to assign a name to an element.

lang

```
lang="language code"
```

This attribute specifies the language in which an element and its values should be rendered.

onclick

```
onclick=script
```

This attribute takes effect when a user clicks the button on a pointing device with the pointer over an element.

b

c

d

ondblclick

```
ondblclick=script
```

This attribute takes effect when a user double-clicks the button on a pointing device with the pointer over an element.

onkeydown

```
onkeydown=script
```

This attribute takes effect when a user presses a key and the pointer is over an element.

onkeypress

```
onkeypress=script
```

This attribute takes effect when a key is either pressed and released while the pointer is over an element.

onkeyup

```
onkeyup=script
```

This attribute takes effect when a user releases a key with the pointer over an element.

onmousedown

```
onmousedown=script
```

This attribute takes effect when a user presses the button on a pointing device while the pointer is over an element.

onmousemove

```
onmousemove=script
```

This attribute is activated when the mouse pointer is moved while it is over an element.

onmouseout

```
onmouseout=script
```

This attribute is activated when the mouse pointer is moved away from an element.

onmouseover

```
onmouseover=script
```

This attribute is activated when the mouse pointer is moved over an element.

onmouseup

```
onmouseup=script
```

This attribute takes effect when the button on a pointing device is released while the pointer is over an element.

style

```
style=style descriptors
```

This attribute applies specific style-sheet information to one particular element.

title

```
title=text
```

This attribute provides annotation information to the element.

Example

The following example code uses the CITE element to provide a reference to the Gettysburg Address.

ON THE CD-ROM

Look for **cite.htm** on the accompanying CD-ROM.

```
<BODY>
It was a fine day in our country's history when President
Abraham Lincoln stood on that knoll overlooking the
devastation wreaked by the Battle of Gettysburg and declared
to our country:
<P>
<CITE title="Gettysburg Address" >
Fourscore and seven years ago, our fathers brought forth on
this continent, a new nation conceived in Liberty, and
dedicated to the proposition that all men are created equal.
<BR>
Now we are engaged in a great civil war, testing whether that
nation or any nation so conceived and so dedicated can long
endure. We are met on a great battle-field, of that war. We
have come to dedicate a portion of that field, as a final
resting place for those who here gave their lives that that
nation might live. It is altogether fitting and proper that we
should do this.
</CITE>
</BODY>
```

CROSS-REFERENCE

See **<EM>**, **<BIG>**, **<CODE>**, **<SAMP>**, **<ABBR>**, and **<ACRONYM>**.

class

Attribute

HTML

The HTML attribute is used to assign a class name or a set of class names to a particular object. You can use the same class name for as many objects as you wish. If you wish to assign multiple class names to a single object, you need to separate the names with a white space character, rather than a comma, which is common for some lists.

This element is used in several different ways by HTML elements. When used to identify a set of style sheets, the `class` attribute is used to identify which style sheet rules should be used for those particular elements. User agents also use the `class` attribute for general information processing and for adjustments made by some scripts.

The syntax for this attribute is

```
class = cdata-list
```

Values
cdata-list

This is a list of characters, or strings, that are used to identify specific classes of elements.

Elements

A	ACRONYM	ADDRESS	APPLET
AREA	B	BGSOUND	BIG
BLOCKQUOTE	BODY	BR	BUTTON
CAPTION	CENTER	CITE	CODE
COL	COLGROUP	COMMENT	DD
DEL	DFN	DIR	DIV
DL	DT	EM	EMBED
FIELDSET	FONT	FORM	FRAME
FRAMESET	H1–H6	HR	I
IFRAME	IMG	INPUT	INS
KBD	LABEL	LEGEND	LI
LINK	LISTING	MAP	MARQUEE
MENU	OBJECT	OL	OPTION
P	PLAINTEXT	PRE	Q
S	SAMP	SELECT	SMALL

SPAN	STRIKE	STRONG	STYLE
SUB	SUP	TABLE	TBODY
TD	TEXTAREA	TFOOT	THEAD
TR	TT	U	UL
VAR	XMP		

CROSS-REFERENCE
See **classid** and **className**.

classid

Attribute

HTML

This attribute is used to identify the location of an object's implementation. It can be used as an alternative to the `data` attribute, depending on the type of object being placed.

```
<OBJECT classid = uri ... >
```

JAVASCRIPT
```
[ sID = ] object.classid
```

This JavaScript attribute is used to retrieve the class identifier for a specified object. It is more closely related to the `class` HTML attribute.

Values
uri

This URI identifies the location of the object being used.

Elements
OBJECT

CROSS-REFERENCE
See **data**, **className**, and **class**.

className

Property

DHTML

This property is used to specify the class of an identified object or to set the class of that object. This class is generally associated with a particular style rule in a style sheet.

The syntax of this command is

```
object.className [ = Class ]
```

Parameters

Class

This string is used to specify the class or style rule that is being applied to this string.

Elements

A	ACRONYM	ADDRESS	APPLET
AREA	B	BASE	BASEFONT
BGSOUND	BIG	BLOCKQUOTE	BODY
BR	BUTTON	CAPTION	CENTER
CITE	CODE	COL	COLGROUP
DD	DEL	DFN	DIR
DIV	DL	DT	EM
EMBED	FIELDSET	FONT	FORM
FRAME	FRAMESET	HEAD	H1–H6
HR	HTML	I	IFRAME
IMG	INPUT	INS	ISINDEX
KBD	LABEL	LEGEND	LI
LISTING	MAP	MARQUEE	MENU
OBJECT	OL	OPTION	P
PLAINTEXT	PRE	Q	S
SAMP	SELECT	SMALL	SPAN
STRIKE	STRONG	SUB	SUP
TABLE	TBODY	TD	TEXTAREA
TFOOT	THEAD	TR	TT
U	UL	VAR	XMP

Objects
nextid

CROSS-REFERENCE
See **class**, **classid**, and **Style Sheet**.

clear

Attribute

CSS

This attribute controls whether an element allows a floating object on either its left or right side so that text can be properly placed around the floating object. This property is only valid for block-level elements.

The syntax for this attribute is

```
clear: none | left | right | both
```

JAVASCRIPT
```
object.style.clear [ = sClear]
```

This property is used to set or retrieve the value of the clear attribute of a specified object.

Values
none

Floating objects are allowed on both sides. This is the default value.

left

Floating objects are not allowed on the left side.

right

Floating objects are not allowed on the right side.

both

Floating objects are not allowed on either side, but they are allowed above the element.

Example
The following example uses both the clear attribute and the clear property to specify placement of text relative to floating images.

The sample below uses a call to an embedded style sheet to move the text below the floating objects when italic text is encountered.

```
<HEAD>
<STYLE>
    BLOCKQUOTE { clear:"right"}
</STYLE>
</HEAD>

<BODY>
<IMG src="circle.jpg" style="float:left"
onclick="this.style.clear='left'">
<BLOCKQUOTE>
When someone blunders, we say that he makes a misstep. Is it
then not clear that all the ills of mankind, all the tragic
misfortunes that fill our history books, all the political
blunders, all the failures of the great leaders have arisen
merely from a lack of skill in dancing. - Moliere
</BLOCKQUOTE>
</BODY>
```

Elements

A	ADDRESS	APPLET	B
BIG	BLOCKQUOTE	BUTTON	CAPTION
CENTER	CITE	CODE	COL
COLGROUP	DD	DFN	DIR
DIV	DL	DT	EM
EMBED	FIELDSET	FONT	FORM
FRAME	FRAMESET	HEAD	H1–H6
HR	HTML	I	IFRAME
IMG	INPUT	INS	ISINDEX
KBD	LABEL	LEGEND	LI
LISTING	MAP	MARQUEE	MENU
OBJECT	OL	OPTION	P
PLAINTEXT	PRE	Q	S
SAMP	SELECT	SMALL	SPAN
STRIKE	STRONG	SUB	SUP
TABLE	TBODY	TD	TEXTAREA
TFOOT	THEAD	TR	TT
U	UL	VAR	XMP

CROSS-REFERENCE
See **clear (HTML Attribute)**, **Float**, and **Inline Element**.

clear

Attribute

HTML

This attribute is used to identify which floating objects aren't to be repositioned when a line break is encountered.

The syntax for this command is

```
clear = all | left | right | none
```

JAVASCRIPT

```
br.clear [ = sValue ]
```

The `clear` property in JavaScript code enables you to set or retrieve the value of this property for the given BR element.

Values

all

Floating objects are allowed only above the current line.

left

The BR element is moved below any floating object on the left side.

right

The BR element is moved below any floating object on the right side.

none

Floating objects are allowed on all sides.

Elements
BR

CROSS-REFERENCE
See **clear (CSS Attribute)**, **clear (DHTML Method)**, **style**, **Float**, and **Inline Element**.

clear

Method

DHTML

The `clear` method in JavaScript can be used either to clear a selection or to remove the document from your screen.

The syntax for this command usually given as follows:

```
object.clear()
```

Objects

document   selection

CROSS-REFERENCE
See **clear (DHTML Method)** and **go**.

clearInterval

Method

DHTML

This method is used to clear the interval that was first set using the `setInterval` method. This can be used to clear out an interval-controlled loop or to clear out a code monitoring statement.

The syntax of this command is

```
object.clearInterval(intervalID)
```

Parameters
intervalID

This required parameter identifies the interval to be cleared.

Objects

window

CROSS-REFERENCE
See **setInterval**.

clearRequest

Method

DHTML

This script method is used to clear a request to access the `userprofile` of the current document.

The syntax of this command is

```
object.clearRequest()
```

Objects

userprofile

 CROSS-REFERENCE
See **addReadRequest**, **doReadRequest**, and **getAttribute**.

clearTimeout

Method

DHTML

This method is used to clear the timeout that was first set using the `setTimeout` method.

The syntax of this command is

```
object.clearTimeout(timoutID)
```

Parameters
timeoutID

This required parameter identifies the timeout to be cleared.

Objects

window

 **CROSS-REFERENCE**
See **setTimeout**.

click

Method

DHTML

This scripting method is used to simulate the clicking of the mouse over a particular object. This causes the `onclick` attribute to fire and trigger the script associated with the event.

The syntax for this command is

```
object.click()
```

Elements

A	ADDRESS	APPLET	AREA
B	BIG	BLOCKQUOTE	BODY
BR	BUTTON	CAPTION	CENTER
CITE	CODE	DD	DFN
DIR	DIV	DL	DT
EM	EMBED	FIELDSET	FONT
FORM	H1–H6	HR	I
IMG	INPUT	KBD	LABEL
LEGEND	LI	LISTING	MAP
MARQUEE	MENU	OBJECT	OL
OPTION	P	PLAINTEXT	PRE
S	SAMP	SELECT	SMALL
SPAN	STRIKE	STRONG	SUB
SUP	TABLE	TBODY	TD
TEXTAREA	TFOOT	TH	THEAD
TR	TT	U	UL
VAR	XMP		

CROSS-REFERENCE
See **onclick** and **ondblclick**.

Client Application

Concept

CROSS-REFERENCE
See **User Agent** and **Web Browser**.

Client Pull

Concept

In an attempt to provide more capability to our HTTP exchanges, client pull and server push were developed. In the case of client pull, the server sends information, including a set of instructions, to the client. After a specified amount of time, the client acts on those instructions. In some cases, this means reloading information or loading a whole new page or changing specific features of a document. When this is attempted through server push, the connection is held open for an indefinite period of time until the server is sure that it is done sending data to the client or until the client terminates the connection. This is a waste of bandwidth and slows the operation of your system. In client pull, the connection isn't held open. The client opens a new connection whenever it is supposed to retrieve new data. Of course, this is slower, with time being wasted resetting the connection each time new data is required.

Server push uses a variation of MIME to incorporate multiple instructions within a single message. Client pull uses an HTTP response header, the equivalent of an HTML tag, to tell the client what task to perform after a specified time delay.

One use of client pull is to force a document to be automatically reloaded on a regular basis. The following code forces a document to be refreshed every five seconds.

```
<META http-equiv="Refresh" content=5>
<title>Client Pull Test Document 1</title>
<h1>This is First Test Document!</h1>
Here's some text to test with. Isn't this exciting. <p>
```

With this example, the META tag is used to tell the browser that it should act as if it has received a "Refresh: 5" HTTP command. This header tells the client to reload the document after five seconds has elapsed. If you wish the document to be refreshed every minute, you must use the following META command:

```
<META http-equiv="Refresh" content=60>
```

This command is treated as an HTTP "Refresh: 60" response header.

You should be aware of a few things when using these types of commands. The "Refresh" directive does not loop. In each new document retrieval, the Refresh command is reissued, creating a looping effect. In other words, the command says to get a new document in five seconds, not to get a new copy of the document every five seconds from now until eternity. Once you have given the user agent a directive, it does it after the specified amount of time. To end the "infinite reload" situation implemented above, you can click the Back button, load a different URL in the current window, or close the current window.

You can avoid the infinite reload situation by instructing the current document to load another document in its stead. To create this situation, the HTTP response header "Refresh: 5; http://myWebsite.com/nextchap. html" loads the document nextchap.html instead of the current document. You need to use a full URL when you are specifying the document to load. The corresponding META tag would be

```
<META http-equiv="Refresh" Content="5;
URL=http://myWebsite.com/nextchap.html">
```

Example

In the following example, the two documents load each other in succession. No matter which document you start with, your browser will flip back and forth between them indefinitely.

Document 1

```
<META http-equiv="Refresh" content="10;
URL=http://myWebsite/doc2.html">
<TITLE>Little Jack Horner</TITLE >
<H1>Little Jack Horner</H1>
Little Jack Horner<BR>
Sat in a corner <BR>
Eating of Christmas pie.<BR>
He stuck in his thumb<BR>
And pulled out a plum<BR>
And said "What a good boy am I."<P>
```

Document 2

```
<META http-equiv="Refresh" content="10;
URL=http://myWebsite/doc1.html">
<TITLE>Hickory Dickory Dock</TITLE>
<H1> Hickory Dickory Dock </H1>
Hickory Dickory Dock<BR>
The mouse ran up the clock<BR>
The clock struck 1<BR>
The mouse ran down<BR>
Hickory Dickory Dock <P>
```

CROSS-REFERENCE
See **Server Push**, **<META>**, and **http-equiv**.

clientHeight

Property

DHTML

This document object property is used to find the height, in pixels, of a specified object. It does not take into account the margin, border, scroll bar, or padding applied to that object.

```
[ Height = ] object.clientHeight
```

Parameters
Height

This is an integer variable that holds the height of an object in pixels.

Elements

A	ADDRESS	APPLET	B
BIG	BLOCKQUOTE	BODY	BUTTON
CAPTION	CENTER	CITE	CODE
COL	COLGROUP	DD	DFN
DIR	DIV	DL	DT
EM	EMBED	FIELDSET	FORM
HEAD	H1–H6	HTML	I
IMG	INPUT	ISINDEX	KBD
LABEL	LEGEND	LI	LISTING
MARQUEE	MENU	META	OBJECT
OL	OPTION	P	PLAINTEXT
PRE	S	SAMP	SCRIPT
SELECT	SMALL	SPAN	STRIKE
STRONG	STYLE	SUB	SUP
TABLE	TBODY	TD	TEXTAREA
TFOOT	TH	THEAD	TR
TT	U	UL	VAR
XMP			

CROSS-REFERENCE
See **height**, **width**, **clientWidth**, and **clientInformation**.

clientInformation

Property

DHTML

This document object property is used to retrieve information about the user agent being used. It specifically collects the information contained within the navigator object, which generally includes the browser name and version and feature settings.

The syntax of this command is

```
[ oNavigator = ] object.clientInformation
```

Parameters
oNavigator

This variable contains the navigator object containing information about the browser viewing the document.

Objects
window

CROSS-REFERENCE
See **navigator**, **User Agent**, and **Web Browser**.

clientLeft

Property

DHTML

This property retrieves the distance between the offsetleft and the true left side of the object in question. This distance is the width of any border around the object.

The syntax to use this property is

```
[ Distance = ] object.clientLeft
```

Parameters
Distance

This is an integer variable holding distance measurement in pixels.

Elements

A	ADDRESS	APPLET	B
BIG	BLOCKQUOTE	BODY	BUTTON
CAPTION	CENTER	CITE	CODE
COL	COLGROUP	DD	DFN
DIR	DIV	DL	DT
EM	EMBED	FIELDSET	FORM
HEAD	H1–H6	HTML	I
IMG	INPUT	ISINDEX	KBD
LABEL	LEGEND	LI	LISTING
MARQUEE	MENU	META	OBJECT
OL	OPTION	P	PLAINTEXT
PRE	S	SAMP	SCRIPT
SELECT	SMALL	SPAN	STRIKE
STRONG	STYLE	SUB	SUP
TABLE	TBODY	TD	TEXTAREA
TFOOT	TH	THEAD	TR
TT	U	UL	VAR
XMP			

CROSS-REFERENCE
See **clientHeight**, **clientWidth**, **offsetLeft**, **clientTop**, and **offsetTop**.

Client-Side Image-Maps

Concept

CROSS-REFERENCE
See **Image-Maps** and **<MAP>**.

clientTop

Property

DHTML

This property retrieves the distance between the `offsettop` and the true top side of the object in question. This distance is the width of any border around the object.

The syntax to use this property is

```
[ Distance = ] object.clientTop
```

Parameters

Distance

This is an integer variable holding distance measurement in pixels.

Elements

A	ADDRESS	APPLET	B
BIG	BLOCKQUOTE	BODY	BUTTON
CAPTION	CENTER	CITE	CODE
COL	COLGROUP	DD	DFN
DIR	DIV	DL	DT
EM	EMBED	FIELDSET	FORM
HEAD	H1–H6	HTML	I
IMG	INPUT	ISINDEX	KBD
LABEL	LEGEND	LI	LISTING
MARQUEE	MENU	META	OBJECT
OL	OPTION	P	PLAINTEXT
PRE	S	SAMP	SCRIPT
SELECT	SMALL	SPAN	STRIKE
STRONG	STYLE	SUB	SUP
TABLE	TBODY	TD	TEXTAREA
TFOOT	TH	THEAD	TR
TT	U	UL	VAR
XMP			

CROSS-REFERENCE

See **clientHeight**, **clientWidth**, **offsetLeft**, **clientLeft**, and **offsetTop**.

clientWidth

Property

DHTML

This document property is used to find the width, in pixels, of a specified object. It does not take into account the margin, border, scroll bar, or padding applied to that object.

```
[ Height = ] object.clientWidth
```

Parameters
Height

This is an integer variable that holds the height of an object in pixels.

Elements

A	ADDRESS	APPLET	B
BIG	BLOCKQUOTE	BODY	BUTTON
CAPTION	CENTER	CITE	CODE
COL	COLGROUP	DD	DFN
DIR	DIV	DL	DT
EM	EMBED	FIELDSET	FORM
HEAD	H1–H6	HTML	I
IMG	INPUT	ISINDEX	KBD
LABEL	LEGEND	LI	LISTING
MARQUEE	MENU	META	OBJECT
OL	OPTION	P	PLAINTEXT
PRE	S	SAMP	SCRIPT
SELECT	SMALL	SPAN	STRIKE
STRONG	STYLE	SUB	SUP
TABLE	TBODY	TD	TEXTAREA
TFOOT	TH	THEAD	TR
TT	U	UL	VAR
XMP			

CROSS-REFERENCE
See **height**, **width**, **clientHeight**, and **clientInformation**.

clientX

Property

DHTML

This property can be used to retrieve the *x*-coordinate of the cursor location where the mouse was clicked in relation to the viewable area of the client window.

The syntax for using this property is

```
[XPos = ] object.clientX
```

Parameters
XPos

This integer variable is used to specify the *x*-coordinate (in pixels) of the mouse cursor position.

Objects
events

CROSS-REFERENCE
See clientY.

clientY

Property

DHTML

This property can be used to retrieve the *y*-coordinate of the cursor location where the mouse was clicked in relation to the viewable area of the client window.

The syntax for using this property is

```
[YPos = ] object.clientY
```

Parameters
YPos

This integer variable is used to specify the *y*-coordinate (in pixels) of the mouse cursor position.

Objects

events

CROSS-REFERENCE
See **clientX**.

clip

Attribute

CSS

The Cascading Style Sheets `clip` attribute identifies the portion of an object's content that is visible when rendered by a user agent. Generally, the clipping region matches the outside borders of the element's box, but the region can be altered. This property applies only to elements with an `overflow` attribute that is set to a value other than **visible.**

```
clip =shape | auto | inherit
```

Values

auto

This value sets the clipping region to the outside border of the object's containment box.

shape

In the CSS2 specification, `rect` is the only valid shape that can be used with this attribute. To use this specification, the **top, bottom, left,** and **right** offsets must be specified. These offsets are calculated in relation to their respective box sides and can be either in the form of a *length* value or auto. You can use negative lengths.

NOTE
If the resulting clipped object still exceeds the boundaries of the viewable area of the user agent's window, the operating environment of the user agent may clip the contents to match the available window size.

Elements

BODY	BLOCKQUOTE	BUTTON	CAPTION
CENTER	COL	COLGROUP	DIV
FIELDSET	FORM	FRAME	FRAMESET
H1–H6	HEAD	HR	IFRAME
INPUT	LABEL	LAYER	LEGEND
LI	MAP	MARQUEE	OBJECT
OL	P	PRE	Q
SCRIPT	SELECT	SPAN	TABLE
TD	TEXTAREA	TFOOT	TH
THEAD	TR	UL	

CROSS-REFERENCE
See **visibility**.

close

Method

DHTML

This method is used to close either a window or a document's data stream. If you attempt to close a window that has not been opened with a script, the user is provided with a confirmation dialog box.

The syntax for this command is

```
object.close()
```

Objects

document   window

CROSS-REFERENCE
See **closed**.

closed

Property

DHTML

This property identifies whether a particular window is open or closed on the desktop.

The syntax for this command is

```
[booleanTF = ] window.closed
```

Parameters

booleanTF

If the value of this Boolean variable is **false,** the window is open. If the value of this variable is **true,** the window is closed. The default value of this variable is false.

Objects

window

CROSS-REFERENCE
See **close** and **window**.

<CODE>

Element

HTML

Start Tag: Required
End Tag: Required

This element forces its contents to be displayed in a monospaced font similar to that used in displaying computer code. This element should be used to identify the segments of computer programming code that you see in this book.

Attributes

class

```
class="cdata-list"
```

This attribute is used to assign a class name to an element. User agents employ classes to group specific types of information for later use.

dir

```
dir = LTR | RTL | [CS | CI | CN | CA | CT]
```

This attribute defines the direction of the text flow in a document so that a user agent can correctly display it to the reader. This attribute can also be used to specify information about the case of the characters.

id

```
id="name"
```

This attribute is used to assign a name to an element.

lang

```
lang="language code"
```

This attribute specifies the language in which an element and its values should be rendered.

onclick

```
onclick=script
```

This attribute takes effect when a user clicks the button on a pointing device with the pointer over an element.

ondblclick

```
ondblclick=script
```

This attribute takes effect when a user double-clicks the button on a pointing device with the pointer over an element.

onkeydown

```
onkeydown=script
```

This attribute takes effect when a user presses a key and the pointer is over an element.

onkeypress

```
onkeypress=script
```

This attribute takes effect when a key is either pressed and released while the pointer is over an element.

onkeyup

```
onkeyup=script
```

This attribute takes effect when a user releases a key with the pointer over an element.

onmousedown

```
onmousedown=script
```

This attribute takes effect when a user presses the button on a pointing device while the pointer is over an element.

onmousemove

```
onmousemove=script
```

This attribute is activated when the mouse pointer is moved while it is over an element.

onmouseout

```
onmouseout=script
```

This attribute is activated when the mouse pointer is moved away from an element.

onmouseover

```
onmouseover=script
```

This attribute is activated when the mouse pointer is moved over an element.

onmouseup

```
onmouseup=script
```

This attribute takes effect when the button on a pointing device is released while the pointer is over an element.

style

```
style=style descriptors
```

This attribute applies specific style-sheet information to one particular element.

title

```
title=text
```

This attribute provides annotation information to the element.

Example

The following example shows how to use CODE to display a set of programming code within the contents of an HTML document.

ON THE CD-ROM

Look for **code.htm** on the accompanying CD-ROM.

```
<html>
<head>
<title>Learning to use CODE</title>
<meta http-equiv="Content-Type" content="text/html;
charset=iso-8859-1">
</head>

<body bgcolor="#FFFFFF">
<p>When creating HTML documents, you should always specify the
full framework
  for the document, even when you can leave segments off. For
  example:</p>
<p><code>&lt;HTML&gt;<br>
  &lt;HEAD&gt;<br>
  &lt;/HEAD&gt;</p>
<p>&lt;BODY&gt;<br>
  Text of the body goes here!!!<br>
  &lt;/BODY&gt;<br>
  &lt;/HTML&gt; </p> </code>
</body>
</html>
```

CROSS-REFERENCE
See **<ABBR>**, **<ACRONYM>**, **<CITE>**, **<KBD>**, and **<VAR>**.

code

Attribute

HTML

This attribute is used with HTML applets to identify either the name of the class file containing the applets' compiled subclass or the path to get the class file itself. The value of this attribute is interpreted in reference to the value of the `APPLET` element's `codebase` attribute. Either the `code` or the `object` attribute must be present in the `APPLET` element's start tag.

The syntax for this attribute is

```
code=cdata
```

JAVASCRIPT

```
[ sURL = ] object.code
```

Scripts use this document object property to retrieve the URL of the file containing the compiled Java class.

Values
cdata

This string is used to identify either the name of the class file or its name and location.

Example
The following example code uses the `codebase` and `code` attributes of the `APPLET` element to locate the class to be used by this applet.

```
<APPLET code="jinx.class"
codebase="http://www.jinx.com/classes">
</APPLET>
```

Elements
APPLET

CROSS-REFERENCE
See **codebase**.

<CODEBASE>

Element

OSD

This element is used in the Open Software Description to identify the location of the archive where software to be distributed resides. You can specify more than one `CODEBASE` for each implementation of the software. When more than one location is specified, they are all used to balance out the load on the network system. This element is required and is treated as an error in the same manner as if it did exist but had an invalid `href` attribute.

Attributes
filename

```
filename=string
```

This attribute contains the name of the file contained within the archive that is the OSD.

href

```
href=url
```

This attribute identifies the full address of the archive file to be found.

size

```
size=max-KB
```

This is the maximum allowable size, in kilobytes, of the file to be downloaded. If the file is larger than this, it is not downloaded.

Elements

This element is a child of IMPLEMENTATION.

Example

The following example code uses the CODEBASE element to identify the program being distributed through the network.

```
<IMPLEMENTATION>
  <OS value="WinNT">
    <OSVERSION value="4" />
  </OS>
  <OS value="Win95" />
  <CODEBASE size=1024KB
href="http://www.software.com/newsoftware.cab" />
</IMPLEMENTATION>
```

CROSS-REFERENCE
See **code** and **codebase**.

codebase

Attribute

HTML

This attribute is used to identify the location of the class file that is used to implement the OBJECT or APPLET element.

The syntax of this attribute is

```
codebase= url
```

JAVASCRIPT
```
[ url = ] object.codeBase
```

This document object property retrieves the URL identifying where to find the implementation of the object.

Parameters

url

 This is the full URL from which the component should be downloaded.

Example

The code below uses the codebase attribute to specify the download location for the Jinx class.

```
<APPLET codebase="http://www.jinx.com/classes/jinx.class">
</APPLET>
```

Elements

APPLET   OBJECT

CROSS-REFERENCE
See **code** and **object**.

codetype

Attribute

HTML

This attribute is used to identify the content type of the data that is being downloaded for the object. Although this attribute is not required, it is recommended when using the classid attribute. It enables the user agent to avoid loading information for content types that are unsupported. When this attribute is not included, it defaults to the value of the type attribute.

The syntax for this attribute is

```
codetype = content-type
```

JAVASCRIPT
```
object.codeType [ = sType ]
```

This script property is used to set or retrieve the MIME type for the program associated with the object being accessed.

Values
content-type

The value of this variable identifies the specific type of content to be downloaded for the object.

Elements
OBJECT

CROSS-REFERENCE
See **code**, **type**, **object**, and **codebase**.

<COL>

Element

HTML

Start Tag: Required
End Tag: Forbidden

This element is used to group columns on a table. It is an empty element that simply provides the document author a means of applying attributes to all cells in a table column at the same time, rather than to each cell individually. The COLGROUP element groups the columns together structurally if that is necessary.

Attributes
align

```
align = left|center|right|justify|char]
```

This attribute specifies the alignment and justification of text in the columns. **Left** forces the data to be flush left and left-justified. This is the default value for table data. **Center** forces the data to be centered within the columns. This is the default value for table headers. **Right** forces the data to be flush right and right-justified. **Justify** aligns the text to both the left and right margins. **Char** forces the text to be aligned around a specific character.

char

```
char=character
```

This attribute enables you to specify a particular character to serve as an alignment point within a table and its subdivisions.

charoff

`charoff=length`

This attribute is used to offset the first occurrence of the alignment character specified by the `char` attribute.

class

`class="cdata-list"`

This attribute is used to assign a class name to an element. User agents employ classes to group specific types of information for later use.

dir

`dir = LTR | RTL | [CS | CI | CN | CA | CT]`

This attribute defines the direction of the text flow in a document so that a user agent can correctly display it to the reader. This attribute can also be used to specify information about the case of the characters.

id

`id="name"`

This attribute is used to assign a name to an element.

lang

`lang="language code"`

This attribute specifies the language in which an element and its values should be rendered.

onclick

`onclick=script`

This attribute takes effect when a user clicks the button on a pointing device with the pointer over an element.

ondblclick

`ondblclick=script`

This attribute takes effect when a user double-clicks the button on a pointing device with the pointer over an element.

onkeydown

`onkeydown=script`

This attribute takes effect when a user presses a key and the pointer is over an element.

onkeypress

```
onkeypress=script
```

This attribute takes effect when a key is either pressed and released while the pointer is over an element.

onkeyup

```
onkeyup=script
```

This attribute takes effect when a user releases a key with the pointer over an element.

onmousedown

```
onmousedown=script
```

This attribute takes effect when a user presses the button on a pointing device while the pointer is over an element.

onmousemove

```
onmousemove=script
```

This attribute is activated when the mouse pointer is moved while it is over an element.

onmouseout

```
onmouseout=script
```

This attribute is activated when the mouse pointer is moved away from an element.

onmouseover

```
onmouseover=script
```

This attribute is activated when the mouse pointer is moved over an element.

onmouseup

```
onmouseup=script
```

This attribute takes effect when the button on a pointing device is released while the pointer is over an element.

span

```
span=number
```

This attribute is used to identify the number of columns that are included in the COL element. This number must be an integer greater than 0.

style

```
style=style descriptors
```

This attribute applies specific style-sheet information to one particular element.

title

```
title=text
```

This attribute provides annotation information to the element.

valign

```
valign = top | middle | bottom | baseline
```

This attribute specifies the vertical alignment of text in columns. **Top** forces the data to line up from the top of the column. **Middle** forces the data to be centered vertically within the columns. This is the default value. **Bottom** forces the data to be flush against the bottom of the cells. **Baseline** forces the first line of text in columns using that value to be aligned on the same baseline.

width

```
width = length
```

This attribute is used to specify the width of each column being displayed.

Example

This sample uses the COL and COLGROUP elements to apply style sheet attributes to a set of specific cells.

 ON THE CD-ROM

Look for **col.htm** on the accompanying CD-ROM.

```
<TABLE>
<COLGROUP>
    <COL valign="baseline" style="color: red; font-family:verdana;">
    <COL span="2" align="left">
</COLGROUP>
<TR>
    <TD> testing </TD>
    <TD> testing </TD>
    <TD> testing </TD>
</TR>
<TR>
    <TD> testing </TD>
    <TD> testing </TD>
    <TD> testing </TD>
</TR>
</TABLE>
```

CROSS-REFERENCE
See **<COLGROUP>**.

<COLGROUP>

Element

HTML

Start Tag: Required
End Tag: Optional

This element is used to create a group of columns. This group is used to apply attributes to a variety of columns at a single pass or to organize individual columns using the `COL` element and apply attributes to them alone.

Attributes
align

```
align = left | center | right | justify | char
```

This attribute specifies the alignment and justification of text in the columns. **Left** forces the data to be flush left and left-justified. This is the default value for table data. **Center** forces the data to be centered within the columns. This is the default value for table headers. **Right** forces the data to be flush right and right-justified. **Justify** aligns the text to both the left and right margins. **Char** forces the text to be aligned around a specific character.

char

```
char=character
```

This attribute enables you to specify a particular character to serve as an alignment point within a table and its subdivisions.

charoff

```
charoff=length
```

This attribute is used to offset the first occurrence of the alignment character specified by the `char` attribute.

class

```
class="cdata-list"
```

This attribute is used to assign a class name to an element. User agents employ classes to group specific types of information for later use.

dir

```
dir = LTR | RTL | [CS | CI | CN | CA | CT]
```

This attribute defines the direction of the text flow in a document so that a user agent can correctly display it to the reader. This attribute can also be used to specify information about the case of the characters.

id

```
id="name"
```

This attribute is used to assign a name to an element.

lang

```
lang="language code"
```

This attribute specifies the language in which an element and its values should be rendered.

onclick

```
onclick=script
```

This attribute takes effect when a user clicks the button on a pointing device with the pointer over an element.

ondblclick

```
ondblclick=script
```

This attribute takes effect when a user double-clicks the button on a pointing device with the pointer over an element.

onkeydown

```
onkeydown=script
```

This attribute takes effect when a user presses a key and the pointer is over an element.

onkeypress

```
onkeypress=script
```

This attribute takes effect when a key is either pressed and released while the pointer is over an element.

onkeyup

```
onkeyup=script
```

This attribute takes effect when a user releases a key with the pointer over an element.

onmousedown

> onmousedown=*script*

This attribute takes effect when a user presses the button on a pointing device while the pointer is over an element.

onmousemove

> onmousemove=*script*

This attribute is activated when the mouse pointer is moved while it is over an element.

onmouseout

> onmouseout=*script*

This attribute is activated when the mouse pointer is moved away from an element.

onmouseover

> onmouseover=*script*

This attribute is activated when the mouse pointer is moved over an element.

onmouseup

> onmouseup=*script*

This attribute takes effect when the button on a pointing device is released while the pointer is over an element.

span

> span=*number*

This attribute is used to identify the number of columns that are included in the COL element. This number must be an integer greater than 0.

style

> style=*style descriptors*

This attribute applies specific style-sheet information to one particular element.

title

> title=*text*

This attribute provides annotation information to the element.

valign

```
valign = top | middle | bottom | baseline
```

This attribute specifies the vertical alignment of text in columns. **Top** forces the data to align downward from the top of the column. **Middle** forces the data to be centered vertically within the columns. This is the default value. **Bottom** forces the data to be flush against the bottom of the cells. **Baseline** forces the first line of text in columns using that value to be aligned on the same baseline.

width

```
width = length
```

This attribute is used to specify the width of each column being displayed.

Example

Here, the COLGROUP element creates a group of columns that can all be used to share attributes.

ON THE CD-ROM

Look for **colgroup.htm** on the accompanying CD-ROM.

```
<TABLE>
<COLGROUP span="3" style="color: red; font:verdana;"
align="center" valign="top"></COLGROUP>
<TR>
<TD> red </TD>
<TD> green </TD>
<TD> blue </TD>
</TR>
<TR>
<TD> red </TD>
<TD> green </TD>
<TD> blue </TD>
</TR>
</TABLE>
```

CROSS-REFERENCE
See **<COL>**.

collapse

Method

DHTML

This method is used to move the insertion point for text to the beginning or the end of the current range.

The syntax of this command is

```
object.collapse([bStart])
```

Parameters
bStart

This optional parameter indicates whether the insertion point is moved to the beginning or end of the text range. If this value is **true** (default), the insertion point moves to the beginning of the range. A value of **false** moves the insertion point to the end of the range.

Objects
TextRange

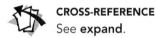 **CROSS-REFERENCE**
See **expand**.

Collapsing Margins

Concept

CSS

In Cascading Style Sheets, it is possible for vertical margins to combine, or collapse together, to create a single margin between two or more boxes or borders that are either next to each other or nested. Horizontal margins should never collapse.

Vertical margins may collapse to the width of the combined borders of block boxes. Adjoining floating boxes do not have collapsing borders; neither do absolutely positioned elements.

 CROSS-REFERENCE
See **margin**, **padding**, **Box**, **Block**, and **Border**.

Collections

Concept

Collections are compiled sets of objects that have been gathered by a scripting engine from within a document or application. A collection generally uses a zero-based index value to identify the individual objects within its array. That same name or ID can reference objects with specific names or identification.

Document Object Collections

All	anchors	Applets	areas
bookmarks(IE5)	boundelements(IE5)	Cells	children
Elements	embeds	Filters	forms
Frames	images	Imports	links
MimeTypes(IE5)	options	Plugins	rows
Rules	scripts	StyleSheets	tBodies
TextRectangle(IE5)			

 CROSS-REFERENCE
See **method** and **Attribute**.

color

Attribute

CSS

This attribute is used to identify the foreground color for the text content of an element.

The syntax of this command is

```
color: colorname | RGBcolor
```

Values

colorname

This is one of the valid color names specified by the HTML 4.0 standard or, if the element is viewed with Internet Explorer 4.0, one of Microsoft's identified color names.

RGBcolor

The name of the color is returned in hexadecimal format representing the RGB value of the color.

Example

The following style sheet applies color to two types of objects, using both methods of identifying color. It forces all uses of the acronym tag to take on the RGB hex value #FF0000, all quotes to appear in red, and all EM elements to appear in rgb(255,0,0). All of these values are the same. They all force these elements to be displayed in red.

```
<style type="text/css">
<!-
acronym {  font-family: Arial, Helvetica, sans-serif;
           color: #FF0000}
q        {  text-decoration: underline;
           color: red}
em       {  color: rgb( 255,0,0)}
->
</style>
```

Elements

A	ABBR	ACRONYM	ADDRESS
APPLET	AREA	B	BASE
BASEFONT	BDO	BIG	BLOCKQUOTE
BODY	BR	BUTTON	CAPTION
CENTER	CITE	CODE	COL
COLGROUP	DD	DEL	DFN
DIR	DIV	DL	DT
EM	EMBED	FIELDSET	FONT
FORM	FRAME	FRAMESET	H1–H6
HEAD	HR	HTML	I
IFRAME	IMG	INPUT	INS
ISINDEX	KBD	LABEL	LEGEND
LI	LINK	MAP	MARQUEE
MENU	META	NOFRAMES	NOSCRIPT
OBJECT	OL	OPTGROUP	OPTION
P	PARAM	PRE	Q
S	SAMP	SCRIPT	SELECT
SMALL	SPAN	STRIKE	STRONG
STYLE	SUB	SUP	TABLE
TBODY	TD	TEXTAREA	TFOOT
TH	THEAD	TITLE	TR
TT	U	UL	VAR
XMP			

CROSS-REFERENCE
See **Appendix A, bgcolor, color (HTML Attribute)**, and **colorDepth**.

color

Attribute

HTML

This attribute is used to identify the color to be used for the text of an object. The syntax of this command is

```
color= colorname | RGBcolor
```

JAVASCRIPT
```
object.color [ = sColor ]
```

This script property is used to set the color of an object.

Values
colorname

This is one of the valid color names specified by the HTML 4.0 standard or, if the object is viewed with Internet Explorer 4.0, one of Microsoft's identified color names.

RGBcolor

The name of the color is returned in hexadecimal format representing the RGB value of the color.

Example
The following example document uses the color attribute of the BASFFONT and FONT elements.

ON THE CD-ROM
Look for **color.htm** on the accompanying CD-ROM.

```
<html>
<head>
<title>Varied Colors</title>
<meta http-equiv="Content-Type" content="text/html; charset=
iso-8859-1">
</head>

<body bgcolor="#FFFFFF">
<p align="center">
```

```
<font size="+7" color="#FF9900">H</font>
<font size="+7" color="#FF0000">E</font>
<font size="+7" color="#0000FF">A</font>
<font size="+7" color="#006600">T</font>
<font size="+7" color="#660099">H</font>
<font size="+7" color="#FFFF00">E</font>
<font size="+7" color="#FF33FF">R</font>
<font size="+7" color="#00CCFF">'s</font>
<font size="+7">
  <font color="#FF9900">P</font>
<font color="#FF0000">L</font>
<font color="#0000FF">A</font>
<font color="#006600">C</font>
<font color="#660099">E</font>
</font>
</p>
<p align="center">
<font size="+7" color="#99FF00">ON</font>
<font size="+7" color="#00FF99">THE</font>
<font color="#00FF00">NET</font>
</p>
</body>
</html>
```

Elements

BASEFONT   FONT

CROSS-REFERENCE

See **Appendix A**, **bgcolor**, **color (CSS Attribute)**, and **colorDepth**.

colorDepth

Property

DHTML

This script property is used to retrieve the number of bits per pixel used in colors on the user agent. By using a script to retrieve this information, the document author can select an appropriate color to send to the browser.

The syntax of this command is

```
[BitsPerPixel =] object.colorDepth
```

Parameters
BitsPerPixel

This parameter contains the number 1, 4, 8, 15, 16, 24, or 32 that identifies the number of bits per pixel used in the off-screen buffer or by the user agent.

Objects

screen

CROSS-REFERENCE
See **Appendix A**, **bgcolor**, and **color (HTML Attribute)**.

cols

Attribute

HTML

This attribute is used by two elements in relatively different ways. The TEXTAREA and the FRAMESET elements both use this attribute to control the visible area of columns on your screen.

For the TEXTAREA element, this attribute is used to set the visible width of the text range. Because users can enter lines that are longer than the visible width, user agents should provide a means of scrolling through the contents of the control. One method used by user agents to provide this functionality is to wrap text lines to keep long lines visible without scrolling.

When used with the TEXTAREA element, the syntax for this attribute is

```
cols= number
```

When used with the FRAMESET element, the cols attribute identifies the width of each column that defines the frames. This is a comma-separated list of absolute dimensions or percentages used as guides for rendering the borders of the frames.

When used with the FRAMESET element, the syntax for this attribute is

```
cols= length list
```

JAVASCRIPT

```
[ iCount = ] object.cols
```

This script property is used to retrieve the width of the object in characters.

Values
length list

This is the absolute or percentage value representing the width of the columns used in the FRAMESET.

number

This is the width in pixels of the visible area of the text range.

Example

The following code shows you how to use the cols attribute to set up absolute values for the size of frames drawn by the FRAMESET element.

```
<frameset cols="166,478" rows="*" bordercolor="#9900CC"
border="3" framespacing="3">
  <frame src="leftdocument.html">
  <frame src="rightdocument.html">
</frameset>
```

CROSS-REFERENCE
See **<COL>**, **<COLGROUP>**, **colspan**, **rows**, and **rowspan**.

colspan

Attribute

HTML

This HTML attribute is used to specify the number of columns TD or TH cells are supposed to span.

The syntax for this attribute is

```
colspan= number
```

JAVASCRIPT

```
object.colSpan [ = Count ]
```

This script property is used to set or retrieve the number of columns in the <TABLE> that a single object should span. It can be changed only after the document has been loaded.

Values

number

> This is the total number of columns that this particular cell should encompass. The default value of this attribute is 1. If this value is 0, the cell encompasses all the cells from the current cell to the end of the row.

Example

The six-by-six table created by the following sample code displays a variety of values for the `colspan` attribute.

ON THE CD-ROM

Look for **colspan.htm** on the accompanying CD-ROM.

```
<body bgcolor="#FFFFFF">
<table border="1" width="75%">
  <tr>
    <td colspan="2" bgcolor="#FFFF00"> </td>
    <td bgcolor="#33FFFF"> </td>
    <td colspan="3" bgcolor="#0000FF"> </td>
  </tr>
  <tr>
    <td bgcolor="#33FFFF"> </td>
    <td colspan="2" bgcolor="#FFFF00"> </td>
    <td bgcolor="#33FFFF"> </td>
    <td bgcolor="#33FFFF"> </td>
    <td bgcolor="#33FFFF"> </td>
  </tr>
  <tr>
    <td bgcolor="#33FFFF"> </td>
    <td bgcolor="#33FFFF"> </td>
    <td colspan="2" bgcolor="#FFFF00"> </td>
    <td bgcolor="#33FFFF"> </td>
    <td bgcolor="#33FFFF"> </td>
  </tr>
  <tr>
    <td height="22" bgcolor="#33FFFF"> </td>
    <td height="22" bgcolor="#33FFFF"> </td>
    <td height="22" bgcolor="#33FFFF"> </td>
    <td colspan="3" bgcolor="#0000FF" height="22"> </td>
  </tr>
  <tr>
    <td colspan="3" bgcolor="#0000FF"> </td>
    <td bgcolor="#33FFFF"> </td>
    <td colspan="2" bgcolor="#FFFF00"> </td>
  </tr>
```

```
<tr>
  <td bgcolor="#33FFFF"> </td>
  <td colspan="0" bgcolor="#FF99FF"> </td>
</tr>
</table>
</body>
```

Elements

TD   TH

CROSS-REFERENCE
See **<COL>**, **<COLGROUP>**, **cols**, **rows**, and **rowspan**.

<COMMENT>

Element

CROSS-REFERENCE
See **<!— —>**.

Comments

Concept

Whenever you are developing a program or writing a marked-up document for consumption by other individuals, you should add notations to your program that make it easier for other individuals to understand how your program works. Comments are imperative in some applications such as JavaScripts where the document creator is doing pure programming. In other applications such as HTML documents and XML, it is important that you provide comments on the various sections of your marked-up text to make it easier for you, or another document author, to adjust the contents of the document at a later date. Comments are not required by the rules of programming, although programming convention strongly encourages them.

Comments in each language appear in a different format. Some of the common formats found within Internet Web documents appear below:

■ HTML Comments

```
<!- Add your comment here. ->
```

■ JavaScript Comments

```
/** Add your comment here*
/** for multiple lines *
// Add your comment here for comments on code lines
```

CROSS-REFERENCE
See <!— —>.

Common Gateway Interface

Concept

CROSS-REFERENCE
See **CGI**.

compact

Attribute

HTML

This attribute is used to force a list to be compacted, shrinking the size of the space between the lines and characters until the list is displayed in its most space-efficient size.

This attribute has no value associated with it. The syntax for using it is

```
compact
```

JAVASCRIPT
```
dl.compact [ = bCompactList]
```

This script property is used either to set or to retrieve information on how the extra space between list objects should be treated. If this value is **true,** the extra space is compacted.

Example
The following code uses the compact attribute to shrink the size of the list in the first instance of the chart, while leaving it uncompacted in the second instance.

ON THE CD-ROM

Look for **compact.htm** on the accompanying CD-ROM.

```
<UL compact>
    <LI>Laughter is a tranquilizer with no side effects. - Unknown
    <LI>More than kisses, letters mingle souls. - John Donne
    <LI>The best way to get a bad law repealed is to enforce it
    strictly. - A. Lincoln
    <LI>You've got to dance like nobody's watching, and love like
    it's never going to hurt. - Unknown
</UL>

<UL>
    <LI>Laughter is a tranquilizer with no side effects. - Unknown
    <LI>More than kisses, letters mingle souls. - John Donne
    <LI>The best way to get a bad law repealed is to enforce it
    strictly. - A. Lincoln
    <LI>You've got to dance like nobody's watching, and love like
    it's never going to hurt. - Unknown
</UL>
```

Elements

DIR   DL   MENU   OL
UL

compareEndPoints

Method

DHTML

This method is used to compare the end point of a specified TextRange object
with the end point of another identified range. Since each text range includes
two end points, one at the beginning of the range, the other at the end, an end
point can most easily be identified as the space between two characters.

The syntax used to express this method is

```
Result = object.compareEndPoints(Type, Range)
```

Parameters

Type

This required parameter identifies the end point on the object range and the end point of the **Range** parameter to compare. If set to **StartToEnd**, it compares the start of the TextRange object to the end of the TextRange parameter. **StartToStart** compares the start of the TextRange object to the start of the TextRange parameter. **EndToStart** compares the end of the TextRange object to the start of the TextRange parameter. **EndToEnd** compares the end of the TextRange object to the end of the TextRange parameter.

Range

This required parameter is used to identify the range to be compared to the current TextRange object.

Result

This integer-based parameter has three possible return values:

−1 The object's end point is further to the left than the end point of **Range.**

0 The object's end point is at the same location as the end point of **Range.**

1 The object's end point is further to the right than the end point of **Range.**

Objects

TextRange

CROSS-REFERENCE
See **setEndPoints**.

complete

Property

DHTML

This document object property is used to identify whether a specified object has been completely loaded into the current user agent.

The syntax associated with this property is

```
[bComplete = ] object.complete
```

Parameters

bComplete

This Boolean variable is by default **false,** implying that the window has not completed loading. A value of **true** shows that the specified window is completely loaded.

Example

The following script example uses the complete property to enable a control, in this case a text field, after the document has completely loaded.

ON THE CD-ROM

Look for **complete.htm** on the accompanying CD-ROM.

```
<SCRIPT>
function checkComplete() {
    var checkText = window.complete;
    if (checkText == "false")
        {
        alert("STOP!! The window is still loading.");
        }
    else
        {
        alert("OK!! The window is done loading.");
        oTextFld.disabled = false;
        }
    }
</SCRIPT>
<BODY onload=checkComplete()>
Please type your name in this field, after the page has
completely loaded:
<INPUT id=oTextFld type=text disabled>
</BODY>
```

Objects

window

Computed Value

Concept

There are two types of values used in Cascading Style Sheets and HTML documents: absolute and relative. Absolute values are not specified in relation to anything else, such as a color name (blue) or a set dimension (1 cm). Relative values are specified in relation to another object such as a percentage of the window of your user agent.

Relative values are computed values. They are percentages that must be multiplied by a reference value such as the size of the viewable area of a user agent window or the outside border of an image. They are values with relative units such as em, ex, and px that are made absolute by computing their actual size based on the size of a font selection or screen pixel. Some relative values use words such as "smaller," "higher," and "auto." When these types of designators are used, the user agent must compute the dimensions of your objects based upon the algorithms included with the definition of that property. Most of the objects used on an HTML document are rendered using inherited values, such as the line-height for a section of text or the cell dimensions on a table.

CROSS-REFERENCE
See **specified values** and **actual values**.

Conditional

Concept

When you are developing a program, you will find that you need certain actions to take place when specific conditions exist. Conditional statements give you this ability. When you have properly formatted conditional statements in your programs, you can use them to cause the program to interact with the user differently each time it is loaded.

Example

The most common form of conditional statement is the `if` statement. This type of statement enables you to perform different tasks based upon the current state of a specified, or combination of specified, conditions. In the following pseudocode, a test is performed to see if a specific job is completed, and then a document is loaded.

```
if jobdone=true then
    load document(my document.txt)
else
    load document(old docs.txt)
end if
```

CROSS-REFERENCE
See **variable**, **identifier**, **function**, and **expression**.

confirm

Method

DHTML

This document method is used to display a Confirm dialog box containing a specified message and both an OK and Cancel button.

The syntax for this method is

```
choice = object.confirm([Message])
```

Parameters

choice

This is a Boolean variable that tracks the choice made in the dialog box. If the value is **true**, the OK button was selected. If the value is **false**, the Cancel button was selected.

Message

This is a string containing the text that you wish to appear within the Confirmation dialog.

Objects

window

 CROSS-REFERENCE
See **alert**.

Conformance

Concept

Everything on the Internet, or that reads information from the Internet, deals with specifications. There are specifications that identify how HTML files should be written, how they should be read, and how they should be rendered. The same sorts of specifications exist for Cascading Style Sheets, XML, and channels, to name a few. Each of these specifications requires user agents to follow to some degree the rules identified within the specification. When a user agent follows the specification, it is said to conform to it.

Strict conformance to a specification is often unattainable, so software often has multiple levels of conformance. This allows the software to work with new specifications without having to match every rule in the first stage of its development cycle.

CROSS-REFERENCE
See **specification**.

Containing Block

Concept

CSS

Each object has a containing box. This box is often used to assist in the computation of relative values used when rendering an object. The containing block of an object is defined by the user agent to contain the root element (BODY for most HTML documents). The user agent's available visible area determines this block's size. All other elements are placed within this root containing block unless they are absolutely positioned. Absolutely positioned elements can be forced outside of the containing block. Fixed position elements have their containing block established by the user agent, not the containing block of their parent elements.

Consider the following example script.

```
<HTML>
<HEAD>
    <TITLE>A look at Containing Blocks</TITLE>
</HEAD>
<BODY id="body">
    <DIV id="div1">
        <P id="p1">This is a test. This is a test of the
American Broadcasting system.</P>
        <P id="p2">This is a
            <EM id="em1"> test. </EM>
            This is a test of the
            <STRONG id="strong1"><EM id="em2">American </EM>
Broadcasting</STRONG> system.</P>
    </DIV>
</BODY>
</HTML>
```

The code in this script creates containment blocks in the fashion specified in Table C-8.

Table C-8 Containment Block Construction Using Block and In-Line Elements

Element Name	Containment Block Creator
Body	User Agent
Div1	Body
P1	Div1
P2	Div1
Em1	P2
Strong1	P2
Em2	P2

CROSS-REFERENCE
See **position**, **Block**, and **Box**.

contains

Method

DHTML

This object method is used to discover whether an object contains the specified element.

The syntax of this method is

```
Found=object.contains(ElementName)
```

Parameters
ElementName

This is the name of the element being searched for.

Found

If the value of this Boolean variable is **true**, the element was found. If the value is **false,** the element was not found.

Elements

A	ADDRESS	APPLET	AREA
B	BASE	BASEFONT	BIG
BLOCKQUOTE	BODY	BR	BUTTON
CAPTION	CENTER	CITE	CODE
COL	COLGROUP	DD	DFN
DIR	DIV	DL	DT
EM	EMBED	FIELDSET	FONT
FORM	FRAME	FRAMESET	H1–H6
HEAD	HR	HTML	I
IFRAME	IMG	INPUT	KBD
LABEL	LEGEND	LI	LINK
MAP	MARQUEE	MENU	META
OBJECT	OL	OPTION	P
PRE	Q	S	SAMP
SCRIPT	SELECT	SMALL	SPAN
STRIKE	STRONG	STYLE	SUB
SUP	TABLE	TBODY	TD
TEXTAREA	TFOOT	TH	THEAD
TITLE	TR	TT	U
UL	VAR	XMP	

CROSS-REFERENCE
See **innerHTML**, **innerText**, and **element**.

content

Attribute

CSS

This attribute is used with the `:before` and the `:after` pseudo-elements to insert content into a document before or after a specific element.

The syntax used to implement this attribute is

```
content: [ string | uri | counter | attr(X) | open-quote |
close-quote | no-open-quote | no-close-quote ]+ | inherit
```

Values
attr(X)

This function is used to insert the value of the specified attribute before or after the element it is being applied to.

counter

This function can be expressed as either **counter()** or **counters()** and has two distinct forms: **counter(name)** or **counter(name, style).** The default style is decimal.

no-open-quote, no-close-quote

These don't insert any characters, but they increment the level of nesting as if quotes were used.

open-quote, close-quote

The quote character is inserted in place of these strings.

string

This adds text content to your elements.

uri

This is the URI of an external resource that is inserted by the pseudo-element. If this resource can't be supported, it is ignored.

Example
This code places a small blue ball behind every paragraph tag.

```
<HTML>
   <HEAD>
      <TITLE> Insert Before </TITLE>
      <STYLE type="text/css">
         BR:before {content:"blueball.gif"}
       </STYLE>
   </HEAD>
   <BODY>
      This is line 1.<BR>
      This is line 2.<BR>
   </BODY>
</HTML>
```

NOTE
Internet Explorer does not support this attribute.

Elements
    :before   :after

CROSS-REFERENCE
See **elements**, **pseudo-elements**, and **pseudo-classes**.

content

Attribute

HTML

This attribute is used to set the contents for meta-information to be associated with the HTTP response header in an `http-equiv` attribute. It also provides the meta content that needs to be associated with the `name` attribute.

This attribute can be expressed using the following syntax:

```
content= string
```

JAVASCRIPT
    `meta.content [ = sDescription ]`

This script property is used either to set or to retrieve the meta contents of an `http-equiv` statement.

Values
string

This string contains the contents being applied to the `http-equiv` header.

Example
In this example, the `content` attribute is used to force the user agent to reload a new document after ten seconds. The second `MFTA` element provides some keywords that a server can use to identify the topics discussed on the page.

```
<META http-equiv="REFRESH" content="10;
url(http://www.catsback.com)">
<META http-equiv ="keywords" content ="fish, bass, panfish,
fly-fishing, fly">
```

Elements
    META

CROSS-REFERENCE
See **name**, **http-equiv**, and **Client Pull**.

Content Model

Concept

Each element has a set of allowable contents. The DTD identifies the type of content that can be used with any particular element. Some elements allow only text content, and others don't allow any. The content model specifies within the DTD the content that is allowable for that element.

 **CROSS-REFERENCE**
See **%contentType**.

Content Types

Concept

 **CROSS-REFERENCE**
See **%contentType** and **Mime Types**.

Continuous

Media Group

CSS

Cascading Style Sheets, level 2, has defined the following media groups:

- Visual/Aural/Tactile
- Continuous/Paged
- Grid/Bitmap
- Interactive/Static

Each media group is used to describe specific types of media. Many media types are identified as part of these groups. The continuous media group is used to identify specific types of media that don't have a set dimension. Aural information is considered a continuous medium. Other continuous media types include your computer screen, TTY, Braille devices, and your TV.

 CROSS-REFERENCE
See **Media Type** and **Media Group**.

Controls

Concept

Interactive controls can be added to HTML documents in a variety of ways. Adding controls is just one of the ways to add interactivity to your documents, but it is a very common way to do so. Typical forms in HTML documents are designed to collect information so that the server, or the site manager, can perform some task with it, such as sending information, registering for a prize, or simply adding a comment to a Web site's guest book.

Buttons

Buttons are used to start an activity. Most forms have a button that submits their information and a reset button to reset their contents. Other times, a button is used to start a movie running or to start some other activity on your screen.

Checkboxes

Checkboxes are used to provide a means of selecting multiple options in answer to a single question. Checkboxes are often used to provide a list of magazines or newsletters that you wish to receive or to select your favorite colors from a chart. Checkboxes can also be used to start activity on your documents.

Radio buttons

Radio buttons are used when a document author wants to provide you a list of selections, but only wants one selection to be picked. Radio buttons are often used when you are asking for an individual's age or income range on a form.

Menus

Menus are used to provide options from which the reader gets to choose.

Text input

Text fields contain information that is being collected in a string format. This could be a name, an e-mail address, or a description of a problem.

File select

This is a list of filenames from which a user can select so that the contents of the file is submitted with the form.

Hidden controls

Hidden controls provide information to the form-processing engine that needs to be included but that the document author does not want to have altered by the reader.

Object controls

Objects such as movies, images, or sounds can be placed within a form to help provide information to the form-processing engine.

 CROSS-REFERENCE
See **<INPUT>**, **<FORM>**, **checked**, and **<OBJECT>**.

cookie

Property

DHTML

This script property is used to control the string value of a cookie. Cookies are small pieces of information stored by the browser that have been requested by particular Web sites.

```
object.cookie [ = "name=value; [expires=date;
domain=domainname; path=path; secure;] "]
```

Parameters

name=value;

Every cookie has a `name=value` pair assigned to it. This information is used to look up the cookie so that all the cookies that should be applied to a single page are found and used.

expires=date;

The expiration date of a cookie can be in the future, in the past, or nonexistent. If a cookie doesn't have an expiration date, it expires when the browser is closed. If it is set in the future, the cookie is saved until that date. If it is sent in the past, the cookie is deleted. The date used should be in GMT format.

domain=domainname;

Setting the domain name option allows sites that have more than one server to use the same cookie.

path=path;

This path is used by all the documents in the same domain when they need to share cookie information. This helps you avoid setting eight cookies for a single domain.

secure;

> This specification means that the information in this cookie can be accessed only from within a secure environment.

Objects

> document

CROSS-REFERENCE
See **cookieEnabled**.

cookieEnabled

Property

DHTML

This property is used to identify whether client-side cookies are enabled in the browser.

The syntax for using this command is

```
[Enabled = ] object.cookieEnabled
```

Parameters

Enabled

> If this Boolean variable is set to **false**, the browser does not support cookies. If it is set to **true**, the browser does support cookies.

Objects

> scripting

CROSS-REFERENCE
See **cookie**.

Coordinates

Concept

CROSS-REFERENCE
See **Cartesian Positioning Points**.

coords

Attribute

HTML

This attribute is used to set the coordinates of a hyperlink AREA within an image map.

The syntax of this command is

```
coords= coordinates
```

JAVASCRIPT

```
object.coords [ = sCoords ]
```

This script parameter is used either to set or to retrieve the value of the coordinates used for an <AREA> element.

Values
coordinates

```
coordinates= "x1,y1,x2,y2..."
```

The number of coordinate pairs that you use is dependent upon the shape attribute. *x1,y1* are the coordinates of the upper-left corner of the rectangle when shape=rect, and *x2,y2* are the coordinates of the lower-right coordinates of the rectangle. If shape=circ, you use "*x1,y1,r*", where *x1,y1* are the coordinates of the center of the circle and *r* is the circle's radius. If shape=poly, you use "*x1,y1,x2,y2,x3,y3...*", where each coordinate pair is one of the vertices of the polygon.

Example

The following example code uses an image map to enable the user to explore a fish tank. By clicking on the fish, the user would be able to go to a page about that fish if each of the links were active.

ON THE CD-ROM

Look for **coords.htm** on the accompanying CD-ROM.

```
<html>
<head>
<title>Looking at Coordinates</title>
<meta http-equiv="Content-Type" content="text/html; charset=iso-
8859-1">
</head>
```

```
<body bgcolor="#FFFFFF">
<img src="bground.gif" usemap="#fishtank"> <map name="fishtank">
  <area shape="poly" coords="164,174,228,123,308,123,337,93,385,
  104,425,96,453,164,403,182,369,222,277,226,192,225,163,175">
  <area shape="circle" coords="494,264,78" href="fish4.html">
  <area shape="rect" coords="203,230,411,319" href="fish4.html">
  <area shape="poly" coords="101,93,154,161,72,176,26,123,67,92,
  102,94" href="fish5.html">
  <area shape="poly" coords="106,89,156,160,247,102,194,37,105,89"
  href="fish3.html">
  <area shape="rect" coords="232,2,340,69" href="fish1.html">
  <area shape="circle" coords="91,304,44" href="fish1.html">
  <area shape="default" href="fish6.html">
</map>
</body>
</html>
```

Elements

A   AREA

CROSS-REFERENCE
See **<MAP>**, **image map**, **<LINK>**, and **images**.

Core

Concept

Just as the core of an apple is in its center and supports the apple as it grows, the core of the DOM is the center support of the developments for DHTML on the Web. The DOM Core is used to provide the minimal set of objects and interfaces for implementing, accessing, and manipulating objects within a document. The main goal of the DOM Core is to provide a strong and complete enough foundation for higher-level implementations and development to take place.

The Core of the DOM specifically provides a common API for software developers and Web script authors to manipulate HTML and XML content inside conforming user agents. Primary document structures and some DTDs are provided as a way for authors to create, from scratch, entire Web documents within memory.

CROSS-REFERENCE
See **Document Object Model** and **Style Sheets**.

Counter

Concept

CSS

Many documents require each line or paragraph to be numbered. For example, many legal documents have line numbers identifying each line. With the advent of Cascading Style Sheets, you can automatically number information within your HTML document. For example, you can have heading numbers automatically incremented or set back to zero for you.

Cascading Style Sheets counters use two separate identifiers to control the incrementing and resetting of a counter: `counter-increment` and `counter-reset`. Counters are by default decimal numbers and can be accessed using the notation `'counter(id)'` or `'counter(id,list-style-type)'`. Counters can be nested. If you need to refer to a counter using the same name, the notation is `'counters(id;string)'`.

Example

The following style sheet automatically numbers paragraphs (P) for each chapter (H1). The paragraphs are numbered with roman numerals followed by a period and a space:

```
P {counter-increment: par-num}
H1 {counter-reset: par-num}
P:before {content: counter(par-num, lower-roman) ". "}
```

CROSS-REFERENCE
See **<LI>**, **<OL>**, and **<UL>**.

cpuClass

Property

DHTML

This object property is used to retrieve a string showing the CPU class of the computer viewing the document.

The syntax for this property is

```
[ sCPU = ] object.cpuClass
```

Values
x86

This value identifies an Intel processor.

68K

This value identifies a Motorola processor.

Alpha

This value identifies a Digital processor.

PPC

This value identifies a Motorola processor.

Other

This value identifies other CPU classes.

Objects
navigator

CROSS-REFERENCE

See **appCodeName**, **appMinorVersion**, **appName**, **appVersion**, **browserLanguage**, **clientInformation**, **systemLanguage**, **userAgent**, and **userLanguage**.

createCaption

Method

DHTML

This method is used to create a `CAPTION` for a `TABLE` inside a scripted document. The syntax for using this method is

```
Caption = object.createCaption()
```

Parameters
Caption

This parameter represents the contents of the current caption. If the caption has no contents, this creates a blank caption that you can then complete.

Elements
TABLE

CROSS-REFERENCE
See **CAPTION**, **createTFoot**, **createTHead**, **deleteCaption**, **deleteTFoot**, and **deleteTHead**.

createElement

Method

DHTML

This method is used to create an instance of the specified element for the specified tag in a scripted document.

The syntax for using this method is

```
element = object.createElement(Tag)
```

Parameters

element

This is a pointer to the element that has been created.

Tag

This string contains the name of the tag to be created.

Elements
IMG   AREA   OPTION

Objects
document

CROSS-REFERENCE
See **add**, **createCaption**, **createRange**, **createStyleSheet**, **createTFoot**, and **createTHead**.

createRange

Method

DHTML

This script is used to create a TextRange object from the current selection.

The syntax of this command is

```
object.createRange()
```

Objects
> selection

CROSS-REFERENCE
See **createCaption**, **createElement**, **createStyleSheet**, **createTFoot**, and **createTHead**.

createStyleSheet

Method

DHTML

This method is used to create a new style sheet from within a scripted document. The syntax of this command is

```
stylesheet=object.createStyleSheet([sURL] [,iIndex])
```

Parameters

iIndex

This is an integer-based index value that specifies the object's position in a collection.

stylesheet

This is a pointer to the style sheet that has been created.

sURL

This optional parameter is a string indicating how the style sheet should be added to the document. If a filename is specified for the URL, the style sheet is added as a `LINK` object. If the URL contains style information, it is added to the `STYLE` object.

Objects
> document

CROSS-REFERENCE
See **createCaption**, **createElement**, **createRange**, **createTFoot**, and **createTHead**.

createTextRange

Method

DHTML

This script is used to create a `TextRange` object from the current object. The syntax of this command is

```
TextRange=object.createTextRange()
```

Parameters
TextRange

This is a pointer to the `TextRange` that has been created.

Elements

BODY BUTTON   INPUT TEXTAREA

Objects

TextRange

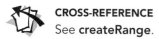

CROSS-REFERENCE
See **createRange**.

createTFoot

Method

DHTML

This method is used to create a `TFOOT` element for a `TABLE` inside a scripted document.

The syntax for using this method is

```
TFoot = object.createTFoot()
```

Parameters
TFoot

This is the contents of the current `TFOOT`. If no `TFOOT` exists, this creates a blank `TFOOT` element that you can then complete.

Elements
TABLE

CROSS-REFERENCE
See **<TFOOT>**, **createCaption**, **createTHead**, **deleteCaption**, **deleteTFoot**, and **deleteTHead**.

createTHead

Method

DHTML

This method is used to create a THEAD element for a TABLE inside a JavaScript. The syntax for using this method is

```
THead = object.createTHead()
```

Parameters
THead

This is the contents of the current THEAD. If no THEAD exists, this creates a blank THEAD element that you can then complete.

Elements
TABLE

CROSS-REFERENCE
See **<THEAD>**, **createCaption**, **createTFoot**, **deleteCaption**, **deleteTFoot**, and **deleteTHead**.

Crop Marks

Concept

Crop marks are used to identify where the page should be cut.

CROSS-REFERENCE
See **Cross Marks** and **marks**.

Cross Marks

Concept

Cross marks are marks used as registration marks. They are also used to align printed sheets.

CROSS-REFERENCE
See **Crop Marks** and **marks**.

cssText

Property

DHTML

This object property is used to specify the persisted representation of the style rule.

The syntax of this property is

```
object.cssText [ = Txt ]
```

Values

Txt

This is a string value holding the text of the style rule.

Objects

stylesheet

CROSS-REFERENCE
See **Style Sheet** and **<STYLE>**.

ctrlKey

Property

DHTML

This property identifies the current state of the Ctrl key.

The syntax of this property is

```
[ bEvent = ] object.ctrlKey
```

Values
bEvent

If the value of this Boolean variable is **false,** the CTRL key is not down. If the value is **true,** the key is currently pressed.

Objects
event

cue

Attribute

CSS

This property is used as a shorthand for setting the `'cue-before'` and `'cue-after'` attributes. When two values are given, the first is applied to `'cue-before'` and the second is applied to `'cue-after'`. If only one value is supplied, it applies to both attributes.

```
cue: [ 'cue-before' || 'cue-after' ] | inherit
```

Values
cue-after

This identifies the URL of the sound to be loaded after the element has been loaded.

cue-before

This identifies the URL of the sound to be loaded before the element has been loaded.

Example
The following rules are equivalent:

```
IMG {cue-before: url("cat.au"); cue-after: url("cat.au") }
IMG {cue: url("cat.au") }
```

Elements
This attribute applies to all HTML elements.

CROSS-REFERENCE
See **cue-after, cue-before, :after,** and **:before.**

cue-after

Attribute

CSS

This attribute is used to play a sound after an element to bring attention to it within an aural setting. If the user agent does not support aural objects, it should provide a warning message or sound to delimit the object.

The syntax for this command is

```
cue-after: uri | none | inherit
```

Values

uri

This is the address of the auditory resource. If the URI points to any resource other than an audio file, the resource should be ignored and the attribute treated as if it had the value **none.**

none

No auditory element is specified.

Elements

This attribute applies to all HTML elements.

 CROSS-REFERENCE

See **cue**, **cue-before**, **:after**, and **:before**.

cue-before

Attribute

CSS

This attribute is used to play a sound before an element to bring attention to it within an aural setting. If the user agent does not support aural objects, it should provide a warning message or sound to delimit the object.

The syntax for this command is

```
cue-before: uri | none | inherit
```

Values

uri

This is the address of the auditory resource. If the URI points to any resource other than an audio file, the resource should be ignored and the attribute treated as if it had the value **none.**

none

No auditory element is specified.

Example

The following statements use the cue-before attribute to play a sound to correspond with an image before and after it is loaded.

```
IMG {cue-before: url("howl.aiff"); cue-after: url("wolf.wav")}
MAP {cue-before: url("tiger.au"); cue-after: url("growl.au")}
```

Elements

This attribute applies to all HTML elements.

CROSS-REFERENCE

See **cue**, **cue-after**, **:after**, and **:before**.

cursor

Attribute

CSS

This attribute is used to identify the type of cursor that a user agent should display when a reader moves the mouse over a particular object on the HTML document. A cursor is the visible representation of your mouse's logical position that is displayed on the viewable area of your computer monitor or another viewing screen.

The syntax enabling this attribute is

```
cursor: "auto" | "crosshair" | "default" | "hand" | "move" |
"e-resize" | "ne-resize" | "nw-resize" "n-resize" | "se-
resize" | "sw-resize" | "s-resize" | "w-resize" | "text" |
"wait" | "help" }
```

JAVASCRIPT

```
object.style.cursor [ = sCursor]
```

This JavaScript property can be used to set or retrieve the value of the `cursor` Cascading Style Sheets attribute.

Values

auto

With this setting, the browser determines the cursor to display based on the current context. This is the default value.

crosshair

This identifies a simple crosshair cursor.

default

This identifies the platform-dependent default cursor, which is usually an arrow.

hand

This identifies a hand cursor.

move

This changes the cursor to crossed arrows, indicating something to be moved.

n-resize, ne-resize, nw-resize, s-resize, se-resize, sw-resize, e-resize, w-resize

These change the arrow to one indicating an edge to be moved.

text

This changes the cursor to a text I-beam cursor.

wait

This forces the cursor to be an hourglass, which indicates that the program is busy and the user should wait.

help

This identifies an arrow with question mark indicating that Help is available.

Example

The following example automatically changes your cursor when you place it over any `H1` element.

```
<html>
<head>
<style>
H1 {cursor: "wait"}
</style>
<title>Cursor</title>
```

```
</head>
<body>
<H1 id=hh>The heading</h1>
<P>Watch your mouse change as you pass your mouse over the
line above.</P>
</body>
</html>
```

Elements

A	ADDRESS	APPLET	B
BIG	BLOCKQUOTE	BODY	BUTTON
CAPTION	CENTER	CITE	CODE
COL	COLGROUP	DD	DEL
DFN	DIR	DIV	DL
DT	EM	EMBED	FIELDSET
FORM	H1–H6	HR	HTML
I	IFRAME	IMG	INPUT
KBD	LABEL	LEGEND	LI
LISTING	MARQUEE	MENU	OBJECT
OL	P	PLAINTEXT	PRE
S	SAMP	SMALL	SPAN
STRIKE	STRONG	SUB	SUP
TABLE	TBODY	TD	TEXTAREA
TFOOT	TH	THEAD	TR
TT	U	UL	VAR
XMP			

Objects

style

CROSS-REFERENCE
See **style**.

data

Attribute

HTML

The OBJECT element uses this attribute to point to the source of the object's data (often an image, video, or audio resource).

The syntax of this attribute is

```
data=uri
```

JAVASCRIPT

```
[ sURL = ] object.data
```

This JavaScript property retrieves the URL that is referencing the object's data resource.

Values

uri

This URI, which can be either relative or absolute, points to various resources on the Internet or local system. If the URI is relative, it is interpreted in relation to the value of the codebase attribute.

Example

The following example code shows how to use the data attribute to load a particular file of a specified type for the OBJECT element.

```
<OBJECT data="earth.mpeg" type="application/mpeg"></OBJECT>
```

Elements

OBJECT

CROSS-REFERENCE

See **code**, **<APPLET>**, and **codebase**.

Data Cell

Concept

A *data cell* is a segment of a table set aside to hold information. It does not contain any information labeling the cells. The HTML element TD automatically identifies the cell as a data cell. You can use style sheets to adjust the visual appearance of data cells without affecting the header cell styles or information.

CROSS-REFERENCE
See <TD>.

Data Type

Concept

A variety of data types are defined within a document type definition. The following data types (you'll also see the term written *datatypes*) are used in SGML documents to identify value content ranges for elements and attributes used within the documents.

CDATA

Character data is a sequence of informational characters that originate with the document character set and can include special character entities.

ID

This identifier begins with a letter (A–Z or a–z) followed by any number of letters, digits (0–9), hyphens (-), underscores (_), periods (.), and colons (:).

IDREF

This is a reference to an Id token or a list of Id tokens (when **Idrefs** is the data type).

NAME

This identifier begins with a letter (A–Z or a–z) followed by any number of letters, digits (0–9), hyphens (-), underscores (_), periods (.), and colons (:).

NUMBER

This token must contain at least one number between zero and nine. The NUMBER data type includes hex numbers, but the HTML 4.0 specification does not define hex numbers as such.

Text Strings

These tokens store easily readable character-based text strings.

URI

This token represents an address that identifies where within the scope of the network system the object exists.

CROSS-REFERENCE
See **%CharacterData**, **%Text**, and **%URI**.

dataFld

Property

DHTML

This property sets which field of a given data source (as specified by the `datasrc` property) to bind to the given object. It can also retrieve the current setting.

The syntax of this command is

```
object.dataFld [ = Field ]
```

Parameters
Field

This string identifies the field name of the resource.

Elements

A	APPLET	BODY	BUTTON
DIV	FRAME	IFRAME	IMG
INPUT	LABEL	MARQUEE	OBJECT
SELECT	SPAN	TEXTAREA	

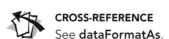

CROSS-REFERENCE
See **dataFormatAs**.

dataFormatAs

Property

DHTML

This document object property sets how the data supplied to the object is rendered. It can also retrieve the current setting.

The syntax for implementing this property is

```
object.dataFormatAs [ = text | html ]
```

Parameters

text

This denotes that the data is rendered as text.

html

This denotes that the data is rendered as HTML.

Elements

BODY	BUTTON	DIV	INPUT
LABEL	MARQUEE	SELECT	SPAN

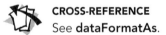

CROSS-REFERENCE
See **dataFormatAs**.

dataPageSize

Property

DHTML

This property sets or retrieves the number of records displayed in a table bound to a data source. Your script can use the nextPage and previousPage properties to move between the pages of records contained within the table.

The syntax for using this property is

```
object.dataPageSize [ = Size ]
```

Parameters

Size

This integer value specifies the number of records in the table.

Elements

TABLE

CROSS-REFERENCE
See **nextpage** and **previouspage**.

dataSrc

Property

DHTML

Script developers use this document object property to collect or set the source of data for data binding.

You can access this property using the following syntax:

```
object.dataSrc [ = ID ]
```

Parameters
ID

This string specifies the identifier of the data source.

Elements

A	APPLET	BODY	BUTTON
DIV	FRAME	IFRAME	IMG
INPUT	LABEL	MARQUEE	OBJECT
SELECT	SPAN	TABLE	TEXTAREA

CROSS-REFERENCE
See **src**, **URI**, and **URL**.

datetime

Attribute

HTML

This attribute specifies the date and time an object was changed.

The syntax for using this attribute is

```
datetime=datetime
```

Values

datetime

This string represents a date-and-time combination in the following format:
`YYYY-MM-DDThh:mm:ssTZD`

Elements

DEL INS

CROSS-REFERENCE
See **%datetime**.

<DD>

Element

HTML

Start Tag: Required
End Tag: Optional

This element marks up the definition of a term (`DT` element) used within a definition list (`DL`). A `DD` element can contain any combination of text or images that provide meaning to the term the element marks up.

Attributes

class

`class="cdata-list"`

This attribute assigns a class name to an element. User agents use classes to group specific types of information and use them later.

dir

`dir = LTR | RTL`

This attribute defines the direction of the text flow in a document so a user agent can correctly display it to the reader.

id

`id="name"`

This attribute assigns a name to an element.

lang

> lang="*language code*"

This attribute specifies the language that renders an element and its values.

onclick

> onclick=*script*

This attribute takes effect when a user clicks the button on a pointing device while the pointer is over an on-screen element.

ondblclick

> ondblclick=*script*

This attribute takes effect when a user double-clicks the button on a pointing device while the pointer is over an on-screen element.

onkeydown

> onkeydown=*script*

This attribute takes effect when a user presses a key while the pointer is over an on-screen element.

onkeypress

> onkeypress=*script*

This attribute takes effect when a user either presses and releases a key while the pointer is over an on-screen element.

onkeyup

> onkeyup=*script*

This attribute takes effect when a user releases a key while the pointer is over an on-screen element.

onmousedown

> onmousedown=*script*

This attribute takes effect when a user presses the button on a pointing device while the pointer is over an on-screen element.

onmousemove

> onmousemove=*script*

This attribute becomes active when a user moves the mouse while the pointer is over an on-screen element.

onmouseout

```
onmouseout=script
```

This attribute becomes active when a user moves the mouse pointer away from an on-screen element.

onmouseover

```
onmouseover=script
```

This attribute becomes active when a user moves the mouse pointer over an on-screen element.

onmouseup

```
onmouseup=script
```

This attribute takes effect when a user releases the button on a pointing device while the pointer is over an on-screen element.

style

```
style=style descriptors
```

This attribute applies specific style-sheet information to one particular element.

title

```
title=text
```

This attribute provides annotation information for the element.

Example

The following segment of code uses the DD element to identify a variety of definitions for a list of terms.

ON THE CD-ROM

Look for **dd.htm** on the accompanying CD-ROM.

```
<html>
<head>
<title>Looking At DT</title>
<meta name="generator" content ="NetObjects ScriptBuilder">
</head>

<body bgcolor="#FFFFFF">
<h1>My Favorite Animals</h1>
<dl> bat
  <dd>A nocturnal frugivorous or insectivorous flying
mammals.</dd>
```

```
<dt>fox</dt>
<dd>A sly stealthy carnivorous canine.</dd>
<dt>giraffe</dt>
<dd>An extraordinarily tall, long-legged and long-necked
herbivore that roams the plains of Africa.</dd>
<dt>hamster</dt>
<dd>A lovely cuddly rodent. </dd>
<dt>Tasmanian devil</dt>
<dd>A powerful heavily built carnivorous terrestrial
Tasmanian marsupial about the size of a badger.</dd>
<dt>wolf</dt>
<dd>A large predatory canine that lives and hunts in
packs.</dd>
<dt>wolverine</dt>
<dd>A carnivorous solitary mammal that is part of the weasel
family.</dd>
</dl>
</body>
</html>
```

CROSS-REFERENCE
See **<DL>**, **<DT>**, **<LI>**, **<OL>**, and **<UL>**.

Declaration

Concept

CSS

When a document author is creating a style sheet, it is important that she identify the specific rules and values properly for each element. The individual declaration for a rule must use the proper syntax as displayed below:

```
element  { attribute: value}
```

You can also create a declaration block to apply a series of attribute values to a single element. The proper syntax for using a declaration block follows:

```
element  { attribute: value;
          attribute: value;
          attribute: value;
          ….
          attribute: value}
```

CROSS-REFERENCE
See **elements**, **attributes**, **properties**, **values**, and **rules**.

declare

Attribute

HTML

This attribute makes the current OBJECT definition a declaration only. The object is available only when represented by another OBJECT definition that refers to the original OBJECT's declaration. Use the following syntax with this attribute:

```
declare
```

Elements

OBJECT

defaultCharset

Property

DHTML

This property identifies the default character set of the document. The syntax you need if you want to use this property is

```
object.defaultCharset [ = Charset ]
```

Parameters

Charset

This string variable either holds or specifies the default character set. The default value of this variable is ISO-8859-1.

Elements

META

Objects

document

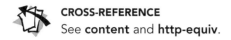

CROSS-REFERENCE
See **content** and **http-equiv**.

defaultChecked

Property

DHTML

This property tracks whether a particular check box or radio button is selected by default.

The syntax to use this property is

```
object.defaultChecked [ = Checked ]
```

Parameters
Checked

This Boolean variable is set to **true** when the check box or radio button is selected by default and set to **false** when it is not selected.

Elements
INPUT type=Checkboxes   INPUT type=radio

CROSS-REFERENCE
See **checked**, **<INPUT>**, **<OPTION>**, and **<SELECT>**.

defaultSelected

Property

DHTML

This property sets whether an identified option is selected by default. It can also retrieve the current setting. Resetting the value of a form's default does not affect how the form is submitted, but it will affect the default settings of the control when the form is reset.

The syntax to access this parameter is

```
object.defaultSelected [ = Selected ]
```

Parameters
Selected

This Boolean variable is set to **true** when the option is selected by default and set to **false** when it is not selected.

Element

OBJECT

CROSS-REFERENCE
See **selected** and **checked**.

defaultStatus

Property

DHTML

This property sets the default message displayed in the status bar at the bottom of the window. It can also retrieve the status bar message.

The syntax to access this parameter is

```
object.defaultStatus [ = Message ]
```

Parameters
Message

This string contains the message to display in the status bar.

Objects

window

CROSS-REFERENCE
See **status bar**, **Web browser**, and **user agent**.

defaultValue

Property

DHTML

This property sets the initial contents of the object. It can also retrieve the object's current contents. Resetting the value of a form's default does not affect how the form is submitted, but it will affect the default settings of the control when the form is reset.

The syntax of this command is

```
object.defaultValue [ = Value ]
```

Parameters

Value

This string specifies the initial value of the control.

Elements

INPUT   TEXTAREA

CROSS-REFERENCE
See **defaultSelected**.

defer

Attribute

HTML

This attribute shows the user agent that a script is not going to generate any document content and can, therefore, continue parsing and rendering a document.

Use the following syntax with this attribute:

```
defer
```

JAVASCRIPT
```
script.defer [ = bDefer ]
```

This scripting property either sets the defer attribute or identifies whether defer was set in the original HTML source document.

Elements

SCRIPT

CROSS-REFERENCE
See **write** and **writeln**.

definition-src

Descriptor

CSS

This descriptor helps identify the location of the font definitions used during font matching. Loading the font definitions from a URL saves network space when multiple style sheets use the same definition.

```
definition-src: <uri>
```

CROSS-REFERENCE
See **@font-face**, **font-style**, and **font-family**.

<DEL>

Element

HTML

Start Tag: Required
End Tag: Required

DEL marks the portions of a document that have been deleted with respect to a different version of the same document. This enables you to see what changes have been made within a document so they are not lost immediately. This element may serve as either a block-level or inline element. DEL can contain a series of words within a single paragraph or a series of blocks such as tables, paragraphs, images, or lists. User agents must provide an obvious means of visually determining which text has been deleted. Some agents mark deleted text in a special color or with other special markings (such as strikethrough); some do not show it at all.

Attributes
cite

```
cite=uri
```

This URI points to the location of information about why the document was changed. This information could be another document or simply a message.

class

> `class="cdata-list"`

This attribute assigns a class name to an element. User agents use classes to group specific types of information and use them later.

datetime

> `datetime=datetime`

This attribute specifies the date and time an object was changed.

id

> `id="name"`

This attribute assigns a name to an element.

lang

> `lang="language code"`

This attribute specifies the language that renders an element and its values.

onclick

> `onclick=script`

This attribute takes effect when a user clicks the button on a pointing device while the pointer is over an on-screen element.

ondblclick

> `ondblclick=script`

This attribute takes effect when a user double-clicks the button on a pointing device while the pointer is over an on-screen element.

onkeydown

> `onkeydown=script`

This attribute takes effect when a user presses a key while the pointer is over an on-screen element.

onkeypress

> `onkeypress=script`

This attribute takes effect when a user either presses and releases a key while the pointer is over an on-screen element.

onkeyup

`onkeyup=`*`script`*

This attribute takes effect when a user releases a key while the pointer is over an on-screen element.

onmousedown

`onmousedown=`*`script`*

This attribute takes effect when a user presses the button on a pointing device while the pointer is over an on-screen element.

onmousemove

`onmousemove=`*`script`*

This attribute becomes active when a user moves the mouse while the pointer is over an on-screen element.

onmouseout

`onmouseout=`*`script`*

This attribute becomes active when a user moves the mouse pointer away from an on-screen element.

onmouseover

`onmouseover=`*`script`*

This attribute becomes active when a user moves the mouse pointer over an on-screen element.

onmouseup

`onmouseup=`*`script`*

This attribute takes effect when a user releases the button on a pointing device while the pointer is over an on-screen element.

style

`style=`*`style descriptors`*

This attribute applies specific style-sheet information to one particular element.

title

`title=`*`text`*

This attribute provides annotation information for the element.

Example

The author of the following HTML document uses the DEL and INS elements to edit the information and provide notes as to the reasons for the changes.

ON THE CD-ROM

Look for **del.htm** on the accompanying CD-ROM.

```
<HTML>
<HEAD>
   <TITLE>DEL/INS Trials and Tribulations</TITLE>
   <META name="generator" content="Adobe PageMill">
</HEAD>

<BODY>
Cat's Back Consulting was developed to provide rural
businesses with access to professional advertising on the
<DEL topic="Change in terminology to remove lingo">Net</DEL>
<INS>Internet</INS>. Located in the far northeastern corner
of Oregon, high in the snowcapped Wallowa Mountains, Cat's
Back Consulting (CBC) knows and understands the problems and
pleasures associated with rural living.</P>
   <P>
It is hard turning majestic scenery, abundant wildlife,
sparkling water, and friendly people into food on your table.
As we say around here &quot;You can't eat the mountains&quot;,
but you can expand your business potential by hiring Cat's
Back Consulting to host your company's Web site. From your
<DEL cite="boringterms.html">business Web site</DEL><INS>home
on the Internet</INS> you can reach a potential customer
market of over <DEL datetime="
1998-11-08T09:15:30-05:00">40</DEL><INS>60</INS> million
people in a medium that is growing roughly 10% each month.</P>
   <P>
</BODY>
</HTML>
```

CROSS-REFERENCE

See **<INS>**.

deleteCaption

Method

DHTML

This method deletes the `CAPTION` for a `TABLE` inside a scripted document. The syntax for using this method is

```
object.deleteCaption()
```

Elements

TABLE

CROSS-REFERENCE
See **<CAPTION>**, **createTFoot**, **createTHead**, **createCaption**, **deleteTFoot**, and **deleteTHead**.

deleteCell

Method

DHTML

This method deletes the `TD` for a `TABLE` inside a scripted document. The syntax for using this method is

```
object.deleteCell(Index)
```

Parameters

Index

This identifies the specific cell to delete in the identified row of the current table.

Elements

TR

CROSS-REFERENCE
See **<CAPTION>**, **createTFoot**, **createTHead**, **createCaption**, **deleteRow**, **deleteCaption**, **deleteTFoot**, and **deleteTHead**.

deleteRow

Method

DHTML

This method deletes the TR from a TABLE inside a scripted document.
The syntax for using this method is

```
object.deleteRow(Index)
```

Parameters

Index

This identifies the row to delete from the current table.

Elements

TABLE

CROSS-REFERENCE
See <CAPTION>, **createTFoot**, **createTHead**, **createCaption**, **deleteCaption**,
deleteTFoot, **deleteCell**, and **deleteTHead**.

deleteTFoot

Method

DHTML

This method deletes the TFOOT element of the TABLE inside a particular scripted
document.
The syntax for using this method is

```
object.deleteTFoot()
```

Elements

TABLE

CROSS-REFERENCE
See **<TFOOT>**, **createCaption**, **createTHead**, **deleteCaption**, **deleteCell**,
deleteRow, and **deleteTHead**.

deleteTHead

Method

DHTML

This method deletes the THEAD element for the TABLE inside a particular scripted document.

The syntax for using this method is

```
object.deleteTHead()
```

Elements

TABLE

CROSS-REFERENCE
See **<THEAD>**, **createCaption**, **createTFoot**, **deleteCaption**, **deleteTFoot**, and **createTHead**.

<DEPENDENCY>

Element

OSD

This element identifies a dependent relationship between various components of distributed software.

Attributes
action

```
action=(assert | install)
```

If the value of this attribute is assert, the client should ignore the SOFTPKG element entirely unless the dependent material is already on the machine. If the value is install, the client gets the dependent material and then installs the software.

Example
In the following sample code, the DEPENDENCY element links required information to the IMPLEMENTATION element.

```
<IMPLEMENTATION>
    <IMPLETYPE value="VB" />
```

```
<CODEBASE href="program.cab />
<DEPENDENCY action="install">
    <CODEBASE href="http://workaholic.com/addins.cab? />
</DEPENDENCY>
</IMPLEMENTATION>
```

CROSS-REFERENCE
See **<IMPLEMENTATION>** and **<SOFTPKG>**.

Deprecation

Concept

Deprecated elements or attributes have been replaced by newer constructs within updated standards. Many of the elements discussed in the standards have been deprecated and should be marked as such within the standard specification. Although the elements that have been deprecated may be removed from future versions of a standard, such as HTML, user agents should continue to support them for backward compatibility.

Elements that have been deprecated in the HTML 4.0 specification include

APPLET	BASEFONT	CENTER	DIR
FONT	ISINDEX	MENU	STRIKE
U			

CROSS-REFERENCE
See **DTD**.

Descendant

Concept

CROSS-REFERENCE
See **child element**.

Descent

Descriptor

CSS

This descriptor defines the maximum unaccented depth for a font. Intelligent font matching utilities compare this depth with other font characteristics when attempting to match a font family.

The syntax is

```
descent: number
```

Value
number

This is an integer value with a unit identifier.

CROSS-REFERENCE
See **@font-face** and **ascent**.

<DFN>

Element

HTML

Start Tag:	Required
End Tag:	Required

This element identifies the defining instance of a term. For example, if you discuss the RGB color system in a chapter about computer graphics, you would use the DFN element to identify the first time you define the term. This makes it visually easier for users to find the definition when they skim the chapter for information.

Attributes
class

```
class="cdata-list"
```

This attribute assigns a class name to an element. User agents use classes to group specific types of information and use them later.

id

```
id="name"
```

This attribute assigns a name to an element.

lang

```
lang="language code"
```

This attribute specifies the language that renders an element and its values.

onclick

```
onclick=script
```

This attribute takes effect when a user clicks the button on a pointing device while the pointer is over an on-screen element.

ondblclick

```
ondblclick=script
```

This attribute takes effect when a user double-clicks the button on a pointing device while the pointer is over an on-screen element.

onkeydown

```
onkeydown=script
```

This attribute takes effect when a user presses a key while the pointer is over an on-screen element.

onkeypress

```
onkeypress=script
```

This attribute takes effect when a user either presses and releases a key while the pointer is over an on-screen element.

onkeyup

```
onkeyup=script
```

This attribute takes effect when a user releases a key while the pointer is over an on-screen element.

onmousedown

```
onmousedown=script
```

This attribute takes effect when a user presses the button on a pointing device while the pointer is over an on-screen element.

onmousemove

```
onmousemove=script
```

This attribute becomes active when a user moves the mouse while the pointer is over an on-screen element.

onmouseout

```
onmouseout=script
```

This attribute becomes active when a user moves the mouse pointer away from an on-screen element.

onmouseover

```
onmouseover=script
```

This attribute becomes active when a user moves the mouse pointer over an on-screen element.

onmouseup

```
onmouseup=script
```

This attribute takes effect when a user releases the button on a pointing device while the pointer is over an on-screen element.

style

```
style=style descriptors
```

This attribute applies specific style-sheet information to one particular element.

title

```
title=text
```

This attribute provides annotation information for the element.

Example

In the following example code, the DFN element identifies the defining instances of the terms *comment* and *RGB*.

 ON THE CD-ROM
Look for **dfn.htm** on the accompanying CD-ROM.

```
<HTML>
<HEAD>
  <TITLE>Using DFN</TITLE>
  <META name="generator" content="Macromedia Dreamweaver">
```

```
</HEAD>

<BODY>
This notation represents an HTML comment. <DFN>Comments</DFN>
are used to provide instructions within an HTML document for
the programmer, and anyone performing follow-up maintenance.
Comments can include information on <DFN>RGB</DFN> (Red-Green-
Blue) color schematics, explaining how the RGB values
correspond to matching Hex numbers.
</BODY>
</HTML>
```

CROSS-REFERENCE
See **<EM>**, **<STRONG>**, **<ABBR>**, and **<ACRONYM>**.

dialogArguments

Property

DHTML

This property collects the name of the variable or array of variables passed into the modal dialog window.

The syntax of this property is

```
object.dialogArguments [ = Variables ]
```

Parameters
Variables

This variable can be a string, numeric, object, or array value containing arguments.

Objects

window

CROSS-REFERENCE
See **dialogHeight**, **dialogLeft**, **dialogTop**, and **dialogWidth**.

dialogHeight

Property

DHTML

This property either sets or identifies the height of the current dialog window if the window was created using the modal dialog method.

The syntax for this command is

```
object.dialogHeight [ = Height ]
```

Parameters

Height

This integer variable specifies the height in ems.

Object

window

CROSS-REFERENCE
See **dialogTop**, **dialogLeft**, and **dialogWidth**.

dialogLeft

Property

DHTML

This property either sets or identifies the left coordinate of the current dialog window if the window was created using the modal dialog method.

The syntax for this command is

```
object.dialogLeft [ = Left ]
```

Parameters

Left

This integer variable specifies the dialog's left coordinate in ems.

Example

The following example code creates a modal dialog window located in the upper left corner of the visible area of your user agent.

```
<HTML>
<HEAD>
```

```
    <TITLE>Modal Dialog</TITLE>
<script>
function domodal() {
action=window.showModalDialog('pages.htm',"","dialogLeft:0;
dialogTop:0");
}
</script>
</HEAD>
<BODY onload="domodal();">
This produces a modal dialog box.
</BODY>
</HTML>
```

Objects

window

CROSS-REFERENCE
See **dialogWidth**, **dialogTop**, and **dialogHeight**.

dialogTop

Property

DHTML

This property either sets or identifies the top coordinate of the current dialog window if the window was created using the modal dialog method.

The syntax used for this command is

```
object.dialogTop [ = Top ]
```

Parameters
Top

This integer variable specifies the dialog's top coordinate in ems.

Objects

window

CROSS-REFERENCE
See **dialogWidth**, **dialogLeft**, and **dialogHeight**.

dialogWidth

Property

DHTML

This property either sets or identifies the width of the current dialog window if the window was created using the modal dialog method.
The syntax used for this command is

```
object.dialogWidth [ = Width ]
```

Parameters
Width

This integer variable specifies the width in ems.

Objects

window

CROSS-REFERENCE
See **dialogTop**, **dialogLeft**, and **dialogHeight**.

<DIR>

Element

HTML

Start Tag: Required
End Tag: Required

This element creates multicolumn directory lists. It has been deprecated in favor of the UL element because in practice most user agents render this element the same as a UL.

Attributes
class

```
class="cdata-list"
```

This attribute assigns a class name to an element. User agents use classes to group specific types of information and use them later.

dir

```
dir = LTR | RTL
```

This attribute defines the direction of the text flow in a document so that a user agent can correctly display it to the reader.

id

```
id="name"
```

This attribute assigns a name to an element.

lang

```
lang="language code"
```

This attribute specifies the language that renders an element and its values.

onclick

```
onclick=script
```

This attribute takes effect when a user clicks the button on a pointing device while the pointer is over an on-screen element.

ondblclick

```
ondblclick=script
```

This attribute takes effect when a user double-clicks the button on a pointing device while the pointer is over an on-screen element.

onkeydown

```
onkeydown=script
```

This attribute takes effect when a user presses a key while the pointer is over an on-screen element.

onkeypress

```
onkeypress=script
```

This attribute takes effect when a user either presses and releases a key while the pointer is over an on-screen element.

onkeyup

```
onkeyup=script
```

This attribute takes effect when a user releases a key while the pointer is over an on-screen element.

onmousedown

```
onmousedown=script
```

This attribute takes effect when a user presses the button on a pointing device while the pointer is over an on-screen element.

onmousemove

```
onmousemove=script
```

This attribute becomes active when a user moves the mouse while the pointer is over an on-screen element.

onmouseout

```
onmouseout=script
```

This attribute becomes active when a user moves the mouse pointer away from an on-screen element.

onmouseover

```
onmouseover=script
```

This attribute becomes active when a user moves the mouse pointer over an on-screen element.

onmouseup

```
onmouseup=script
```

This attribute takes effect when a user releases the button on a pointing device while the pointer is over an on-screen element.

style

```
style=style descriptors
```

This attribute applies specific style-sheet information to one particular element.

title

```
title=text
```

This attribute provides annotation information to the element.

Example

The following example code uses the DIR element to create a directory of information.

```
<DIR style="color: red">
   <LI> Cats
   <LI> Dogs
```

```
        <LI> Monkeys
    </DIR>
```

CROSS-REFERENCE
See **<MENU>**, **<DD>**, **<DL>**, **<DT>**, **<OL>**, **<LI>**, and **<UL>**.

dir

Attribute

HTML

This attribute controls the direction of text flow within directionally neutral text. Some languages have an inherent text flow to them, but a user agent should not use the `lang` specification to identify that flow. Unicode specifications assign directionality to characters and an algorithm for determining the proper direction for text flow. In instances when a document doesn't contain a displayable right-to-left character, the user agent is not required to apply the directional algorithm; but when right-to-left characters are discovered, the user agent must use the algorithm.

The syntax of this attribute is

```
dir=LTR | RTL
```

JAVASCRIPT
```
object.dir [= sDir ]
```

These script parameters retrieve the value of the `dir` attribute or set it for an element if necessary.

Value
LTR

This displays all text left-to-right, which is normal for many European languages.

RTL

This displays all text right-to-left, which is normal for many Asian and Middle Eastern languages.

Example
Within this Hebrew statement, the direction of the text and the language are appropriately specified for true rendering of Hebrew characters.

```
<Q lang="he" dir="rtl"> ...ani metureft alicha...</Q>
```

Elements

A	ABBR	ACRONYM	ADDRESS
AREA	B	BDO	BGSOUND
BIG	BLOCKQUOTE	BODY	BUTTON
CAPTION	CENTER	CITE	CODE
COL	COLGROUP	DD	DEL
DFN	DIR	DIV	DL
DT	EM	EMBED	FIELDSET
FONT	FORM	HEAD	H1–H6
HR	HTML	I	IMG
INPUT	INS	KBD	LABEL
LEGEND	LI	LINK	MAP
MARQUEE	MENU	NOFRAMES	NOSCRIPT
OBJECT	OL	OPTGROUP	OPTION
P	PRE	Q	S
SAMP	SELECT	SMALL	SPAN
STRIKE	STRONG	STYLE	SUB
SUP	TABLE	TBODY	TD
TEXTAREA	TFOOT	TH	THEAD
TITLE	TR	TT	U
UL	VAR	XMP	

CROSS-REFERENCE
See **<BDO>** and **lang**.

direction

Attribute

CSS

This attribute controls the direction of text flow within block elements and the direction of embedded objects. It also overrides the Unicode bidirectional algorithm.

The syntax of this attribute is

```
direction=LTR | RTL
```

Value
LTR

This displays all text left-to-right, which is normal for many European languages.

RTL

This displays all text right-to-left, which is normal for many Asian and Middle Eastern languages.

Elements

A	ABBR	ACRONYM	ADDRESS
AREA	B	BDO	BGSOUND
BIG	BLOCKQUOTE	BODY	BUTTON
CAPTION	CENTER	CITE	CODE
COL	COLGROUP	DD	DEL
DFN	DIR	DIV	DL
DT	EM	EMBED	FIELDSET
FONT	FORM	HEAD	H1–H6
HR	HTML	I	IMG
INPUT	INS	KBD	LABEL
LEGEND	LI	LINK	MAP
MARQUEE	MENU	NOFRAMES	NOSCRIPT
OBJECT	OL	OPTGROUP	OPTION
P	PRE	Q	S
SAMP	SELECT	SMALL	SPAN
STRIKE	STRONG	STYLE	SUB
SUP	TABLE	TBODY	TD
TEXTAREA	TFOOT	TH	THEAD
TITLE	TR	TT	U
UL	VAR	XMP	

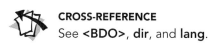

CROSS-REFERENCE
See <BDO>, **dir**, and **lang**.

direction

Property

HTML

This property sets the direction for the scrolling action of the MARQUEE element. It can also retrieve the value of this attribute.

The syntax of this property is

```
object.direction [ = sDirection ]
```

Parameters

sDirection

This string variable has four possible values: **left, right, up,** and **down.**

Elements

MARQUEE

 CROSS-REFERENCE
See **dir.**

disabled

Attribute

HTML

This Boolean attribute disables (or makes unavailable) form controls, applets, and other interactive objects. When this value is set for an element, the element cannot receive focus or input, is skipped in tabbing navigation, and cannot submit its value to a form engine.

The syntax of this command is

```
disabled
```

 NOTE
User agents are not told how to treat a disabled object. Some "gray out" the object, some do not display the field at all, and others leave an apparent "dead spot" on your screen.

JAVASCRIPT

```
object.disabled [ =booleanVar ]
```

This JavaScript property can set the object as disabled, activate it, or find the current state of the object.

Example

In this example, the INPUT text element has been disabled. This field cannot receive user input, and its default value cannot be submitted with the form.

```
<INPUT disabled name="fred" value="stone" type="text">
```

Elements

BUTTON	INPUT	OPTGROUP	OPTION
SELECT	TEXTAREA		

CROSS-REFERENCE
See **selected** and **readonly**.

Disabled Controls

Concept

CROSS-REFERENCE
See **disabled**.

<DISKSIZE>

Element

OSD

This element, a child of IMPLEMENTATION, identifies the amount of disk space required for this software.

Attributes
Value

This number, in kilobytes, specifies the disk space required by the software installation.

Example

```
<IMPLEMENTATION>
   <IMPLETYPE value="VB" />
   <CODEBASE href="program.cab />
   <DISKSIZE value="65KB">
</IMPLEMENTATION>
```

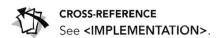

CROSS-REFERENCE
See **<IMPLEMENTATION>**.

Display

Attribute

CSS

This attribute identifies the type of element displayed. User agents must deal differently with elements to display them in a block versus inline, and so on. A block element is drawn by breaking out space around the element, forcing the element to provide a buffer around the object it contains. Inline elements work without setting aside separate space.

```
display: inline | block | list-item | run-in | compact |
marker | table | inline-table | table-row-group | table-
header-group | table-footer-group | table-row |
table-column-group | table-column | table-cell | table-caption
| none | inherit
```

Values
block

This identifies an element that creates a principal block box when rendered.

inline

This identifies an element that generates an inline box when rendered.

list-item

This identifies an element that creates a block box and a list-item-styled inline box.

marker

This identifies an element that creates generated contents either before or after a box. This value is only used with :before and :after pseudo-elements attached to block-level elements.

none

This identifies an element that creates no boxes within the formatting structure of the document and, therefore, has no effect on the document layout.

compact

These values identify either a block or an inline box, depending upon context. Properties used on items declared as these types take effect based upon their final rendered status.

table

inline-table

table-row-group

table-column

table-column-group

table-header-group

table-footer-group

table-row

table-cell

table-caption

These values cause an element to behave like a specific part of a table. For more information on individual table parts, see TABLE.

Example
The following style sheet declaration identifies how a series of elements is displayed.

```
FRAME { display: block }
TD { display: table-cell }
BIG { display: inline }
LI { display: list-item }
IMG { display: none } /* Don't display images */
```

CROSS-REFERENCE
See **<TABLE>**, **Block-Level Element**, **inline element**, **lists**, **:before**, and **:after**.

display

Property

DHTML

Use this property to discover how an object is rendered.
The syntax for using this property is

```
object.style.display [ = sDisplay]
```

Parameters
sDisplay

This string can have a variety of values, depending upon the user agent accessing the script. If the value is **none,** the object is not rendered.

Internet Explorer allows alternative values also. **Block** identifies the creation of a block-level element. An **inline** value identifies an inline box sized by the dimensions of the contents. If the value is **list-item,** a block-level box with a list-item marker has been applied to the object.

Elements

BODY	BUTTON	DIV	IFRAME
IMG	INPUT	ISINDEX	MARQUEE
SELECT	SPAN	TABLE	TD
TEXTAREA	TR		

Objects

style

CROSS-REFERENCE
See **visibility**.

<DIV>

Element

HTML

Start Tag: Required
End Tag: Required

The DIV element works with the id and class attributes to provide a generic mechanism for providing structure within a document. DIV is a block-level element that places no other visual structure on the screen. Authors can then use this element with a style sheet to tailor that block to their needs. Authors can make DIV elements into floating objects or layers, or they can use the elements as identifiable blocks of information to be manipulated by a script.

Attributes

align

```
align=center | justify | left | right
```

This attribute controls the horizontal and vertical alignment of text and objects within the bounds of the document margins.

class

```
class="cdata-list"
```

This attribute assigns a class name to an element. User agents use classes to group specific types of information and use them later.

href

```
href= uri
```

This attribute identifies the referenced Internet site in relation to the current document.

id

```
id="name"
```

This attribute assigns a name to an element.

lang

```
lang="language code"
```

This attribute specifies the language that renders an element and its values.

onclick

```
onclick=script
```

This attribute takes effect when a user clicks the button on a pointing device while the pointer is over an on-screen element.

ondblclick

```
ondblclick=script
```

This attribute takes effect when a user double-clicks the button on a pointing device while the pointer is over an on-screen element.

onkeydown

```
onkeydown=script
```

This attribute takes effect when a user presses a key while the pointer is over an on-screen element.

onkeypress

```
onkeypress=script
```

This attribute takes effect when a user either presses and releases a key while the pointer is over an on-screen element.

onkeyup

```
onkeyup=script
```

This attribute takes effect when a user releases a key while the pointer is over an on-screen element.

onmousedown

```
onmousedown=script
```

This attribute takes effect when a user presses the button on a pointing device while the pointer is over an on-screen element.

onmousemove

```
onmousemove=script
```

This attribute becomes active when a user moves the mouse while the pointer is over an on-screen element.

onmouseout

```
onmouseout=script
```

This attribute becomes active when a user moves the mouse pointer away from an on-screen element.

onmouseover

```
onmouseover=script
```

This attribute becomes active when a user moves the mouse pointer over an on-screen element.

onmouseup

```
onmouseup=script
```

This attribute takes effect when a user releases the button on a pointing device while the pointer is over an on-screen element.

style

```
style=style descriptors
```

This attribute applies specific style-sheet information to one particular element.

title

```
title=text
```

This attribute provides annotation information for the element.

Example
The following code uses the DIV element to identify a series of paragraphs that are then adjusted with the use of JavaScript and its associated buttons.

ON THE CD-ROM
Look for **div.htm** on the accompanying CD-ROM.

```
<HTML>
<HEAD>
<TITLE> Looking At DIV </TITLE>
<META name="generator" content="Macromedia Dreamweaver">
</HEAD>
  <STYLE TYPE="text/css">
  <!-
    #layer1 {position:absolute; top: 160px; left:40px; height:
350; width:650px; overflow: auto;}
    #layer2 {position:absolute; top: 60px; left:35px; height:
50; width:650px; overflow: auto;}
  ->
  </STYLE>
<SCRIPT LANGUAGE="JavaScript">
          <!-
          var bName = navigator.appName;
          var bVer = parseInt(navigator.appVersion);
```

```
                   var NS4 = (bName == "Netscape" && bVer >= 4);
                   var IE4 = (bName == "Microsoft Internet Explorer" &&
           bVer >= 4);
           // ->
           </SCRIPT>

           <SCRIPT LANGUAGE="JavaScript">
           <!-
           function D1stuff() {
               RStuff.innerHTML = savcR;
           }

           function D2stuff() {
               RStuff.innerHTML = saveE;
           }

           function D3stuff() {
               RStuff.innerHTML = saveC;
           }

           function D4stuff() {
               RStuff.innerHTML = saveA;
           }

           function doOver() {
               RStuff.innerHTML = saveR;
           }
           //-->
           </SCRIPT>
           <BODY bgcolor=ffffff>
           <p>
           <IMG SRC="bookback.gif"><br>
           <center>
           <BUTTON onClick="doOver()"><B>RESET</B></BUTTON>
           </center>
           <Span id="layer1">
           <DIV id="RStuff">
           This is the first DIV statement in Layer 1
           </DIV>
           </span>
           <span id="layer2">
           <BUTTON onClick="D1stuff()">Load DIV 1</BUTTON>
           <BUTTON onClick="D2stuff()">Load DIV 2</BUTTON>
           <BR>
```

```
<BUTTON onClick="D3stuff()">Load DIV 3</BUTTON>
<BUTTON onClick="D4stuff()">Load DIV 4</BUTTON>
</span>
<DIV id="EStuff">
This is the contents of Div 2
</DIV>
<DIV id="PStuff">
The Contents of DIV 3
</DIV>
<Div id="AStuff">
The Contents of DIV 4
</DIV>
<SCRIPT LANGUAGE="JavaScript1.1">
<!—
    var saveR = "";
    var saveE= "";
    var saveC="";
    var saveA="";

if (IE4) { saveR = RStuff.innerHTML };
if (IE4) { saveE = EStuff.innerHTML };
if (IE4) { saveC = PStuff.innerHTML };
if (IE4) { saveA = AStuff.innerHTML };
if (!IE4) {NewWindow=window.open("resumens.html")};
//—>
</SCRIPT>
</BODY>
</HTML>
```

CROSS-REFERENCE
See **<SPAN>**.

<DL>

Element

HTML

Start Tag: Required
End Tag: Required

This element creates a definition list (DL). A definition list contains a variety of DT and DD elements that identify the terms and their definitions respectively.

Attributes

class

> class="*cdata-list*"

This attribute assigns a class name to an element. User agents use classes to group specific types of information and use them later.

id

> id="*name*"

This attribute assigns a name to an element.

lang

> lang="*language code*"

This attribute specifies the language that renders an element and its values.

onclick

> onclick=*script*

This attribute takes effect when a user clicks the button on a pointing device while the pointer is over an on-screen element.

ondblclick

> ondblclick=*script*

This attribute takes effect when a user double-clicks the button on a pointing device while the pointer is over an on-screen element.

onkeydown

> onkeydown=*script*

This attribute takes effect when a user presses a key while the pointer is over an on-screen element.

onkeypress

> onkeypress=*script*

This attribute takes effect when a user either presses and releases a key while the pointer is over an on-screen element.

onkeyup

> onkeyup=*script*

This attribute takes effect when a user releases a key while the pointer is over an on-screen element.

onmousedown

    onmousedown=script

This attribute takes effect when a user presses the button on a pointing device while the pointer is over an on-screen element.

onmousemove

    onmousemove=script

This attribute becomes active when a user moves the mouse while the pointer is over an on-screen element.

onmouseout

    onmouseout=script

This attribute becomes active when a user moves the mouse pointer away from an on-screen element.

onmouseover

    onmouseover=script

This attribute becomes active when a user moves the mouse pointer over an on-screen element.

onmouseup

    onmouseup=script

This attribute takes effect when a user releases the button on a pointing device while the pointer is over an on-screen element.

style

    style=style descriptors

This attribute applies specific style-sheet information to one particular element.

title

    title=text

This attribute provides annotation information for the element.

Example

The following sample code uses the DL element to identify a list to format in the manner of a glossary.

ON THE CD-ROM

Look for **dl.htm** on the accompanying CD-ROM.

```
<html>
<head>
<title>DL and Mythical Creatures</title>
</head>

<body bgcolor="#FFFFFF">
<h1>My Favorite Creatures</h1>
<dl>
<dt>banshee</dt>
<dd>A female spirit in Gaelic folklore whose appearance of
wailing warns a family that one of them will soon die.</dd>
<dt>basilisk</dt>
<dd>A legendary reptile whose breath or look would turn any
living thing to stone.</dd>
<dt>chimera</dt>
<dd>A fire breathing female monster in Greek mythology, that
sported the head of a lion, a goat's body, and a serpent's
tail.</dd>
<dt>djinn</dt>
<dd>A spirit whom, according to Muslim demonology, inhabits
the earth, assumes various forms, and has supernatural
powers.</dd>
<dt>harpy</dt>
<dd>A creature in Greek mythology that is part woman and part
bird with a foul evil disposition.</dd>
<dt>hydra</dt>
<dd>In Greek mythology this many headed serpent destroyed
whole islands, until  killed by Hercules.</dd>
<dt>kraken</dt>
<dd>A gigantic Scandinavian sea monster often thought to be
similar to a squid,  that devoured whole ships.</dd>
</dl>
</body>
</html>
```

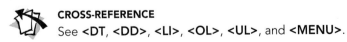

CROSS-REFERENCE
See **<DT**, **<DD>**, **<LI>**, **<OL>**, **<UL>**, and **<MENU>**.

Document Tree

Concept

A document can be described so many different ways. In general, a document is a type of information-sharing device that interested parties access visually or through a speech synthesizer. Documents are generally meant to be shared, and one way to do that is to use the Internet.

Cascading Style Sheets and the Document Object Model (DOM) work together to provide a version of a document that is organized in an easily read, universal format, which a variety of software clients developed by individual corporations worldwide can read and understand.

Each document, when rendered by a user agent, creates a *document tree* that enables you to trace the logical structure of the document. Each document tree has a root element, which, in the case of an HTML document, is the HTML element. The document tree is composed of child elements, descendants, ancestors, and parents. In a document, each child element should have exactly one parent, except for the root, which has no parents. Not all child elements have siblings; those that do have siblings have them because they share the same direct parent. A parent element is an ancestor to all of its child elements and their children. All of the children, and the children's children, of an element are that element's descendants. To make this simpler to understand, let's look at it graphically.

For example, evaluate the following HTML document:

```
<HTML>
<TITLE>Example Document showing its structure</TITLE>
<STYLE type="text/css">
<!-
   H1  { color: purple }
->
</STYLE>
<BODY>
   <H1>Document Trees</H1>
   <P>Here are some of my favorite one liners.
   <UL>
      <LI>The only substitute for good manners is fast reflexes.
      <LI>When everything's coming your way, you're in the wrong
lane.
      <LI>If I worked as much as others, I would do as little as
they.
```

```
        <LI>Everyone has a photographic memory. Some don't have
film.
        <LI> Eagles may soar, but weasels don't get sucked into
jet engines.
        <LI> Early bird gets the worm, but the second mouse gets
the cheese.
</UL>
    <DIV>
        <P> Peter Piper Picked a Peck of Pickled Peppers<BR>
        If Peter Piper Picked a Peck of Pickled Peppers, <BR>
        How many Pecks of Pickled Peppers, did Peter Piper
Pick?</P>
        <IMG src="turtle.gif" alt="Look at our green turtle.">
    </DIV>
</BODY>
</HTML>
```

This listing results in the document tree shown in Figure D-1.

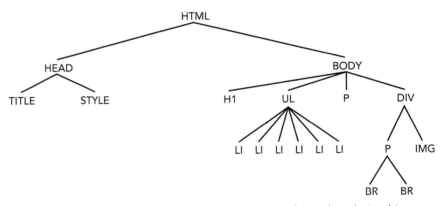

Figure D-1 The inverted tree structure of a document shows the relationships among the various objects, or nodes, of an HTML source document.

 NOTE
If a HEAD or BODY element is not a part of the document, it is inferred during the parsing of the document. This forces these elements to become part of the document tree and ancestors of other elements.

Table D-1 lists the relationships between each of the elements identified in Figure D-1.

Table D-1 Object Relationships Within the HTML Document Structure

Element	Parent	Ancestors	Siblings	Children	Descendants
HTML	N/A			HEAD	
BODY	HEAD				
BODY					
TITLE					
STYLE					
H1					
P					
UL					
LI					
DIV					
IMG					
BR					
HEAD	HTML	HTML	BODY	TITLE	
STYLE	TITLE				
STYLE					
BODY	HTML	HTML	HEAD	H1	
P					
UL					
DIV	H1				
P					
UL					
LI					
DIV					
IMG					
BR					
TITLE	HEAD	HEAD			
HTML	STYLE				
STYLE	HEAD	HEAD			
HTML	TITLE				
H1	BODY	BODY			
HTML	P				
UL					
DIV					
P	BODY	BODY			
HTML	H1				
UL					
DIV					

Continued

Table D-1 *Continued*

Element	Parent	Ancestors	Siblings	Children	Descendants
UL	BODY	BODY			
HTML	H1				
P					
DIV	LI(6)	LI(6)			
DIV	BODY	BODY			
HTML	H1				
UL					
DIV	P				
IMP	P				
IMG					
BR(2)					
LI(6)	UL	UL			
BODY					
HTML	LI(5)				
P	DIV	DIV			
BODY					
HTML	IMG	BR(2)	BR(2)		
IMG	DIV	DIV			
BODY					
HTML	P				

CROSS-REFERENCE
See **child**, **sibling**, **parent**, **descendant**, and **progenitor**.

Document Type Definition

Concept

A *Document Type Definition* (DTD) is composed of the individual element and attribute type declarations. Each declaration is identified with the following syntax:

```
<!ELEMENT elementname sTag eTag content>
```

elementname

This is the name of the element, for example, HR or IMG.

sTag

This character identifies whether the start tag is required, Optional, or Forbidden. If the value of this parameter is a hyphen, the start tag is required, an O signals an optional tag, and an F signals a forbidden tag.

eTag

This character identifies whether the end tag is required, Optional, or Forbidden. If the value of this parameter is a hyphen, the start tag is required; an O signals an optional tag.

content

This identifies the valid contents of the element. Allowable contents for an element make up the *content model*. An element's content model is specified with the following syntax:

(...)	Delimits a group.
A | B	Either A or B occurs, but not both.
A , B	Both A and B occur, in that order.
A & B	Both A and B occur, in any order.
A?	A occurs zero times or one time.
A*	A occurs zero or more times.
A+	A occurs one or more times.

NOTE

Some elements have no contents; to declare the content model for these *empty elements*, use the keyword EMPTY (see Example 2).

Example 1

The following example declares the UL element. The two hyphens show that both the start tags and end tags are required, and the content model shows that the UL element contains at least one LI element.

```
<!ELEMENT UL - - (LI)+>
```

Example 2

The following example declares the IMG element. The first hyphen shows that the start tag is required; the O shows that the end tag is optional. The content model shows that this element is empty, which forces the optional state of the end tag to forbidden.

```
<!ELEMENT IMG - O EMPTY>
```

CROSS-REFERENCE

See **<!DOCUMENT>** and **content model**.

Document Object Model

Concept

The *Document Object Model* (DOM) is a platform- and language-independent interface system that provides programs and scripts a means of dynamically accessing and updating the contents, structure, and style of a document. The DOM standard provides developers a consistent model to use when putting together the objects found in XML and HTML documents. It also provides them a standard interface to use for accessing and manipulating the objects and the relationships between those objects. Vendors can support the DOM as an alternative interface for their proprietary Application Programming Interfaces (APIs), and content authors, such as Web programmers, can design documents based on the DOM rather than on a specific vendor's program. Altogether, this extends the interoperability of the Web. Without an understanding of the DOM, HTML scriptwriters have difficulty designing pages that can take full advantage of the capabilities of the Web and our current Web browsers.

The DOM is the API for both HTML and XML. It defines the logical structures of either of these types of documents. The DOM began as a means of ensuring that JavaScript scripts and Java programs would be shareable across user agents. It has developed into a means of forcing consistency among Web browsers' interpretations of various objects and elements. It is the standard model for using all programming languages on the Internet.

The DOM treats documents in a manner very close to the structure of the document itself. This structure is referred to as a document tree and creates a hierarchical structure representing the relationships between each object on the document. The DOM does not force the document to be implemented in any way, so user agents can use the most convenient method. Although implementation is up to the user agent, any agent using the DOM to create a rendering of the same document will create the same structure model with the same objects and relationships.

The DOM is a true object model that has been identified with the traditional object-oriented design methods. All of the documents are rendered using objects, and the model defines the structure of the document, the behavior of the document, and the individual objects that it contains. In this manner the DOM is used to identify the following:

- Objects and interfaces used when rendering and manipulating the document
- Behavior and attributes of the objects and interfaces
- Relationships between the interfaces and objects

The current DOM specification consists of the DOM Core and the DOM HTML. The Core represents the functionality required for XML documents, which in turn serves as the basis for the HTML DOM. All implementations of the DOM must support the interfaces shown as "fundamental" within the Core specification. Each additional specification identifies additional functionality needed for that particular type of document.

CROSS-REFERENCE
See **Document Tree** and **Document Type Definition**.

domain

Property

DHTML

This document object property sets or retrieves the security domain of the current document. When first returned, this property contains the name of the server that hosts the page. This property enables secure transmissions between servers using the same domain name. Generally, the pages you would find on `home.catsback.com` and `www.catsback.com` cannot communicate with each other. By setting the domain to `catsback.com`, you can securely communicate with them both of them.

The syntax of this property is

```
object.domain [ = stringDomain ]
```

Parameters
stringDomain

This string identifies the domain suffix.

Object

document

CROSS-REFERENCE
See **URI** and **URL**.

doReadRequest

Method

DHTML

This scripting method performs the requests located in the read-requests queue. If the site doesn't currently have read access, the user is prompted with a list of requested attributes that either allow or deny access to the site.

The syntax to implement this method is

```
bSuccess = object.doReadRequest(vUsageCode [,vFriendlyName]
[,vDomain] [,vPath] [,vExpiration] [,vReserved])
```

Parameters

bSuccess

The value of this parameter is true if the process was successful; otherwise it is false.

vUsageCode

This required parameter tells the user what type of access has been requested. Possible values are

- 0   For system administration.
- 1   For research and/or product development.
- 2   For completion and support of current transaction.
- 3   For customizing the contents or design of a site.
- 4   For improving the contents of a site. This includes advertisements.
- 5   For notifying visitors about site updates.
- 6   For contacting visitors for marketing purposes.
- 7   For linking to collected information.
- 8   For other general purposes.
- 9   For sharing with others interested in the customization and improvement of the site contents and design.
- 10   For sharing with others (who may be in contact) interested in marketing ideas.
- 11   For sharing with others (who may be in contact) interested in marketing ideas.
- 12   For sharing with others for general purposes.

vFriendlyName

This optional parameter is the name of the party requesting access to the private information. In addition to this name, the URL that starts the script that requests the profile access must appear.

vDomain

This optional parameter identifies both the page that the user's choice is applied to and the current page.

vPath

This parameter identifies the path to the user's choice.

vExpiration

This optional parameter identifies the length of time the site will be requesting access to particular attributes.

vReserved

This optional parameter is reserved.

Object

userprofile

CROSS-REFERENCE
See **addReadRequest**, **clearRequest**, and **getAttribute**.

drop caps

Concept

CROSS-REFERENCE
See **:first-letter**.

DSSSL

Language

The Document Style Semantics and Specification Language (DSSSL) is a standard used in processing SGML documents. SGML is the Standard Generalized Markup Language that describes documents in regard to their logical, rather than presentational, structure. DSSSL describes how the structure is presented visually, converted, or processed. Whereas SGML is a document structure language, DSSSL is a document processing language especially designed for presenting or transforming documents.

DSSSL both displays HTML (or other) documents and converts them from their original version to another. For instance, an HTML document could be converted to XML, Microsoft Word, or Adobe FrameMaker. DSSSL defines how these conversions should be written and how you convert markup tags from one language to another.

CROSS-REFERENCE
See **SGML**, **XSL**, and **CSS**.

<DT>

Element

HTML

Start Tag: Required
End Tag: Optional

This element marks up the term associated with a definition used within a definition list (DL). The contents of a DT element are an inline element only capable of containing text.

Attributes
class

```
class="cdata-list"
```

This attribute assigns a class name to an element. User agents use classes to group specific types of information and use them later.

dir

```
dir = LTR | RTL
```

This attribute defines the direction of the text flow in a document so that a user agent can display it correctly.

id

```
id="name"
```

This attribute assigns a name to an element.

lang

```
lang="language code"
```

This attribute specifies the language that renders an element and its values.

onclick

```
onclick=script
```

This attribute takes effect when a user clicks the button on a pointing device while the pointer is over an on-screen element.

ondblclick

```
ondblclick=script
```

This attribute takes effect when a user double-clicks the button on a pointing device while the pointer is over an on-screen element.

onkeydown

```
onkeydown=script
```

This attribute takes effect when a user presses a key while the pointer is over an on-screen element.

onkeypress

```
onkeypress=script
```

This attribute takes effect when a user either presses and releases a key while the pointer is over an on-screen element.

onkeyup

```
onkeyup=script
```

This attribute takes effect when a user releases a key while the pointer is over an on-screen element.

onmousedown

```
onmousedown=script
```

This attribute takes effect when a user presses the button on a pointing device while the pointer is over an on-screen element.

onmousemove

```
onmousemove=script
```

This attribute becomes active when a user moves the mouse while the pointer is over an on-screen element.

onmouseout

```
onmouseout=script
```

This attribute becomes active when a user moves the mouse pointer away from an on-screen element.

onmouseover

```
onmouseover=script
```

This attribute becomes active when a user moves the mouse pointer over an on-screen element.

onmouseup

```
onmouseup=script
```

This attribute takes effect when a user releases the button on a pointing device while the pointer is over an on-screen element.

style

```
style=style descriptors
```

This attribute applies specific style-sheet information to one particular element.

title

```
title=text
```

This attribute provides annotation information to the element.

Example

The following segment of code uses the DT element to identify a variety of terms for a definition list.

ON THE CD-ROM

Look for **dt.htm** on the accompanying CD-ROM.

```
<html>
<head>
<title>Looking At DT</title>
<meta name="generator" contents="NetObjects ScriptBuilder">
</head>

<body bgcolor="#FFFFFF">
<h1>My Favorite Quotations</h1>
<dl>
  <dt>On Courage</dt>
```

```
<dd>Remember, no one can make you feel inferior without your
consent.- <b>Eleanor Roosevelt</b></dd>
   <dt>On Love</dt>
   <dd>To receive everything, one must open one's hands and
give.- <b>Taisen Deshimaru</b></dd>
   <dt>On Persistence</dt>
   <dd>What doesn't kill me makes me stronger. - <b>Albert
Camus</b></dd>
   <dt>On Creativity</dt>
   <dd>Learning is movement from moment to moment. - <b>J.
Krishnamurti</b></dd>
   <dt>On Friends</dt>
   <dd>Believe me, a thousand friends suffice thee not; In a
single enemy thou hast more than enough. - <b>Ali Ben Abi
Taleb</b></dd>
   </dl>
   </body>
   </html>
```

CROSS-REFERENCE
See **<DL>**, **<DT>**, **<LI>**, **<OL>**, and **<UL>**.

DTD

Concept

CROSS-REFERENCE
See **Document Type Definition**.

duplicate

Method

DHTML

This scripting method returns a duplicate TextRange to the script.
The syntax for this method is

```
TextRange = object.duplicate()
```

Parameters

TextRange

This is the duplicated TextRange object.

Objects

TextRange

 **CROSS-REFERENCE**
See **<TEXTAREA>**.

Dynamic HTML

Concept

Dynamic HTML (or *DHTML*) is apparently a very misunderstood term. DHTML is an all-encompassing term that includes the HTML 4.0 specification, Cascading Style Sheets, the Document Object Model, and enough JavaScript/JScript/ECMAScript/VBScript to create a totally interactive Web site. DHTML is where advanced Web development is going. DHTML sites use an extended set of HTML elements and attributes in conjunction with style sheet elements, all of which can be modified by scripting languages. This combination of features enables you to create pages that come alive with moving text and objects and interactive contents.

The following example document shows how a combination of JavaScript, HTML, and Cascading Style Sheets create an interactive page for sharing and displaying information in an attractive, yet informative, manner.

 ON THE CD-ROM
Look for **dhtml.htm** on the accompanying CD-ROM.

```
<html>
<head>
<title>DHTML Example</title>
<style type="text/css">
<!-
h1 {  font-family: Arial, Helvetica, sans-serif; font-size:
xx-large; font-style: italic; color: #FFFF00}
->
</style>
  <script language="JavaScript">
<!-
function MM_initTimelines() {
```

```
    //MM_initTimelines() Copyright 1997 Macromedia, Inc. All
rights reserved.
    var ns = navigator.appName == "Netscape";
    document.MM_Time = new Array(1);
    document.MM_Time[0] = new Array(5);
    document.MM_Time["Timeline1"] = document.MM_Time[0];
    document.MM_Time[0].MM_Name = "Timeline1";
    document.MM_Time[0].fps = 15;
    document.MM_Time[0][0] = new String("sprite");
    document.MM_Time[0][0].slot = 1;
    if (ns)
        document.MM_Time[0][0].obj = document.Layer4;
    else
        document.MM_Time[0][0].obj = document.all ?
document.all["Layer4"] : null;
    document.MM_Time[0][0].keyFrames = new Array(1, 5, 10, 15,
20);
document.MM_Time[0][0].values = new Array(2);
    document.MM_Time[0][0].values[0] = new
Array(288,324,361,395,416,405,385,359,329,293,255,221,190,163,
147,164,193,224,256,288);
    document.MM_Time[0][0].values[0].prop = "left";
    document.MM_Time[0][0].values[1] = new
Array(92,121,151,183,224,260,291,318,342,355,343,321,294,263,2
26,191,163,139,116,92);
    document.MM_Time[0][0].values[1].prop = "top";
    if (!ns) {
        document.MM_Time[0][0].values[0].prop2 = "style";
        document.MM_Time[0][0].values[1].prop2 = "style";
    }
    document.MM_Time[0][1] = new String("sprite");
    document.MM_Time[0][1].slot = 2;
    if (ns)
        document.MM_Time[0][1].obj = document.Layer2;
    else
        document.MM_Time[0][1].obj = document.all ?
document.all["Layer2"] : null;
    document.MM_Time[0][1].keyFrames = new Array(1, 10, 20,
30, 40);
    document.MM_Time[0][1].values = new Array(2);
    document.MM_Time[0][1].values[0] = new
Array(169,181,192,203,214,226,238,252,268,288,306,323,339,353,
367,379,391,401,409,413,410,403,393,382,370,357,344,328,312,29
4,276,261,247,234,222,210,199,187,176,164);
```

```
    document.MM_Time[0][1].values[0].prop = "left";
    document.MM_Time[0][1].values[1] = new
Array(206,190,174,158,141,125,110,95,83,77,83,93,106,120,135,1
51,168,185,204,223,242,259,276,291,305,319,331,342,351,355,350
,339,326,312,298,283,268,253,238,223);
    document.MM_Time[0][1].values[1].prop = "top";
    if (!ns) {
        document.MM_Time[0][1].values[0].prop2 = "style";
        document.MM_Time[0][1].values[1].prop2 = "style";
    }
    document.MM_Time[0][2] = new String("sprite");
    document.MM_Time[0][2].slot = 3;
    if (ns)
        document.MM_Time[0][2].obj = document.Layer3;
    else
        document.MM_Time[0][2].obj = document.all ?
document.all["Layer3"] : null;
    document.MM_Time[0][2].keyFrames = new Array(1, 20, 40,
60, 80);
    document.MM_Time[0][2].values = new Array(2);
    document.MM_Time[0][2].values[0] = new
Array(417,411,405,400,394,389,384,378,373,367,361,355,349,343,
336,329,322,314,305,295,286,276,268,259,251,243,235,228,221,21
4,207,200,194,188,182,176,172,168,164,163,164,167,170,175,180,
185,191,197,203,210,217,224,231,238,246,254,262,271,280,289,29
8,307,315,322,329,336,343,349,355,361,367,373,378,384,389,395,
400,406,412,418);
    document.MM_Time[0][2].values[0].prop = "left";
    document.MM_Time[0][2].values[1] = new
Array(223,230,238,246,254,262,270,277,285,293,301,308,316,323,
330,336,343,348,352,354,353,350,346,341,336,331,325,319,312,30
5,298,291,284,276,268,260,252,243,234,224,214,205,196,188,180,
172,164,156,149,142,135,129,123,117,111,106,101,97,94,93,94,98
,103,108,114,121,127,134,141,148,156,163,170,177,185,192,200,2
07,214,221);
    document.MM_Time[0][2].values[1].prop = "top";
    if (!ns) {
        document.MM_Time[0][2].values[0].prop2 = "style";
        document.MM_Time[0][2].values[1].prop2 = "style";
    }
    document.MM_Time[0][3] = new String("sprite");
    document.MM_Time[0][3].slot = 4;
    if (ns)
        document.MM_Time[0][3].obj = document.Layer5;
```

```
    else
        document.MM_Time[0][3].obj = document.all ?
document.all["Layer5"] : null;
    document.MM_Time[0][3].keyFrames = new Array(1, 10, 20,
30, 40);
    document.MM_Time[0][3].values = new Array(2);
    document.MM_Time[0][3].values[0] = new
Array(295,277,258,239,220,201,183,167,152,144,149,159,171,185,
200,216,233,251,269,289,309,327,345,361,376,391,404,416,425,43
0,425,414,400,386,371,356,341,325,310,295);
    document.MM_Time[0][3].values[0].prop = "left";
    document.MM_Time[0][3].values[1] = new
Array(355,341,328,315,302,288,273,258,240,219,199,182,166,151,
137,125,113,103,95,92,96,104,115,127,140,154,169,185,203,222,2
41,257,271,284,297,308,320,331,343,355);
    document.MM_Time[0][3].values[1].prop = "top";
    if (!ns) {
        document.MM_Time[0][3].values[0].prop2 = "style";
        document.MM_Time[0][3].values[1].prop2 = "style";
    }
    document.MM_Time[0][4] = new String("behavior");
    document.MM_Time[0][4].frame = 81;
    document.MM_Time[0][4].value =
"MM_timelineGoto('Timeline1','1')";
    document.MM_Time[0].lastFrame = 81;
    for (i=0; i<document.MM_Time.length; i++) {
        document.MM_Time[i].ID = null;
        document.MM_Time[i].curFrame = 0;
        document.MM_Time[i].delay =
1000/document.MM_Time[i].fps;
    }
}
//-->
</script>
  <script language="JavaScript">
<!--
function MM_timelineGoto(tmLnName, fNew, numGotos) { //v1.2
  //Copyright 1997 Macromedia, Inc. All rights reserved.
  var
i,j,tmLn,props,keyFrm,sprite,numKeyFr,firstKeyFr,lastKeyFr,pro
pNum,theObj;
  if (document.MM_Time == null) MM_initTimelines(); //if
*very* 1st time
  tmLn = document.MM_Time[tmLnName];
```

```
    if (numGotos != null)
      if (tmLn.gotoCount == null) tmLn.gotoCount = 1;
      else if (tmLn.gotoCount++ >= numGotos) {tmLn.gotoCount=0;
return}
  jmpFwd = (fNew > tmLn.curFrame);
  for (i = 0; i < tmLn.length; i++) {
     sprite = (jmpFwd)? tmLn[i] : tmLn[(tmLn.length-1)-i];
//count bkwds if jumping back
     if (sprite.charAt(0) == "s") {
        numKeyFr = sprite.keyFrames.length;
        firstKeyFr = sprite.keyFrames[0];
        lastKeyFr = sprite.keyFrames[numKeyFr - 1];
        if ((jmpFwd && fNew<firstKeyFr) || (!jmpFwd &&
lastKeyFr<fNew)) continue; //skip if untouchd
        for (keyFrm=1; keyFrm<numKeyFr &&
fNew>=sprite.keyFrames[keyFrm]; keyFrm++);
        for (j=0; j<sprite.values.length; j++) {
           props = sprite.values[j];
           if (numKeyFr == props.length) propNum = keyFrm-1
//keyframes only
           else propNum = Math.min(Math.max(0,fNew-
firstKeyFr),props.length-1); //or keep in legal range
           if (sprite.obj != null) {
              if (props.prop2 == null) sprite.obj[props.prop] =
props[propNum];
              else        sprite.obj[props.prop2][props.prop] =
props[propNum];
  } } } }
  tmLn.curFrame = fNew;
  if (tmLn.ID == 0) eval('MM_timelinePlay(tmLnName)');
}
//-->
</script>
  <script language="JavaScript">
<!-
function MM_timelinePlay(tmLnName, myID) { //v1.2
  //Copyright 1997 Macromedia, Inc. All rights reserved.
  var
i,j,tmLn,props,keyFrm,sprite,numKeyFr,firstKeyFr,propNum,theOb
j,firstTime=false;
  if (document.MM_Time == null) MM_initTimelines(); //if
*very* 1st time
  tmLn = document.MM_Time[tmLnName];
```

```
   if (myID == null) { myID = ++tmLn.ID; firstTime=true;}//if
new call, incr ID
  if (myID == tmLn.ID) { //if Im newest

setTimeout('MM_timelinePlay("'+tmLnName+'",'+myID+')',tmLn.del
ay);
    fNew = ++tmLn.curFrame;
    for (i=0; i<tmLn.length; i++) {
      sprite = tmLn[i];
      if (sprite.charAt(0) == 's') {
        if (sprite.obj) {
          numKeyFr = sprite.keyFrames.length; firstKeyFr =
sprite.keyFrames[0];
          if (fNew >= firstKeyFr && fNew <=
sprite.keyFrames[numKeyFr-1]) {//in range
            keyFrm=1;
            for (j=0; j<sprite.values.length; j++) {
              props = sprite.values[j];
              if (numKeyFr != props.length) {
                if (props.prop2 == null)
sprite.obj[props.prop] = props[fNew-firstKeyFr];
                else
sprite.obj[props.prop2][props.prop] = props[fNew-firstKeyFr];
              } else {
                while (keyFrm<numKeyFr &&
fNew>=sprite.keyFrames[keyFrm]) keyFrm++;
                if (firstTime ||
fNew==sprite.keyFrames[keyFrm-1]) {
                  if (props.prop2 == null)
sprite.obj[props.prop] = props[keyFrm-1];
                  else
sprite.obj[props.prop2][props.prop] = props[keyFrm-1];
      } } } } }
      } else if (sprite.charAt(0)=='b' && fNew ==
sprite.frame) eval(sprite.value);
      if (fNew > tmLn.lastFrame) tmLn.ID = 0;
  } }
}
//-->
</script>
</head>

<body bgcolor="#000000" onLoad="MM_timelinePlay('Timeline1')">
```

```
<div id="Layer1" style="position:absolute; left:187px;
top:128px; width:301px; height:301px; z-index:1"><img
src="blackcirc.gif"></div>
<div id="Layer2" style="position:absolute; left:169px;
top:206px; width:106px; height:100px; z-index:2"><img
src="bluecirc.gif" width="100" height="100"
name="Image1"></div>
<div id="Layer3" style="position:absolute; left:417px;
top:223px; width:112px; height:104px; z-index:3"><img
src="greencirc.gif" width="100" height="100"></div>
<div id="Layer4" style="position:absolute; left:288px;
top:92px; width:108px; height:96px; z-index:4"><img
src="redcirc.gif" width="100" height="100"></div>
<div id="Layer5" style="position:absolute; left:295px;
top:355px; width:104px; height:104px; z-index:5"><img
src="yellcirc.gif" width="100" height="100"></div>
<div id="Layer6" style="position:absolute; left:265px;
top:165px; width:169px; height:105px; z-index:6"><font
color="#000000" size="+3">Watch
  for your destiny. <br>
  It may be swirling around you.</font></div>

</body>
</html>
```

CROSS-REFERENCE
See **Document Object Model, Cascading Style Sheets, JavaScript, JScript, ECMAScript, VBScript,** and **HTML.**

dynsrc

Property

DHTML

This document object attribute either sets or retrieves a video clip or VRML world to display in the window.
The syntax is

```
object.dynsrc [ = sURL ]
```

Parameters

sURL

This string identifies the URL of the video source.

Elements

IMG

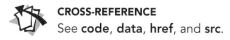

CROSS-REFERENCE

See **code**, **data**, **href**, and **src**.

E

<EarliestTime>

Element

CDF

Start Tag: Required
End Tag: Forbidden

This is simply the earliest time during the specified Channel delivery schedule that the channel information can be sent. This element can only be used as a child of the CHANNEL element.

Attributes

day

day="*number*"

This integer represents the day of the month the channel document should be delivered.

hour

hour="*number*"

This is the hour of the day in a 24-hour format.

min

min="*number*"

This is an integer between 1 and 60, representing a minute interval during a single hour.

Example

This example channel, located at http://mychannels.com/channels.cdf, must be delivered between midnight and noon on the first of each month.

```
<CHANNEL href="http://mychannels.com/channels.cdf ">
  <SCHEDULE>
    <INTERVALTIME Day=30 />
```

```
        <EARLIESTTIME Hour=0 />
        <LATESTTIME Hour=12 />
    </SCHEDULE>
  </CHANNEL>
```

Elements
    CHANNEL

CROSS-REFERENCE
See **Channel Definition Format**, **<LATESTTIME>**, **<StartDate>**, **<Enddate>**, and **<INTERVALTIME>**.

EBNF

Metasyntax

CROSS-REFERENCE
See **Extended Backus-Naur Form**.

ECMAScript

Language

The European Computer Manufacturing Association (http://www.ecma.ch) officially accepted the ECMAScript standard in June 1997 after working on it for eight months. This standard, designated ECMA-262, is primarily a derivative of Netscape's JavaScript and Microsoft's JScript, containing extensions and constructs from other scripting languages used in the industry. The ECMA, a European organization for standardizing information and communications systems founded in 1961, worked with Netscape, Microsoft, Borland, Sun, the Internet Engineering Task Force, and the World Wide Web Consortium, to name a few, while developing this open-standard scripting language.

The ECMA standard defines all of the types, values, objects, properties, and functions used in the scripting language. It also defines all of the program syntax that is required for proper interpretation of the script. When developing the specifications for this scripting language, ECMA compiled a series of "future reserved words," allowing the language to grow easily within established bounds.

ECMAScript is an object-oriented scripting language. Like all other scripting languages, it relies on its environment (your HTML document and

Web browser, for example) to provide it with any external data that may be needed. ECMAScript was designed for performing computations and manipulating objects within its environment (in most cases, HTML documents and viewers). Both programmers and nonprogrammers can use its relaxed, Java-like syntax and structure to customize, manipulate, and automate the Web environment. Because ECMAScript was originally designed as a Web scripting language, it can be used across a variety of host systems. You do not have to have a UNIX box or an NT machine to be able to use and benefit from the development of ECMAScript.

Your Web browser provides ECMAScript with a complete environment to manipulate, including such objects as windows, menus, dialog boxes, text areas, anchors, frames, cookies, and an input/output source. As with JavaScript and JScript, the ECMAScript code is contained within the HTML documents processed by the Web browser. Because of the amount of document manipulation done by a Web browser, ECMAScript is able to interact with your browser each time a document is opened or closed; each time an item receives focus or the focus is changed; and each time a form is submitted, a mouse is moved, or an error is encountered. Because the script is responsive to all user interactions, there is no need to have a main program.

The Web server provides an additional environment for working with information requests, clients, and files. The servers provide you with a mechanism for sharing data. The combination of client-side and server-side scripting enables you to distribute the workload and provide a completely customized interface for your Web applications.

An ECMAScript object is organized into a series of properties. Each property has a series of attributes that determine how the property can be used. If a property's attribute designates it as read-only, you cannot change the value of that property through the ECMAScript. Properties can hold other objects, values, or methods. If a property holds a value, it will be one of the built-in types such as Boolean, Null, Number, String, or Undefined. A method is simply a function that has been associated with the object through the property. If the property holds another object, it will be one of the built-in objects such as Array, Boolean, Date, Global, Math, Number, Object, or String. ECMAScript also uses a set of operators that enable you to compare and relate data or objects as required by your script. The relaxed format of ECMAScript's syntax intentionally resembles Java and makes it an easy-to-use scripting language. One example of this is found with variables. In ECMAScript, you are not required to declare each of your variables or to have them assigned to a specific value type.

Microsoft, Netscape, Sun, Borland, and IBM have all announced their support for ECMAScript and have begun implementing support for it in their products. Within a short time, you may be seeing less and less true JavaScript and JScript and more and more ECMAScript.

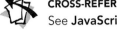

CROSS-REFERENCE
See **JavaScript**, **JScript**, **W3C**, **IETF**, and **Open Standards**.

Element

Concept

Elements are representations of structures and behaviors that have been out-lined for a particular SGML-based language's document type definition (DTD). Elements can be used to identify particular types of paragraphs, hypertext links, lists, tables, forms, frames, and images, to name a few.

When an element is being defined in the DTD, the element definition lists a start tag, an end tag, and the contents of the element. The start tag of an element is enclosed in angle brackets (`element-name`), whereas the end tag is enclosed in angle brackets with the name of the element being preceded by a forward slash (`/element-name`). Not all elements require an end tag. Some have the end tag built into the start tag. With others, the end tag is either optional or forbidden.

Elements such as `LI` and `P` have optional end tags because the interpretation of the next matching start tag serves as the sign of the beginning of a new section. Tags such as `BR` and `HR` have no content, and therefore end tags are forbidden for use with them. The `HEAD` and `BODY` elements do not necessarily require start tags, although conventions specify their use for marking proper document structure. The HTML DTD identifies the start and end tag requirements for each element.

Some of these element declarations also list the attributes that are supported by the element. These attributes are then defined in more detail in a separate section of the DTD.

Example
Examples of a variety of start and end tags are shown in the following HTML document segment.

```
<HEAD>
   <TITLE>My sample text</TITLE>
</HEAD>
<P> This is a short paragraph so you can see what a paragraph
would look like on an HTML document. I could keep typing, but
I'd rather get on with the rest of the example. That is if you
don't mind?
<BR>
<HR>
<P> As you can see from the above line, and code, the HR
element does not need an end tag to function properly.
```

HTML 4.0 Elements

A	ABBR	ACRONYM	ADDRESS
APPLET	AREA	B	BASE
BASEFONT	BDO	BIG	BLOCKQUOTE
BODY	BR	BUTTON	CAPTION
CENTER	CITE	CODE	COL
COLGROUP	DD	DEL	DFN
DIR	DIV	DL	DT
EM	FIELDSET	FONT	FORM
FRAME	FRAMESET	H1–H6	HEAD
HR	HTML	I	IFRAME
IMG	INPUT	INS	ISINDEX
KBD	LABEL	LEGEND	LI
LINK	MAP	MENU	META
NOFRAMES	NOSCRIPT	OBJECT	OL
OPTGROUP	OPTION	P	PARAM
PRE	Q	SAMP	SCRIPT
SELECT	SMALL	SPAN	STRIKE
STRONG	STYLE	SUP	TABLE
TBODY	TD	TEXTAREA	TFOOT
TH	THEAD	TR	TT
U	UL	VAR	

Channel Definition Format Elements

ABSTRACT	AUTHOR	AUTHORIZATION
CATEGORY	CATEGORYDEF	CATEGORYNAME
CHANNEL	COPYRIGHT	DESCRIPTION
EARLIESTTIME	ENDDATE	HREF
INTERVALTIME	INTROURI	ISCLONEABLE
ISVISIBLE	ITEM	KEYWORDS
LASTMOD	LATESTTIME	LOGO
MIMETYPE	MINSTORAGE	POSTURL
PRECACHE	PRIORITY	PUBLICATIONDATE
PUBLISHER	RATINGS	SCHEDULE
STARTDATE	TITLE	TRACKING
TYPE	USAGE	USERSCHEDULE

Open Software Description Elements

ABSTRACT	CODEBASE	DEPENDENCY
DISKSIZE	IMPLEMENTATION	IMPLTYPE
LANGUAGE	LICENSE	MEMSIZE
OS	OSVERSION	PROCESSOR
SOFTPKG	TITLE	VM

CROSS-REFERENCE
See **Attribute**, **Document Type Definition**, **Variable**, **value**, and **Appendix E**.

Element Type

Declaration

XML

When you are defining elements in XML documents, you must identify the elements in a specific format in a document declaration. Each element type declaration is used to constrain the contents of the element, and it also identifies which other elements can be placed within a parent element's bounds. An element declaration appears in the following form:

```
<!ELEMENT name contentspec>
```

Parameters

name

The name of an element is the identifier that separates it from all other elements in a particular type of document. No element can be declared more than once.

contentspec

The contentspec of an element can have the values **ANY, EMPTY, <Mixed>,** or **<Children>**. A value of **ANY** lets you have anything, both children and text, as the contents of the element. A value of **EMPTY** forces the element to have no contents. Most empty elements have only a start tag. If the value is **<Mixed>**, that element can contain both characters and specified child elements. If the value is **<Children>**, you can include only specified children within the contents of the element.

Examples

The following examples of element declarations show some common HTML tags being identified using XML's Extended Backus-Naur Form.

```
<!ELEMENT br EMPTY>
<!ELEMENT p (#PCDATA|emph)* >
<!ELEMENT %name.para; %content.para; >
<!ELEMENT container ANY>
```

CROSS-REFERENCE
See **Extended Backus-Naur Form**, **elements**, **Attribute**, and **DTD**.

elementFromPoint

Method

DHTML

This document object method is used to identify the element found at specified *iX* and *iY* coordinates. These coordinates are provided in pairs, where (0,0) is the top-left corner of the client area. For this method to function properly, the element located at the designated coordinates must support and respond to mouse events.

The syntax of this command is

```
oElement = object.elementFromPoint(iX, iY)
```

Parameters
iX

This required parameter supplies the X-offset, in pixels.

iY

This required parameter supplies the Y-offset, in pixels.

Objects

document

CROSS-REFERENCE
See **clientX** and **clientY**.

elements

Collection

DHTML

This document object collection creates a list, in source order, of all the objects in a specified form. This collection can contain any combination of INPUT, SELECT, and TEXTAREA objects.

This command can be used in either of these fashions:

```
[ collElements = ] object.elements
[ oObject = ] object.elements(vIndex)
```

Parameters
collElements

This variable refers to the array of elements contained by the object.

oObject

This variable refers to an individual item in the array.

vIndex

This parameter is required and contains the number or string identifying the element or collection to retrieve. When a number is specified, the method returns the element in the zero-based collection at the identified position. When a string identifier is used and multiple elements with the same name or id attributes match the string, this method returns a collection of those matched elements.

Elements
FORM

 CROSS-REFERENCE
See **Element**, **<FORM>**, **<INPUT>**, **<SELECT>**, and **<TEXTAREA>**.

elevation

Attribute

CSS

This controls the apparent height of the speaker in reference to your position. This attribute is available only on aural style sheets and takes effect when a speech synthesizer is used to "read" information. Since you cannot predetermine the number and location of speakers in use by the document reader, this attribute simply identifies the desired end result. As the document author, you can't really force a specific result in all cases.

The syntax of this attribute is

```
elevation: angle | below | level | above | higher | lower |
inherit
```

Values

above

This value places the speaker directly above you. This produces the same effect as 90deg.

angle

This value can be an angle between –90 and 90 degrees. 0deg places the speaker on the same level as the listener, -90deg is directly below, and 90deg is directly overhead.

below

This value places the speaker directly below you. This produces the same effect as a setting of -90deg.

higher

This value adds 10 degrees to the current elevation.

level

This value places the speaker level with you. This produces the same effect as 0deg.

lower

This value subtracts 10 degrees from the current elevation.

Example

When specifying an elevation for your text to be read from, it is best to do it in the style sheet as shown in the following code segment.

```
<STYLE type="text/css">
   H1 { elevation: above }
H6 { elevation: below }
   P  { elevation: level }
   SUP { elevation: 60deg }
   SUB { elevation: -60deg}
</STYLE>
```

Elements
This attribute is available for all HTML elements.

CROSS-REFERENCE
See **Aural Style Sheets**.

<EM>

Element

HTML

This element is used to indicate emphasis in text. When used with a speech synthesizer and an aural style sheet, it can add special stress to a word or phrase. In a visual medium, it changes your text to italics.

Attributes
class
```
class="cdata-list"
```
This attribute is used to assign a class name to an element. User agents employ classes to group specific types of information for later use.

id
```
id="name"
```
This attribute is used to assign a name to an element.

lang
```
lang="language code"
```
This attribute specifies the language in which an element and its values should be rendered.

onclick
```
onclick=script
```
This attribute takes effect when a user clicks the button on a pointing device with the pointer over an element.

ondblclick
```
ondblclick=script
```
This attribute takes effect when the button on a pointing device is double-clicked over an element.

onfocus

`onfocus=`*script*

This attribute takes effect when an element receives focus from either a mouse or another pointing device or through tabbing navigation.

onkeydown

`onkeydown=`*script*

This attribute takes effect when a key is pressed with the pointer over an element.

onkeypress

`onkeypress=`*script*

This attribute takes effect when a key is pressed and released with the pointer over an element.

onkeyup

`onkeyup=`*script*

This attribute takes effect when a key is released with the pointer over an element.

onmousedown

`onmousedown=`*script*

This attribute takes effect when the button on a pointing device is pressed with the pointer over an element.

onmousemove

`onmousemove=`*script*

This attribute is activated when the mouse pointer is moved while it is over an element.

onmouseout

`onmouseout=`*script*

This attribute is activated when the mouse pointer is moved away from an element.

onmouseover

`onmouseover=`*script*

This attribute is activated when the mouse pointer is moved over an element.

d
e
f

onmouseup

`onmouseup=script`

This attribute takes effect when the button on a pointing device is released with the pointer over an element.

style

`style=style descriptors`

This attribute is used to apply specific style-sheet information to one particular element.

title

`title=text`

This attribute provides annotation information to the element.

Example

The following script shows how a speech synthesizer adds emphasis to the specific words identified by the EM tag. This example will not render on the screen because it is aural.

```
<html>
<head>
<title>Looking at Emphasis</title>
<style type="text/css"
@media: aural  {
    em  {elevation: above;
         voice-family: male;
         pitch: low; }
}
</style>
</head>

<body bgcolor="#FFFFFF">
This is a test. <em>This</em> is only a test.
</body>
</html>
```

CROSS-REFERENCE
See **Aural Style Sheets**, **<B>**, **<STRONG>**, and **<BIG>**.

<EMBED>

Element

HTML

Start Tag: Required
End Tag: Required

This element is used to incorporate documents, video, music, and other types of files into the BODY of an HTML document. This element must occur within the BODY tags. You should be aware that any individual who views your document must have an application capable of reading the type of file that you have embedded before they can access that data.

Attributes

accesskey

```
accesskey="character"
```

You can assign an access key to an element. This key enables you to put the focus on an element quickly. In the case of a form element, the user is immediately able to input information. In the case of a link, the link is activated and followed.

 NOTE
If the embedded object does not use an interface, this attribute will not function.

align

```
align= absbottom | absmiddle | baseline | bottom | left |
middle | right | texttop | top
```

This attribute is used to specify the specific position of the EMBED object with respect to the document margins.

alt

```
alt=text
```

This attribute provides you with alternative text to display when a user agent cannot show the applet.

autostart

```
autostart= true | false
```

This attribute is used to automatically start the embedded object playing if it is supported by an application on the viewer's computer system.

bgcolor

```
bgcolor=colorname | RGBcolor
```

This attribute controls the color of the background of the element. You can use either the color name or the hex value of the color. You can use bgcolor when embedding MIDI players and some other objects. The effect of this attribute is dependent upon the type of object being used.

class

```
class="cdata list"
```

This attribute is used to assign a class name to an element. User agents employ classes to group specific types of information for later use.

code

```
code=filename
```

This is the name of the file containing the data to display.

codebase

```
codebase=uri
```

This is the location of the embedded object's base directory, which is used for a reference for all other addresses.

dir

```
dir = LTR | RTL | [CS | CI | CN | CA | CT]
```

This attribute defines the direction of the text flow in a document so that a user agent can display it correctly. This attribute can also be used to specify information about the case of the characters.

height

```
height=objectHeight
```

This attribute serves as a reference to set the height of the embedded object.

hspace

```
hspace=number
```

The value of this attribute is used to specify the horizontal margins of the object's box.

id

```
id="name"
```

This attribute is used to assign a name to an element.

lang

    lang="*language code*"

This attribute specifies the language in which an element and its values should be rendered.

language

    language=javascript | jscript | vbscript | vbs

This attribute specifies the language in which any associated script is written.

loop

    loop=*number*

This is the total number of times the element loops.

name

    name="*appname*"

This attribute specifies the identifying name for your application or object.

pluginspage

    pluginspage=*url*

This is the location of an application that supports the file type that has been embedded.

src

    src=*url*

This is the location of the file containing the data to display.

style

    style=*style descriptors*

This attribute is used to apply specific style-sheet information to one particular element.

tabindex

    tabindex=*number*

This attribute provides the position of the current element within the overall tabbing order of the document.

d
e
f

title

```
title=text
```

This attribute provides annotation information to the element.

units

```
units= px | em | pt | ex | cm | in | mm | xx
```

This attribute identifies the units used by the height and width attributes.

vspace

```
vspace=number
```

The value of this attribute is used to specify the vertical margins of the object's box.

width

```
width=number
```

This is the width of the object's box in pixels or as a percentage of the entire screen width.

NOTE

Not all of these attributes work in Netscape Communicator.

Example

The following code uses EMBED to incorporate a MIDI file into a document.

```
<HTML>
<HEAD>
   <TITLE> Embedding Popular Objects</TITLE>
<HEAD>
<BODY>
   <EMBED src="crow.mid" autostart="true" loop="5" height="0"
   width="0" loop="true">
   </EMBED>

</BODY>
</HTML>
```

CROSS-REFERENCE

See **<BGSOUND>**, **<APPLET>**, and **<OBJECT>**.

embeds

Collection

DHTML

This document object collection creates a list of all the `EMBED` objects found within the current document.

This collection can be used in the following ways:

```
[ collEmbeds = ] object.embeds
[ oObject = ] object.embeds(vIndex [, iSubIndex] )
```

Parameters
collEmbeds

This variable refers to the array of elements contained by the object.

oObject

This variable refers to an individual item in the array.

vIndex

This parameter is required and contains the number or string identifying the element or collection to retrieve. When a number is specified, the method returns the element in the zero-based collection at the identified position. When a string identifier is use and multiple elements with the same `name` or `id` attributes match the string, this method returns a collection of those matched elements.

iSubIndex

This optional parameter is used to identify the position of the element being retrieved when `vIndex` is a string. `ISubIndex` becomes the index of the specific item in the collection of matching elements identified by the `vIndex` string contents.

Objects
document

CROSS-REFERENCE
See **<EMBED>**.

empty

Method

DHTML

This method is used in object-based documents to deselect the currently active object, set the selection type to none, and then set the item property to null.

The syntax for this method is

```
object.empty()
```

Objects

selection

 CROSS-REFERENCE
See **:active**, **id**, and **name**.

Empty-Element Tags

Concept

HTML, XML

Some HTML and XML elements are not allowed to have any content. These tags are considered *empty* because they do not contain any child elements or textual information. Two examples of empty HTML elements are HR and BR. Neither of these elements is allowed to contain any content. They, like all empty elements, are also forbidden to have end tags. The document type definition (DTD) indicates whether the end tag is allowed and what type of element is being used. If the element is not empty, the DTD identifies what is allowable for its content.

 CROSS-REFERENCE
See **Element**, **Element Type**, and **Document Type Definition**.

encoding

Property

DHTML

This method is used either to set or retrieve the MIME-encoding specification for the selected form object.

The syntax for this command is

```
object.encoding [ = sType ]
```

Parameters

sType

This variable identifies a string used to specify the format of the data being submitted by the form. The default value of this string is as follows:

```
"application/x-www-form-urlencoded".
```

Elements

FORM

 **CROSS-REFERENCE**
See **action**.

Enddate

Attribute

CDF

Start Tag: Required
End Tag: Forbidden

This is simply the last day during the specified channel delivery schedule that the channel information can be sent. This element can be used only as a child of the SCHEDULE element.

The syntax of this command is

```
Enddate="yyyy-mm-dd"
```

where *yyyy* is the four-digit year, *mm* is the two-digit month, and *dd* is the two-digit day of the date that the channel is no longer sent.

Example

This example channel, located at `http://mychannels.com/channels.cdf`, must be delivered between midnight and noon on the first of each month between January and August in the year 1999.

```
<CHANNEL HREF="http://mychannels.com/channels.cdf ">
   <SCHEDULE startdate="1999-01-01" enddate="1999-08-24">
      <INTERVALTIME Day=30 />
      <EARLIESTTIME Hour=0 />
      <LATESTTIME Hour=12 />
   </SCHEDULE>
</CHANNEL>
```

Elements
CHANNEL

CROSS-REFERENCE
See **Channel Definition Format**, **<LATESTTIME>**, **<StartDate>**, **<EarliestTime>**, and **<INTERVALTIME>**.

End Tags

Concept

XML, HTML

All elements have start tags, but they don't all have end tags. End tags are the closing portion of the element. Within the end tag, the name of the element is preceded by a forward slash. Not all elements use end tags. For some of these, such as the P element, the end tag is optional. For others, such as the BR and HR elements, the end tag is forbidden. Each element entry in this book specifies whether the end tag is required, optional, or forbidden.

CROSS-REFERENCE
See **Empty-Element Tags**, **Element**, and **Document Type Definition**.

Entity Declaration

Concept

XML

In XML, entity declarations identify various storage units, or entities, that are used within the XML data system. All entities have a name and a document entity. The document entity is used by the XML processing system as a starting point. The entity declaration statements allow the XML parser to identify the entities used in a document. If the same entity name is identified twice, the first to be defined is considered the true element.

XML uses EBNF notation to identify entities in one of the following ways:

```
<!ENTITY name entitydefinition>
<!ENTITY name parsed-entity-definition>
```

CROSS-REFERENCE
See **Entity Reference**.

Entity Reference

Concept

XML

An *entity reference* enables you to identify and use the contents of an entity. An entity reference uses comma- or semicolon-separated lists to display the entity contents. A general entity reference can appear in either the document DTD or the document itself, whereas a parameter entity reference can appear only in the DTD. Entity references are displayed using the following notation:

```
<!- declare the parameter entity "ISOLat4"... ->
<!ENTITY % ISOLat4
SYSTEM "http://www.xml.com/iso/isolat4-xml.entities" >
<!- ... now reference it. ->
%ISOLat4;
```

CROSS-REFERENCE
See **Entity Declaration**.

Enumerated Attribute Types

Concept

XML

Enumerated attribute types provide you with a limited list of notations or named tokens. These types of attributes limit the ability of the XML parser to interpret their contents but simultaneously give you, the document author, more finite control over your document because all user agents are required to display correctly the specified types associated with this type of attribute.

CROSS-REFERENCE
See **Attribute** and **Entity Declaration**.

Errors

Concept

An *error* is any type of mistake or other circumstance that should not have occurred. Some errors are simple but annoying, and others are fatal. Errors always occur. There is no way to avoid them entirely. Users of the Internet get very used to them, but they don't normally like them. As a document author, you really need to avoid the most common error found on the Web: the broken link. Although this type of error does not adversely affect the functioning of your viewer's system, it does create a less than positive opinion of the Web site's development and maintenance staff.

Although broken links are the most common error encountered on the Web, the growth of JavaScripts and the disparity of the browser market make other errors almost as frequent and just as irritating. Most JavaScript errors occur when a script is written using the proprietary commands of one browser's language but the users wish to view the document in a different browser. Microsoft's JScript and Netscape's JavaScript are varied enough to create more hassles for the Web document author than the constant improvements in HTML and the slow speed at which Web browsing individuals actually update their software.

CROSS-REFERENCE
See **Fatal Error**.

event

Property

DHTML

Object-based scriptlets use the `event` property to retrieve the name of the `event` for which the script is written.

The syntax of this command is

```
[ sEvent = ] object.event
```

Values
sEvent

This string variable is used to hold the name of the event that activated the script. If the current script was started by an `onblur` event, the value of this string is as follows:

```
"onblur()".
```

Example

The following example demonstrates the use of the `event` attribute and the `event` property by identifying the event that started the click.

ON THE CD-ROM

Look for *filename.htm* on the accompanying CD-ROM.

```
<HTML>
<HEAD>
<META NAME="GENERATOR" Content="NetObjects ScriptBuilder 2.0">
<TITLE>Scripting Buttons</TITLE>
</HEAD>
<BODY>

<BUTTON id="flipButton"onclick="this.innerText='Flip Flop the
Day is Shot!'">Flip</BUTTON>
<BUTTON onclick="flipButton.innerText='Flop Flip my Day is
Hip'">Reset</BUTTON>

</BODY>
</HTML>
```

Elements
SCRIPT

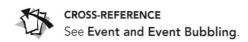

CROSS-REFERENCE
See **Event and Event Bubbling**.

Event

Concept

Whenever a mouse is clicked or moved or a button or key is pressed, an event occurs. An event is simply any sort of activity that can be used to trigger a reaction in the user agent or server that is involved in the sharing of a document. All information controlling the effect of the event is contained within the document being displayed. This information can direct the user agent to find a specific JavaScript or JScript included in the document, to run a specific function, or to go to the server and collect more information. Each activity can be used to cause a variety of events to fire. The clicking of your mouse can activate either the `onclick` or the `ondblclick` events. Moving your mouse can activate the `onmousedown`, `onmousemove`, `onmouseover`, `onmouseout`, and `onmouseup` events.

Events work in the following fashion:

1. The user performs an action such as pressing a key or moving or clicking the mouse. It is also possible to schedule an event from a page's loading, unloading, or having its current state change.

2. An event associated with the active object is fired. This object gets to handle the event first through its event handler instructions.

3. The event is passed up to each parent object, in succession, until it is received by the document or until one of the parent object's event handlers cancels the process of the event. This is known as event bubbling.

4. A default action, unrelated to the event bubbling, occurs. This action must be cancelled in a script if you wish to avoid having it occur.

Events

onabort	onafterupdate	onbeforeunload
onbeforeupdate	onblur	onbounce
onchange	onclick	ondataavailable
ondatasetchanged	ondatasetcomplete	ondblclick
onerror	onerrorupdate	onfilterchange
onfinish	onfocus	onhelp
onkeydown	onkeypress	onkeyup

onload	onmousedown	onmousemove
onmouseout	onmouseover	onmouseup
onreadystatechange	onreset	onresize
onrowenter	onrowexit	onscroll
onselect	onselectstart	onstart
onsubmit	onunload	

CROSS-REFERENCE
See **event** and **Event Bubbling**.

Event Bubbling

Concept

When an event occurs on a document, it can bubble. *Event bubbling* is the process of passing the event parameters through the document object hierarchy until the event is either closed or reaches the base document object.

CROSS-REFERENCE
See **Event** and **event**.

execCommand

Method

DHTML

Scripted documents use the execCommand method to execute a command over a given selection or text range. This command should not be invoked until after the complete HTML document has been loaded.

The syntax for this command is

```
bSuccess = object.execCommand(sCommand [,bUserInterface]
[,vValue])
```

Parameters
sCommand

This required parameter identifies the command that needs to be executed.

bUserInterface

This optional parameter indicates whether a user interface needs to be displayed if the command supports one. Valid values for this parameter are **true** or **false**, with the default value being **false**.

vValue

This optional parameter can be a string, a number, or another value, depending on the contents of the *sCommand* parameter.

Objects

Document   TextRange

CROSS-REFERENCE
See **execScript**, **queryCommandEnabled**, **queryCommandIndeterm**, **queryCommandState**, **queryCommandSupported**, and **queryCommandValue**.

execScript

Method

DHTML

This command enables document authors to execute a specific script in a specific scripting language.

The syntax of this method is

```
window.execScript(sExpression, sLanguage)
```

Parameters

sExpression

This required parameter identifies the specific code to be executed.

sLanguage

This required parameter is used to identify the scripting language in which the code is executed. The default value is **JScript** in Internet Explorer and **JavaScript** in Netscape Navigator.

Objects

window

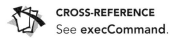

CROSS-REFERENCE
See **execCommand**.

expand

Method

DHTML

Scripted objects can use the `expand` method to increase the specified text range so that partial units are completely enclosed.

The syntax of this method is

```
bSuccess = object.expand(unit)
```

Parameters
bSuccess

This variable is set to **true** if the text range was expanded successfully and to **false** if it failed for any reason.

unit

This required parameter is used to identify the number of units, or characters, by which to expand the range. If the value of this parameter is **character,** it expands the range by one character. A value of **word** expands the text range to include the full word that is currently only partially included in the text range. If the value of this parameter is **sentence**, it expands the text range to include the current sentence as identified by a period or other punctuation mark. A value of **textedit** expands the text range to include the entire possible range of characters.

Example
The following code segment creates a range from the current selection and then uses `expand` to expand the range so that any word partially enclosed by the range becomes entirely enclosed in the range.

```
var SelectedTextRange = document.selection.createRange();
SelectedTextRange.expand("word");
```

Objects
TextRange

CROSS-REFERENCE
See **collapse**.

expando

Property

DHTML

This document object property is used to control whether arbitrary variables can be created within an object. You can use this command either to set or retrieve the state of this script property. As a document author, you can extend the properties available with a particular object by creating arbitrary properties with values.

The syntax of this command is

```
object.expando [ = bExpand ]
```

Parameters
bExpand

If this value is **true,** you can create arbitrary variables; if it is **false,** you cannot create arbitrary variables. The default value of this parameter is **true.**

Objects

Document

CROSS-REFERENCE
See **Variable, Properties,** and **Attribute.**

Extended Backus-Naur Form (EBNF)

Metasyntax

This form is used to provide notations on the syntax of the various elements and attributes available within a programming language. The Extended Backus-Naur Form is any variation on the basic *Backus-Naur Form (BNF)* that uses square brackets to enclose optional items, curly brackets to enclose a list of alternatives, and special suffixes such as the asterisk (*) and plus sign (+) to note various sequences of items. This is one of the most commonly used metasyntax notations, and it is used to identify HTML- and XML-based documents. It is also used to identify the syntax of Java and JavaScript.

CROSS-REFERENCE
See **ECMAScript, JavaScript, JScript,** and **VBScript.**

External Entity

Declaration

XML

Entities are simply storage units. If a storage unit is contained within a document that is referencing it, it is considered an internal entity. If a storage unit is not contained within the current document, it is considered an external entity. An external entity declaration uses either a `PUBLIC` or `SYSTEM` identification that lets the user agent know whether the source information can be found on a public or local system. A *name* is provided for the entity that identifies the address where the document is found.

The syntax for an external entity declaration is

```
<!ENTITY PUBLIC|SYSTEM name>
```

CROSS-REFERENCE
See **<!DOCTYPE>**, **Document Type Definition**, **Entity Declaration**, and **Entity Reference**.

External Style Sheets

Concept

When you are writing a document, you may not necessarily want your style sheet to be attached to the HTML code. There are many benefits to attaching, but not including, style sheets within your documents.

- By separating your style sheets from your HTML code, you can create a single style sheet for use with dozens of pages. In this fashion, you do not need to "recreate the wheel" multiple times, and you can easily make all the pages for a single site flow together.
- You can change a single document, the style sheet, and affect multiple documents or sites simultaneously. You no longer have to open 50 files to make minute changes.
- User agents can load style sheets based upon the media descriptions, so you do not have to have a strictly visual user agent dig through the style code for an aural user agent.

HTML document authors have a wide variety of options when working with external style sheets. You can associate as many external style sheets to your HTML document as you need. The user agent, as directed by the Cascading

Style Sheets rules provided in the specification, controls the interaction between your style sheets.

You also have the option of identifying mutually exclusive, or alternate, style sheets. These style sheets are automatically used based upon the user's screen settings. For example, an author can specify a specific style sheet for use with small screens (640 × 480 resolution), or one for individuals with bad eyesight (large fonts). The user agent should provide a mechanism for the users to select between the available alternate style sheets. As the document author, you can specify a preferred style sheet. User agents should apply the author's preferences in the event that the user does not select one of the other alternatives.

You can identify preferred and alternate style sheets through the LINK element. The value of the title attribute should be used by the user agents to provide a list entry from which the user can select. If you set the title attribute of a style sheet whose rel attribute is set to stylesheet, this identifies the style sheet as your preferred style sheet. Whether a style sheet has a title or not, if the rel attribute is set to alternate stylesheet, it is treated as an alternative by the user agent. In the following lines of example code, the first statement identifies the preferred style sheet, and the remaining lines of code identify alternate style sheets:

```
<LINK href="mainstyle.css" title="Main Sheet" rel="stylesheet"
type="text/css">
<LINK href="stylea.css" title="Aural" rel="alternate
stylesheet" type="text/css">
<LINK href="stylev.css" title="Visual" rel="alternate
stylesheet" type="text/css">
<LINK href="stylet.css" title="TTY" rel="alternate stylesheet"
type="text/css">
```

You can group multiple alternate style sheets together under a single style name. When the user then selects a name from a list of available style sheets, the user agent must apply all the style sheets with that name.

When creating your documents, if you wish to identify a style sheet to apply in addition to a preferred or alternate style sheet, you need a persistent style sheet. These style sheets are identified solely by the rel attribute's value of **stylesheet** and the lack of a title attribute setting.

CROSS-REFERENCE

See **Cascading Style Sheets, Style Sheet, @media**, and **@-rules**.

F

face

Attribute

HTML

This attribute is used to identify a list of font names that the user agent should search for, in order, when attempting to match its rendering of a document to the author's intended display layout.

The syntax of this attribute is

```
face=stringfontname
```

Values

stringfontname

This string contains the name of the specific font that should be used to display the text on the reader's screen.

Example

The following code creates a visual list of a variety of font faces. If your readers' user agent has access to all these font faces, they will be able to see how a font looks before they use it.

ON THE CD-ROM

Look for **face.htm** on the accompanying CD-ROM.

```
<html>
<head>
<title>Adjusting Font Faces</title>
</head>

<body bgcolor="#FFFFFF">
<p><font face="Arial, Helvetica, sans-serif">Arial</font></p>
<p><font face="Bookman Old Style">Bookman Old Style</font></p>
<p><font face="Comic Sans MS">ComicSans</font></p>
<p><font face="Courier New, Courier, mono">Courier</font></p>
<p><font face="cursive">Cursive</font></p>
```

```
<p><font face="fantasy">Fantasy</font></p>
<p><font face="Georgia, Times New Roman, Times,
serif">Georgia</font></p>
<p><font face="Haettenschweiler">Haettenschweiller</font></p>
<p><font face="Impact">Impact</font></p>
<p><font face="Lucida Console">Lucida Console</font></p>
<p><font face="monospace">Monospace</font></p>
<p><font face="Times New Roman, Times, serif">Times New
Roman</font></p>
<p><font face="Verdana, Arial, Helvetica, sans-
serif">Verdana</font></p>
</body>
</html>
```

Elements

FONT   BASEFONT

CROSS-REFERENCE
See **font-family**, **style**, **variant**, **weight**, **size**, **set**, and **adjust**.

family-name

Value

CSS

This value is used to designate the name of a font family. It is most often applied to the font-family attribute although it is also used to identify the fonts used to display the caption, menu, status-line, and message box text. Some font family-names include: "Baskerville," "Symbol," and "Times New Roman." It is generally a good rule to put all font-family names in quotation marks. If the quotation characters are omitted, any whitespace characters that may come before or after the font name are ignored. In addition, any sequence of whitespace characters inside the font name is converted to a single space.

CROSS-REFERENCE
See **font-family**, **font**, and **<FONT>**.

Fatal Error

Concept

This is a type of error that simply makes it impossible to continue your work. It is therefore one of the most irritating errors to encounter. Only on very rare occasions will an HTML document ever cause a user agent to experience a fatal error. When it does happen, generally a script (either on the client or server side) is interfering with the user agent's operation. These random errors make it imperative that you, the document author, test your code on as many system configurations as possible. Just as a document formatted to print on a dot-matrix printer may not print properly in a laser printer, a script that runs properly on Windows user agents might not function with Macintosh or UNIX user agents.

 CROSS-REFERENCE
See **Errors**.

fgColor

Property

DHTML

This script property is used to set and/or retrieve the text color of a document.
The syntax for this command is

```
document.fgColor [=RGBcolor]
```

Example
The following example code changes the color of the text as you move your mouse pointer over it.

```
<html>
<head>
<title>Color Change</title>
</head>
<body bgcolor="#ffffff">
<p onmouseout="document.fgColor='#ff0000';"
onmouseover="document.fgColor='#0000ff';">Run your cursor over
this text!</p>
</body>
</html>
```

Parameters
RGBcolor

The name of the color is returned in hexadecimal format representing the RGB value of the color.

Object

document

CROSS-REFERENCE
See **color**, **bgcolor**, and **Appendix B**.

Fictional Tag Sequence

Concept

CSS

A *fictional tag sequence* is used with Cascading Style Sheets specification's pseudo-elements to create an effect on a segment of code that is not otherwise individually identified. These pseudo-elements identify the first line of a paragraph or the first letter of a phrase. Items can be conceptually different depending upon the user agent that is rendering them.

NOTE
In the 4.0 versions of our Internet Web browsing software these types of sequences are not supported, but they are planned for the upcoming versions.

CROSS-REFERENCE
See **:first-line** and **:first-letter**.

<FIELDSET>

Element

HTML

Start Tag: Required
End Tag: Required

This element is used to identify a specific section of a form. For instance FIELDSET can be used to set apart the personal information gathering section of a form from an individual's employment history. You can use the border style sheet attributes to create a visual disparity between each portion of a form, or use the bgcolor attributes to adjust the background.

NOTE

The FIELDSET element is not supported in Netscape Navigator 4.0.

Attributes

class

```
class="cdata-list"
```

This attribute is used to assign a class name to an element. User agents employ classes to group specific types of information for later use.

id

```
id="name"
```

This attribute is used to assign a name to an element.

lang

```
lang="language code"
```

This attribute specifies the language in which an element and its values should be rendered.

onclick

```
onclick=script
```

This attribute takes effect when a user clicks the button on a pointing device with the pointer over an element.

ondblclick

```
ondblclick=script
```

This attribute takes effect when the button on a pointing device is clicked twice with the pointer over an element.

onkeydown

```
onkeydown=script
```

This attribute takes effect when a key is pressed over an element.

onkeypress

`onkeypress=script`

This attribute takes effect when a key is pressed and released with the pointer over an element.

onkeyup

`onkeyup=script`

This attribute takes effect when a key is released with the pointer over an element.

onmousedown

`onmousedown=script`

This attribute takes effect when the button on a pointing device is pressed over an element.

onmousemove

`onmousemove=script`

This attribute is activated when the mouse is moved while the pointer is over an element.

onmouseout

`onmouseout=script`

This attribute is activated when the mouse pointer is moved away from an element.

onmouseover

`onmouseover=script`

This attribute is activated when the mouse is moved over an element.

onmouseup

`onmouseup=script`

This attribute takes effect when the button on a pointing device is released with the pointer over an element.

style

`style=style descriptors`

This attribute is used to apply specific style-sheet information to one particular element.

title

```
title=text
```

This attribute serves to provide annotation information to the element to which it is being applied.

Example

The following sample code uses the FIELDSET element to set apart various parts of an employment application form. It then uses specific style descriptors to create a more visually enhanced difference between the individual segments of information being gathered.

ON THE CD-ROM

Look for **fieldset.htm** on the accompanying CD-ROM.

```html
<html>
<head>
<title>Fieldset Examples</title>
</head>

<body bgcolor="#FFFFFF">
<h1>Application for Employment</h1>
<form method="post" action="">
  <fieldset style="border: 1 red; bgcolor: gray;" >
  <legend><h2>Personal Information</h2></legend>
  <p>Name:
    <input type="text" name="name" size="50">
    (last, first, mi)</p>
  <p>Address:
    <input type="text" name="address" size="60">
  </p>
  <p>City, ST, Zip:
    <input type="text" name="costzip" size="50">
  </p>
  <p>Email Address:
    <input type="text" name="email" size="50">
  </p>
  </fieldset>
  <fieldset style="border: "inset green"; bgcolor: silver;" >
  <legend><h2>Educational History</h2></legend>
  <table border="1" width="85%">
    <tr>
      <td> </td>
      <td>Name</td>
      <td>Date Graduated</td>
```

```
      <td>Degree Received</td>
   </tr>
   <tr>
     <td>Highschool</td>
     <td>
       <input type="text" name="hiname">
     </td>
     <td>
       <input type="text" name="hidate">
     </td>
     <td>
       <input type="text" name="hideg">
     </td>
   </tr>
   <tr>
     <td>College/University</td>
     <td>
       <input type="text" name="collname">
     </td>
     <td>
       <input type="text" name="colldate">
     </td>
     <td>
       <input type="text" name="colldeg">
     </td>
   </tr>
   <tr>
     <td>Technical School</td>
     <td>
       <input type="text" name="techname">
     </td>
     <td>
       <input type="text" name="techdate">
     </td>
     <td>
       <input type="text" name="techdeg">
     </td>
   </tr>
   <tr>
     <td>Graduate School</td>
     <td>
       <input type="text" name="gradname">
     </td>
     <td>
```

```
      <input type="text" name="graddate">
    </td>
    <td>
      <input type="text" name="graddeg">
    </td>
  </tr>
</table>
</fieldset>
<fieldset style="border: "outset purple"; bgcolor: ivory;" >
<legend><h2>Employment History</h2></legend>
<p>Company Name:
  <input type="text" name="CoName1" size="50"
maxlength="100">
</p>
<p>Supervisor:
  <input type="text" name="Supr1" size="50" maxlength="50">
  Phone:
  <input type="text" name="phone1" size="15" maxlength="15">
</p>
<p>Can We Contact Your Supervisor:
  <input type="radio" name="contact" value="contactYes"
checked>
  Yes
  <input type="radio" name="contact" value="ContactNo">
  No</p>
<p>Job Description:
  <textarea name="JobDesc" cols="75" rows="7"></textarea>
</p>
<hr>
<p>Company Name:
  <input type="text" name="CoName2" size="50"
maxlength="100">
</p>
<p>Supervisor:
  <input type="text" name="Supr2" size="50" maxlength="50">
  Phone:
  <input type="text" name="phone2" size="15" maxlength="15">
</p>
<p>Can We Contact Your Supervisor:
  <input type="radio" name="contact2" value="contactYes22"
checked>
  Yes
  <input type="radio" name="contact2" value="ContactNo2">
  No</p>
```

```
      <p>Job Description:
        <textarea name="jobdesc2" cols="70" rows="7"></textarea>
      </p>
      </fieldset>
  </form>
  <p>  </p>
  </body>
  </html>
```

CROSS-REFERENCE
See **<LEGEND>** and **<FORM>**.

File select

Value

HTML

This is one of the available options for form control input fields. The file select field allows you to select a file whose contents will be submitted to the form-processing engine along with the contents of the remaining form fields. Using this type of form control gives you an additional source for a variety of information. One way to use this capability is to sort specific types of information into files. This allows you to provide selectable white paper information to customers, or download specific chapters of a book that you are trying to sell to a publishing house.

CROSS-REFERENCE
See **<FORM>**, **<INPUT>**, **buttons**, **checkboxes**, **radio buttons**, **menus**, **text input**, **hidden controls**, and **object controls**.

FileCreatedDate

Property

DHTML

This DOM property is used to retrieve the date that a file was created. It can not be used to alter the date in any way, simply read it from the drive.

The syntax of this command is

```
[ sDate = ] img.fileCreatedDate
```

Parameters

sDate

This string contains the creation date of the file you are referencing. This string is in the format of "Monday, January 1, 1999."

Object

document

Element

IMG

CROSS-REFERENCE
See **fileModifiedDate** and **fileSize**.

fileModifiedDate

Property

DHTML

This property is used to retrieve the date that a file was last modified. It can not be used to alter the date in any way, simply read it from the drive.

The syntax of this command is

```
[ sDate = ] object.fileModifiedDate
```

Parameters

sDate

This string contains the latest modification date of the file you are referencing. This string is in the format of "Monday, January 1, 1999."

Example

The following example code collects information about the document and displays it on the document itself.

```
<html>
<head>
<title>ModiJ+14
```

```
fied Date</title>
</head>
<body bgcolor="#ffffff"onload="fileinfo()">
<script>
function fileinfo() {
document.writeln("document.fileModifiedDate=" +
document.fileModifiedDate + "<BR>");

document.writeln("document.fileCreatedDate=" +
document.fileCreatedDate + "<BR>");
document.writeln("document.fileSize=" + document.fileSize +
"<BR>");

document.writeln("document.fileUpdatedDate=" +
document.fileUpdatedDate + "<BR>");

}
</script>
</body>
</html>
```

Object

> document

Element

> IMG

CROSS-REFERENCE
See **fileUpdatedDate**, **fileSize**, and **fileCreatedDate**.

fileSize

Property

DHTML

This document object property is used to retrieve the size of the file specified. It can not be used to alter the size in any way, simply read it from the drive.

The syntax of this command is

```
[ iSize = ] object.fileSize
```

Parameters

iSize

This integer contains the size of the file being referenced.

Object

document

Element

IMG

CROSS-REFERENCE

See **fileCreationDate**, **fileUpdatedDate**, and **fileModifiedDate**.

fileUpdatedDate

Property

DHTML

This document object property is used to retrieve the date that a file was last updated. It can not be used to alter the date in any way, simply read it from the drive.

The syntax of this command is

```
[ sDate = ] object.fileUpdatedDate
```

Parameters

sDate

This string contains the date the file you are referencing was last updated. This string is in the format of *Monday, January 1, 1999.*

Object

document

Element

IMG

CROSS-REFERENCE

See **fileCreationDate**, **fileSize**, and **fileModifiedDate**.

Filter

Attribute

CSS

This attribute is used to apply a single, or multiple, filters to information. There are three types of filters that can be selected from: Visual Filters, Reveal Transition Filters, and Blend Transition Filters. Each of these filters has a variety of effects that can be used to create advanced multimedia effects on your pages.

The syntax of this attribute is

```
filter: filterstyle (filterproperties)
```

NOTE

This attribute appears to only be available in Internet Explorer.

JAVASCRIPT

```
object.style.filter [=sfilter]
```

This Cascading Style Sheet attribute can be set or retrieved using the object Filter property.is

Elements

BODY	BUTTON	DIV	HTML
IMG	INPUT	MARQUEE	SPAN
TABLE	TD	TEXTAREA	TFOOT
TH	THEAD	TR	

NOTE

When using this attribute with SPAN or DIV, you must specify at least one of the three required CSS attributes: height, width, or position (absolute or relative).

CROSS-REFERENCE

See **filter** and **filters**.

Filters

Collection

DHTML

This JavaScript command can be used to retrieve a collection of filters that have been applied to the specified object.

They syntax for this command can be either of the following

```
collFilters = ] object.filters
[ oObject = ] object.filters(iIndex)
```

Parameters

collFilters

This is a reference to an array of elements contained by the object.

oObject

This is a reference to an individual item in the array of elements contained by the object.

iIndex

This is an integer that indicates the specific item to be returned.

Elements

BODY	BUTTON	DIV	FIELDSET
HTML	IMG	INPUT	MARQUEE
NEXTID	SPAN	TABLE	TD
TEXTAREA	TFOOT	TH	THEAD
TR			

NOTE
When using this attribute with the SPAN or DIV you must specify at least one of the three required CSS attributes: `height`, width, or `position` (absolute or relative).

CROSS-REFERENCE
See **Filter**.

findText

Method

DHTML

This method searches for a specific text string in a document, then positions the start and end points of a specified range to encompass the search string. The syntax for this command is

```
booleanFound = object.findText(sText [, iSearchScope] [,
iFlags])
```

Parameters

sText

This parameter is required. It specifies the text string to find.

iSearchScope

This parameter is optional. This is used to set the direction of the search from the starting point of the range. A positive integer indicates a forward search; a negative integer indicates a backward search. A range can be either degenerate or nondegenerate. If the range is degenerate your marker is set between two distinct characters. If the range is nondegenerate the end points of the range will be an actual character.

The findText method behaves differently depending upon the state (degenerate or nondegenerate) of that range.

- If the range is degenerate, a large positive number causes the text on the right of the range to be searched. Conversely, passing the method a large negative number causes the text on the range's left to be searched.
- A value of 0 causes nondegenerate ranges to only search the selected text.
- A positive value causes nondegenerate ranges to search the text to the right of the start of the range.
- A negative value causes nondegenerate ranges to search the text to the left of the end of the range.

NOTE

For all intents and purposes, the largest positive and negative number is 9999999 and -9999999, respectively. When passing information to *iSearchScope* you should avoid using numbers larger than these, since such values may not be compatible with future versions of user agents.

iFlags

This parameter is optional. This parameter is set to one or more of the following flags which indicate the type of search to be performed:

- 2 - Match whole words only.
- 4 - Match case.

booleanFound

This Boolean will be TRUE if the search text is found, and FALSE otherwise.

Example

The following example finds a specific string specified by the reader, and selects it.

```
<BODY>
<P> This is the time that all good men must come to the aid of
their country. The quick brown fox jumped over the lazy dog.
This is a test of the American Broadcasting System.</P>
<FORM>
Enter a string to search for:
<INPUT id=SearchStr value="" type=text>
<SUBMIT id=submit onclick="sText=searchStr.value;
textRange.findText(sText )">
</BODY>
```

Objects

TextRange

 **CROSS-REFERENCE**
See **setTextRange**.

first-child

Pseudo-Class

CSS

 CROSS-REFERENCE
See **:first-child**.

First-Letter

Pseudo-Element

 CROSS-REFERENCE
See **:first-letter**.

First-Line

Pseudo-Element

CSS

 CROSS-REFERENCE
See **:first-line**.

Fixed Positioning

Concept

CSS

 CROSS-REFERENCE
See **Absolute Positioning**.

Float

Attribute

CSS

This attribute is used to specify whether a containment box should float to the left, right or not at all. This can be set for all elements that are not absolutely positioned.

The following rules govern the behavior of floating boxes, as shown in Figure F-1.

- Neither the left outer edge of a left-floating box, nor the right outer edge of a right-floating box, may be located outside its left or right borders.

- If a left-floating box is preceded by other left-floating boxes, then for each such earlier box, either the left outer edge of the current box must be to the right outer edge of the earlier boxes, or its top must extend lower than the bottom of the earlier box. This rule must be reversed for right-floating boxes.

- A floating box must be placed as high as possible on the document.

- The outside most top edge of a floating box can not be higher than the top of that box's containing block.

- The right outside edge of a left-floating box cannot be located to the right of the left outer edge of any right-floating box located to the right of it. Similar rules hold true for right-floating elements.

- The top of a floating box may not be higher than the top of any block or floated box created by an element found earlier in the HTML document.

- The top of an element's floating box may not be higher than the top of an inline box created by an element located earlier in the document.

- A left-floating box may not stick out on the right edge unless it is currently as far to the left as possible. A correlating rule holds true for right-floating elements.

- A left-floating box must be placed as far to the left as possible, and a right-floating box as far to the right as possible.

The syntax for this command is

```
float: left | right | none | inherit
```

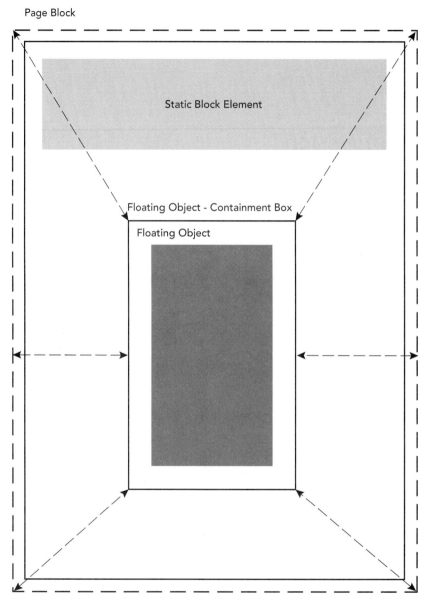

Figure F-1 The containment block of a floating image, the page block, and actual floating area are all shown with the available area for the floating box.

Value

left

This setting causes the box to rest against the left side of the document, and the content is allowed to float past it on the right side of the box.

none

The box is not floated.

right

This setting causes the box to rest against the right side of the document, and the content is allowed to flow past it on the left side of the box.

Elements

This attribute is available for all elements that are not positioned absolutely.

CROSS-REFERENCE

See **inline**, **Floating Text**, and **Absolute Positioning**.

Floating Text

Concept

CSS

Imagine a boat anchored to a very still lake. The boat isn't going to move from where it is set, but hundreds of fish can swim under it as they like. This is how floating text works. The floating text is like that boat. It can be placed in a stationary position, and have images and text floating around and under it as if it wasn't even located on the page.

CROSS-REFERENCE

See **clear**, **inline**, **float**, and **Absolute Positioning**.

Focus

Method

DHTML

This method is fired by an `onfocus` event, and will switch focus to a specific control and executes the code specified by `onfocus`

The syntax of this command is

```
object.focus()
```

Elements

A	APPLET	AREA	BODY
BUTTON	CAPTION	EMBED	FIELDSET
FRAME	HTML	IFRAME	INPUT
MARQUEE	OBJECT	SELECT	TABLE
TD	TEXTAREA		

Objects

window

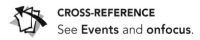 **CROSS-REFERENCE**
See **Events** and **onfocus**.

<FONT>

Element

HTML

Start Tag: Required
End Tag: Required

This element is used to set specific display properties for the text that is being rendered by your audience's user agents. Although not all user agents can support all `FONT` attributes, specifically agents such as speech-synthesizers, the user agent may use the characteristics described by the `FONT` element to alter the voice used when reading that particular segment of the text.

Attributes
class

```
class="cdata-list"
```

This attribute is used to assign a class name to an element. User agents employ classes to group specific types of information for later use.

color

```
color= colorname | #RGBcolor
```

This attribute controls the color of the rendered font. Not all user agents and operating systems will render the same color exactly the same. *Colorname* is one of the valid color names specified by the HTML 4 standard, or if viewed with Internet Explorer 4, one of Microsoft's identified color names. *#RGBcolor* is either a three or six digit hexadecimal number that is used to represent the Red-Green-Blue (RGB) value of the color.

dir

```
dir = LTR | RTL | [CS | CI | CN | CA | CT]
```

This attribute defines the direction of the text flow in a document, so a user agent can display it correctly.

face

```
face= cdata
```

This attribute defines a comma-separated list of font names that the user agent should search for in an attempt to match fonts before rendering the text.

id

```
id="name"
```

This attribute is used to assign a name to an element.

lang

```
lang="language code"
```

This attribute specifies the language in which an element and its values should be rendered.

size

```
size=length
```

This attribute modifies the font size identified with the BASEFONT element.

style

```
style=style descriptors
```

This attribute is used to apply specific style-sheet information to one particular element.

title

```
title=text
```

This attribute serves to provide annotation information to the element to which it is being applied.

Example
The following document provides an example of various font sizes, colors, and faces.

ON THE CD-ROM

Look for **font.htm** on the accompanying CD-ROM.

```
<html>
<head>
<title>Adjusting Fonts</title>
</head>

<body bgcolor="#FFFFFF">
<p><font face="Arial, Helvetica, sans-serif">Arial</font></p>
<p><font face="Bookman Old Style" size="6">Bookman Old
Style</font></p>
<p align="center"><font face="Comic Sans MS" size="+4
color="#CC0099""><b>ComicSans</b></font></p>
<p><font face="Courier New, Courier, mono"
size="+6"><i>Courier</i></font></p>
<p align="left"><font face="cursive"
color="#CC3300"><i>Cursive</i></font></p>
<h1><font face="fantasy">Fantasy</font></h1>
<p><font face="Georgia, Times New Roman, Times, serif"
size="+3">Georgia</font></p>
<p><font face="Haettenschweiler" size="3"
color="#FF6600">Haettenschweiller</font></p>
<p><font face="Impact" size="+1">Impact</font></p>
<blockquote>
   <p><font face="Lucida Console" size="+4"
color="#00FF99">Lucida Console</font></p>
</blockquote>
<p><font face="monospace" size="-2">Monospace</font></p>
```

```
<blockquote>
  <p><font face="Times New Roman, Times, serif"><i>Times New
Roman</i></font></p>
</blockquote>
<p><font face="Verdana, Arial, Helvetica, sans-
serif"><b>Verdana</b></font></p>
</body>
</html>
```

CROSS-REFERENCE
See **<BASEFONT>**.

Font

Attribute

CSS

This Cascading Style Sheets attribute is used as shorthand notation for setting the attributes that affect the font used to render text on a page. These attributes include: `font-style`, `font-variant`, `font-weight`, `font-size`, `line-height`, and `font-family`.

When using this attribute to set the font properties, they will all be first reset to their initial values, including some of the other font attributes including `caption`, `menu`, and `message-box`. Then the properties that have been given a specific value are set.

The syntax of this attribute is

```
font: [ [ <'font-style'> || <'font-variant'> || <'font-
weight'> ]? <'font-size'> [ / <'line-height'> ]?
<'font-family'> ] | caption | icon | menu | message-box |
small-caption | status-bar | inherit
```

Values
caption

This is the font that is used for captioned controls such as buttons and drop.

font-family

This attribute is used to define either the **family-name** or the **generic-family** that will be used when displaying this text.

font-size

This controls the size of the font to be rendered. It can be an **absolute-size**, a **relative-size**, a **length**, or a **percentage**.

font-style

This specifies whether the font being rendered should be displayed in a **normal**, **italic**, or **oblique** manner. **Normal** is the default.

font-variant

This controls whether the font is rendered in a **normal** or a **small-caps** style. **Normal** is the default.

font-weight

This value is used to control the thickness of the font. Valid options of this attribute are: **normal**, **bold**, **bolder**, **lighter**, or a numerical value between **100** and **900**.

icon

This is the font that will be used to label all icons on documents.

line-height

This attribute controls the height of the line that the font is being displayed on. It can be set to **normal**, a **number**, a **length**, or a **percentage**.

menu

This font is used when rendering menus and drop-down menu lists.

message-box

This font is used to display text in dialog boxes.

small-caption

This font is used for labeling captions on small controls.

status-bar

This font is used when displaying messages in the status bars in user agent windows.

Example

The following style-sheet segments show how the shorthand font attribute can be used in place of specifying each individual font-related attribute.

```
<STYLE type="text/css">
   button { font: italic smallcaps lighter 12pt  "Comic Sans"
"Times New Roman" "sans serif" "sans serif" "helvetica" "small
fonts" "Festive"
         }
</STYLE>
<STYLE type="text/css">
 button { font-style: italic;
          font-variant: smallcaps;
          font-weight: lighter;
          font-size: 12pt;
          font-family:  "Comic Sans";
          caption: "Times New Roman" ;
          icon: "sans serif";
          menu: "sans serif";
          messagebox: "helvetica";
          small-caption: "small fonts";
          status-line: "Festive" ;
         {
</STYLE>
```

Elements
This attribute is available for all elements.

CROSS-REFERENCE
See **<FONT>** and **<STYLE>**.

Font Encoding

Concept

Every font has a *font-encoding table* associated with it. This table creates a correlation between the character glyph and the character that it is representing. If the language being encoded has multiple options for the character, as many fonts provide, you are unfortunately unable to select from the available characters, the default character always being used. In languages like Hebrew and Arabic that use either two or four glyphs to represent a single character, depending upon its location in the word in which it is being used. This creates incorrectly displayed and printed documents.

CROSS-REFERENCE
See **Font** and **Character Tables (Appendix C)**.

Font Sets

Concept

CSS

A *font set* is a list of font names, generally of a similar style and size, that can be used by a user agent to find a specific glyph that is needed for displaying characters on documents.

 CROSS-REFERENCE
See **font-family**, **family-name**, and **generic-family**.

font-family

Attribute

CSS

This attribute is used to specify a prioritized list of font family names and/or generic family names that can be searched by a user agent to match character glyphs. Because all fonts may not contain glyphs to display all the characters in a document, and not all fonts are available on all systems, this attribute allows you to identify a specific list of fonts, generally of the same style and size, which are searched in sequence by the user agent for a glyph for a specific character. This list is called a font set.

The syntax of this command is

```
font-family:   [[ <family-name> | <generic-family> ],]*
[<family-name> | <generic-family>] | inherit
```

 NOTE
This style sheet setting can be modified using the Java Script command font-family. The syntax for the fontfamily command is

```
object.style.fontFamily[=stringFamilyName]
```

Values
family-name

This is the name of the font family to use. Some font family-names include: "Bookman," "Lucida," and "Times New Roman." Include all font family names within quotes. If the quotation characters are omitted, any whitespace characters before or after the font name is ignored. In addition, any sequence of whitespace characters inside the font name is converted to a single space.

generic-family

Generic family names are: serif, sans-serif, cursive, fantasy, and monospace. Because they are keywords, they can not be included within quotation marks.

Example

The following style sheet designation identifies a variety of font family names and generic families.

```
<STYLE type="text/css">
 button { font-family:  "Comic Sans";  }
 p       { font-family: "Times New Roman" ; }
 sup    { font-family: sans-serif; }
 H1     { font-family: sans-serif; }
 H2     { font-family: "helvetica"; }
 tfoot  { font-family: "small fonts"; }
 q      {font-family: "Festive" ; }
</STYLE>
```

Elements

This attribute is available for all elements.

CROSS-REFERENCE
See **font**, **<FONT>**, and **<STYLE>**.

font-size

Attribute

CSS

This attribute is used to identify the size of the font. The interpretation of this setting is based upon the user agent, and the attributes of the BASEFONT element.

The syntax of this attribute is

```
font-size: <absolute-size> | <relative-size> | <length> |
<percentage> | inherit
```

NOTE
    object.style.fontSize[=stringSize]
This style sheet setting can be modified using the Java Script command fontSize.

Values
absolute-size

If an absolute-size is specified (**xx-small** | **x-small** | **small** | **medium** | **large** | **x-large** | **xx-large**) there will be a scaling factor of 1.2 between each size. For example, if a **medium** font is actually 12pt, then a **large** font would be 14.4 pt and a **small** font would be 10pt. This table is somewhat modifiable by the user agent, to ensure the best quality and availability of characters. It will also change from one font family to another.

relative-size

If a relative-size is specified (**larger** | **smaller**) it is always in relation to the parent element's font size. So, if the parent element's font is medium, **'larger'** changes the size of the current element to large. In addition, when the parent element's size isn't similar to a table entry, the user agent can adjust either the table entries to match, or adjust the font to fit the table.

length

This is used to specify a positive integer representing an absolute font size. This value is independent of the font table. You can use a specific length when you want a font size such as 38pt or 42pt.

percentage

This percentage value is used to identify an absolute font size in relation to the parent element's font size. You can create more robust documents and cascadable style sheets using percentages.

Example
The following style sheet designation identifies a variety of font sizes and methods of implementing a range of sizes.

```
<STYLE type="text/css">
button { font-size:  "large";  }
p       { font-size: "medium." ; }
sup     { font-size: "25%"; }
H1      { font-size: "xx-large"; }
H2      { font-size: "larger"; }
tfoot   { font-size: "smaller"; }
q       {font-size: "24pt" ; }
</STYLE>
```

Elements
This attribute is available for all elements.

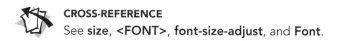

CROSS-REFERENCE
See **size**, **<FONT>**, **font-size-adjust**, and **Font**.

font-size-adjust

Attribute

CSS

This attribute allows you to control the aspect value of elements that preserve the x-height of the first choice font in the substitute font when using the font-family attribute. The legibility of a font is generally less dependent upon the size of the font, than on the value of its x-height. The aspect value of a font is the result of the font-size divided by the x-height. The higher this number, the more likely it is that a font will be legible when the font is a small size. The lower the aspect value, the more likely it is that the font will become illegible as it is shrunk. When user agents perform straightforward font substitutions that rely solely on the font-size alone, the likelihood that the resulting rendering of the font will be illegible is greatly increased.

The popular fonts Verdana and Times New Roman provide a good example of this legibility issue. Verdana has an aspect value of .58, while Times New Roman has an aspect value of .46. Therefore, Verdana will remain legible at smaller sizes than Times New Roman, but may appear too large if substituted directly for Times New Roman at a preselected font size.

Values

none

The font's x-height is not preserved.

number

This is used to identify the aspect value of the first choice font, and directs the user agent to scale the substitution font accordingly. This system helps you force legibility across all platforms, and all supporting user agents.

```
y(a/a') = c
```

where:

```
y = 'font-size' of first-choice font
a' = aspect value of available font
c = 'font-size' to apply to available font
```

Example

The following style sheet code segment identifies a variety of font families and uses the font-size-adjust attribute to maintain the legibility of your fonts while implementing a range of sizes.

```
<STYLE type="text/css">
 button { font-size-adjust:  ".56";  }
         font-family: "Verdana, Times New Roman, Helvetica,
Arial " ; }
 sup    { font-size-adjust: ".46" }
         font-family: "Times New Roman, Goudy Old Style,
serif, fantasy"; }
</STYLE>
```

Elements

This attribute is available for all elements.

 CROSS-REFERENCE
See **font-size** and **size**.

fontSmoothingEnabled

Property

DHTML

This script property can be used to set or retrieve the current status of the font smoothing setting often found in a browser's options or preferences. Font smoothing is a means of making the text on your screen appear smooth-edged, no matter the size of the font or resolution of the screen.

The syntax for this command is

```
object.fontSmoothingEnabled [ = bEnabled ]
```

Parameters
bEnabled

This parameter is a Boolean value that is used to identify the current font smoothing setting. If it is set to false, the default, smoothing is disabled. If it is set to true, then smoothing has been enabled.

Objects

screen

CROSS-REFERENCE
See **font**, **<FONT>**, and **user agents**.

font-stretch

Attribute

CSS

This attribute is used to control the kerning of your font, or in other words, it controls the amount of space found between each individual character of the font.

The syntax of this command is

```
font-stretch: normal | wider | narrower | ultra-condensed |
extra-condensed | condensed | semi-condensed | semi-expanded |
expanded | extra-expanded | ultra-expanded | inherit
```

Values

ultra-condensed

extra-condensed

condensed

semi-condensed

normal

semi-expanded

expanded

extra-expanded

ultra-expanded

These values are organized from most condensed to least condensed. Each of them is a small change in the horizontal spacing of your text.

wider

This value is relative to the parent element, and expands the spacing one stop without increasing it above the "ultra-expanded" level.

narrower

This value is relative to the parent element, and decreases the spacing one step without decreasing it below the "ultra-condensed" level.

Example
The following style sheet designation identifies a variety of font kernings.

```
<STYLE type="text/css">
 button { font-stretch:  "ultra-expanded";   }
 p       { font-stretch: "expanded." ; }
 sup     { font-stretch: "ultra-condensed" }
 H1      { font-stretch: "xx-large"; }
 H2      { font-stretch: "wider"; }
 tfoot   { font-stretch: "narrower"; }
 q       {font-stretch: "normal" ; }
</STYLE>
```

Elements
This attribute is available for all elements.

CROSS-REFERENCE
See **font** and **size**.

font-style

Attribute

CSS

This attribute can be used to specify the style of font being used. You can specify normal, opaque, or italic fonts.
The syntax of this attribute is

```
font-style: normal | italic | oblique | inherit
```

JAVASCRIPT
```
object.style.fontStyle[=stringstyle]
```

This style sheet setting can be modified using the JavaScript command fontStyle.

Values
normal

This font does not display any style changes.

italic

This font is displayed with an italic or cursive slant to each character.

oblique

This font is used to specify a font that has been classified as "oblique" in the font database. This generally includes oblique, slanted, or inclined fonts.

Elements
This attribute is available for all elements.

CROSS-REFERENCE
See **font-variant**, **font-weight**, and **font**.

font-variant

Attribute

CSS

This attribute is used to set up small caps with fonts that support them. Small caps are an effect that is achieved by replacing all lowercase letters with lower-case-height capital letters.

The syntax for this attribute is

```
font-variant: normal | small-caps | inherit
```

JAVASCRIPT
```
object.fontVariant [=fontVariant]
```

This property enables you to control the variant of your font through a script.

Values
normal

This value does not change from the standard font characters.

small-caps

This value specifies to use small capital letters in the place of the standard lower case letters within the specified text.

Example
The following style sheet changes the lower case letters in all the level 1 headings to small caps.

```
<STYLE type="text/css">
H1     { font- variant: "small-caps"; }
</STYLE>
```

Elements

This attribute is available for all HTML elements.

 CROSS-REFERENCE

See **font-weight**, **font-style**, and **Font**.

font-weight

Attribute

CSS

This attribute is used to specify the weight, or thickness, or the font used to display the specified text.

The syntax of this attribute is

```
font-weight: 100 | 200 | 300 | 400 | 500 | 600 | 700 | 800 |
900 | normal | bold | bolder | lighter | inherit
```

Values

100 to 900

The numerical values form an ordered sequence in which each integer identifies a font weight that is at least as dark as its predecessor in all user agent. In most agents each digit will make an incremental increase in the weight of the font, without using a predetermined weight.

normal

This value is typically the same as a value of 400.

bold

This value is typically the same as a value of 700.

bolder

This value is used to apply the next weight to a font that is darker than the inherited one. If the inherited value is less than 900 the value will increase by 100. If the value is 900, the value will not increase.

lighter

This value is used to apply the previous weight to a font that is lighter than the inherited one. If the inherited value is greater than 100 the value will decrease by 100. If the value is 100, the value will not decrease.

Example
The following style sheet designation identifies a variety of font weights.

```
<STYLE type="text/css">
 button { font-weight:  "600";  }
 p       { font-weight: "normal." ; }
 sup     { font-weight: "lighter" }
 H1      { font-weight: "900"; }
 H2      { font-weight: "bolder"; }
 tfoot   { font-weight: "300"; }
 q       {font-weight: "400" ; }
</STYLE>
```

Elements
This attribute is available for all elements.

CROSS-REFERENCE
See **Font**, **font-style**, **font-variant**, and **<FONT>**.

<FORM>

Element

HTML
Start Tag: Required
End Tag: Required

The FORM element is used to contain the specific controls used by a document author to gather information from the document reader. The controls are generally accompanied by a series of textual labels that provide instruction or information about the intended contents of the form control. The form is used to specify:

- The layout of the form.
- The program which will process the form data.
- The method used to send the information collected in the form to the server.
- The server must first accept a character encoding which before it can handle the form data.

JAVA SCRIPT

```
object.form
```

The form JavaScript property can also affect this element. It is used to identify the form a specific object is associated with.

Attributes
accept-charset

```
accept-charset="charset-list"
```

This attribute is used to specify a list of character encoding that is used to control data input acceptability by the server processing the form. Either spaces or commas can separate the character values in this list. This list of values is interpreted by the server as an exclusive-or list. The default value for this attribute is a reserved string with the contents of "UNKNOWN".

action

```
action=uri
```

This attribute is used to specify the URL that the form data will be submitted to. It can be either an HTTP form processing program or an email URL.

class

```
class="cdata-list"
```

This attribute is used to assign a class name to an element. User agents employ classes to group specific types of informationspecific types of information for later use.

dir

```
dir = LTR | RTL | [CS | CI | CN | CA | CT]
```

This attribute defines the direction of the text flow in a document, so a user agent can display it correctly.

enctype

```
enctype=content-type
```

This attribute is used to specify the type of encoding used when submitting the form to your processing agent if the method attribute is set to **post.** The default value for this attribute is application/x-www-form-urlencoded.

NOTE
If the form includes an INPUT element with type="file" then you need to set the enctype attribute to multipart/form-data.

id

    id="*name*"

This attribute is used to assign a name to an element.

lang

    lang="*language code*"

This attribute specifies the language in which an element and its values should be rendered.

method

    method=get | post

This attribute is used to specify how the information will be shared with the processing agent.

onclick

    onclick=*script*

This attribute takes effect when a user clicks the button on a pointing device with the pointer over an element.

ondblclick

    ondblclick=*script*

This attribute takes effect when the button on a pointing device is clicked twice over an element.

onkeydown

    onkeydown=*script*

This attribute takes effect when a key is pressed over an element.

onkeypress

    onkeypress=*script*

This attribute takes effect when a key is pressed and released with the pointer over an element.

onkeyup

    onkeyup=*script*

This attribute takes effect when a key is released with the pointer over an element.

onmousedown

```
onmousedown=script
```

This attribute takes effect when the button on a pointing device is pressed with the pointer over an element.

onmousemove

```
onmousemove=script
```

This attribute is activated when the mouse is moved while the pointer is over an element.

onmouseout

```
onmouseout=script
```

This attributed is activated when the mouse pointer is moved away from an element.

onmouseover

```
onmouseover=script
```

This attribute is activated when the mouse is moved over an element.

onmouseup

```
onmouseup=script
```

This attribute takes effect when the button on a pointing device is released with the pointer over an element.

onreset

```
onreset=script
```

This event is toggled whenever the form **reset** button is pressed.

onsubmit

```
onsubmit=script
```

This event is toggled whenever the form **submits** button is pressed.

style

```
style=style descriptors
```

This attribute is used to apply specific style-sheet information to one particular element.

target

```
target=frame-target
```

This attribute is used to specify the destination frame of the link's reference document.

title

```
title=text
```

This attribute serves to provide annotation information to the element to which it is being applied.

Example

This example creates an order form that can be used to order up to ten T-shirts of a single size and color. With a bit of modification, you can allow to place multiple orders for a variety of other services.

ON THE CD-ROM

Look for **form.htm** on the accompanying CD-ROM.

```
<HTML>
<HEAD>
   <TITLE>Form Layout and Design</TITLE>
</HEAD>
<BODY bgcolor="#FFFF99" text="#000000">
<H1 align="center"><font color="#0000FF">Marios Shirt
Emporium</font></H1>
<FORM>
  Make your first selection:<BR>
<INPUT NAME="size" TYPE="radio" VALUE="sm">:Small
<INPUT NAME="size" TYPE="radio" VALUE="md">:Medium
<INPUT NAME="size" TYPE="radio" VALUE="lg">:Large
<INPUT NAME="size" TYPE="radio" VALUE="x">:X-Large
<INPUT NAME="size" TYPE="radio" VALUE="xx">
  :XX-Large
  <P>Colors:
    <select name="select" size="1">
      <option value="red">Red</option>
      <option value="blue">Blue</option>
      <option value="green">Green</option>
      <option value="black">Black</option>
      <option value="yellow">Yellow</option>
      <option value="white">White</option>
      <option value="gray">Gray</option>
  </select>
```

```
<P>Number :
  <select name="select2" size="1">
    <option value="1">1</option>
    <option value="2">2</option>
    <option value="3">3</option>
    <option value="4">4</option>
    <option value="5">5</option>
    <option value="6">6</option>
    <option value="7">7</option>
    <option value="8">8</option>
    <option value="9">9</option>
    <option value="10">10</option>
  </select>
<HR>
<TABLE>
  <TR>
    <TD>Name:</TD>
    <TD>
      <INPUT TYPE="text" NAME="name" SIZE="50">
    </TD>
  </TR>
  <TR>
    <TD>E-mail:</TD>
    <TD>
      <INPUT TYPE="text" NAME="email" SIZE="50">
    </TD>
  </TR>
  <TR>
    <TD>Street Address:</TD>
    <TD>
      <INPUT TYPE="text" NAME="street1" SIZE="50">
    </TD>
  </TR>
  <TR>
    <TD></TD>
    <TD>
      <INPUT TYPE="text" NAME="street2" SIZE="50">
    </TD>
  </TR>
  <TR>
    <TD>City:</TD>
    <TD>
      <INPUT TYPE="text" NAME="city" SIZE="50">
    </TD>
```

```
      </TR>
      <TR>
        <TD>State:</TD>
        <TD>
          <INPUT TYPE="text" NAME="state" SIZE="5"
maxlength="2">
        </TD>
      </TR>
      <TR>
        <TD>Zip:</TD>
        <TD>
          <INPUT TYPE="text" NAME="zip" SIZE="15"
maxlength="10">
        </TD>
      </TR>
    </TABLE>
    <P>
    <HR>
    <DL>
      <DT>How would you like to pay for this?
      <DD>
        <INPUT NAME="pay" TYPE="radio" VALUE="cash" checked>
Cash
      <DD>
        <INPUT NAME="pay" TYPE="radio" VALUE="check">    Check
      <DD>
        <INPUT NAME="pay" TYPE="radio" VALUE="debit">    Debit
Card
        <DL>
          <DT>Credit Card
          <DD>
            <INPUT NAME="pay" TYPE="radio" VALUE="mc">
Mastercard
          <DD>
            <INPUT NAME="pay" TYPE="radio" VALUE="visa">   Visa
          <DD>
            <INPUT NAME="pay" TYPE="radio" VALUE="disc">
Discover
          <DD>
            <INPUT NAME="pay" TYPE="radio" VALUE="ae">
American Express
          <dt>Number:
            <input type="text" name="textfield" size="40"
value="1111-1111-1111-1111" maxlength="30">
```

```
        </dt>
      </DL>
    <dd>Exp:
      <input type="text" name="text" maxlength="5"
value="00/99">
      </dd>
    </DL>
    <P>
      <INPUT TYPE="submit">
      <INPUT TYPE="reset" VALUF="Clear that form!">
  </FORM>
  </BODY>
  </HTML>
```

CROSS-REFERENCE
See **<INPUT>**, **<FIELDSET>**, and **<LEGEND>**.

Formatting

Concept

Formatting—at its most basic—is the organization of text and images on a page or other media with the goal of providing the most visually pleasing, and legible means of dispersing your information. When you are formatting HTML pages, you have two different types of items to work with. Inline objects, which are normally text based, and Block objects.

Inline Objects

Inline object boxes are laid out horizontally in a row (as shown in Figure F-2), starting from the top of the containing box of the surrounding page or block element. Between these boxes, a variety of horizontal margins, borders, and padding spaces are implemented. You can also align these types of boxes vertically in a variety of ways including character baselines, box bottoms, or box tops.

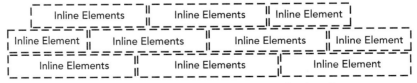

Figure F-2 Inline elements build on each other likes a brick wall.

A series of horizontal boxes that create a full line make up a *line box*. There is one line box for each horizontal line of text on a document. To make this more understandable, you can think of this paragraph as a vertical stack of line boxes, and each line in the paragraph an individual line box containing a series of words. As with text in a paragraph, line boxes cannot have any vertical overlap or separation.

The width of each line box is determined by the containing block of the page or block element that contains it. The height of the line box is determined by the line height and vertical alignment of the boxes it contains. The height of each line box on a document is generated independently of each other, therefore, one line box may be 150 pixels high due to a tall image, while another is only 20 pixels high and contain only text. Generally line boxes are horizontally justified, meaning that their left edge is flush with the left edge of the containing block, and the right edge is flush with the right edge of the containment block. If a line box is in the vicinity of a floating box, one or more edges of the line box may be bordered by the floating box, not the containment block.

Sometimes the total width of the boxes inside a line box, is less than the total available width for that line. In these instances, the `text-align` property will control the distribution of the elements found on that line. Some user agents can also stretch the inline boxes, if the text-align property is set to "justify."

At other times the width of the inline box will be greater than that of the line box. When this occurs the inline box will be split across multiple lines, just as a words are wrapped down your page.

Block Context

Block context boxes are laid out vertically one on top of the other. The first block is laid in the top left corner of the containing block, then the second block is placed below it, also flush against the left edge of the containing block. The vertical distance between blocks is defined by each individual block's margin and padding properties.

CROSS-REFERENCE
See **alignment**, **blocks**, **boxes**, and **inline objects**.

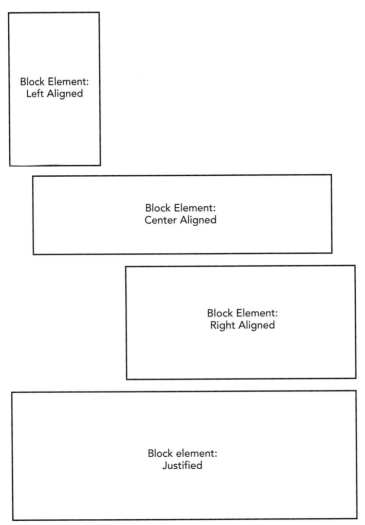

Figure F-3 Block elements build on each other likes the blocks in a pyramid.

forms

Collection

DHTML

This document object collection contains, in source-code order, all the STYLE objects located within the document. This collection is indexed first by name, then by form identifier. When duplicate names are identified, a collection of those named items is created, which is then referenced by the ordinal position of the item in the document.

The syntax of this command can be either of the following:

```
[ collForms = ] object.forms
[ oObject = ] object.forms(vIndex [, iSubIndex] )
```

Parameters

collForms

This variable refers to the array of elements contained by the object.

oObject

This variable refers to an individual item in the array.

vIndex

This parameter is required, and contains the number or string identifying the element or collection to retrieve. When a number is specified, the method returns the element in the zero-based collection at the identified position. When a string identifier is used, and there are multiple elements with the same name or id attributes matching the string, this method returns a collection of those matched elements.

iSubIndex

This optional parameter is used to identify the position of the element being retrieved, when vIndex is a string. ISubIndex becomes the index of the specific item in the collection of matching elements identified by the vIndex string contents.

Object

    document

CROSS-REFERENCE
See **<FORM>** and **form**.

Forward

Method

DHTML

This method is used to load the next URL in the History list into the user agent's viewing window. This method recreates the same effect as the user clicking the Forward button in the user agent. The `forward` method also creates the same effect as `history.go(1)`. You can not use the forward method to travel past the end of the History list. When the end is reached you will simply stay on that page.

The syntax for implementing this method is

```
object.forward()
```

Objects

history

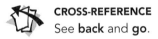

CROSS-REFERENCE
See **back** and **go**.

Fragment identifier

Concept

Some documents contain named anchors that serve as targets for other links and URLs. When this target is used in an URL, it is proceeded by a # symbol and the name of the anchor, which is also referred to as a fragment identifier. An URI pointing to an anchor named `famtrips` could look like this

```
http://catsback.com/outbackranch/vacations.htm#famtrips
```

CROSS-REFERENCE
See **<A>**, **anchor**, **url**, **uri**, and **identifier**.

<FRAME>

Element

HTML

Start Tag: Required
End Tag: Forbidden

This element is used to identify the specific contents and appearance of a single frame within a FRAMESET. A frame is a singular pane, as you would see in an old farmhouse window, that is set aside from the reminder of the window by a border, which may or may not be visible. Frames can be used to organize information into table of contents and its related information. Frames allow you to keep one document loaded all of the time, while rotating through a variety of other documents within a second pane of your window.

Attributes

class

```
class="cdata-list"
```

This attribute is used to assign a class name to an element. User agents employ classes to group specific types of informationspecific types of information for later use.

frameborder

```
frameborder= 1 | 0
```

This attribute is used to control whether the frame is displayed with a border. If the value is 1, there will be a border drawn between this frame and all others. If the value is 0, no frame will be drawn.

id

```
id="name"
```

This attribute is used to assign a name to an element.

longdesc

```
longdesc=uri
```

This attribute provides a link to a file that contains a thorough description of the frame, and its intended uses. This description is particularly useful for non-visual user agents and should be used to add detail to the information contained within the title attribute.

marginheight

`marginheight= `*`pixels`*

This attribute specifies the distance between the content of a frame and its top and bottom margins. The value of this attribute must be greater than one pixel, although the default value is dependent upon the user agent displaying the document.

marginwidth

`marginwidth=`*`pixels`*

This attribute specifies the distance between the content of a frame and its left and right margins. The value of this attribute must be greater than one pixel, although the default value is dependent upon the user agent displaying the document.

name

`name=`*`cdata`*

This attribute assigns a name to the current frame. This attribute is required, in order for other links to load information into the frame.

noresize

This attribute is used to tell the user agent to prohibit the document viewers from being able to change the dimensions of the frame.

scrolling

`scrolling= auto | no | yes`

This attribute controls how the window is or isn't scrolled. If the value is **auto**, then the user agent will provide scroll bars when necessary. When set to **no**, the frame can not be scrolled, and when set to **yes**, the frame will always be displayed with scroll bars.

src

`src=`*`uri`*

This attribute is used to identify the initial contents of the frame.

style

`style=`*`style descriptors`*

This attribute is used to apply specific style-sheet information to one particular element.

target

title

```
title=text
```

This attribute serves to provide annotation information to the element to which it
is being applied.

Example

The following FRAMES example, creates a standard three frame window. The
documents that make up the contents of each of these windows are located on
the CD, along with this main framed page.

ON THE CD-ROM

Look for **frame.htm** on the accompanying CD-ROM.

```
<html>
<head>
    <title>Frameset 1</title>
</head>

<frameset rows="15%,85%">
    <frame src="frbanner.htm" name="banner" marginwidth="1"
marginheight="1">
    <frameset cols="35%,65%">
        <frame src="frconten.htm" name="contents"
marginwidth="1" marginheight="1">
        <frame src="frmain.htm" name="main" marginwidth="1"
marginheight="1">
    </frameset>
</frameset>
<noframes>
    <body>
        <p>
        <p>This web page uses frames, but your browser doesn't
support them.</p>
    </body>
</noframes>
</html>
```

CROSS-REFERENCE

See **<FRAMESET>**, **frameborder**, and **frames**.

frameBorder

Attribute

HTML

This attribute is used to identify whether a frame had a visible border or not. The syntax of this attribute is

```
frameborder= 1 | 0
```

 JAVA SCRIPT
```
object.frameborder [=frameborder]
```

This property is used to set the borders visibility from within a script.

Values
1

A value of one forces a frame to be drawn with a border along each edge of the identified frame.

0

This value prohibits any borders from being drawn around the frame.

Example
The following segments of code draws two sets of frames, one without borders, the other with borders.

```
<frameset cols="35%,65%">
   <frame src="frconten.htm" name="contents" frameborder=1>
   <frame src="frmain.htm" name="main" frameborder=1>
</frameset>

<frameset cols="35%,65%">
   <frame src="frconten.htm" name="contents" frameborder=0>
   <frame src="frmain.htm" name="main" frameborder=0>
</frameset>
```

Elements

FRAME   IFRAME

 CROSS-REFERENCE
See **<FRAMESET>**, **<FRAME>**, and **Frames**.

Frames

Collection

DHTML

The object collection, frames, provides you with a list of all the window objects defined by a document or by the document associated with a given window. If your document contains IFRAME elements, the list will contain an entry for each set of IFRAME tags. If your document contains FRAMESET elements, the collection will contain an entry for each set of FRAME tags. No matter how your document is written, the order of the collection will be based upon the order of the elements in your source code.

This command can be used in either of these fashions:

```
[collFrames = ] object.frames
[ oObject = ] object.frames(vIndex [, iSubIndex] )
```

Values
collFrames

This refers to the array of elements contained by the object.

vIndex

This parameter is required, and contains the number or string identifying the element or collection to retrieve. When a number is specified, the method returns the element in the zero-based collection at the identified position. When a string identifier is used, and there are multiple elements with the same name or id attributes matching the string, this method returns a collection of those matched elements.

iSubIndex

This optional parameter is used to identify the position of the element being retrieved, when vIndex is a string. ISubIndex becomes the index of the specific item in the collection of matching elements identified by the vIndex string contents.

Objects

document   window

CROSS-REFERENCE
See **<FRAME>**, **<FRAMESET>**, and **<IFRAME>**.

<FRAMESET>

Element

HTML

Start Tag: Required
End Tag: Required

This element is used with create a layout of frames, either in columns or rows, that divides the user's screen, and can display multiple documents.

Attributes

class

```
class="cdata-list"
```

This attribute is used to assign a class name to an element. User agents employ classes to group specific types of information for later use.

cols

```
cols=number-list
```

This is a comma-separated list of the size of each column to be created by the FRAMESET element and its associated FRAME tags. This list can contain percentages, pixels, or relative widths, and any combination thereof. The default value of this attribute is 100%.

id

```
id="name"
```

This attribute is used to assign a name to an element.

onload

```
onload=script
```

This event fires when all the frames in a FRAMESET or the entire contents of a window have completely loaded.

onunload

```
onunload=script
```

This event becomes active when a document is closed out of a window. This can occur when a new document replaces it, or it is simply removed as in the case of loading a full page over a complete set of frames.

rows

```
rows=number-list
```

This is a comma-separated list of the size of each row to be created by the FRAMESET element and its associated FRAME tags. This list can contain percentages, pixels, or relative lengths, and any combination thereof. The default value of this attribute is 100%.

style

```
style=style descriptors
```

This attribute is used to apply specific style-sheet information to one particular element.

title

```
title=text
```

This attribute serves to provide annotation information to the element to which it is being applied.

Example

The following FRAMES example, creates a standard three frame window. The documents that make up the contents of each of these windows are located on the CD-ROM, along with this main framed page.

ON THE CD-ROM

Look for **frameset.htm** on the accompanying CD-ROM.

```
<html>
<head>
    <title>Building a bit with Frames</title>
</head>

<frameset rows="15%,85%">
    <frame src="frbanner.htm" name="banner" marginwidth="1"
marginheight="1">
    <frameset cols="35%,65%">
        <frame src="frconten.htm" name="contents"
marginwidth="1" marginheight="1">
        <frame src="frmain.htm" name="main" marginwidth="1"
marginheight="1">
    </frameset>
</frameset>
<noframes>
    <body>
```

```
        <p>
        <p>Uhh Ohh…  Your browser doesn't support frames, and
this document uses them. You can access the individual pages
of the frame by loading the following documents:
        <p><a href="frcontent.html">Contents</a>
        <p><a href="frbanner.html">Banner</a>
        <p><a href="frmain.html">Main Page</a>
      </body>
    </noframes>
  </html>
```

CROSS-REFERENCE
See **<FRAME>**, **frameBorder**, and **Frames**.

FrameSpacing

Property

DHTML

This JavaScript command is used to set and/or retrieve the number of pixels of reserved space between frames. The frameSpacing size does not include the width of the frame border. If you set framespacing on nested frames, it will be applied to all contained FRAMESET objects unless the nested FRAMESET defines different frame spacing.

The syntax for this command is

```
object.frameSpacing [ = sPixels ]
```

Parameters
sPixels

String specifying the spacing, in pixels. The default value is 2.

Elements

FRAMESET   IFRAME

CROSS-REFERENCE
See **frameborder**, **<FRAME>**, **<IFRAME>**, and **<FRAMESPACING>**.

Frequency

Attribute

CSS

This Cascading Style Sheets attribute allows you to control the average pitch, in hertz (Hz) of the speaking voice used in speech synthesizers. Frequency values, which are identified as `frequency` in the command syntax for various aural Cascading Style Sheets command, are formatted as a positive `number` immediately followed by a frequency unit identifier. Frequency unit identifiers can be either **Hz:** (Hertz) or **kHz:** (kiloHertz).

Table F-1 should help you understand the sound induced by a particular frequency setting.

Table F-1 Frequency Ranges of Common Sounds

Instrument/Voice	Approximate Start of Range (Hz)	Approximate End of Range (Hz)
Soprano	250	1500
Contralto	175	900
Tenor	100	575
Baritone	80	375
Bass	60	450
Piccolo	600	4250
Flute	250	2075
Oboe	200	1500
English Horn	175	900
Clarinet	150	1900
Alto Saxophone	150	800
Bassoon	55	600
Trumpet	200	1000
Tuba	50	450
Harp	30	3000
Guitar	70	1000
Violin	200	3500
Viola	125	1500
Cello	60	1000
Bass Violin	35	250

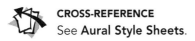

CROSS-REFERENCE
See **Aural Style Sheets**.

FromElement

Property

DHTML

Every time your mouse pointer moves over an element or object on your HTML page, the `onmouseover` and `onmouseout` events fire. This JavaScript property is used to retrieve the name of the object the cursor is leaving during these events.

This command should be expressed in the following manner:

```
[ oObject = ] event.fromElement
```

Parameters
oObject

This is the name of the element over which the mouse pointer is moving.

Example
In the following example, the alert returns `"Ohh La La Baby...Was that Good for you?"` when the mouse pointer is moved over the button.

```
<SCRIPT language="JavaScript">
function testMouse(oObject) {
   if(!oObject.contains(event.fromElement)) {
      alert("Ohh La La Baby...Was that Good for you?");
   }
}
</SCRIPT>
<BODY>
   <BUTTON id=oButton onmouseover="testMouse(this)">Don't
Click Me! Just Mouse Over Me!</BUTTON>
</BODY>
```

Object

event

CROSS-REFERENCE
See **onmouseover** and **onmouseout**.

Gamma Correction

Concept

CSS

You probably hear the term *gamma correction* every time someone talks about images on the Internet. At its most basic, gamma correction is used to control the brightness of images so that they are displayed accurately on the computer screen. Images that have not been properly corrected can appear either bleached out, or too dark, on your computer screen. When creating graphics for the Internet, you may also need to adjust the Red-Green-Blue (RGB) ratio of an image.

Gamma correction is easier to understand if you look at the images displayed on your computer screen.

Practically every computer monitor has a gamma of 2.5. This means that their intensity to voltage curve is roughly a function of the power 2.5. This means that if you send your monitor a message for a specific pixel to have an intensity of 1, that pixel will automatically have an intensity of x^2.5 applied to it. Because the range of voltage is between 0 and 1, this means that your pixel's intensity is lower than you wish. To correct this, the voltage to the monitor has to be "gamma-corrected."

The easiest way to correct this problem is to increase the voltage before it gets to the monitor. Since we know the relationship between the voltage sent to the monitor and the brightness, or intensity, that it produces, we can adjust the signal to remove the effect of the monitor's gamma. When this is done properly, the output of your computer system should accurately reflect the images you have input. Of course, when you are gamma-correcting an image the light in your computer room, the brightness and contrast settings on your monitor, and your personal taste will also play a role.

When we attempt to do gamma correction for the Web, we run into problems with platforms. Some UNIX machines will automatically correct for gamma variance within their video cards, just as the Macintosh does, while most PCs do not. This means that when something looks good on your PC, it will be too light on your Mac, and when something looks good on your Mac, it will be too dark on your PC. This means that if you are placing a graphic on the Internet for all platforms to view, you will be out of luck part of the time; not everyone will view it correctly. Currently, none of the graphic formats used on the Web can encode gamma-correction information. But there is always hope for the future.

CROSS-REFERENCE
See **GIF**, **JPEG**, **Multimedia**, **<IMG>**, **images**, and **RGB**.

generic-family

Value

CSS

Generic family names are used by the `font-family` and `face` attributes to provide an ordered list of fonts for a user agent to search through when performing font matching. These are used as a fallback mechanism for document authors and user agents. The generic font families provide you with at least some means of preserving some of your intended style when none of the specific fonts can be found.

There are five generic families that have been defined: serif, sans-serif, cursive, fantasy, and monospace. These font family names are treated as keywords and must not be placed in quotation marks within your source documents.

Serif

The particular glyphs that are used in a serif font have finishing strokes on each character. These strokes, whether flared or tapered, must be included for a font to be considered as part of the generic serif family. Serif fonts are generally proportionately spaced; therefore a "w" will take up more room on the document, or screen than an "i." Serif fonts will also generally use both thick and thin lines, or *strokes*, in a single glyph, a trait normally not seen in sans-serif fonts.

Table G-1 Examples of Serif Fonts

Language	Font Name
Latin	Bitstream Cyberbit, Bodoni, Garamond, ITC Stone Serif, Minion Web, MS Georgia, and Times New Roman
Greek	Bitstream Cyberbit
Cyrillic	Adobe Minion Cyrillic, Bitstream Cyberbit, ER Bukinst, Excelsior Cyrillic Upright, and Monotype Albion 70
Hebrew	Bitstream Cyberbit, New Peninim, and Raanana
Japanese	Futo Min A101, Kyokasho ICA, Ryumin Light-KL
Arabic	Bitstream Cyberbit
Cherokee	Lo Cicero Cherokee

Sans-serif

The character glyphs in sans-serif fonts don't have feet, or *serifs*, on them. They have stroke endings that are plain — without any flaring or other ornamentation. Sans-serif fonts are generally proportionately spaced; therefore a *w* will take up more room on the document or screen than an "i." Unlike serif fonts, sans-serif fonts generally do not have a variation between the thickness of the strokes that make up the glyphs.

Table G-2 Examples of Sans-Serif Fonts

Language	Font Name
Latin	Akzi-denz Grotesk, Futura, Gill Sans, Helvetica, ITC Avante Garde Gothic, ITC Stone Sans, MS Arial, MS Trebuchet, MS Verdana, and Univers
Greek	Attika, Helvetica Greek, Monotype Gill Sans 571, MS Tahoma, and Typiko New Era
Cyrillic	Bastion, ER Univers, Helvetica Cyrillic, and Lucida Sans Unicode
Hebrew	Arial Hebrew and MS Tahoma
Japanese	Heisei Kaku Gothic W5 and Shin Go
Arabic	MS Tahoma

Cursive

The character glyphs in cursive fonts will generally have either joining strokes or other cursive characteristics in addition to those of an italic type. Since the characters are either partially or completely connected, the resultant type often appears more like true pen or brush handwriting than do printed letters.

f
g
h

Table G-3 Examples of Cursive Fonts

Language	Font Name
Latin	Adobe Poetica, Caflisch Script, Ex-Ponto, Sanvito, Snell-Roundhand, and Zapf Chancery
Cyrillic	ER Architekt
Hebrew	Corisiva
Arabic	Deco Type Naskh, and Monotype Urdu 507

Fantasy

Fantasy fonts are decorative characters. They are not picture fonts (such as Wingdings) that only contain only pictures.

Table G-4 Examples of Fantasy Fonts

Language	Font Names
Latin	Alpha Geometrique, Critter, Cottonwood, FB Reactor, Studz

Monospace

Monospace fonts simply require that all glyphs have a fixed base width. This creates the same effect as an old manual typewriter. The code examples in this book use a monospace font.

Table G-5 Examples of Sans-Serif Fonts

Language	Font Names
Latin	Courier, Everson Mono, MS Courier New, Prestige
Greek	Everson Mono and MS Courier New
Cyrillic	ER Kurier, Everson Mono
Japanese	Osaka Monospaced
Cherokee	Everson Mono

generic-voice

Value

CSS

This value represents one of three possible voice families that are used when attempting to match a voice to an aural style sheet. Possible values are **male**, **female**, and **child**.

 CROSS-REFERENCE
See **voice-family**.

GET

Concept

When you have created a form and placed it on the Internet, that form has to be sent or collected by the form-processing engine. The method attribute of the FORM element specifies the HTTP method used to send the form to the processing agent. GET is one of the values that this attribute can accept.

When you use the HTTP GET method, the form data is appended to the URI that has been specified with the action attribute. This limits you to using ASCII characters in your form collections. The contents of the form will be separated by the URI by a question mark (?), and then this combined URI is sent to the processing agent.

This method should only be used when the form has no side effects such as modifying a database or service subscription. If you are simply searching for information in a database, or adding information to a database, that operation does not actually modify the format of the database being used.

 CROSS-REFERENCE
See **<FORM>** and **Post**.

getAttribute

Method

DHTML

This document object method is used to retrieve the value of the specified HTML document object attribute.

The syntax for this method is

```
vAttrValue = object.getAttribute(sAttrName [, iFlags] )
```

Parameters

sAttrName

This attribute is required to identify the name of the attribute whose value is being collected.

sAttrValue

This variable contains the string, number, or Boolean value of the attribute if it is found. If the attribute does not exist, the value of this variable will be null.

iFlags

This optional attribute controls how the search is performed. The available values for this attribute are **0** (search is not case-sensitive), **1** (search is case-sensitive), **2** (returns the value as it was set in the script or document).

Elements

A	ADDRESS	APPLET	AREA
B	BASE	BASEFONT	BGSOUND
BIG	BLOCKQUOTE	BODY	BR
BUTTON	CAPTION	CENTER	CITE
CODE	COL	COLGROUP	COMMENT
DD	DFN	DIR	DIV
DL	DT	EM	EMBED
FIELDSET	FONT	FRAME	FRAMESET
HEAD	H1-H6	HR	HTML
I	IFRAME	IMB	INPUT
KBD	LABEL	LEGEND	LI
LINK	MAP	MARQUEE	MENU
META	NEXTID	OBJECT	OL
OPTION	P	PLAINTEXT	PRE

S	SAMP	SCRIPT	SELECT
SMALL	SPAN	STRIKE	STRONG
STYLE	SUB	SUP	TABLE
TBODY	TD	TEXTAREA	TFOOT
TH	THEAD	TITLE	TR
TT	U	UL	VAR
WBR	XMP		

Objects

style

CROSS-REFERENCE
See **Attribute**, **id**, and **name**.

getBookmark

Method

DHTML

This object method retrieves a bookmark, as a string, that can be used with `moveToBookmark` to navigate through a series of bookmarks and URLs.
The syntax of this method is

```
sBookmark = object.getBookmark()
```

Object

TextRange

CROSS-REFERENCE
See **bookmark** and **URL**.

GIF

Concept

A GIF, at its most basic, is an image format. It happens to be an image format that uses a built-in LZW compression algorithm that has been patented by Unisys Corporation. Since 1995, all commercial vendors who incorporate

GIF-LZW creators or viewers in their software must have a license for its use. To avoid paying this license fee, many vendors are starting to use the Portable Network Graphic (PNG) format. The problem with this is that GIFs allow you to create animations through the timed rotation of flat GIF images; PNG does not.

A GIF image contains a global palette containing 2, 4, 8, 16, 32, 64, 128, or 256 colors. This palette is used by all the images contained within the GIF file. If a color appears in the GIF, then it is also in the palette. If your GIF file contains multiple images, then an individual image may use a local palette. However no image in the file can reference more than one palette—which limits the colors in the image to 256. When creating an animated GIF wherein many of the images use a local palette, your viewers may see color shifts in your display. This may cause some eyestrain for viewers, or simply cause them to feel uncomfortable enough to quit viewing the document with the varied color scheme.

The current GIF standard is GIF98a. Within these types of files you can encode multiple images, control the position of images, use LZW compression, control delay time between the display of images, wait for and accept user input, specify specific transparency colors, include comments, and display text.

You can find specific information about the GIF file structure—and their individual information blocks—at the Unisys Web site (`http://www.unisys.com`).

CROSS-REFERENCE
See **JPG**, **IMG**, and **PNG**.

Glyph

Concept

CSS

Glyphs are the artistic representation of characters that are used to display information on any visual medium. All of the characters in the alphabet, whether that alphabet is English, Greek, or Swahili, are created by glyphs that we have come to recognize as representing specific letters and the sounds that they make. A font is a set of glyphs, all using a similar style, that is used to represent all the characters in an alphabet, and the other common symbols associated with that language.

CROSS-REFERENCE
See **characters**, **family-name**, **font**, **generic-name**, and **Appendix B**.

go

Method

DHTML

This document object method is used to load a specified URL from the History list. If you attempt to go past the beginning or end of the history list, you will not generate an error; you will simply be left on the current page.

The syntax for using this method is

```
object.go(iIndex | sUrl)
```

Parameters
iIndex

This is the relative position (index) of the URL in the History list.

sUrl

This is a string that can be matched to all or part of an URL in the History list.

Object

history

 CROSS-REFERENCE
See **back** and **forward**.

grid

Media group

CSS

Cascading Style Sheets level 2 has defined the following media groups:

- Visual/Aural/Tactile
- Continuous/Paged
- Grid/Bitmapped
- Interactive/Static

Each media group describes a specific type of medium. There are many media types that are identified as part of these groups. The *grid media group* identifies types of media that use a grid to mark out the dimensions of an image or text. Grid media include TTY machines, Braille print, and embossed print.

CROSS-REFERENCE
See **media groups** and **media types**.

Grouping

Concept

CSS

Why reinvent the wheel — especially when you are coding a style sheet? When several elements share the same attribute declarations, you can group them into a comma-separated list.

Example

In this example, we use grouping to condense three rules with identical declarations into a single statement.

This means that the statements

```
H1  { font-family: sans-serif }
Q   { font-family: sans-serif }
BIG { font-family: sans-serif }
```

can be expressed as

```
H1, Q, BIG { font-family: sans-serif }
```

CROSS-REFERENCE
See **shorthand**, **blocks**, and **declarations**.

<H1 — H6>

Element

HTML

Start Tag: Required
End Tag: Required

The heading tags, H1 through H6 enable document authors to provide labeling information about the sections of their documents. Each level of heading—H1 being the highest—can be used by some user agents to automatically create a table of contents for a document, or to manually create an outline for your next best-selling book. Most visual user agents will display the most important user heading (H1) in a larger, bolder font than the least important (H6) headers will use. This system helps the document reader to identify the main sections of the document with ease, while being able to glean the most important facts from the remainder of the text by simply skimming the other headings.

 NOTE
When you create your documents, please remember that the user agents will only automatically create a Table of Contents for you if you use the appropriate tags at each level of the document tree.

Attributes
align

```
align=center | justify | left | right
```

This attribute controls the horizontal and vertical alignment of text and objects within the bounds of the document margins.

class

```
class="cdata-list"
```

This attribute is used to assign a class name to an element. User agents employ classes to group specific types of information for later use.

dir

```
dir = LTR | RTL | [CS | CI | CN | CA | CT]
```

This attribute defines the direction of the text flow in a document so a user agent can display it correctly.

id

```
id="name"
```

This attribute is used to assign a name to an element.

lang

```
lang="language code"
```

This attribute specifies the language in which an element and its values should be rendered.

onclick

```
onclick=script
```

This attribute takes effect when a user clicks the button on a pointing device with the pointer over an element.

ondblclick

```
ondblclick=script
```

This attribute takes effect when the button on a pointing device is double-clicked with the pointer over an element.

onkeydown

```
onkeydown=script
```

This attribute takes effect when a key is pressed over an element.

onkeypress

```
onkeypress=script
```

This attribute takes effect when a key is pressed and released with the pointer over an element.

onkeyup

```
onkeyup=script
```

This attribute takes effect when a key is released with the pointer over an element.

onmousedown

`onmousedown=script`

This attribute takes effect when the button on a pointing device is pressed with the pointer over an element.

onmousemove

`onmousemove=script`

This attribute is activated when the mouse is moved while the pointer is over an element.

onmouseout

`onmouseout=script`

This attribute is activated when the mouse pointer is moved away from an element.

onmouseover

`onmouseover=script`

This attribute is activated when the mouse pointer is moved over an element.

onmouseup

`onmouseup=script`

This attribute takes effect when the button on a pointing device is released with the pointer over an element.

style

`style=style descriptors`

This attribute is used to apply specific style-sheet information to one particular element.

title

`title=text`

This attribute serves to provide annotation information to the element to which it is being applied.

Example
The following example uses all of the heading markers in conjunction with the OL and LI elements to create a staggered outline for a Spanish Inquisition report.

ON THE CD-ROM
Look for **h1toh6.htm** on the accompanying CD-ROM.

```html
<html>
<head>
   <title>The Headings of the Spanish Inquisition</title>
</head>

<body bgcolor="#FFFFFF">
<h1>The Spanish Inquisition</h1>
<ol type="A">
  <li>
    <h2>The Building</h2>
    <ol type>
      <li>
        <h3>The Church</h3>
        <ol type="a">
          <li>
            <h4>The Jews</h4>
          </li>
          <li>
            <h4>The Catholics</h4>
          </li>
        </ol>
      </li>
      <li>
        <h3>The Fear</h3>
        <ol type="a">
          <li>
            <h4>The Women</h4>
              <ol type="i">
                <li>
                  <h5>Witches</h5>
                </li>
                <li>
                  <h5>Devil Worship</h5>
                </li>
              </ol>
          </li>
          <li>
            <h4>The Devil</h4>
          </li>
```

```
                <li>
                    <h4>The Lies</h4>
                </li>
            </ol>
        </li>
        </ol>
    </li>
    <li>
      <h2>The Horror</h2>
    </li>
    <li>
      <h2>The Shame</h2>
    </li>
    </ol>
    </body>
    </html>
```

CROSS-REFERENCE
See **<HEAD>**, **<BODY>**, **<TITLE>**, and **User Agents**.

half-leading

Concept

CSS

A *half-leading* is half of a leading. *Leading* (the name comes from the lead slugs used to space lines of movable print in early publishing) is extra space seen when there is a difference in height between the size of a font character and the height of the line displaying the font. When fonts are smaller than their allotted line height, the font should be centered within the line height, leaving a half-leading on either side of the font. For example, if you have an 18-point font and a 24-point line height, the font would be positioned to leave 3 points of empty space (half-leading) both above and below the text. The full leading would be 6 points.

CROSS-REFERENCE
See **leading** and **line-height**.

hash

Property

DHTML

This document object property is used to retrieve the segment of the URL of a site discussed in an anchor or area's `href` attribute. The only information it reads is the text following the hash or # mark in the address.

They syntax for this command is

```
object.hash [=stringurl]
```

Parameters

stringurl

This string contains the specific information that will be loaded after the hash mark in the document address shown in the `href` attribute.

Elements

A   AREA

Objects

Locations

CROSS-REFERENCE
See **<A>**, **<AREA>**, and **href**.

<HEAD>

Element

HTML

Start Tag: Optional
End Tag: Optional

Each HTML document uses a header to help provide user agents and search engines with important information about the document. The information included within the header does not affect the rendering of the document in any way.

Attributes
profile

```
profile=url
```

This attribute designates the location of one or more meta data profiles. Although, in HTML 4.0, only the first URL listed is considered relevant, future specifications are expected to recognize and implement multiple profiles.

lang

```
lang="language code"
```

This attribute specifies the language in which an element and its values should be rendered.

dir

```
dir = LTR | RTL | [CS | CI | CN | CA | CT]
```

This attribute defines the direction of the text flow in a document so a user agent can display it correctly.

Example
The following code segment shows a variety of information that can be stored within the HEAD tags of a document.

ON THE CD-ROM
Look for **head.htm** on the accompanying CD-ROM.

```
<HEAD>
    <BASE href="http://www.catsback.com">
    <BASEFONT face="cursive" color="purple">
    <TITLE> Looking at Header information</TITLE>
    <META name="keywords" content="http, html, xml, mathml,
    css, dom, headers>
    <BGSOUND src="music.mdi">
    <STYLE type="text/css">
    <!-
      acronym {  font-family: Arial, Helvetica, sans serif;
                 font-style: italic;
                 line-height: 2em;
                 text-decoration: underline;
                 letter-spacing: 1em;
                 color: #660066}
      img        {  left: 5cm}
    </STYLE>
</HEAD>
```

Elements

The following list of elements are valid to appear within the HEAD /HEAD tags.

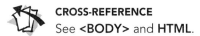

BASE   BASEFONT   BGSOUND   LINK
META   NEXTID   SCRIPT   STYLE
TITLE

CROSS-REFERENCE
See **<BODY>** and **HTML**.

Header Cell

Concept

HTML

A *header cell* is used to provide information about the contents of a table. Headings can be used to identify a column of city names or a row of column totals. Some headings will not be found in "normal" locations of a table and therefore need to be identified as a heading. Visual user agents use the table header cells — such as TH and THEAD — to render information in a fashion that is obviously that of a heading. This helps readers differentiate between normal data and its respective headings. Other user agents, such as speech synthesizers or Braille machines, use the TD and TH element's associated attributes to vocalize information in a more meaningful fashion. This allows non-visual readers to receive the full effect of the information contained within the table.

CROSS-REFERENCE
See **<TD>** and **<TH>**.

headers

Attribute

HTML

This attribute is used by document authors to identify a list of header cells that provide information about the current data cell. This attribute is comprised of a space-separated list of cell names that have already been named using the id attribute. Document authors use the headers attribute to help non-visual user agents provide meaningful information about the headers that should be displayed with each data cell.

Visual user agents use the table header cells, such as TH, to render information in a fashion that is obviously that of a heading. Non-visual user agents like speech synthesizers use the header attribute of the TD and TH elements to vocalize information in a more meaningful fashion.

The header attribute works in conjunction with these elements by identifying specific cells that contain header information rather than data. Each header cell is named using the id attribute that helps differentiate between the headers and data. When there is any confusion between a header cell and a data cell, you should use the TD element and its id and scope attributes to identify to the best of your ability the cell's contents.

The scope attribute can be used instead of header to identify the specific header cells associated with this data cell. You can also use the abbr attribute to specify abbreviated header information for header cells, allowing user agents to render header information more rapidly.

The syntax of this attribute is

```
headers = idrefs
```

Values
idrefs

This is a space-separated list of header names that identify specific headers that refer to the contents of the cell.

Example
The following segment of code shows how the header attribute can be used to add meaning to the contents of the data cells contained within the table.

ON THE CD-ROM

Look for **headers.htm** on the accompanying CD-ROM.

```
<TABLE>
   <TR>
      <TH headers="cars"> Car</TH>
      <TH headers="standing">Standing</TH>
      <TH headers="model"> Model</TH>
      <TH headers="price"> Price</TH>
   </TR>
   <TR>
      <TD headers="cars"> Ford</TD>
      <TD headers="standing"> 1st</TD>
      <TD headers="model"> Probe</TD>
      <TD headers="price"> 19K</TD>
   </TR>
   <TR>
      <TD headers="cars"> Pontiac</TD>
      <TD headers="standing"> 2nd</TD>
```

```
        <TD headers="model"> Grand Am</TD>
        <TD headers="price"> 17K</TD>
     </TR>
     <TR>
        <TD headers="cars"> Dodge</TD>
        <TD headers="standing"> 3rd</TD>
        <TD headers="model"> Stealth</TD>
        <TD headers="price"> 21K</TD>
     </TR>
  </TABLE>
```

Elements

TD   TH

CROSS-REFERENCE
See **scope** and **id**.

Height

Attribute

CSS and HTML

The height of each element's containment block is automatically calculated based on the inherited height of the element's contents. This inherited height is computed based upon three things: the contents of the min-height, max-height, and height properties. Each of these properties can be over ridden with the use of the height Cascading Style Sheet and HTML attributes.

The height attributes are used to override the inherit height of an element's contents, and are therefore accessible throughout the STYLE element for practically every element which can be affected by Cascading Style Sheets. The height attribute specifies the height of the containment block of the element being discussed. In the case of IFRAME, height specifies the height of the inline frame. When used with APPLET, the initial height of the applications area is designated using this attribute. This attribute used with IMG and OBJECT allows you to override the size of the original item. The TD and TH elements use the height attribute to control the size of the cells in the table.

The syntax of this command with HTML elements is

height=*length*

The syntax of the command used with Cascading Style Sheets is

height= *length* | *percentage* | inherit

Values
length

The length is a number followed by a unit identifier to specify either a relative or absolute height change for the element. Valid values for this attribute include such measurements as 3px, 1cm, 5ex, and so on.

percentage

This is the percentage of the item's original containing block that you wish to be used when displaying this object.

Example

The following code segments show how the height attribute is used in a variety of ways to control the display of elements.

ON THE CD-ROM

Look for **height.htm** on the accompanying CD-ROM.

```
<TABLE border="1">
  <TR>
    <TH height="150px"> This is an example of a tall header
    cell.</TH>
    <TH> This header's height has not been adjusted , but
    uses the height of the previous cell..</TH>
  </TR>
  <TR>
    <TDThis height of this cell has not been adjusted.</TD>
    <TD height="4px"> > This cell's height has been
    adjusted.</TD>
  </TR>
</TABLE>
<IMG src="bookfront.gif" height=50>
<!—This shrinks the height of the image by two-thirds.—>
<IMG src="bookfront.gif"> <!— This image is normal —>
```

Elements

APPLET	IFRAME	IMG	OBJECT
TD	TH		

CROSS-REFERENCE

See **length**.

hidden

Properties

DHTML

This property is used in scripted documents to control whether the contents of the EMBED element are hidden or visible. This property can be used by a script to either set or retrieve its contents.

The syntax of this command is:

```
object.hidden(=boolean)
```

Parameters

boolean

This value can be either **true** or **false.** If this value is **true,** the object is invisible. If the value is set to **false,** the object is visible.

Elements
EMBED

CROSS-REFERENCE
See **visibility**.

Hidden Controls

Concept

HTML

When you are working on an HTML input form, you don't always want every field to be visible when the form opens. *Hidden controls* can be used to store information that could otherwise be lost when the form is submitted to the server for processing. This type of control can be used to store practically any type of information that is needed to be processed. This allows you to make sure that every piece of information that needs transferred to the processing system is passed on properly.

Elements
INPUT

CROSS-REFERENCE
See **<FORM>**, **hidden**, **visibility**, and **<INPUT>**.

host

Property

DHTML

This document object property is used to either set or retrieve the value of the `hostname` and `port` of the specified object's `href` attribute.

The syntax of this command is

```
object.host [=stringhost]
```

NOTE
If you wish to set a new location, using the `href` command is considered safer and more appropriate.

Parameters
stringhost

This string contains a concatenation of the `hostname` and `port` identification. If both exist, then the string will appear as

hostname:port

Elements

A   AREA

Objects

location

CROSS-REFERENCE
See **hostname**, **port**, and **href**.

hostname

Property

DHTML

This document object property is used to either set or retrieve the value of the `hostname` portion of an element's `href` attribute.

The syntax of this command is

```
object.hostname [=stringhostname]
```

Parameters

stringhostname

This string contains the domain name or IP address of the location being referenced.

Elements

    A   AREA

Objects

    location

CROSS-REFERENCE
See **host**, **port**, and **href**.

hover

Attribute

CSS

CROSS-REFERENCE
See **:hover**.

<HR>

Element

HTML

Start Tag: Required
End Tag: Forbidden

This element is used to insert a horizontal rule across the body of a document. Only visual user agents employ this command, and the horizontal space between the rule and its preceding and following elements is completely up to the user agent rendering the document. Horizontal rules are used almost exclusively to break up large segments of text into more visually appealing subsections.

Attributes

align

```
align=center | left | right
```

This attribute controls the horizontal alignment of the horizontal rule within the document.

class

```
class="cdata-list"
```

This attribute is used to assign a class name to an element. User agents employ classes to group specific types of information for later use.

dir

```
dir = LTR | RTL | [CS | CI | CN | CA | CT]
```

This attribute defines the direction of the text flow in a document so a user agent can display it correctly.

id

```
id="name"
```

This attribute is used to assign a name to an element.

lang

```
lang="language code"
```

This attribute specifies the language in which an element and its values should be rendered.

noshade

`noshade`

`noshade` is a Boolean attribute that informs the user agent not to draw a shadow below the horizontal rule. By default, most user agents display shadows under these elements. This attribute has been deprecated.

onclick

`onclick=script`

This attribute takes effect when a user clicks the button on a pointing device with the pointer over an element.

ondblclick

`ondblclick=script`

This attribute takes effect when the button on a pointing device is double-clicked with the pointer over an element.

onkeydown

`onkeydown=script`

This attribute takes effect when a key is pressed over an element.

onkeypress

`onkeypress=script`

This attribute takes effect when a key is pressed and released with the pointer over an element.

onkeyup

`onkeyup=script`

This attribute takes effect when a key is released with the pointer over an element.

onmousedown

`onmousedown=script`

This attribute takes effect when the button on a pointing device is pressed with the pointer over an element.

onmousemove

`onmousemove=script`

This attribute is activated when the mouse is moved while the pointer is over an element.

onmouseout

```
onmouseout=script
```

This attribute is activated when the mouse pointer is moved away from an element.

onmouseover

```
onmouseover=script
```

This attribute is activated when the mouse pointer is moved over an element.

onmouseup

```
onmouseup=script
```

This attribute takes effect when the button on a pointing device is released with the pointer over an element.

size

```
size=pixels
```

This attribute is used to specify the height of the rule.

style

```
style=style descriptors
```

This attribute is used to apply specific style-sheet information to one particular element.

title

```
title=text
```

This attribute serves to provide annotation information to the element to which it is being applied.

width

```
width=length
```

This attribute is used to display the overall horizontal space that the rule will take up on your document. This attribute can be a percentage of the visual area of the document, or a specific floating-point integer with its unit designator that can specify either an absolute or relative length for the rule.

Example

The following code example shows you a variety of methods that can be used to draw horizontal rules on your document.

ON THE CD-ROM
Look for **hr.htm** on the accompanying CD-ROM.

```
<HR width="50%" size="2" noshade align="left">
<HR width="250px" size=5" align="center" title="Start of Next
Segment">
<HR style="color:red">
```

CROSS-REFERENCE
See **<IFRAME>**, **<IMG>**, and **<TABLE>**.

href

Attribute

HTML

This attribute is used to identify the referenced Internet site in relation to the current document.

The syntax of this command is

```
href= uri
```

Values
uri

This is an Internet address of the destination identified by this anchor.

Example

The following lines of example code should provide you with a look at how you can use the `href` command to reference all other major types of sites on the Internet.

ON THE CD-ROM
Look for **href.htm** on the accompanying CD-ROM.

```
<A href="mailto:
dectoid@decature.com">dectoid@decature.com</A>
<A href="http://catsback.com/aboutus.html"> About Us</A>
<AREA href="ftp://ftp.papa.indstate.edu" shape="poly"
coords="40,40,146,146,146,0,40,40">
<AREA href="news://news.oregontrail.net" shape="poly"
coords="146,0,146,146,256,40,146,0">
```

Elements

A   AREA   BASE   LINK

CROSS-REFERENCE
See **hreflang**, **host**, **hostname**, **post**, and **src**.

hreflang

Attribute

HTML

This attribute is used to identify the language being used by the destination of the source document's link. This value is used in conjunction with the `href` attribute of the current element.

The syntax of this attribute is

```
hreflang=langcode
```

Values
langcode

This code is one of the recognized language codes identified in the discussion of the `lang` attribute.

Example

The following statement uses the `hreflang` attribute to specify to the user agent that the next document is written in Spanish.

```
<A href="spindex.html" hreflang="sp"> Spanish Index </A>
```

Elements

A   LINK

CROSS-REFERENCE
See **href**, **host**, **hostname**, **lang**, **post**, and **src**.

hspace

Attribute

HTML

This attribute is used to designate how much horizontal white space will be allowed to the left and right of the containment block of an APPLET, IMG, or OBJECT element.

The syntax of this command is

```
hspace=length
```

Values
length

This is any floating-point integer with a designated unit identifier that can be used to define either an absolute or a relative amount of white space around the designated object.

Elements

APPLET   IMG   OBJECT

CROSS-REFERENCE
See **vspace** and **white space**.

<HTML>

Element

HTML

Start Tag: Optional
End Tag: Optional

This element is used to identify the type of document being displayed. You do not need to specify the HTML element tags in order for your user agent to view the document, although you do need those tags to conform to strict HTML 4 document standards.

Attributes
dir

```
dir = LTR | RTL | [CS | CI | CN | CA | CT]
```

This attribute defines the direction of the text flow in a document so a user agent can display it correctly.

lang

```
lang="language code"
```

This attribute specifies the language in which an element and its values should be rendered.

version

```
version=cdata
```

This attribute has been deprecated in favor of the DTD statement. This attribute was used to specify the HTML version that should be used to control the rendering of the current document.

Example

The following code shows you the basic layout of the HTML elements, with child HEAD and BODY elements.

ON THE CD-ROM

Look for **html.htm** on the accompanying CD-ROM.

```
<!DOCTYPE HTML PUBLIC "-//W3C//DTD HTML 4.0//EN"
"http://www.w3.org/TR/REC-html/strict.dtd">
<HTML lang="en-us">
  <HEAD>
     <TITLE> A Document's Title.</TITLE>
  </HEAD>
  <BODY>
     This is the body.
  </BODY>
</HTML>
```

CROSS-REFERENCE

See **<!DOCTYPE>**, **<HEAD>**, and **<BODY>**.

HTML — HyperText Markup Language

HyperText Markup Language (HTML) is a derivative language based on SGML (Standard Generalized Markup Language). HTML uses a series of elements, attributes, character references, and comments to identify individual sections and presentation layouts in a document. A basic HTML document would have the following structure:

```
<HTML>
  <HEAD>
    <TITLE> This is the title.</TITLE>
  </HEAD>
  <BODY>
    This is the body.
  </BODY>
</HTML>
```

The document has two sections: the *head* (identified by the <HEAD> / </HEAD> markers), and the *body* (identified by the <BODY>/</BODY> markers). In HTML, information about the entire document is contained within the head section, and consists mostly of style sheet specifications (style), the document title, and meta information. The body of the document contains the information displayed for the reader.

 CROSS-REFERENCE
See **HTML, CSS, XML, DOM, CDF, MathML,** and **SGML.**

HTML Extension

Concept

A variety of file extensions can be used for Web-based HTML files. The following three extensions are the most popular in current use on the Web:

- **htm** — identifies standard HTML files. When documents are created on 16-bit computer systems, they are limited to a three-character file extension.

- **html** — identifies a standard HTML file that can be read on a machine not limited to three-character file extensions.

- **shtml** — identifies server-parsed HTML code. This code must be interpreted by the HTTP server before the user agents can display their contents.

- **asp** — used with Active Server Pages, which are used by the Internet Information Server. ASP pages can combine HTML and server scripts in a single document, giving developers control over how the server interacts with the user agent.

CROSS-REFERENCE
See **CGI**.

HTTP — HyperText Transfer Protocol

Language

The *HyperText Transfer Protocol (HTTP)* is used by client-server TCP/IP-compliant servers to exchange HTML-formatted information through the World Wide Web. This protocol controls the interpretation of each element by user agents, as well as how to display the documents. By default, HTTP servers use port 80 for both sending and receiving documents.

Using HTTP to access information on the Internet entails a series of steps that must be completed. These steps provide a way for information to be queried, collected, and (in the case of errors) to be sent at appropriate events. Each step, or *event*, can direct the information exchange between the server and the client.

CROSS-REFERENCE
See **URL**.

http-equiv

Attribute

HTML

This attribute, when used with the `META` element, takes the place of the `name` attribute. HTTP servers use `http-equiv` to collect information from the document for inclusion in the HTTP server response headers.

The syntax of this attribute is

```
http-equiv="stringID"
```

Values
stringID

This value holds the name, or *label*, of the information identified in the META element's `content` attribute.

Examples

The following lines of code provide some examples of how the http-equiv attribute can be used to provide information to the HTTP server.

ON THE CD-ROM

Look for **httpequiv.htm** on the accompanying CD-ROM.

```
<META http-equiv= "Publication_Date" content= "December 1997">
<META http-equiv= "Author" content= "Heather Williamson">
<META http-equiv= "Custodian Contact" content= "Heather
Williamson, phone, fax, email">
<META http-equiv= "Custodian Contact Position" content=
"Developer: Business Marketing Unit">
<META http-equiv= "Owner" content= "Jenine Williamson">
<META http-equiv= "Reply to" content=
"HTMLMaster@catsback.com">
```

Elements

META

CROSS-REFERENCE

See **id** and **name**.

Hyphenation

Concept

HTML uses two types of hyphens: a plain hyphen and a soft hyphen. Although a plain hyphen is interpreted by the user agent as another character "-" (- or -), the soft hyphen "­" (­ or ­) provides the user agent with a directive as to where line breaks can occur.

When soft hyphens are included in a document, there are two rules that the user agent must follow:

- If a line is broken at the soft hyphen, a hyphen character must be displayed at the end of the first line.
- If a line is not broken at the soft hyphen, the user agent must not display a hyphen character.

CROSS-REFERENCE

See **Characters** and **Language**.

<I>

Element

HTML

Start Tag: Required
End Tag: Required

This element is used to create italicized text within the middle of your paragraphs. If you are attempting to provide emphasis through the use of italics, you should use the `EM` tag. If you are defining the first instance of a word, you need to use the `DEF` tags.

Attributes
class

```
class="cdata-list"
```

This attribute is used to assign a class name to an element. User agents employ classes to group specific types of information for later use.

id

```
id="name"
```

This attribute is used to assign a name to an element.

lang

```
lang="language code"
```

This attribute specifies the language in which an element and its values should be rendered.

onclick

```
onclick=script
```

This attribute takes effect when the button on a pointing device is clicked while the pointer is over an on-screen element.

527

ondblclick

```
ondblclick=script
```

This attribute takes effect when the button on a pointing device is double-clicked while the pointer is over an on-screen element.

onkeydown

```
onkeydown=script
```

This attribute takes effect when a key is pressed while the pointer is over an on-screen element.

onkeypress

```
onkeypress=script
```

This attribute takes effect when a key is pressed and released while the pointer is over an on-screen element.

onkeyup

```
onkeyup=script
```

This attribute takes effect when a key is released while the pointer is over an on-screen element.

onmousedown

```
onmousedown=script
```

This attribute takes effect when the button on a pointing device is pressed while the pointer is over an on-screen element.

onmousemove

```
onmousemove=script
```

This attribute is activated when the mouse pointer is moved while it is over an on-screen element.

onmouseout

```
onmouseout=script
```

This attribute is activated when the mouse pointer is moved away from an on-screen element.

onmouseover

```
onmouseover=script
```

This attribute is activated when the mouse pointer is moved over an on-screen element.

onmouseup

```
onmouseup=script
```

This attribute takes effect when the button on a pointing device is released while the pointer is over an on-screen element.

style

```
style=style descriptors
```

This attribute is used to apply specific style-sheet information to one particular element.

title

```
title=text
```

This attribute provides annotation information to the element.

Example

The following example code uses the I element to italicize the names of a series of reference materials that are included on a book-purchasing list for a college's independent study course.

ON THE CD-ROM

Look for **i.htm** on the accompanying CD-ROM.

```
<HTML>
<HEAD>
  <TITLE>Web Development - Independent Study - Book
List</TITLE>
</HEAD>
<BODY>
  <H1>CS220 - Web Development (IS)</H1>
  <P>Instructor: <EM>Mike Williams</EM><BR>
 Schedule: M-W-F 9-10:45am (includes Lab) or T-Th 1-2:45pm
w/Lab W 4:00-5:45pm
   <P>
  <H2>Required Book List</H2>
  <P><I>HTML Master Reference</I> H. Williamson, IDG Books
Worldwide, 1999<BR>
  <I>JAVA Master Reference</I>A. Griffith, IDG Books
Worldwide, 1998<BR>
  <I>JavaScript Bible, 3rd Edition</I> D. Goodman, IDG Books
Worldwide, 1998<BR>
</BODY>
</HTML>
```

CROSS-REFERENCE
See **<B>**, **<EM>**, **<CITE>**, **<STRONG>**, and **<BIG>**.

IANA — Internet Assigned Numbers Authority

Concept

The Internet Assigned Numbers Authority is a nonprofit organization composed of board members from across the globe; it works to help the Internet police itself. The IANA issues IP addresses, such as 233.233.233.2, and assists in distributing domain names, such as ofc.org, for companies and other organizations that wish to be connected to the Internet.

CROSS-REFERENCE
See **Unicode**, **Unisys**, **RFC**, **characters,** and **MathML**.

ID

Datatype

This datatype is used by the Document Type Definition (DTD) to identify all element or attribute contents of this type as a string containing only the letters of the alphabet in either lower- or uppercase, numbers, and the punctuation characters, including a hyphen, an underscore, a colon, or a period.

CROSS-REFERENCE
See **DTD**, **<IDREF>**, **<IDREFS>**, **name**, **number**, **string**, **uri,** and **datatype**.

id

Attribute

HTML

This attribute is used to identify the name or identifier of a particular object. The id and name attributes can be used together but should contain the same contents if they are. A variety of JavaScripts and VBScripts can access the contents of an element and its attributes through identifying it by its name.

The syntax of this attribute is

```
id=name
```

Values

name

This is a string that provides an identifiable name for the element.

Example

In this example, the id attribute is provided for a series of SPAN elements, which are placed at various positions on your screen by the use of positioning attributes within a style sheet.

ON THE CD-ROM

Look for **id.htm** on the accompanying CD-ROM.

```
<HTML>
<HEAD>
  <TITLE>Controlling Layers using ID</TITLE>
  <STYLE type="text/css">
  <-!
  #topbox {position: absolute;
          top: 100px;
          left: 100px;
          width: 200px;
          height: 200px }
  #bottombox {position: absolute;
            top: 350px;
            left: 200px;
            width: 200px;
            height: 200px }
  ->
  </STYLE>
</HEAD>
<BODY>
  <SPAN id="topbox">
  <IMG src="mural.jpg" alt="A mural for all the seasons."
width=200 height=200>
  </SPAN>
  <SPAN id="bottombox">
  <H1>Ski Mount Howard</H1>
  <P>Visit the great ski slopes of the high mountains of North
Eastern Oregon. Take a gondola ride, ski the slopes, drink
some hot cocoa, and enjoy the beauty of the Eagle Cap
Wilderness.
  </SPAN>
</BODY>
</HTML>
```

Elements
This attribute is available with all HTML elements.

CROSS-REFERENCE
See **id**, **<IDREF>**, **<IDREFS>**, and **name**.

ID Selector

Concept

CROSS-REFERENCE
See **id**, **ID**, **identifier**, **IDREF**, and **name**.

Identifier

Concept

CSS

An identifier is used within a program to provide a means of referencing either a constant or a variable. An identifier is used to name elements, classes, and attributes. Identifiers can contain only the alphabetic characters, the numbers from zero to nine, and some special ISO 10646 characters, including the hyphen.

CROSS-REFERENCE
See **attribute**, **constant**, **element**, **ID**, **value**, and **variable**.

IDL — Interface Definition Language

Concept

DOM

Practically everything on the Internet has a specification identifying how it should be done, created, or made to look and perform. Interfaces are no different. The Interface Description Language (IDL) used the Open Software Foundation (OSF) Distributed Computing Environment (DCE) specification as its foundation for describing interfaces, operations, and attributes used in the definition of remote procedure calls.

Using IDL, designers can create definitions for custom interfaces by creating an interface definition file. The interface definition uses the IDL to define the datatypes and functions of the interface, while the definition file itself contains information about the interaction between the client application and the server. The definition file contains three specific definitions:

- **Language binding** — This definition is used to specify a particular programming model using a specified programming language that will be exposed to the application.

- **Application binary interface** — This definition identifies how interface consumers and providers work together on a specified platform.

- **Network interface** — This definition identifies how client applications will be able to access server objects through a network.

Once the interface definition file is completed, the IDL compiler is run. This generates the interface headers and any source code necessary to build the interface proxy and stub defined in the definition file. The header is made available to user agents so that they can use the interface. The interface proxy and stub are used to create DLLs to be distributed with the client applications (proxies) and server objects (stubs) using the interface.

In this way, IDL is a tool that makes developing interfaces easier for a programmer. Although this is not the only way to develop interfaces for the Component Object Model (COM), it does make the development of interfaces convenient and makes the interfaces themselves easy to share with other programmers.

One of the results of running the IDL compiler is the IDL file. This file contains the complete specification for the interface, including datatypes and function sets.

CROSS-REFERENCE
See **user agent** and **Document Object Model**.

IDREF

Datatype

CSS

This datatype is used by the DTD to identify the contents of an element or attribute as a URI that references the location of other contents the user agent needs to access.

CROSS-REFERENCE
See **datatype, id, IDREFS, name, number, string,** and **uri.**

IDREFS

Datatype

CSS

This datatype is used by the DTD to identify the contents of an element or attribute as a comma-delimited string of URIs; this string references a series of locations that should be accessed to find other contents required by the user agent.

CROSS-REFERENCE
See **name, number, string, id, IDREF, uri,** and **datatype.**

IETF — Internet Engineering Task Force

Concept

The Internet Engineering Task Force (IETF) is a large international community of network designers, operators, vendors, and researchers who wish to focus their energies on the evolution of the Internet architecture and its operation. The members of the IETF form a loosely organized group that consistently makes contributions to the engineering and development of the Internet and its supporting technologies.

There are three IETF meetings each year to discuss its mission, and the closest equivalent to becoming an IETF "member" is to attend the meetings and to be on the IETF mailing list. Although the IETF does not make standards, it proposes many ideas to typical standards organizations; often these are accepted.

This group's main focus is to develop Internet standards specifications to address a variety of problems on the Internet in ways that include

- Working with proposed solutions to operational and technical problems
- Recommending standardizations for protocols and protocol usage on the Internet to the Internet Engineering Steering Group (IESG)

- Assisting in the development or usage of protocols and architectures that solve technical problems on the Internet
- Assisting in transferring technology to the Internet community from the Internet Research Task Force (IRTF)

Each IETF working group is assigned a particular area of interest and is managed by Area Directors. These directors are members of the IESG. The Internet Architecture Board (IAB) provides architectural oversight and also governs appeals when a complaint is issued against the IESG. The IAB and IESG have been chartered by the Internet Society (ISOC) for these purposes. The General Area Director serves as the chair of both the IESG and the IETF.

CROSS-REFERENCE
See **ISO.**

<IFRAME>

Element

HTML

Start Tag: Required
End Tag: Required

This element is used to identify an inline frame. An inline frame is placed within an object block or a block of text. The process used to insert an IFRAME element is similar to that of using the OBJECT element. You can use IFRAME to insert a new HTML document in the middle of the current document. You can align the IFRAME's contents, which have been designated by its src attribute, with the surrounding text. This element should only be displayed by user agents that either do not support frames or that have been configured not to display them.

Attributes
align

```
align=left | center | right | justify
```

This attribute controls the visual alignment of the inline frame within its bounding box.

class

```
class="cdata-list"
```

This attribute is used to assign a class name to an element. User agents employ classes to group specific types of information for later use.

frameborder

```
frameborder= 1 | 0
```

This attribute controls whether the frame is displayed with a border. If the value is 1, a border is drawn between this frame and all others. If the value is 0, no frame is drawn.

height

```
height=number
```

This attribute specifies the height of the frame being displayed. If this value is not provided, the inline frame is displayed fully sized.

id

```
id="name"
```

This attribute is used to assign a name to an element.

lang

```
lang="language code"
```

This attribute specifies the language in which an element and its values should be rendered.

longdesc

```
longdesc=uri
```

This attribute provides a link to a file that contains a thorough description of the frame and its intended uses. This description is particularly useful for nonvisual user agents and should be used to add detail to the information contained within the title attribute.

marginheight

```
marginheight=pixels
```

This attribute specifies the distance between the content of a frame and its top and bottom margins. The value of this attribute must be greater than one pixel, although the default value is dependent upon the user agent displaying the document.

marginwidth

```
marginwidth=pixels
```

This attribute specifies the distance between the content of a frame and its left and right margins. The value of this attribute must be greater than one pixel, although the default value is dependent upon the user agent displaying the document.

name

```
name=cdata
```

This attribute assigns a name to the current frame. This attribute is required for other links to load information into the frame.

scrolling

```
scrolling= auto | no | yes
```

This attribute controls how the window is or isn't scrolled. If the value is **auto,** the user agent provides scroll bars when necessary. When the value is **no,** the frame cannot be scrolled. When the value is **yes,** the frame is always displayed with scroll bars.

src

```
src=uri
```

This attribute is used to identify the initial contents of the frame.

style

```
style=style descriptors
```

This attribute is used to apply specific style-sheet information to one particular element.

title

```
title=text
```

This attribute provides annotation information to the element.

target

```
target=name | _blank | _self | _parent | _top
```

This is the name of the frame or of the window level into which the linked document or image is loaded.

width

> width=number

This attribute specifies the width of the frame being displayed. If this value is not provided, the frame is displayed fully sized.

Example
This example document uses the IFRAME element to insert the contents of the listed page within the current document.

 ON THE CD-ROM
Look for **iframe.htm** on the accompanying CD-ROM.

```
<html>
<head>
   <title> Using IFRAME</title>
</head>

<body>
   <h1> The Fox and the Turtle </h1>
   <p> The turtle won over the rabbit in round one. Who will
win in round 2?
   </p>
   <iframe width="200" height="150" frameborder="1"
src="turtle.html">
   <img alt="Fox or turtle- who shall win" src="foxturt.gif">
   </iframe>
   <p>Only time will tell.….
   </p>
</body>
</html>
```

 CROSS-REFERENCE
See **<FRAME>**and **frame target.**

Image Map

Concept

An image map is essentially what it sounds like, an image with a map of shapes laid over the top of it. Each shape is used to create a link to another page or section of the current document. In most cases, the image is composed of a flat GIF or JPEG file, although it is possible to create an image map out of an animated GIF image. The AREA and the A elements define the outlines of the "map" overlay for the image and provide the address for the link to take the user to.

 CROSS-REFERENCE
See **<IMG>**, **<MAP>**, **<A>**, **<AREA>**, **GIF,** and **JPEG.**

Images

Concept

"A picture is worth a thousand words," and the Internet takes this idea to heart. You could describe an image as any graphical element used, in this case, on a Web page. Images are used all over the Web to provide "eye candy" and alternative means of explaining concepts, describing an event, or identifying people, places, and things. Images can be used on a Web page to provide a means of traveling through a Web site or as buttons, logos, family photos, or cards to tell people that you are thinking of them.

 CROSS-REFERENCE
See **<IMG>**, **<MAP>**, **GIF,** and **JPEG.**

images

Collection

DHTML

This object collection creates a list of all the IMG objects found within the current document.

This collection can be used in the following ways:

```
[ collImages = ] document.images
[ oObject = ] document.images(vIndex [, iSubIndex] )
```

Parameters
collImages

This variable refers to the array of elements contained by the object.

oObject

This variable refers to an individual item in the array.

vIndex

This parameter is required and contains the number or string identifying the element or collection to retrieve. When a number is specified, the method returns the element in the zero-based collection at the identified position. When a string identifier is used and multiple elements with the same name or id attributes match the string, this method returns a collection of those matched elements.

iSubIndex

This optional parameter is used to identify the position of the element being retrieved when vIndex is a string. ISubIndex becomes the index of the specific item in the collection of matching elements identified by the vIndex string contents.

Objects

document

 CROSS-REFERENCE
See **<IMG>, images, <MAP>, GIF,** and **JPEG.**

<IMG>

Element

HTML

Start Tag: Required
End Tag: Forbidden

This element is used to display flat graphics, animated GIFs, and videos on your HTML document. You can use images as the foundation of image maps or any other graphical navigational tool. Some images on HTML documents use IMG objects to display company logos, sidebars, menus, buttons, icons, graphical additions, rules for visually breaking apart documents, or even family reunion photographs.

Attributes
align

```
align=bottom | middle | top
```

This attribute is used to control the visual alignment of the image within its bounding box. If the value of this attribute is **bottom,** the lower edge of the contents is aligned to the bottom of the object. When the value is **middle,** the contents are aligned to the middle of the object block. If the value is **top,** the top edge of the contents is aligned to the top of the containment block.

alt (required for HTML 4.0 compliance)

    alt=*string*

This text appears in place of the image on text-only browsers, when a mouse is moved across the image in a compatible user agent, or to provide information to speech synthesizers to make the document accessible for all ranges of viewers.

border

    border=*<number>*

This attribute is used to control the outline of each image.

class

    class="*cdata-list*"

This attribute is used to assign a class name to an element. User agents employ classes to group specific types of information for later use.

dir

    dir = LTR | RTL

This attribute defines the direction of the text flow in a document so that a user agent can correctly display it to the reader.

height

    height=*<number>*

This attribute specifies the height of the image being displayed. If this value is not provided, the image is displayed fully sized.

hspace

    hspace=*length*

This attribute specifies the amount of white space to insert to the left and right of the image box.

id

    id="*name*"

This attribute is used to assign a name to an element.

ismap

    ismap

This attribute is used to identify and implement server-side image maps.

lang

`lang="`*`language code`*`"`

This attribute specifies the language in which an element and its values should be rendered.

longdesc

`longdesc=`*`url`*

This attribute specifies a link to the long description of the image. The description to which this link directs your users should provide a supplement to the contents of the `alt` attribute. If this attribute is used with an image map, it should be used to provide information about the contents of the map.

onclick

`onclick=`*`script`*

This attribute takes effect when the button on a pointing device is clicked while the pointer is over an on-screen element.

ondblclick

`ondblclick=`*`script`*

This attribute takes effect when the button on a pointing device is double-clicked while the pointer is over an on-screen element.

onkeydown

`onkeydown=`*`script`*

This attribute takes effect when the button on a pointing device is double-clicked while the pointer is over an on-screen element.

onkeypress

`onkeypress=`*`script`*

This attribute takes effect when a key is pressed and released while the pointer is over an on-screen element.

onkeyup

`onkeyup=`*`script`*

This attribute takes effect when a key is pressed and released while the pointer is over an on-screen element.

onmousedown

`onmousedown=`*`script`*

This attribute takes effect when the button on a pointing device is pressed while the pointer is over an on-screen element.

onmousemove

`onmousemove=`*`script`*

This attribute is activated when the mouse pointer is moved while it is over an on-screen element.

onmouseout

`onmouseout=`*`script`*

This attribute is activated when the mouse pointer is moved away from an on-screen element.

onmouseover

`onmouseover=`*`script`*

This attribute is activated when the mouse pointer is moved over an on-screen element.

onmouseup

`onmouseup=`*`script`*

This attribute takes effect when the button on a pointing device is released while the pointer is over an on-screen element.

src (required)

`src=`*`uri`*

This attribute is used to store the address for the image. This can be either an absolute or a relative reference.

style

`style=`*`style descriptors`*

This attribute is used to apply specific style-sheet information to one particular element.

title

`title=`*`text`*

This attribute provides annotation information to the element.

usemap

> usemap=*uri*

This attribute is used to associate an image map created with the MAP element with the current image. The value of this attribute must match the value of the name attribute of the MAP element.

vspace

> vspace=*length*

This attribute specifies the amount of white space to insert above and below the image box.

width

> width=<*number*>

This attribute specifies the width of the image being displayed. If this value is not provided, the image is displayed fully sized.

Example

The following example combines a series of images into a larger image, with a floating layer containing an animated GIF centered over the combined image.

ON THE CD-ROM

Look for **img.htm** on the accompanying CD-ROM.

```
<html>
<head>
<title>IMG Example</title>
</head>

<body bgcolor="#FFFFFF">
<div id="Layer1" style="position:absolute; left:242px;
top:283px; width:133px; height:136px; z-index:1">
   <img src="spiderani.gif" width="101" height="128">
</div>
<img src="tietop.gif" width="600" height="200"> <br>
<img src="tieleft.gif" width="300" height="200">
<img src="tieright.gif" width="300" height="200"><br>
<img src="tiebottom.gif" width="600" height="200">
</body>
</html>
```

CROSS-REFERENCE

See **image map**, **<MAP>**, **<AREA>**, **<A>**, **JPEG**, and **GIF**.

<IMPLEMENTATION>

Element

OSD

This element is a child of SOFTPKG and is used to describe the current implementation of the software package that resides on the network.

Example
The following example shows how to use the IMPLEMENTATION element to define the specific operating system and memory requirements of the software that is being made available for installation.

```
<SOFTPKG>
<IMPLEMENTATION>
    <CODEBASE href="http://www.mysoftware.com/soft.cab" />
    <OS value="WinNT" />
    <MEMSIZE value="1024Kb" />
</IMPLEMENTATION>
</SOFTPKG>
```

Elements
The following elements are child elements of IMPLEMENTATION.

CODEBASE	DEPENDENCY	DISKSIZE	IMPLTYPE
LANGUAGE	MEMSIZE	OS	PROCESSOR
VM			

CROSS-REFERENCE
See **<SOFTPKG>**.

<IMPLTYPE>

Element

OSD

This element is a child of IMPLEMENTATION and is used to identify the type of installation being performed.

Attributes

Value

This is the name of the type of implementation being installed. For a Java applet, this is **Java.**

Example

The following example shows how to use the IMPLTYPE element to define the type of software that is being installed.

```
<SOFTPKG>
<IMPLEMENTATION>
    <IMPLTYPE value="java" />
    <CODEBASE href="http://www.mysoftware.com/soft.cab" />
    <OS value="WinNT" />
    <MEMSIZE value="1024Kb" />
</IMPLEMENTATION>
</SOFTPKG>
```

CROSS-REFERENCE
See **\<SOFTPKG >**and **\<IMPLEMENTATION>.**

imports

Collection

DHTML

This object collection creates a list of all the imported style sheets found within the current document. Imported style sheets are incorporated into the current document by using the @import Cascading Style Sheets attribute.

This collection can be used in the following ways:

```
[ collImports = ] object.imports
[ oObject = ] object.imports(vIndex [, iSubIndex] )
```

Parameters

collImports

This variable refers to the array of elements contained by the object.

oObject

This variable refers to an individual item in the array.

vIndex

This parameter is required and contains the number or string identifying the element or collection to retrieve. When a number is specified, the method returns the element in the zero-based collection at the identified position. When a string identifier is used and multiple elements with the same name or id attributes match the string, this method returns a collection of those matched elements.

iSubIndex

This optional parameter is used to identify the position of the element being retrieved when vIndex is a string. ISubIndex becomes the index of the specific item in the collection of matching elements identified by the vIndex string contents.

Objects

stylesheets

 CROSS-REFERENCE
See **@import** and **style sheets.**

indeterminate

Property

DHTML

This sets or retrieves whether a checkbox is in an indeterminate state. An indeterminate box will be checked and dimmed. It can be used to indicate whether the user has acted on a control. An indeterminate control is not a disabled control. Indeterminate controls can be altered and can receive the focus of the user or a script. When a user adjusts an indeterminate control, its state is changed, and it is toggled to a fully checked state.

The syntax of this command is

```
object.indeterminate [ = Dim ]
```

Values
Dim

This Boolean attribute is used to identify when a box is checked and dimmed (**true**) or not dimmed (**false**).

Elements

INPUT (type=checkbox)

Objects

checkbox

CROSS-REFERENCE
See <INPUT> and **checked**.

index

Property

DHTML

This property is used in scripts to collect the ordinal number of a line item within the collection or list of `OPTION` element values.

The syntax required for using this property is

`[iIndex = ] object.index`

Values
iIndex

This integer specifies the ordinal position of the object.

Elements

OPTION

CROSS-REFERENCE
See **collections** and **z-index**.

inherit

Value

CSS

The computed value of each Cascading Style Sheets attribute can be used by child elements using the same attribute. `Inherit` is normally the default value of the attributes, although you can set it explicitly by using the value of `inherit`.

Example

In the sample code below, the "color" and "background" properties are set on the P and the BODY elements explicitly. On all elements contained within the P block, the background will be yellow with black text. On all other elements, the color value will be inherited from the BODY element and the background will be white.

```
<STYLE type="text/css">
<!—
P       { color: black;
          background: yellow }
BODY    { color: black;
          background: white }
—>
</STYLE>
```

 CROSS-REFERENCE
See **Parent, Ancestor, Computed Value,** and **Child**.

Inheritance

Concept

CSS

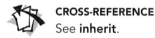 **CROSS-REFERENCE**
See **inherit**.

Initial Caps

Concept

CSS

Previous to the Cascading Style Sheets, level 2, specification, there was no way to identify individually the first letter or line of a paragraph. The only way to create an initial cap or a drop cap effect was to use an image within a table or a floating image. Now, with the advent of the :first-letter pseudo-element, you can create the effect of an initial capital letter.

When you create an `initial cap` with the `:first-letter` pseudo-element, it works like an inline element or a floating element when its `float` element is set to anything other than **none**.

CROSS-REFERENCE
See **:first-letter**, **:first-line**, and **drop caps**.

Initial Containing Block

Concept

CSS

Each object has a containing box. This box is often used to assist in the computation of relative values used when rendering an object. The initial containing block is defined by the user agent to contain the root element (`<BODY>` for most HTML documents). The size of this area is determined by the user agent's available visible area. All other elements are organized within the initial block but can be forced outside of it at need. Fixed-position elements have their containing block established by the user agent, not the initial containing block of the document.

CROSS-REFERENCE
See **containment block, block level elements, inline elements,** and **root containment block.**

Initial Structure Model

Concept

The Document Object Model provides for a main predefined, or initial, document structure that guides the layout and incorporation of objects being placed within the document's structure. The initial structure of a document consists of a single root, generally the `HTML` element for HTML documents. This root is then used to spawn a series of branches, which hold the main-level elements such as `BODY` and `HEAD` for HTML documents. This structure expands with each comment, script, or other element that is added to the document.

CROSS-REFERENCE
See **Document Object Model**.

Initial Value

Concept

CSS

The initial value, or original starting value, of most elements' attributes is inherited from the user agent's style sheet and is then altered based upon any style sheet attributes or element attributes contained within the document. The initial value of an option can be changed multiple times before it is rendered, or it can be displayed and then altered through the use of scripts.

 CROSS-REFERENCE
See **inherit** and **Cascading Style Sheets**.

Inline Element

Concept

CSS

Inline elements are those objects that do not create a new block of content. With inline elements, the content is dispersed within the existing block. The `display` attribute can be used to create an inline element from a user-defined tag. Inline elements create boxes that may be within an existing block box. These types of elements are stacked one upon the other until their contents have been displayed.

 CROSS-REFERENCE
See **block element**, **containment block**, and **display**.

Inline-Table

Concept

CSS

As with standard block tables, inline-tables consist of a number of rows and cells, headings, footers, and captions. The primary difference between a block table and an inline-table is the lack of the inline-table's containment block.

Both of these tables maintain the same rectangular appearance, but the inline-table is treated as any other inline element, and not as a block object of its own.

HTML Master Reference HTML Master Reference HTML Master Reference
HTML Master Reference HTML Master Reference HTML Master Reference
HTML Master Reference HTML Master Reference HTML Master Reference
HTML Master Reference HTML Master Reference HTML Master Reference

TABLE as a Block Element

HTML Master Reference HTML Master Reference HTML Master Reference
HTML Master Reference HTML Master Reference HTML Master Reference
HTML Master Reference HTML Master Reference HTML Master Reference
HTML Master Reference HTML Master Reference HTML Master Reference

TABLE as an Inline Element

HTML Master Reference
HTML Master Reference
HTML Master Reference
HTML Master Reference
HTML Master Reference
HTML Master Reference
HTML Master Reference

HTML Master Reference HTML Master Reference HTML Master Reference
HTML Master Reference HTML Master Reference HTML Master Reference
HTML Master Reference HTML Master Reference HTML Master Reference
HTML Master Reference HTML Master Reference HTML Master Reference

Figure I-1 The block aspect of a normal table prohibits the display of text around its borders, whereas an inline-table can have text information appearing to its sides without using layers or absolute positioning.

CROSS-REFERENCE
See **display**, **<TABLE>,** and **inline element**.

innerHTML

Property

DHTML

This document object property is used to retrieve the contents of the HTML document—including HTML tags—between the current object's start and end tag. The syntax for this command is

```
object.innerHTML [=string]
```

Parameters
string

This string contains the contents of the HTML document between the identified object tags.

Example
The following sample code automatically changes the text of the P element to the identified strings, based upon the action of the viewer's mouse.

ON THE CD-ROM

Look for **innerhtml.htm** on the accompanying CD-ROM.

```
<P onmouseover="this.innerHTML='<BIG>The clock struck 1. The
mouse ran down.</BIG>'"
    onmouseout="this.innerHTML='<I>Hickory Dickory
Dock.</I>'">
<I>Hickory Dickory Dock. The Mouse Ran up the Clock.</I></P>
```

Elements

A	ACRONYM	ADDRESS	B
BIG	BLOCKQUOTE	BODY	BUTTON
CAPTION	CENTER	CITE	CODE
DD	DEL	DFN	DIR
DIV	DL	DT	EM
FIELDSET	FONT	FORM	H1–H6
I	IFRAME	INS	KBD
LABEL	LEGEND	LI	LISTING
MARQUEE	MENU	NEXTID	OL
P	PRE	Q	S
SAMP	SMALL	SPAN	STRIKE
STRONG	SUB	SUP	TT
U	UL	VAR	

CROSS-REFERENCE

See **innerText**, **insertAdjacentHTML**, **outerText**, **outerHTML**, and **<TEXTAREA>**.

innerText

Property

DHTML

This script property is used either to set or retrieve the text contents of the HTML document between the current object's start and end tag.

The syntax for this command is

```
object.innerText [=string]
```

Parameters

string

This string contains the text found between the start and end tags or the text to be placed there.

Example

The following sample code automatically changes the text of the P element to the identified strings, based upon the action of the viewer's mouse.

ON THE CD-ROM

Look for **innertext.htm** on the accompanying CD-ROM.

```
<P ID=oPara>Make a Wish!!!</P>
:
<BUTTON onclick="oPara.innerText='Ahh.. you told me what it
was! It will not happen now.'">Tell me your wish.</BUTTON>
<BUTTON onclick="oPara.innerText='Cool.. the first star came
out tonight.'">Wish on a Star.</BUTTON>
```

Elements

<!— —>	A	ACRONYM	ADDRESS
B	BIG	BLOCKQUOTE	BODY
BR	BUTTON	CAPTION	CENTER
CITE	CODE	DD	DEL
DFN	DIR	DIV	DL
DT	EM	FIELDSET	FONT
FORM	H1–H6	I	IFRAME
INS	KBD	LABEL	LEGEND
LI	LISTING	MAP	MARQUEE
MENU	NEXTID	OL	P

PLAINTEXT	PRE	Q	S
SAMP	SMALL	SPAN	STRIKE
STRONG	SUB	SUP	TD
TEXTAREA	TH	TITLE	TR
TT	U	UL	VAR
XMP			

CROSS-REFERENCE
See **innerHTML**, **insertAdjacentHTML**, **outerText**, **outerHTML**, and
<TEXTAREA>.

<INPUT>

Element

HTML

Start Tag: Required
End Tag: Forbidden

This element is used within a FORM to create fields and controls that can be
used to collect information from a document viewer. This information can be
used to change a page automatically, request information, update a database,
or do any one of a hundred other tasks that can be optimized through reader
input on the Internet.

Attributes
accept

```
accept = content-type-list
```

This attribute contains a comma-separated list of MIME content types that the
server processing the form will handle correctly.

accesskey

```
accesskey="character"
```

You can assign an access key to an element. This key allows you to put the focus
on an element quickly. In the case of a form element, the user is immediately able
to input information. In the case of a link, the link is activated and followed.

align

```
align=bottom | middle | top
```

This attribute is used to control the visual alignment of the image within its bounding box. If the value of this attribute is **bottom,** the lower edge of the contents is aligned to the bottom of the object. When the value is **middle,** the contents are aligned to the middle of the object block. If the value is **top,** the top edge of the contents is aligned to the top of the containment block.

alt

```
alt=string
```

This text appears in place of the image on text-only browsers, when a mouse is moved across the image in a compatible user agent, or to provide information to speech synthesizers to make the document accessible for all ranges of viewers.

checked

```
checked
```

This Boolean attribute is used to specify whether an INPUT element, when it is either a radio button or a checkbox, is selected. This attribute can only be used in conjunction with a **type='radio'** or a **type='checkbox'** INPUT attribute.

class

```
class="cdata-list"
```

This attribute is used to assign a class name to an element. User agents employ classes to group specific types of information for later use.

disabled

```
disabled
```

This is a Boolean attribute that, when set, will disable the button, disallowing any user input.

id

```
id="name"
```

This attribute is used to assign a name to an element.

lang

```
lang="language code"
```

This attribute specifies the language in which an element and its values should be rendered.

maxlength

```
maxlength = number
```

This is the maximum number of characters that the user may enter when the type attribute is set to either **text** or **password**. This can be a number greater than the value of the size attribute.

name

```
name=cdata
```

This attribute is used to give the INPUT element a name that is used as an identifier when it is identified for the FORM.

onblur

```
onblur=script
```

This attribute becomes active when an element loses the focus either through the actions of a mouse or another pointing device or by tabbing navigation.

onchange

```
onchange = script
```

If a control's value is changed while the control has input focus, this event occurs when the control loses the focus.

onclick

```
onclick=script
```

This attribute takes effect when the button on a pointing device is clicked while the pointer is over an on-screen element.

ondblclick

```
ondblclick=script
```

This attribute takes effect when the button on a pointing device is double-clicked while the pointer is over an on-screen element.

onfocus

```
onfocus=script
```

This attribute takes effect when an element receives focus from either a mouse or another pointing device or through tabbed navigation.

onkeydown

```
onkeydown=script
```

This attribute takes effect when the button on a pointing device is double-clicked while the pointer is over an on-screen element.

onkeypress

```
onkeypress=script
```

This attribute takes effect when a key is pressed and released while the pointer is over an on-screen element.

onkeyup

```
onkeyup=script
```

This attribute takes effect when a key is pressed and released while the pointer is over an on-screen element.

onmousedown

```
onmousedown=script
```

This attribute takes effect when the button on a pointing device is pressed while the pointer is over an on-screen element.

onmousemove

```
onmousemove=script
```

This attribute is activated when the mouse pointer is moved while it is over an on-screen element.

onmouseout

```
onmouseout=script
```

This attribute is activated when the mouse pointer is moved away from an on-screen element.

onmouseover

```
onmouseover=script
```

This attribute is activated when the mouse pointer is moved over an on-screen element.

onmouseup

```
onmouseup=script
```

This attribute takes effect when the button on a pointing device is released while the pointer is over an on-screen element.

onselect

```
onselect = script
```

This event occurs when a user selects text within a text field.

readonly

```
readonly
```

This Boolean attribute prohibits change in a control. A reader cannot modify the contents of the control in any way, although the control can still receive the focus and is included in the tabbing order.

size

```
size = cdata
```

This attribute is used to specify the initial width of the control for the user agent. The width is given in pixels for all control types except **text** or **password**, for which the width is considered to be the number of characters to display.

src

```
src=uri
```

This attribute is used to identify the initial contents of the object when the type is identified as an image for this INPUT object.

style

```
style=style descriptors
```

This attribute is used to apply specific style-sheet information to one particular element.

title

```
title=text
```

This attribute provides annotation information to the element.

tabindex

```
tabindex=number
```

This attribute provides the position of the current element within the overall tabbing order of the document.

type

```
type = text | password | checkbox | radio | submit | reset |
file | hidden | image | button
```

This attribute specifies the type of control to create. Its default value is "text."

usemap

```
usemap=uri
```

This attribute is used to associate an image map created with the MAP element with the current image. The value of this attribute must match the value of the name attribute of the MAP element.

value

```
value = cdata
```

This attribute is used to identify the initial value of the form control. This is optional for all control types except **radio.**

Example

The following example code uses INPUT tags to create a form that collects information on people interested in fishing.

ON THE CD-ROM

Look for **input.htm** on the accompanying CD-ROM.

```
<html>
<head>
<title>The Fishing Club Information Sheet</title>
<meta http-equiv="Content-Type" content="text/html;
charset=iso-8859-1">
<meta name="generator" content="Macromedia Dreamweaver">
</head>

<body bgcolor="#FFFFFF">
<h1 align="center"><font color="#FF0000">The Fishing
Club</font></h1>
<h3 align="center">Fishing Survey and Request for Membership
Information </h3>
<form method="post" action="">
  <p align="left">Name:
    <input type="text" name="name" size="75">
    <br>
    Address:
    <input type="text" name="address" size="75">
    <br>
    City, State, Zip:
    <input type="text" name="cstz" size="75">
  </p>
  <p align="left">Email:
    <input type="text" name="email" size="75">
```

```
   <br>
   Daytime Phone:
   <input type="text" name="phone" size="25">
   Best Time to Call:
   <input type="text" name="calltime" size="25">
</p>
<p align="left">Best days for property tour:
   <select name="tripdays" size="3" multiple>
     <option value="Sat">Saturday</option>
     <option value="Sun">Sunday</option>
     <option value="Mon">Monday</option>
     <option value="Tue">Tuesday</option>
     <option value="Wed">Wednesday</option>
     <option value="Thur">Thursday</option>
     <option value="Fri">Friday</option>
   </select>
   <br>
   Other comments or questions:<br>
   <textarea name="textfield" cols="75" rows="3"></textarea>
</p>
<hr>
<p align="left">How many days a year would you like to fish?
   <input type="radio" name="FishingDays" value="0to5"
checked>
   0-5
   <input type="radio" name="FishingDays" value="5to10">
   5-10
   <input type="radio" name="FishingDays" value="10-15">
   10-15
   <input type="radio" name="FishingDays" value="15-20">
   15-20
   <input type="radio" name="FishingDays" value="20to25">
   20 -25
   <input type="radio" name="FishingDays" value="over25">
   Over 25</p>
<ol>
   <li>Where do you like to fish, and how?<br>
     <textarea name="textarea" cols="75" rows="4"></textarea>
   </li>
   <li>What irritates you most about the places you fish?<br>
     <textarea name="textarea" rows="3" cols="75"></textarea>
   </li>
   <li>Describe your dream fishing trip:<br>
     <textarea name="textarea" cols="75" rows="3"></textarea>
```

h
i
j

```
      </li>
      <li>Your Age:
        <input type="radio" name="yourage" value="under21"
checked>
      under 21
        <input type="radio" name="yourage" value="21to30">
      21-30
        <input type="radio" name="yourage" value="31to40">
      31-40
        <input type="radio" name="yourage" value="41to50">
      41-50
        <input type="radio" name="yourage" value="51to60">
      51-60
        <input type="radio" name="yourage" value="61to70">
      61-70
        <input type="radio" name="radiobutton"
value="radiobutton">
      Over 70<br>
      Spouse's Age:
        <input type="radio" name="spouseage" value="under21"
checked>
      under 21
        <input type="radio" name="spouseage" value="21to30">
      21-30
        <input type="radio" name="spouseage" value="31to40">
      31-40
        <input type="radio" name="spouseage" value="41to50">
      41-50
        <input type="radio" name="spouseage" value="51to60">
      51-60
        <input type="radio" name="spouseage" value="61to70">
      61-70
        <input type="radio" name="spouseage"
value="radiobutton">
      Over 70<br>
      Kid(s) Age(s):
        <input type="checkbox" name="checkbox" value="0to5">
      0-5
        <input type="checkbox" name="checkbox" value="5to10">
      5-10
        <input type="checkbox" name="checkbox" value="10-15">
      10-15
        <input type="checkbox" name="checkbox" value="15-20">
      15-20
```

```
      <input type="checkbox" name="checkbox" value="over21">
      Over 21</li>
   <li>Occupation - Yours:
      <input type="text" name="text" size="50">
      <br>
      Spouses:
      <input type="text" name="text" size="50">
   </li>
 </ol>
</form>
</body>
</html>
```

 CROSS-REFERENCE
See **type**, **<FORM>**, and **<LABEL>**.

inRange

Method

DHTML

This method is used to identify whether an identified range is contained within another.

The syntax for this command is

```
bFound = object.inRange(oRange)
```

Parameters
bFound

This Boolean attribute is **true** if the range is contained within another range. It is **false** otherwise.

oRange

This required element is used to identify the referenced `TextRange` object.

Objects

textRange

 **CROSS-REFERENCE**
See **isEqual**.

<INS>

Element

HTML

Start Tag: Required
End Tag: Required

INS is used to mark up portions of a document that has been inserted with respect to a different version of the same document. This allows you to see what changes have been made within a document, so they are not lost immediately. This element may serve as either a block level or inline element. INS can contain a series of words within a single paragraph or a series of blocks such as tables, paragraphs, images, or lists. User agents are required to provide an obvious means of visually determining which text has been inserted. Some mark text in a special color or with other special markings.

Attributes

cite

cite=*uri*

This uri points to the location of information about why the document was changed. This could be another document or simply a message.

class

class="*cdata-list*"

This attribute is used to assign a class name to an element. User agents employ classes to group specific types of information for later use.

datetime

datetime=*datetime*

This attribute is used to specify the date and time when a change was made to an object.

id

id="*name*"

This attribute is used to assign a name to an element.

lang

lang="*language code*"

This attribute specifies the language in which an element and its values should be rendered.

onclick

```
onclick=script
```

This attribute takes effect when the button on a pointing device is clicked while the pointer is over an on-screen element.

ondblclick

```
ondblclick=script
```

This attribute takes effect when the button on a pointing device is double-clicked while the pointer is over an on-screen element.

onkeydown

```
onkeydown=script
```

This attribute takes effect when the button on a pointing device is double-clicked while the pointer is over an on-screen element.

onkeypress

```
onkeypress=script
```

This attribute takes effect when a key is pressed and released while the pointer is over an on-screen element.

onkeyup

```
onkeyup=script
```

This attribute takes effect when a key is pressed and released while the pointer is over an on-screen element.

onmousedown

```
onmousedown=script
```

This attribute takes effect when the button on a pointing device is pressed while the pointer is over an on-screen element.

onmousemove

```
onmousemove=script
```

This attribute is activated when the mouse pointer is moved while it is over an on-screen element.

onmouseout

```
onmouseout=script
```

This attribute is activated when the mouse pointer is moved away from an on-screen element.

h
i
j

onmouseover

```
onmouseover=script
```

This attribute is activated when the mouse pointer is moved over an on-screen element.

onmouseup

```
onmouseup=script
```

This attribute takes effect when the button on a pointing device is released while the pointer is over an on-screen element.

style

```
style=style descriptors
```

This attribute is used to apply specific style-sheet information to one particular element.

title

```
title=text
```

This attribute provides annotation information to the element.

Example

The author of the following HTML document uses the DEL and INS elements to edit the information and provide notes as to the reasons for the changes.

ON THE CD-ROM

Look for **ins.htm** on the accompanying CD-ROM.

```
<HTML>
<HEAD>
   <TITLE>DEL/INS Trials and Tribulations</TITLE>
</HEAD>

<BODY>
Cat's Back Consulting was developed to provide rural
businesses with access to professional advertising on the
<DEL>Net</DEL> <INS topic="Change in terminology to remove
lingo">Internet</INS>. Located in the far northeastern corner
of Oregon, high in the snowcapped Wallowa Mountains, Cat's
Back  Consulting (CBC) knows and understands the problems and
pleasures associated with rural living.</P>
   <P>
```

```
It is hard turning majestic scenery, abundant wildlife,
sparkling water, and friendly people into food on your table.
As we say around here &quot;You can't eat the mountains&quot;,
but you can expand your business potential by hiring Cat's
Back Consulting to host your company's Web site. From your
<DEL> business Web site</DEL><INS cite="boringterms.html">home
on the Internet</INS> you can reach a potential customer
market of over <DEL>40</DEL><INS datetime="
1998-11-08T09:15:30-05:00">60</INS> million people in a medium
that is growing roughly 10% each month.</P>
    <P>
</BODY>
</HTML>
```

CROSS-REFERENCE
See **<DEL>**.

insertAdjacentHTML

Method

DHTML

This method is used to insert the supplied HTML text into the element at the specified location. In the event that the text contains HTML tags, the elements are interpreted and formatted as they are inserted.

The syntax for this method is

```
object.insertAdjacentHTML(sWhere, sText)
```

Parameters
sWhere

This required parameter is used to identify the position into which the HTML text needs to be inserted. This position can be one of the following: **beforeBegin** inserts the text immediately before the element; **afterBegin** inserts the text directly after the element's start tag; **beforeEnd** inserts the text immediately before the end tag of the element; **afterEnd** inserts the text immediately after the element's end tag.

sText

This required parameter contains the HTML text being inserted. The string can be a combination of text and HTML tags. If the text is not well-formed, valid HTML, this method will fail.

Elements

<!— —>	A	ADDRESS	AREA
B	BASEFONT	BIG	BLOCKQUOTE
BODY	BUTTON	CAPTION	CENTER
CITE	CODE	DD	DFN
DIR	DIV	DL	DT
EM	FIELDSET	FONT	FORM
FRAMESET	H1–H6	HR	I
IFRAME	IMG	INPUT	KBD
LABEL	LEGEND	LI	LISTING
MAP	MARQUEE	MENU	OL
OPTION	P	PLAINTEXT	PRE
S	SAMP	SELECT	SMALL
SPAN	STRIKE	STRONG	STYLE
SUB	SUP	TD	TEXTAREA
TH	TT	U	UL
VAR	XMP		

CROSS-REFERENCE
See **innerHTML**, **insertAdjacentText**, **outerText**, **outerHTML**, and **<TEXTAREA>**.

insertAdjacentText

Method

DHTML

This method is used to insert the supplied text into the element at the specified location. In the event that the text contains HTML tags, the elements will be ignored and formatted as text when placed into the document.

The syntax for this method is

```
object.insertAdjacentText(sWhere, sText)
```

Parameters
sWhere

This required parameter is used to identify the position into which the HTML text needs to be inserted. This position can be one of the following: **beforeBegin** inserts the text immediately before the element; **afterBegin** inserts the text directly after the element's start tag; **beforeEnd** inserts the text immediately before the end tag of the element; **afterEnd** inserts the text immediately after the element's end tag.

sText

This required parameter contains the text being inserted.

Elements

<!— —>	A	ADDRESS	AREA
B	BASEFONT	BIG	BLOCKQUOTE
BODY	BUTTON	CAPTION	CENTER
CITE	CODE	DD	DFN
DIR	DIV	DL	DT
EM	FIELDSET	FONT	FORM
FRAMESET	H1–H6	HR	I
IFRAME	IMG	INPUT	KBD
LABEL	LEGEND	LI	LISTING
MAP	MARQUEE	MENU	OL
OPTION	P	PRE	S
SAMP	SELECT	SMALL	SPAN
STRIKE	STRONG	STYLE	SUB
SUP	TD	TEXTAREA	TH
TT	U	UL	VAR
XMP			

 CROSS-REFERENCE
See **innerHTML**, **insertAdjacentHTML**, **outerText**, **outerHTML**, and **<TEXTAREA>**.

insertCell

Method

DHTML

This method is used to create a new cell within a table and add it to the `cells` collection.

The syntax for using this method is

```
oTD = object.insertCell([iIndex])
```

Parameters

iIndex

This optional parameter is used to identify the location to insert the cell in the TR. The default value is –1, which appends the new cell to the end of the cells collection.

oTD

This is the TD cell that is created if the insert is completed successfully.

Elements

TR

CROSS-REFERENCE
See **deleteCell** and **insertRow**.

insertRow

Method

DHTML

This method is used to insert a TR into a TABLE inside a JavaScript. The syntax for using this method is

```
oTR=object.insertRow(Index)
```

Parameters

Index

This identifies the location of the row to be inserted into the current table. The default value of -1 places the row at the end of the rows collection.

oTR

This is the TR element that is created if the insert is completed successfully.

Elements

TABLE   TBODY   TFOOT   THEAD

CROSS-REFERENCE
See **<CAPTION>**, **createTFoot**, **createTHead**, **createCaption**, **deleteCaption**, **deleteTFoot**, **deleteCell**, and **deleteTHead**.

Integer

Concept

CSS

Some values use an integer type, rather than a real number or a length. Integers are very similar to real numbers in that they are specified in decimal notation only. An integer can only be a whole number consisting of a series of digits from 0 to 9. Numbers can have digits following a decimal point. An integer can be signed by being preceded by a plus (+) or minus (–) character.

 CROSS-REFERENCE
See **number** and **length**.

Interactive

Media Group

CSS

Cascading Style Sheets, level 2, has defined the following media groups:

- Visual/Aural/Tactile
- Continuous/Paged
- Grid/Bitmap
- Interactive/Static

Each media group is used to describe a specific type of medium. Many media types are identified as part of these groups. The interactive media group is used to identify media that allow the user to provide immediate feedback. When viewed on a computer screen or a Web TV, the Internet is considered an interactive media type. A computer game is interactive in the same way. An ATM uses a digital display in an interactive fashion.

CROSS-REFERENCE
See **media group** and **media type**.

Internationalization

Concept

The idea supporting internationalization on the Web is one similar to the emerging idea of the global community. Internationalization is intended to be a means of providing information in languages other than those that use the English and Latin alphabets, which are so prevalent on the Internet.

HTML can be internationalized by allowing the characters making up the document context to represent other alphabets and by setting the language of the text fragment explicitly. The base character set of HTML documents was originally specified to be ISO Latin 1, but now it is ISO 10646 or Unicode, which contains approximately 34,000 of the world's characters. HTML uses the SPAN and Q elements, along with the lang, dir, and align attributes, to enable fragments of text to be displayed in a certain language or writing style.

You can also create separate versions of a document in multiple languages. The user agent can use the LINK tag to access and automatically load these separate versions. The various languages that you create documents for may need to use bidirectional text, which has been provided for with the BDO, PRE, and dir elements and attributes.

HTTP servers can also assist with internationalization by identifying the character encoding used before it is sent to the user agent. HTTP can also share the character encoding schemes that the client understands with the server and inform the server which document to send to a client.

CROSS-REFERENCE
See **Cascading Style Sheets, dir, lang, <SPAN>, <Q>**, and **align**.

<INTERVALTIME>

Element

CDF

This element is used to identify the amount of time between each repetition of sending the channel contents to its subscribers.

Attributes
day

```
day="number"
```

This integer represents the number of days between times that the channel document should be delivered.

hour

```
hour="number"
```

This specifies the additional hours of the interval in a 24-hour format.

min

```
min="number"
```

This is an integer between 1 and 60 representing a minute interval between deliveries of the channel.

Example
This example channel, located at `http://mychannels.com/channels.cdf`, must be delivered between midnight and noon every 30 days.

```
<CHANNEL href="http://mychannels.com/channels.cdf ">
    <SCHEDULE>
        <INTERVALTIME Day=30 />
        <EARLIESTTIME Hour=0 />
        <LATESTTIME Hour=12 />
    </SCHEDULE>
</CHANNEL>
```

Elements

CHANNEL

CROSS-REFERENCE
See **<USERSCHEDULE>**, **<EARLIESTTIME>**, and **<LATESTTIME>**.

Inter-Word Space

Concept

This is the term used for the amount of space that has been set aside between words. In most English/Latin texts, the inter-word space is the width of a space character. In other languages, it may be the width of another special character, zero, or nonexistent.

CROSS-REFERENCE
See **kerning, padding, margins, borders, containment block**, and **inline element**.

Intrinsic Dimensions

Concept

CSS

Intrinsic dimensions of an image or some other object are the natural, unaltered dimensions of the object. Dimensions can be affected by a variety of attributes, including `width` and `height`.

CROSS-REFERENCE
See **width, height, hspace, vspace**, and **margins**.

isEqual

Method

DHTML

This method is used to identify whether a specified text range is equal to the current range.

The syntax for this method is

```
bEqual = TextRange.isEqual(oCompareRange)
```

Parameters
bEqual

This Boolean parameter is **true** if the ranges are equal and **false** otherwise.

oCompareRange

This object identifies the text range being compared to the current one.

Objects

textRange

CROSS-REFERENCE
See **inRange**.

<ISINDEX>

Element

HTML

Start Tag: Required
End Tag: Optional

This element has been deprecated, but it is used to create a single-line text-input control. This element has been replaced with the `INPUT type=text` element.

Attributes

class

```
class="cdata-list"
```

This attribute is used to assign a class name to an element. User agents employ classes to group specific types of information for later use.

dir

```
dir = LTR | RTL
```

This attribute defines the direction of the text flow in a document so that a user agent can correctly display it to the reader.

id

```
id="name"
```

This attribute is used to assign a name to an element.

lang

```
lang="language code"
```

This attribute specifies the language in which an element and its values should be rendered.

prompt

```
prompt=string
```

This is a string containing the information used as a prompt for the text field.

style

```
style=style descriptors
```

This attribute is used to apply specific style-sheet information to one particular element.

title

```
title=text
```

This attribute provides annotation information to the element.

Example

The following statement uses the ISINDEX element to create a single-line text box for collecting information.

```
<ISINDEX prompt="Enter your password here:">
```

 CROSS-REFERENCE
See **<INPUT>**, **<FORM>**, and **type**.

ismap

Attribute

HTML

This attribute is used to identify whether an image is used as a server-side image map. When this attribute is supplied, the image is presumed to be part of a server-side image map.

The syntax for this command is

```
ismap
```

 JAVA SCRIPT
```
[ Map = ] img.isMap
```

This JavaScript property is used to discover, through the use of the Boolean Map variable, whether a specific image is used as a server-side image map.

Example

The following line of code uses ismap to mark the image being displayed as part of a server-side image map.

```
<IMG src="gullagoola.jpg" ismap alt="Server side map of Gulla
Goola Amusement Park">
```

Elements

IMG

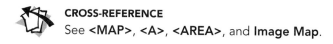

CROSS-REFERENCE
See **<MAP>**, **<A>**, **<AREA>**, and **Image Map**.

ISO

Concept

ISO is the International Organization for Standardization, composed of national-standards bodies from over 100 countries. This organization is not related to any governmental body. Its mission is to promote the development of standards and their related activities throughout the world, with a focus on facilitating the international exchange of goods and services. ISO also assists in developing cooperation in intellectual, scientific, technological, and economic global communities. The work of the ISO results in a series of international agreements published as international standards.

CROSS-REFERENCE
See **IETF** and **IANA**.

isSubscribed

Method

DHTML

This method is used to identify whether a user has subscribed to a specified channel.

The syntax of this method is

```
bSubscribed = object.isSubscribed (sURLToCDF)
```

Parameters
bSubscribed

This Boolean value contains **true** if the channel has been subscribed to; otherwise it contains **false**.

sURLToCDF

This required parameter contains the URL of the Channel Definition Format file that needs to be checked to verify the subscription.

Objects

external

CROSS-REFERENCE
See **CDF**.

isTextEdit

Property

DHTML

This property is used to identify whether the current text object can be used to create a `TextRange` object. Only the `BODY`, `BUTTON`, `TEXTAREA`, and `INPUT` `type="text"` elements can be used to create a text range.

The syntax for this command is

```
[Edit = ] object.isTextEdit
```

Parameters
Edit

This Boolean parameter is **true** if the TextRange can be created and **false** if it cannot be created.

Elements

<!— —>	A	ACRONYM	ADDRESS
AREA	B	BASE	BASEFONT
BGSOUND	BIG	BLOCKQUOTE	BODY
BR	BUTTON	CAPTION	CENTER
CITE	CODE	COL	COLGROUP
DD	DEL	DFN	DIR
DIV	DL	DT	EM
EMBED	FIELDSET	FONT	FORM
FRAME	FRAMESET	H1–H6	HEAD
HR	HTML	I	IFRAME
IMG	INPUT	INS	KBD
LABEL	LEGEND	LI	LINK
LISTING	MAP	MARQUEE	MENU
META	NEXTID	OBJECT	OL

OPTION	P	PLAINTEXT	PRE
Q	S	SAMP	SCRIPT
SELECT	SMALL	SPAN	STRIKE
STRONG	STYLE	SUB	SUP
TABLE	TBODY	TD	TEXTAREA
TFOOT	TH	THEAD	TITLE
TR	TT	U	UL
VAR	XMP		

CROSS-REFERENCE
See **inRange** and **isEqual**.

<ITEM>

Element

CDF

This element is used to identify a specific item within a channel. This item is generally a specific Web page or another presentation device.

Attributes
href

```
href=url
```

This required attribute is used to identify the location of the channel so that the user agent can properly navigate itself through the channel's information.

lastmod

```
lastmod=date
```

This attribute is used to specify the date that the channel item was last modified in GMT time. The current default format for a date/time string is

```
YYYY-MM-DDThh:mm:ssTZD
```

where

```
YYYY = four-digit year
MM = two-digit month (01=January, etc.)
DD = two-digit day of month (01 through 31)
hh = two digits of hour (00 through 23) (am/pm NOT allowed)
mm = two digits of minute (00 through 59)
ss = two digits of second (00 through 59)
```

which displays 9:30 p.m. on January 16, 1999, in the following manner:

```
1999-01-16T21:30:00
```

level

```
level=n
```

This is the number of levels that a user agent should go down to look for information on the site. This is also the number of layers to go to when precaching information.

precache

```
precache=yes | no
```

This tells the user agent to save copies of all the documents and images that are read on the channel on the local machine. If this attribute is omitted or set to **yes,** information is cached. If it is set to **no,** information is not cached, and the `level` attribute is ignored.

Example

The following example code identifies a particular document within this channel.

```
<CHANNEL href="http://mychannels.com/channels.cdf ">
    <ITEM href="http://mychannels.com/interests.html"
precache="yes" level="4">
        <ABSTRACT value="The latest information on Jelly Bellies" />
</ITEM>
</CHANNEL>
```

Elements

CHANNEL

CROSS-REFERENCE
See **<ABSTRACT>**, **<LOG>**, **<LOGO>**, **<TITLE>**, and **<USAGE>**.

item

Method

DHTML

This method is used to retrieve a specific object from an identified collection as specified by the `vIndex` parameter.

This collection can be used in the following way:

```
[ oElement = ] object.item(vIndex [, iSubIndex] )
```

Parameters

oElement

This variable refers to an individual item in the array.

vIndex

This parameter is required and contains the number or string identifying the element or collection to retrieve. When a number is specified, the method returns the element in the zero-based collection at the identified position. When a string identifier is used and multiple elements with the same name or id attributes match the string, this method returns a collection of those matched elements.

iSubIndex

This optional parameter is used to identify the position of the element being retrieved when vIndex is a string. ISubIndex becomes the index of the specific item in the collection of matching elements identified by the vIndex string contents.

Objects

all	anchors	applets	areas
bookmarks	boundElements	cells	children
elements	embeds	filters	forms
frames	images	imports	links
options	plugins	rows	rules
scripts	styleSheets	tbodies	textRange

CROSS-REFERENCE

See **element**, **collection**, and **object**.

Java

Language

Around 1990, a small collection of programmers working at Sun Microsystems developed a programming language, temporarily labeled "Oak" after the trees seen outside the engineers' windows. The original plan for Oak was to use it for consumer electronics devices such as interactive television boxes and VCRs. When the Internet market exploded, rather than the Interactive TV market, these engineers grabbed Oak off the shelves and began developing a Web browser then called WebRunner, which was shortly followed by the development of the ancestor of Java applets, an animated mini-application to work with WebRunner.

By the end of 1994, Oak was a sophisticated language used to develop applets that could run anywhere, on anything, through the implementation of a virtual machine. By this time it could also be used to animate Web pages.

Then a new problem arose. The Oak and WebRunner trademarks had already been taken. Eventually a committee came up with the name "Java," probably over a cup of hot coffee. No matter the name, Java is likely the most hyped technology in the history of computing.

Java borrows quite a bit of its syntax and structure from C++. It has become an industrial-strength programming language with one claim to individuality that makes people take notice: the Java Virtual Machine.

Unlike most other programming languages, Java is not compiled. The Java Virtual Machine works like a go-between, interpreting Java programs for the computer on which it is running. This makes it possible for Java to be used on any operating system. This means that the developer only needs to write one version of a program, instead of three. Similarly, users don't have to worry about their applications not running on their computers, or any other device, for that matter.

In 1996, with the release of Netscape Navigator 2.0, Java began its explosion onto the Web. This browser provided a means for Java applets to be experienced and enjoyed by the masses. The improved functionality that Java gave to Web developers encouraged the growth of Java over the Web. Of course, its "write once, run anywhere" promise motivated developers to fall in love with this new programming language.

Within corporate computing departments, Java was seen as one solution for Information Systems (IS) departments, enabling them to keep one centrally stored software archive that is available to all the systems connected to the server. This allows every user of the network to install or upgrade software without any direct interaction with IS personnel. Java allows developers to create robust client server applications, and full-blown productivity programs just as you can with C or C++.

There are a few problems with counting on Java for your applications. If an application is not 100% pure Java, then it will run only on one operating system. The lack of some features, such as its own printing mechanism, forces some Java developers to create a core program, with multiple modules that can access various operating system printing features.

Another of Java's main drawbacks is that it requires a very powerful machine to run with acceptable performance on a desktop PC. Although 16-bit operating systems can run Java software, they run it quite slowly. Acceptable performance can be achieved on chips running 32-bit operating systems.

Although Java was designed to work in networked environments, and security was made a top priority, it still has a high risk of being interfered with. Sun made every attempt to completely secure Java but the researchers at Princeton University and the University of Washington, have found a few holes in Java's defenses. Sun has promptly closed all the leaks that these researchers have found, and so far there have been no reports of any criminal activity with data through a Java security hole. Even though Java is not impregnable, like most programming systems, it is fundamentally more secure than other type of executable code including ActiveX.

Java uses a security model wherein an applet runs within a confined environment a *sandbox*. Within this environment, it is supposed to be impossible for an applet to be programmed to corrupt data, delete files, or reformat a hard drive. This is due to the confined environment the application runs in, disallowing any contact with any area of memory or files not actually used by the applet. Of course this limits the functionality of the applet. To undo some of the damage this limitation does, Sun is trying to allow applets to perform specific tasks outside of the sandbox. These tasks could include writing data to a hard disk. This does lessen the security of the sandbox, it does allow for greater trust of your applet providers. Developers can now stamp their applets with digital certificates that identify the author. This means that if an applet damages a user's system, that user can identify the applet's publisher quickly and efficiently. The browsers also are now capable of letting users know when an applet is from and unknown source. This allows users to find applets from trusted vendors, thereby reducing their risk.

Future plans for Java include returning to Sun's original idea of using it to control consumer electronic devices such as cellular phones and TV Internet terminals. In order to bring this goal into existence, Sun is developing chips designed to solely read Java code. The ultimate goal of these chips is to run Java applets faster, with less cost, than other CPUs.

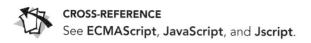

CROSS-REFERENCE
See **ECMAScript**, **JavaScript**, and **Jscript**.

javaEnabled

Method

DHTML

This element is used to identify whether or not the current user's browser can work with Java applications, and is set up to do so.

The syntax that allows you to use this method is as follows:

```
Enabled = object.javaEnabled()
```

Parameters

enabled

The value of this attribute is **true** if Java is enabled and **false** otherwise.

Object

navigator

CROSS-REFERENCE
See **appCodeName**, **appMinorVersion**, **appName**, **appVersion**, **browserLanguage**, **clientInformation**, **systemLanguage**, **userAgent**, and **userLanguage**.

JavaScript

Language

JavaScript is not Java, but they are related, even if loosely. Both of these languages are developing with both Sun's and Netscape's help, and are object-based, but only Java is a true programming language. JavaScript is just that, a scripting language that can be used to add client side controls for interactive Web pages, or as a server-side script for Active Server Pages being distributed by the Microsoft Internet Information Server. Using JavaScript, document authors can check that forms are properly filled out before they are submitted, they can send information to Java applets, use browser plug-ins, alter the contents of a document, or even simply identify user agents and proactively load copies of documents that work best for that browser.

JavaScript is an interpreted scripting language that has been designed to be simple enough that practically anyone with an interest, and some time, can learn to program with it. One of JavaScript's largest failings rests in the hands of corporate decision. JavaScript is not supported the same way Netscape and Microsoft browsers. Microsoft has their own flavor of JavaScript, called JScript, that includes commands which are not supported by Netscape, while at the same time, not supporting some of the Netscape commands.

In the mid-1990s, Netscape was pressing forward with JavaScript, promoting it as an "open Internet-scripting language standard" before handing it over to the ECMA, a European standards body. One of their current tasks is to synchronize their version of JavaScript with the new ECMAScripting standard that the ECMA produced. If the prayers of many Web developers are answered, then both Netscape and Microsoft will fully adopt the ECMAScript standard without adding all the personalized enhancements.

CROSS-REFERENCE
See **ECMAScript**, **Java**, and **JScript**.

JPG/JPEG

Concept

The Joint Photographic Experts Group (JPEG) was the original committee that designed the standard JPEG image compression algorithm. This format is capable of compressing full-color or gray-scale images with over 1.6 million colors. This gives the digital images a natural "real-world" sort of impression to your photographs. This format doesn't work well with cartoons or line drawn illustrations. It cannot compress black and white images, nor does it support animations or transparencies.

There is also a format known as progressive JPEG. This format is really a standard JPEG file that has had the compressed image data arranged into scans. This allows your document viewers to see a rough version of an image that will slowly improve in quality as your user agent downloads more data. This main advantage of using progressive JPEG files is also coupled with a somewhat smaller file size, allowing the information to load faster.

CROSS-REFERENCE
See **GIF** and **image**.

JScript

Language

The easiest way to describe JScript is "JavaScript with a twist." JScript is Microsoft's proprietary version of ECMAScript and JavaScript. JScript 3.0 is a full implementation of the ECMAScript specification, with additional enhancements used only with Internet Explorer. JScript, like JavaScript, shares some similarities with Java, but is not simply a cut-down version of that language. JScript is a true object-oriented scripting language.

CROSS-REFERENCE
See **ECMAScript**, **Java**, and **JavaScript**.

<KBD>

Element

HTML

Start Tag: Required
End Tag: Required

This element is used to identify text that should be entered by the user. It is most often used for instructions that are found on the Web. This element's content is generally shown by a user agent in a monospaced font.

Attribute

class

```
class="cdata-list"
```

This attribute is used to assign a class name to an element. User agents employ classes to group specific types of information for later use.

id

```
id="name"
```

This attribute is used to assign a name to an element.

lang

```
lang="language code"
```

This attribute specifies the language in which an element and its values should be rendered.

onclick

```
onclick=script
```

This attribute takes effect when a user clicks the button on a pointing device with the pointer over an element.

589

ondblclick

```
ondblclick=script
```

This attribute takes effect when the button on a pointing device is double-clicked with the pointer over an element.

onkeydown

```
onkeydown=script
```

This attribute takes effect when a key is pressed with the pointer over an element.

onkeypress

```
onkeypress=script
```

This attribute takes effect when a key is pressed and released with the pointer over an element.

onkeyup

```
onkeyup=script
```

This attribute takes effect when a key is released with the pointer over an element.

onmousedown

```
onmousedown=script
```

This attribute takes effect when the button on a pointing device is pressed with the pointer over an element.

onmousemove

```
onmousemove=script
```

This attribute is activated when the mouse is moved while the pointer is over an element.

onmouseout

```
onmouseout=script
```

This attribute is activated when the mouse pointer is moved away from an element.

onmouseover

```
onmouseover=script
```

This attribute is activated when the mouse pointer is moved over an element.

onmouseup

```
onmouseup=script
```

This attribute takes effect when the button on a pointing device is released with the pointer over an element.

style

```
style=style descriptors
```

This attribute is used to apply specific style-sheet information to one particular element.

title

```
title=text
```

This attribute serves to provide annotation information to the element.

Example

The following sample script provides instructions on how to open the text file autoexec.bat using the DOS Edit program. All of the commands that the user needs to type are displayed using the KBD tags.

ON THE CD-ROM

Look for **kbd.htm** on the accompanying CD-ROM.

```html
<html>
<head>
<title>keyboard code</title>
</head>

<body bgcolor="#FFFFFF">
<h1>Opening a file in DOS Edit</h1>
<ol>
  <li>At the <b>C:\&gt;</b> prompt type: <kbd>edit</kbd></li>
  <li>Open the <b>File</b> menu, and select <b>Open</b>.</li>
  <li>In the filename field type: <kbd>autoexec.bat</kbd></li>
  <li>Click the <b>Open</b> button.</li>
</ol>
</body>
</html>
```

CROSS-REFERENCE

See **<CITE>**, **<CODE>**, and **<VAR>**.

keyCode

Property

DHTML

This property is used to either set or retrieve the UNICODE key code that is associated with the key that caused an event to fire.

The syntax of this command is

```
event.keycode= string
```

Parameters

string

This string contains the UNICODE code for the key that triggered the event. There is no default value for this parameter. If no key caused the event, then the value of this string is 0.

Objects

event

CROSS-REFERENCE
See **events**, **onkeydown**, **onkeyup**, and **onkeypress**.

<LABEL>

Element

HTML

Start Tag: Required
End Tag: Required

Many form elements have labels that can be applied to them with their value attribute. The LABEL element is provided for use with FORM items that do not have an explicit label already applied to them. Each LABEL element is attached to exactly one form control. The LABEL element will automatically pass on focus to its associated element whenever it receives the focus of the document reader. Labels may be treated by a user agent in a variety of ways, such as being read by a speech synthesizer or being displayed graphically.

Attributes

accesskey

    accesskey="character"

You can assign an access key to an element. This key allows you to put quick focus on an element. In the case of a form element, the user is immediately able to input information. In the case of a link, the link is activated and followed.

class

    class="cdata-list"

This attribute is used to assign a class name to an element. User agents employ classes to group specific types of information for later use.

dir

    dir = LTR | RTL | [CS | CI | CN | CA | CT]

This attribute defines the direction of the text flow in a document so a user agent can display it correctly. It can also be used to specify information about the case of the characters.

for

> for="*idref*"

This attribute is used to explicitly associate the label with a form control. In a form, the value of this attribute must match the value of an id attribute of another form control. If this attribute is absent, the label being defined is associated with an element's contents.

id

> id="*name*"

This attribute is used to assign a name to an element.

lang

> lang="*language code*"

This attribute specifies the language in which an element and its values should be rendered.

onblur

> onblur=*script*

This attribute activates when an element loses the focus either through the actions of a mouse (or other pointing device), or by tabbing navigation.

onclick

> onclick=*script*

This attribute takes effect when a user clicks the button on a pointing device with the pointer over an element.

ondblclick

> ondblclick=*script*

This attribute takes effect when the button on a pointing device is double-clicked with the pointer over an element.

onfocus

> onfocus=*script*

This attribute is in effect when an element receives focus from either a mouse or another pointing device, or through tabbed navigation.

onkeydown

> onkeydown=*script*

This attribute takes effect when a key is pressed while the pointer is over an element.

onkeypress

> onkeypress=*script*

This attribute takes effect when a key is pressed and released with the pointer over an element.

onkeyup

> onkeyup=*script*

This attribute takes effect when a key is released with the pointer over an element.

onmousedown

> onmousedown=*script*

This attribute takes effect when the button on a pointing device is pressed with the pointer over an element.

onmousemove

> onmousemove=*script*

This attribute is activated when the mouse is moved while the pointer is over an element.

onmouseout

> onmouseout=*script*

This attributed is activated when the mouse pointer is moved away from an element.

onmouseover

> onmouseover=*script*

This attribute is activated when the mouse pointer is moved over an element.

onmouseup

> onmouseup=*script*

This attribute takes effect when the button on a pointing device is released with the pointer over an element.

style

> style=*style descriptors*

This attribute is used to apply specific style-sheet information to one particular element.

k
l
m

tabindex

```
tabindex=number
```

This attribute provides the position of the current element within the overall tabbing order of the document.

title

```
title=text
```

This attribute serves to provide annotation information to the element.

Examples

The following form uses the LABEL element to request information for its particulat fields. Currently no visual change can be seen by using the LABEL element (in comparison to the typical method of just inserting text before the INPUT tab), but this may change. This also allows you to make an indelible (unbreakable) link your between your label and your form control.

ON THE CD-ROM

Look for **label.htm** on the accompanying CD-ROM.

```
<HTML>
   <HEAD>
      <TITLE> Labels used in a form.</TITLE>
   </HEAD>
   <BODY>
      <FORM action="...." method="post">
      <P>
      <LABEL for="firstname">First name: </LABEL>
      <INPUT type="text" id="firstname"><BR>
      <LABEL for="lastname">Last name: </LABEL>
      <INPUT type="text" id="lastname"><BR>
      <LABEL for="email">email: </LABEL>
      <INPUT type="text" id="email"><BR>
      <INPUT type="radio" name="sex" value="Male"> Male<BR>
      <INPUT type="radio" name="sex" value="Female">
Female<BR>
      <INPUT type="submit" value="Send">
      <INPUT type="reset">
      </P>
      </FORM>
   </BODY>
</HTML>
```

This example uses a table to align two text input controls and their associated labels. Each label is associated with only one text input field.

```
<HTML>
  <HEAD>
    <TITLE> Label within a Table</TITLE>
  </HEAD>
  <BODY>
    <FORM action="..." method="post">
    <TABLE>
      <TR>
      <TD><LABEL for="email">E-mail Address</LABEL>
      <TD><INPUT type="text" name="email" id="email">
      </TR>
      <TR>
      <TD><LABEL for="waddy">Web Address</LABEL>
      <TD><INPUT type="text" name="webaddy" id="waddy">
      <TR>
    </TABLE>
    </FORM>
  </BODY>
</HTML>
```

It is also possible to directly link a LABEL element to a control element by embedding the control within the label. When you are doing this, the LABEL element can only contain a single control element. (You cannot use this system for linking a control with its label if a table is being used for formatting and the label appearing in one cell but the control appears in another.)

```
<HTML>
  <HEAD>
    <TITLE> Embedded Labels and Controls</TITLE>
  </HEAD>
  <BODY>
    <FORM action="..." method="post">
    <P>
    <LABEL>
    First Name
    <INPUT type="text" name="firstname">
    </LABEL>
    <LABEL>
    <INPUT type="text" name="lastname">
```

```
      Last Name
      </LABEL>
      </P>
      </FORM>
   <BODY>
</HTML>
```

lang

Attribute

HTML

In short, the `lang` attribute allows the document author to specify the language to be used in a document, or on a specified element. This attribute can be used in a variety of ways, including these:

- Define the way a user agent renders special characters and the spacing between them.
- Assist search engines.
- Assist speech synthesizers.
- Assist spell checkers and grammar checkers.

The ultimate goal of this command is to allow user agents to display characters in a more meaningful way to the culture that is reading the language represented. The user agent must display all the characters in the document, no matter the `lang` attribute's value. By identifying the language, it allows the user agent to avoid presenting "junk" to the individual reading the document. By identifying the language, the user agent should be able to acquire the utilities needed to correctly display the document, or at least provide the reader with useable error messages explaining why the document is not legible.

Some of the language codes being used don't follow the accepted two-letter codes shown in the chart later in this section. Some of them, like the ones that follow here, use a slightly different system to discuss the language being represented.

- `"en-UK"` — The United Kingdom version of English.
- `"en-cockney"` — The Cockney version of English.
- `"i-navajo"` — The Navajo language spoken by certain Native Americans.
- `"x-klingon"` — The primary tag "x" indicates an experimental language tag. In this case, it refers to the popular *Star Trek*-invented Klingon language.

Computer languages are explicitly prohibited from acquiring a language code. Table L-1 lists legitimate language code.

Table L-1 Accepted Country Language Codes

Language	Language Code	Language Family
Abkhazian	ab	Ibero-Caucasian
Afan (Oromo)	om	Hamitic
Afar	aa	Hamitic
Afrikaans	Af	Germanic
Albanian	sq	Indo-European (Other)
Amharic	am	Semitic
Arabic	Ar	Semitic
Armenian	hy	Indo-European (Other)
Assamese	as	Indian
Aymara	ay	Amerindian
Azerbaijani	az	Turkic/Altaic
Bashkir	ba	Turkic/Altaic
Basque	eu	Basque
Bengali; Bangla	bn	Indian
Bhutani	dz	Asian
Bihari	bh	Indian
Bislama	bi	[Not Given]
Breton	br	Celtic
Bulgarian	bg	Slavic
Burmese	my	Asian
Byelorussian	be	Slavic
Cambodian	km	Asian
Catalan	ca	Romance
Chinese	zh	Asian
Corsican	co	Romance
Croatian	hr	Slavic
Czech	cs	Slavic
Danish	da	Germanic
Dutch	nl	Germanic
English	en	Germanic
Esperanto	eo	International Aux.
Estonian	et	Finno-Ugric
Faroese	fo	Germanic
Fiji	fj	Oceanic/Indonesian

Continued

Table L-1 *Continued*

Language	Language Code	Language Family
Finnish	fi	Finno-Ugric
French	fr	Romance
Frisian	fy	Germanic
Galician	gl	Romance
Georgian	ka	Ibero-Caucasian
German	de	Germanic
Greek	el	Latin/Greek
Greenlandic	kl	Eskimo
Guarani	gn	Amerindian
Gujarati	gu	Indian
Hausa	ha	Negro-African
Hebrew	he	Semitic
Hindi	hi	Indian
Hungarian	hu	Finno-Ugric
Icelandic	is	Germanic
Indonesian	id	Oceanic/Indonesian
Interlingua	ia	International Aux.
Interlingue	ie	International Aux.
Inuktitut	iu	[Not Given]
Inupiak	ik	Eskimo
Irish	ga	Celtic
Italian	it	Romance
Japanese	ja	Asian
Javanese	Jv	Oceanic/Indonesian
Kannada	kn	Dravidian
Kashmiri	ks	Indian
Kazakh	kk	Turkic/Altaic
Kinyarwanda	rw	Negro-African
Kirghiz	ky	Turkic/Altaic
Kurundi	rn	Negro-African
Korean	ko	Asian
Kurdish	ku	Iranian
Laothian	lo	Asian
Latin	la	Latin/Greek
Latvian; Lettish	lv	Baltic
Lingala	ln	Negro-African
Lithuanian	lt	Baltic
Macedonian	mk	Slavic

Language	Language Code	Language Family
Malagasy	mg	Oceanic/Indonesian
Malay	ms	Oceanic/Indonesian
Malayalam	ml	Dravidian
Maltese	mt	Semitic
Maori	mi	Oceanic/Indonesian
Marathi	mr	Indian
Moldavian	mo	Romance
Mongolian	mn	[Not Given]
Nauru	na	[Not Given]
Nepali	ne	Indian
Norwegian	no	Germanic
Occitan	oc	Romance
Oriya	or	Indian
Pashto; Pushto	ps	Iranian
Persian (Farsi)	fa	Iranian
Polish	pl	Slavic
Portuguese	pt	Romance
Punjabi	pa	Indian
Quechua	qu	Amerindian
Rhaeto-Romance	rm	Romance
Romanian	ro	Romance
Russian	ru	Slavic
Samoan	sm	Oceanic/Indonesian
Sangho	sg	Negro-African
Sanskrit	sa	Indian
Scots Gaelic	gd	Celtic
Serbian	sr	Slavic
Serbo-Croatian	sh	Slavic
Sesotho	st	Negro-African
Setswana	tn	Negro-African
Shona	sn	Negro-African
Sindhi	sd	Indian
Singhalese	si	Indian
Siswati	ss	Negro-African
Slovak	sk	Slavic
Slovenian	sl	Slavic
Somali	so	Hamitic
Spanish	es	Romance
Sudanese	su	Oceanic/Indonesian

Continued

k
l
m

Table L-1 *Continued*

Language	Language Code	Language Family
Swahili	sw	Negro-African
Swedish	sv	Germanic
Tagalog	tl	Oceanic/Indonesian
Tajik	tg	Iranian
Tamil	ta	Dravidian
Tatar	tt	Turkic/Altaic
Telugu	te	Dravidian
Thai	th	Asian
Tibetan	bo	Asian
Tigrinya	ti	Semitic
Tonga	to	Oceanic/Indonesian
Tsonga	ts	Negro-African
Turkish	tr	Turkic/Altaic
Turkmen	tk	Turkic/Altaic
Twi	tw	Negro-African
Uigur	ug	[Not Given]
Ukrainian	uk	Slavic
Urdu	ur	Indian
Uzbek	uz	Turkic/Altaic
Vietnamese	vi	Asian
Volapuk	vo	International Aux.
Welsh	cy	Celtic
Wolof	wo	Negro-African
Xhosa	xh	Negro-African
Yiddish	yi	Germanic
Yoruba	yo	Negro-African
Zhuang	za	[Not Given]
Zulu	zu	Negro-African

Examples

In this example, the paragraph has mixed Greek and English text. In this instance, the user agent will attempt to render all the English content, and then make its best attempt to display the Greek characters in the statement even though they are not English characters.

```
<P><BLOCKQUOTE lang="en">She was a member of &Alpha;&Lambda
&Delta; during her Freshman  year of college.</BLOCKQUOTE>
```

The following code shows a short document written in Hebrew, with the lang attributes being applied to the HEAD and BODY portions of the document. This document will be displayed using roman characters with the appropriate Hebrew inflections on a user agent that supports the Hebrew language.

 ON THE CD-ROM

Look for lang.htm on the accompanying CD-ROM.

```
<HTML>
   <HEAD lang="he">
      <TITLE> Hebrew Language Document </TITLE>
   </HEAD>
   <BODY lang="he">
      <H1> A Song for Peace</H1>
      <P> tnu lashemsh la'a lot<BR>
      laboker lehair<BR>
      hazaka shebatfilot<BR>
      otanu lo tahzir<BR>
      <P> Mi asher kava nero<BR>
      U'VeAfar nitman<BR>
      Bechi mar lo yairo<BR>
      lo yahziro lechan<BR>
      <P> Ish otanu lo yashiv<BR>
      mibor tachtit afel<BR>
      kan lo yoilu<BR>
      lo shirei hanitzahon <BR>
      Velo shirei hallel<BR>
      <P> Lachen rak shiru shir lashalom<BR>
      al tilchashu tfila<BR>
      lachren rak shiru shir lashalom<BR>
      bitzeaka gdola<BR>
      <P>tnu lashemesh lahador<BR>
      mibaad laprachim<BR>
      al tabitu leachor<BR>
      hanichu laholchim<BR>
      <P>s'eu einayim betikva<BR>
      lo derech kavanot<BR>
      shiru shir la'ahava<BR>
      velo lamilhamot<BR>
      <P>al tagidu yom yavo<BR>
      havi'u et hayom<BR>
      ki lo halom hu<BR>
      uv'hol hakikarot<BR>
     hari'u lashalom<BR>
      <P align="right"> <I> - Unknown - </I>
```

```
        </BODY>
    </HTML>
```

Elements

A	ABBR	ACRONYM	ADDRESS
AREA	B	BDO	BIG
BLOCKQUOTE	BODY	BUTTON	CAPTION
CENTER	CITE	CODE	COL
COLGROUP	DD	DEL	DFN
DIR	DIV	DL	DT
EM	FIELDSET	FONT	FORM
H1–H6	HEAD	HTML	I
IMG	INPUT	INS	ISINDEX
KBD	LABEL	LEGEND	LI
LINK	MAP	MENU	META
NOFRAMES	NOSCRIPT	OBJECT	OL
OPTGROUP	OPTION	P	PRE
Q	S	SAMP	SELECT
SMALL	SPAN	STRIKE	STRONG
STYLE	SUB	SUP	TABLE
TBODY	TD	TEXTAREA	TFOOT
TH	THEAD	TITLE	TR
TT	U	UL	VAR

CROSS-REFERENCE
See %LangCodes and Language Identification.

lang

Property

DHTML

This property is used to specify the language that will be used in the text of the document. Just as with the lang HTML attribute, the value of this attribute is one of the ISO standard language abbreviations. Because this property has both read and write values, you can use it to retrieve the current lang value or to set the lang value for an HTML element.

The syntax for this scripting command is

```
object.lang[=slang]
```

Parameters
slang

This string holds the name of the language to be applied, or that has been applied to the selected object.

Example

The following code displays a statement that has been written in Hebrew, and then uses JavaScript to discover its lang specification, switch the specification to English, and write a line showing us the original specification setting.

ON THE CD-ROM

Look for **lang2.htm** on the accompanying CD-ROM.

```
<HTML>
    <HEAD>
        <TITLE>JavaScript Set and Retrieve Lang </TITLE>
    </HEAD>
    <BODY lang="he">
        <P> Mi asher kava nero<BR>
        U'VeAfar nitman<BR>
        Bechi mar lo yairo<BR>
        lo yahziro lechan<BR>
        <SCRIPT language="JavaScript">
            {
            OrigLang=document.body.lang;
            document.writeln("<P lang='en'>This document was
written in: "+OrigLang);
            }
        </SCRIPT>
    </BODY>
</HTML>
```

Elements

A	ACRONYM	ADDRESS	APPLET
AREA	B	BIG	BLOCKQUOTE
BODY	BUTTON	CAPTION	CENTER
CITE	CODE	DD	DEL
DFN	DIR	DIV	DL

DT	EM	EMBED	FIELDSET
FONT	FORM	FRAME	FRAMESET
H1–H6	I	IFRAME	IMG
INPUT	INS	KBD	LABEL
LEGEND	LI	LISTING	MAP
MARQUEE	MENU	OBJECT	OL
OPTION	P	PLAINTEXT	PRE
Q	S	SAMP	SELECT
SMALL	SPAN	STRIKE	STRONG
SUB	SUP	TABLE	TBODY
TD	TEXTAREA	TFOOT	TH
THEAD	TITLE	TR	TT
U	UL	VAR	XMP

 CROSS-REFERENCE
See lang (HTML Attribute).

langcode

Attribute

XML

This XML attribute identifies the language being used in the document. The value of this attribute can be any one of the following:

- Any two-letter language code as defined by ISO639 that discusses the "Codes for the representation of names of languages."

- Any language identifier that has been registered with the Internet Assigned Numbers Authority (IANA). All of these identifiers begin with the prefix "i-" or "I-".

- Any language identifier that has been created by a document author, or that has been agreed upon between parties for private use are also available. These created language codes must begin with the prefix "x-" or "X-" to make sure that they don't conflict with future names standardized or registered with IANA.

The langcode values are not case-sensitive, unlike most other XML values, although they are typically displayed in lowercase. Country codes are typically displayed in uppercase.

The `langcode` **format is**

```
langcode::= ISO639Code | IANACode | UserCode
```

CROSS-REFERENCE
See language identification, lang, and languageID.

language

Property

DHTML

This property is used to identify the language that the script is written in. This is a read-only property for accessing the language of a script from within itself, or another script.

It uses the following syntax:

```
object.language=scriptname
```

There are only four values currently available for this property:

- javascript   Specifies JavaScript
- jscript   Specifies JavaScript
- vbs   Specifies VBScript
- vbscript   Specifies VBScript

Example

The following code is used to specify the scripting language being used in SCRIPT element.

ON THE CD-ROM
Look for **language.htm** on the accompanying CD-ROM.

```
<SCRIPT language= "javascript">
   {
   document.writeln ("This is a test of the American
Broadcasting system.");
   }
</SCRIPT>
```

Elements

A	ACRONYM	ADDRESS	APPLET
AREA	B	BIG	BLOCKQUOTE
BODY	BR	BUTTON	CAPTION
CENTER	CITE	CODE	DD
DEL	DFN	DIR	DIV
DL	EM	EMBED	FIELDSET
FONT	FORM	FRAME	FRAMESET
H1–H6	I	IFRAME	IMG
INPUT	INS	KBD	LABEL
LEGEND	LI	LISTING	MAP
MARQUEE	OBJECT	OL	OPTION
P	PLAINTEXT	PRE	Q
S	SAMP	SCRIPT	SELECT
SMALL	SPAN	STRIKE	STRONG
SUB	SUP	TABLE	TBODY
TD	TEXTAREA	TFOOT	TH
THEAD	TR	TT	U
UL	VAR	XMP	

CROSS-REFERENCE
See JavaScript, JScript, and VBScript.

<LANGUAGE>

Element

OSD

Start Tag: Required
End Tag: Forbidden

In the Open Software Description, the LANGUAGE element is used within the IMPLEMENTATION OSD element to specify the required natural language of the software application being specified. There can be multiple instances of this command within a single IMPLEMENTATION statement. If this element is not specified, then it is assumed that this software runs on all language platforms.

Attribute
value

```
value="language code"
```

The single attribute of the OSD LANGUAGE element specifies the language code to be used. These codes are the same as what has been detailed in the discussion of the lang attribute.

Example
The following code lists the discussed software as being valid for English and French platforms, but should not be used on any other platform.

```
<IMPLEMENTATION>
    <LANGUAGE value= "en" />
    <LANGUAGE value= "fr" />
</IMPLEMENTATION>
```

CROSS-REFERENCE
See lang, <IMPLEMENTATION>, and <OSD>.

Language

Concept

There are many different languages being used on computer systems across the globe. Software has to be adjusted to work with each of these language bases. For example, Microsoft has English, German, Japanese, French, and other versions of their popular operating systems. For each of these internationalized operating systems, you must have software that is designed to work with it properly. Not only does this process of internationalization (or localization) not force everyone across the globe to learn to read English, it provides a fuller computer experience for all global users.

By identifying specific languages in your documents, in the case of HTML and Cascading Style Sheets, you can give your user agent the chance to display readable material and not "garbage" to the viewer. An identified language gives the user agent the chance to acquire the utilities it needs to correctly present the document, or provide the reader with a useable error message explaining why the document is not readable. In the case of OSD, identifying the natural language of a software product gives the user's operating environment the information it needs to decide whether it can use the software that has been made available to it.

CROSS-REFERENCE
See Internationalization.

Language Binding

Concept

Language binding is a term used for describing the interaction that occurs to force a specific implementation of an interface in a specific programming language. This specific implementation is controlled through the Interface Definition Language (IDL), which defines interfaces used when accessing and operating upon objects within a software environment. You might also think of this as a way of forcing an interface to always be used for a specific implementation of a program. Think of this as always adding the cream and sugar to your coffee. You can't drink it otherwise.

One example of language binding can be seen with the Java implementation for the Document Object Model IDL. In this instance, the DOM IDL would use the concrete Java classes that are used to provide the software functionality that has been exposed through the interface.

 CROSS-REFERENCE
See Interface Definition Language (IDL).

Language Identification

Concept

XML

XML documents provide you with the ability to specify languages to be used for displaying a document. The process involved in identifying the language controls the display of the characters on the document depending upon the type of user agent reading it, and that agent's base language. When the language is identified, it allows the user agent to avoid presenting "garbage" to the reader. By identifying the language, the user agent will be able to acquire the utilities it needs to correctly present the document, or at least provide the reader with a useable error message explaining why the document is not readable.

LanguageID

This identifier is used within an XML statement to set the language to be used. This identifier is a combination of the Langcode and the Subcode.

Langcode

This attribute is used to identify the language being used in the document.

ISO639Code

The specific codes registered with the ISO for identifying specific languages in use on public networks.

IanaCode

The specific codes used by the IANA for identifying specific languages that have been registered with the IANA.

UserCode

Personalized language codes that have been created for identifying a specific user agent.

SubCode

Subcodes are used to identify specific languages within an existing category. For example, Klingon is a specific type of usercode language.

Definition

```
LanguageID::=Langcode (- Subcode)
        Langcode::= ISO639Code | IANACode | UserCode
        Subcode::= ([a-z] | [A-Z])+
                ISO639Code::= ([a-z] | [A-Z]) ([a-z] | [A-Z])
                IANACode::= ('i' | 'I') '-' ([a-z] | [A-Z])+
                UserCode::= ('x' | 'X') '-' ([a-z] | [A-Z])+
```

Example

```
<p xml:lang="en">Peter Piper picked a peck of pickled
peppers.</p>
<p xml:lang="en-GB">Is that flavour vanilla?</p>
<p xml:lang="en-US">Is that flavor vanilla?</p>
<p xml:lang="he"> Ganna Gidel dgnim bagan, diganim gadlu bgan
shell hagannan.</p>
```

CROSS-REFERENCE
See lang and langcode.

languageID

Attribute

XML

The `languageID` attribute contains the information that is assigned to the `xml:lang` declaration when it is used within an element. This attribute's value holds the combination of the `langcode` and `subcode` values.

```
languageID::=langcode (- subcode)
```

CROSS-REFERENCE
See Language Identification.

<LASTMOD>

Element

CDF

Start Tag: Required
End Tag: Forbidden

This element contains the last date that the document was modified. This value can be used to decide when to send out a new copy of the channel documentation, or to decide if a new copy needs to be retrieved. This element can only be used within a `CHANNEL` or an `ITEM` element block.

Attribute
value

```
value="date code"
```

This attribute specifies the date, in YYYY.MM.DDTHH:MM-SSSS format, of the last time that the document was modified.

Example
The following example sets the last modified date for a channel located at http://mychannels.com/channels.cdf.

```
<CHANNEL HREF="http://mychannels.com/channels.cdf ">
    <LASTMOD value="1999.01.10T00:15-0300" />
</CHANNEL>
```

Elements

CHANNEL   ITEM

CROSS-REFERENCE
See Channel Definition Format (CDF), and %datetime.

lastModified

Property

DHTML

This property is read-only and applies to the document object. It can be used within a script to control document manipulation options based upon the currency of the document. You cannot change the value of this attribute.

```
document.lastModified
```

Objects
document

The document object represents the current HTML document being displayed by the user agent.

Examples
The following example uses the lastModified attribute to display a message to the document reader if that date can not be found.

ON THE CD-ROM
Look for **lastmod.htm** on the accompanying CD-ROM.

```
<HTML>
  <HEAD>
    <TITLE> lastModified Script Attribute</TITLE>
    <SCRIPT Language="javascript">
    {
      if (document.lastModified =="")
        alert ("This document was created by Cleopatra. I
think!")
    }
    </SCRIPT>
    </HEAD>
    <BODY>
```

```
        <H1> Welcome to Caesar's Egyptian palace.</H1>
    </BODY>
</HTML>
```

In the following code, the `lastModified` attribute is checked and written to the page to inform the user of the last time the document had been edited.

ON THE CD-ROM
Look for **lastmod2.htm** on the accompanying CD-ROM.

```
<HTML>
    <HEAD>
        <TITLE> lastModified Script Attribute: Take 2</TITLE>
    </HEAD>
    <BODY>
        <P>Check out the date of this last edit!
        <SCRIPT Language="javascript">
        {
                if (document.lastModified =="")
                    document.write ("Last Modification Date
Unknown!<BR>");
                else {
                    LastEditDate = document.lastModified;
                    document.write (LastEditDate);
                }
        }
            </SCRIPT>
    </BODY>
</HTML>
```

CROSS-REFERENCE
See JavaScript and DHTML.

<LATESTTIME>

Element

CDF

Start Tag: Required
End Tag: Forbidden

This is simply the latest time during the specified Channel delivery schedule that the channel information will be sent. This element can only be used as a child of the SCHEDULE element.

Attributes
day

    day="number"

This integer represents the day of the month the channel document should be delivered.

hour

    hour="number"

This is the hour of the day in a 24-hour format.

min

    min="number"

This is an integer between 1 and 60 representing a minute interval during a singular hour.

sec

    sec="number"

This is an integer between 1 and 60 representing a second interval during a singular specified minute.

Example
This example channel, at http://mychannels.com/channels.cdf must be delivered between midnight and noon on the first of each month.

```
<CHANNEL HREF="http://mychannels.com/channels.cdf ">
  <SCHEDULE>
    <INTERVALTIME Day=30 />
    <EARLIESTTIME Hour=0 />
    <LATESTTIME Hour=12 />
  </SCHEDULE>
</CHANNEL>
```

Element

SCHEDULE

CROSS-REFERENCE
See Channel Definition Format.

<LAYER>

Element

HTML—Netscape Only

Start Tag: Required
End Tag: Required

This element is the Netscape alternative to the Cascading Style Sheet layering method using multidimensional styles. The `LAYER` element provides you with the ability to view pages using precisely positioned overlapping layers of transparent or opaque content. Web developers can use JavaScript to move, hide, reorder, and/or modify specific layers of content. Using JavaScript and HTML combined, you can create highly interactive animations on your Web pages. One application of joining technologies is to create a series of overlapping layers that can be dynamically peeled away revealing the underlying content. This system works for diagrams and displays showing engineering schematics. It can also be used to tell a story in a new way.

The `LAYER` tag has a variety of attributes that you can control, including transparency and opaqueness. Transparent layers show the contents of the layers below it, as if you were writing on glass. Background images and colors can be defined for your layers, just as they are for the main body of an HTML document. Of course, setting those background attributes will hide the layers that lie below it.

Unlike the `SPAN` command which uses a layering order and an x,y positioning system to designate the order and location of a particular block element, the `LAYER` command has an intrinsic order and position for an entire series of blocks. This z-order layering system is referred to as the "stacking order." In this system, Layer A serves as a base. Layer B is above A. Layer C is above B, and so on. The `LAYER` command allows you to place layers within layers. This allows you to create a layer that contains an additional layer.

The `LAYER` tag is placed inside the `BODY` of the page. When you use this tag, you do not need to define the layer before identifying the content. The `LAYER` command is not standard, and only recent Netscape browsers are capable of reading the CSS standard commands. **This command is not recommended.**

Attributes
above

    above="layername"

This attribute specifies the name of the layer that will be immediately on top of the layer being specified. If you use the `above` attribute, you cannot use the `z-index` or `below` attributes for this layer being created. Before you can use this attribute, the layer you are specifying must have already been created.

background

```
background="url"
```

This attribute specifies the URL of the background image used on this layer. By default, a layer is transparent, so setting this attribute will make the layer opaque.

below

```
below="layername"
```

This attribute specifies the name of the layer that will be immediately below the layer being specified. If you use the below attribute, you cannot use the z-index or above attributes for this layer being created. Before you can use this attribute, the layer you are specifying must have already been created.

bgcolor

```
bgcolor="rgbColor | colorname"
```

This attribute specifies either the name of the standard color for the background, or the RGB value of the color to be used in the background of the layer. By setting a background color on a layer, you will lose that layer's inherent transparency.

clip

```
clip="x1_offset, y1_offset, x2_offset, y2_offset"
```

This attribute specifies the dimensions of the portion of the layer that should be displayed by your user agent. Any portion of text or images outside of these dimensions will be treated as transparent objects. Each number specified in the clip attribute must be an integer.

The *x1_offset* and the *y1_offset* specify which upper-left coordinates of the text and images should be displayed. The *x2_offset* and *y2_offset* specify the lower-right corner of the image to be displayed. If either set of offsets is not specified, they will default to the outer edges of the layer. For example, if you do not specify an *x1_offset* and *y1_offset* pair, it will default to (0,0). If you do not specify a *x2_offset* and *y2_offset* pair, it will default to the lower right corner of the layer.

If the clip attribute is omitted in its entirety, the entire layer will be visible.

height

```
height=layerHeight
```

This attribute serves as a reference for the length of the layer being displayed.

left

```
left=xPosition
```

This is the leftmost position of the layer. If a specific number of pixels have been specified, this attribute will be the number of pixels from the left margin of your browser screen. If a percentage is entered at this attribute, your layers will move by that percentage of the total screen size to the right of your left browser margin.

name

```
name="layername"
```

This attribute specifies the identifying name for your layer. When you use multiple layers and wish a script to interact with them individually, specify identifying names for each layer.

src

```
src="url"
```

This attribute automatically places all of the content on the page referenced into the layer being created.

top

```
top=yPosition
```

This attribute specifies either the pixel or relative location of the top edge of your layer. If a specific number of pixels have been specified, your layer will begin that number of pixels down from the top edge of your browser window. If a percentage has been specified, your layer will begin that percentage of your browser screen down from the top of your browser window.

visibility

```
visibility= "show | hide | inherit"
```

This attribute is used to specify whether the layer is initially displayed through the user agent. Show specifies that the layer should be visible. Hide designates that the layer should be considered invisible. The inherit value indicates that this layer will use the same visibility value as its parent layer. By default, this attribute is set to inherit.

width

```
width=layerWidth
```

This attribute specifies the total width of your layer. This number must be either an integer value (signed or unsigned) or a percentage. By setting the width of your layer, you can control how the text on your screen is wrapped within a specific layer.

z-index

```
z-index=layerZ
```

This attribute is used to specify the stacking order of the layers. If you do not specify this attribute, the layers will be stacked in the order of their creation. Layers with higher numbered z-index values will be placed above layers with lower values. If you use the z-index attribute when creating a layer, neither the above nor below attributes can be used.

Examples

The following example creates multiple layers, in a book form, and uses scripting to move the layers off of each other one at a time, so you can read the remainder of the text in the "book."

ON THE CD-ROM

Look for **layer.htm** on the accompanying CD-ROM.

```
<HTML>
   <HEAD>
      <TITLE> Netscape Layer Tag</TITLE>
   </HEAD>
   <BODY>
      <P>The cover image should rotate for you every 5 seconds.
      <BR>
       So sit back and enjoy.</P>
      <LAYER name="bookback" top=75 left=25 visibility=show>
         <IMG SRC="bookback.gif">
      </LAYER>
      <LAYER name="quotes" top=100 left=50 visibility=show>
         Laughter is a tranquilizer with no side effects. <BR>
                - Unknown
         <P>More than kisses, letters mingle souls. <BR>
               - John Donne
         <P>The best way to get a bad law repealed <BR>
                is to enforce it strictly.<BR>
                -Abraham Lincoln
      </LAYER>
      <LAYER name="bookfront" top=75 left=25 visibility=hide>
         <IMG SRC="bookfront.gif">
      </LAYER>
      <SCRIPT language="javascript">
       {
       bookfront = document.layers['bookfront'];
       setInterval ("showcover()", 5000);
       function showcover()          {
```

k
l
m

```
                    if (bookfront.visibility=="hide")        {
                       bookfront.visibility="show";
                      } else {
                        bookfront.visibility="hide";
                         }
                    }
                  }
              </SCRIPT>
            </BODY>
          </HTML>
```

CROSS-REFERENCE
See <DHTML>, <SPAN>, JavaScript, and **Style Sheets**.

Leading

Concept

CSS2

Leading is a term used to refer to the difference in height between the size of a font character and the height of the line that font is displayed on. When fonts are smaller than their line height, they should be split over the line height leaving a half-leading on either side of the font. For example, if you have an 18-point font, and a 24-point line height, the font would be positioned so 3 points of empty space would appear both above and below the text.

CROSS-REFERENCE
See **half-leading** and **line-height**.

left

Attribute

CSS

The left Cascading Style Sheet attribute specifies the distance between the left edge of the object box and the left edge of the containing block.

    left=length | percentage | auto | inherit

Values
length

> This is the amount of the offset in pixels. This value is any whole signed or unsigned integer.

percentage

> This is the percentage of offset from the edge of the reference side of the containing block. The percentage is based upon the visible area of the page in your user agent.

auto

> This is the default setting, and automatically calculates the offset based upon the width and height of the object box.

inherit

> The value for this distance is inherited from its parent elements.

Elements
This attribute is available for all HTML elements.

CROSS-REFERENCE
See @page, margin, padding, and containing block.

left

Property

DHTML

This property is used in conjunction with a style sheet to either set or retrieve the position of an element in relation to the left edge of the document being displayed. This property can be used with a variety of HTML elements.

```
object.style.left[=length]
```

The value of this readable and writable property is a string element containing a floating-point integer with a unit designator as used with the length Cascading Style Sheets value.

Examples
This example uses the left property to retrieve the value of leftmost position of an image.

```
<HTML>
  <HEAD>
    <TITLE>JavaScript Retrieve Left </TITLE>
    <STYLE type="text/css">
    <!-
       IMG   {left: 5cm}
    ->
    </STYLE>
  </HEAD>
  <BODY>
    <IMG id="turtle" src="turtle.gif" alt="A lovely green
box turtle." tyle="left: 5cm">
    <SCRIPT language="JavaScript">
       {
       turtleImg=document.images['turtle'];
       turtleLeft=turtleImg.style.left;
       document.writeln("The left edge of this image is
located at: "+turtleLeft);
       }
    </SCRIPT>
  </BODY>
</HTML>
```

NOTE
This property works with Internet Explorer and is not part of the Netscape JavaScript command language.

Example 2
This example uses the left property to set the position of the same image.

```
<HTML>
  <HEAD>
    <TITLE>JavaScript Set Left </TITLE>
  </HEAD>
  <BODY>
    <IMG id="turtle" src="turtle.gif" alt="A lovely green
box turtle." Style="left:100px">
    <SCRIPT language="JavaScript">
```

```
          {
          turtleImg=document.images[0];
          turtleImg.style.left="250px";
          }
        </SCRIPT>
      </BODY>
    </HTML>
```

Elements

A	ADDRESS	APPLET	B
BIG	BLOCKQUOTE	CENTER	CITE
CODE	DD	DFN	DIR
DIV	DL	DT	EM
EMBED	FIELDSET	FORM	H1–H6
HR	I	IFRAME	IMG
INPUT	KDB	LABEL	LEGEND
LI	LISTING	MARQUEE	MENU
OBJECT	OL	P	PRE
S	SAMP	SELECT	SMALL
SPAN	STRIKE	STRONG	SUB
SUP	TABLE	TEXTAREA	TT
U	UL	VAR	XMP

CROSS-REFERENCE
See left (Cascading Style Sheets), length, and style.

leftMargin

Property

DHTML

This property sets the left margin for the entire page being viewed. It overrides the existing margin properties that have been established using either a stylesheet or defaults found within a user agent. This property is both readable and writable, and can be used to dynamically adjust your page on the fly.

```
object.leftMargin[=length]
```

The value of length follows the same rules as the string value of the length Cascading Style Sheet value.

Examples

This example uses the leftMargin property to retrieve the value of the page's left margin.

ON THE CD-ROM

Look for **leftMargin.htm** on the accompanying CD-ROM.

```
<HTML>
  <HEAD>
    <TITLE>JavaScript Retrieve LeftMargin </TITLE>
    <STYLE type="text/css">
      @page  {margin-left: 5em}
    </STYLE>
  </HEAD>
  <BODY style="margin-left: 5em" name="poems">
    <H1> A little Ditty!!!</H1>
    This little ditty is silly.<BR>
    This little ditty ain't dirty.<BR>
    It doesn't say nothin'. <BR>
    Just sits here as somethin'<BR>
    Waiting for you to go nilly.<P>
    <SCRIPT language="JavaScript">
       {
      PoemEdge=document.leftMargin;
      document.writeln("The left edge of this page is located
      at: "+PoemEdge);
       }
    </SCRIPT>

  </BODY>
</HTML>
```

The following code uses the leftMargin property to set the document's left margin.

ON THE CD-ROM

Look for **leftMargin2.htm** on the accompanying CD-ROM.

```
<HTML>
  <HEAD>
    <TITLE>JavaScript Set LeftMargin </TITLE>
    <SCRIPT language="JavaScript">
```

```
                {
                document.leftMargin="5em";
                }
            </SCRIPT>
        </HEAD>
        <BODY name="poems">
            <H1> A little Ditty!!!</H1>
            This little ditty is silly.<BR>
            This little ditty ain't dirty.<BR>
            It doesn't say nothin'. <BR>
            Just sits here as somethin'<BR>
            Waiting for you to go nilly.<P>
        </BODY>
        </HTML>
```

Elements

> BODY

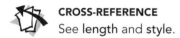

CROSS-REFERENCE
See length and style.

<LEGEND>

Element

HTML

Start Tag:	Required
End Tag:	Required

The LEGEND element works in conjunction with the FIELDSET element to provide a caption for a group of joined form controls. This caption makes it easier to organize and access groups of controls when they have not been grouped visually.

Attributes
accesskey

```
accesskey="character"
```

You can assign an access key to an element. This key allows you to quickly put the focus on an element. In the case of a form element, the user is immediately able to input information. In the case of a link, the link is activated and followed.

align

```
align=top | bottom | center | left | right
```

This attribute is used to specify the specific position of the legend with respect to the area of the fieldset. Possible values for this attribute are: top, bottom, center, left, and right.

class

```
class="cdata-list"
```

This attribute is used to assign a class name to an element. Classes are used by user agents to group specific types of information, saving them for later use.

dir

```
dir = LTR | RTL | [CS | CI | CN | CA | CT]
```

This attribute defines the direction of the text flow in a document so a user agent can display it correctly.

id

```
id="name"
```

This attribute is used to assign a name to an element.

lang

```
lang="language code"
```

This attribute specifies the language in which an element and its values should be rendered.

onclick

```
onclick=script
```

This attribute takes effect when a user clicks the button on a pointing device with the pointer over an element.

ondblclick

```
ondblclick=script
```

This attribute takes effect when the button on a pointing device is double-clicked with the pointer over an element.

onkeydown

```
onkeydown=script
```

This attribute takes effect when a key is pressed while the pointer is over an element.

onkeypress

```
onkeypress=script
```

This attribute takes effect when a key is pressed and released with the pointer over an element.

onkeyup

```
onkeyup=script
```

This attribute takes effect when a key is released with the pointer over an element.

onmousedown

```
onmousedown=script
```

This attribute takes effect when the button on a pointing device is pressed with the pointer over an element.

onmousemove

```
onmousemove=script
```

This attribute is activated when the mouse is moved while the pointer is over an element.

onmouseout

```
onmouseout=script
```

This attributed is activated when the mouse pointer is moved away from an element.

onmouseover

```
onmouseover=script
```

This attribute is activated when the mouse pointer is moved over an element.

onmouseup

```
onmouseup=script
```

This attribute takes effect when the button on a pointing device is released with the pointer over an element.

style

```
style=style descriptors
```

This attribute is used to apply specific style-sheet information to one particular element.

title

```
title=text
```

This attribute serves to provide annotation information to the element.

Example

The following code uses the LEGEND element to provide information about the groups of controls used in this form.

ON THE CD-ROM

Look for **legend.htm** on the accompanying CD-ROM.

```
<HTML>
    <HEAD>
        <TITLE> The Legend Tag</TITLE>
    </HEAD>
    <BODY>
        <FORM action="..." method="post">
        <FIELDSET border="inset">
        <LEGEND align="top"> <H1>Personal Information:</H1></LEGEND><P>
        <LABEL for="lastname"> Last Name:</LABEL>
        <INPUT type="text" id="lastname"><BR>
        <LABEL for="firstname"> First Name:</LABEL>
        <INPUT type="text" id="firstname"><BR>
        <LABEL for="address">Address:</LABEL>
        <INPUT type="text" id="address" size=75><BR>
        <LABEL for="city"> City, State, Zip:</LABEL>
        <INPUT type="text" id="city">,  
        <INPUT type="text" id="state" size=5 maxlength=2>   
        <INPUT type="text" id="zip" size=10 maxlength=10><BR>
        <INPUT type="radio" name="sex" value="Male">Male<BR>
        <INPUT type="radio" name="sex" value="Female">Female<P>
        </FIELDSET>
        <FIELDSET border="inset" bgcolor="green">
        <LEGEND align="right"> <H1>Personal Favorites:</H1></LEGEND><P>
        <LABEL for="cardgame"> Card Game:</LABEL>
        <INPUT type="text" id="cardgame"><BR>
        <LABEL for="boardgame"> Board Game:</LABEL>
        <INPUT type="text" id="boardgame"><BR>
        <LABEL for="activity">Activity:</LABEL>
        <INPUT type="text" id="activity"><BR>
        <LABEL> Favorite Color:<BR>
            <INPUT type="radio" name="color" value="Blue">Blue<BR>
            <INPUT type="radio" name="color" value="Green">Green<BR>
            <INPUT type="radio" name="color" value="Orange">Orange<BR>
```

```
            <INPUT type="radio" name="color" value="Purple">Purple<BR>
            <INPUT type="radio" name="color" value="Yellow">Yellow<BR>
            <INPUT type="radio" name="color" value="Red">Red<BR>
            <INPUT type="radio" name="color" value="Brown">Brown<BR>
            <INPUT type="radio" name="color" value="Black">Black<BR>
        </LABEL>
        <INPUT type="submit" value="send">
        <INPUT type="reset">
        </FIELDSET>
        </FORM>
    </BODY>
</HTML>
```

CROSS-REFERENCE
See <FIELDSET> and <FORM>.

Length

Concept

CSS

While reading the specifications of many different Cascading Style Sheets attributes, you will find that they show length as part of their optional values. This length refers to the various signed or unsigned integers and unit identifiers that can be used for that value. The default sign for all lengths is positive (+), although many elements will allow you to have negative (–) signed numbers for the length. Negative integers do create many design and formatting problems when used with some user agents.

Lengths can be either relative or absolute. Relative lengths use a reference to another automatically scaled property when defining their resultant distance. Style sheets that use relative lengths are easier to convert between media styles. For instance, if you set all of your distances based upon pixels (px), the height of the element's text (em), or the height of the letter 'x' (ex), your display medium will show them correctly. The 'em' unit can be used to measure items both horizontally and vertically, while the 'ex' measurement allows only height measurement. Both of these measurements refer to the font size of the element, unless they are used within a font-size attribute where they will increase the size of the font being used.

Pixels are a relative length, because they are dependent upon the resolution of the viewing device, which for Web pages is most often a computer display, but could also be a WebTV device or other handheld display. If the density of the pixels is widely divergent from that of a computer screen, the user agent should re-scale the pixel values of the style sheet to create a more accurate display on the device being used.

Absolute lengths are those that are displayed in actual measurements such as inches (in), centimeters (cm), millimeters (mm), points (pt), or picas (pc). In some cases, the user agent can not support the dimension that has been specified. In these cases, the user agent will do its best to approximate the distance that has been specified.

Examples

In the following line, the height of the line used for all BLOCKQUOTE elements will be 40% larger than the font size of the standard BLOCKQUOTE element.

```
BLOCKQUOTE {line-height: 1.4em}
```

In the following statement, the situation differs. The font size used to display the BLOCKQUOTE will be 40% larger than what the BLOCKQUOTE would normally inherit.

```
BLOCKQUOTE {font-size: 1.4em}
```

These next few lines of example code use absolute lengths to control how a series of headers and other objects are going to be displayed in the document.

```
H1      {line-height: 18pt}       /* point - 1pt = 1/72 inch */
DIV     {margin: .9in}            /* inches */
P       {word-spacing: 5mm}       /* millimeters */
BIG     {letter-spacing: 1cm}     /* centimeters */
B       {letter-spacing: 4pc}     /* picas - 1pc = 12pt */
```

CROSS-REFERENCE
See Cascading Style Sheets.

length

Property

DHTML

This property gives you the number of elements in a set collection.
The syntax for this command is

```
object.length
```

For the `areas` and `options` collections, as well as for the `SELECT` element, this property is both readable and writable. This ability allows you to change the number of elements there are within image maps and select boxes on forms. For all other objects and collections, this property is read only.

Example

The following code segment finds the total number of objects on your document, including frames, links, images, applets, and forms.

```
<SCRIPT language="javascript">
{
    totalElements=document.all.length;
    document.writeln("There are "+totalElements+" elements on
this page.");
}
</SCRIPT>
```

NOTE
Netscape Navigator does not support any properties for the `all` collection used in this example.

Collections

Anchors	Applets	areas	embeds
Forms	Frames	images	imports
Links	Plugins	scripts	styleSheets

Objects

All   history   window

Elements

SELECT

CROSS-REFERENCE
See Image Map, options, collections, and JavaScript.

k
l
m

letterSpacing

Property

DHTML

This property is used to either set or retrieve the amount of space between the individual letters of an element. If you set this element to 3 px, it will place 3 pixels between each character. For this property not to affect the end of the last word of a paragraph or sentence, you will need to place that character outside of the element brackets identifying the string you are changing.

The syntax for this command is

```
object.letterSpacing[=length]
```

Elements

A	ADDRESS	B	BIG
BLOCKQUOTE	BODY	CAPTION	CENTER
CITE	CODE	COL	COLGROUP
DD	DFN	DIR	DIV
DL	DT	EM	FIELDSET
FORM	H1–H6	HTML	I
INPUT	KBD	LABEL	LEGEND
LI	LISTING	MARQUEE	MENU
OL	P	PLAINTEXT	PRE
S	SAMP	SMALL	SPAN
STRIKE	STRONG	SUB	SUP
TABLE	TBODY	TD	TEXTAREA
TFOOT	TH	THEAD	TR
TT	U	UL	VAR
XMP			

CROSS-REFERENCE

See letter-spacing (Attribute) and length (Attribute).

letter-spacing

Attribute

CSS

This attribute is used to set the amount of space between the individual characters in an element that displays text. You can set this value in the style sheet, or you can set it using the `style` attribute within a specific command.

```
letter-spacing: normal | length | auto | inherit
```

Values
normal

This is the default value and allows the user agent to control the space between individual characters so the user agent can justify text.

length

This value specifies a set distance between characters in the text. This may be altered based upon the user agent's interpretation of the measurement.

auto

This value allows the text to be spaced so the complete text associated with an element can be placed on a single line.

inherit

The value for this distance is inherited from its parent elements.

Example
The following example code shows a stylesheet that sets different letter-spacing for various elements that could appear in a document.

```
<STYLE type="text/css">
<!-
    H1 { letter-spacing: 2px}
    H2 { letter-spacing: auto }
    B   { letter-spacing: 1mm}
    P   { letter-spacing: normal}
->
</STYLE>
```

Elements
This attribute applies to all HTML elements.

CROSS-REFERENCE
See letterspacing (Property), text-align, Cascading Style Sheets, and length (Attribute).

<LI>

Element

HTML

Start Tag: Required
End Tag: Optional

This element is used to identify a single list item. This tag is used with both the UL and the OL tags to create lists of specific style, whether they are ordered or unordered. Lists can be of any length, and styles start or stop at any number. You can create ordered lists with a series of unordered elements, or vice versa, depending upon your documentation needs.

Attributes

class

```
class="cdata-list"
```

This attribute is used to assign a class name to an element. Classes are used by user agents to group specific types of information.

compact

```
class=compact
```

This attribute is freely interpreted by the user agent, but it should instruct the user agent to display the list in a compact manner.

dir

```
dir = LTR | RTL | [CS | CI | CN | CA | CT]
```

This attribute defines the direction of the text flow in a document so a user agent can display it correctly.

id

```
id="name"
```

This attribute is used to assign a name to an element.

lang

```
lang="language code"
```

This attribute specifies the language in which an element and its values should be rendered.

onclick

```
onclick=script
```

This attribute takes effect when a user clicks the button on a pointing device with the pointer over an element.

ondblclick

```
ondblclick=script
```

This attribute takes effect when the button on a pointing device is double-clicked with the pointer over an element.

onkeydown

```
onkeydown=script
```

This attribute takes effect when a key is pressed while the pointer is over an element.

onkeypress

```
onkeypress=script
```

This attribute takes effect when a key is pressed and released with the pointer over an element.

onkeyup

```
onkeyup=script
```

This attribute takes effect when a key is released with the pointer over an element.

onmousedown

```
onmousedown=script
```

This attribute takes effect when the button on a pointing device is pressed with the pointer over an element.

onmousemove

```
onmousemove=script
```

This attribute is activated when the mouse is moved while the pointer is over an element.

onmouseout

> `onmouseout=script`

This attribute is activated when the mouse pointer is moved away from an element.

onmouseover

> `onmouseover=script`

This attribute is activated when the mouse pointer is moved over an element.

onmouseup

> `onmouseup=script`

This attribute takes effect when the button on a pointing device is released with the pointer over an element.

style

> `style=style descriptors`

This attribute is used to apply specific style-sheet information to one particular element.

title

> `title=text`

This attribute serves to provide annotation information to the element it is being applied to.

type

> `type= disc | circle | square | 1 | a | A | I | i`

This deprecated attribute is used to designate the type of bullet or number to be used when displaying the list. Although this attribute is only used by visual user agents, you may encounter it; Table L-1 shows you what to expect.

Table L-1: Bullet Types Determined by the type Attribute

Type	Example	Description
Disc	●	Solid black dot — default
Circle	○	Outlined circle
Square	□	Outlined square
1	1, 2, 3, ...	Arabic numbers
A	a, b, c, ...	Lowercase roman alpha characters
A	A, B, C, ...	Uppercase roman alpha characters

Type	Example	Description
I	i, ii, iii, …	Lowercase roman numerals
I	I, II, III	Uppercase roman numerals

value

```
value=number
```

This attribute is used to set the value of the element. Although you will always specify this element in an integer form, it may display in another format.

Example

The following code creates two lists, one ordered and the other unordered, both using the LI element to highlight important information.

 ON THE CD-ROM

Look for **li.htm** on the accompanying CD-ROM.

```
<HTML>
   <HEAD>
      <TITLE> List Tag</TITLE>
   </HEAD>
   <BODY>
      <H1>Quotes you can't forget!</H1>
      <UL compact>
         <LI>Laughter is a tranquilizer with no side effects. -
         Unknown
         <LI>More than kisses, letters mingle souls. - John Donne
         <LI>Life - the universally fatal, sexually transmitted
         disease. - Unknown
         <LI>The best way to get a bad law repealed is to enforce
         it strictly. - A. Lincoln
          <LI>You've got to dance like nobody's watching, and
          love like it's never going to hurt. - Unknown
      <LI>
      </UL>
      <P>
      <H1>My Favorite Animals</H1>
      <OL>
         <LI value=10>Horses
         <LI>Dogs
         <LI value=21>Cats
         <LI dir=RTL>Cows
         <LI type="I" value = 15>Pigs
```

```
        <LI>Chickens
      </OL>
    </BODY>
  </HTML>
```

CROSS-REFERENCE
See <OL>, <UL>, and **Lists**.

<LICENSE>

Element

OSD

This command provides the user with the location of the software license or copyright notice. The user agent can then use this information to retrieve the license or copyright during installation, or at any time that it is needed.

Attribute
href

```
href="url"
```

This attribute contains the URL of the license or copyright agreement that is associated with the package currently being discussed.

Example
The following example shows how the license information would be displayed in OSD code.

```
<SOFTPKG>
  <LICENSE
href="http://www.oursoftware.com/osplicense.html"/>
</SOFTPKG>
```

CROSS-REFERENCE
See **OSD**.

Line Break

Concept

A *line break* is simply a break in your text. It can be composed of a carriage return, line feed, or both carriage return and line feed. In your HTML source code, line breaks are used to provide readability to your text. In a displayed HTML document, the BR and P elements are used to force line breaks where they are needed. Line breaks can be automatically inserted by user agents based upon the size of the viewable area your readers are using. If you wish to prohibit a line break from appearing at a specific point you can use the ** ** non breaking space code to prevent a user from creating a break at that point.

 CROSS-REFERENCE
See <BR>, Appendix C (Character Tables), and <P>.

line-height

Attribute

CSS

This Cascading Style Sheets attribute is used to specify the height of a specific line that either text or graphics will be displayed upon. The line-height property can be used to control the amount of extra space provided for text, or it can be used to create a shadow effect with your characters. This value is interpreted differently by varying user agents, so test thoroughly when using this attribute.

```
line-height: normal | number | length | percentage | inherit
```

Values

normal

This value informs user agents to use the computed value of the line height, based on the size of the font being used on that line. This value works the same as the number value.

number

The computed line-height is this number multiplied by the absolute height of the property. Negative values are not allowed.

length

This value is used to set the absolute height of the line. Negative values are not allowed.

percentage

This value allows the document author to control the height of the line, by forcing the user agent to multiply this percentage to the height of the font being used. You can use negative values. For example, a value of "−50%" will lower the baseline of the specified element so it is now located where the midline of the next line should have been.

inherit

This value forces the element to use the line-height value it received from its parent elements.

Examples

The following example creates a shadow of the text shown in the stacked H1 elements.

ON THE CD-ROM
Look for **lineheight.htm** on the accompanying CD-ROM.

```
<HTML>
<HEAD>
    <TITLE> Line-Height Creating Shadows </TITLE>
</HEAD>
<BODY>
    <H1> Only the Shadow Knows!!! </H1>
    <H1 style="color: red" line-height: 3pt"> Only the Shadow
    Knows!!!</H1>
</BODY>
</HTML>
```

Elements

This attribute applies to all HTML elements.

CROSS-REFERENCE
See **lineHeight (Property)**.

lineHeight

Property

DHTML

This property is used within scripts to set or retrieve the distance between lines in a paragraph. You can create various effects by using a variety of line height values, although negative values are not allowed according to the W3C specification. Internet Explorer supports negative values. This value is measured from the bottom of the font descender, to the top of the internal leading of the font. The format for specifying line height is shown below.

```
object.style.lineHeight[=lineHeight]
```

Elements

A	ADDRESS	B	BIG
BLOCKQUOTE	BODY	CAPTION	CENTER
CITE	CODE	COL	COLGROUP
DD	DFN	DIR	DIV
DL	DT	EM	FIELDSET
FORM	H1–H6	HTML	I
INPUT	KBD	LABEL	LEGEND
LI	LISTING	MARQUEE	MENU
OL	P	PLAINTEXT	PRE
S	SAMP	SMALL	SPAN
STRIKE	STRONG	SUB	SUP
TABLE	TBODY	TD	TEXTAREA
TFOOT	TH	THEAD	TR
TT	U	UL	VAR
XMP			

CROSS-REFERENCE
See line-height (Attribute), Leading, half-leading, and font size.

link

Property

DHTML

This property is used to set or retrieve the color of links in a document. It is used with the style property and works in conjunction with your stylesheets. The color specified can be written as either a standard color name, or as one of the RGB color values. The color specified using this property will be active when the link is not being activated in some way, or has not been visited. You can use this property in conjunction with the link pseudo-classes (active, visited, and hover) to control the color of your links at all stages of activity.

The syntax for this command is

```
object.style.link[=color]
```

Object

body

CROSS-REFERENCE
See :active, :hover, :visited, aLink, and vLink.

<LINK>

Element

HTML

Start Tag: Required
End Tag: Forbidden

The LINK element is used within the HEAD document block to identify a link. It can not be used in any other section of the document. This element is used to convey relationship information between documents. Multiple LINK elements can be used in each document.

The LINK element can also provide a variety of information to search engines. For example, authors can use this element to provide information about documents written in other languages, or to versions of the document that have been specifically formatted for another media, such as print. This element can also be used by search engines to find the starting page of a collection of documents.

Attributes
charset

```
charset=charset
```

This attribute is used to specify the character encoding of the resource that has been identified by the link.

class

```
class="cdata-list"
```

This attribute is used to assign a class name to an element. Classes are used by user agents to group specific types of information.

dir

```
dir = LTR | RTL | [CS | CI | CN | CA | CT]
```

This attribute defines the direction of the text flow in a document so a user agent can display it correctly.

href

```
href="url"
```

This attribute is used to specify the location of the document or resource to which this link refers.

hreflang

```
hreflang=langcode
```

This attribute specifies the language used by the document or recourse that has been identified by the `href` attribute.

id

```
id="name"
```

This attribute is used to assign a name to an element.

lang

```
lang="language code"
```

This attribute specifies the language in which an element and its values should be rendered.

media

```
media=media-descriptors
```

This attribute is used to specify the intended media type of the document link. The value of this element is a comma-separated list of the valid media types.

onclick

```
onclick=script
```

This attribute takes effect when a user clicks the button on a pointing device with the pointer over an element.

ondblclick

```
ondblclick=script
```

This attribute takes effect when the button on a pointing device is double-clicked with the pointer over an element.

onkeydown

```
onkeydown=script
```

This attribute takes effect when a key is pressed while the pointer is over an element.

onkeypress

```
onkeypress=script
```

This attribute takes effect when a key is pressed and released with the pointer over an element.

onkeyup

```
onkeyup=script
```

This attribute takes effect when a key is released with the pointer over an element.

onmousedown

```
onmousedown=script
```

This attribute takes effect when the button on a pointing device is pressed with the pointer over an element.

onmousemove

```
onmousemove=script
```

This attribute is activated when the mouse is moved while the pointer is over an element.

onmouseout

```
onmouseout=script
```

This attributed is activated when the mouse pointer is moved away from an element.

onmouseover

```
onmouseover=script
```

This attribute is activated when the mouse pointer is moved over an element.

onmouseup

```
onmouseup=script
```

This attribute takes effect when the button on a pointing device is released with the pointer over an element.

rel

```
rel=linktype
```

This attribute describes the relationship between the current document and the document that has been specified by the `href` attribute. The value of this attribute is a space-separated list of the *linktypes*.

rev

```
rev=linktype
```

This attribute is used to describe the reverse link from the document specified in the `href` attribute, to the current document. The value of this attribute is a space-separated list of *linktypes*.

style

```
style=style descriptors
```

This attribute is used to apply specific style-sheet information to one particular element.

target

```
target=frame-target
```

This attribute specifies the destination frame of the link's reference document.

title

```
title=text
```

This attribute serves to provide annotation information to the element it is being applied to.

k

l

m

type

```
type=content-type
```

This attribute is used to specify the MIME type of the document being linked to.

Example

This example uses the LINK element to explain the relationship between the current document, woods.html, and the other documents in its collection.

ON THE CD-ROM

Look for **link.htm** on the accompanying CD-ROM.

```
<HTML>
<HEAD>
    <TITLE>Tiger Woods Tourney Results</TITLE>
    <LINK rel="Alternative"
            title="Tiger Woods Tourney Results - Spanish"
            href="woods-sp.html"
            hreflang="sp">
    <LINK rel="Index"
            href="../results.html"
            type="text/html"
            media="screen">
    <LINK rel="Next"
            href="nicholson.html"
            type="text/html"
            media="screen">
    <LINK rel="Prev"
            href="rodriguez.html"
            type="text/html"
            media="screen">
</HEAD>
<BODY>
    <H1> Tiger Woods Tourney Results</H1>
    <P> His performance was so outstanding we have decided to
    not display his records in an attempt to be mindful of the
    other players' feelings.
        <P align="right"> <CITE> - The Tourney Committee</CITE>
</BODY>
</HTML>
```

CROSS-REFERENCE

See %mediadesc, %linktypes, <HEAD>, MIME Types, profile, and <A>.

linkColor

Property

DHTML

This property allows you to set or retrieve the color of the links in the document. You can specify the color of your links using either the color name or the RGB value of the color.

The syntax for this command is

```
object.linkColor[=color]
```

Objects

document

 CROSS-REFERENCE
See Link (Property), Color, alinkColor, and vlinkColor.

links

Collection

DHTML

This collection creates an array out of all the A elements, using the href attribute and all the AREA elements found within a HTML document. You can use this command to select a specific link found within your document and perform a function with it, or alter it in some way. This collection only works with the document object.

This collection is automatically ordered first by name, and then by the element ordinal number. If multiple elements share the same name, they will be placed in their own collection, and must be identified by the ordinal number.

The syntax for this command is

```
object.links(index)
```

The value of the *index* can be either an integer identifying the element to be retrieved, or the name of the element. Since the indexes for collections are zero-based, the first element in the collection will have the ordinal number 0. For example, if the *index* value were 3, this command would retrieve the fourth A or AREA element in the document. If the *index* value were 'Adobe', it would retrieve the link with the id="Adobe" attribute set.

Example

The following lines of code show you how to display the href and id values of a link identified by its ordinal number.

```
<SCRIPT language="JavaScript">
    {
    alert(document.links(3).href);
    alert(document.links(3).id);
    }
</SCRIPT>
```

Elements

    A   AREA

CROSS-REFERENCE
See link, <LINK>, <A>, <AREA>, and Ordinal Number.

List Item

Concept

CROSS-REFERENCE
See Lists, <LI>, <OL>, and <UL>.

Lists

Concept

Lists are used in many media to create a pleasing visual impression to an otherwise daunting set of information. Items found in a list can be either ordered (numbered—OL) or unordered (bulleted—UL). In HTML, the individual items found on a list are identified using the LI element and its associated properties. A list item is any item that is displayed in such a way as to create the visual impression of an organized list.

Examples

Ordered lists are commonly used to display information that must be done in a specific order. For example, the following code list shows step-by-step instructions that you might write down for someone who has never started a car before.

```
1. Find your car keys.
2. Find your driver's license.
3. Find your car.
4. Walk to your car's left side.
5. Stand by the door closest to the front of the car.
6. Grasp the handle of your car door, and open the door.
7. Sit in the first seat you see just inside this door. There
   should be a large round object in front of you at chest
   height.
8. Close the door.
9. Behind the round object, your steering wheel, is a column.
   On that column is a small round metal object with a small
   centimeter-long slit. Find that slit.
10. Place the large key on your key ring into that slit.
Etc.
```

Unordered lists are commonly used to display information that is important, but does not need to be acted on in any particular order. An example of this could be a series of quotes that you want to share with your friends.

```
◆ More than kisses, letters mingle souls. - John Donne

◆ The best way to get a bad law repealed is to enforce it
  strictly. - Abraham Lincoln

◆ To be, or not to be, that is the question.
  - W. Shakespeare

◆ There's no such thing as a free lunch. - R. Heinlein

◆ Great art requires great suffering. - Vincent Van Gogh

◆ Keep 'em — I can always make more! - Caterina Sforza in
  reference to her children

◆ Could I write all, the world would turn to stone. -
  Caterina Sforza
```

CROSS-REFERENCE

See <LI>, <OL>, and <UL>.

list-style

Attribute

CSS

This attribute provides a shorthand for setting the three divergent attributes of a list. This is a space-delineated list.

```
list-style= list-style-image | list-style-type | list-style-
position | inherit
```

Values

list-style-type

This value is set to one of the valid list types and forces the lists to be displayed using that particular list marker.

list-style-image

This value will contain the URL of the image that should be used as the marker for these types of lists.

list-style-position

This value designates the position of the list on the document.

inherit

This value forces the user agent to use the same settings as the lists parent element.

Example

The following example lines of code display the various types of options that are available when controlling the appearance of your lists.

```
UL { list-style: lower-roman inside } /* Any UL*/
UL + UL { list-style: circle outside } /* Any UL child of a UL*/
UL + OL { list-style: decimal inside } /* Any OL child of a UL*/
UL + LI { list-style: url(blueball.png) outside} /* Any LI child
of an UL */
OL.alpha LI { list-style: lower-roman } /* Any LI descendant of
an OL */
OL.alpha + LI { list-style: lower-alpha } /* Any LI child of an
OL */
```

Elements

    LI   OL   UL

 CROSS-REFERENCE
See liststyle.

list-style-image

Attribute

CSS

If you wish to use an image for your list-item marker, this attribute provides you with that functionality. If the image is available, it will replace the default `list-style-type` attribute settings. If it is not available, the `list-style-type` attribute will be used instead.

```
list-style-image= url | none | inherit
```

Values

url

This value specifies the address of the image to be used as the marker for the list.

none

No marker is used, unless a marker has been identified in the `list-style-type` attribute.

inherit

The marker displayed is inherited from the element's parent.

Elements

    LI   OL   UL

 **CROSS-REFERENCE**
See list-style and listStyleImage.

list-style-position

Attribute

CSS

This attribute is used to choose the position of the list, item marker in relation to the actual text of the line item.

```
list-style-position – inside | outside | inherit
```

Values
inside

The marker is placed inside of the object box that is created for the list item.

outside

The marker is placed outside of the object box that is created for the list item.

inherit

If the attribute is set to this value, then the position of the list will be a copy of its parent.

Example
The following code creates two short lists. In the first list (UL), the list-item marker is placed outside of the line item's object box; in the second (OL), it is placed within the item box.

ON THE CD-ROM
Look for **liststylepos.htm** on the accompanying CD-ROM.

```
<HTML>
<HEAD>
  <TITLE> Line-Item Marker Position </TITLE>
  <STYLE type="text/css">
  <!–
    UL {list-style-position: outside}
    OL {list-style-position: inside}
  –>
  </STYLE>
</HEAD>
<BODY>
  <H2> This is the UL list.</H2>
  <UL>
    <LI>This is the first item on the first list.
```

```
      <LI>This is the second item on the first list.
   </UL>
   <H2> This is the OL list.</H2>
   <OL>
      <LI> This is the first item on the second list.
      <LI> This is the second item on the second list.
   </OL>
</BODY>
</HTML>
```

Elements

LI   OL   UL

CROSS-REFERENCE
See list-style and listStyleposition.

list-style-type

Attribute

CSS

This attribute is used to identify the type of list-item marker that will be used in the lists. By default, this setting is *disc* for an UL list, and *decimal* for an OL list.

```
list-style-type= disc | circle | square | decimal | lower-roman
| upper-roman | lower-alpha | upper-alpha | none | inherit
```

Values
disc

A solid round dot. Exact representation is user-agent dependent.

circle

An outlined circle. Exact representation is user- agent dependent.

square

An outlined square. Exact representation is user-agent dependent.

decimal

All decimal numbers beginning with 1 by default.

lower-roman

The lower Roman numerals. For example: i, ii, iii, iv, v, vi...

upper-roman

The upper Roman numerals. For example: I, II, III, IV, V, VI...

lower-alpha

The lowercase characters of the ASCII character set.

upper-alpha

The uppercase characters of the ASCII character set.

none

No marker is used.

inherit

The marker displayed is inherited from the element's parent. Table L-2 shows some types of markers.

Table L-2: Types of Markers

Type	Example	Description
disc	●	Solid black dot — default
circle	○	Outlined circle
square	□	Outlined square
decimal	1, 2, 3, …	Arabic numbers
lower-alpha	A, b, c, …	Lowercase roman alpha characters
upper-alpha	A, B, C, …	Uppercase roman alpha characters
lower-roman	i, ii, iii, …	Lowercase Roman numerals
upper-roman	I, II, III	Uppercase Roman numerals

Elements

LI   OL   UL

CROSS-REFERENCE
See **list-style** and **listStyletype (Property)**.

listStyle

Property

DHTML

This property is used to set or retrieve the listStyleType, listStyleImage, and the listStylePosition property simultaneously. The value of this property can specify either an URL for an image, or the style of list marker to use.
The syntax for this command is

```
object.style.listStyle[=URL | type designator]
```

Elements

LI   OL   UL

CROSS-REFERENCE
See list-style, style, <LI>, <OL>, and <UL>.

listStyleImage

Property

DHTML

This property is used to either set or retrieve the image that is used as the list-item marker. If the image is available, it will replace the existing list marker. The syntax for this property is

```
object.style.listStyleImage[=listStyleImage]
```

Example
The following example retrieves the value of the listStyleImage list marker.

ON THE CD-ROM
Look for **listStyleimage.htm** on the accompanying CD-ROM.

```
<HTML>
  <HEAD>
    <TITLE>JavaScript listStyleImage </TITLE>
  </HEAD>
  <BODY>
<H1>My Favorite Animals</H1>
```

```
                    <UL onmouseover="this.style.listStyleImage='url
                    (blueball.gif)" onmouseout="this.style.listStyleType=
                    'circle'">
                       <LI>Horses
                       <LI>Dogs
                       <LI>Cats
                       <LI>Cows
                       <LI>Pigs
                       <LI>Chickens
                    </UL>
              </BODY>
              </HTML>
```

Elements

LI   OL   UL

CROSS-REFERENCE
See list-style-image, style, <LI>, <OL>, and <UL>.

listStylePosition

Property

DHTML

This property is used to either set or retrieve the position of the list-item
marker in relation to the content it is marking. You can only use this property
on elements that are using the display attribute of your list item. The syntax
for this command is

Object.style.listStylePosition*[=listStylePosition]*

Elements

LI   OL   UL

CROSS-REFERENCE
See list-style-position, style, <LI>, <OL>, and <UL>.

listStyleType

Property

DHTML

This property will either set or return the type of marker that is being used to set off the individual items in a list. The default value for this option is *disc*. The syntax of this command is

```
object.style.listStyleType[=listStyleType]
```

Example

The following example retrieves the value of the listStyleType list marker.

ON THE CD-ROM

Look for **liststyletype.htm** on the accompanying CD-ROM.

```
<HTML>
   <HEAD>
      <TITLE>JavaScript listStyleType </TITLE>
   </HEAD>
   <BODY>
      <H1>My Favorite Animals</H1>

<UL onmouseover="this.style.listStyleType='circle'" onmouseout
="this.style.listStyleType='disc'">
  <LI>Camels
  <LI>Giraffes
  <LI>Zebras
  <LI>Elephants
  <LI>Gazelles
  <LI>Monkeys
</UL>

   </BODY>
</HTML>
```

Elements

LI   OL   UL

CROSS-REFERENCE

See **list-style-type, style, <LI>, <OL>,** and **<UL>**.

Literal

Concept

A *literals* is a constant that has been made available to a program through the execution of a segment of code. Literals are generally read-only, meaning that they can not be changed or altered by the program that uses them. On the other hand, *variables* can be altered. MathML uses both string and numeric literals for displaying information on HTML documents.

 CROSS-REFERENCE
See Variable and MathML.

location

Property

DHTML

This property returns the location of the document's current URL. This property can be both read and written to, so you can change your document locations on the fly if need be. The other properties that can be used to find information on the current URL include hash, host, hostname, href, pathname, port, protocol, and search.

The syntax is

```
object.location [=location]
```

Objects

document

 CROSS-REFERENCE
See hash, host, hostname, href, pathname, port, protocol, and search.

<LOG>

Element

CDF

Start Tag: Required
End Tag: Forbidden

The Channel Definition Format uses the LOG element to track the number of page hits that an individual channel receives. This is a child element of the CHANNEL or ITEM element, and can only record the hits on the document or item identified by those elements.

Attribute
Value

```
Value="document:view"
```

This attribute specifies the events to be logged for this channel.

Example
The following channel code specifies a that a log be created at the specified target.

```
<CHANNEL href="mychannel.cdf">
  <LOGTARGET href="mylogfile.txt" method="post" scope="all">
    <PURGETIME hour="24" />
  </LOGTARGET>
  <LOG value="document:view" />
</CHANNEL>
```

Element

CHANNEL   ITEM

CROSS-REFERENCE
See Channel Definition Format and <LOGTARGET>.

<LOGIN>

Element

CDF

Start Tag: Required
End Tag: Forbidden

The LOGIN element is used by the Channel Definition Format to force a channel visitor to provide login information. This information is later used for unattended channel updates. This element has no valid attributes or properties.

```
<LOGIN />
```

CROSS-REFERENCE
See CDF.

<LOGO>

Element

CDF

Start Tag: Required
End Tag: Forbidden

This element is used to specify the size and location of a channel logo. The logo can be a valid GIF, JPEG, or icon file.

Attributes

href

```
href="url"
```

This attribute is used to specify the location of the image that should be used for this channel logo.

style

```
style= "icon | image | image-wide"
```

This attribute is used to specify the size of the image that has been identified as the channel logo. If *icon* is identified, the image will be rendered 16 px high by 16 px wide. The *image* designation displays a logo 32 px high by 80 px wide. The *image-wide* designation renders the logo 32 px high by 194 px wide.

Example

The following code assigns a logo to the specified channel, and provides the user agent with its size and location.

```
<CHANNEL href="mychannel.cdf">
  <LOGO href="mylogo.gif" style="image-wide" />
</CHANNEL>
```

CROSS-REFERENCE
See <CDF>.

<LOGTARGET>

Element

CDF

Start Tag: Required
End Tag: Optional

This element specifies where a client's page-hit log file should be uploaded using the Extended Log File Format. The client will only log the page hits for the URLs which this channel has been authorized to track. This means that the page URL must be part of the `LOGTARGET href` attribute, or the `CHANNEL` URL.

Attributes
href

```
href="url"
```

This attribute is required for this element, and specifies the URL of the location where the log file should be sent.

method

```
method= post | get
```

This attribute is required for this element. By selecting either *post* or *put* for the element you can decide how your information will be delivered to your target directory.

scope

```
scope= all | offline | online
```

This attribute allows you to specify which events to log. If you select *all*, you will record both the *offline* hits that are read from the local cache, and the *online* hits that are read while a user is browsing.

Example
The following channel code specifies the target and method used to create a log file. It also starts that log, and specifies when it should be purged.

```
<CHANNEL href="mychannel.cdf">
   <LOGTARGET href="http://myserver/logfiles" method="post"
scope="all">
      <PURGETIME hour="24" />
   </LOGTARGET>
   <LOG />
</CHANNEL>
```

Element

    CHANNEL

CROSS-REFERENCE
See CDF, <LOG>, and <PURGETIME>.

longdesc

Attribute

HTML

This attribute is valid for three HTML elements: FRAME, IFRAME, and IMG. The FRAME and IFRAME elements treat this attribute somewhat differently than the IMG element.

When used with the FRAME and IFRAME elements, the longdesc attribute provides a long description of the contents of the frame. This definition is used to supplement the contents of the title attribute used with these elements. This information is particularly useful for non-visual user agents, as it provides them with a means of understanding the intended organization of the document.

When used with the IMG element, the longdesc attribute specifies a link to the long description of the image. The description that is linked directs your users to, and should provide a supplement, to the contents of the alt attribute. If this attribute is used with an image map, it should be used to provide information about the contents of the map.

No matter which element you are using the longdesc tag with, its syntax is

```
longdesc = "url"
```

Elements

    FRAME   IFRAME   IMG

CROSS-REFERENCE
See alt and title.

loop

Property

DHTML

This property specifies how many times a sound or video clip will be repeated, or how many times a MARQUEE will display its contents. You can use this property to both set and retrieve the number of times the element should repeat itself. The number of loops can be any value of −1 or greater. The syntax for the loop command is

```
object.loop=number
```

Example

The following lines of code show you how the loop property can be used in a MARQUEE to control the number of times the text is displayed.

```
<MARQUEE loop> once  </marquee><br>
<MARQUEE loop=-1> infinitely </marquee><br>
<MARQUEE loop=0> once </marquee> <br>
<MARQUEE loop=> zero </marquee> <br>
<MARQUEE loop=10> ten </marquee> <br>
```

 NOTE

MARQUEE is only available in Internet Explorer. The loop attribute is not implemented properly.

Elements

   BGSOUND   IMG   MARQUEE

lowsrc

Property

DHTML

This property is used to specify in image to use on low-resolution monitors. You can use it to either retrieve or set the value of an image. If you wish to change the value of the lowsrc property, you will need to do so before setting the src value. If an image is currently being loaded into the image cell, it will override any other changes that you try to make.

The syntax for `lowsrc` is

```
object.lowsrc[=url]
```

Example
The following code is used to display a smaller ball if the screen resolution is 640480 or lower.

```
<IMG src="bigball.gif" lowsrc="blueball.gif">
```

Elements

IMG

 **CROSS-REFERENCE**
See Resolution.

Macros

Concept

Anyone who has tried to automate a function in a program has probably found macros to be a lifesaver. *Macros* are small programs, self-contained by the software application for which they were developed, that are used to perform a specific action or accomplish a task automatically. Because macros are program-specific, they cannot be run outside of their originating host package.

CROSS-REFERENCE

See **Scripting, Scripts, JavaScript, VBScript,** and **ECMAScript**.

<maction>

Element

MathML

Start Tag: Required
End Tag: Required

This MathML element is used to bind a particular action to an expression. For example, you may wish your readers to be able to toggle between a shorthand and longhand expression. You might also wish to provide specific information on the status line or as a tool tip that would help your reader understand what is happening with your equation. The maction element provides you with all of these capabilities. As the document author, you simply need to decide how the information is best displayed and set the element's attributes accordingly.

Attributes
actiontype (required)

```
actiontype="toggle | statusline | tooltip | highlight | menu"
```

The `actiontype` attribute specifies the type of action that has been specifically tied to an expression. If the user agent reading the MathML expression does not recognize the specified `actiontype`, the agent should render the subexpressions based upon the number specified in the `selection` attribute. Because MathML-compliant user agents are not required to recognize any of the following `actiontypes`, a user agent can implement MathML just by implementing the default behavior described in the previous sentence.

The available values for this attribute vary depending upon the user agent rendering the document. The following list of values is simply for illustration purposes and should not be considered all-inclusive.

```
<maction actiontype="toggle" selection="1">
  (expression 1)
  (expression 2)...
</maction>
```

An `actiontype` value of **toggle** gives the user the ability to alternately display the series of expressions identified in the `maction` element. This enables the reader to click on an expression and reveal a series of underlying expressions. One common use of this element is outlined in Example 1, which shows how you can use toggle to show each stage in the development of an expression. Because various expressions can be different sizes, you may need to use some type of panning mechanism to view the expressions fully.

```
<maction actiontype="statusline">
  (expression)
  (message) …
</maction>
```

If the value of `actiontype` is **statusline,** your readers can receive extra information about your expression on the user agent's status line. The expression is displayed normally on your document, but when selected, your status-line message appears. In most cases, the `mtext` element containing the status line message uses straight ASCII text.

```
<maction actiontype="tooltip">
  (expression)
  (message) …
</maction>
```

When `actiontype` is set to **tooltip,** the user agent displays a pop-up "tooltip" box when the mouse is held over the expression for a long enough delay time. In most cases, the mtext element containing the tool-tip box message uses straight ASCII text, although some user agents may provide for more advanced text display.

```
<maction actiontype="highlight" other="color= red">
   (expression)
</maction>
```

If the value of actiontype is **highlight,** the changes in the other attribute are made when the mouse is held over the expression long enough for a mouse-over event to be activated. The other attribute is used in this case to pass nonstandard information to the user agent.

```
<maction actiontype="menu" selection="1">
   (menu item 1)
   (menu item 2)...
</maction>
```

If the value of actiontype is **menu,** the user agent is instructed to create a pop-up menu. This value enables you to create a one-to-many relationship between the options in the menu. You can even use nested maction commands to create menus with subitems on them.

selection

selection=*positive-integer*

This attribute identifies the number of expressions that are available when the actiontype is set to **toggle** or **menu.** The value of this attribute specifies the first subexpression to view among those displayed by this element. The number must be between 1 and the total number of subexpressions identified by maction. If the number specified in the selection attribute does not correspond to a valid subexpression, it creates an error. When this attribute is not specified, it defaults to the value of 1.

The value of this attribute affects not only the maction element, but also all the elements it contains, by controlling their display order.

other

other="*style-despcriptor*"

This attribute can be used to control how the expression appears from strictly a style standpoint when it is selected. You can use this attribute to change the color and font of an expression. This attribute is most often used with the **highlight** actiontype attribute.

Example 1
The following example code shows you how to create a MathML expression that can be toggled between steps for solving the following equation:

```
<math>
    <maction actiontype="toggle" selection="1">
<mtd>
    <mrow>
        <mrow>
            <maligngroup/>
            <mn> 8.5 </mn>
            <mo> &InvisibleTimes; </mo>
            <maligngroup/>
            <mi> x </mi>
        </mrow>
        <maligngroup/>
        <mo> + </mo>
        <mrow>
            <maligngroup/>
            <mn> 2 </mn>
            <mo> &InvisibleTimes; </mo>
            <maligngroup/>
            <mi> y </mi>
        </mrow>
    </mrow>
    <maligngroup/>
    <mo> = </mo>
    <maligngroup/>
    <mn> 0 </mn>
</mtd>
<mtd>
    <mrow>
        <mrow>
            <maligngroup/>
            <mn> 6 </mn>
            <mo> &InvisibleTimes; </mo>
            <maligngroup/>
            <mi> x </mi>
        </mrow>
        <maligngroup/>
        <mo> - </mo>
        <mrow>
            <maligngroup/>
            <mn> 1</mn>
            <mo> &InvisibleTimes; </mo>
```

```
            <maligngroup/>
            <mi> y </mi>
        </mrow>
    </mrow>
    <maligngroup/>
    <mo> = </mo>
    <maligngroup/>
    <mrow>
        <mn> 2 </mn>
    </mrow>
</mtd>
    </maction>
</math>
```

Example 2

The following example code shows you how to create nested pop-up menu items for your expressions.

```
<math>
    <maction actiontype="menu" selection="1">
        <mtext> Menu option 1 </mtext>
        <mtext> Menu option 2 </mtext>
        <maction actiontype="menu" selection="1">
            <mtext> Option A </mtext>
            <mtext> Option B </mtext>
        </maction>
        <mtext> Menu option 3 </mtext>
    </maction>
</math>
```

<maligngroup/>

Element

MathML

Start Tag: Required
End Tag: Forbidden

When you work with mathematical equations, alignment is crucial. By changing the alignment of an equation set, you can change the numbers that the equation works with. When you specify an alignment using MathML, you need to specify the points that are to be aligned in each equation and the beginning of the alignment group. You must also specify which parts of the equation do not have any alignment needs. The maligngroup element provides you with part of this function. This tag is displayed as a zero-width element on your documents, so you need not worry about the tag changing the appearance of the remaining text of your document.

The alignment groups start at the first maligngroup element. You need to place the maligngroup element before each group of characters that you wish to have aligned in your document. You can use this element only within an existing alignment structure such as the mtable or mrow elements. Any other use of the maligngroup element is ignored.

Attributes
groupalign

```
groupalign= left | right | center | decimalpoint
groupalign-list= (groupalign) (groupalign) (groupalign) ...
```

This attribute identifies the arrangement of a group's alignment points when the malignmark element is not used. By default, the value of this property is inherited from this element's parent.

When using groupalign in your maligngroup element, you need to specify an alignment property for just that individual group. If you specify the groupalign in one of the parent elements, you need to specify the alignment of each group that occurs in its expression.

If the value of groupalign is **left, right,** or **center,** the point that is aligned is defined as the group's left, right, or midpoint, respectively.

If the value of groupalign is **decimalpoint,** the point that is aligned is defined as the right edge of the character directly to the left of the decimal point. The decimal point in this case is the first period (.) that is found in the first mn element in the equation. If your mn element is contained within a maction element block, the decimal point is applied only to the expression that is identified in the maction selection= attribute. If any character other than a period (.) is used as a decimal point, you should precede it with the malignmark/ element rather than use the groupalign attribute.

Example

Let's take the following equations and align them so they can be properly worked in our HTML documents.

```
8.5x + 2y = 0
6x - 1y = 2
```

The code for properly aligning these two equations follows:

```
<mtable groupalign="decimalpoint left left decimalpoint left
left decimalpoint">
<mtd>
    <mrow>
```

```
   <mrow>
      <maligngroup/>
      <mn> 8.5 </mn>
      <mo> &InvisibleTimes; </mo>
      <maligngroup/>
      <mi> x </mi>
   </mrow>
   <maligngroup/>
   <mo> + </mo>
   <mrow>
      <maligngroup/>
      <mn> 2 </mn>
      <mo> &InvisibleTimes; </mo>
      <maligngroup/>
      <mi> y </mi>
   </mrow>
</mrow>
<maligngroup/>
<mo> = </mo>
<maligngroup/>
<mn> 0 </mn>
</mtd>
<mtd>
   <mrow>
      <mrow>
         <maligngroup/>
         <mn> 6 </mn>
         <mo> &InvisibleTimes; </mo>
         <maligngroup/>
         <mi> x </mi>
      </mrow>
      <maligngroup/>
      <mo> - </mo>
      <mrow>
         <maligngroup/>
         <mn> 1</mn>
         <mo> &InvisibleTimes; </mo>
         <maligngroup/>
         <mi> y </mi>
      </mrow>
   </mrow>
   <maligngroup/>
   <mo> = </mo>
   <maligngroup/>
   <mrow>
```

```
            <mn> 2 </mn>
        </mrow>
    </mtd>
</mtable>
```

Elements

The `maligngroup/` element can be contained within the following elements:

maction   mfenced   mphantom   mrow

mstyle   semantics

Element

MathML

Start Tag: Required
End Tag: Forbidden

This element is used with the `maligngroup/` element when no `groupalign` attribute has been specified or when a special character needs to be used as an alignment marker.

Attributes
edge

```
edge= left | right
```

This attribute specifies whether the left or right edge of an element or a character should be used for the alignment point. If `malignmark` is set to **left**, the alignment point is the right edge of the character immediately to the left of the `malignmark` element. If `malignmark` is set to **right**, the alignment point is the left edge of the element immediately to the right of the marker.

Example

```
<mtd>
    <mrow>
        <mrow>
            <maligngroup/>
            <mn> 1<malignmark/ edge="left">.8 </mn>
            <mo> &InvisibleTimes; </mo>
            <maligngroup/>
            <mi><malignmark/ edge="right"> x </mi>
        </mrow>
```

```
         <maligngroup/>
         <mo> <malignmark/ edge="right">+ </mo>
         <mrow>
             <maligngroup/>
             <mn> 18 <malignmark/ edge="left"></mn>
             <mo> &InvisibleTimes; </mo>
             <maligngroup/>
             <mi> <malignmark/ edge="right">y </mi>
         </mrow>
      </mrow>
      <maligngroup/>
      <mo><malignmark/ edge="right"> = </mo>
      <maligngroup/>
      <mrow>
          <mn> <malignmark/ edge="right">1099 </mn>
      </mrow>
   </mtd>
```

Elements

The `malignmark/` element can be contained within the following elements:

    maligngroup/

<MAP>

Element

HTML

    Start Tag: Required
    End Tag: Required

This element is required when you identify the name and areas of a client-side image map. You can create a map using an `OBJECT`, `IMG`, or `INPUT` element. Each map element contains one or more `AREA` or `A` elements that identify the geometrical regions that work as hot spots for linking to other documents. Image maps make it more difficult for individuals using text-only user agents or handicapped viewers to discern your links. If you use an image map in a document, you should also use separate individual links to make navigation easier for these groups.

Attributes

class

```
class="cdata-list"
```

This attribute is used to assign a class name to an element. User agents employ classes to group specific types of information for later use.

dir

```
dir = LTR | RTL | [CS | CI | CN | CA | CT]
```

This attribute defines the direction of the text flow in a document so a user agent can display it correctly. It can also be used to specify information about the case of the characters.

id

```
id="name"
```

This attribute is used to assign a name to an element.

lang

```
lang="language code"
```

This attribute specifies the language in which an element and its values should be rendered.

name

```
name=cdata
```

This attribute is used to give the MAP a name that is used as an identifier when automating your map data or outlining your map areas.

onclick

```
onclick=script
```

This attribute takes effect when a user clicks the button on a pointing device with the pointer over an element.

ondblclick

```
ondblclick=script
```

This attribute takes effect when the button on a pointing device is double-clicked with the pointer over an element.

onkeydown

```
onkeydown=script
```

This attribute takes effect when a key is pressed while the pointer is over an element.

onkeypress

```
onkeypress=script
```

This attribute takes effect when a key is pressed and released with the pointer over an element.

onkeyup

```
onkeyup=script
```

This attribute takes effect when a key is released with the pointer over an element.

onmousedown

```
onmousedown=script
```

This attribute takes effect when the button on a pointing device is pressed with the pointer over an element.

onmousemove

```
onmousemove=script
```

This attribute is activated when the mouse is moved while the pointer is over an element.

onmouseout

```
onmouseout=script
```

This attribute is activated when the mouse pointer is moved away from an element.

onmouseover

```
onmouseover=script
```

This attribute is activated when the mouse pointer is moved over an element.

onmouseup

```
onmouseup=script
```

This attribute takes effect when the button on a pointing device is released with the pointer over an element.

l
m
n

style

```
style=style descriptors
```

This attribute is used to apply specific style-sheet information to one particular element.

title

```
title=text
```

This attribute provides annotation information to the element.

Example

The following image map is used to navigate a technical support site for a small consulting firm. The animation does not alter the effectiveness of the image map.

ON THE CD-ROM
Look for **map.htm** on the accompanying CD-ROM.

```
<HTML>
<HEAD>
   <TITLE>Animated GIF Imagemap</TITLE>
</HEAD>
<BODY>
   <P>
   <MAP name="animap">
    <AREA href="email.html" shape="poly" coords="40,40,146,146,
    0,146,40,40">
    <AREA href="fax.html" shape="poly" coords="40,40,146,146,
    146,0,40,40">
    <AREA href="faq.html" shape="poly" coords="146,0,146,146,
    256,40,146,0">
    <AREA href="online.html" shape="poly"    coords="256,40,146,
    146,299,146,256,40">
    <AREA href="news.html" shape="poly" coords="299,146,146,146,
    260,260,299,146">
    <AREA href="dbase.html" shape="poly" coords="260,260,146,
    146,146,299,260,260">
    <AREA href="write.html" shape="poly" coords="146,299,146,
    146,40,260,146,299">
    <AREA href="call.html" shape="poly" coords="40,260,146,146,
    0,146,40,260">
   </MAP>
   <IMG src="tswheelani.gif" type="image/gif" usemap="#animap">
</BODY>
</HTML>
```

CROSS-REFERENCE
See **<AREA>** and **Image Map**.

margin

Attribute

CSS

This Cascading Style Sheets attribute is used to control the margins on the page block. It can be used with all the HTML elements. This attribute is used as a shorthand for setting the `margin-top`, `margin-bottom`, `margin-right`, and `margin-left` properties for your stylesheet.

The syntax for this command is

```
margin: margin-width[1,4] | inherit
```

Values
margin-width[1,4]

The **margin-width** is a length value representing either an absolute or a relative number using a specific unit value. You can have up to four lengths listed for this value. If there is a single value assigned for `margin`, it is used for all the margins of the document. If there are two values, the first is used for the top and bottom margins, and the second is used for the right and left document margins. In the case of three identified values, the first is the top, the second is the right and left margins, and the third is used for the bottom margin. If all four values have been set, the first is the top margin, the second is the right side, the third is the bottom, and the fourth creates the left document margin.

inherit

If the value of `margin` is set to inherit, it uses the value of the parent element. If the `margin` is applied to a whole document through an `@page` element, inherit becomes an invalid value.

Example
The following groups of examples are equal statements.

This group uses three values in the margin statement to set dimensions for all four sides of the document. As you can see, the `2cm` setting is applied to both the right and left margins.

```
BODY { margin:  1cm 2cm 3cm }

BODY {margin-top: 1cm
```

```
    margin-right: 2cm
    margin-left: 2cm
    margin-bottom: 3cm  }
```

This second group uses a single setting in the margin statement to control the margins of the entire document. As you can see, the 2pc setting is applied to all the margins of the page.

```
@page { margin: 2pc }

@page {margin-top: 2pc
       margin-right: 2pc
       margin-left: 2pc
       margin-bottom: 2pc }
```

This third group has two values in the margin statement that are used to set the top and bottom and the left and right margins separately for a particular block element. As you can see, the 1ex setting is applied to the top and bottom margins of the object, and the 2ex setting is applied to the right and left margins of the object.

```
blockquote { margin: 1ex 2ex }

blockquote {margin-top: 1ex
       margin-right: 2ex
       margin-left: 2ex
       margin-bottom: 1ex }
```

Elements

The margin attribute is available for all HTML elements.

 CROSS-REFERENCE
See **length**, **margin-bottom**, **margin-left**, **margin-right**, and **margin-top**.

margin-bottom

Attribute

CSS

This attribute is used to set the bottom margin of the box generated by an HTML element.

The syntax of this attribute is

```
margin-bottom: margin-width | inherit
```

Values
margin-width

> The margin-width is a length value representing either an absolute or a relative number using a specific unit value.

inherit

> If the value of margin is set to inherit, it uses the value of the parent element. If the margin is applied to a whole document through an @page element, inherit is an invalid value.

Elements
This attribute can be applied to all HTML elements.

CROSS-REFERENCE
See **length**, **margin (CSS Attribute)**, **margin-left**, **margin-right**, and **margin-top**.

margin-left

Attribute

CSS

This attribute is used to set the left margin of the box generated by an HTML element.

The syntax of this attribute is

```
margin-left: margin-width | inherit
```

Values
margin-width

> The margin-width is a length value representing either an absolute or a relative number using a specific unit value.

inherit

> If the value of margin is set to inherit, it uses the value of the parent element. If the margin is applied to a whole document through an @page element, inherit is an invalid value.

Elements
This attribute can be applied to all HTML elements.

CROSS-REFERENCE
See **length**, **margin** (CSS attribute), **margin-bottom**, **margin-right**, and **margin-top**.

margin-right

Attribute

CSS

This attribute is used to set the right margin of the box generated by an HTML element.

The syntax of this attribute is

```
margin-right: margin-width | inherit
```

Values
margin-width

The margin-width is a length value representing either an absolute or a relative number using a specific unit value.

inherit

If the value of margin is set to inherit, it uses the value of the parent element. If the margin is applied to a whole document through an @page element, inherit is an invalid value.

Elements
This attribute can be applied to all HTML elements.

CROSS-REFERENCE
See **length**, **margin** (CSS attribute), **margin-bottom**, **margin-left**, and **margin-top**.

margin-top

Attribute

CSS

This attribute is used to set the top margin of the box generated by an HTML element.

The syntax of this attribute is

```
margin-top: margin-width | inherit
```

Values
margin-width

The margin-width is a length value representing either an absolute or a relative number using a specific unit value.

inherit

If the value of margin is set to inherit, it uses the value of the parent element. If the margin is applied to a whole document through an @page element, inherit is an invalid value.

Elements
This attribute can be applied to all elements.

CROSS-REFERENCE

See **length**, **margin (CSS Attribute)**, **margin-bottom**, **margin-left**, and **margin-right**.

marks

Attribute

CSS

Cascading Style Sheets provides a method for a document author to force marks to appear on a page delineating where the paper should be cut and/or how pages should be aligned. These marks are added outside of the page box. The user agent controls the rendering of the marks, which are only displayed on absolute page boxes. Relative page boxes are aligned against a target page, in most cases forcing the marks off the edge of the page.

The marks attribute can only be used with the @page element. Its syntax follows.

```
@page { marks: crop | cross | inherit | none }
```

Values
crop

These marks identify the edges along which to cut the paper.

cross

These marks, also known as *registration marks*, are used to align pages after printing.

inherit

> The document inherits its specific dimensions and marks from the user agent displaying the author's information.

none

> No marks are displayed, or used, on the document.

Example

The following statement shows how to use the marks command to create a series of marks around the text of a document.

ON THE CD-ROM

Look for **mark.htm** on the accompanying CD-ROM.

```
<HTML>
    <HEAD>
        <TITLE>The Mark Attribute</TITLE>
        <STYLE type="text/css">
            @page {marks: cross crop }
        </STYLE>
    </HEAD>
    <BODY>
        This text is displayed with a series of cropping
        and cross marks that make it easier for your
        reader's equipment to find the outer edges of
        the printed area of your documents.<BR>
    </BODY>
</HTML>
```

Elements

@page

Markup Characters

Concept

Markup characters are used by markup languages to identify specific pieces of information. In the case of HTML, the angle brackets (< >) are used to identify an element and its respective attributes, and the ampersand (&) and semicolon (;;) are used to identify a specific character reference. Each markup language uses its own set of characters to identify the elements used in that language.

CROSS-REFERENCE

See **Markup Language** and **Extended Backaus-Naur Form**.

Markup Language

Concept

A *markup language* is any language that can be used to create documents in which the formatting is controlled by a series of tags or elements. The two most popular markup languages are currently HTML and SGML. Markup languages are used in practically every type of information-sharing system available.

When you create a document in a markup language, you specify the structural, presentational, and semantic information in addition to, and alongside, the content you are displaying in the document. Most markup languages share the following characteristics:

- A *declaration* of the specific markup characters and delimiters that are used in the language.

- A *document type definition* (DTD), which defines the syntax of the markup elements and their respective attributes. This document can also include additional reference information such as character tables.

- A *description of the semantics of the language,* including any restrictions on arguments that can't be expressed within the DTD.

Markup languages are generally designed to be malleable so they can grow as their respective industries change and develop. Take the case of HTML. As a derivative language based on SGML, HTML uses a series of elements, attributes, character references, and comments to identify individual sections and presentation layouts in a document. A basic HTML document has the following structure:

```
<HTML>
   <HEAD>
      <TITLE> This is the title.</TITLE>
   </HEAD>
   <BODY>
      This is the body.
   </BODY>
</HTML>
```

The document has two sections: the *head* (identified by the `<HEAD>` / `</HEAD>` markers), and the *body* (identified by the `<BODY>` / `</BODY>` markers). In HTML, information about the entire document is contained within the head section. This information consists mostly of style sheet specifications, the document title, and meta information. The body of the document contains the contents of the document that are displayed for the reader.

684 • Markup Language

CROSS-REFERENCE
See **HTML**, **Markup Characters**, **XML**, and **SGML**.

markupdecl

Attribute

XML

This attribute of the XML `DTD` statement is used to identify the type of elements, attributes, entities, and notations that are used within this type of document. This statement is part of the `doctypedecl` employed by a user agent to identify the standards and declarations that are valid for use in the document.

The `markupdecl` code syntax is

```
markupdecl=elementdecl | attlistdecl | entitydecl |
notationdecl | PI | Comment
```

CROSS-REFERENCE
See **Document Type Definition**.

<MARQUEE>

Element

HTML — Internet Explorer Only

Start Tag: Required
End Tag: Required

This element is used to create a scrolling object containing text information that can be displayed on an author's HTML document. `MARQUEE` is supported only by Internet Explorer.

Attributes
behavior

```
behavior=alternate | scroll | slide
```

This attribute controls how the text in your `marquee` moves across your screen. **Alternate** forces the text to rotate first to the left and then to the right.

Scroll forces the text to scroll in the direction specified in the `direction` attribute. The text scrolls off one end of the `marquee` and then starts over at the other end.

Slide forces the text to scroll in the direction specified in the `direction` attribute. The text stops when it reaches the end of the `marquee` box.

bgcolor

`bgcolor=colorname | RGBcolor`

This attribute controls the color of the background of the element. You can use either the color name or the hex value of the color.

class

`class="cdata-list"`

This attribute is used to assign a class name to an element. User agents employ classes to group specific types of information for later use.

datafld

`datafld=colname`

This contains the name of the column of information that is the source for information found in the `marquee`.

dataformatas

`dataformatas=html | text`

This attribute indicates whether the data is from a plain text or an HTML source.

datasrc

`datasrc=#id`

This attribute provides the name of the data source that is supplying information to this element.

direction

`direction=down | left | right | up`

The value of this attribute controls the direction of the scrolling text.

height

`height=number`

The value of this attribute controls the height of the `marquee` either in pixels or as a percentage of the total screen height.

hspace

`hspace=number`

The value of this attribute specifies the horizontal margins of the `marquee` box.

id

id="*name*"

This attribute is used to assign a name to an element.

lang

lang="*language code*"

This attribute specifies the language in which an element and its values should be rendered.

language

language=javascript | jscript | vbscript | vbs

loop

loop=*number*

This is the total number of times the element loops.

onafterupdate

onafterupdate=*script*

This attribute becomes active after an onbeforeupdate element fires. Once started, this event cannot be cancelled.

onblur

onblur=*script*

This element becomes active after a button, a checkbox, or another input element loses the input focus.

onbounce

onbounce=*script*

This event fires when the behavior property of this element is set to **alternate** and the text of the marquee reaches a side.

onclick

onclick=*script*

This attribute takes effect when a user clicks the button on a pointing device with the pointer over an element.

ondblclick

`ondblclick=script`

This attribute takes effect when the button on a pointing device is double-clicked with the pointer over an element.

ondragstart

`ondragstart=script`

This attribute becomes active when a user begins to drag a selected element.

onfinish

`onfinish=script`

This attribute fires when the looping process triggered by the `loop` attribute finishes.

onfocus

`onfocus=script`

When an element receives the focus of either the mouse or the cursor, this element becomes active.

onhelp

`onhelp=script`

This attribute fires when a user accesses the help menu or presses the F1 key.

onkeydown

`onkeydown=script`

This attribute takes effect when a key is pressed while the pointer is over an element.

onkeypress

`onkeypress=script`

This attribute takes effect when a key is pressed and released with the pointer over an element.

onkeyup

`onkeyup=script`

This attribute takes effect when a key is released while the pointer is over an element.

onmousedown

`onmousedown=script`

This attribute takes effect when the button on a pointing device is pressed with the pointer over an element.

onmousemove

`onmousemove=script`

This attribute is activated when the mouse is moved while the pointer is over an element.

onmouseout

`onmouseout=script`

This attribute is activated when the mouse pointer is moved away from an element.

onmouseover

`onmouseover=script`

This attribute is activated when the mouse pointer is moved over an element.

onmouseup

`onmouseup=script`

This attribute takes effect when the button on a pointing device is released with the pointer over an element.

onresize

`onresize=script`

The script contents of this attribute fire when a resize operation begins.

onrowenter

`onrowenter=script`

Whenever a row changes and new information is available, this attribute becomes active.

onrowexit

`onrowexit=script`

This attribute becomes active just before your data source control changes away from the current information row.

onselectstart

`onselectstart=script`

This attribute fires when a user first selects the element.

onstart

`onstart=script`

This attribute becomes active at the beginning of a loop cycle or at the start of another bounce cycle when the `behavior` of the `marquee` is set to **alternate**.

scrollamount

`scrollamount=number`

This value represents the distance in pixels that text scrolls between subsequent drawings of the `marquee` element.

scrolldelay

`scrolldelay=milliseconds`

This is the speed, in milliseconds, at which the `marquee` scrolls.

style

`style=style descriptors`

This attribute is used to apply specific style-sheet information to one particular element.

title

`title=text`

This attribute provides annotation information to the element.

truespeed

`truespeed`

This attribute forces the time specified in the `scrolldelay` attribute to be used when selecting the timing on the `marquee`'s movements. This forces the scroll to take up to 60 milliseconds.

vspace

`vspace=number`

The value of this attribute specifies the vertical margins of the `marquee` box.

width

```
width=number
```

This is the width of the marquee box in pixels or as a percentage of the entire screen width.

Example

The following example displays the Octogenarian League Baseball Scores for their final tournament.

 ON THE CD-ROM

Look for **marquee.htm** on the accompanying CD-ROM.

```
<HTML>
    <HEAD>
        <TITLE>The OLB using a Marquee</TITLE>
    </HEAD>
    <BODY>
        <H1> Octogenarian League Baseball</H1>
        <DIV align="center">
        <MARQUEE> 1999 Octogenarian League Top Teams:
            Tinsel Town Toon-Smiths 12- 0,
            Cartesian Cantelopers 11-1,
            Twilled Tulip Trimmers 11- 1,
            MASH Monsters 10 - 2
        </MARQUEE>
        </DIV>
    </BODY>
</HTML>
```

<math>

Element

MathML

Start Tag: Required
End Tag: Required

To include MathML expressions in an HTML document, you must specify a single top-level math element. This element must serve as the bounds on all other MathML content. Both math tags must always be expressed, and it is illegal for one math element to contain another. You can have any number of child elements contained within your math tags.

Attributes
class

```
class="cdata-list"
```

This attribute is used to assign a class name to an element. User agents employ classes to group specific types of information for later use. Although this is not implemented, it has been provide for future Cascading Style Sheets compatibility.

macros

```
macros="URL URL..."
```

This attribute enables the document author to use external macro files. Although macros currently are not part of the MathML specification, they are expected in the future.

mode

```
mode="display | inline "
```

This attribute controls the rendering of the math expression. The default value is inline.

style

```
style=style descriptors
```

This attribute is used to apply specific style-sheet information to one particular element. This attribute has been added for future Cascading Style Sheets compatibility.

Example

The following code shows how the math element is used within an HTML document to display a MathML expression.

ON THE CD-ROM

Look for **math.htm** on the accompanying CD-ROM.

```
<HTML>
<HEAD>
   <TITLE> Embedding MathML in and HTML document </TITLE>
</HEAD>
<BODY>
   The following equations are displayed using MathML.
   <math style=display>
 <mtable>
    <mtd>
    <mrow>
      <mrow>
```

```
                <maligngroup/>
                <mn> 1<malignmark/ edge="left">.8 </mn>
                <mo> &InvisibleTimes; </mo>
                <maligngroup/>
                <mi><malignmark/ edge="right"> x </mi>
            </mrow>
            <maligngroup/>
            <mo> <malignmark/ edge="right">+ </mo>
            <mrow>
                <maligngroup/>
                <mn> 18 <malignmark/ edge="left"></mn>
                <mo> &InvisibleTimes; </mo>
                <maligngroup/>
                <mi> <malignmark/ edge="right">y </mi>
            </mrow>
        </mrow>
        <maligngroup/>
        <mo><malignmark/ edge="right"> = </mo>
        <maligngroup/>
        <mrow>
            <mn> <malignmark/ edge="right">1099 </mn>
        </mrow>
    </mtd>
        </mtable>
        </math>
    </BODY>
    </HTML>
```

CROSS-REFERENCE
See **MathML**.

Mathematics

Concept

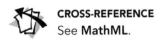

CROSS-REFERENCE
See **MathML**.

mathline

Descriptor

CSS

This attribute is used to set the mathematical baseline for a font. This attribute is used for alignment by ideographic scripts, whereas the lower baseline is used by Latin, Greek, and Cyrillic scripts. This attribute must be used with the `units-per-em` descriptor. If this descriptor is not used, the user agent uses the font's baseline for alignment. This descriptor is used only for visual media.

```
mathline=number
```

NOTE
Ideographic scripts are those characters used in mathematical equations that represent specific functions such as the square root sign, a division marker, or an area-based range marker.

CROSS-REFERENCE
See **Alignment**, **baseline**, **centerline**, and **topline**.

MathML

Language

Mathematics has been a hot topic for the world since history was first recorded. It has taken us only ten years to be able to display math efficiently on the most popular information dispersal tool of the 20th Century. With the completion of the MathML specification, mathematicians and scientists around the world can finally display mathematical equations in a meaningful manner without creating bulky graphics files or displaying their work in a sloppy manner using tables and spaces.

The main goal of the MathML committee was to create a language that would enable mathematics to be viewed and processed on the Web in the same manner that HTML has enabled text to be displayed. MathML is an XML application designed for controlling both the vertical and horizontal alignment of characters in equations displayed on HTML pages. MathML enables document authors to describe all mathematical notation and content while correctly representing both its structure and content.

Commands

MathML currently uses over 100 commands to show mathematical notation correctly. The 28 commands that are listed below are used to control its presentation but not necessarily the meaning of its content. You can study the remaining MathML commands at the World Wide Web Consortium's (W3C) Web site (www.w3.org/TR/PR-math).

\<maction\>

This command is used to bind actions to a subexpression.

\<maligngroup/\>

This command is used to set up alignment markers for equations using multiple expressions.

\<malignmark/\>

This command is used to set up alignment markers for individual characters within expressions.

\<merror\>

This command enables the author to enclose a syntax error message from the preprocessor.

\<mfenced\>

This command is used to surround math content with a pair of fences.

\<mfrac\>

This command enables you to form a fraction from two subexpressions.

\<mi\>

This element is used to mark any identifier such as x, y, or z.

\<mmultiscripts\>

You can attach prescripts and tensor indices to base values with this element.

\<mn\>

This element is used to note a decimal number.

\<mo\>

This element is used to note an operator, fence, or separator (+, –, *, /, and so on).

\<mover\>

Using mover, you can attach an overscript to base.

\<mpadded\>

Using mpadded, you can adjust the space around document content.

\<mphantom\>

This element makes its contents invisible while preserving its size.

\<mroot\>

Authors can use mroot to form a radical.

\<mrow\>

Using mrow, authors group subexpressions horizontally.

\<ms\>

This element creates a string literal of its contents.

\<mspace/\>

This element inserts a space into your expression.

\<msqrt\>

Authors can use msqrt to create a square root form of a radical.

\<mstyle\>

This element is used to change the style of your expression.

\<msub\>

You can attach subscript to base with this element.

\<msubsup\>

This element is used to attach a subscript-superscript pair to a base.

\<msup\>

You can attach superscript to a base with this element.

\<mtable\>

This element marks the start and finish of a table or matrix.

\<mtd\>

This element marks a single entry in a table or matrix.

\<mtext\>

This element notes standard text information found within your expressions.

<mtr>

This element marks a single row in a table or matrix.

<munder>

You can attach an underscript to a base with this element.

<munderover>

You can attach underscript-overscript to a base with this element.

Example

The following example shows how to use some MathML elements in an HTML document to display math functions and processes correctly.

ON THE CD-ROM

Look for **mathml.htm** on the accompanying CD-ROM.

```
<HTML>
<HEAD>
    <TITLE> Embedding MathML in and HTML document </TITLE>
</HEAD>
<BODY>
    <!-- This equation is  (a+b)^2. -->
    <H3> (a+b)<sup>2</sup> expressed using MathML </H3>
    <math style=display>
        <mtable>
          <mtd>
           <msup>
           <mfenced>
           <mrow>
              <mi>a</mi>
              <mo>+</mo>
             <mi>b</mi>
           </mrow>
           </mfenced>
           <mn>2</mn>
           </msup>
       </mtd>
   </mtable>
</math>

    <!-- This equation is  ( x^2 + 8x +8 =0) -->
    <H3> x<sup>2</sup> + 8x + 8 = 0  expressed using MathML </H3>
    <math style=display>
       <mtable>
```

```
    <mrow>
        <mrow>
            <msup>
                <mi>x</mi>
                <mn>2</mn>
            </msup>
            <mo>+</mo>
            <mrow>
                <mn>8</mn>
                <mo>&InvisibleTimes;</mo>
                <mi>x</mi>
            </mrow>
            <mo>+</mo>
            <mn>8</mn>
        </mrow>
        <mo>=</mo>
        <mn>0</mn>
    </mrow>
   </mtable>
</math>

</-- This equation is x= (-b &plusmn; &sqrt; (b<sup>2</sup> -
4ac) ) / 2a -->
<H3> x= (-b &plusmn; &sqrt; (b<sup>2</sup> - 4ac) ) / 2a
expressed using MathML </H3>
<math style=display>
    <mtable>
        <mrow>
            <mi>x</mi>
            <mo>=</mo>
            <mfrac>
            <mrow>
              <mrow>
                <mo>-</mo>
                <mi>b</mi>
              </mrow>
              <mo>&PlusMinus;</mo>
              <msqrt>
                  <mrow>
                    <msup>
                        <mi>b</mi>
                        <mn>2</mn>
                    </msup>
                    <mo>-</mo>
```

```
              <mrow>
                 <mn>4</mn>
                 <mo>&InvisibleTimes;</mo>
                 <mi>a</mi>
                 <mo>&InvisibleTimes;</mo>
                 <mi>c</mi>
              </mrow>
           </mrow>
        </msqrt>
     </mrow>
     <mrow>
        <mn>2</mn>
        <mo>&InvisibleTimes;</mo>
        <mi>a</mi>
     </mrow>
     </mfrac>
   </mrow>
</mtable>
</math>

</- This equation is A= [ x y] over [ z u ] ->
<IMG src="mathml.gif"> <FONT size=+3>expressed using MathML
</FONT><P>
<math style=display>
   <mtable>
      <mrow>
         <mi>A</mi>
         <mo>=</mo>
         <mfenced open="[" close="]">
            <mtable>
               <mtr>
                  <mtd><mi>x</mi></mtd>
                  <mtd><mi>y</mi></mtd>
               </mtr>
               <mtr>
                  <mtd><mi>z</mi></mtd>
                  <mtd><mi>w</mi></mtd>
               </mtr>
            </mtable>
         </mfenced>
      </mrow>
   </mtable>
</math>
</BODY
</HTML>
```

CROSS-REFERENCE
See **<math>**, **<mtable>**, and **<mtd>**.

max-height

Attribute

CSS

This attribute is used to constrain the height of an element's box on your HTML documents.

The syntax for this command is

```
max-height: none | length | percentage | inherit
```

Values

none

There is no limit to the height of the box used by this element.

length

This value specifies a fixed maximum computed height for the box of the element.

percentage

This value is used for computing the height of the box and is based upon the containing block of the element.

inherit

This value specifies that the maximum height of this block should be inherited from the parent element.

Example

In the following code examples, the maximum height is set to control the development of specific block elements in a document.

```
<STYLE type="text/css">
   BLOCKQUOTE  {max-height: 3px }
   IMG  {max-height: 150% }
   OBJECT {max-height: 15pc }
</STYLE>
```

Elements

This attribute is applied to all HTML elements.

CROSS-REFERENCE
See **height**, **max-width**, **min-height**, and **min-width**.

max-width

Attribute

CSS

This attribute is used to constrain the width of an element's containment block on HTML documents.

The syntax for this command is

```
max-width: none | length | percentage | inherit
```

Values

none

There is no limit to the width of the box used by this element.

length

This value specifies a fixed maximum computed width for the box of the element.

percentage

This value is used for computing the width of the box and is based upon the containing block of the element.

inherit

This value specifies that the maximum width of this block should be inherited from its parent element.

Example

In the following code example, the maximum width has been set to control the rendering of specific block elements in a document.

```
<STYLE type="text/css">
   H1  {max-width: 20px }
   PRE {max-width: 150% }
   IMG {max-width: 15pc }
</STYLE>
```

Elements
This attribute is applied to all HTML elements.

CROSS-REFERENCE
See *width*, *max-height*, *min-height*, and *min-width*.

maxLength

Property

DHTML

This document object property attribute applies to the number of characters that can be entered into an INPUT box. Although this value cannot be negative, it can be greater than the actual size of the box. If the maxLength value is greater than the field size, the text area should scroll automatically as the reader types. By default, this attribute has no limit. You can both set and retrieve the size of a text INPUT field using this attribute.

```
object.maxLength=number.
```

Example
The following sample script sets the number of characters that can be entered into the "First Name" field on an HTML form.

```
<HTML>
<HEAD>
  <TITLE> Setting maxLength </TITLE>
</HEAD>
<BODY>
THis is a test <br>
<FORM name="testform" action="http://myweb.website.com"
method="POST">
First Name:
<input type="Text" name="fname" value="fred">
</form>
<SCRIPT language="javascript">
   {
   testform.elements('fname').maxLength = 15
   }
</SCRIPT>

</BODY>
```

</HTML> Elements
INPUT

CROSS-REFERENCE
See **<INPUT>** and **size**.

Media

Concept

You use a variety of media every day. While watching television, you are using both aural and visual media. When you are reading a newspaper, you get the sense of paged and tactile media. While reading this book you are using both paged and tactile media; and if you use the accompanying CD-ROM, you will experience the joy of page-based visual media. When you are reading documents off the Internet, you are experiencing visual, aural, and paged media at an awesome rate. As the Web grows, you can design pages that can incorporate multiple visual and auditory effects; these, in turn, affect how well your chosen medium communicates. At their most basic, media are simply devices used to provide information to those who need it and to facilitate communications.

CROSS-REFERENCE
See **Media Groups**, **Media Types**, and **@media**.

Media Groups

Concept

CSS

Every Cascading Style Sheets attribute in the specification identifies the specific media type(s) to which that attribute can be applied by a conforming user agent. Each of these attribute definitions specifies its own valid group of mediad. The valid media groups, which may have attributes designed for them, are as follows:

- Visual/Aural/Tactile
- Continuous/Paged
- Grid/Bitmap
- All

The media groups are so closely interconnected that if an attribute is not specified explicity for one or the other of these groups, that attribute is valid for all the related groups. Table M-1 helps you see how the specified media types are tied into specific media groups.

Table M-1 Media Groups

Media Groups/ Media Types	Visual/Aural/ Tactile	Continuous/ Paged	Interactive/ Static	Grid/ Bitmap
All				
Aural	Aural	Continuous	Both	N/A
Braille	Tactile	Continuous	Both	Grid
Embossed	Tactile	Paged	Both	Grid
Handheld	Visual	Both	Both	Both
Print	Visual	Paged	Static	Bitmap
Projection	Visual	Paged	Static	Bitmap
Screen	Visual	Continuous	Both	Bitmap
TTY	Visual	Continuous	Both	Grid
TV	Aural/Visual	Both	Both	Both

CROSS-REFERENCE
See **@media**, **Media Types**, and **Media**.

Media Types

Concept

CSS

Ten types of media have been identified with Cascading Style Sheets. User agents need not support all these types of media; if they do support a particular medium, however, they must support its corresponding media group.

All

This value designates that the following style sheet is suitable for all devices.

Aural (continuous, aural)

This value designates that the following style sheet is to be used with speech synthesizers.

Braille (continuous, tactile)

This value designates that the following style sheet is to be used with Braille tactile feedback devices.

Embossed (paged, tactile)

This value designates that the following style sheet is to be used with paged Braille printers.

Handheld (visual)

This value designates that the following style sheet is to be used with handheld devices such as Windows CE palmtops, monochromatic monitors, and Palm Pilots.

Print (paged, visual)

This value designates that the following style sheet is to be used with all printed and opaque material and for documents that are viewed onscreen in print preview mode.

Projection (paged, visual)

This value designates that the following style sheet is to be used with projected presentations. The presentation can be either on a projector or printed to transparencies.

Screen (continuous, visual)

This value designates that the following style sheet is to be used primarily for color computer screens.

TTY (continuous, visual)

This value designates that the following style sheet is to be used for teletypes and terminals that use a fixed-pitch character grid. Document developers should avoid using pixel units with the TTY media type.

TV (aural, visual)

This value designates that the following style sheet is to be used with television-type devices that use a low resolution, are color, and have a limited ability to scroll.

CROSS-REFERENCE
See **Aural Style Sheets**, **Paged**, **Continuous**, **Tactile**, **Aural**, **Visual**, and **Media Groups**.

<MEMSIZE>

Element

OSD

Start Tag: Required
End Tag: Forbidden

The MEMSIZE element is used to specify the total amount of run-time memory that a specified software application requires.

Attributes
value

    value=KB-number

This is the number of bytes of memory, in kilobytes, required for this program while it is being executed.

Elements
MEMSIZE is a child element of IMPLEMENTATION.

 **CROSS-REFERENCE**
See **<DISKSIZE>**.

<MENU>

Element

HTML

Start Tag: Required
End Tag: Required

The MENU element was used to create a menu listing of items that, with some user agents, would be displayed differently than the UL and OL elements. This element has been deprecated in favor of the UL and OL elements.

Attributes
class

    class="cdata-list"

This attribute is used to assign a class name to an element. User agents employ classes to group specific types of information for later use.

dir

```
dir = LTR | RTL | [CS | CI | CN | CA | CT]
```

This attribute defines the direction of the text flow in a document so a user agent can display it correctly. This attribute can also be used to specify information about the case of the characters.

id

```
id="name"
```

This attribute is used to assign a name to an element.

lang

```
lang="language code"
```

This attribute specifies the language in which an element and its values should be rendered.

onclick

```
onclick=script
```

This attribute takes effect when a user clicks the button on a pointing device with the pointer over an element.

ondblclick

```
ondblclick=script
```

This attribute takes effect when the button on a pointing device is double-clicked with the pointer over an element.

onkeydown

```
onkeydown=script
```

This attribute takes effect when a key is pressed while the pointer is over an element.

onkeypress

```
onkeypress=script
```

This attribute takes effect when a key is pressed and released with the pointer over an element.

onkeyup

```
onkeyup=script
```

This attribute takes effect when a key is released with the pointer over an element.

onmousedown

```
onmousedown=script
```

This attribute takes effect when the button on a pointing device is pressed with the pointer over an element.

onmousemove

```
onmousemove=script
```

This attribute is activated when the mouse is moved while the pointer is over an element.

onmouseout

```
onmouseout=script
```

This attribute is activated when the mouse pointer is moved away from an element.

onmouseover

```
onmouseover=script
```

This attribute is activated when the mouse pointer is moved over an element.

onmouseup

```
onmouseup=script
```

This attribute takes effect when the button on a pointing device is released with the pointer over an element.

style

```
style=style descriptors
```

This attribute is used to apply specific style-sheet information to one particular element.

title

```
title=text
```

This attribute provides annotation information to the element.

Example

The following code creates a menu with six options, each of which would open an additional page of information about the listed topic if the site were complete.

ON THE CD-ROM

Look for **menu.htm** on the accompanying CD-ROM.

```
<HTML>
    <HEAD>
        <TITLE>HTML Menus </TITLE>
    </HEAD>
    <BODY>
        <SCRIPT language="javascript">
        {
        function OnOil (){
            // enter code to open document here//
            }
        function OnLotion (){
            // enter code to open document here//
            }
        function OnSuits (){
            // enter code to open document here//
            }
        function OnUmbrellas (){
            // enter code to open document here//
            }
        function OnTowels (){
            // enter code to open document here//
            }
        function OnToys (){
            // enter code to open document here//
            }
        }
        </SCRIPT>
        <H1> Our HOTTEST Beach Supplies</H1>
        <MENU>
            <LI onclick ="OnOil()"> Tanning Oil
            <LI onclick ="OnLotion()"> Tanning Lotions
            <LI onclick ="OnSuits()"> Bathing Suits
            <LI onclick ="OnUmbrellas()"> Beach Umbrellas
            <LI onclick ="OnTowels()"> Beach Towels
            <LI onclick ="OnToys()"> Sand Toys
    </BODY>
</HTML>
```

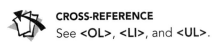

CROSS-REFERENCE

See **<OL>**, **<LI>**, and **<UL>**.

<merror>

Element

MathML

Start Tag: Required
End Tag: Required

This element displays its contents as an "error message." This can be done in a variety of ways, including displaying the contents in a vivid color, blinking the contents, or altering the background color of the element's contents. This element was designed to provide MathML-generating programs a standard way of reporting syntax errors in data. Although the function of the merror element was outlined, there are no rules as to the format of the error messages it can contain. Let's assume that application developers will make their error messages as easy for viewers to read as possible.

The merror element can contain any expression or expression sequence. If it contains more than one argument or expression, its entire contents are treated as a single mrow element.

Attributes
color

```
color= #rgb | #rrggbb | color-name
```

This attribute sets the color for the text revealed by the element. By default, this value is inherited from the document.

fontfamily

```
fontfamily= string | css-fontfamily
```

This attribute identifies the font family in which the math error message should be displayed. By default, this value is inherited from the document.

fontsize

```
fontsize= number v-unit
```

This attribute controls the size of the font you have selected, just as this attribute does for a standard HTML element. By default, this value is inherited from the document.

fontstyle

```
fontstyle= normal | italic
```

This attribute identifies the content of the element as either normal text or italicized text.

fontweight

```
fontweight= normal | bold
```

This attribute controls the weight of the characters being displayed. By default, this value is inherited.

 **CROSS-REFERENCE**
See **MathML**.

<META>

Element

HTML

Start Tag: Required
End Tag: Forbidden

Although the HTML META tag is not required on your pages, it is probably the most important tag to be placed on your HTML header. META tags provide information about your page to the servers and search engines on the Internet. They do not affect the document content or layout. These tags can be used to inform a viewer's browser when a document has expired so it can be refreshed automatically. They can inform your visitors about you, the document author, providing them with names and e-mail addresses for making comments on the page. META tags allow search engine spiders to sort through your information and include the terms that you find most important within their indexed lists. You won't always see this information listed in each HTML file, but it can be used to help both search engines and Web servers report information about your site.

There are three rules for using META tags:

1. The tag must appear between HEAD and /HEAD tags.
2. You must place the META tag after the background tags.
3. The start tag is required; the end tag is forbidden.

Attributes

content

```
content="text-string"
```

This attribute specifies the value of the previously designated property. The contents of this attribute vary depending upon the assigned name of the property.

dir

```
dir=LTR | RTL | [CS | CI | CN | CA | CT]
```

This attribute defines the direction of the text flow in a document so a user agent can display it correctly. It can also be used to specify information about the case of the characters.

http-equiv

```
http-equiv="text-identifier"
```

This attribute is generally interchangeable with the `name` attribute. HTTP servers can use this attribute's contents to gather specific information about your page for inclusion in an HTTP response message header. The label applied to these properties needs to be specified in your document profile. Some of the commonly used labels are listed below:

```
Custodian
Custodian Contact
Description
Expires
Keywords
Owner
Owner Contact
Publication Date
Refresh
Reply to
```

lang

```
lang="language-code"
```

This attribute identifies the base language used for an element's content. The language specification can be used to assist search engines, speech synthesizers, spelling checkers, and grammar checkers. It can also assist Web browsing software in determining glyph values for typography, choosing quotation marks, hyphenation, and even spacing.

name

```
name="text-identifier"
```

This attribute specifies the name that a property is using. Although there is no list of valid property names, many are commonly used. You can specify the property names to be used in your document profile. The most common are listed below.

```
Author
Copyright
Description
```

```
Date
Keywords
```

scheme

This attribute specifies a specific method of interpreting the Meta data, which has been previously specified in your document profile.

Example

The following examples of available META tags provide the retrieving server or user agent most of the information that you would want to know for tracking information about a particular HTML document:

```
<META NAME="Author" CONTENT="Heather Williamson">
<META HTTP-EQUIV = "Expires" CONTENT="Thu, 1 Jan 1998 12:00:00
PST">
<META NAME= "description" CONTENT ="Come visit us to find
great summer and winter activities.">
<META NAME= "keywords" CONTENT= "hunting, fishing,
backpacking, cross-country skiing, horseback riding, llama
treks">
<META http-equiv= "Publication_Date" CONTENT= "December 1997">
<META http-equiv= "Custodian" CONTENT= "Heather Williamson">
<META http-equiv= "Custodian Contact" CONTENT= "Heather
Williamson, phone, fax, email">
<META http-equiv= "Custodian Contact Position" CONTENT=
"Developer: Business Marketing Unit">
<META http-equiv= "Owner" CONTENT= "Jenine Williamson">
<META http-equiv= "Reply to" CONTENT=
"HTMLMaster@catsback.com">
```

The lines just displayed would return the following information as part of an HTTP response to a GET or HEAD request for that document:

```
Author: Heather Williamson
Expires: Thu, 1 Jan 1998 12:00:00 PST
Description: Come visit us to find great summer and winter
activities.
Keywords: hunting, fishing, backpacking, cross-country skiing,
horseback riding, llama treks
Publication_Date: December 1997
Custodian: Heather Williamson
Custodian Contact: Heather Williamson, phone, fax, email
Custodian Contact Position: Developer: Business Marketing Unit
Owner: Jenine Williamson
Reply to: HTMLMaster@catsback.com
```

CROSS-REFERENCE
See **Profile**.

Meta Data

Concept

Meta data is information about a specific document, rather than part of its content. Although the World Wide Web Consortium (W3C) does not specify a set of legal meta-data properties, document authors can create a set of properties and legal values for those properties in a profile. Profiles can be designed for any function from helping search engines recognize and index documents to assisting specialized document filters to save and sort the information found in a document correctly.

Generally, two steps are required to specify meta data:

1. Either declare a property and a value for that property through the META element within a document, or use the LINK element to link to the data found outside of the document.

2. Reference a profile where the property and its legal values are defined. If you use this method to declare your meta data, your profile applies to all META and LINK elements in your document.

User agents are not required to support meta data statements. Any interpretation of meta data by a user agent is strictly up to the user agent.

CROSS-REFERENCE
See **<META>**.

Meta Tags

Concept

CROSS-REFERENCE
See **<META>**.

method

Attribute

HTML

This attribute is used within a FORM element to control how information is submitted from the specified form.

The syntax of this command is

```
method= get | post
```

JAVASCRIPT

```
object.method=[sMethod]
```

This property is used to set the method property for a selected form object.

Values

get

This value specifies the HTTP get method, in which the form data set is appended to the URI specified by the FORM's action attribute and this new URI is sent to the processing agent. The get method should be used when the form cannot cause any side effects to the URL. Many application designers use the get method to complete database searches. If you choose to use the HTTP get method, you are limited to transmitting ASCII characters.

post

This HTTP post method combines the entire form and form data and sends it directly to the processing agent. This allows you to include more than just ASCII characters in your form processes. Post is normally used when you want to write information to a database or send information over e-mail.

Elements

FORM

CROSS-REFERENCE
See <INPUT>.

<mfenced>

Element

MathML

Start Tag: Required
End Tag: Required

This element is used to provide a way to express the common equation break-downs involving fences such as braces, brackets, and parentheses. It has also been expanded to include separators such as commas that often occur between arguments. The mfenced element is used to represent a pair of fences. If you need to show a single fence character, use the mo element instead.

An mfenced element is capable of containing no or multiple arguments enclosed in an mrow statement. For nested parenthetical statements, the use of nested mrow elements is required around the mfenced expressions.

Attributes

A generic mfenced element, with all of its attributes specified, is similar to the following code segment.

```
<mfenced open="opening-fence"
         close="closing-fence"
         separators="sep#1 sep#2 ... sep#(n-1)" >
    arg#1
    ...
    arg#n
</mfenced>
```

close

```
close="string"
```

This string represents the symbol to use as your fence. Valid characters for this string are ")", "]", and "}".

color

```
color= #rgb | #rrggbb | color-name
```

This attribute sets the color for the text revealed by the element. By default, this value is inherited from the document.

fontfamily

```
fontfamily= string | css-fontfamily
```

This attribute identifies the font family in which the fenced statement should be displayed. By default, this value is inherited from the document.

fontsize

```
fontsize= number v-unit
```

This attribute controls the size of the font you have selected, just as this attribute does for a standard HTML element. By default, this value is inherited from the document.

fontstyle

```
fontstyle= normal | italic
```

This attribute identifies the content of the element as either normal text or italicized text. The content is italicized by default.

fontweight

```
fontweight= normal | bold
```

This attribute controls the weight of the characters being displayed. By default, this value is inherited.

open

```
open="string"
```

This string represents the symbol to use as your fence. Valid characters for this string are "(", "[", and "{".

separator

```
separator= "character"
```

This character, or string of characters, represents the symbol to use as a separator in your equations. Common separator characters are ",", ";", and "|". If a statement has too many separator characters, the extra characters are ignored; conversely, if there are too few characters, the last one is repeated as necessary for the equation.

Examples

The following MathML code displays $(x+y)$ correctly.

```
<mfenced>
    <mrow>
        <mi> x </mi>
        <mo> + </mo>
        <mi> y </mi>
    </mrow>
</mfenced>
```

NOTE

In the statement given here, the mrow element is necessary so that the default separator attribute of the mfenced element does not incorrectly display the statement as (x, +, y).

In the following two statements, you do not need to use the mrow element because there should be a separator between the listed items. Note also that because the open bracket is specified but the close bracket isn't, your statement is closed with the default parenthesis, as follows: [1,0)

```
<mfenced open="[">
    <mn> 1 </mn>
    <mn> 0 </mn>
</mfenced>
```

f(*x,y*)

```
<mrow>
    <mi> f </mi>
    <mo> &ApplyFunction; </mo>
    <mfenced>
        <mi> x </mi>
        <mi> y </mi>
    </mfenced>
</mrow>
```

CROSS-REFERENCE

See **<mrow>** and **<mo>**.

<mfrac>

Element

MathML

Start Tag: Required
End Tag: Required

The mfrac element is used to display fractions, although you can use it to mark up any fractionlike object such as a binomial coefficient.

Attributes

color

```
color= #rgb | #rrggbb | color-name
```

This attribute sets the color for the text revealed by the element. By default, this value is inherited from the document.

fontfamily

```
fontfamily= string | css-fontfamily
```

This attribute identifies the font family in which the fraction should be displayed. By default, this value is inherited from the document.

fontsize

```
fontsize= number v-unit
```

This attribute controls the size of the font you have selected, just as this attribute does for a standard HTML element. By default, this value is inherited from the document.

fontstyle

```
fontstyle= normal | italic
```

This attribute identifies the content of the element as either normal text or italicized text. The content is italicized by default.

fontweight

```
fontweight= normal | bold
```

This attribute controls the weight of the characters being displayed. By default, this value is inherited.

linethickness

```
linethickness=number [ v-unit ] | thin | medium | thick
```

This attribute controls the thickness of the horizontal fraction bar, or *rule*, used to render fractions. A linethickness="0" statement creates a fraction without a visible bar. The value of linethickness can be a number, a number with a unit of length, or one of the following keywords: **medium** is equal to 1, **thin** is less than 1 (although the user agent decides upon the rendered thickness), and **thick** is greater than 1 (again, the user agent decides upon the rendered thickness).

Examples

The following code is used to create a properly displayed fraction 1/2.

```
<mrow>
   <mfrac linethickness="1">
      <mn> 1 </mn>
      <mn> 2 </mn>
   </mfrac>
</mrow>
```

The following code creates a multidimensional fraction:

```
<mfrac linethickness="2">
   <mfrac>
      <mi> x </mi>
      <mi> y </mi>
   </mfrac>
   <mfrac>
      <mi> a </mi>
      <mi> b </mi>
   </mfrac>
</mfrac>
```

<mi>

Element

MathML

Start Tag: Required
End Tag: Required

This element is used to represent a symbolic name or text that represents an identifier. Identifiers can be designated in part or whole as variables, function names, or symbolic constants. Because mi is a presentation element, its content should be rendered as an identifier, although individual user agents may function differently. You need to be aware that not all math identifiers are represented by the mi element. If a variable is either subscripted or primed, it is represented using the msub or msup elements.

In addition to this rule, the names of symbolic constants should be displayed using the mi element as shown in the following three examples:

<mi> &pi; </mi>

<mi> sin </mi>

<mi> &ExponentialE; </mi>

Attributes

color

```
color= #rgb | #rrggbb | color-name
```

This attribute sets the color for the text revealed by the element. By default, this value is inherited from the document.

fontfamily

```
fontfamily= string | css-fontfamily
```

This attribute identifies the font family in which the math identifier should be displayed. By default, this value is inherited from the document.

fontsize

```
fontsize= number v-unit
```

This attribute controls the size of the font you have selected, just as this attribute does for a standard HTML element. By default, this value is inherited from the document.

fontstyle

```
fontstyle= normal | italic
```

This attribute identifies the content of the element as either normal text or italicized text. If the content of the mi element is a character, the content is italicized by default. If the contents are numerical, they are displayed normally.

fontweight

```
fontweight= normal | bold
```

This attribute controls the weight of the characters being displayed. By default, this value is inherited.

Examples

The following statements show some of the ways that the mi attribute can be used to display information that should be treated as a constant, variable, or function.

```
<mi>: <mi> x </mi>
<mi> D </mi>
<mi> cos </mi>
<mi></mi>
<mtext>/** This element is allowed with no content. **/
</mtext>
```

With MathML, identifiers are designed to include function names such as "sin," "cos," and "tan." Using MathML, you can write expressions such as "tan *x*" using the ⁡ operator as shown in the following code.

```
<mrow>
<mi> tan </mi>
<mo> &ApplyFunction; </mo>
<mi> x </mi>
</mrow>
```

NOTE
Some functions will not be displayed properly in Amaya, W3C's browser for testing MathML, although all of the examples conform to the MathML specification.

CROSS-REFERENCE
See **<mo>**.

MIME

Concept

MIME (Multipurpose Internet Mail Extensions) is the format originally designed for Internet mail to allow the transmission of binary, audio, video, and graphics files as attachments to e-mail messages. MIME has also been used to identify specific document and file types used on the World Wide Web. With the MIME standard, new file formats can be accommodated by simply updating the user agent's list of MIME-Type pairs and the appropriate software for handling each type.

CROSS-REFERENCE
See **MIME Types** and **type**.

MIME Types

Concept

Table M-2 is not even remotely a complete list of MIME types. Because this list changes on a daily basis, you should simply use it as a preliminary guide. If you have any other questions about MIME types, you should consult the MIME resource center located at http://www.oac.uci.edu/indiv/ehood/MIME.

Table M-2 MIME Types and Their Associated Functions

Type	Subtype	Description
text	plain	Plain ASCII text file.
	richtext	Text file using the RTF extensions.
	enriched	
	tab-separated-values	
	html	HTML-formatted file.
	sgml	SGML-formatted file.
	uri-list	List of Uniform Resource Locators.
	rfc822-headers	RFC822-formatted text headers.
	css	Cascading Style Sheets document.
multipart	mixed	Contains multiple types of information.
	alternative	
	digest	
	parallel	
	appledouble	
	header-set	
	form-data	Results of a FORM submittal.
	related	
	report	
	voice-message	Multipart voice message.
	signed	
	encrypted	Encrypted message with unencrypted material.
	byteranges	
message	rfc822	RFC822-formatted encapsulated message.
	partial	Part of a larger message.
	external-body	The body of the message is not included, only referenced.
	news	NNTP News-formatted information.
	http	HTTP-formatted information packets.
	delivery-status	
	disposition-notification	
application	octet-stream	
	postscript	Adobe Postscript document.
	oda	
	slate	
	wita	

Type	Subtype	Description
	dec-dx	DEC document.
	dca-rft	
	activemessage	
	rtf	Rich Text Format.
	applefile	Apple-formatted document.
	mac-binhex40	Macintosh BinHex-compressed file.
	wordperfect5.1	WordPerfect 5.1-formatted document.
	pdf	Adobe PDF-formatted document.
	zip	Zipped file.
	macwriteii	Mac Write II-formatted document.
	msword	Microsoft Word-formatted document.
	remote-printing	
	mathematical	
	cybercash	Cybercash document.
	commonground	
	iges	
	riscos	
	eshop	
	x400-bp	
	sgml	SGML-formatted file.
	pgp-encrypted	PGP-encrypted document.
	pgp-signature	PGP-encrypted signature.
	pgp-keys	PGP encryption key.
	vnd.framemaker	Adobe FrameMaker-formatted document.
	vnd.ms-excel	Microsoft Excel-formatted document.
	vnd.ms-powerpoint	Microsoft PowerPoint-formatted presentation.
	vnd.ms-project	Microsoft Project-formatted document.
	vnd.ms-works	Microsoft Works-formatted document.
	vnd.ms-artgalry	Microsoft Art Gallery-formatted display.
	vnd.truedoc	TrueDoc-formatted document.
	vnd.webturbo	
	vnd.hp-HPGL	HTGL-formatted document.
	vnd.hp-PCL	PCL-formatted document.
	vnd.hp-PCLXL	PCLXL-formatted document.
	pkcs7-mime	
	pkcs10	

Continued

l
m
n

Table M-2 *Continued*

Type	Subtype	Description
image	jpeg	JPEG image.
	gif	Graphic Interchange Format.
	ief	Image Exchange Format.
	tiff	Tag Image File Format.
	cgm	Computer Graphics Metafile.
	png	PNG formatted graphic.
audio	basic	
	32kadpcm	
	vnd.qeclp	
video	mpeg	MPEG-formatted video.
	quicktime	Apple QuickTime Format.
	vnd.motorola video	Motorola-formatted video.
	vnd.motorola.vidoep	Motorola-formatted video.
	vrml	Virtual Reality Markup Language.

CROSS-REFERENCE
See **MIME** and **type**.

min-height

Attribute

CSS

This attribute is used to constrain the height of an element's containing block on your HTML documents.

The syntax for this command is

```
min-height: length | percentage | inherit
```

Values

length

This value specifies a fixed minimum computed height for the box of the element.

percentage

This value is used for computing the minimum allowable height of the box and is based upon the containing block of the element.

inherit

This value specifies that the minimum height of this block should be inherited from the parent element.

Example

In the following code example, the minimum height is set to control the display of specific block elements in a document.

```
<STYLE type="text/css">
    H6   {min-height: 1px }
    B    {min-height: 50% }
    AREA {min-height: 1pc }
</STYLE>
```

Elements

This attribute is applied to all HTML elements.

CROSS-REFERENCE
See **height**, **max-width**, **max-height**, and **min-width**.

min-width

Attribute

CSS

This attribute is used to constrain the width of an element's containing block on HTML documents.

The syntax for this command is

```
min-width: length | percentage | inherit
```

Values

length

This value specifies a fixed minimum computed width for the box of the element.

percentage

This value is used for computing the minimum allowable width of the box and is based upon the containing block of the element.

inherit

This value specifies that the minimum width of this block should be inherited from the parent element.

Example

In the following code example, the minimum width is set to control the development of specific block elements in a document through the document's style sheet.

```
<STYLE type="text/css">
   AREA  { min-width: 10px }
   PRE   { min-width: 75% }
   H2 { min-width: 1pc }
</STYLE>
```

Elements

This attribute is applied to all elements.

 CROSS-REFERENCE
See **width**, **max-width**, **max-height**, and **min-height**.

Mixed-Content Declaration

Concept

XML

When you are defining elements using XML, you often need to define an element that must contain both character data and child elements. The only way to do this is to use *mixed-content declaration* to identify the specific types of child elements that are valid within the statement. Using these types of declarations, you can control the identity of the child elements, but you can't control their number or their order.

```
Mixed:: { #PCDATA (Name) | (Name) | (Name) ...}
```

 **CROSS-REFERENCE**
See **Declaration**.

<mmultiscripts>

Element

MathML

Start Tag: Required
End Tag: Required

This element is used to display presubscripts and tensor notations. If you wish to render any number of vertically aligned pairs of subscripts and superscripts attached to a single base expression, you have to use `mmultiscripts`. You can use postscripts and prescripts, the former appearing to the right of your base expression and the latter to the left. Any missing sub- or superscript must be represented by an empty `none/` element.

Generally, in an `mmultiscripts` element arrangement, the argument sequence is composed of a base expression and then zero or more pairs of vertically aligned subscripts and superscripts.

Attributes

color

```
color= #rgb | #rrggbb | color-name
```

This attribute sets the color for the text revealed by the element. By default, this value is inherited from the document.

fontfamily

```
fontfamily= string | css-fontfamily
```

This attribute identifies the font family in which the numeral should be displayed. By default, this value is inherited from the document.

fontsize

```
fontsize= number v-unit
```

This attribute controls the size of the font you have selected, just as this attribute does for a standard HTML element. By default, this value is inherited from the document.

fontstyle

```
fontstyle= normal | italic
```

This attribute identifies the content of the element as either normal text or italicized text.

fontweight

```
fontweight= normal | bold
```

This attribute controls the weight of the characters being displayed. By default, this value is inherited.

subscriptshift

```
subscriptshift= number
```

This attribute controls the minimal distance that the subscript's baseline is shifted down.

superscriptshift

```
superscriptshift= number
```

This attribute controls the minimal distance that the superscript's baseline is shifted up.

Example

The following example code shows both a prescript and a postscript, using subscripts without matching superscripts to represent the equation:

$${}_0F_5(:a;d)$$

```
<mrow>
    <mmultiscripts>
        <mi> F </mi>
        <mn> 5 </mn>
        <none/>
        <mprescripts/>
        <mn> 0 </mn>
        <none/>
    </mmultiscripts>
    <mo> &ApplyFunction; </mo>
<mrow>
<mo> ( </mo>
<mrow>
    <mo> ; </mo>
    <mi> a </mi>
    <mo> ; </mo>
    <mi> d </mi>
</mrow>
<mo> ) </mo>
</mrow>
```

CROSS-REFERENCE
See **<msub>**, **<msup>**, and **<msubsup>**.

<mn>

Element

MathML

Start Tag: Required
End Tag: Required

The mn element is used to display a *numeric literal* or other data that should be displayed as a number. A numeric literal is simply a sequence of digits, possibly including a decimal point, that represents an unsigned integer or a real number. Because the true definition of a number depends upon the context in which it is used, negative numbers, complex numbers, ratios, and numeric constants should be displayed using other MathML tags such as the mfrac or the mi elements.

Attributes

color

```
color= #rgb | #rrggbb | color-name
```

This attribute sets the color for the text revealed by the element. By default, this value is inherited from the document.

fontfamily

```
fontfamily= string | css-fontfamily
```

This attribute identifies the font family in which the numeral should be displayed. By default, this value is inherited from the document.

fontsize

```
fontsize= number v-unit
```

This attribute controls the size of the font you have selected, just as this attribute does for a standard HTML element. By default, this value is inherited from the document.

fontstyle

```
fontstyle= normal | italic
```

This attribute identifies the content of the element as either normal text or italicized text.

fontweight

```
fontweight= normal | bold
```

This attribute controls the weight of the characters being displayed. By default, this value is inherited.

Examples

The following lines of code show a variety of ways to display numerical values using the mn element, which forces these values to be treated as a number.

```
<mn> 16 </mn>
<mn> 16,000,000 </mn>
<mn> 4.1e9 </mn>
<mn> MCMLXIX </mn>
<mn> 0.987 </mn>
<mn> 0xDEAF </mn>
<mn> twenty five </mn>
```

 CROSS-REFERENCE
See **<mfrac>**, **<mrow>**, **<mi>**, and **<mo>**.

<mo>

Element

MathML

Start Tag: Required
End Tag: Required

If you need to identify an operator in MathML, use the mo element. MathML includes a sophisticated mechanism allowing you to deal with the complicated nature of mathematical notation of operators. Because of this built-in flexibility, you can use the mo operator to include tildes, braces, brackets, parentheses, or other notations not normally thought of as operators. Table M-3 shows some of these common operators.

Table M-3 Common Mathematical Operators Used in Popular Formulas

Symbol or Code	Description
+	Addition
-	Subtraction

Symbol or Code	Description
/	Division
*	Multiplication
&lt;	Less than
&gt;	Greater than
&le;	Less than or equal to
&ge;	Greater than or equal to
&not;	Not sign
&plusmn;	Vertical plus/minus sign
&times;	Multiplication symbol
&divide;	Division symbol

Although the `mo` element has been designed to render mathematical operators, it can't display all operators without help. In some cases, it needs the assistance of elements such as `msub`, `msup`, or `mfrac`.

Some operators are invisible yet require specific spacing or other layout effects within the representation of an equation. These operators have specific entity references that are displayed within the `mo` element. Some of these "invisible operators" are

- **&InvisibleTimes (⁢)**, which is used for equations such as $2x$, where the multiplication of 2 and x is implied rather than outwardly stated using the multiplication sign (*)

- **&ApplyFunction (⁡)**, which is used for equations such as f(x) and sin x, where you need to apply the listed function to the numerical identifier

- **&InvisibleComma (⁣)**, which is used in statements such as m 12, where a comma is implied but not necessarily stated in normal mathematical notation

Attributes
accent

```
accent= true | false
```

This attribute is used to designate whether this operator is treated as a diacritical mark when it is used as either an underscript or an overscript. The default value for this element is false.

color

```
color= #rgb | #rrggbb | color-name
```

This attribute sets the color for the text revealed by the element. By default, this value is inherited from the document.

fence

```
fence= true | false
```

This attribute is used only for nonvisual user agents. The default value for this element is false.

fontfamily

```
fontfamily= string | css-fontfamily
```

This attribute identifies the font family in which the operator should be displayed. By default, this value is inherited from the document.

fontsize

```
fontsize= number v-unit
```

This attribute controls the size of the font you have selected, just as this attribute does for a standard HTML element. By default, this value is inherited from the document.

fontstyle

```
fontstyle= normal | italic
```

This attribute identifies the content of the element as either normal text or italicized text.

fontweight

```
fontweight- normal | bold
```

This attribute controls the weight of the characters being displayed. By default, this value is inherited.

form

```
form= prefix | infix | postfix
```

This attribute specifies the form to use when displaying the content of the element. If this element is not specified, there are rules that govern how it is applied by the user agent. If the form is **prefix,** it is applied before the next element in the statement. If the form is **infix** it is applied in the middle of the next element. If the form is set to **postfix,** it is applied after the following element.

largeop

```
largeop= true | false
```

This attribute specifies whether the operator should be drawn larger than the other elements. The default value of this attribute is false.

lspace

```
lspace= number h-unit
```

This attribute is used to designate the amount of space around an embellished operator. Unless otherwise specified, the value of this attribute is given in em units; the .27777em is the default value.

maxsize

```
maxsize= number [ v-unit | h-unit ] | infinity
```

This element is used to designate the maximum amount of stretch in an element in any direction. The default value of this attribute is infinity.

minsize

```
minsize= number [ v-unit | h-unit ]
```

This element is used to designate the minimum amount of stretch in an element in any direction. The default value of this attribute is 1.

movablelimits

```
movablelimits= true | false
```

This attribute is used to define whether underscripts and overscripts should be displayed as standard subscripts and superscripts. The default value of this attribute is false.

rspace

```
rspace= number h-unit
```

This attribute is used to designate the amount of space around an embellished operator. Unless otherwise specified, this attribute's value is in em units, and the default value of this attribute is (.27777em).

separator

```
separator= true | false
```

This attribute controls the placement of infix operators when the expression has to be broken into multiple lines. The default value of this attribute is false.

stretchy

```
stretchy= true | false
```

This attribute is used to designate whether the rendered operator can be stretched to the size of other elements on the document. The default value of this attribute is false.

symmetric

```
symmetric= true | false
```

This attribute controls the display of a character on the midline of its axis. If symmetric is **true**, the character is balanced about the midline. The default value of this attribute is true.

Example

```
<mo> + </mo>   /** Addition sign **/
<mo> &InvisibleTimes; </mo>   /** Multiply **/
<mo> &lt; </mo>  /** Less Than **/
<mo> &le; </mo>  /** Less Than or Equal To **/
<mo> ++ </mo>
<mo> &sum; </mo>
<mo> .NOT. </mo>
<mo> and </mo>
```

CROSS-REFERENCE
See Appendix C: Character Charts.

Model

Concept

A model in computer terminology is the same as it is in our everyday language. At its most basic, a model is a mock-up or description that is provided for individuals to gain a better understanding of the process or device that they are examining. A model can be a chart, graph, sketch, or paragraphic description. The model most often referred to in HTML programming is the Document Object Model (DOM). The DOM is a document outlining the structure and style associated with HTML documents and Cascading Style Sheets. It is used by developers and users of these languages as a guide for ensuring that all their documents maintain a specific set of standards and guides.

CROSS-REFERENCE
See Document Object Model.

move

Property

DHTML

This document object property is used to move a specified text range to a new location. When enacted, it collapses the text range, moves it, and then reinstates the contents of the text block.

The syntax of this command is

```
long= object.move(unit, [count])
```

Parameters
unit

This string specifies one of the following text areas to move. If *unit* is **character,** you move one or more characters as designated by the *count* parameter. If *unit* is **word,** you move one or more words as designated by the *count* parameter. **Sentence** specifies that you move one or more sentences or blocks of words designated as a collection by terminating punctuation characters. The setting of **textedit** moves the specified text range to the start or end of the original text range. If *count* is positive, the text moves to the end; if count is negative, it moves to the start of the range.

count

Although this property is optional, it specifies the number of units that should be moved. The default value of this property is 1, and the range includes both positive and negative integers.

Objects
TextRange

CROSS-REFERENCE
See **moveEnd** and **moveStart.**

moveBy

Method

DHTML

This document object method is used to move the position of the window on your reader's computer screen in relation to the x and y offset values that you specify.

The syntax of this command is

```
object.moveBy(x,y)
```

Parameters

x

This long value sets the horizontal scroll in pixels.

y

This long value sets the vertical scroll in pixels.

Objects

window

CROSS-REFERENCE
See moveTo.

moveEnd

Property

DHTML

This document object property is used to alter the range of the selected area by moving the end of the range.

The syntax of this command is

```
long=object.moveEnd(unit[,count])
```

Properties

unit

This string specifies one of the following text areas to move. If *unit* is **character**, you move one or more characters as designated by the *count* parameter. If *unit* is **word**, you move one or more words as designated by the *count* parameter.

Sentence specifies that you move one or more sentences or blocks of words designated as a collection by terminating punctuation characters. The setting of **textedit** moves the specified text range to the start or end of the original text range. If *count* is positive, the text moves to the end; if count is negative, it moves to the start of the range.

count

Although this property is optional, it specifies the number of units that should be moved. The default value of this property is 1, and the range includes both positive and negative integers.

Objects

TextArea

 CROSS-REFERENCE
See **move**, **moveStart**, and **<TEXTAREA>**.

<mover>

Element

MathML

Start Tag: Required
End Tag: Required

The mover element enables you to create an *overscript* within your expression. Overscripts can be used as either accent marks or limits. One of the most common uses of an overscript is with the repetitive character mark commonly seen in the results of long division expressions.

Attributes

accent

```
accent = true | false
```

The accent attribute controls whether *overscript* is drawn as an "accent" or as a limit. An accent mark is the same size as the base and is drawn closer to the base than a limit mark.

fontfamily

```
fontfamily= string | css-fontfamily
```

This attribute identifies the font family in which the script should be displayed. By default, this value is inherited from the document.

fontsize

```
fontsize= number v-unit
```

This attribute controls the size of the font you have selected, just as this attribute does for a standard HTML element. By default, this value is inherited from the document.

fontstyle

```
fontstyle= normal | italic
```

This attribute identifies the content of the element as either normal text or italicized text. The content is italicized by default.

fontweight

```
fontweight= normal | bold
```

This attribute controls the weight of the characters being displayed. By default, this value is inherited.

Example

The following example code, along with Figures M-1 and M-2, displays two versions of two equations. The first of each set is drawn as an accent mark; the second is drawn as a limit.

$$\hat{z} \quad \text{vs} \quad \hat{z}$$

Figure M-1 Using the accent attribute can create the impression of a true accent mark or a limit mark.

```
<mrow>
   <mover accent="true">
      <mi> z </mi>
      <mo> &hat; </mo>
   </mover>
   <mtext>   vs   </mtext>
   <mover accent="false">
      <mi> z </mi>
      <mo> &hat; </mo>
   </mover>
</mrow>
```

$$\overline{a+b-c} \quad \text{vs} \quad \overline{a+b-c}$$

Figure M-2 You can also use an accent to create the impression of a variety of equations.

```
<mrow>
    <mover accent="true">
        <mrow>
            <mi> a </mi>
            <mo> + </mo>
            <mi> b </mi>
            <mo> - </mo>
            <mi> c </mi>
        </mrow>
        <mo> &OverBar; </mo>
    </mover>
    <mtext>   vs   </mtext>
    <mover accent="false">
        <mrow>
            <mi> a </mi>
            <mo> + </mo>
            <mi> b </mi>
            <mo> - </mo>
            <mi> c </mi>
        </mrow>
        <mo> &OverBar; </mo>
    </mover>
</mrow>
```

moveStart

Method

DHTML

This document object method is used to alter the range of the selected area by moving the start of the range.

The syntax of this command is

```
long=object.moveStart(unit[,count])
```

Properties
unit

This string specifies one of the following text areas to move. If *unit* is **character,** you move one or more characters as designated by the *count* parameter. If *unit* is **word,** you move one or more words as designated by the *count* parameter. **Sentence** specifies that you move one or more sentences or blocks of words designated as a collection by terminating punctuation characters. The setting of **textedit** moves the specified text range to the start or end of the original text range. If *count* is positive, the text moves to the end; if count is negative, it moves to the start of the range.

count

Although this property is optional, it specifies the number of units that should be moved. The default value of this property is 1, and the range includes both positive and negative integers.

Objects
TextArea

 CROSS-REFERENCE
See **move, moveEnd,** and **<TEXTAREA>**.

moveTo

Method

DHTML

This document object method is used to move the position of the window on your reader's computer screen to the specified *x* and *y* pixel position.
The syntax of this command is

```
object.moveTo(x,y)
```

Parameters
x

This long value sets the horizontal position in pixels.

y

This long value sets the vertical position in pixels.

Objects
window

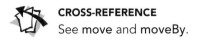

CROSS-REFERENCE
See **move** and **moveBy**.

moveToBookmark

Method

DHTML

This document object method moves the selected bookmark to the specified text range location.

The syntax of this method is

```
bSuccess = object.moveToBookmark(sBookmark)
```

Parameters
bSuccess

This returns **true** if the bookmark was moved and **false** if it wasn't.

sBookmark

This string identifies the bookmark to move. This is a required parameter.

Objects
TextRange

CROSS-REFERENCE
See **moveTo** and **moveBy**.

moveToElementText

Method

DHTML

Scripts using this document object method allow the document creator to alter the start and end positions of a text range so that it encompasses all of the text in a specified element. This selection process works in a fashion similar to a paragraph selection in a word processor.

The syntax of this command is

```
object.moveToElementText(element)
```

This method has a single parameter, *element*, which is used to identify the specific object that should be selected.

Objects

TextRange

CROSS-REFERENCE
See **move**, **moveBy**, **moveTo**, and **moveToPoint**.

moveToPoint

Method

DHTML

This document object method element allows the document author to move the start and end positions of a text range to specified points. The point references are in pixels and are relative to the upper left-hand corner of the document window. This method only moves an empty text range, although you can use the `expand` or `moveEnd` commands to adjust the range.

The syntax of this command is

```
object.moveToPoint(x,y)
```

Parameters

x

This long value sets the horizontal scroll in pixels.

y

This long value sets the vertical scroll in pixels.

Objects

TextRange

CROSS-REFERENCE
See **move**, **moveTo**, **moveBy**, and **moveToElementText**.

<mpadded>

Element

MathML

Start Tag: Required
End Tag: Required

The mpadded element enables you to control the overall size and dimensions taken up by its contents. Although this element does not stretch or shrink the content of the tags, it does create the appearance of bounds around the expression it contains. This enables you to control more accurately how the user agent displays your content. You can use the mpadded element to contain as many expressions as you need. If the element's content contains multiple expressions, they are all treated as if they were bound by an inferred mrow command.

Attributes

depth

```
depth= [ + | - ] number ( % [ pseudo-unit ] | pseudo-unit | v-
unit )
```

This attribute controls the amount of vertical space between the bottom of the bounding box and the baseline of the element's content. The length of the space is specified as either an increment () or a decrement () of the number of pseudo-units specified.

height

```
height= [ + | - ] number ( % [ pseudo-unit ] | pseudo-unit |
v-unit )
```

This attribute controls the amount of vertical space between the baseline and the top of the bounding box. The length of the space is specified as either an increment () or a decrement () of the number of pseudo-units specified.

lspace

```
lspac= [ + | - ] number ( % [ pseudo-unit ] | pseudo-unit | h-
unit )
```

This attribute provides document authors with the ability to add space between the left edge of the element's bounding box and the edge of its contents box. Lspace is the only attribute that does not correspond to a real property of a bounding box. It is computed during each instance of mpadded, and provided solely as a way to add space on the left edge of the element's content.

width

```
width= [ + | - ] number ( % [ pseudo-unit ] | pseudo-unit | h-
unit )
```

This attribute controls the horizontal width of the element's bounding box. When the lspace attribute is not specified, the left edge of a bounding box is drawn flush with the left edge of the element's content. This enables you to add space to only the right side of the box. The length of the space is specified as either an increment () or a decrement () of the number of pseudo-units specified.

Example

The following code examples show how the mpadded attributes can be used to control the bounding box dimensions.

```
<mpadded width="+9em"> ... </mpadded>
<mpadded lspace="+70%"> ... </mpadded>
<mpadded height="-3em"> ... </mpadded>
<mpadded width="- 1 height"> ... </mpadded>
<mpadded depth="90%"> ... </mpadded>
<mpadded width="10% width"> ... </mpadded>
<mpadded height="8 width"> ... </mpadded>
<mpadded length="3.0 width"> ... </mpadded>
<mpadded> ... </mpadded>
```

CROSS-REFERENCE
See length, <mtext>, and <mspace/>.

<mphantom>

Element

MathML

Start Tag: Required
End Tag: Required

"Only the phantom knows . . ." As with the radio show character, the mphantom element can't be seen by the viewer, but it maintains the size and dimensions that its content would normally require. One use for mphantom is to align segments of expressions by invisibly copying their subexpressions. The expressions contained within mphantom tags should use the same spacing rules as those contained in an mrow element. This element can accept an unlimited number of expressions.

NOTE

If you wish both to make an expression invisible and to control its size, you can wrap it in both an `mphantom` and an `mpadded` element.

Attributes

fontfamily

```
fontfamily= string | css-fontfamily
```

This attribute identifies the font family in which the expression should be displayed. By default, this value is inherited from the document.

fontsize

```
fontsize= number v-unit
```

This attribute controls the size of the font you have selected, just as this attribute does for a standard HTML element. By default, this value is inherited from the document.

fontstyle

```
fontstyle= normal | italic
```

This attribute identifies the content of the element as either normal text or italicized text.

fontweight

```
fontweight= normal | bold
```

This attribute controls the weight of the characters being displayed. By default, this value is inherited.

Example

The following code example uses the `mphantom` element as a means of ensuring the alignment of corresponding variables in the numerator and denominator of a fraction. The goal is to create an equation. This method forces the following equation to render as it is displayed here

```
a + b + c
─────────
a     + c
```

rather than here

```
a + b + c
─────────
  a + c
```

The following code is the MathML representation of this equation.

```
<mfrac>
    <mrow>
        <mi> a </mi>
        <mo> + </mo>
        <mi> b </mi>
        <mo> + </mo>
        <mi> c </mi>
    </mrow>
    <mrow>
        <mi> a </mi>
        <mphantom>
            <mo form="infix"> + </mo>
            <mi> b </mi>
        </mphantom>
        <mo> + </mo>
        <mi> c </mi>
    </mrow>
</mfrac>
```

 CROSS-REFERENCE
See <mfrac>, <mspace/>, and <mpadded>.

<mroot>

Element

MathML

Start Tag: Required
End Tag: Required

This element is used to construct radicals with indices, such as a cube root. This element requires two arguments. The first is the base value being evaluated. The second is the index value with which the base is being evaluated.

The syntax for this element is

```
<mroot> base index </mroot>
```

Attributes
fontfamily

```
fontfamily= string | css-fontfamily
```

This attribute identifies the font family in which the operator should be displayed. By default, this value is inherited from the document.

fontsize

```
fontsize= number v-unit
```

This attribute controls the size of the font you have selected, just as this attribute does for a standard HTML element. By default, this value is inherited from the document.

fontstyle

```
fontstyle= normal | italic
```

This attribute identifies the content of the element as either normal text or italicized text.

fontweight

```
fontweight= normal | bold
```

This attribute controls the weight of the characters being displayed. By default, this value is inherited.

Example

The following code shows the equation $(a+b)^2$ being evaluated for its cube root.

```
<math style=display>
<mtable>
    <mtd>
        <mroot>
            <msup>
            <mfenced>
            <mrow>
                <mi>a</mi>
                <mo>+</mo>
                <mi>b</mi>
            </mrow>
            </mfenced>
            <mn>2</mn>
            </msup>
            <mn> 3</mn>
        </mroot>
    </mtd>
</mtable>
</math>
```

CROSS-REFERENCE
See <msqrt>.

<mrow>

Element

MathML

Start Tag: Required
End Tag: Required

At its most basic, the mrow element is used to group together any number of subexpressions. These expressions generally consist of a series of mo elements (operators) acting upon a series of expressions that function as operands. The mrow element creates horizontally grouped rows of arguments. This element enables user agents to insert line breaks automatically into an expression without forcing document authors to specify explicitly how and where the breaks should occur on various sizes of displays.

Other elements, such as mfenced or msqrt, automatically treat their arguments as if they were contained in an mrow element. Similarly, if an mrow element contains a single argument, that element is treated as if it were alone. If an mrow element contains multiple arguments, they need to be grouped in the same logical way they would be on paper by a mathematician. This grouping is necessary to ensure that the expression is read properly in audio renderings by user agents. If the mrow elements are not grouped properly, you could easily change the expression "A plus B squared" into something more closely resembling "A plus B multiplied by 2." Proper grouping also enables user agents to insert line breaks when needed, and at appropriate locations, so as not to distort the meaning of the equation.

Attributes
fontfamily

```
fontfamily= string | css-fontfamily
```

This attribute identifies the font family in which the operator should be displayed. By default, this value is inherited from the document.

fontsize

```
fontsize= number v-unit
```

This attribute controls the size of the font you have selected, just as this attribute does for a standard HTML element. By default, this value is inherited from the document.

fontstyle

```
fontstyle= normal | italic
```

This attribute identifies the content of the element as either normal text or italicized text.

fontweight

```
fontweight= normal | bold
```

This attribute controls the weight of the characters being displayed. By default, this value is inherited.

Examples

You can display a standard algebraic equation such as $2x + y + 3z = 0$ in MathML using the following nested mrow elements.

```
<mrow>
   <mrow>
      <mn> 2 </mn>
      <mo> &InvisibleTimes; </mo>
      <mi> x </mi>
   </mrow>
   <mo> + </mo>
   <mi> y </mi>
   <mo> + </mo>
   <mrow>
      <mn> 3 </mn>
      <mo> &InvisibleTimes; </mo>
      <mi> z </mi>
   </mrow>
   <mo> = </mo>
   <mn> 0 </mn>
</mrow>
```

Another example of nesting mrow elements might not be as obvious. In the expression (x,y), the commas and the parentheses do not work on the arguments of the expression in the same fashion.

```
<mrow>
   <mo> ( </mo>
   <mrow>
      <mi> x </mi>
      <mo> , </mo>
      <mi> y </mi>
   </mrow>
   <mo> ) </mo>
</mrow>
```

<ms>

Element

MathML

Start Tag: Required
End Tag: Required

This element is used to represent string literals commonly found in algebraic systems or those that are interpreted through a programming system. Generally, string literals are displayed between quotation marks for easy identification.

NOTE

You should never use the ms tag to display ordinary text that has been embedded in a mathematical expression. Text of this sort should be displayed using the mtext element or, in some rare cases, the mo or mi tags. The strings encoded in the ms tags are Unicode strings rather than ASCII strings.

Attributes

fontfamily

```
fontfamily= string | css-fontfamily
```

This attribute identifies the font family in which the literal should be displayed. By default, this value is inherited from the document.

fontsize

```
fontsize= number v-unit
```

This attribute controls the size of the font you have selected, just as this attribute does for a standard HTML element. By default, this value is inherited from the document.

fontstyle

```
fontstyle= normal | italic
```

This attribute identifies the content of the element as either normal text or italicized text.

fontweight

```
fontweight= normal | bold
```

This attribute controls the weight of the characters being displayed. By default, this value is inherited.

lquote

```
lquote=string
```

This attribute gives you, the document author, the ability to change the quotation marks used on the left side of the string literal. The default value for this attribute is **"**, which is used to display a double quotation mark.

rquote

```
rquote= string
```

This attribute gives you, the document author, the ability to change the quotation marks used on the right side of the string literal. The default value for this attribute is **"**, which is used to display a double quotation mark.

 CROSS-REFERENCE
See <mi>, <mo>, and <mn>.

<mspace/>

Element

MathML

Start Tag: Required
End Tag: Forbidden

A document author can use the `mspace/` element to display blank spaces of any desired dimension within an expression. Because the space is controlled by setting attributes and the default value for each of its attributes is either `0em` or `0ex`, this element is not useful without its attributes specified. `mspace/` is not the only element that can be used to create space within an equation. The other elements that can be used to create spaces and control equation alignment include

- `mtext`
- `maligngroup/`
- `malignmark/`
- an `mstyle`, `mphantom`, or `mpadded` element whose subexpressions are designed to assist with expression alignment
- `maction` elements whose selected subexpression exists and is designed to create spaces
- `mrow` elements whose direct subexpressions are designed to assist with expression alignment

The `mspace/` element uses the following syntax:

```
<mspace width= "n h-units" height="n v-units" depth="n v-
units" />
```

Attributes
depth

```
depth= number v-unit
```

This attribute controls the depth taken up by this element. The default value of this attribute is 0cx.

height

```
height= number v-unit
```

This attribute controls the vertical height of the space reserved by this element. The default value for this attribute is 0ex.

width

```
width = number  h-unit
```

This attribute controls the horizontal width of the space reserved by this element. The length of the space is specified as an increment of the number of horizontal units specified. The default value of this attribute is 0em.

 CROSS-REFERENCE
See <maligngroup/>, <mphantom>, and <mtext>.

<msqrt>

Element

MathML

Start Tag: Required
End Tag: Required

This element evaluates the given equation for its square root. If the `msqrt` element tags enclose more than one argument, the entire contents are treated as if they were contained within a single `mrow` element.

The syntax for this element is

```
<msqrt> base </msqrt>
```

Attributes
fontfamily

```
fontfamily= string | css-fontfamily
```

This attribute identifies the font family in which the operator should be displayed. By default, this value is inherited from the document.

fontsize

```
fontsize= number v-unit
```

This attribute controls the size of the font you have selected, just as this attribute does for a standard HTML element. By default, this value is inherited from the document.

fontstyle

```
fontstyle= normal | italic
```

This attribute identifies the content of the element as either normal text or italicized text.

fontweight

```
fontweight= normal | bold
```

This attribute controls the weight of the characters being displayed. By default, this value is inherited.

Example

The following code shows the equation $(a+b)^3$ being evaluated for its square root.

```
<math style=display>
<mtable>
   <mtd>
      <msqrt>
         <msup>
         <mfenced>
         <mrow>
            <mi>a</mi>
            <mo>+</mo>
           <mi>b</mi>
         </mrow>
         </mfenced>
         <mn>3</mn>
         </msup>
      </msqrt>
```

```
        </mtd>
      </mtable>
    </math>
```

CROSS-REFERENCE
See \<mroot>.

\<mstyle>

Element

MathML

Start Tag: Required
End Tag: Required

The mstyle element enables the document creator to force style changes that control how the contents of an element are rendered. This element can use any attribute accepted by any MathML presentation element. Because this element enables you to use any of the attributes valid for other presentation elements, you can use it to change the default value of any of its child elements.

NOTE
There is one exception to the rule that mstyle can use all the attributes of the other presentation elements. The only element whose attributes mstyle can't use are those of mpadded. If mpadded's width, height, and depth attributes are specified, they apply only to the mspace/ element. If mpadded's lspace attribute is set, it applies only to the mo element.

Attributes
background

```
background= #rgb | #rrggbb | transparent | html-color-name
```

The value of this attribute controls the color of the background of the box surrounding the objects contained within the mstyle tags. The default value of this attribute is transparent.

NOTE
MathML visual display rules don't outline the precise region whose background is affected by the background attribute. If the content of this element neither has negative spacing nor is overlapped by other content, the background attribute should be applied to all the content between the mstyle tags.

color

```
color= #rgb | #rrggbb | html-color-name
```

This attribute allows you to control the color of the tokens displayed within the child elements of mstyle.

depth

```
depth= number v-unit
```

This attribute controls the depth taken up by this element. The default value of this attribute is 0ex.

displaystyle

```
displaystyle= true | false
```

This attribute is used by other elements to control how their attribute setting is rendered by various types of user agents in a variety of situations. This attribute has the greatest effect on the largeop and movablelimits attributes of the mo element.

fontfamily

```
fontfamily= string | css-fontfamily
```

This attribute identifies the font family in which the element's contents should be displayed. By default, this value is inherited from the document.

fontsize

```
fontsize= number v-unit
```

This attribute controls the size of the font you have selected, just as this attribute does for a standard HTML element. By default, this value is inherited from the document.

fontstyle

```
fontstyle= normal | italic
```

This attribute identifies the content of the element as either normal text or italicized text.

fontweight

```
fontweight= normal | bold
```

This attribute controls the weight of the characters being displayed. By default, this value is inherited.

height

```
height= number v-unit
```

This attribute controls the vertical height of the space reserved by this element. The default value for this attribute is 0ex.

lquote

```
lquote=string
```

This attribute gives you, the document author, the ability to change the quotation marks used on the left side of the string literal. The default value for this attribute is **"**, which is used to display a double quotation mark.

lspace

```
lspace= [ + | - ] number ( % [ pseudo-unit ] | pseudo-unit |
h-unit )
```

This attribute provides document authors with the ability to add space between the left edge of the element's bounding box and the edge of its contents box. (This attribute is used only by the mo element when identified in the mstyle tag.)

rquote

```
rquote= string
```

This attribute gives you, the document author, the ability to change the quotation marks used on the right side of the string literal. The default value for this attribute is **"**, which is used to display a double quotation mark.

scriptlevel

```
scriptlevel= ['+' | '-'] unsigned-integer
```

This attribute controls the size of the font used to display various levels of a script. If the script level is a high number, the font is small.

scriptsizemultiplier

```
scriptsizemultiplier= number
```

This attribute works with scriptlevel to control the size of the font displayed at various levels of a script. Whenever the scriptlevel is altered, the current size of the font is multiplied by the value of scriptsizemultiplier raised to the power of the change in the script level. The default value of this attribute is 0.71.

scriptminsize

```
scriptminsize= number v-unit
```

This attribute is used to set the minimum size of a script font. The default value for this attribute is 8pt.

width

```
width = number h-unit
```

This attribute controls the horizontal width of the space reserved by this element. The length of the space is specified as an increment of the number of horizontal units specified. The default value of this attribute is 0em.

Example

The following example code enables you to display a series of similar equations over different backgrounds with varying text colors. One application of this effect could be to post results of final exams or practice exams in an educational environment.

ON THE CD-ROM

Look for **mstyle.htm** on the accompanying CD-ROM.

```
<HTML>
<HEAD>
<TITLE> MathML Styles </TITLE>
</HEAD>
<BODY>
<H1> Diff-EQ Practice Quiz</H1>
<math>
<mtable>
<mtr>
<mtext> 1.</mtext>
<mstyle fontcolor=#FF0000 background=#0000FF>
   <mrow>
      <mi>y</mi>
      <mo>&InvisibleTimes</mo>
      <mfenced>  <mi>t</mi>  </mfenced>
   </mrow>
   <mo> = </mo>
   <mrow>
      <mrow>
         <mfrac> <mn>5</mn><mn>2</mn></mfrac>
         <mo>&InvisibleTimes</mo>
         <msup>
            <mi>e</mi>
            <mi>t</mi>
         </msup>
      </mrow>
      <mo> - </mo>
      <mrow>
         <mn>2</mn>
         <mo>&InvisibleTimes</mo>
         <msup>
```

```
            <mi>e</mi>
            <mrow>
                <mn>2</mn>
                <mo>&InvisibleTimes</mo>
                <mi>t</mi>
            </mrow>
        </msup>
    </mrow>
    <mo>+</mo>
    <mrow>
        <mfrac> <mn>1</mn><mn>2</mn></mfrac>
        <mo>&InvisibleTimes</mo>
        <msup>
            <mi>e</mi>
            <mrow>
                <mn>3</mn>
                <mo>&InvisibleTimes</mo>
                <mi>t</mi>
            </mrow>
        </msup>
    </mrow>
  </mrow>
</mstyle>
</mtr>
<mtr>
<mtext> 2.</mtext>
<mstyle fontcolor=#FFFFFF background=#0000FF>
    <mrow>
        <mfrac>
            <mrow>
                <mi> d </mi>
                <mo>&InvisibleTimes</mo>
                <mi>y</mi>
            </mrow>
            <mrow>
                <mi> d </mi>
                <mo>&InvisibleTimes</mo>
                <mi>t</mi>
            </mrow>
        </mfrac>
        <mo>=</mo>
        <mn> 1</mn>
    </mrow>
</mstyle>
</mtr>
```

```
<mtr>
<mtext> 3. </mtext>
<mstyle fontcolor=#FF0000 background=#0000FF>
    <mrow>
        <mi>y</mi>
        <mo>&InvisibleTimes</mo>
        <mfenced>  <mi>t</mi>  </mfenced>
    </mrow>
    <mo> = </mo>
    <mrow>
        <mfrac> <mn>1</mn><msqrt><mi>t</mi></msqrt></mfrac>
        <mo>&InvisibleTimes</mo>
        <mrow>
            <mi> sin </mi>
            <mo>&InvisibleTimes</mo>
            <mi>t</mi>
        </mrow>
    </mrow>
</mstyle>
</mtr>
</mtable>
</math>
</BODY>
</HTML>
```

CROSS-REFERENCE
See <STYLE>, Cascading Style Sheets, and Style Sheet.

<msub>

Element

MathML

Start Tag: Required
End Tag: Required

This element is used to create a subscript attached to either an identifier or a number. Whenever you use the msub element, you increase the script level by one. This causes the attributes controlling the font size of the subscript to be set automatically.

The syntax for msub is

```
<msub> base subscript</msub>
```

Attributes
fontfamily

```
fontfamily= string | css-fontfamily
```

This attribute identifies the font family in which the element's contents should be displayed. By default, this value is inherited from the document.

fontsize

```
fontsize= number v-unit
```

This attribute controls the size of the font you have selected, just as this attribute does for a standard HTML element. By default, this value is inherited from the document.

fontstyle

```
fontstyle= normal | italic
```

This attribute identifies the content of the element as either normal text or italicized text.

fontweight

```
fontweight= normal | bold
```

This attribute controls the weight of the characters being displayed. By default, this value is inherited.

subscriptshift

```
subscriptshift= number v-unit
```

This attribute specifies the minimum distance to shift the baseline of the *subscript* down.

 CROSS-REFERENCE
See <mstyle>, <msup>, and <msubsup>.

<msubsup>

Element

MathML

Start Tag: Required
End Tag: Required

This element enables you to control the distance between the base and the subscript and superscript. As with the `msub` element, the `msubsup` element increases the `scriptlevel` by one, causing an automatic shift in the size of the rendered font.

The syntax for the `msubsup` element is

```
<msubsup>base subscript superscript</msubsup>
```

Attributes

fontfamily

```
fontfamily= string | css-fontfamily
```

This attribute identifies the font family in which the element's contents should be displayed. By default, this value is inherited from the document.

fontsize

```
fontsize= number v-unit
```

This attribute controls the size of the font you have selected, just as this attribute does for a standard HTML element. By default, this value is inherited from the document.

fontstyle

```
fontstyle= normal | italic
```

This attribute identifies the content of the element as either normal text or italicized text.

fontweight

```
fontweight= normal | bold
```

This attribute controls the weight of the characters being displayed. By default, this value is inherited.

subscriptshift

```
subscriptshift= number v-unit
```

This attribute controls the minimum amount of downward shift that occurs in the baseline of the *subscript*.

superscriptshift

```
superscriptshift= number v-unit
```

This attribute controls the minimum amount of upward shift that occurs in the baseline of the *superscript*.

Example

The following code uses the `msubsup` element to place limits on an integral (see the results in Figure M-3).

$$\int_0^1 e^x dx$$

Figure M-3 The equation created by placing limits on an integral

The equation as displayed in MathML code looks like the following example:

```
<mrow>
    <msubsup>
        <mo> &int; </mo>
        <mn> 0 </mn>
        <mn> 1 </mn>
    </msubsup>
    <mrow>
        <msup>
            <mi> &ExponentialE; </mi>
            <mi> x </mi>
        </msup>
        <mo> &InvisibleTimes; </mo>
        <mrow>
            <mo> &DifferentialD; </mo>
            <mi> x </mi>
        </mrow>
    </mrow>
</mrow>
```

CROSS-REFERENCE
See <msup> and <msub>.

<msup>

Element

MathML

Start Tag: Required
End Tag: Required

This element enables the document author to control the placement and content of a superscript. Whenever you use the `msup` element, you increase the script level by one, which automatically sets the attributes that control the font size of the superscript.

The syntax for `msup` is

```
<msup> base superscript </msup>
```

Attributes
fontfamily

```
fontfamily= string | css-fontfamily
```

This attribute identifies the font family in which the element's contents should be displayed. By default, this value is inherited from the document.

fontsize

```
fontsize= number v-unit
```

This attribute controls the size of the font you have selected, just as this attribute does for a standard HTML element. By default, this value is inherited from the document.

fontstyle

```
fontstyle= normal | italic
```

This attribute identifies the content of the element as either normal text or italicized text.

fontweight

```
fontweight= normal | bold
```

This attribute controls the weight of the characters being displayed. By default, this value is inherited.

superscriptshift

```
superscriptshift= number v-unit
```

This attribute specifies the minimum distance to shift the baseline of the *superscript* up.

CROSS-REFERENCE
See <msub>, <mstyle>, and <msubsup>.

<mtable>

Element

MathML

Start Tag: Required
End Tag: Required

The mtable element is used to lay out a matrix or a table. The mtr and mtd elements are used within mtable tags to provide a designation of each row and table cell. An mtable element that doesn't use mtr tags is treated as a one-column row (which essentially infers the mtr designation). Similarly, if an expression is not included in an mtd element, that expression is treated as a single-table entry (the mtd tags are inferred). When a series of rows that have a nonstandard number of columns is specified for a table, the short rows are padded on the right side with empty implied mtd elements. This forces the number of columns in all rows to match across the table.

Attributes
align

```
align= (top | bottom | center | baseline | axis) [ rownumber ]
```

This attribute specifies how the table should be aligned in relation to its environment. If the value of this attribute is **axis,** the table is aligned by the table's horizontal center axis (the line on which the minus sign lies) in relation to its environment. A value of **center** or **baseline** implies that the center of the table should be aligned to the environment's baseline. A value of **top** or **bottom** forces the top or bottom, respectively, to the environment's baseline. This attribute can also be used to align a specific row rather than the complete table. The top row is designated with 1, and the bottom row is the *n*th row of the table. The default value of this attribute is **axis.**

columnalign

```
columnalign =(left | center | right) +
```

This attribute controls how each column is aligned. The default value of this attribute is center.

columnlines

```
columnlines =(none | solid | dashed) +
```

This attribute controls the type of visual lines that appear between the columns of the table or matrix. This value defaults to none.

columnspacing

```
columnspacing= ( number h-unit ) +
```

This attribute controls the amount of visual space that appears between the columns of the table or matrix. This value defaults to 0.8em.

displaystyle

```
displaystyle= true | false
```

This attribute is used by other elements to control how their attribute setting is rendered by various types of user agents in a variety of situations. This attribute has the greatest effect on the largeop and movablelimits attributes of the mo element.

equalcolumns

```
equalcolumns= true | false
```

This attribute forces the columns used in the matrix to be the same size. The default value of this attribute is true.

equalrows

```
equalrows= true | false
```

This attribute forces the rows used in the matrix to be the same size. The default value of this attribute is true.

frame

```
frame= none | solid | dashed
```

This attribute controls the type of visual lines that appear before and after the first row and column of the table or matrix. This value defaults to none.

framespacing

```
framespacing= number h-unit number v-unit
```

This attribute controls the amount of visual space that appears before and after the first and last row and column of the table or matrix. This value defaults to 0.4em 0.5ex.

groupalign

```
groupalign = left | right | center | decimalpoint
groupalign-list= (groupalign) (groupalign) (groupalign)...
```

This attribute identifies the arrangement of a group's alignment points when the malignmark element is not used. By default, the value of this property is inherited from this element's parent.

When using `groupalign` in your `maligngroup` element, you need to specify an alignment property for just that individual group. If you specify the `groupalign` in one of the parent elements, you need to specify the alignment of each group that occurs in its expression.

If the value of `groupalign` is **left, right,** or **center,** the point that is aligned is defined as the group's left, right, or midpoint, respectively.

If the value of `groupalign` is **decimalpoint,** the point that is aligned is defined as the right edge of the character directly to the left of the decimal point. The decimal point in this case is the first period (.) that is found in the first mn element in the equation. If your mn element is contained within an `maction` element block, the decimal point is applied only to the expression that has been identified in the `maction selection=...` attribute. If any character other than a period (.) is used as a decimal point, you should precede it with the `malignmark/` element rather than use the `groupalign` attribute.

rowalign

```
rowalign= (top | bottom | center | baseline | axis) +
```

This attribute controls how elements are aligned within their rows. The default value for this attribute is baseline.

rowlines

```
rowlines =(none | solid | dashed) +
```

This attribute controls the type of visual lines that appear between the rows of the table or matrix. This value defaults to none.

rowspacing

```
rowspacing =( number v-unit ) +
```

This attribute controls the amount of visual space that appears between each row of the table or matrix. This value defaults to 1.0ex.

alignmentscope

```
alignmentscope =(true | false) +
```

This attribute controls whether an element can be used for aligning elements. If the value of `alignmentscope` is **false,** it prohibits the columns of the table from being used as alignment markers. The default value of this attribute is **true.**

Example

The following code shows a three-by-three matrix laid out using MathML.

NOTE

You must display the parentheses bordering the matrix in mo elements because they are not automatically displayed as part of mtable.

```
<mrow>
    <mo> ( </mo>
    <mtable>
        <mtr> <mn>1</mn> <mn>2</mn> <mn>6</mn> </mtr>
        <mtr> <mn>-1</mn> <mn>1</mn> <mn>4</mn> </mtr>
        <mtr> <mn>1</mn> <mn>0</mn> <mn>1</mn> </mtr>
    </mtable>
    <mo> ) </mo>
</mrow>
```

CROSS-REFERENCE
See <mtr> and <mtd>.

<mtd>

Element

MathML

Start Tag: Required
End Tag: Required

This tag is used to identify a single entry in a matrix or a table that is a direct subexpression of an mtr element. You can place any number of arguments in a single mtd element block. All of the arguments are treated as a single mtd expression.

NOTE

You must explicitly declare mtd elements if you wish them to use attributes that vary from those they would inherit from their parent mtr or mtable.

Attributes
rowspan

```
rowspan=number
```

This attribute allows the expression identified by the mtd element to take up the specified number of rows. This value corresponds to the rowspan attribute in HTML 4.0. The default value for this attribute is 1.

columnspan

```
columnspan=number
```

This attribute allows the expression identified by the mtd element to take up the specified number of columns. This value corresponds to the colspan attribute in HTML 4.0. The default value for this attribute is 1.

rowalign

```
rowalign= top | bottom | center | baseline | axis
```

This attribute is used to override the horizontal alignment specified by the mtable or mtr element.

columnalign

```
columnalign= left | center | right
```

This attribute is used to override the vertical alignment specified by the mtable or mtr element.

groupalign

```
groupalign= left | right | center | decimalpoint
groupalign-list= (groupalign)  (groupalign) (groupalign)...
```

This attribute identifies the arrangement of a group's alignment points when the malignmark element is not used. By default, the value of this property is inherited from this element's parent.

If you specify the groupalign in one of the parent elements, you need to specify the alignment of each group that occurs in its expression. If the value of groupalign is **left, right,** or **center,** the point that is aligned is defined as the group's left, right, or midpoint, respectively.

If the value of groupalign is **decimalpoint,** the point that is aligned is defined as the right edge of the character directly to the left of the decimal point. The decimal point in this case is the first period (.) that is found in the first mn element in the equation. If your mn element is contained within an maction element block, the decimal point is applied only to the expression that has been identified in the maction selection= attribute. If any character other than a period (.) is used as a decimal point, you should precede it with the malignmark/ element rather than use the groupalign attribute.

Example
The code in this example uses the mtd element as a frame to create the following expression:

```
8.5x + 2y + z = 199
<mtable>
   <mtd>
      <mrow>
```

```
        <mn> 8.5</mn>
        <mo> &InvisibleTimes; </mo>
        <mi> x </mi>
    </mrow>
    <mo> + </mo>
    <mrow>
        <mn> 2</mn>
        <mo> &InvisibleTimes; </mo>
        <mi> y </mi>
    </mrow>
    <mo> + </mo>
    <mrow>
        <mi> z </mi>
    </mrow>
    <mo> = </mo>
    <mrow>
        <mn> 199</mn>
    </mrow>
    </mtd>
  </mtable>
```

Elements
This element needs to be used within a block created by one of the following elements:

> mtable   mtr

CROSS-REFERENCE
See **<mstyle>**.

<mtext>

Element

MathML

Start Tag: Required
End Tag: Required

This element's main job is to display text that needs to be displayed as itself, not as part of an equation. Most often, this element is used to show commentary text that explains the mathematical process being displayed. You can use mtext to assist with controlling the spacing of characters by using invisible characters to create what is referred to as "renderable whitespace." These types of characters are used to provide delays or affect the rhythm of speech in audio renderers. Some of the invisible characters that can affect spacing are listed below.

- **
** starts a new line without indenting
- **&IndentingNewLine;** starts a new line with an indent
- **** does not allow a linebreak to occur at this location
- **&GoodBreak;** specifies an acceptable location for a line break if needed
- **&BadBreak;** specifies that this is a bad location for a line break to occur if one is needed on this line

Attributes

fontfamily

```
fontfamily= string | css-fontfamily
```

This attribute identifies the font family in which the element's contents should be displayed. By default, this value is inherited from the document.

fontsize

```
fontsize= number v-unit
```

This attribute controls the size of the font you have selected, just as this attribute does for a standard HTML element. By default, this value is inherited from the document.

fontstyle

```
fontstyle= normal | italic
```

This attribute identifies the content of the element as either normal text or italicized text.

fontweight

```
fontweight= normal | bold
```

This attribute controls the weight of the characters being displayed. By default, this value is inherited.

Examples

The following example code shows a variety of ways that you can use mtext to display text that adds meaning to or descriptions of the equations shown or that alters the spacing used in the equations.

```
<mtext> Algorithm 3: </mtext>
<mtext>   </mtext>
<mtext>    </mtext>
<mtext> /* a comment */ </mtext>
```

CROSS-REFERENCE
See **\<mstyle\>**.

\<mtr\>

Element

MathML

Start Tag: Required
End Tag: Required

As with the TR element used in standard HTML, the mtr element represents a single row in a table or matrix. You can use the mtr element only as a subexpression of mtable. As with TR, each argument of mtr is placed in its individual column, starting with the left-most column. This element can be inferred, and in such instances, it can have only a single argument. This creates a single-column table.

When a series of rows that have a nonstandard number of columns is specified for a table, the short rows are padded on the right side with empty implied mtd elements. This forces the number of columns in all rows to match across the table. You can use the rowspan and columnspan attributes to force your mtr elements to take up more columns than normal. This limits the number of inferred mtd elements that need to be created.

Attributes
rowalign

```
rowalign= top | bottom | center | baseline | axis
```

This attribute is used to override the horizontal alignment specified by the mtable element.

columnalign

```
columnalign= left | center | right
```

This attribute is used to override the vertical alignment specified by the mtable element.

groupalign

```
groupalign= left | right | center | decimalpoint
groupalign-list= (groupalign) (groupalign) (groupalign)...
```

This attribute identifies the arrangement of a group's alignment points when the malignmark element is not used. By default, the value of this property is inherited from this element's parent.

If you specify the groupalign in one of the parent elements, you need to specify the alignment of each group that occurs in its expression. If the value of groupalign is **left, right,** or **center,** the point that is aligned is defined as the group's left, right, or midpoint, respectively.

If the value of groupalign is **decimalpoint,** the point that is aligned is defined as the right edge of the character directly to the left of the decimal point. The decimal point in this case is the first period (.) that is found in the first mn element in the equation. If your mn element is contained within an maction element block, the decimal point is applied only to the expression that has been identified in the maction selection= attribute. If any character other than a period (.) is used as a decimal point, you should precede it with the malignmark/ element rather than use the groupalign attribute.

Example

The code in this example uses the mtr element as a frame to create the matrix displayed in Figure M-4.

$$\begin{pmatrix} x & 0 & x \\ 0 & x & 2 \\ 1 & 0 & 0 \end{pmatrix}$$

Figure M-4 A standard three-by-three matrix used for evaluating x

```
<mrow>
   <mo> ( </mo>
   <mtable>
      <mtr> <mi>x</mi > <mn>0</mn> <mi>x</mi > </mtr>
      <mtr> <mn>0</mn> < mi >x</mi > < mi >2x</mi > </mtr>
      <mtr> <mn>1</mn> <mn>0</mn> <mn>0</mn> </mtr>
   </mtable>
   <mo> ) </mo>
</mrow>
```

Elements

mtable

CROSS-REFERENCE
See **<mstyle>**.

<MULTICOL>

Element

HTML — Netscape Browsers Only

Start Tag: Required
End Tag: Required

This tag is used in Netscape browsers, versions 3.0 and greater, to create an area of a document that uses multiple equal-width columns.

The syntax of the command is

```
<MULTICOL cols="columns" attributes...> ... </MULTICOL>
```

Attributes

cols

```
cols="number"
```

This required attribute specifies the number of text columns for the text display. Netscape Navigator makes an attempt at flowing information equally through the columns so they are each about the same height.

gutter

```
gutter= "number"
```

This attribute identifies the forced distance, in pixels, between each column. The default value is 10 pixels.

width

```
width= "number"
```

This attribute specifies the width, in pixels, of the available space to display the columns. If this value isn't present, it is calculated from the gutter width and the specified number of columns that need to be displayed. If this attribute is not specified, the column width is adjusted to fill the available space on the document.

Example

The following example code shows you how to use MULTICOL to display three columns of text. This effect can be used to create a short newsletter-styled article as shown below.

ON THE CD-ROM
Look for **multicol.htm** on the accompanying CD-ROM.

```
<HTML>
  <HEAD>
```

```
<TITLE> Multicol Example for Netscape Users</TITLE>
</HEAD>
<BODY BACKGROUND="catsrow.gif" BGCOLOR=#FFFFFF LINK=#0000FF
VLINK=#800080>
<P>
<IMG SRC="CBClogo.gif" ALIGN=BOTTOM WIDTH=500 HEIGHT=135 BORDER=0
VSPACE=0 HSPACE=0>
<MULTICOL COLS="3" WIDTH="500" >

<P>
 Cat's Back Consulting was developed to provide rural businesses
with access to professional advertising on the Internet. Located
in the far north eastern corner of Oregon, high in the snowcapped
Wallowa Mountains, Cat's Back Consulting (CBC) knows and
understands the problems and pleasures associated with rural
living.</P>
 <P>
 It is hard turning majestic scenery, abundant wildlife, sparkling
water, and friendly people into food on your table. As we say
around here &quot;You can't eat the mountains&quot;, but you can
expand your business potential by hiring Cat's Back Consulting to
host your company's web site. From your business web site you can
reach a potential customer market of over 40 million people in a
medium that is growing roughly 10% each month.</P>
 <P>
 Cat's Back Consulting can do whatever is required to build your
company's presence on the Internet in a professional manner,
whether it is as simple as creating a new logo or as complicated
as creating your market image from the ground up. Cat's Back will
convert your business brochure into a professional image on the
Internet, then track that site giving you detailed feed back
reports.</P>
 <P>
 While you are working hard building your local market, Cat's Back
will register your business Web site with 25 different search
engines organized to give you the greatest exposure possible. What
does that mean for your company? Only the greatest exposure for
the smallest fee. For the cost of one advertisement in a monthly
magazine, your company's products will be seen in 25 different
&quot;magazines&quot; everyday of the year.</P>
</MULTICOL>
</BODY>
</HTML>
```

CROSS-REFERENCE
See <TABLE>.

Multimedia Effects

Concept

Multimedia is a term you see bandied about in reference to Internet Web pages, applied to anything that uses more than one media type. (It is almost as popular a term as *interactive*.) For example, a multimedia Web site includes sound, visual graphics, animation, and text. With the development and growing implementation of JavaScript and DHTML, Web viewers will see multimedia elements occurring on even the most common pages.

There are many ways to implement multimedia on your Web pages. Those noted here are just a few of the more popular.

Animated GIFs

Animated GIFs are probably the most universally acceptable form of providing animation on a page. All current Microsoft-, Netscape-, and Mosaic-based Web browsers support these types of files. Animated GIF files are created by placing multiple flat GIF images together in a specific pattern to create an image that moves or a banner that flickers. You can use GIFs to place an animated cartoon character on a Web page or simply to create a neat eye-catching icon to light up an element of your page.

Audio Effects

Since the advent of popular multimedia games and computers, the majority of desktop computer systems have sound cards and speakers. This makes the perfect audience for incorporating sound into Web pages. Many site creators use MIDI or WAV files to create a bit more atmosphere at their Web sites. For example, many e-mall sites play background music similar to what you would hear piped into an actual mall. Sites that are advertising music groups can play snippets of their music. Celtic sites can play Celtic music. The goal with using audio is to create atmosphere, or to assist in marketing, not to drive your viewers away with a headache.

Layers Animation

With the advent of Cascading Style Sheets and their movable and positionable layers, you can create marquee-type movements of text by using the built-in components of a manipulable style sheet. You can create images that rotate in circles and text that slides around. You can put puzzles together or show all the layers of an apple. You can even display your resume to prospective employers in a creative fashion.

Scripting

Everything from JavaScript to VBScript and ActiveX controls can be used to alter the way text and images appear on your Web documents. Scripts can be used for simple processes (such as making buttons "push") or more complicated effects involving the interaction of multiple transparent layers (for example, showing how to build a skyscraper from the ground up). You can create puzzles that users can slide together or develop a neat little program that automatically grades an online quiz.

VRML

The Virtual Reality Modeling Language is used to create virtual 3D worlds on the Internet. There are many complete sites totally devoted to the development and display of these types of environments. One of these, Active Worlds™ (`http://www.activeworlds.com`), is so advanced that it uses its own browser software to assist visitors. You can even build your own homestead on these sites and create an avatar-based family or group of friends.

multiple

Property

DHTML

This property is used in scripts to indicate that multiple items in the list can be selected. It works only with the `SELECT` element.

The syntax of this property is

```
object.multiple[ = multiple]
```

Elements
SELECT

CROSS-REFERENCE
See **<FORM>** and **<INPUT>**.

<munder>

Element

MathML

Start Tag: Required
End Tag: Required

This attribute is used to attach an underscript to a base character, an equation, or a value.

The syntax for munder is

```
<munder> base underscript </munder>
```

Attributes
accentunder

```
accentunder= true | false
```

The accentunder attribute controls whether *underscript* is drawn as an "accent" or as a limit. An accent mark is the same visual size as the base and is drawn closer to the base than a limit mark. The default value of this attribute is false, unless you are applying the underscript to the mo element, where the default value is the same as the value of the accent attribute.

fontfamily

```
fontfamily= string | css-fontfamily
```

This attribute identifies the font family in which the script should be displayed. By default, this value is inherited from the document.

fontsize

```
fontsize= number v-unit
```

This attribute controls the size of the font you have selected, just as this attribute does for a standard HTML element. By default, this value is inherited from the document.

fontstyle

```
fontstyle= normal | italic
```

This attribute identifies the content of the element as either normal text or italicized text. The content is italicized by default.

fontweight

```
fontweight= normal | bold
```

This attribute controls the weight of the characters being displayed. By default, this value is inherited.

Examples
The following example code displays two versions of an equation. The first set is drawn as an accent mark; the second is drawn as a limit. Figure M-5 displays the results.

$$a + b - c \quad \text{vs} \quad a + b - c$$

Figure M-5 Results of the code that displays two versions of an equation

```
<mrow>
    <munder accentunder="true">
        <mrow>
            <mi> a </mi>
            <mo> + </mo>
            <mi> b </mi>
            <mo> - </mo>
            <mi> c </mi>
        </mrow>
        <mo> &UnderBrace; </mo>
    </munder>
    <mtext>   vs   </mtext>
    <munder accentunder="false">
        <mrow>
            <mi> a </mi>
            <mo> + </mo>
            <mi> b </mi>
            <mo> - </mo>
            <mi> c </mi>
        </mrow>
        <mo> &UnderBrace; </mo>
    </munder>
</mrow>
```

CROSS-REFERENCE
See **<mover>**, **<msub>**, **<msup>**, and **<munderover>**.

<munderover>

Element

MathML
Start Tag: Required
End Tag: Required

The `munderover` element provides document authors with a means of applying both an overscript and an underscript to a base simultaneously. This element places the underscript and overscript vertically, spacing them equally in relation to the base to which they are applied.

```
<munderover> base underscript overscript </munderover>
```

NOTE

If you use the `mover` and/or `munder` (instead of `munderover`) to specify the vertical spacing of underscript and overscript, a slight difference occurs between those settings. Although this difference is too small to be noticed on a low-resolution display, it does show up on high-resolution devices such as printers (or when you use large fonts). You may find it more accurate to attach both the underscript and overscript to the same base.

Attributes

accent

```
accent = true | false
```

The `accent` attribute controls whether *overscript* is drawn as an "accent" or as a limit. An accent mark is the same size as the base and is drawn closer to the base than a limit mark.

accentunder

```
accentunder= true | false
```

The `accentunder` attribute controls whether *underscript* is drawn as an "accent" or as a limit. An accent mark is the same visual size as the base and is drawn closer to the base than a limit mark. The default value of this attribute is false, unless you are applying the underscript to the `mo` element, where the default value is the same as the value of the `accent` attribute.

fontfamily

```
fontfamily= string | css-fontfamily
```

This attribute identifies the font family in which the scripts should be displayed. By default, this value is inherited from the document.

fontsize

```
fontsize= number v-unit
```

This attribute controls the size of the font you have selected, just as this attribute does for a standard HTML element. By default, this value is inherited from the document.

fontstyle

```
fontstyle= normal | italic
```

This attribute identifies the content of the element as either normal text or italicized text. The content is italicized by default.

fontweight

```
fontweight= normal | bold
```

This attribute controls the weight of the characters being displayed. By default, this value is inherited.

CROSS-REFERENCE

See **\<munder\>**, **\<mover\>**, **\<msub\>**, and **\<msup\>**.

NAME

Datatype

The DTD uses this datatype to identify all element or attribute contents of this type as a string, only containing the letters of the alphabet in either lower or upper case, numbers, and the punctuation characters including a hyphen, underscore, colon, or period. This is the same as the ID datatype.

CROSS-REFERENCE
See **<ID>**, **<IDREF>**, **<IDREFS>**, **URL**, **URI**, **<number>**, **string**, and **datatype**.

name

Attribute

HTML

This attribute used to assign a name to a control, applet, frame, http header command, local document link, and image map. Used with an A element, name serves as an identifier for link destinations.

When defining a name for your anchor, object, or applet the name should be unique, and should not differ solely by case if you wish to use them as identifiers within JavaScripts.

Because both the id and name attributes use the same name space, you can't use one to define a "titlepage" anchor and the other to define a "Titlepage" anchor. When deciding whether to use the id or the name attributes to set the name for your anchor, you need to consider a few things. On one hand, the id attribute can be used to invoke a style sheet or work with a script process, although it might not be supported in all older user agents. On the other hand, the name attribute enables you to create richer names for your object. When considering which attribute to use, take the object's intended uses into account, as well as who will be viewing it.

The syntax of this command is

```
name=cdata
```

Values
cdata

This string identifies the name of an object. This name is accessible through the DOM, and through object-based scripts such as JavaScript.

Example

The following sample code shows how the name attribute can be used with a series of A elements to create links to document sections from a Table of Contents.

 ON THE CD-ROM

Look for **name.htm** on the accompanying CD-ROM.

```
<html>
<head>
<title>Named Anchors and Nursery Rhymes</title>
</head>

<body bgcolor="#FFFFFF">
<h1>Mother Goose</h1>
<ul>
   <li><a href="#BoPeep">Little Bo Peep </a></li>
   <li><a href="#BoyBlue">Little Boy Blue</a></li>
   <li><a href="#PatACake">Pat-a-Cake</a></li>
   <li><a href="#ManandMaid">A Man and a Maid</a></li>
   <li><a href="#JackSprat">Jack Sprat</a></li>
</ul>
<h2>Little Bo Peep <a name="BoPeep"></a></h2>
<p>little Bo-Peep has lost her sheep,<br>
   And can't tell where to find them;<br>
   Leave them alone, and they'll come home,<br>
   And bring their tails behind them.</p>
<p>Little Bo-Peep fell fast asleep,<br>
   And dreamt she heard them bleating;<br>
   But when she awoke, she found it a joke,<br>
For still they all were fleeting.</p>
<p>Then up she took her little crook,<br>
   Determined for to find them;<br>
   She found them indeed, but it made her heart bleed,<br>
   For they'd left all their tails behind 'em!</p>
<p>It happened one day, as Bo-Peep did stray<br>
   Unto a meadow hard by -<br>
   There she espied their tails, side by side,<br>
```

```
  All hung on a tree to dry.</p>
<p>She heaved a sigh and wiped her eyes,<br>
  And over the hillocks she raced;<br>
  And tried what she could, as a shepherdess should,<br>
  That each tail should be properly placed.</p>
<p> </p>
<h2>Little Boy Blue<a name="BoyBlue"></a></h2>
<p>Little Boy Blue, come, blow your horn!<br>
  The sheep's in the meadow, the cow's in the corn.<br>
  Where's the little boy that looks after the sheep?<br>
  Under the haystack, fast asleep!</p>
<p> </p>
<h2>Pat-a-Cake<a name="PatACake"></a></h2>
<p>Pat-a-cake, pat-a-cake,<br>
  Baker's man!<br>
  Bake me a cake,<br>
  As fast as you can.</p>
<p>Pat it, and prick it,<br>
  And mark it with a B,<br>
  Put it in the oven<br>
  For Baby and me.</p>
<p> </p>
<h2>A Man and a Maid<a name="ManandMaid"></a></h2>
<p>There was a little man,<br>
  Who wooed a little maid,<br>
  And he said, &quot;Little maid, will you wed, wed, wed?<br>
  I have little more to say,<br>
  So will you, yeah or nay,<br>
  For least said is soonest mended-ded, ded, ded.&quot;</p>
<p>The little maid replied,<br>
  &quot;Should I be your little bride,<br>
  Pray what must we have for to eat, eat, eat?<br>
  Will the flame that you're so rich in<br>
Light a fire in the kitchen?<br>
  Or the little god of love turn the spit, spit,
spit?&quot;</p>
<p> </p>
<h2>Jack Sprat<a name="JackSprat"></a></h2>
<p>Jack Sprat could eat no fat.<br>
  His wife could eat no lean.<br>
  And so between the two of them,<br>
  They licked the platter clean.</p>
<p> </p>
</body>
</html>
```

m
n
o

Elements

A	APPLET	BUTTON	FRAME
IFRAME	INPUT	MAP	META
OBJECT	PARAM	SELECT	TEXTAREA

CROSS-REFERENCE
See **NAME, ID,** and **id**.

names

Concept

XML

In XML, a name identifies an individual element or token placed on an application or document. All names start with a letter, number, hyphen, underscore, colon, or full stop. All names beginning with the letters *xml* in any form are reserved for future versions of this standard.

CROSS-REFERENCE
See **name, nmtokens,** and **tokens**.

navigate

Method

DHTML

Scripts uses this method to navigate through the URL specified by *sURL*. The syntax of this command is

```
object.navigate(sURL)
```

Parameters
URL
This required parameter holds the URL of the document to be displayed.

Objects
window

CROSS-REFERENCE
See **URI**, **URL**, **href**, **code**, **codebase**, and **src**.

nextPage

Method

DHTML

This document object method displays the next page of records in the table's data set. Use of this method requires prior use of the dataPageSize property to set the number of records that the table should display.

The syntax needed to use this method is

```
object.nextPage()
```

Elements

TABLE

CROSS-REFERENCE
See **previousPage** and **go**.

nmtoken

Concept

XML

This method represents the individual characters, or *tokens*, that form an identifiable name for an individual XML element (or attribute of an XML document) when you combine them in a string.

CROSS-REFERENCE
See **name**.

<NOBR>

Element

HTML

Start Tag: Required
End Tag: Optional

Use this HTML element to keep a line of text from breaking automatically when a user agent would normally wrap its text.

NOTE

The HTML 4.0 specification does not include this element; it may no longer be supported by user agents.

Attribute
class

class="*cdata-list*"

This attribute assigns a class name to an element. By means of classes, user agents group specific types of information for later use.

id

id="*name*"

This attribute assigns a name to an element.

lang

lang="*language code*"

This attribute specifies the language that renders an element and its values.

onclick

onclick=*script*

This attribute acts upon an on-screen element under the pointer when a user clicks the button on a pointing device.

ondblclick

ondblclick=*script*

This attribute takes effect when a user double-clicks the button on a pointing device while the pointer is over an element.

onkeydown

    `onkeydown=script`

This attribute takes effect when a user presses a key while the pointer is over an element.

onkeypress

    `onkeypress=script`

This attribute takes effect when a key is pressed and released while the pointer is over an element.

onkeyup

    `onkeyup=script`

This attribute takes effect when a key is released while the pointer is over an element.

onmousedown

    `onmousedown=script`

This attribute takes effect when the button on a pointing device is pressed while the pointer is over an element.

onmousemove

    `onmousemove=script`

A user activates this attribute by moving the mouse while the pointer is over an element.

onmouseout

    `onmouseout=script`

This attribute becomes active when the mouse is moved away from an element.

onmouseover

    `onmouseover=script`

This attribute becomes active when a user moves the mouse pointer over an element.

onmouseup

    `onmouseup=script`

This attribute takes effect when a user releases the button on a pointing device while the pointer is over an element.

style

```
style=style descriptors
```

This attribute applies specific style-sheet information to one particular element.

title

```
title=text
```

This attribute provides annotation information to the element.

Example

In the following example, the WBR element is inserted to provide a soft line break between lines in a poem depending on how narrow the window gets. Without the WBR, the contents of a NOBR will not break.

ON THE CD-ROM

Look for **nobr.htm** on the accompanying CD-ROM.

```
<NOBR>Peter Piper Picked a Peck of Pickled Peppers <WBR> If
Peter Piper Picked a Peck of Pickled Peppers, <WBR> How Many
Pecks of Pickled Peppers did Peter Piper Pick?<WBR> Peter
Piper Picked a Peck of Pickled Peppers <WBR> If Peter Piper
Picked a Peck of Pickled Peppers, <WBR> How Many Pecks of
Pickled Peppers did Peter Piper Pick?<WBR> Peter Piper Picked
a Peck of Pickled Peppers <WBR> If Peter Piper Picked a Peck
of Pickled Peppers, <WBR> How Many Pecks of Pickled Peppers
did Peter Piper Pick?</NOBR>
```

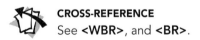

CROSS-REFERENCE

See **\<WBR\>**, and **\<BR\>**.

Node

Concept

DOM

A *node* is a joint within a binary document tree. This is generally an element that serves as a parent to another element or a series of elements. Each node can have one or more child elements that may serve as either an additional node or as a leaf. A *leaf* is a terminating element at the end of a branch of the inverted document tree created when a document's structure is diagrammed.

CROSS-REFERENCE
See **node list**, **node type**, **document tree**, **ancestry**, **child**, **parent**, and **descendants**.

Node List

Concept

DOM

Each node can be added to a list, or grouping, often referred to as a *node list*. This grouping of nodes can be used for altering large portions of the nodes in a single sweep, often through the use of a script.

CROSS-REFERENCE
See **node list**, **node type**, **document tree**, **ancestry**, **child**, **parent**, and **descendants**.

Node Type

Concept

DOM

Various types of nodes are used in creating documents. By far the most prevalent are the *element nodes* formed by block or inline elements found within your documents. Other types of nodes include: document, attribute, processing instructions, comments, text, CDATA sections, document fragments, entities, entity reference, and document types.

CROSS-REFERENCE
See **node list**, **node**, **document tree**, **ancestry**, **child**, **parent**, and **descendants**.

<NOFRAMES>

Element

HTML

Start Tag: Required
End Tag: Required

This element identifies content that should be displayed on user agents that do not support FRAMEs. User agents must display the contents of the NOFRAMES element if it has been configured to not display frames, or if it is incapable of displaying frames.

Attributes

class

```
class="cdata-list"
```

This attribute assigns a class name to an element. By means of classes, user agents group specific types of information for later use.

id

```
id="name"
```

This attribute assigns a name to an element.

lang

```
lang="language code"
```

This attribute specifies the language that renders an element and its values.

style

```
style=style descriptors
```

This attribute applies specific style-sheet information to one particular element.

title

```
title=text
```

This attribute provides annotation information to the element.

Example

The following segment of FRAMESET and NOFRAMES code provides a newsletter's table of contents to those viewers using browsers that can't see the split-screen TOC and articles.

ON THE CD-ROM
Look for **noframes.htm** on the accompanying CD-ROM.

```
<html>
<head>
<title>Fishing Club News Letter</title>
</head>

<frameset cols="25%,75%">
```

```
        <frame marginwidth="2" marginheight="2" name="TOCBar"
         scrolling="AUTO" src="TOC.htm" frameborder="0">
        <frame marginwidth="2" marginheight="2" name="Articles"
         scrolling="AUTO" src="page1.htm" frameborder="0">
<noframes>
    <body>
    <h1><b>You currently need frames support to see the
newsletter... but... Here is the TOC just in case.</b></h1>
    <p> </p>
    <p><font size="5" face="Arial">Inside This Issue:<br>
</font>
    <a href="page1.html" target="Articles">
        <font size="1" face="Arial">Pond Added East of
Salem<br>
        Who are these Guys?!?!<br></font>
    </a>
    <p>
    <a href="page2.html" target="Articles">
     <font size="1" face="Arial">Trout Tournament Planned<br>
      Washougahal Boundaries Defined<br>
      Remember New Lock Combinations<br>
      Four Fliers Enclosed<br>
      Send Photos: Reap Rewards<br></font>
    </a>
    <a href="page3.html" target="Articles">
        <font size="1" face="Arial">1998 Still Water
Regulations<br>
      Hotline Number Changes<BR></font>
    </a>
    <a href="page4.html" target="MsgBody">
        <font size="1" face="Arial">SLOW DOWN!<br>
      Picnic Scheduled<br>
      2nd Annual Bass Tournament Planned<br>
      Library has good videos<br>
      Annual meeting date set<br></font>
    </a>
<hr>
<font size="4" face="Arial"
<a href="page9.html" target="Articles">Members Page</a><br>
Property Page<br>
<a href="prostaff.html" target=" Articles ">ProStaff
Page</a><br>
<a href="pondregs.html" target=" Articles ">Pond
Regulations</a><br>
```

```
<a href="page14.html" target=" Articles ">Events
Calendar</a><br>
</body>
    </noframes>
</frameset>
</html>
```

CROSS-REFERENCE
See **<FRAMES>**, **<FRAMESET>**, and **<IFRAME>**.

nohref

Attribute

HTML

This attribute informs a user agent that the current object has no associated link.

This Boolean statement has very simple syntax:

```
nohref
```

JAVASCRIPT
```
area.noHref [ = bHref ]
```

This JavaScript property can be used to either set or retrieve whether mouse clicks in a specified region cause an action.

Examples

The following example code uses the `nohref` attribute to keep a map area from linking to another HTML document.

```
<AREA shape="poly" coords="0,0,50,100,125,200,250,0,0,0" nohref>
```

Elements

AREA

CROSS-REFERENCE
See **href**, **code**, **codebase**, and **src**.

<NOLAYER>

Element

HTML — Netscape browsers only

Start Tag: Required
End Tag: Required

This element serves by Netscape to provide access to content for users with browsers that do not support the LAYER tag. Browsers that do not support the LAYER tag will display the content of the layers, but without their positioning information. In non-Netscape browsers the information is displayed sequentially. This element works like the NOFRAME and NOSCRIPT elements.

Attributes

class

```
class="cdata-list"
```

This attribute assigns a class name to an element. By means of classes, user agents group specific types of information for later use.

id

```
id="name"
```

This attribute assigns a name to an element.

lang

```
lang="language code"
```

This attribute specifies the language that renders an element and its values.

style

```
style=style descriptors
```

This attribute applies specific style-sheet information to one particular element.

title

```
title=text
```

This attribute provides annotation information to the element.

Example

The following example code loads an HTML document into a layer on the browser. If the browser does not support the LAYER tag, then the information will be displayed in succession with the contents of the NOLAYER tag following.

m

n

o

ON THE CD-ROM
Look for **nolayer.htm** on the accompanying CD-ROM.

```
<LAYER top="100" src="book.html"></LAYER>
<LAYER top="200" src="turtle.html"></LAYER>
<NOLAYER>
Take a look at this page using Netscape Navigator 4.0 or
later. You might be pleasantly surprised.
</NOLAYER>
```

CROSS-REFERENCE
See **<LAYER>**, **<SPAN>**, **<DIV>**, and **positioning**.

noResize

Attribute

HTML

This HTML attribute prevents site visitors from resizing frame windows. If this attribute is present, the FRAME cannot be resized.

The syntax of this Boolean attribute is

```
noresize
```

JAVASCRIPT
```
object.noResize [ = bResize ]
```

This parameter controls the resizability of a frame from within a JavaScript.

Example

The following HTML source code uses the noresize attribute to prohibit a document reader from altering the size of a document author's specified frame.

ON THE CD-ROM
Look for **noresize.htm** on the accompanying CD-ROM.

```
<frameset cols="168,577" rows="*">
  <frame src="Untitled-1" noresize>
  <frame src="UntitledFrame-2" noresize>
</frameset>
```

Elements

FRAME

CROSS-REFERENCE
See **<IFRAME>** and **border**.

Normalization

Concept

Normalization is a term that serves in many areas of the computer technical age. It is often used to refer to the way a database is organized to hold the most information in the least amount of space. Databases on the Internet can be normalized in the same fashion. A normalized database has no duplicate fields in the tables, unless they are key fields used strictly to link related information. The table structure shown in Figure N-1 is just one way that the following sample customer support database could be organized.

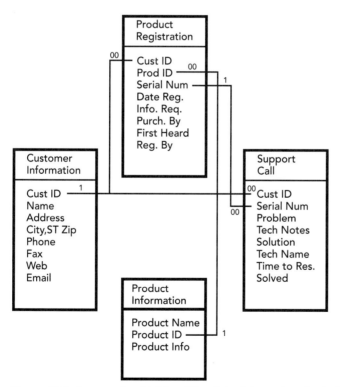

Figure N-1 A normalized table will be linked through a single field to all other tables in the relational database. SQL databases on the Internet can be created in this fashion, while most CGI-based flat databases cannot.

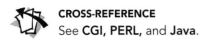

CROSS-REFERENCE
See **CGI, PERL,** and **Java**.

<NOSCRIPT>

Element

HTML

Start Tag: Required
End Tag: Required

This element provides alternative content when a script cannot execute. Only user agents that support scripts can display this element, and only in the following situations:

- The user agent's configuration does not allow it to run scripts.
- The user agent doesn't recognize the scripting language identified by the SCRIPT element.
- A user agent that does not support client-side scripts is required to render the contents of this element.

Attributes

class

```
class="cdata-list"
```

This attribute assigns a class name to an element. By means of classes, user agents group specific types of information for later use.

id

```
id="name"
```

This attribute assigns a name to an element.

lang

```
lang="language code"
```

This attribute specifies the language that renders an element and its values.

style

```
style=style descriptors
```

This attribute applies specific style-sheet information to one particular element.

title

```
title=text
```

This attribute provides annotation information to the element.

Example

The following script uses the NOSCRIPT tag to write a string to the user's screen, even if the script support is turned off in the browser, or if the browser does not support the script language used.

ON THE CD-ROM

Look for **noscript.htm** on the accompanying CD-ROM.

```
<SCRIPT type="JavaScript">
    document.writeln("This is the Hottest! Script Spot ever!
(says the script)">
</SCRIPT>
<NOSCRIPT>
<P> This is the Hottest! Script Spot ever! (says noscript)</P>
</NOSCRIPT>
```

CROSS-REFERENCE

See **<SCRIPT>** and **<NOFRAME>**.

noShade

Attribute

HTML

When this attribute is applied to an HR element, it removes the two-color gradiated look of the line and replaces it with a solid-color line.

The syntax for this command is

```
<HR noShade...>
```

JAVASCRIPT

```
hr.noShade [ = bShade ]
```

This JavaScript command controls how the HR element is displayed. It can also be used to identify how it is currently displayed.

Example

The following example code controls the way the HR element appears on a series of successive lines.

ON THE CD-ROM
Look for **noshade.htm** on the accompanying CD-ROM.

```
<BODY>
   This is the first line of text.
   <HR  size=3 >
   This is the second line of text.
   <HR size =3 noshade>
</BODY>
```

Elements

> HR

CROSS-REFERENCE
See **color** and **border**.

Notation

Concept

All programs, including HTML and XML documents, use a specific method of identifying information. This means of identification is called *notation*. In HTML document notation, for example, angle brackets (<>) identify the start and end tags of individual elements. An end tag is further identified by a forward slash (/) following the first angle bracket. Attributes are also identified by their position within the angle brackets of a start tag. The contents of most attributes are contained within a quotation marks (" ").

Some values of attributes also require special notation. Attributes with string values, for example, must enclose those values (but not most other numbers and lengths) in quotation marks. Other values, such as hexadecimal numbers, require one of several notations to accompany them—for example, a pound sign (#) in front of a six-digit hex number, or an RGB prefix and enclosing parenthesis for the number, as in RGB(*xxx*).

The DTD also uses notation to identify whether a specific element or attribute requires start tags and end tags, allows content of a specific type, allows content at all, or whether an attribute can be used with a specific element. Without this notation, a user agent cannot properly display information from a particular document in a format that is universal to all documents. Without specific document notation, user agents cannot treat XML documents as different from HTML, or interpret CSS or XSL style-sheet notation.

CROSS-REFERENCE
See **elements**, **start tags**, **tags**, and **end tags**.

Notation Declaration

Concept

XML

All languages, including XML, use notations to identify formats in which to display information; they assist user agents in rendering the information correctly. A *notation declaration* provides a name for a notation, and can also appear on lists of declarations for entities or attributes. It also provides an external identifier that the user agent or XML processor can use to locate a helper application that can read the information in the notation.

CROSS-REFERENCE
See **notation**.

noWrap

Attribute

HTML

This attribute serves in HTML documents to prohibit information from wrapping around the screen. It can be used to help force a strict format on information provided within tables, and in paragraphs. Its presence prevents the text from wrapping.

This attribute is implemented by issuing the following command:

```
nowrap
```

JAVASCRIPT
```
object.noWrap [ = bWrap ]
```

This JavaScript property sets a browser to keep words from wrapping on-screen.

Example
The following example script uses the nowrap attribute to control wrapping in both a DIV information block and a table cell.

```
<HTML>
<HEAD>
   <TITLE> Using NoWrap to Change Text</TITLE>
</HEAD>
<BODY>
   <DIV align="center">
   This is a horse. Of course, the horse, is the famous Mister
Ed. This is a horse. Of course, the horse, is the famous
Mister Ed. This is a horse. Of course, the horse, is the
famous Mister Ed. This is a horse. Of course, the horse, is
the famous Mister Ed. This is a horse. Of course, the horse,
is the famous Mister Ed.
   </DIV
<DIV align="center" nowrap>
   This is a horse. Of course, the horse, is the famous Mister
Ed. This is a horse. Of course, the horse, is the famous
Mister Ed. This is a horse. Of course, the horse, is the
famous Mister Ed. This is a horse. Of course, the horse, is
the famous Mister Ed. This is a horse. Of course, the horse,
is the famous Mister Ed.
   </DIV
   <TABLE>
      <TR>
         <TD> This is a horse. Of course, the horse, is the
famous Mister Ed.</TD>
         <TD> This is a horse. Of course, the horse, is the
famous Mister Ed.</TD>
         <TD> This is a horse. Of course, the horse, is the
famous Mister Ed.</TD>
      </TR>
      <TR>
         <TD> This is a horse. Of course, the horse, is the
famous Mister Ed.</TD>
         <TD> This is a horse. Of course, the horse, is the
famous Mister Ed.</TD>
         <TD> This is a horse. Of course, the horse, is the
famous Mister Ed.</TD>
      </TR>
   </TABLE>
</BODY>
</HTML>
```

NOTE

This attribute takes effect on the TD and TH elements only if you are using the Internet Explorer 4 and Navigator 4 browsers. Finalization of the DOM, though not yet implemented, makes this attribute valid for all the elements listed.

Elements

BODY   DD   DIV   DT
TD   TH

CROSS-REFERENCE

See **width** and **height**.

NUMBER

Datatype

This datatype serves by the DTD to identify all element or attribute contents of this type as a number, only containing the digits from zero to nine.

CROSS-REFERENCE

See **<ID>**, **<IDREF>**, **<IDREFS>**, **URL**, **URI**, *number*, and **datatype**.

number

Value

CSS

Some values use a *number type* instead of an integer or a length. As with an integer, a number is specified in a decimal value. Unlike an integer (which can only be a whole number consisting of digits between 0 and 9), real numbers can have digits following a decimal point. This means that while the expression 99.99 is a valid number, it is not a valid integer. A number can be signed, or preceded by a + or ? sign to indicate whether it is greater than or less than zero.

CROSS-REFERENCE

See **integer** and **length**.

<OBJECT>

Element

HTML

Start Tag: Required
End Tag: Required

This element is used to identify objects that are not part of the normal rendering scheme of the user agent. Normal objects include items such as GIF and JPG images, text files, colors and fonts, and hyperlinks. Objects they may not naturally support include VRML files, proprietary plug-in formats such as Flash movies, or odd document types. When a user agent encounters an OBJECT element it must first attempt to render its content itself. If it does not recognize the content, then it evaluates the contents for PARAM and MAP elements.

When you use the OBJECT command you, as the document author, generally need to specify three specific types of information for the user agent:

1. Identify the location of the applet's executable code.
2. Identify the location of the information or data file to be displayed.
3. Identify the location of any additional values or parameters that are required by the object at runtime.

You might not need to specify all pieces of information simultaneously, so it is possible to have the parameters of your OBJECT altered with a script. In some cases the user agent will know how to implement the object (for example, Flash movies with Microsoft Internet Explorer 5). If specific runtime values are needed, the PARAM element is used to provide those runtime data parameters that are required by the data object.

The OBJECT element can appear within the BODY or the HEAD sections of an HTML document. If you place the OBJECT in the HEAD section, you should be sure that the object does not require its contents to be rendered.

Attributes

align

```
align= bottom | middle | top
```

This attribute is used to control the visual alignment of the object within its bounding box. If the value of this attribute is `bottom`, the alignment begins at the bottom of the box and works upward.

archive

```
archive=uri-list
```

This attribute is used to identify the list of URI or the resources that contain the classes and resources that need to be preloaded by the user agent. Each URI is separated by a comma.

border

```
border=number
```

This attribute is used with many HTML elements to specify the width in pixels of any border surrounding an object on an HTML page.

class

```
class="cdata-list"
```

This attribute is used to assign a class name to an element. User agents employ classes to group specific types of information for later use.

classid

```
classid=uri
```

This attribute is used to identify the location of an objects implementation. It can be used as an alternative to the `data` attribute, depending on the type of object being placed.

codebase

```
codebase=URI
```

This attribute is used to specify the base URI for the applet being specified. When it is not specified, it defaults to the same URI that is used for the containing document. You can only refer to the current directory and its subdirectories in this attribute. Any other values are invalid.

codetype

```
codetype=content-type
```

This attribute is used to identify the content type of the data that is being down-loaded for the object. Although this attribute is not required, it is recommended when you use the `classid` attribute.

data

```
data=uri
```

This attribute is used by the `OBJECT` element to point to the source of the object's data. This is often an image, video, or audio resource.

declare

```
declare
```

This attribute is used to make the current `OBJECT` definition, a declaration only. The object will only be available when it is also represented by another `OBJECT` definition that refers to the original `OBJECT`'s declaration.

dir

```
dir = LTR | RTL
```

This attribute defines the direction of the text flow in a document so a user agent can display it correctly.

height

```
height=length
```

This attribute is used to specify the height of the applet's display area.

hspace

```
hspace=length
```

This attribute specifies the amount of white space to insert to the left and right of the applet box.

id

```
id="name"
```

This attribute is used to assign a name to an element.

lang

```
lang="language code"
```

This attribute specifies the language that should be used to render an element.

name

```
name=cdata
```

This attribute is used to assign a name to a control, applet, frame, http header command, local document link, and image map.

onclick

```
onclick=script
```

This attribute takes effect when a user clicks the button on a pointing device with the pointer over an element.

ondblclick

```
ondblclick=script
```

This attribute takes effect when the button on a pointing device is double-clicked with the pointer over an element.

onkeydown

```
onkeydown=script
```

This attribute takes effect when a key is pressed while the pointer is over an element.

onkeypress

```
onkeypress=script
```

This attribute takes effect when a key is pressed and released with the pointer over an element.

onkeyup

```
onkeyup=script
```

This attribute takes effect when a key is released with the pointer over an element.

onmousedown

```
onmousedown=script
```

This attribute takes effect when the button on a pointing device is pressed with the pointer over an element.

onmousemove

> onmousemove=*script*

This attribute is activated when the mouse pointer is moved while the pointer is over an element.

onmouseout

> onmouseout=*script*

This attribute is activated when the mouse pointer is moved away from an element.

onmouseover

> onmouseover=*script*

This attribute is activated the mouse pointer is movedwhen the mouse pointer is moved over an element.

onmouseup

> onmouseup=*script*

This attribute takes effect when the button on a pointing device is released with the pointer over an element.

standby

> standby=text

This is the message that a user agent can display while waiting for the object to load.

style

> style=*style descriptors*

This attribute is used to apply specific style-sheet information to one particular element.

tabindex

> tabindex=*number*

This attribute provides the position of the current element within the overall tabbing order of the document.

n
o
p

title

    title=*text*

This attribute serves to provide annotation information to the element.

type

    type=content-type

This attribute is used to specify the MIME type of the document being linked to.

usemap

    usemap=*uri*

This attribute is used to associate an image map created with the MAP element with the current object. The value of this attribute must match the value of the name attribute of the MAP element.

vspace

    vspace=*length*

This attribute specifies the amount of white space to insert to above and below the applet box.

width

    width=*length*

This attribute is used to specify the width of the applet's display area.

Example

The following HTML sample code inserts a small Flash movie into an otherwise plain document. This movie really only has one scene, but incorporates additional multiple scene movies within it.

ON THE CD-ROM

Look for **object.htm** on the accompanying CD-ROM.

```
<html>
<head>
<title>Inserting Flash Objects</title>
<meta name="GENERATOR" content="Macromedia Dreamweaver">
</head>

<body bgcolor="#00CCFF">
<h1 align="center">
<font color="#003300">Hmm.. a Flying Fish, or a Swimming
Plane</font></h1>
```

```
<p align="center">
<object classid="clsid:D27CDB6E-AE6D-11cf-96B8-444553540000"
codebase="http://active.macromedia.com/flash2/cabs/swflash.cab
#version=2,0,0,0" width="600" height="400">
    <param name="SRC" value="fishplane.swf">
    <embed src="fishplane.swf"
pluginspage="http://www.macromedia.com/shockwave/download/"
width="600" height="400"></embed>
  </object> </p>
</body>
</html>
```

CROSS-REFERENCE
See **<PARAM>**, **<EMBED>**, and **<APPLET>**.

object

Attribute

HTML

This HTML attribute is used to name a resource for the APPLET element that identifies the serialized representation of the applet's current state. The value of this attribute is interpreted in relation to the value of the codebase attribute of the APPLET. This representation contains information about the applet's class name, but not its implementation. The class name is used to find the implementation in a class file or an archive. Either a code or an object attribute must be present in the APPLET element. If both exist, but have different values, an error will develop.

The syntax of this command is

```
object= cdata
```

Values
cdata

This string is used to either identify the name of the class file or its name and location.

Example
The following example code uses the codebase and code attributes of the APPLET element to locate the class to be used by this applet.

```
<APPLET object="jinx.class"
codebase="http://www.jinx.com/classes">
</APPLET>
```

Elements
APPLET

CROSS-REFERENCE
See **code**, **codebase**, and **codetype**.

Object

Property

DHTML

This object property is used to retrieve an object for further manipulation by the script.

The syntax for this property is

```
[oObject=]object.Object
```

Parameters
oObject

This is the actual object that has been selected.

Elements
OBJECT

CROSS-REFERENCE
See **collection** and **item**.

Object Controls

Concept

CROSS-REFERENCE
See **Form Controls**.

Object Hierarchy

Concept

 CROSS-REFERENCE
See **Document Tree**, **Ancestors**, **Descendants**, **Children**, **Parents**, and **Document Object Model**.

Objects

Concept

Within HTML and XML documents, each element's start and end tag set is used to create a complete object which can be assigned space, borders, a containment area, a position in the document tree, and a series of controllable attributes. Objects are essentially the building blocks of documents. Objects can be either inline or block level, and are used to create the full formatting of the document. User agents are provided with instructions that tell them how to deal with all the objects so they will be displayed in a similar fashion across all the available user agents.

 CROSS-REFERENCE
See **elements**, **attributes**, and **containment blocks**.

Obsolete Elements

Concept

Obsolete elements are those that have been removed completely from the HTML specification. These elements may be supported in the current browser base, but there is no assurance that they will continue to be supported. Document authors should remove all obsolete elements from their documents so they will continue to be viewable by future user agents.

 **CROSS-REFERENCE**
See **Deprecated**.

offscreenBuffering

Property

DHTML

This object property is used to set or retrieve off-screen buffering for information contained within the current user agent's window. *Buffers* are areas of memory where information is stored so it can be accessed rapidly. Often such information is not currently visible, or currently is in use by the user agent. A buffer enables you to view a long HTML page, without having to wait while your computer loads the information from storage on the drive, or refreshes information from the server.

The syntax for this command is

```
object.offscreenBuffering [ = auto | true | false ]
```

Parameters

auto

This value allows the user agent to decide when off-screen buffering should be used.

false

A value of false forces off-screen buffering to be disabled.

true

A value of true forces off-screen buffering to be enabled.

Objects

window

CROSS-REFERENCE

See **onload**, **onunload**, and **onbeforeunload**.

offsetHeight

Property

DHTML

This object property is used to identify the height of an object, in relation to the top left corner of the document. You can use a combination of the

`offsetHeight`, `offsetLeft`, `offsetTop` and `offsetWidth` properties to identify the exact location and dimensions of any object on a document.

The syntax for this command is

Height`=object.offsetHeight`

Parameters

Height

This is the height of the object in pixels.

Elements

A	ACRONYM	ADDRESS	APPLET
AREA	B	BIG	BLOCKQUOTE
BODY	BR	BUTTON	CAPTION
CENTER	CITE	CODE	COL
COLGROUP	DD	DEL	DFN
DIR	DIV	DL	DT
EM	EMBED	FIELDSET	FONT
FORM	FRAME	H1–H6	HR
I	IFRAME	IMG	INPUT
INS	KBD	LABEL	LEGEND
LI	LISTING	MAP	MARQUEE
MENU	NEXTID	OBJECT	OL
OPTION	P	PLAINTEXT	PRE
Q	S	SAMP	SELECT
SMALL	SPAN	STRIKE	STRONG
SUB	SUP	TABLE	TBODY
TD	TEXTAREA	TFOOT	TH
THEAD	TR	TT	U
UL	VAR	XMP	

CROSS-REFERENCE

See **offsetLeft**, **offsetParent**, **offsetTop**, **offsetWidth**, **height**, **left**, **Parent**,
top, and **width**.

offsetLeft

Property

DHTML

This property is used to identify the left most edge of an object, in relation to the top left corner of the current object's parent. You can use a combination of the offsetHeight, offsetLeft, offsetTop and offsetWidth properties to identify the exact location and dimensions of any object on a document.

The syntax for this command is

```
Coords=object.offsetLeft
```

Parameters
Coords

This is an integer representing the left edge of the object.

Elements

A	ACRONYM	ADDRESS	APPLET
AREA	B	BIG	BLOCKQUOTE
BODY	BR	BUTTON	CAPTION
CENTER	CITE	CODE	COL
COLGROUP	DD	DEL	DFN
DIR	DIV	DL	DT
EM	EMBED	FIELDSET	FONT
FORM	FRAME	H1–H6	HR
I	IFRAME	IMG	INPUT
INS	KBD	LABEL	LEGEND
LI	LISTING	MAP	MARQUEE
MENU	NEXTID	OBJECT	OL
OPTION	P	PLAINTEXT	PRE
Q	S	SAMP	SELECT
SMALL	SPAN	STRIKE	STRONG
SUB	SUP	TABLE	TBODY
TD	TEXTAREA	TFOOT	TH
THEAD	TR	TT	U
UL	VAR	XMP	

CROSS-REFERENCE
See **offsetHeight**, **offsetParent**, **offsetTop**, **offsetWidth**, **height**, **left**, **parent**, **top**, and **width**.

offsetParent

Property

DHTML

This object property is used to identify the parent element of an object that is being used as the reference point for identifying the `offsetLeft` and `offsetTop` properties. The majority of the time the parent is the `BODY` element.

The syntax for this command is

```
Element=object.offsetParent
```

Parameters
Element

This is the name of the element which is providing the offset values for the left and top offset properties.

Elements

A	ACRONYM	ADDRESS	APPLET
AREA	B	BIG	BLOCKQUOTE
BODY	BR	BUTTON	CAPTION
CENTER	CITE	CODE	COL
COLGROUP	DD	DEL	DFN
DIR	DIV	DL	DT
EM	EMBED	FIELDSET	FONT
FORM	FRAME	H1–H6	HR
I	IFRAME	IMG	INPUT
INS	KBD	LABEL	LEGEND
LI	LISTING	MAP	MARQUEE
MENU	NEXTID	OBJECT	OL
OPTION	P	PLAINTEXT	PRE
Q	S	SAMP	SELECT
SMALL	SPAN	STRIKE	STRONG
SUB	SUP	TABLE	TBODY

n
o
p

TD	TEXTAREA	TFOOT	TH
THEAD	TR	TT	U
UL	VAR	XMP	

CROSS-REFERENCE
See **offsetLeft**, **offsetTop**, **left**, and **top**.

offsetTop

Property

DHTML

This object property is used by scripted documents to identify the top most edge of an object, in relation to the top left corner of the current object's parent. You can use a combination of the `offsetHeight`, `offsetLeft`, `offsetTop` and `offsetWidth` properties to identify the exact location and dimensions of any object on a document.

The syntax for this command is

```
Coords=object.offsetTop
```

Parameters
Coords

This is an integer representing the top edge of the object.

Elements

A	ACRONYM	ADDRESS	APPLET
AREA	B	BIG	BLOCKQUOTE
BODY	BR	BUTTON	CAPTION
CENTER	CITE	CODE	COL
COLGROUP	DD	DEL	DFN
DIR	DIV	DL	DT
EM	EMBED	FIELDSET	FONT
FORM	FRAME	H1–H6	HR
I	IFRAME	IMG	INPUT
INS	KBD	LABEL	LEGEND
LI	LISTING	MAP	MARQUEE
MENU	NEXTID	OBJECT	OL
OPTION	P	PLAINTEXT	PRE

Q	S	SAMP	SELECT
SMALL	SPAN	STRIKE	STRONG
SUB	SUP	TABLE	TBODY
TD	TEXTAREA	TFOOT	TH
THEAD	TR	TT	U
UL	VAR	XMP	

CROSS-REFERENCE

See **offsetHeight**, **offsetLeft**, **offsetParent**, **offsetWidth**, **height**, **left**, **parent**, **top**, and **width**.

offsetWidth

Property

DHTML

This property is used to identify the width of an object, in relation to the top left corner of the document. You can use a combination of the `offsetHeight`, `offsetLeft`, `offsetTop`, and `offsetWidth` properties to identify the exact location and dimensions of any object on a document.

The syntax for this command is

```
Width=object.offsetWidth
```

Parameters
Width

This is the width of the object in pixels.

Elements

A	ACRONYM	ADDRESS	APPLET
AREA	B	BIG	BLOCKQUOTE
BODY	BR	BUTTON	CAPTION
CENTER	CITE	CODE	COL
COLGROUP	DD	DEL	DFN
DIR	DIV	DL	DT
EM	EMBED	FIELDSET	FONT
FORM	FRAME	H1–H6	HR
I	IFRAME	IMG	INPUT
INS	KBD	LABEL	LEGEND

LI	LISTING	MAP	MARQUEE
MENU	NEXTID	OBJECT	OL
OPTION	P	PLAINTEXT	PRE
Q	S	SAMP	SELECT
SMALL	SPAN	STRIKE	STRONG
SUB	SUP	TABLE	TBODY
TD	TEXTAREA	TFOOT	TH
THEAD	TR	TT	U
UL	VAR	XMP	

CROSS-REFERENCE
See **offsetLeft**, **offsetParent**, **offsetTop**, **offsetHeight**, **height**, **left**, **parent**, **top**, and **width**.

offsetX

Property

DHTML

This script property is used to retrieve the horizontal coordinate of the mouse's position in relation to the object that fired the identified event. The coordinates of this property match those identified by the `offsetLeft` property of the object. You can then use the `offsetParent` object to find the container object that defines the coordinate system being measured.

The syntax of this property is

```
Coords=event.offsetX
```

Parameters
Coords

This is an integer representing horizontal coordinates in pixels.

Objects
events

CROSS-REFERENCE
See **offsetTop**, **offsetLeft**, **offsetParent**, and **offsetY**.

offsetY

Property

DHTML

This object property is used to retrieve the vertical coordinate of the mouse's position in relation to the object that fired the identified event. The coordinates of this property match those identified by the `offsetTop` property of the object. You can then use the `offsetParent` object to find the container object that defines the system being measured.

The syntax of this property is

```
Coords=event.offsetY
```

Parameters
Coords

This is an integer representing vertical coordinates in pixels.

Example

The following example code collects the coordinates that a user clicks on when the pointer is over an image, and then displays them within a TEXTAREA and on the user agent's status bar.

```
<html>

<head>
<title>Coords</title>
<script language="JavaScript">
<!-
function showit(obj) {
  CoordsY=event.offsetY;
  CoordsX=event.offsetX;
  mytext="Click coordinates: Y=" + CoordsY + "  X=" + CoordsX
  thetextarea.value=mytext
  window.status=mytext
}
// ->
</script>
</head>

<body>
  <p align="center"><strong><font color="#FF0000">Click the
  image to See the mouse coordinates.</font></strong></p>
  <p align="center">
```

```
<input name="theimage" type="image" src="turtle.gif"
onclick="showit(this);" width="97" height="78">
</p>
<p align="center">
<textarea name="thetextarea" rows="2" cols="20">
Click coordinates:
</textarea>
</p>
</body>
</html>
```

Objects

events

CROSS-REFERENCE
See **offsetTop**, **offsetLeft**, **offsetParent**, and **offsetX**.

<OL>

Element

HTML

Start Tag: Required
End Tag: Required

This element is used to identify an ordered list. Ordered lists use numbers, symbols, or letters to identify the various items within the list. As the document author you can control the beginning serial number of your list, its text direction, and the type of number or letter being displayed as an item identifier.

Attributes
class

```
class="cdata-list"
```

This attribute is used to assign a class name to an element. User agents employ classes to group specific types of information for later use.

compact

```
compact
```

This attribute is freely interpreted by the user agent, but it should instruct the user agent to display the list in a compact manner.

dir

```
dir = LTR | RTL
```

This attribute defines the direction of the text flow in a document so a user agent can display it correctly.

id

```
id="name"
```

This attribute is used to assign a name to an element.

lang

```
lang="language code"
```

This attribute specifies the language in which an element and its values should be rendered.

onclick

```
onclick=script
```

This attribute takes effect when a user clicks the button on a pointing device with the pointer over an element.

ondblclick

```
ondblclick=script
```

This attribute takes effect when the button on a pointing device is double-clicked with the pointer over an element.

onkeydown

```
onkeydown=script
```

This attribute takes effect when a key is pressed while the pointer is over an element.

onkeypress

```
onkeypress=script
```

This attribute takes effect when a key is pressed and released with the pointer over an element.

onkeyup

```
onkeyup=script
```

This attribute takes effect when a key is released with the pointer over an element.

n
o
p

onmousedown

```
onmousedown=script
```

This attribute takes effect when the button on a pointing device is pressed with the pointer over an element.

onmousemove

```
onmousemove=script
```

This attribute is activated when the mouse pointer is moved while the pointer is over an element.

onmouseout

```
onmouseout=script
```

This attribute is activated when the mouse pointer is moved away from an element.

onmouseover

```
onmouseover=script
```

This attribute is activated the mouse pointer is movedwhen the mouse pointer is moved over an element.

onmouseup

```
onmouseup=script
```

This attribute takes effect when the button on a pointing device is released with the pointer over an element.

start

```
start=number
```

This is the number that you wish the initial item in the list to be identified with.

style

```
style=style descriptors
```

This attribute is used to apply specific style-sheet information to one particular element.

title

```
title=text
```

This attribute serves to provide annotation information to the element.

type

```
type= 1 | a | A | I | i
```

This deprecated attribute is used to designate the type of bullet or number to be used when displaying the list. This attribute is used only by visual user agents; Table O-1 summarizes its available values.

Table O-1 Available Type Values for the OL Element

Type	Example	Description
1	1, 2, 3, …	Arabic numbers
a	a, b, c, …	Lowercase roman alpha characters
A	A, B, C, …	Uppercase roman alpha characters
i	i, ii, iii, …	Lowercase Roman numerals
I	I, II, III	Uppercase Roman numerals

value

```
value=number
```

This attribute is used to set the value of the element. Although you should always specify this element in an integer form, it may display in another format.

Example

The following code creates an ordered list identifying popular farm animals. The list is told to start numbering at 13, as if it is a continuation of a previous list, and the numbering is all displayed in lower roman numerals.

 ON THE CD-ROM

Look for **ol.htm** on the accompanying CD-ROM.

```
<HTML>
  <HEAD>
    <TITLE> Ordered Lists </TITLE>
  </HEAD>
  <BODY>
    <H1>Farm Animals</H1>
    <OL type="i" start="13" >
      <LI>Horses
      <LI>Dogs
      <LI>Cats
      <LI>Cows
      <LI>Pigs
      <LI>Chickens
```

n
o
p

```
            </OL>
          </BODY>
        </HTML>
```

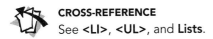

CROSS-REFERENCE
See **<LI>**, **<UL>**, and **Lists**.

onabort

Attribute/Event

HTML — Internet Explorer Only

This attribute is activated when an image-loading process has been aborted. A user can abort the loading of an image by clicking on an anchor to load another page, pressing the stop button on the browser, or by using some other navigational means of loading another document.

The syntax of this command is

```
onabort=script
```

JAVASCRIPT
```
object.onabort=handler
```

This event can also be used as a JavaScript command to set this attribute for specific images.

Values
script

This is either a name of a script function or a section of scripting code that should run with this event it fired.

Example
The following example document uses the onabort attribute to display a screen message whenever you have interrupted the loading of an image.

ON THE CD-ROM
Look for **onabort.htm** on the accompanying CD-ROM.

```
<html>
<head>
<title> This is my test page</title>
</head>
<body>
```

```
<IMG alt="Simple green turtle" src="halloween.gif"
onabort="alert("You have halted the loading of this
image.");">
</body>
</html>
```

Elements
> IMG

CROSS-REFERENCE
See **events**, **onload**, **onclose**, **onupdate**, **onclick**, **ondblclick**, **onerror**, **onfinish**,
onfocus, **onmousedown**, **onmouseover**, **onmouseup**, **onresize**, **onselect**, and
onunload.

onafterupdate

Attribute/Event

HTML — Internet Explorer Only

This event is fired after information contained within a document has been
completed, and the document has been completely updated.
The syntax used with this event is

```
onafterupdate=script
```

JAVASCRIPT
```
object.onafterupdate=handler
```

This event can also be used as a JavaScript command to set this attribute for
specific documents.

Values
script
> This is either a name of a script function or a section of scripting code that should
> run with this event it fired.

Elements

APPLET	BODY	BUTTON	CAPTION
DIV	EMBED	FIELDSET	IMG
INPUT	MAP	MARQUEE	NEXTID
OBJECT	SELECT	TABLE	TD
TEXTAREA	TR		

CROSS-REFERENCE
See **onbeforeupdate** and **onupdate**.

onbeforeunload

Attribute/Event

HTML — Internet Explorer Only

This attribute is fired directly before an HTML page is unloaded. This event can be triggered by an `open` scripting method or by changing the current documents shown in a `FRAMESET`.

The syntax used with this event is

```
onbeforeunload=script
```

JAVASCRIPT
```
object.onbeforeunload=handler
```

This event can also be used as a JavaScript command to set this attribute for specific documents or framesets.

Values
script

This is either a name of a script function or a section of scripting code that should run with this event it fired.

Elements
FRAMESET   IMG

CROSS-REFERENCE
See **onload** and **onunload**.

onbeforeupdate

Attribute/Event

HTML — Internet Explorer

This event is fired before information contained within a document has been loaded and or updated.

The syntax used with this event is

```
onbeforeupdate=script
```

JAVASCRIPT

```
object.onbeforeupdate=handler
```

This event can also be used as a JavaScript command to set this attribute for specific documents.

Values
script

This is either a name of a script function or a section of scripting code that should run with this event it fired.

Elements

APPLET	BODY	BUTTON	CAPTION
DIV	EMBED	FIELDSET	IMG
INPUT	MAP	MARQUEE	NEXTID
OBJECT	SELECT	TABLE	TD
TEXTAREA	TR		

CROSS-REFERENCE
See **onafterupdate** and **onupdate**.

onblur

Attribute/Event

HTML

This attribute activates when an element loses the focus, whether from the action of a pointing device or by tabbing navigation. You can activate it by clicking on a page's background, pressing the Tab key on your keyboard, using the blur JavaScript method, or by opening a different application or window.

The syntax for this command is

```
onblur=script
```

JAVASCRIPT

```
object.onblur=script
```

This JavaScript statement enables you to set the actions taken when an onblur event is encountered.

Values
script

This is either a name of a script function or a section of scripting code that should run with this event it fired.

Example
The following sample script uses an alert box to pop up the name of an element each time you tab past it when navigating through a document.

ON THE CD-ROM
Look for **onblur.htm** on the accompanying CD-ROM.

```
<HTML>
<HEAD>
  <TITLE>Using OnBlur</TITLE>
</HEAD>
<BODY>
<FORM>
<INPUT TYPE=text NAME=BirthDate VALUE="Birthdate"
onblur="alert(event.srcElement.name)">
<INPUT TYPE=text NAME=HoroscopeSign VALUE=" Horoscope Sign"
onblur="alert(event.srcElement.name)">
<INPUT TYPE=text NAME=FavGod VALUE="Favorite Greek God"
onblur="alert(event.srcElement.name)">
</FORM>
</BODY>
</HTML>
```

NOTE
The preceding example works only in Internet Explorer.

Elements
A	AREA	BUTTON	INPUT
LABEL	SELECT	TEXTAREA	

CROSS-REFERENCE
See **focus**, **onchange**, **onfocus**, and **navigate**.

onbounce

Attribute/Event

HTML — Internet Explorer Only

This even is activated when the `behavior` property of a `MARQUEE` object has been set to **alternate,** and the contents of the marquee reach one side and are bouncing back to the other side of the object's containment block.

The syntax for this command is

```
onbounce=script
```

 JAVASCRIPT

```
marquee.onbounce=script
```

In JavaScript, this statement enables you to set the actions taken when a MAR-QUEE banner changes direction.

Values

script

This is either a name of a script function or a section of scripting code that should run with this event it fired.

Example

This sample script shows how you can use the `onbounce` attribute to play a WAV each time the marquee changes direction.

 ON THE CD-ROM

Look for **onbounce.htm** on the accompanying CD-ROM.

```
<MARQUEE behaviour="alternate" bgcolor="red" direction="left"
loop= 10 onbounce="document.jukebox.play(ping.wav)">
Ping Pong
</MARQUEE>
<EMBED name="jukebox" src="ping.wav" hidden="true"
autostart="false">
```

Elements

MARQUEE

 **CROSS-REFERENCE**
See **behavior.**

onchange

Attribute/Event

HTML

This event is activated when an object's or document's contents change or are updated. You can invoke this event by altering the text within an object and then leaving it, or by selecting another option in a SELECT or INPUT object.

The syntax for this command is

```
onchange=script
```

JAVASCRIPT

```
object.onchange=script
```

In JavaScript, this statement enables you to set the actions taken when an object is altered.

Values
script

This is either a name of a script function or a section of scripting code that should run with this event it fired.

Elements

INPUT   SELECT   TEXTAREA

CROSS-REFERENCE

See **onupdate**, **onafterupdate**, and **onbeforeupdate**.

onclick

Attribute/Event

HTML

This attribute is activated when a user clicks the mouse over the top of an element, or other object. It can also be invoked when a user presses the Enter key within a form, press the access key for a form control, or by selecting an item inside a list box or a combo box.

The syntax for this command is

```
onclick=script
```

JAVASCRIPT

```
object.onclick=script
```

A user fires this event by activating an object (normally by clicking the mouse button or pressing Enter).

Values
script

This is either a name of a script function or a section of scripting code that should run with this event it fired.

Elements

A	ABBR	ACRONYM	ADDRESS
ADDRESS	AREA	B	BIG
BLINK	BLOCKQUOTE	BODY	BUTTON
CAPTION	CENTER	CITE	CODE
COL	COLGROUP	DD	DEL
DFN	DIR	DIV	DL
DT	EM	FIELDSET	FORM
H1–H6	HR	I	IMG
INPUT	INS	KBD	LABEL
LEGEND	LI	LINK	MAP
MARQUEE	MENU	NOFRAMES	NOSCRIPT
OBJECT	OL	OPTGROUP	OPTION
P	PRE	Q	S
SAMP	SELECT	SMALL	SPAN
STRIKE	STRONG	SUB	SUP
TABLE	TBODY	TD	TEXTAREA
TFOOT	TH	THEAD	TR
TT	U	UL	VAR

CROSS-REFERENCE
See **ondblclick** and **click**.

ondataavailable

Attribute/Event

HTML — Internet Explorer Only

This attribute is invoked when data arrives from a data source objects in an asynchronous fashion.

The syntax for this command is

```
ondataavailable=script
```

 JAVASCRIPT

```
object. ondataavailable =script
```

This event is used to control the actions taken when a user receives information from an object.

Values

script

This is either a name of a script function or a section of scripting code that should run with this event it fired.

Elements

APPLET   IMG   MAP   OBJECT

 CROSS-REFERENCE

See **Data**, **Server Push**, **Client Pull**, **ondatasetchanged**, **ondatasetcomplete**, and **Downloading**.

ondatasetchanged

Attribute/Event

HTML — Internet Explorer Only

This attribute is invoked when data that has been assigned to a data source objects has been altered or changed in any fashion. This is invoked when information is run through a filter, when a new dataset is loaded, or an existing dataset has been made available.

The syntax for this command is

```
ondatasetchanged=script
```

JAVASCRIPT

```
object.ondatasetchanged =script
```

This JavaScript event is used to control the actions taken when an object's dataset has been altered.

Values
script

This is either a name of a script function or a section of scripting code that should run with this event it fired.

Elements

APPLET   IMG   MAP   OBJECT

CROSS-REFERENCE
See **Data**, **Dataset**, **Server Push**, **Client Pull**, **Downloading**, **ondataavailable**, and **ondatasetcomplete**.

ondatasetcomplete

Attribute/Event

HTML — Internet Explorer Only

This attribute is invoked when data has been made completely available from a data source object.

The syntax for this command is

```
ondatasetcomplete=script
```

JAVASCRIPT

```
object.ondatasetcomplete =script
```

This JavaScript event is used to control the actions taken when an object's dataset has been completely loaded and made available to the user agent and user.

Values
script

This is either a name of a script function or a section of scripting code that should run with this event it fired.

APPLET   NEXTID   OBJECT

CROSS-REFERENCE
See **Data**, **Dataset**, **Server Push**, **Client Pull**, **Downloading**, **ondataavailable**, and **ondatasetchanged**.

ondblclick

Attribute/Event

HTML

This attribute is activated when a user double-clicks the left mouse button with the pointer over an element or other object.

The syntax for this command is

```
ondblclick=script
```

JAVASCRIPT
```
object.ondblclick=script
```

This JavaScript event forces a specific action to be taken when a user activates an object through double-clicking the mouse.

Values
script

This is either a name of a script function or a section of scripting code that should run with this event it fired.

Elements

A	ABBR	ACRONYM	ADDRESS
ADDRESS	AREA	B	BIG
BLINK	BLOCKQUOTE	BODY	BUTTON
CAPTION	CENTER	CITE	CODE
COL	COLGROUP	DD	DEL
DFN	DIR	DIV	DL
DT	EM	FIELDSET	FORM
C	HR	I	IMG
INPUT	INS	KBD	LABEL
LEGEND	LI	LINK	MAP
MARQUEE	MENU	NOFRAMES	NOSCRIPT
OBJECT	OL	OPTGROUP	OPTION
P	PRE	Q	S

SAMP	SELECT	SMALL	SPAN
STRIKE	STRONG	SUB	SUP
TABLE	TBODY	TD	TEXTAREA
TFOOT	TH	THEAD	TR
TT	U	UL	VAR

CROSS-REFERENCE
See **onclick** and **click**.

ondragstart

Attribute/Event

HTML — Internet Explorer Only

This attribute is activated when a user first starts to drag a selection of text or an object across the document.

The syntax for this command is

```
ondragstart=script
```

 JAVASCRIPT
```
object.ondragstart=script
```

This JavaScript event forces a specific action to be taken when a user drags any text or objects across (or onto) a document.

n
o
p

Values
script

This is either a name of a script function or a section of scripting code that should run with this event it fired.

Elements

A	ABBR	ACRONYM	ADDRESS
ADDRESS	AREA	B	BIG
BLINK	BLOCKQUOTE	BODY	BUTTON
CAPTION	CENTER	CITE	CODE
COL	COLGROUP	DD	DEL
DFN	DIR	DIV	DL
DT	EM	FIELDSET	FORM
H1–H6	HR	I	IMG

INPUT	INS	KBD	LABEL
LEGEND	LI	LINK	MAP
MARQUEE	MENU	NOFRAMES	NOSCRIPT
OBJECT	OL	OPTGROUP	OPTION
P	PRE	Q	S
SAMP	SELECT	SMALL	SPAN
STRIKE	STRONG	SUB	SUP
TABLE	TBODY	TD	TEXTAREA
TFOOT	TH	THEAD	TR
TT	U	UL	VAR

CROSS-REFERENCE
See **onclick** and **ondblclick**.

onerror

Attribute/Event

HTML — Internet Explorer Only

This attribute is activated when an error is encountered within a document. Errors generally occur when you first load an object, or in a script when the document is being parsed.

The syntax for this command is

```
onerror=script
```

JAVASCRIPT

```
object.onerror=script
```

This JavaScript event forces a specific action to be taken when an error is encountered while an object is being loaded.

Values
script

This is either a name of a script function or a section of scripting code that should run with this event it fired.

Example

This example code traps an error that has been purposefully inserted into the script on line 10. It then displays an alert box identifying the error, the line, and the URL of the error.

```
<HEAD>
<SCRIPT language="JavaScript">
  function traperror(msg,url,line)
  { alert(msg + "\n" + url + "\nLine: " + line);
  return true;
  // Suppresses IE error messaging.
  }

  onerror=traperror;
  This.Entry.should_cause_a_scripting_error = 5;
</SCRIPT>
</HEAD>
<BODY onerror="errortrap()">
</BODY>
```

Elements

IMG   LINK   OBJECT   SCRIPT
STYLE

CROSS-REFERENCE
See **onerrorupdate**.

onerrorupdate

Attribute/Event

HTML — Internet Explorer Only

This attribute is activated when an `onbeforeupdate` attribute cancels the loading of a document's objects. When this happens, the `onerrorupdate` runs instead of the `onafterupdate` option.

The syntax for this command is

`onerrorupdate=script`

JAVASCRIPT
`object.onerrorupdate=script`

This JavaScript event forces a specific action to be taken when the onbeforeupdate event cancels the loading of a document or its objects.

Values
script

This is either a name of a script function or a section of scripting code that should run with this event it fired.

Elements

A	APPLET	MAP	NEXTID
OBJECT	SELECT	TEXTAREA	

CROSS-REFERENCE
See **onerrorupdate**, **onupdate**, **onbeforeupdate**, and **onafterupdate**.

onfilterchange

Attribute/Event

HTML — Internet Explorer Only

This event is invoked when a visual filter on data is altered or updated. The syntax for this command is

```
onfilterchange=script
```

JAVASCRIPT
```
object.onfilterchange=script
```

This JavaScript event forces a specific action to be taken when the visual filter of a document has been altered.

Values
script

This is either a name of a script function or a section of scripting code that should run with this event it fired.

Elements

BODY	BUTTON	DIV	FIELDSET
IMG	INPUT	MARQUEE	NEXTID
SPAN	TABLE	TD	TEXTAREA
TH	TR		

CROSS-REFERENCE
See **filter** and **onchange**.

onfinish

Attribute/Event

HTML — Internet Explorer Only

This HTML event is used by Microsoft browsers to perform a specified action when a looping process for a MARQUEE has completed. This attribute needs a valid value that is greater than one, but less than infinity, for the loop attribute of the MARQUEE element before it will fire.

The syntax for this command is

```
onfinish=script
```

JAVASCRIPT

```
marquee.onfinish=script
```

This JavaScript event forces a specific action to be taken when the MARQUEE has finished looping.

Values
script

This is either a name of a script function or a section of scripting code that should run with this event it fired.

Example
This sample script shows how you can use the onfinish attribute to play a WAV when the marquee has completed its loops.

ON THE CD-ROM
Look for **onfinish.htm** on the accompanying CD-ROM.

```
<HTML>
<HEAD>
<META NAME="GENERATOR" Content="NetObjects ScriptBuilder 2.0">
<TITLE>OnFinish Events</TITLE>
</HEAD>
<BODY>
<MARQUEE behavior="alternate" bgcolor="blue" direction="left"
loop="3" onfinish="alert('Marquee is done.')">
Ping Pong
```

n
o
p

```
</MARQUEE>

</BODY>
</HTML>
```

Elements
MARQUEE

CROSS-REFERENCE
See **behavior**, **onbounce**, **onstart**, and **loop**.

onfocus

Attribute/Event

HTML

This attribute is in effect when an element element receives focus, whether from the action of a pointing device or by tabbing navigation. It is also activated when an object receives the focus through a scripted focus method.

The syntax for this command is

```
onfocus=script
```

JAVASCRIPT
```
object.onfocus=script
```

This JavaScript event forces a specific action to be taken when an object receives the focus of the cursor.

Values
script

This is either a name of a script function or a section of scripting code that should run with this event it fired.

Example
This example places the focus on the Submit button when the document is first loaded.

ON THE CD-ROM
```
Look for onfocus.htm on the accompanying CD-ROM.<BODY
onload="btnSubmit.focus()">
<INPUT type=text name=email value="Email Address">
```

```
<INPUT type=text name=web value="Web Address">
<INPUT type=submit name=btnSubmit>
</BODY>
```

Elements

A	AREA	BUTTON	INPUT
LABEL	SELECT	TEXTAREA	

CROSS-REFERENCE
See **<INPUT>**, **focus**, and **accesskey**.

onhelp

Attribute/Event

HTML—Internet Explorer Only

This event is invoked whenever a user access the help menu through the F1 key while the browser is the active window.

The syntax for this command is

```
onhelp=script
```

JAVASCRIPT
```
object.onhelp=script
```

This JavaScript event forces a specific action to be taken whenever a user access the help documents through the F1 key.

Values
script

This is either a name of a script function or a section of scripting code that should run with this event it fired.

Elements

A	ADDRESS	APPLET	AREA
B	BIG	BLOCKQUOTE	BUTTON
CAPTION	CENTER	CITE	CODE
DD	DFN	DIR	DIV
DL	DT	EM	EMBED
FIELDSET	FONT	FORM	H1–H6
HR	I	IMG	INPUT

KBD	LABEL	LEGEND	LI
LISTING	MAP	MARQUEE	MENU
NEXTID	OL	P	PLAINTEXT
PRE	S	SAMP	SELECT
SMALL	SPAN	STRIKE	STRONG
SUB	SUP	TABLE	TBODY
TD	TEXTAREA	TFOOT	TH
THEAD	TR	TT	U
UL	VAR	XMP	

CROSS-REFERENCE
See **window** and **document**.

onkeydown

Attribute/Event

HTML

This attribute takes effect when a key is pressed on the keyboard. The syntax for using this command is

```
onkeydown=script
```

JAVASCRIPT
```
object.onkeydown=handler
```

When a user presses a key while the pointer is over a specified object, this event fires before the key is released. It returns the value of the particular key the user has pressed.

Values
script

This is either a name of a script function or a section of scripting code that should run with this event it fired.

Elements

A	ABBR	ACRONYM	ADDRESS
ADDRESS	AREA	B	BIG
BLINK	BLOCKQUOTE	BODY	BUTTON
CAPTION	CENTER	CITE	CODE
COL	COLGROUP	DD	DEL
DFN	DIR	DIV	DL
DT	EM	FIELDSET	FORM
H1–H6	HR	I	IMG
INPUT	INS	KBD	LABEL
LEGEND	LI	LINK	MAP
MARQUEE	MENU	NOFRAMES	NOSCRIPT
OBJECT	OL	OPTGROUP	OPTION
P	PRE	Q	S
SAMP	SELECT	SMALL	SPAN
STRIKE	STRONG	SUB	SUP
TABLE	TBODY	TD	TEXTAREA
TFOOT	TH	THEAD	TR
TT	U	UL	VAR

CROSS-REFERENCE
See **onkeypress** and **onkeyup**.

onkeypress

Attribute/Event

HTML

This attribute takes effect when a key is pressed and released on the keyboard. The syntax for using this command is

```
onkeypress=script
```

JAVASCRIPT
```
object.onkeypress=handler
```

When a user presses a key with the pointer over a specified object, this event fires before the key is released. It returns the value of the key that the user pressed.

Values

script

This is either a name of a script function or a section of scripting code that should run with this event it fired.

Elements

A	ABBR	ACRONYM	ADDRESS
ADDRESS	AREA	B	BIG
BLINK	BLOCKQUOTE	BODY	BUTTON
CAPTION	CENTER	CITE	CODE
COL	COLGROUP	DD	DEL
DFN	DIR	DIV	DL
DT	EM	FIELDSET	FORM
H1–H6	HR	I	IMG
INPUT	INS	KBD	LABEL
LEGEND	LI	LINK	MAP
MARQUEE	MENU	NOFRAMES	NOSCRIPT
OBJECT	OL	OPTGROUP	OPTION
P	PRE	Q	S
SAMP	SELECT	SMALL	SPAN
STRIKE	STRONG	SUB	SUP
TABLE	TBODY	TD	TEXTAREA
TFOOT	TH	THEAD	TR
TT	U	UL	VAR

CROSS-REFERENCE
See **onkeydown** and **onkeyup**.

onkeyup

Attribute/Event

HTML

This attribute takes effect when a key is released on the keyboard.
The syntax for using this command is

```
onkeyup=script
```

 JAVASCRIPT

```
object.onkeyup=handler
```

As a user presses and releases a key while a specified object is selected, this
event fires when the key is released. It returns the value of the key that was
pressed.

Values

script

This is either a name of a script function or a section of scripting code that should
run with this event it fired.

Elements

A	ABBR	ACRONYM	ADDRESS
ADDRESS	AREA	B	BIG
BLINK	BLOCKQUOTE	BODY	BUTTON
CAPTION	CENTER	CITE	CODE
COL	COLGROUP	DD	DEL
DFN	DIR	DIV	DL
DT	EM	FIELDSET	FORM
H1–H6	HR	I	IMG
INPUT	INS	KBD	LABEL
LEGEND	LI	LINK	MAP
MARQUEE	MENU	NOFRAMES	NOSCRIPT
OBJECT	OL	OPTGROUP	OPTION
P	PRE	Q	S
SAMP	SELECT	SMALL	SPAN
STRIKE	STRONG	SUB	SUP
TABLE	TBODY	TD	TEXTAREA
TFOOT	TH	THEAD	TR
TT	U	UL	VAR

n
o
p

CROSS-REFERENCE
See **onkeydown** and **onkeypress**.

onLine

Property

DHTML

This property is used within a script to identify whether the navigator viewing the document is being viewed online or offline. When a browser is offline it is generally viewing documents that have been downloaded previously, and saved for this purpose.

The syntax of this parameter is

```
[bOnline=] navigator.onLine
```

Parameters
bOnline

This Boolean variable is set to `true` when the user agent is currently connected to a network, and `false` when it is not.

Example
The following code alerts you to whether you are online (`true`), or offline (`false`) when the document is loaded. You can use the Work Offline option on Internet Explorer's File menu to alter your results. You will need to reload the document after each change to your online status.

```
<html>
<head>
<title>onLine example</title>
</head>
<body onload="alert("Are we online? "+navigator.onLine)">
</body>
</html>
```

Objects
navigator

CROSS-REFERENCE
See **navigator** and **user agent**.

onload

Attribute/Event

HTML

This attribute is invoked when a document or FRAMESET has completely loaded within the visual area of the user agent.

The syntax for using this command is

```
onload=script
```

JAVASCRIPT

```
object.onload=handler
```

This property returns the handler of the object, after it is loaded.

Values

script

This is either a name of a script function or a section of scripting code that should run with this event it fired.

Example

The following example code displays a message in the user agent's status window identifying when a document has been fully loaded.

ON THE CD-ROM

Look for **onload.htm** on the accompanying CD-ROM.

```
<SCRIPT>function bdyLoaded()
{ alert("The document has been loaded");}
</SCRIPT>
<BODY onload="bdyLoaded">
  The body text goes here.
</BODY>
```

Elements

FRAMESET   BODY

CROSS-REFERENCE

See **onunload**.

onmousedown

Attribute/Event

HTML

This attribute takes effect when the button on a pointing device is pressed with the pointer over an element.

```
onmousedown=script
```

JAVASCRIPT

```
object.onmousedown=handler
```

This event fires when the mouse button has been pressed, but before it is released, over the specified object.

Values

script

This is either a name of a script function or a section of scripting code that should run with this event it fired.

Example

The following example uses the onmousedown event to identify the type of element that the mouse was pressed over.

ON THE CD-ROM

Look for **onmousedown.htm** on the accompanying CD-ROM.

```
<BODY onmousedown="alert(event.srcElement.tagName)">
<TABLE BORDER=1>
  <TH>Click the items below with your mouse.</TH>
  <TR><TD><BUTTON>Click right here</BUTTON></TD></TR>
  <TR><TD><INPUT type=text value="Click Me"></TD></TR>
  <TR><TD><IMG src="clickme.gif" alt="Click here"></TD></TR>
</TABLE>
</BODY>
```

Elements

A	ABBR	ACRONYM	ADDRESS
ADDRESS	AREA	B	BIG
BLINK	BLOCKQUOTE	BODY	BUTTON
CAPTION	CENTER	CITE	CODE
COL	COLGROUP	DD	DEL
DFN	DIR	DIV	DL

DT	EM	FIELDSET	FORM
H1–H6	HR	I	IMG
INPUT	INS	KBD	LABEL
LEGEND	LI	LINK	MAP
MARQUEE	MENU	NOFRAMES	NOSCRIPT
OBJECT	OL	OPTGROUP	OPTION
P	PRE	Q	S
SAMP	SELECT	SMALL	SPAN
STRIKE	STRONG	SUB	SUP
TABLE	TBODY	TD	TEXTAREA
TFOOT	TH	THEAD	TR
TT	U	UL	VAR

CROSS-REFERENCE

See **onmousemove**, **onmouseover**, **onmouseout**, and **onmouseup**.

onmousemove

Attribute/Event

HTML

This attribute takes effect when a pointing device is moved over an element.

```
onmousemove=script
```

JAVASCRIPT

```
object.onmousemove=handler
```

This event fires when the mouse pointer is moved off or over the specified object.

Values
script

This is either a name of a script function or a section of scripting code that should run with this event it fired.

Example
The following example uses the `onmousemove` event to identify the name of the element that the mouse pointer was moved over.

ON THE CD-ROM
Look for **onmousemove.htm** on the accompanying CD-ROM.

```
<HTML>
<HEAD>
<META NAME="GENERATOR" Content="NetObjects ScriptBuilder 2.0">
<TITLE>onMouseMove</TITLE>
</HEAD>
<BODY>
<BODY>
<TABLE border=1 >
  <TH name="Table Header"
onmousemove="alert(event.srcElement.name)">Click the items
below with your mouse.</TH>
  <TR>
    <TD name="r1c1"
onmousemove="alert(event.srcElement.name)">
      <BUTTON name=redbutton>Click right here</BUTTON>
    </TD>
  </TR>
  <TR>
    <TD name="r2c1"
onmousemove="alert(event.srcElement.name)">
      <INPUT name=clicktext type=text value="Click Me">
    </TD>
  </TR>
  <TR>
    <TD name="r3c1"
onmousemove="alert(event.srcElement.name)">
      <IMG name=clickgif src="clickme.gif" alt="Click here">
    </TD>
  </TR>
</TABLE>
</BODY>

</BODY>
</HTML>
```

Elements

A	ABBR	ACRONYM	ADDRESS
ADDRESS	AREA	B	BIG
BLINK	BLOCKQUOTE	BODY	BUTTON
CAPTION	CENTER	CITE	CODE
COL	COLGROUP	DD	DEL

DFN	DIR	DIV	DL
DT	EM	FIELDSET	FORM
H1–H6	HR	I	IMG
INPUT	INS	KBD	LABEL
LEGEND	LI	LINK	MAP
MARQUEE	MENU	NOFRAMES	NOSCRIPT
OBJECT	OL	OPTGROUP	OPTION
P	PRE	Q	S
SAMP	SELECT	SMALL	SPAN
STRIKE	STRONG	SUB	SUP
TABLE	TBODY	TD	TEXTAREA
TFOOT	TH	THEAD	TR
TT	U	UL	VAR

CROSS-REFERENCE

See **onmousedown**, **onmouseover**, **onmouseout**, and **onmouseup**.

onmouseout

Attribute/Event

HTML

This attribute takes effect when a pointing device is moved away from an element.

```
onmouseout=script
```

JAVASCRIPT

```
object.onmouseout=handler
```

This event fires when the mouse pointer is moved away from a specified object over which it was placed.

Values

script

This is either a name of a script function or a section of scripting code that should run with this event it fired.

Example

The following example uses the onmouseout event to identify the name of the element that the mouse was removed from in the status window of the user agent.

ON THE CD-ROM

Look for **onmouseout.htm** on the accompanying CD-ROM.

```
<HTML>
<HEAD>
<META NAME="GENERATOR" Content="NetObjects ScriptBuilder 2.0">
<TITLE>onmouseout example</TITLE>
</HEAD>
<BODY>
<BODY >
<TABLE name="Our Table" border=1
onmouseout="alert(event.srcElement.name)">
  <TH name="Table Header">Click the items below with your
  mouse.</TH>
  <TR name="Row 1">
    <TD name="R1C1">
      <BUTTON name=redbutton>The Red Button (ok.. so it isn't
      really red!)</BUTTON>
    </TD>
  </TR>
  <TR name="Row 2">
    <TD name="R2C1">
      <INPUT name=clicktext type=text value="Click Me">
    </TD>
  </TR>
  <TR name="Row 3">
    <TD name="R3C1">
      <IMG name=clickgif src="clickme.gif" alt="Click here">
    </TD>
  </TR>
</TABLE>

</BODY>
</HTML>
```

Elements

A	ABBR	ACRONYM	ADDRESS
ADDRESS	AREA	B	BIG
BLINK	BLOCKQUOTE	BODY	BUTTON

CAPTION	CENTER	CITE	CODE
COL	COLGROUP	DD	DEL
DFN	DIR	DIV	DL
DT	EM	FIELDSET	FORM
H1–H6	HR	I	IMG
INPUT	INS	KBD	LABEL
LEGEND	LI	LINK	MAP
MARQUEE	MENU	NOFRAMES	NOSCRIPT
OBJECT	OL	OPTGROUP	OPTION
P	PRE	Q	S
SAMP	SELECT	SMALL	SPAN
STRIKE	STRONG	SUB	SUP
TABLE	TBODY	TD	TEXTAREA
TFOOT	TH	THEAD	TR
TT	U	UL	VAR

CROSS-REFERENCE

See **onmousedown**, **onmousemove**, **onmouseover**, and **onmouseup**.

onmouseover

Attribute/Event

HTML

This attribute takes effect when a pointing device is moved onto an element.

```
onmouseover=script
```

JAVASCRIPT

```
object.onmouseover=handler
```

This event fires when the mouse pointer is moved over the specified object, and before it has been moved away.

Values
script

This is either a name of a script function or a section of scripting code that should run with this event it fired.

Example

The following example uses the onmouseover event to identify the name of the element that the mouse pointer was moved over. The name will appear in the text box following the table.

 ON THE CD-ROM

Look for **onmouseover.htm** on the accompanying CD-ROM.

```
<HTML>
<HEAD>
<META NAME="GENERATOR" Content="NetObjects ScriptBuilder 2.0">
<TITLE>onMouseover</TITLE>
<script language="JavaScript">
<!-
function showus(obj) {
  mytext=event.srcElement.name
  thetextarea.value=thetextarea.value+"\n"+mytext
  window.status=mytext
}
// ->
</script>
</HEAD>
<BODY>
<TABLE BORDER=0">
  <TH>Drag your mouse around.</TH>
  <TR>
    <TD>
      <BUTTON name="redbutton"
onmouseover="showus(this)">Click right here</BUTTON>
    </TD>
  </TR>
  <TR>
    <TD>
      <INPUT name=clicktext type=text value="Click Me"
onmouseover="showus(this)">
    </TD>
  </TR>
  <TR>
    <TD>
      <IMG name=clickgif src="clickme.gif" alt="Click here"
onmouseover="showus(this)">
    </TD>
  </TR>
</TABLE>
<TEXTAREA name="thetextarea" rows="10" cols="20">
```

```
        Moved Over Elements:
        </TEXTAREA>

      </BODY>
      </HTML>
```

Elements

A	ABBR	ACRONYM	ADDRESS
ADDRESS	AREA	B	BIG
BLINK	BLOCKQUOTE	BODY	BUTTON
CAPTION	CENTER	CITE	CODE
COL	COLGROUP	DD	DEL
DFN	DIR	DIV	DL
DT	EM	FIELDSET	FORM
H1–H6	HR	I	IMG
INPUT	INS	KBD	LABEL
LEGEND	LI	LINK	MAP
MARQUEE	MENU	NOFRAMES	NOSCRIPT
OBJECT	OL	OPTGROUP	OPTION
P	PRE	Q	S
SAMP	SELECT	SMALL	SPAN
STRIKE	STRONG	SUB	SUP
TABLE	TBODY	TD	TEXTAREA
TFOOT	TH	THEAD	TR
TT	U	UL	VAR

 CROSS-REFERENCE

See **onmousedown**, **onmousemove**, **onmouseover**, and **onmouseup**.

onmouseup

Attribute/Event

HTML

This attribute takes effect when the button on a pointing device is released with the pointer over an element.

```
onmouseup=script
```

JAVASCRIPT

```
object.onmouseup=handler
```

This event fires when the mouse button is released after being pressed with the pointer over the specified object, and before it has been moved away.

Values
script

This is either a name of a script function or a section of scripting code that should run with this event it fired.

Example
The following example uses the onmouseup event to play a wav file every time the mouse pointer is moved over a specific element on the document.

ON THE CD-ROM

Look for **onmouseup.htm** on the accompanying CD-ROM.

```
<HTML>
<HEAD>
<META NAME="GENERATOR" Content="NetObjects ScriptBuilder 2.0">
<TITLE>Using onmouseup to play midis</TITLE>
</HEAD>
<SCRIPT>
<!-
function playSound()  {
    document.jukebox.play();
}
->
</SCRIPT>
<BODY >
  <INPUT type="button" value="play" onmouseup="playSound()">
  <P>
  <EMBED name="jukebox" src="crow.mid" autostart="false">
</BODY>
</HTML>
```

Elements

A	ABBR	ACRONYM	ADDRESS
ADDRESS	AREA	B	BIG
BLINK	BLOCKQUOTE	BODY	BUTTON
CAPTION	CENTER	CITE	CODE
COL	COLGROUP	DD	DEL
DFN	DIR	DIV	DL

DT	EM	FIELDSET	FORM
H1–H6	HR	I	IMG
INPUT	INS	KBD	LABEL
LEGEND	LI	LINK	MAP
MARQUEE	MENU	NOFRAMES	NOSCRIPT
OBJECT	OL	OPTGROUP	OPTION
P	PRE	Q	S
SAMP	SELECT	SMALL	SPAN
STRIKE	STRONG	SUB	SUP
TABLE	TBODY	TD	TEXTAREA
TFOOT	TH	THEAD	TR
TT	U	UL	VAR

CROSS-REFERENCE

See **onmousedown**, **onmousemove**, **onmouseover**, and **onmouseout**.

onreadystatechange

Attribute/Event

HTML — Internet Explorer Only

Each object has a default state that lets the user agent (and any scripts) know when that object has been completely loaded, or whether it is still initializing, or currently interacting with a user. Whenever the state of an object changes, this event fires.

The syntax for this event is

```
onreadystatechange=script
```

JAVASCRIPT

```
object.onreadystatechange=handler
```

You can change the actions of this object event, even on the fly.

Values
script

This is either a name of a script function or a section of scripting code that should run with this event it fired.

Elements

APPLET   EMBED   FIELDSET   IMG
LINK   OBJECT   SCRIPT   STYLE

 CROSS-REFERENCE
See **onload**, **onunload**, and **readystate**.

onreset

Attribute/Event

HTML

This event is activated when a user presses the reset button on a form, reset a form through a script, or refresh the contents of a page.

The syntax for this event is

```
onreset=script
```

 JAVASCRIPT
```
object.onreset=handler
```
This script event allows you to change the actions of an event on the fly.

Values
script

This is either a name of a script function or a section of scripting code that should run with this event it fired.

Elements
FORM

 CROSS-REFERENCE
See **<INPUT>**, **<BUTTON>**, **submit**, **reset**, and **type**.

onresize

Attribute/Event

HTML

This event is invoked when an object is about to be resized. This happens when a user places the mouse over a border, and clicks the mouse in order to drag the border bigger.

The syntax for this event is

```
onresize=script
```

JAVASCRIPT
```
object.onresize=handler
```

This script event allows you to change the actions of an event on the fly.

Values
script

This is either a name of a script function or a section of scripting code that should run with this event it fired.

Elements

APPLET	BUTTON	CAPTION	DIV
EMBED	FIELDSET	FRAMESET	HR
IMG	MARQUEE	SELECT	TABLE
TD	TEXTAREA	TR	

CROSS-REFERENCE
See **resize**, **drag**, and **size**.

onrowenter

Attribute/Event

HTML—Internet Explorer Only

This event is used to automate a process that has been associated with a change of information within the data cells of a specific row of a table.

The syntax for this event is

```
onrowenter=script
```

JAVASCRIPT

```
object.onrowenter=handler
```

This object event allows you to change the actions of an event on the fly.

Values

script

This is either a name of a script function or a section of scripting code that should run with this event it fired.

Elements

APPLET	BODY	BUTTON	CAPTION
DIV	EMBED	HR	IMG
MAP	MARQUEE	NEXTID	OBJECT
SELECT	TABLE	TD	TEXTAREA
TR			

CROSS-REFERENCE
See **onrowexit** and **row**.

onrowexit

Attribute/Event

HTML—Internet Explorer Only

This event is used to automate a process that has been associated with a change of information within the data cells of a specific row of a table. This event is fired directly after the data has been changed, but before the focus has left that row entirely.

The syntax for this event is

```
onrowexit=script
```

JAVASCRIPT

```
object.onrowexit=handler
```

This event allows you to change the actions of an event on the fly.

Values
script

> This is either a name of a script function or a section of scripting code that should run with this event it fired.

Elements

APPLET	BODY	BUTTON	CAPTION
DIV	EMBED	HR	IMG
MAP	MARQUEE	NEXTID	OBJECT
SELECT	TABLE	TD	TEXTAREA
TR			

CROSS-REFERENCE
See **onrowenter** and **row**.

onscroll

Attribute/Event

HTML — Internet Explorer Only

This event is used to automated a process that has been associated with the movement of the page marker box found within the scroll bar of an object, or a window. This even can be started by dragging the page marker in the scroll bar with your mouse, clicking on a scrolling arrow, clicking on the scroll bar itself, the page is scrolled by a "doscroll" JavaScript event, and either the **page up, page down, arrow up,** or **arrow down** keys are pressed.

The syntax for this event is

```
onscroll=script
```

JAVASCRIPT
```
object.onscroll=handler
```

This object event allows you to change the actions of an event on the fly.

Values
script

> This is either a name of a script function or a section of scripting code that should run with this event it fired.

Elements

APPLET	BODY	DIV	EMBED
MAP	MARQUEE	OBJECT	SELECT
TABLE	TEXTAREA		

CROSS-REFERENCE
See **scroll**.

onselect

Attribute/Event

HTML

When a user changes the current selection this event will fire. The object selection can be changed by dragging the mouse across characters in a text field, or pressing the **Shift** key will moving the cursor over a series of text.

The syntax for this event is

```
onselect=script
```

JAVASCRIPT
```
object.onselect=handler
```

This object event allows you to change the actions of an event on the fly.

Values
script

This is either a name of a script function or a section of scripting code that should run with this event it fired.

Elements
INPUT   TEXTAREA

CROSS-REFERENCE
See **selection**, **textarea**, **textrange**, **onselectstart**, and **object**.

onselectstart

Attribute/Event

HTML — Internet Explorer Only

This event is fired when the mouse is being used to select and object or a segment of text.

The syntax for this event is

```
onselectstart=script
```

JAVASCRIPT

```
object.onselectstart=handler
```

This event allows you to change the actions of an event on the fly.

Values

script

This is either a name of a script function or a section of scripting code that should run with this event it fired.

Elements

A	ACRONYM	ADDRESS	AREA
B	BIG	BLOCKQUOTE	BODY
BUTTON	CAPTION	CENTER	CITE
CODE	DD	DEL	DFN
DIR	DIV	DL	DT
EM	FIELDSET	FONT	FORM
H1–H6	HR	I	IMG
INPUT	KBD	LABEL	LI
LISTING	MAP	MARQUEE	MENU
NEXTID	OBJECT	OL	OPTION
P	PLAINTEXT	PRE	Q
S	SAMP	SELECT	SMALL
SPAN	STRIKE	STRONG	SUB
SUP	TABLE	TBODY	TD
TEXTAREA	TFOOT	TH	THEAD
TR	TT	U	UL
VAR			

n
o
p

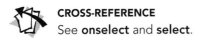

CROSS-REFERENCE
See **onselect** and **select**.

onstart

Attribute/Event

HTML — Internet Explorer Only

This HTML event is used by Microsoft browsers to perform a specified action on when a looping process for a MARQUEE has started. This attribute needs a valid value that is greater than one, but less than infinity, for the loop attribute of the MARQUEE element before it will fire.

The syntax for this command is

```
onstart=script
```

JAVASCRIPT
```
marquee.onstart=handler
```

This script event is used to force a specific action to be taken when the looping of the MARQUEE has started.

Values
script

This is either a name of a script function or a section of scripting code that should run with this event it fired.

Example
This sample script shows how you can use the onstart attribute to play a WAV when the marquee has completed its loops

ON THE CD-ROM
Look for **onfinish.htm** on the accompanying CD-ROM.

```
<HTML>
<HEAD>
<META NAME="GENERATOR" Content="NetObjects ScriptBuilder 2.0">
<TITLE>OnStart Example</TITLE>
</HEAD>
<SCRIPT>
<!-
function playSound() {
    document.jukebox.play();
```

```
}
-->
</SCRIPT>
<BODY>
<MARQUEE behaviour="scroll" bgcolor="blue" direction="left"
loop= 10 onstart="playSound()">
Ping Pong
</MARQUEE>
<EMBED name="jukebox" src="ping.wav" hidden="true"
autostart="false">
</BODY>
</HTML>
```

Elements
MARQUEE

CROSS-REFERENCE
See **behavior**, **onbounce**, **onfinish**, and **loop**.

onsubmit

Attribute/Event

HTML

This event is activated when a user presses the submit button on a form, sub-mitting a form with an image, or through the BUTTON or INPUT object.

The syntax for this event is

```
onsubmit=script
```

JAVASCRIPT
```
object.onsubmit =handler
```
This object event allows you to change the actions of this event on the fly.

Values
script

This is either a name of a script function or a section of scripting code that should run with this event it fired.

Elements
FORM

CROSS-REFERENCE
See <INPUT>, <BUTTON>, **reset**, and **type**.

onunload

Attribute/Event

This attribute is invoked when a document or FRAMESET had completed the unloading process within the visual area of the user agent.

The syntax for using this command is

```
onunload=script
```

JAVASCRIPT

```
object.onunload=handler
```

This event is activated when an object has been completely unloaded.

Values
script

This is either a name of a script function or a section of scripting code that should run with this event it fired.

Example
The following example code displays a message in the user agent's status window that identifies when a document has been fully loaded.

ON THE CD-ROM
Look for **onunload.htm** on the accompanying CD-ROM.

```
<HTML>
<HEAD>
<META NAME="GENERATOR" Content="NetObjects ScriptBuilder 2.0">
<TITLE>Document Title</TITLE>
<SCRIPT>function bdyUnLoaded()
{ alert("The document has been unloaded");}
</SCRIPT>
</head>
<BODY onunload="bdyUnLoaded()">
  The body text goes here.
</BODY>
</HTML>
```

Elements
BODY   FRAMESET

CROSS-REFERENCE
See **onload**.

open

Method

DHTML

This method can be used either to open a window, or open a new document to collect the output of the `write` and `writeln` methods.

```
oNewWindow = window.open([sURL] [, sName] [, sFeatures]
[,bReplace])
document.open(sMimeType [, sReplace])
```

Parameters
sURL

This is the string containing the URL to display in the window being opened. Because this parameter is optional, you can not use this parameter and open the window with a blank document.

sName

This optional parameter provides a name for the window. It is also used for the FORM and the A elements.

sFeatures

This optional parameter decides which window ornaments to display. The following list identifies these features.

fullscreen={ yes | no | 1 | 0 }	This identifies whether the browser is displayed full-screen or in a window. The default is no, which displays the browser in a normal window. Full-screen mode hides the browser's title bar and menus, which confuses some users. (You may want to leave them a note letting them know that they can revert to a normal window by pressing a specific button, or that they can close the window by pressing **Alt+F4**.)
channelmode= { yes | no | 1 | 0 }	Identifies whether the window is displayed in theatre mode showing the channel band.

toolbar={ yes | no | 1 | 0 }	This controls the display of the browser's toolbar.
location= { yes | no | 1 | 0 }	This controls the display of the browser's location input field.
directories = { yes | no | 1 | 0 }	This controls the display of directory buttons. The default is no.
status={ yes | no | 1 | 0 }	This controls the display of the window status bar. The default is yes.
menubar={ yes | no | 1 | 0}	This controls the display of the menu bar. The default is yes.
scrollbars={ yes | no | 1 | 0}	This feature controls the display of the horizontal and vertical scroll bars. The default is yes.
resizable={ yes | no | 1 | 0}	Identifies that resize handles should be displayed on the window.
width=*number*	Identifies the width the window should be drawn, in pixels. The minimum value should be 100.
height=*number*	Identifies the height to which the window should be drawn, in pixels. The minimum value should be 100.
top=*number*	Identifies the top position of the new window, in pixels, relative to the upper-left corner of the screen.
left=*number*	Identifies the left position, in pixels, relative to the upper-left corner of the screen.

bReplace

This is an optional Boolean value that forces the user agent to overwrite the current document in the history list with the one being opened.

NewWindow

This is the new window object that has been created.

sMimeType

This is a required text string that identifies the Mime type to be used for opening the document.

sReplace

This is an optional string with the value of "replace" that forces the user agent to overwrite the current document in the history list with the one being opened.

Objects

document   window

CROSS-REFERENCE
See **onbeforeunload**.

opener

Property

DHTML

This property is used either to set, or to retrieve, the name of the window that opened the current window.

The syntax for this command is

```
object.opener [=sWindow]
```

Parameters
sWindow

This is the string containing the window name being referenced.

Objects

window

CROSS-REFERENCE
See **open** and **window**.

Open Standards

Concept

There is a drive across the Internet for open standards — that is, standards that are open and available for anyone, anywhere, no matter the hardware type, operating system, or software vendor. These universal standards make it easy for software vendors and developers to create software that users around the globe can use without worrying about compatibility issues. One such common issue is whether they can view a document or access a service on both of the communicating computers. Another important question is whether the hardware configurations are even remotely similar for both machines. Open standards are generally decided upon by committees of software vendors, hardware developers, and university technology gurus. Each committee generally focuses on a specific area—such as file transfer protocols, document development, information sharing methods, compression methods—or practically any other way of sharing, formatting, or dispersing information.

CROSS-REFERENCE
See **standards**, **Document Object Model**, **Cascading Style Sheets**, **HTML**, **XML**, **Channel Definition Format**, and **Open Software Description**.

Operators

Concept

Operators are an integral part of any mathematical equation, which is essentially what the assignment of variables is within a script or program. The operator defines how the two separate parts of an equation should interact. Operators can be addition identifiers (+), subtraction signs (-), division and multiplication signs (/, $\star$), parenthesis, brackets, exclamation points, or equal signs to name a few. Operators can be **and, or, nor,** or **xor** symbols also. Operators are used with MathML to assist a compatible user agent in defining the text being displayed, or in a script to merge fields, or set a variable equal to another option.

CROSS-REFERENCE
See **MathML**, **ECMAscript**, **JavaScript**, **VBScript**, and **Java**.

<OPTGROUP>

Element

HTML

Start Tag: Required
End Tag: Required

This element is used to create a group of option controls, complete with label, to provide a visual grouping. Such a group makes your series of options easier to grasp and remember than they would be if displayed in a long list. OPTGROUPs must be specified from within a SELECT statement, and cannot be nested.

Attributes
class

```
class="cdata-list"
```

This attribute is used to assign a class name to an element. User agents employ classes to group specific types of information for later use.

dir

```
dir = LTR | RTL
```

This attribute defines the direction of the text flow in a document so a user agent can display it correctly.

disabled

```
disabled
```

This is a Boolean attribute; when set, it disables the option or option group and disallows any user input.

id

```
id="name"
```

This attribute is used to assign a name to an element.

label

```
label=text
```

This attribute identifies the label to be used with the option group.

lang

```
lang="language code"
```

This attribute specifies the language in which an element and its values should be rendered.

onblur

```
onblur=script
```

This attribute activates when an element loses the focus, whether from the action of a pointing device or by tabbing navigation.

onchange

```
onchange=script
```

This attribute is in effect when an element receives focus, whether from the action of a pointing device or by tabbing navigation.

onclick

> `onclick=`*`script`*

This attribute takes effect when a user clicks the button on a pointing device with the pointer over an element.

ondblclick

> `ondblclick=`*`script`*

This attribute takes effect when the button on a pointing device is double-clicked with the pointer over an element.

onfocus

> `onfocus=`*`script`*

This attribute is in effect when an element receives focus, whether from the action of a pointing device or by tabbing navigation.

onkeydown

> `onkeydown=`*`script`*

This attribute takes effect when a key is pressed while the pointer is over an element.

onkeypress

> `onkeypress=`*`script`*

This attribute takes effect when a key is pressed and released with the pointer over an element.

onkeyup

> `onkeyup=`*`script`*

This attribute takes effect when a key is released with the pointer over an element.

onmousedown

> `onmousedown=`*`script`*

This attribute takes effect when the button on a pointing device is pressed with the pointer over an element.

onmousemove

> `onmousemove=`*`script`*

This attribute is activated when the mouse pointer is moved while the pointer is over an element.

onmouseout

```
onmouseout=script
```

This attribute is activated when the mouse pointer is moved away from an element.

onmouseover

```
onmouseover=script
```

This attribute is activated the mouse pointer is movedwhen the mouse pointer is moved over an element.

onmouseup

```
onmouseup=script
```

This attribute takes effect when the button on a pointing device is released with the pointer over an element.

style

```
style=style descriptors
```

This attribute is used to apply specific style-sheet information to one particular element.

title

```
title=text
```

This attribute serves to provide annotation information to the element.

Example

The following sample code uses the OPTGROUP element to group a series of OPTIONS within a SELECT statement.

ON THE CD-ROM

Look for **optgroup.htm** on the accompanying CD-ROM.

```
<FORM action="" method="POST">
<SELECT name="toys">
  <OPTGROUP label="Favorite Plastic Toys">
    <OPTION selected value="lego">Legos</OPTION>
    <OPTION value="duplo">Duplos</OPTION>
    <OPTION value="barbies">Barbies</OPTION>
    <OPTION value="trains">Toy Trains</OPTION>
    <OPTION value="tonka">Tonka Trucks</OPTION>
    <OPTION value="hotwheels">Hot Wheels</OPTION>
  </OPTGROUP>
```

```
<OPTGROUP label="Favorite Stuffed Toys">
  <OPTION selected value="teddy">Teddy Bears</OPTION>
  <OPTION value="beanie">Beanie Babies</OPTION>
  <OPTION value="cabbage">Cabbage Patch Dolls</OPTION>
  <OPTION value="puppet">Puppets</OPTION>
  <OPTION value="puppy">Stuffed Puppies</OPTION>
  <OPTION value="disney">Disney Characters</OPTION>
  <OPTION value="beanbags">Bean Bag Dolls</OPTION>
  <OPTION value="birds">Squeaky Birds</OPTION>
  <OPTION value="mice">Cuddly Mice</OPTION>
</OPTGROUP>
</SELECT>
<INPUT type=submit name=Submit>
</FORM>
```

NOTE

This element is not currently supported by Internet Explorer 4, the developer's preview of Internet Explorer 5, or Netscape Navigator 4.5. If the OPTGROUP element is used within your code, no errors will be created when you employ these user agents.

CROSS-REFERENCE
See **<SELECT>** and **<OPTION>**.

<OPTION>

Element

HTML

Start Tag: Required
End Tag: Optional

This element is used to describe a single option of a SELECT group. The SELECT object controls how many OPTIONs may be selected from any one group.

Attributes
class

```
class="cdata-list"
```

This attribute is used to assign a class name to an element. User agents employ classes to group specific types of information for later use.

dir

```
dir = LTR | RTL
```

This attribute defines the direction of the text flow in a document so a user agent can display it correctly.

disabled

```
disabled
```

This is a Boolean attribute; when set, it will disable the option or option group, disallowing any user input.

id

```
id="name"
```

This attribute is used to assign a name to an element.

label

```
label=text
```

This attribute identifies the label to be used with the option group.

lang

```
lang="language code"
```

This attribute specifies the language in which an element and its values should be rendered.

name

```
name=cdata
```

This attribute is used to give the MAP a name that will be used as an identifier when automating your map data, or outlining your map areas.

onblur

```
onblur=script
```

This attribute activates when an element loses the focus, whether from the action of a pointing device or by tabbing navigation.

onclick

```
onclick=script
```

This attribute takes effect when a user clicks the button on a pointing device with the pointer over an element.

ondblclick

`ondblclick=script`

This attribute takes effect when the button on a pointing device is double-clicked with the pointer over an element.

onfocus

`onfocus=script`

This attribute is in effect when an element receives focus, whether from the action of a pointing device or by tabbing navigation.

onkeydown

`onkeydown=script`

This attribute takes effect when a key is pressed while the pointer is over an element.

onkeypress

`onkeypress=script`

This attribute takes effect when a key is pressed and released with the pointer over an element.

onkeyup

`onkeyup=script`

This attribute takes effect when a key is released with the pointer over an element.

onmousedown

`onmousedown=script`

This attribute takes effect when the button on a pointing device is pressed with the pointer over an element.

onmousemove

`onmousemove=script`

This attribute is activated when the mouse pointer is moved while the pointer is over an element.

onmouseout

`onmouseout=script`

This attribute is activated when the mouse pointer is moved away from an element.

onmouseover

`onmouseover=script`

This attribute is activated when the mouse pointer is moved over an element.

onmouseup

`onmouseup=script`

This attribute takes effect when the button on a pointing device is released with the pointer over an element.

selected

`selected`

When this option is available it designates the current selection as having been selected.

size

`size = cdata`

This attribute is used to specify the initial width of the control for the user agent. The width is given in pixels for all control `types` except text or password, for which the width is considered to be the number of characters to display.

style

`style=style descriptors`

This attribute is used to apply specific style-sheet information to one particular element.

tabindex

`tabindex=number`

This attribute provides the position of the current element within the overall tabbing order of the document.

title

`title=text`

This attribute serves to provide annotation information to the element.

value

`value = cdata`

This attribute is used to identify the initial value of the form control. This is optional for all control `types` except radio.

n
o
p

Example

This example creates a small form that includes a select box, which enables you to select multiple options from a list.

ON THE CD-ROM

Look for **option.htm** on the accompanying CD-ROM.

```
<FORM action="" method="POST">
<SELECT name="Software" multiple size="4">
    <OPTION selected value="W95">Windows 95</OPTION>
    <OPTION value="W31">Windows 3.1</OPTION>
    <OPTION value="WNT">Windows NT</OPTION>
    <OPTION value="WFWG">Windows for Work Groups</OPTION>
    <OPTION value="UNIX">UNIX</OPTION>
    <OPTION value="LINX">LINUX</OPTION>
    <OPTION value="OS2">OS/2 WARP</OPTION>
    <OPTION value="APPL">Apple</OPTION>
    <OPTION value="MAC">MacIntosh</OPTION>
    <OPTION value="SUN">Sun Unix</OPTION>
    <OPTION value="SOL">Solaris</OPTION>
</SELECT>
<INPUT type=submit name=Submit>
</FORM>
```

CROSS-REFERENCE

See **<INPUT>**, **<SELECT>**, and **<OPTGROUP>**.

options

Collection

DHTML

This object collection creates a list of all the OPTIONS found within the current SELECT object.

This collection can be used in the following ways:

```
[ collOptions = ] document.options
[ oObject = ] document.options(vIndex [, iSubIndex] )
```

Parameters
collOptions

This variable refers to the array of elements contained by the object.

oObject

> This variable refers to an individual item in the array.

vIndex

> This parameter is required, and contains the number or string identifying the element or collection to retrieve. When a number is specified, the method returns the element in the zero-based collection at the identified position. When a string identifier is used, and there are multiple elements with the same name or id attributes matching the string, this method returns a collection of those matched elements.

iSubIndex

> This optional parameter is used to identify the position of the element being retrieved, when vIndex is a string. ISubIndex becomes the index of the specific item in the collection of matching elements identified by the vIndex string contents.

Elements

> SELECT

CROSS-REFERENCE
See <OPTION>.

Ordinal Number

Concept

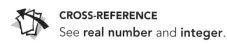

CROSS-REFERENCE
See **real number** and **integer**.

orphans

Attribute

CSS

> This attribute is used to designate the minimum number of lines of a paragraph which are allowed to float at the bottom of a page.

This attribute is used for showing

```
orphans:    integer  |  inherit
```

Values
integer

This is a real number that specifies how many lines are allowed on a page alone.

Example

The following example uses the orphan attribute to force all P elements to force at least three lines of text to appear at the bottom of each printed page of a Web site.

```
<STYLE type="text/css">
<!-
P { orphans: 3 }
->
</STYLE>
```

Elements

BLOCKQUOTE	BODY	BUTTON	CAPTION
CENTER	DD	DIR	DIV
DL	DT	EMBED	FIELDSET
FORM	H1 – H6	HR	IFRAME
IMG	INPUT	ISINDEX	LI
LISTING	MARQUEE	MENU	OBJECT
OL	P	PLAINTEXT	PRE
SPAN	TABLE	TD	TEXTAREA
TH	TR	UL	XMP

CROSS-REFERENCE
See **widow** and **page break**.

<OS>

Element

OSD

This element is a child of IMPLEMENTATION and is used to identify the type of operating system the installation is being performed.

Attributes
Value

This is the name of the type of operating system used for the software being installed.

Example

The following example shows how the OS element is used to define the type of operating system for the software that is being installed.

```
<SOFTPKG>
<IMPLEMENTATION>
   <IMPLTYPE value="java" />
   <CODEBASE href="http://www.mysoftware.com/soft.cab" />
   <OS value="WinNT" />
   <MEMSIZE value="1024Kb" />
</IMPLEMENTATION>
</SOFTPKG>
```

CROSS-REFERENCE
See **<SOFTPKG>**, **<OSVERSION>**, and **<IMPLEMENTATION>**.

OSD — Open Software Description

Concept

In an attempt to make centralized distribution of software and product upgrades easier over the Internet, and other Intranets, Microsoft began the development of an Open Software Description. This format for sharing software is based on the Extensible Markup Language (XML), which allows you to define unique tags used to describe OSD software components, versions, structure, and relationships. OSD can be used in the following ways to assist in the constant distribution of software.

Inform Users Automatically of Upgraded Products

Using OSD, a network administrator can immediately notify all users of a particular type of software, of upgrades to that software. This notification can be mailed directly to them with the automatic update of a channel, or when the user launches the application from a shortcut. The updated version can be held in the user agent's cache and either be installed offline or online whenever the user decides to upgrade.

Extend the Capability to Download Components for Internet Systems

OSD provides software information in a way that allows users to distribute and install programs, which was not previously possible. INF files were previously used to identify installation and dependency information for ActiveX Controls, but these files did not allow for complex dependencies. OSD does. In addition to the software dependencies, you are now able to describe processor types, operating systems, and language for software that is being distributed across a network of varying platforms and machine configurations.

Extend the Channel Definition Format

Using OSD in conjunction with CDF you can expand the vocabulary used to describe a channel, and increase your ability to automatically deliver it across a network. Because of the incorporation of OSD commands within the Channel structure, you can now automatically update a client's software using the same schedule and system that you would update other information such as stock quotes, and business news reports.

 CROSS-REFERENCE
See **Cascading Style Sheets**, **Channel Definition Format**, **XML**, and **Document Object Model**.

<OSVERSION>

Element

OSD

This element is a child of IMPLEMENTATION and is used to identify the type of installation being performed.

Attributes
Value

This is the name of the version of operating system used for installing the software.

Example

The following example shows how the OSVERSION element to define they specific operating system version used for the software that is being installed.

```
<SOFTPKG>
<IMPLEMENTATION>
    <IMPLTYPE value="java" />
    <CODEBASE href="http://www.mysoftware.com/soft.cab" />
```

```
        <OS value="WinNT" />
        <OSVERSION value="4.23" />
        <MEMSIZE value="1024Kb" />
    </IMPLEMENTATION>
    </SOFTPKG>
```

CROSS-REFERENCE
See **<SOFTPKG>**, **<OS>**, and **<IMPLEMENTATION>**.

outerHTML

Property

DHTML

This object property is used to retrieve the contents of the HTML document, including HTML tags, including the current object's start and end tag.

The syntax for this command is

```
object.outerHTML [=string]
```

Parameters
string

This string contains the contents of the HTML document with the identified object tags.

Example

The following sample code automatically changes the text of the P element to the identified strings, based on the action of the viewer's mouse.

ON THE CD-ROM
Look for **outerhtml.htm** on the accompanying CD-ROM.

```
<HTML>
<HEAD>
<META NAME="GENERATOR" Content="NetObjects ScriptBuilder 2.0">
<TITLE>Document Title</TITLE>
</HEAD>
<BODY>
<P onmouseover="this.outerHTML='<BIG>The clock struck 1. The
mouse ran down.</BIG>'">
<I>Hickory Dickory Dock.</I></P>
<P onmouseout="this.outerHTML='<BR><FONT color=red><I>Hickory
Dickory Dock.</I>'">
```

n
o
p

```
<I>The Mouse Ran up the Clock.</I></FONT></P>

</BODY>
</HTML>
```

Elements

A	ACRONYM	ADDRESS	B
BIG	BLOCKQUOTE	BODY	BUTTON
CAPTION	CENTER	CITE	CODE
DD	DEL	DFN	DIR
DIV	DL	DT	EM
FIELDSET	FONT	FORM	H1–H6
I	IFRAME	INS	KBD
LABEL	LEGEND	LI	LISTING
MARQUEE	MENU	NEXTID	OL
P	PRE	Q	S
SAMP	SMALL	SPAN	STRIKE
STRONG	SUB	SUP	TT
U	UL	VAR	

CROSS-REFERENCE

See **innerText**, **insertAdjacentHTML**, **outerText**, **innerHTML**, **TEXTAREA**, and **TextRange**.

outerText

Property

DHTML

This object property is used either to set or retrieve the text contents of the HTML object.

The syntax for this command is

```
object.outerText [=string]
```

Parameters
string

This string contains the text found between the start and end tags, or the text to be placed there.

Example

The following sample code automatically changes the text of the P element to the identified strings, based on the action of the user's mouse.

ON THE CD-ROM

Look for **outertext.htm** on the accompanying CD-ROM.

```
<HTML>
<HEAD>
<META NAME="GENERATOR" Content="NetObjects ScriptBuilder 2.0">
<TITLE>Document Title</TITLE>
</HEAD>
<BODY>
<P ID=oPara>Make a Wish!!!</P>
:
<BUTTON onclick="oPara.outerText='Ahh.. you told me what it
was! Wont happen now.'">Tell me your wish.</BUTTON>
<BUTTON onclick="oPara.outerText='Cool.. the first star came
out tonight.'">Wish on a Star.</BUTTON>

</BODY>
</HTML>
```

Elements

<!— —>	A	ACRONYM	ADDRESS
B	BIG	BLOCKQUOTE	BODY
BR	BUTTON	CAPTION	CENTER
CITE	CODE	DD	DEL
DFN	DIR	DIV	DL
DT	EM	FIELDSET	FONT
FORM	H1–H6	I	IFRAME
INS	KBD	LABEL	LEGEND
LI	LISTING	MAP	MARQUEE
MENU	NEXTID	OL	P
PLAINTEXT	PRE	Q	S
SAMP	SMALL	SPAN	STRIKE
STRONG	SUB	SUP	TD
TEXTAREA	TH	TITLE	TR
TT	U	UL	VAR
XMP			

n
o
p

CROSS-REFERENCE
See **innerHTML**, **insertAdjacentHTML**, **innerText**, **outerHTML**, and **<TEXTAREA>**.

outline

Attribute

CSS

This attribute is used to control the appearance of the outline of each block-level element that can have a border applied to it. Actually a shorthand attribute, `outline` can be used to set the outline width, color, and style for all four edges of a containing box. Unlike the shorthand attributes for margins and padding, the `outline` attribute can only set options for the box as a whole, and not for its individual edges.

The syntax of border is

```
outline=outline-width | outline-style | outline-color |
inherit
```

Values

outline-width

The value in this location is one of the valid properties for the `outline-width` attribute, including medium, thin, thick, or a length.

outline-style

The value in this location is one of the valid properties for the `outline-style` attribute, including none, dotted, dashed, outset, inset, groove, ridge, solid, and double.

outline-color

The value in this location is one of the valid properties for the `outline-color` attribute, which includes either a valid HTML color name, or the three or six hex-digit RGB representation of a color. If this attribute is not supplied the text color will be used automatically.

Example

The following segment of code shows how the outline property can be used in a style sheet to set the appearance of the edges of each type of element

```
<STYLE type="text/css">
<!-
```

```
H1       {  outline: thin dashed red }
BUTTON   {  outline: inset }
->
</STYLE>
```

NOTE

This Cascading Style Sheets attribute is not currently supported by Internet Explorer 4, the developer's preview of Internet Explorer 5, or Netscape Navigator 4.5. If the `outline` attribute is used within your code, no errors will be created when you employ these user agents, but no visual effect will appear.

Elements

A	ABBR	ACRONYM	ADDRESS
APPLET	AREA	B	BASE
BASEFONT	BDO	BIG	BLINK
BLOCKQUOTE	BODY	BR	BUTTON
CAPTION	CENTER	CITE	CODE
COL	COLGROUP	DD	DEL
DFN	DIR	DIV	DL
DT	EM	FIELDSET	FONT
FORM	FRAME	FRAMESET	H1–H6
HEAD	HR	HTML	I
IFRAME	IMG	INPUT	INS
ISINDEX	KBD	LABEL	LEGEND
LI	LINK	MAP	MARQUEE
MENU	META	NOFRAMES	NOLAYER
NOSCRIPT	OBJECT	OL	OPTGROUP
OPTION	P	PARAM	PRE
Q	S	SAMP	SCRIPT
SELECT	SMALL	SPAN	STRIKE
STRONG	STYLE	SUB	SUB
TABLE	TBODY	TD	TEXTAREA
TFOOT	TH	THEAD	TITLE
TR	TT	U	UL
VAR			

CROSS-REFERENCE

See **border**, **margin**, **outline-color**, **outline-style**, and **outline-width**.

outline-color

Attribute

CSS

This attribute is used to set the color of the left, right, top, and bottom outlines of an elements containment box.

The syntax of this attribute is

```
outline-color: colorname | #RGB | invert
```

Values

colorname

This is a string value representing one of the identified color names.

invert

This value forces the outline to invert the color of the pixels on the screen to create a visible border.

#RGB

This is the three or six digit hexadecimal number that is used to represent the Red-Green-Blue value of the selected color.

Example

The following code shows how you can change the color of a block element's border in a style sheet.

ON THE CD-ROM

Look for **outline.htm** on the accompanying CD-ROM.

```
<html>
<head>
<title>Outline Properties</title>
<style type="text/css">
<!—
h1 {  outline-color: #FFCCCC black black;
 outline -style: inset;
      outline-width: thick}
h2 {  border outline-style: groove}
h4 {  outline-color: #FF33CC #FFCCFF}
h5 {  outline: thick #FFFF00 }
—>
</style>
</head>
```

```
<body bgcolor="#FFFFFF">
  <h1>Candy Canes for the Masses </h1>
  <h2>Christmas Cheer Comes to Drysville</h2>
  <h3>Hallowed ground gets Stepped On</h3>
  <h4>He Wished a Horse and Rode</h4>
  <h5>Wyatt OK'd Tombstone's Renovation Projects</h5>
</body>
</html>
```

NOTE

This Cascading Style Sheets attribute is not currently supported by Internet Explorer 4, the developer's preview of Internet Explorer 5, or Netscape Navigator 4.5. If used within your code, no errors will be created when you employ these user agents, but no visual effect will appear.

Elements

A	ABBR	ACRONYM	ADDRESS
APPLET	AREA	B	BASE
BASEFONT	BDO	BIG	BLINK
BLOCKQUOTE	BODY	BR	BUTTON
CAPTION	CENTER	CITE	CODE
COL	COLGROUP	DD	DEL
DFN	DIR	DIV	DL
DT	EM	FIELDSET	FONT
FORM	FRAME	FRAMESET	H1–H6
HEAD	HR	HTML	I
IFRAME	IMG	INPUT	INS
ISINDEX	KBD	LABEL	LEGEND
LI	LINK	MAP	MARQUEE
MENU	META	NOFRAMES	NOLAYER
NOSCRIPT	OBJECT	OL	OPTGROUP
OPTION	P	PARAM	PRE
Q	S	SAMP	SCRIPT
SELECT	SMALL	SPAN	STRIKE
STRONG	STYLE	SUB	SUB
TABLE	TBODY	TD	TEXTAREA
TFOOT	TH	THEAD	TITLE
TR	TT	U	UL
VAR			

n
o
p

CROSS-REFERENCE
See **border**, **margin**, **outline**, **outline-style**, and **outline-width**.

outline-style

Attribute

CSS

This attribute is used to control the style of the outline being displayed for the entire box.

The syntax for this attribute is

```
outline-style: none | hidden | dotted | dashed | solid |
double | grooved | ridge | inset | outset | inherit
```

Values

dashed

The outline is composed of a series of dashes.

dotted

The outline is composed of a series of dots.

double

The outline is composed of two solid lines, with the clear space between the lines being equal to the value of the `outline-width` attribute.

grooved

The outline is displayed to to look like it is drawn into the page.

hidden

There is no outline shown for this element, but the width of the outline is reserved.

inset

The outline is displayed to make the entire box look pressed into the document.

none

There is no outline shown for this box. This value forces the `outline-width` value to be zero.

outset

The outline is displayed to make the entire box look extended out of the document.

ridge

The outline is displayed to make it seem to rise three-dimensionally out of the page.

solid

The outline is composed of a single line.

Example

The following example code uses a style sheet to set the outline styles for a variety of elements in the current document.

```
<STYLE type="text/css">
<!—
   blockquote  { outline-style: solid; }
    p  { outline-style: outset; }
    table  { outline-style: inset; }
    h1        { outline-style: dashed;  }
—>
</STYLE>
```

NOTE

This Cascading Style Sheets attribute is not currently supported by Internet Explorer 4, the developer's preview of Internet Explorer 5, or Netscape Navigator 4.5. If used within your code, no errors will be created when you employ these user agents, but no visual effect will appear.

Elements

A	ABBR	ACRONYM	ADDRESS
APPLET	AREA	B	BASE
BASEFONT	BDO	BIG	BLINK
BLOCKQUOTE	BODY	BR	BUTTON
CAPTION	CENTER	CITE	CODE
COL	COLGROUP	DD	DEL
DFN	DIR	DIV	DL
DT	EM	FIELDSET	FONT
FORM	FRAME	FRAMESET	H1–H6
HEAD	HR	HTML	I
IFRAME	IMG	INPUT	INS

n

o

p

ISINDEX	KBD	LABEL	LEGEND
LI	LINK	MAP	MARQUEE
MENU	META	NOFRAMES	NOLAYER
NOSCRIPT	OBJECT	OL	OPTGROUP
OPTION	P	PARAM	PRE
Q	S	SAMP	SCRIPT
SELECT	SMALL	SPAN	STRIKE
STRONG	STYLE	SUB	SUB
TABLE	TBODY	TD	TEXTAREA
TFOOT	TH	THEAD	TITLE
TR	TT	U	UL
VAR			

CROSS-REFERENCE

See **border**, **margin**, **outline**, **outline-color**, and **outline-width**.

outline-width

Attribute

CSS

This attribute is used to set the width of the outline of a box.
The syntax of this attribute is

```
outline-width: medium | thin | thick | length
```

Values

medium

This displays a medium thickness line, it is roughly 1 pt thick on most user agent displays, and is the default value.

thin

This value displays a width less than medium, generally _ to _ pt. thick on most user agents.

thick

This value displays a width greater than medium, generally 1.5 to 2 pts thick, although it is set by the user agent.

length

This is a floating-point number with either an absolute or relative unit designator following it.

Example

The following example shows a variety of widths that can be used for outlines on specified property boxes.

```
H1 { outline-width:  1pt thin 3pt }
```

NOTE

This Cascading Style Sheets attribute is not currently supported by Internet Explorer 4, the developer's preview of Internet Explorer 5, or Netscape Navigator 4.5. If used within your code, no errors will be created when you employ these user agents, but no visual effect will appear.

Elements

A	ABBR	ACRONYM	ADDRESS
APPLET	AREA	B	BASE
BASEFONT	BDO	BIG	BLINK
BLOCKQUOTE	BODY	BR	BUTTON
CAPTION	CENTER	CITE	CODE
COL	COLGROUP	DD	DEL
DFN	DIR	DIV	DL
DT	EM	FIELDSET	FONT
FORM	FRAME	FRAMESET	H1–H6
HEAD	HR	HTML	I
IFRAME	IMG	INPUT	INS
ISINDEX	KBD	LABEL	LEGEND
LI	LINK	MAP	MARQUEE
MENU	META	NOFRAMES	NOLAYER
NOSCRIPT	OBJECT	OL	OPTGROUP
OPTION	P	PARAM	PRE
Q	S	SAMP	SCRIPT
SELECT	SMALL	SPAN	STRIKE
STRONG	STYLE	SUB	SUB
TABLE	TBODY	TD	TEXTAREA
TFOOT	TH	THEAD	TITLE
TR	TT	U	UL
VAR			

CROSS-REFERENCE
See **border**, **margin**, **outline-color**, **outline-style**, and **outline**.

overflow

Attribute

CSS

This Cascading Style Sheets attribute is used to control how information which more than fills up a designated layer, or containing box should be dealt with.

The syntax for this command is

```
overflow: visible | scroll | hidden | auto
```

JAVASCRIPT

```
object.style.overflow [= string]
```

This property allows you to automatically adjust how overflow of a containment box is dealt with.

Values

auto

This displays the information clipped, and scroll bars are added where necessary.

hidden

The extra content is not shown.

scroll

The extra content is not visible, but scroll bars are added whether they are necessary or not.

visible

The content is not clipped, and is made visible to the reader.

Example

The following example code uses the overflow attribute with a DIV block element to show how information can be displayed with a variety of overflow settings.

ON THE CD-ROM
Look for **overflow.htm** on the accompanying CD-ROM.

```
<HTML>
<HEAD>
  <TITLE> Working with Overflow Text</TITLE>
</HEAD>
<BODY>
<DIV id=quote style="width: 200px; height: 200px; overflow:
auto;">
<P>Cat's Back Consulting was developed to provide rural
businesses with access to professional advertising on the
Internet. Located in the far north eastern  corner of Oregon,
high in the snowcapped Wallowa Mountains, Cat's Back
Consulting (CBC) knows and understands the problems and
pleasures associated  with rural living.</P>
    <P>
It is hard turning majestic scenery, abundant wildlife,
sparkling water, and friendly people into food on your table.
As we say around here &quot;You can't eat the mountains&quot;,
but you can expand your business potential by hiring Cat's
Back Consulting to host your company's web site. From your
home on the Internet you can reach a potential customer market
of over 60 million people in a medium that is growing roughly
10% each month.</P>
</DIV>
<P>
<HR>
<DIV id=quote1 style="width: 200px; height: 200px; overflow:
visible;">
<P>Cat's Back Consulting was developed to provide rural
businesses with access to professional advertising on the
Internet. Located in the far north eastern  corner of Oregon,
high in the snowcapped Wallowa Mountains, Cat's Back
Consulting (CBC) knows and understands the problems and
pleasures associated  with rural living.</P>
    <P>
It is hard turning majestic scenery, abundant wildlife,
sparkling water, and friendly people into food on your table.
As we say around here &quot;You can't eat the mountains&quot;,
but you can expand your business potential by hiring Cat's
Back Consulting to host your company's web site. From your
home on the Internet you can reach a potential customer market
of over 60 million people in a medium that is growing roughly
10% each month.</P>
</DIV>
<P>
```

n
o
p

```
<HR>
<DIV id=quote2 style="width: 200px; height: 200px; overflow:
hidden;">
<P>Cat's Back Consulting was developed to provide rural
businesses with access to professional advertising on the
Internet. Located in the far north eastern  corner of Oregon,
high in the snowcapped Wallowa Mountains, Cat's Back
Consulting (CBC) knows and understands the problems and
pleasures associated  with rural living.</P>
   <P>
It is hard turning majestic scenery, abundant wildlife,
sparkling water, and friendly people into food on your table.
As we say around here &quot;You can't eat the mountains&quot;,
but you can expand your business potential by hiring Cat's
Back Consulting to host your company's web site. From your
home on the Internet you can reach a potential customer market
of over 60 million people in a medium that is growing roughly
10% each month.</P>
</DIV>
</BODY>
</HTML>
```

 NOTE

Netscape does not currently support this Cascading Style Sheets attribute.

Elements

A	ADDRESS	APPLET	B
BIG	BLOCKQUOTE	CENTER	CITE
CODE	DD	DFN	DIR
DIV	DL	DT	EM
EMBED	FIELDSET	FORM	H1–H6
I	IFRAME	IMB	KBD
LABEL	LEGEND	LI	LISTING
MENU	OL	P	PRE
S	SAMP	SELECT	SMALL
SPAN	STRIKE	STRONG	SUB
SUP	TABLE	TEXTAREA	TT
U	UL	VAR	XMP

 CROSS-REFERENCE

See **<LAYER>**, **visible**, **top**, **left**, **width**, **height**, and **<SPAN>**.

owningElement

Property

DHTML

This property is used within scripts to retrieve the name of the next HTML element that occurs within the hierarchy.

The syntax for this command is

```
Element=stylesheet.owningElement
```

Parameters

Element

This is the next element in the hierarchy of the document.

Objects

styleSheet

CROSS-REFERENCE

See **styleSheets**, **element**, and **Document Tree**.

n

o

p

<P>

Element

HTML

Start Tag: Required
End Tag: Optional

This element is used to identify a paragraph within an HTML document. Document authors should not use empty P elements, and all user agents should ignore them. P elements cannot contain block-level elements, including other P elements.

Attributes
align

```
align=left | right | center | inherit
```

This attribute is used to control the visual alignment of the applet within its bounding box unless the value of the attribute is bottom.

class

```
class="cdata-list"
```

This attribute is used to assign a class name to an element. User agents employ classes to group specific types of information for later use.

id

```
id="name"
```

This attribute is used to assign a name to an element.

lang

```
lang="language code"
```

This attribute specifies the language that should be used to render an element and its values.

onclick

`onclick=script`

This attribute takes effect when a user clicks the button on a pointing device with the pointer over an element.

ondblclick

`ondblclick=script`

This attribute takes effect when a user double-clicks the button on a pointing device with the pointer over an element.

onkeydown

`onkeydown=script`

This attribute takes effect when a user presses a key and the pointer is over an element.

onkeypress

`onkeypress=script`

This attribute takes effect when a key is pressed and released while the pointer is over an element.

onkeyup

`onkeyup=script`

This attribute takes effect when a user releases a key with the pointer over an element.

onmousedown

`onmousedown=script`

This attribute takes effect when a user presses the button on a pointing device while the pointer is over an element.

onmousemove

`onmousemove=script`

This attribute is activated when the mouse pointer is moved while it is over an element.

onmouseout

`onmouseout=script`

This attribute is activated when the mouse pointer is moved away from an element.

onmouseover

```
onmouseover=script
```

This attribute is activated when the mouse pointer is moved over an element.

onmouseup

```
onmouseup=script
```

This attribute takes effect when the button on a pointing device is released while the pointer is over an element.

style

```
style=style descriptors
```

This attribute applies specific style-sheet information to one particular element.

title

```
title=text
```

This attribute provides annotation information to the element.

Example

The following example code uses the P element to format a series of short paragraphs and provide them with visual breaks between the segments of text.

ON THE CD-ROM
Look for **p.htm** on the accompanying CD-ROM.

```
<html>
<head>
<title>P in Medieval Paradise</title>
<meta http-equiv="Generator" content="Macromedia Dreamweaver">
</head>

<body bgcolor="#FFFFFF">
<h1>Uppity Women </h1>
<p>Did you know that women had a huge effect on the
development of nations, not only through the sons they have
born and raised, but through the years women have been killed
over their power, and often for simply being a woman. Women
have controlled the lives of many kings, princes, and
dictators through their influence, love, and sometimes
merciless actions.</p>
```

```
<p>In evidence of this I point you to the life story of
Eleanor of Aquitaine. She not only ran off to the crusades in
armor, with a passel of her girlfriends in revealing steel.
She also ruled France as queen for fifteen years, and England
for an additional 50. She consciously married into money and
power, and ruled her kingdoms with a iron but loving hand.</p>
<p>Once Henry II was gone, her second husband, she then
consciously supported her three sons, rescued Richard from a
Vienna prison, rescued John from a rebellion he incited, and
generally stuck around till she was 80 just to keep track of
things. </p>
</body>
</html>
```

CROSS-REFERENCE
See **\<BR\>** and **Block-Level Element**.

padding

Attribute

CSS

This Cascading Style Sheets attribute is used to control the padding on containment blocks of objects. It can be used with all the HTML elements. This attribute is used as a shorthand for setting the `padding-top`, `padding-bottom`, `padding-right`, and `padding-left` properties for your style sheet.

The syntax for this command is

```
padding: padding-width[1,4] | inherit
```

JAVASCRIPT
```
object.style.padding [ = padding-width ]
```

This object attribute sets the padding for the entire object and does not enable you to separate the widths of the padding for each edge.

Values
padding-width[1,4]

The padding-width is a length value representing either an absolute or a relative number and using a specific unit value. You can list up to four lengths for this value. If you assign a single value for `padding`, it is used for all the padding spaces of the object. If you assign two values, the first is used for the top and bottom sides of the object, and the second is used for the right and left object pads. In the case of three identified values, the first is the top, the second is the right and left padding, and the third is used for the bottom padding. If all four values are set, the first is the top padding, the second is the right side, the third is the bottom, and the fourth creates the left object padding.

inherit

If the value of padding is set to inherit, then it equals the value of the parent element. If padding is applied to a whole document through a given @page element, inherit becomes an invalid value.

Examples

The following groups of examples are equal statements.

This group uses three values to set dimensions for all four sides of the object.

```
IMG { padding:  1cm 2 cm 3 cm }
IMG { padding-top: 1cm
      padding-right: 2cm
      padding-left: 2cm
      padding-bottom: 3cm  }
```

This second group uses a single setting to control the padding of the entire document.

```
@page { padding: 2pc }
@page { padding-top: 2pc
      padding-right: 2pc
      padding-left: 2pc
      padding-bottom: 2pc }
```

This third group has two values that are used to set the top and bottom padding and the left and right padding separately for a particular block element.

```
blockquote { padding: 1ex 2ex }
blockquote { padding-top: 1ex
      padding-right: 2ex
      padding-left: 2ex
      padding-bottom: 1ex }
```

Elements

This attribute is available for all HTML elements.

CROSS-REFERENCE

See **length**, **padding-bottom**, **padding-left**, **padding-right**, and **padding-top**.

padding-bottom

Attribute

CSS

This attribute is used to set the bottom padding of the box generated by an HTML element.

The syntax of this attribute is

```
padding-bottom: padding-width | inherit
```

JAVASCRIPT

```
object.style.paddingBottom [ = padding-width ]
```

Using scripts, you can control the width of padding around an object while the document is being accessed.

Values

padding-width

The padding-width is a length value representing either an absolute or a relative number and using a specific unit value. You can list up to four lengths for this value.

inherit

If the value of padding is set to inherit, it uses the value of the parent element. If the padding is applied to a whole document through a given @page element, inherit becomes an invalid value.

Elements

This attribute can be applied to all HTML elements.

CROSS-REFERENCE

See **length**, **padding (CSS attribute)**, **padding-left**, **padding-right**, and **padding-top**.

padding-left

Attribute

CSS

This attribute is used to set the left padding dimension of the box generated by an HTML element.

The syntax of this attribute is

```
padding-left: padding-width | inherit
```

JAVASCRIPT
```
object.style.paddingLeft [ = padding-width ]
```

Values
padding-width

The *padding-width* is a length value representing either an absolute or a relative number and using a specific unit value. You can list up to four lengths for this value.

inherit

If the value of padding is set to inherit, it uses the value of the parent element. If padding is applied to a whole document through a given @page element, inherit becomes an invalid value.

Elements
This attribute can be applied to all HTML elements.

CROSS-REFERENCE
See **length, padding (CSS attribute), padding-bottom, padding-right**, and **padding-top**.

padding-right

Attribute

CSS

This attribute is used to set the right padding of the box generated by an HTML element.

The syntax of this attribute is

```
padding-right: padding-width | inherit
```

JAVASCRIPT
```
object.style.paddingRight [ = padding-width ]
```

Values
padding-width

The *padding-width* is a length value representing either an absolute or a relative number and using a specific unit value. You can list up to four lengths for this value.

inherit

If the value of padding is set to inherit, it uses the value of the parent element. If padding is applied to a whole document through a given @page element, inherit becomes an invalid value.

Elements

This attribute can be applied to all HTML elements.

CROSS-REFERENCE
See **length, padding (CSS attribute), padding-bottom, padding-left,** and **padding-top**.

padding-top

Attribute

CSS

This attribute is used to set the top padding of the box generated by an HTML element.

The syntax of this attribute is

```
padding-top: padding-width | inherit
```

JAVASCRIPT
```
object.style.paddingTop [ = padding-width ]
```

Values
padding-width

The padding-width is a length value representing either an absolute or a relative number and using a specific unit value. You can list up to four lengths for this value.

inherit

If the value of padding is set to inherit, it uses the value of the parent element. If padding is applied to a whole document through a given @page element, inherit becomes an invalid value.

Elements

This attribute can be applied to all HTML elements.

CROSS-REFERENCE
See **length**, **padding (CSS attribute)**, **padding-bottom**, **padding-left**, and **padding-right**.

padding-width

Descriptor

CSS

This value represents either a length or a percentage that is used to set aside the specific amount of padding to be used around a particular object.

The possible values for this descriptor are

```
padding-width=length | percentage
```

Values

length

This value is used to specify a fixed maximum computed height for the padding of the element.

percentage

This value is used for computing the height of the padding and is based upon the containing block of the element.

Example

In the following code examples, the maximum height is set to control the development of specific block elements in a document.

```
<STYLE type="text/css">
   BLOCKQUOTE  {padding: 3px }
   IMG  {padding: 10% }
   OBJECT {padding: 15pc }
</STYLE>
```

CROSS-REFERENCE
See **padding**, **margin**, **padding-left**, **padding-top**, **padding-bottom**, and **padding-right**.

page

Attribute

CSS

This attribute works with all elements, giving them more control over the size and dimensions of their page and the layout of an object on a page. If a block with inline content has a `page` attribute that is different from the preceding block of inline content, a page break is inserted between the blocks.

The syntax of this property is

```
page: identifier | inherit
```

Values
identifier

This is the name of the page, which enables you to access it through the @page element.

Example
In the following example, the two tables are rendered on landscape pages, possibly on the same page if space allows. Because of the layering of the elements in the document, the assignment of the narrow page to the DIV element is overridden and not used.

```
@page narrow {size: 9cm 18cm}
@page rotated {size: landscape}
DIV {page: narrow}
IMG {page: rotated}
```

Usage of the DIV element looks like this with this document:

```
<DIV>
<IMG>...
<IMG>...
</DIV>
```

CROSS-REFERENCE
See **@page**, **page-break** (**-after**, **-before**, **-inside**), and **Page Box**.

Page Box

Concept

CSS

CROSS-REFERENCE
See **@page**.

page-break-after

Attribute

CSS

This attribute is used to force or prohibit the insertion of a page break after the current object.

The syntax of this attribute is

```
page-break-after: auto | always | avoid | left | right |
inherit
```

JAVASCRIPT

```
object.style.pageBreakAfter [ = auto | always | avoid |
left | right]
```

Values

auto

This value neither forces nor prohibits a page break within the current box.

always

This forces a page break always to appear directly after this block.

avoid

This forces a page break placement to be avoided after this object.

left

This forces the insertion of a page break or two to force the next page to be a left-formatted page.

right

This forces the insertion of a page break or two to force the next page to be a right-formatted page.

Example

In the following example code, a style sheet is used to insert a page break after every table and then (after a series of long textual paragraphs) within a document.

```
<STYLE type-"text/css">
<!-
TABLE {page-break-after: always;
       page-break-before: avoid;}
->
</STYLE>
<P style="page-break-after: right">
....
</P>
```

Elements

BLOCKQUOTE	BODY	BUTTON	CAPTION
CENTER	COL	COLGROUP	DIV
FIELDSET	FORM	FRAME	FRAMESET
H1–H6	HEAD	HR	IFRAME
INPUT	LABEL	LAYER	LEGEND
LI	MAP	MARQUEE	OBJECT
OL	P	PRE	Q
SCRIPT	SELECT	SPAN	TABLE
TD	TEXTAREA	TFOOT	TH
THEAD	TR	UL	

CROSS-REFERENCE
See **page-break-before** and **page-break-inside**.

page-break-before

Attribute

CSS

This attribute is used to force or prohibit the insertion of a page break before the current object.

The syntax of this attribute is

```
page-break-before: auto | always | avoid | left | right |
inherit
```

 JAVASCRIPT

```
object.style.pageBreakBefore [ = auto | always | avoid |
left | right]
```

Values

auto

This value neither forces nor prohibits a page break within the current box.

always

This forces a page break always to appear directly before this block.

avoid

This forces a page break placement to be avoided before this object.

left

This forces the insertion of a page break or two to force the next page to be a left-formatted page.

right

This forces the insertion of a page break or two to force the next page to be a right-formatted page.

Example

In the following example code, a style sheet is used to insert a page break before every table and then before a series of long textual paragraphs within a document.

```
<STYLE type="text/css">
<!—
TABLE {page-break-after: avoid;
       page-break-before: always;}
—>
</STYLE>
<P style="page-break-before: left">
….
</P>
```

Elements

BLOCKQUOTE	BODY	BUTTON	CAPTION
CENTER	COL	COLGROUP	DIV
FIELDSET	FORM	FRAME	FRAMESET
H1–H6	HEAD	HR	IFRAME
INPUT	LABEL	LAYER	LEGEND
LI	MAP	MARQUEE	OBJECT
OL	P	PRE	Q
SCRIPT	SELECT	SPAN	TABLE
TD	TEXTAREA	TFOOT	TH
THEAD	TR	UL	

CROSS-REFERENCE
See **page-break-after** and **page-break-inside**.

page-break-inside

Attribute

CSS

This attribute is used to allow or prohibit the insertion of a page break inside the current object.

The syntax of this attribute is

```
page-break-inside: auto | avoid | inherit
```

Values

auto

This value neither forces nor prohibits a page break within the current box.

avoid

This forces a page break placement to be avoided within this object.

Example

In the following example code, a style sheet is used to prohibit a page break from appearing within any table.

```
<STYLE type="text/css">
<!-
TABLE {page-break-inside: avoid; }
->
</STYLE>
```

Elements

BLOCKQUOTE	BODY	BUTTON	CAPTION
CENTER	COL	COLGROUP	DIV
FIELDSET	FORM	FRAME	FRAMESET
H1–H6	HEAD	HR	IFRAME
INPUT	LABEL	LAYER	LEGEND
LI	MAP	MARQUEE	OBJECT
OL	P	PRE	Q
SCRIPT	SELECT	SPAN	TABLE
TD	TEXTAREA	TFOOT	TH
THEAD	TR	UL	

CROSS-REFERENCE
See **page-break-after** and **page-break-before**.

Page-Context

Concept

CSS

Each page identified within an HTML document has a variety of properties applied to it. Each of these properties is applied using the page or the @page attribute. These page properties include the page dimensions, orientation, margins, padding, and font, to name a few. The body of declarations following an @page keyword is considered to be the page context instructions.

 CROSS-REFERENCE
See **@page**, **block**, and **page**.

Paged

Media Group

CSS

Cascading Style Sheets, level 2, has defined the following media groups:

- Visual/Aural/Tactile
- Continuous/Paged
- Grid/Bitmap
- Interactive/Static

Each media group is used to describe specific types of media. Many media types are identified as part of these groups. The paged media group is used to identify specific types of media that have a set dimension. Paged media include books, newspapers, computer printouts, and calendars.

 CROSS-REFERENCE
See **media groups** and **media types**.

palette

Property

DHTML

This property is used within script code to retrieve the color palette used with embedded documents.

```
object.palette [ = sPalette ]
```

Parameters

sPalette

This string represents the palette used to create the document.

Elements

EMBED

CROSS-REFERENCE
See **color**, **<EMBED>**, **<LINK>**, and **import**.

panose-1

Descriptor

CSS

This descriptor is used to identify the Panose-1 number, which consists of ten decimal numbers separated by white space. You cannot separate the digits in this string with a comma because the Panose-1 system indicates a range of matches. The initial value of this descriptor is 0, which allows font matching with any fonts. This setting forces other types of matching criteria to be used.

The syntax for this command is

```
panose-1:   [integer]{10}
```

Values
integer

This is the series of ten digits that identifies the particular typeface style of the current font and that is used with Panose matching to match to other fonts. The following list shows what each byte represents in the matching system used by Panose.

- FamilyType
- SerifStyle
- Weight
- Proportion
- Contrast
- StrokeVariation
- ArmStyle
- Letterform
- Midline
- XHeight

CROSS-REFERENCE
See **font matching** and **@font-face**.

<PARAM>

Element

HTML

Start Tag: Required
End Tag: Forbidden

This element is used to identify the parameters that are associated with an OBJECT or APPLET at run time. Any number of parameters can be contained within an object, and they can occur in any order. The syntax of the names and values is assumed to be understood by the OBJECT or APPLET.

Attributes
id

id="*name*"

This attribute is used to assign a name to an element.

name

```
name=cdata
```

This attributed defines the run-time parameter that the object being inserted is assumed to know.

type

```
type= content-type
```

This attribute specifies the content type of the resource identified with the value attribute.

value

```
value=cdata
```

This attribute is used to set the value of the parameter identified by the name attribute.

valuetype

```
valuetype= data | ref | object
```

This attribute specifies the type of value used in the value attribute. When set to data, the default, the value is implemented by the OBJECT as a string. A value of ref identifies the URI of a run-time value storage resource. When object is used, the value refers to an OBJECT declaration in the same document.

Example

The following sample uses the PARAM element to provide the object element with the name of the Macromedia ~~flash~~ file to display.

ON THE CD-ROM

Look for **param.htm** on the accompanying CD-ROM.

```
<object classid="clsid:D27CDB6E-AE6D-11cf-96B8-444553540000"
codebase="http://active.macromedia.com/flash2/cabs/swflash.cab
#version=2,0,0,0" width="600" height="400">
    <param name="SRC" value="fishplane.swf">
    <embed src="fishplane.swf"
pluginspage="http://www.macromedia.com/shockwave/download/"
width="600" height="400">
    </embed>
  </object>
```

CROSS-REFERENCE
See **plugins**, **<OBJECT>**, and **<APPLET>**.

parent

Property

DHTML

This document object property is used to designate the name of the window that is the parent of the current object.

The syntax of this command is

```
[window=] object.parent
```

Parameters

window

This window is the parent of the current object. If the object is a FRAME element, then the window identified is the one containing the FRAMESET object.

Objects

window

CROSS-REFERENCE
See **document tree**, **object**, **parent element**, **ancestry**, and **descendants**.

Parent Element

Concept

When a user agent converts a document from its document language, it creates a document tree in which every element except one has exactly one parent element. The only exception to this is the root HTML element, which has no parents. A parent element is an ancestor to all of its child elements and their children. To make this simpler to understand, let's look at it graphically.

For example, evaluate the following HTML document:

```
<HTML>
<HEAD>
    <TITLE>Example Document structure</TITLE>
</HEAD>
```

```
<BODY>
    <H1>Document Trees</H1>
    <P>Here are two of my favorite one liners.
    <UL>
        <LI> Eagles may soar, but weasels don't get sucked into
jet engines
        <LI> Early bird gets the worm, but the second mouse gets
the cheese
    </UL>
</BODY>
</HTML>
```

In this code, the HTML is the parent of the HEAD and BODY elements and the ancestor of all the elements used on this document. The HEAD element is the parent of TITLE. The BODY element is the parent of H1, P, and UL. LI is the child of UL.

CROSS-REFERENCE
See **child**, **sibling**, **ancestor**, and **progenitor**.

parentElement

Method

DHTML

This method designates the name of the parent element for the text range. In this case, it is the element that completely encloses the selected text.

The syntax of this command is

```
Element= object.parentElement()
```

Parameters
Element

This is the parent element of the selected text.

Objects

TextRange

CROSS-REFERENCE
See **parentElement**, **Parent Element (Concept)**, and **parent (Element)**.

parentElement

Property

DHTML

This property is used to designate the name of the element that is the parent of the current object.

The syntax of this command is

```
[Element=] object.parentElement
```

Parameters

Element

This element is the parent of the current object.

Elements

<!— —>	A	ACRONYM	ADDRESS
APPLET	AREA	B	BASE
BASEFONT	BGSOUND	BIG	BLOCKQUOTE
BODY	BR	BUTTON	CAPTION
CENTER	CITE	CODE	COL
COLGROUP	DD	DEL	DFN
DIR	DIV	DL	DT
EM	EMBED	FIELDSET	FONT
FORM	FRAME	FRAMESET	H1–H6
HEAD	HR	HTML	I
IFRAME	IMG	INPUT	INS
KBD	LABEL	LAYER	LEGEND
LI	LINK	LISTING	MAP
MARQUEE	MENU	META	NEXTID
OBJECT	OL	OPTION	P
PLAINTEXT	PRE	Q	S
SAMP	SCRIPT	SELECT	SMALL
SPAN	STRIKE	STRONG	STYLE
SUB	SUP	TABLE	TBODY
TD	TEXTAREA	TFOOT	TH
THEAD	TITLE	TR	TT
U	UL	VAR	XMP

CROSS-REFERENCE
See **document tree**, **object**, **parent element**, **ancestry**, and **descendants**.

parentStyleSheet

Property

DHTML

This property is used in a script to identify the name of the style sheet that was used to import other style sheets in effect on this document.

The syntax of this command is

```
[Stylesheet=] stylesheet.parentStyleSheet
```

Parameters

Stylesheet

This is the style sheet that is the importer of the other active style sheets.

Objects

styleSheet

CROSS-REFERENCE
See **Cascading Style Sheets**, **@import**, **@media**, and **<LINK>**.

parentTextEdit

Property

DHTML

Scripted documents use this property to identify the next element that can contain a text range. To find this element, scripted documents search the ancestry of the current element.

The syntax of this command is

```
[Object=] object.parentTextEdit
```

Parameters

Object

This object is the parent of the existing object. If the current object has no parent, this is null.

Elements

<!— —>	A	ACRONYM	ADDRESS
APPLET	AREA	B	BASE
BASEFONT	BGSOUND	BIG	BLOCKQUOTE
BODY	BR	BUTTON	CAPTION
CENTER	CITE	CODE	COL
COLGROUP	DD	DEL	DFN
DIR	DIV	DL	DT
EM	EMBED	FIELDSET	FONT
FORM	FRAME	FRAMESET	H1–H6
HEAD	HR	HTML	I
IFRAME	IMG	INPUT	INS
KBD	LABEL	LAYER	LEGEND
LI	LINK	LISTING	MAP
MARQUEE	MENU	META	NEXTID
OBJECT	OL	OPTION	P
PLAINTEXT	PRE	Q	S
SAMP	SCRIPT	SELECT	SMALL
SPAN	STRIKE	STRONG	STYLE
SUB	SUP	TABLE	TBODY
TD	TEXTAREA	TFOOT	TH
THEAD	TITLE	TR	TT
U	UL	VAR	XMP

 CROSS-REFERENCE
See **parent**, **parentElement**, **parentStyleSheet**, and **parent element**.

parentWindow

Property

DHTML

Scripts use this property to identify the name of the window that contains the current object.

The syntax of this command is

```
[Window=] object.parentWindow
```

Parameters

Window

This is the name of the window that is the parent of the current object.

Objects

document

CROSS-REFERENCE

See **parent**, **Parent Element**, **parentElement**, **parentStyleSheet**, and **parentTextEdit**.

Parsing

Concept

When you are attempting to develop a Web site, the user agent parses, or reads and breaks apart, the information that it receives into the rendering of the Web site that your readers see. Not all user agents interpret the objects contained within an HTML or Cascading Style Sheets document the same, although they all should use the same set of instructions for rendering the data. Parsing the original HTML document enables the user agent to see each object and attribute within the text so that the information can be displayed in the most efficient fashion.

CROSS-REFERENCE

See **interpret** and **document tree**.

Password

Concept

When you are attempting to make sure that your Web site information is secure, or at least safe from the casual hacker, you can password-protect your information. No constructs within HTML or Cascading Style Sheets or the DOM provide direct password protection for your information. Instead, you have to use some other form of password protection such as Java or CGI programs to protect your information. Some programs can password-protect individual lists of documents, whereas others can protect any documents contained within an individual directory. These types of programs are all over the Internet, and many of them are free to download. Matt's Script Archive — http://www.worldwidemart.com/scripts/ — is a good place to go for all sorts of PERL scripts to use with your Web sites. There are also many other companies that produce commercial programs that can be used to protect your information.

The software that is serving your HTML documents plays an important role when you select your password protection scheme. Some UNIX-based servers allow the use of the .htaccess and .htpasswd files to protect information within directories and collect user names and passwords before access can be had to any documents within the protected directory. Windows NT servers use an access-control list to identify the specific directories to which any particular individual may have access. If you do not manage your own server, you will need to discuss the available password protection schemes with your server administrator.

CROSS-REFERENCE
See **Security**.

pasteHTML

Method

DHTML

This object method is used to paste the provided HTML and text information into the selected text range. The new text completely overwrites the existing text.

The syntax of this command is

```
object.pasteHTML(HTMLText)
```

Parameters
HTMLText

This string contains the HTML and text data to place in the text range.

Objects

TextRange

CROSS-REFERENCE
See **<TEXTAREA>**, **innerHTML**, and **outerHTML**.

pathname

Property

DHTML

Scripted documents use this property to identify the filename of the object and the path of the object's location.

The syntax of this command is

```
object.pathname [=string]
```

Parameters
string

This string contains the path to, and filename of, the specified object.

Elements

A   AREA

Objects

location

CROSS-REFERENCE
See **filename** and **location**.

pause

Attribute

CSS

This is a shorthand attribute used for setting the `pause-before` and the `pause-after` attributes used with aural style sheets. If two values are provided, the first is for the `pause-before` setting, and the second for `pause-after`. If only one attribute is given, it applies to both properties.

The syntax for this attribute is

```
pause: [ [time | percentage]{1,2} ] | inherit
```

Values

time

This value is the absolute time that the pause should last in seconds or milliseconds.

percentage

This value is used for computing the length of the pause in relation to the value of the `speech-rate` property.

Example

The following example code enables you to control the dramatic pause before and after the contents of an element are read.

```
<STYLE type="text/css">
   BLOCKQUOTE  {pause: 3ms 6ms }
  DIV {pause: 15% }
</STYLE>
```

Elements

This attribute is available with all HTML Elements.

CROSS-REFERENCE
See **pause-after** and **pause-before**.

pause-after

Attribute

CSS

This attribute is used to control the duration of the pause that occurs after the content of the element is read. This attribute occurs before the content of the cue-after attribute.

The syntax for this attribute is

```
pause-after: [ [time | percentage]{1,2} ] | inherit
```

Values
time

This value is the absolute time that the pause should last in seconds or milliseconds.

percentage

This value is used for computing the length of the pause in relation to the value of the speech-rate property.

Elements
This attribute is available with all HTML elements.

 CROSS-REFERENCE
See **pause** and **pause-before**.

---

pause-before

Attribute

CSS

This attribute is used to control the duration of the pause that occurs before the content of the element is read. This attribute occurs after the content of the cue-before attribute.

The syntax for this attribute is

```
pause-before: time | percentage | inherit
```

Values
time

This value is the absolute time that the pause should last in seconds or milliseconds.

percentage

This value is used for computing the length of the pause in relation to the value of the speech-rate property.

Elements

This attribute is available with all HTML Elements.

CROSS-REFERENCE
See **pause** and **pause-after**.

Percentage

Concept

Percentage values are used to control the width, height, and general size of objects in HTML, Cascading Style Sheets, and XML. Percentages always use a length or another absolute value in their computations. This makes percentages always relative to another object on the document. For every property that allows a percentage to be used, an object or property is identified for that percentage to use as a reference value. In some cases, the reference is inherited from a parent element; in others, the reference is based on the formatting context of the object.

CROSS-REFERENCE
See **Length (Concept)**, **length (Property)**, **Integer (Concept)**, **number**, **Absolute Length**, **Absolute Positioning**, **Absolute Size**, **Absolute Value**, **Relative Positioning**, **Relative Size**, and **Relative Units**.

pitch

Attribute

CSS

The pitch attribute is used with aural style sheets to control the frequency of the speech synthesizer for a particular object or type of object. This enables you to control whether your voice will sound male or female to some degree.

The syntax for this command is

```
pitch: frequency | x-low | low | medium | high | x-high |
inherit
```

Values
frequency

This is the absolute hertz specification that the speech synthesizer should use when reading this text.

x-low, low, medium, high, x-high

These values are mapped by the user agent, based upon the user's environment and selected speech family, to provide a series of frequencies for the user agent to render.

Elements
This attribute applies to all HTML elements.

CROSS-REFERENCE
See **frequency**, **pitch-range**, **volume**, and **Aural Style Sheets**.

pitch-range

Attribute

CSS

This attribute is used to provide a number representing the acceptable variation in the average pitch of the speech synthesizer's voice.

The syntax for this command is

```
pitch-range: number | inherit
```

Values
number

This is a value between 0 and 100 that controls the inflection and variation of the voice used by the speech synthesizer. A value of 0 creates a flat, monotone voice, whereas 50 creates a normal voice. Values above 50 create an animated voice.

Elements
This attribute applies to all HTML elements.

CROSS-REFERENCE
See **frequency**, **pitch**, **volume**, and **Aural Style sheets**.

Pixel

Concept

A *pixel* is a singular unit of measure upon which the dimensions of the viewable area of your computer screen and many objects displayed in that screen are measured. Your computer screen can display 640 by 480 pixels, 800 by 600, 1024 by 768, or even more pixels on your screen, depending upon the resolution of your screen, your video drivers, and your hardware's capabilities. The higher the resolution, the more pixels can be displayed upon your screen.

 CROSS-REFERENCE
See **length** and **resolution**.

pixelHeight

Property

DHTML

Scripts use this property either to set or to retrieve the height of the object in pixels.

The syntax of this command is

```
object.pixelHeight [ = Height ]
```

Parameters
Height
This integer represents the height of the object.

Objects

style

 CROSS-REFERENCE
See **pixel**, **height**, **pixelLeft**, **pixelTop**, and **pixelWidth**.

pixelLeft

Property

DHTML

This property is used with scripted document objects either to set or to retrieve the position of the left edge of the object in pixels.

The syntax of this command is

```
object.pixelLeft [ = Position ]
```

Parameters

Position

This integer represents the position of the left edge of the object.

Objects

style

 CROSS-REFERENCE
See **pixel**, **height**, **pixelHeight**, **pixelTop**, and **pixelWidth**.

pixelTop

Property

DHTML

Scripts use this property either to set or to retrieve the position of the top edge of the object in pixels.

The syntax of this command is

```
object.pixelTop [ = Position ]
```

Parameters

Position

This integer represents the position of the top edge of the object.

Objects

style

CROSS-REFERENCE
See **pixel**, **height**, **pixelHeight**, **pixelLeft**, and **pixelWidth**.

pixelWidth

Property

DHTML

Scripted documents use this property either to set or to retrieve the width of the object in pixels.

The syntax of this command is

```
object.pixelWidth [ = Width ]
```

Parameters
Width

This integer represents the width of the object.

Objects

style

CROSS-REFERENCE
See **pixel**, **height**, **pixelLeft**, **pixelTop**, and **pixelHeight**.

<PLAINTEXT>

Element

HTML — Internet Explorer Only

Start Tag: Required
End Tag: Required

This element is used to render text for Internet Explorer browsers in a fixed-width font without any other processing tags.

NOTE
This element should not be used on documents that may be viewed by users of multiple Web browsers. Instead, you should use the PRE element.

Attributes
class

```
class="cdata-list"
```

This attribute is used to assign a class name to an element. User agents employ classes to group specific types of information for later use.

id

```
id="name"
```

This attribute is used to assign a name to an element.

lang

```
lang="language code"
```

This attribute specifies the language that should be used to render an element and its values.

onclick

```
onclick=script
```

This attribute takes effect when a user clicks the button on a pointing device with the pointer over an element.

ondblclick

```
ondblclick=script
```

This attribute takes effect when a user double-clicks the button on a pointing device with the pointer over an element.

onkeydown

```
onkeydown=script
```

This attribute takes effect when a user presses a key and the pointer is over an element.

onkeypress

```
onkeypress=script
```

This attribute takes effect when a key is pressed and released while the pointer is over an element.

onkeyup

```
onkeyup=script
```

This attribute takes effect when a user releases a key with the pointer over an element.

onmousedown

```
onmousedown=script
```

This attribute takes effect when a user presses the button on a pointing device while the pointer is over an element.

onmousemove

```
onmousemove=script
```

This attribute is activated when the mouse pointer is moved while it is over an element.

onmouseout

```
onmouseout=script
```

This attribute is activated when the mouse pointer is moved away from an element.

onmouseover

```
onmouseover=script
```

This attribute is activated when the mouse pointer is moved over an element.

onmouseup

```
onmouseup=script
```

This attribute takes effect when the button on a pointing device is released while the pointer is over an element.

style

```
style=style descriptors
```

This attribute applies specific style-sheet information to one particular element.

title

```
title=text
```

This attribute provides annotation information to the element.

Example

This example code uses the PLAINTEXT element and the PRE element to display two paragraphs side by side.

ON THE CD-ROM

Look for **plaintext.htm** on the accompanying CD-ROM.

```
<BODY>
<H1> The American Broadcasting System - Take 2 </H1>
<PRE>
This is a test. This is a test of the American Broadcasting
System. If this were not a test this message would be followed
immediately by an important viewer announcement.
</PRE>
<PLAINTEXT>
This is a test. This is a test of the American Broadcasting
System. If this were not a test this message would be followed
immediately by an important viewer announcement.
</PLAINTEXT>
</BODY>
```

CROSS-REFERENCE

See **<PRE>**.

platform

Property

DHTML

This property is used by scripts to find out what platform the browser is operating on.

The syntax of this command is

```
[Win32 | Win16 | WinCE | sOther=] object.platform
```

Parameters

sOther

This string is used to represent the platform that the software is operating on.

Win16

This corresponds to the Windows 16-bit platforms, such as Windows 3.1, Windows for Workgroups, and Windows NT 3.51.

Win32

This is the Windows 32-bit platforms, such as Windows 95, Windows 98, and Windows NT4.

WinCE

This is the operating system designed for Windows-based hand-held computers.

Objects

navigator

CROSS-REFERENCE
See **<OS>**.

play-during

Attribute

CSS

This attribute is used with aural style sheets to specify a sound to play while the contents of an object are spoken.

The syntax of this command is

```
play-during: uri mix? repeat? | auto | none | inherit
```

Values

uri

This is the address of the sound to be played.

mix

This property mixes the sound specified in the parent's play-during attribute with the contents of this object. If this value is not supplied, the new sound replaces the old sound.

repeat

This value repeats the sound for the duration of the element.

auto

The sound of the parent element continues to play.

none

There is silence while this element's contents are read.

Elements

This attribute is available with all HTML elements.

CROSS-REFERENCE
See **cue-after**, **cue**, and **cue-before**.

plugins

Collection

DHTML

This document object collection creates a list of all `plugins` found within the current `navigator` object installation.

This collection can be used in the following ways:

```
[ collPlugins = ] object.plugins
[ oObject = ] object.plugins ( vIndex )
```

Parameters
collPlugins

This variable refers to the array of elements contained by the object.

oObject

This variable refers to an individual item in the array.

vIndex

This parameter is required and contains the number or string identifying the element or collection to retrieve. When a number is specified, the method returns the element in the zero-based collection at the identified position. When a string identifier is used and multiple elements with the same `name` or `id` attributes match the string, this method returns a collection of those matched elements.

Objects

navigator

CROSS-REFERENCE
See **pluginspage**.

pluginspage

Property

DHTML

Scripts use this property to retrieve the address of the plug-in needed to view the embedded data object.

The syntax of this command is

```
[URL =] object.pluginspage
```

Parameters

URL

This is the complete address representing an HTML page that contains various plug-ins needed by this embedded object.

Elements

EMBED

CROSS-REFERENCE
See **plugins**.

PNG

Concept

The Portable Network Graphic (PNG) format is the up-and-coming replacement for the GIF image. Like GIF images, PNG graphics are compressed; but unlike GIF images, PNG graphics are not proprietary and do not require a licensing agreement with CompuServe. The PNG format was developed by an Internet committee for the express purpose of creating a patent-free graphic format to replace GIF images.

PNG images can be 10 to 30 percent more compressed than their GIF counterparts. PNG enables you to set both transparency and opacity on a single color. You can interlace PNG images, as you can GIF images, but PNG images load faster and flow easier than GIFs. You can gamma-correct PNG images for specific platforms, which enables you to create an image specific for Windows viewers and another for Macintoshes. You can also save your images using true color instead of just the 256-color palette or gray-scale options of GIF images.

The one shortcoming of this format is that it doesn't support animations because it cannot contain multiple images. Because the standard is extensible, software developers will be able to create variations of PNG that can contain animations.

 CROSS-REFERENCE
See **GIF**, **JPEG**, **image**, **Image Map**, and **<MAP>**.

port

Property

DHTML

Scripted documents use this property either to set or to retrieve the port number in the address of an object.

The syntax of this command is

```
[string =] object.port
```

Parameters
string

This is the port-number portion of an object's URL.

Example
The following example code uses an alert box to let you know the port number of the current connection and to take you to the IDG Books Worldwide Web site.

```
<html>
<head>
  <title>Port example</title>
</head>

<body>
  <a href="http://www.idgbooks.com"
nClick="alert(this.port);">

  <p>Click me for port identification, and a little trip to
IDG Books.</a> </p>
</body>
</html>
```

Elements

    A   AREA

Objects

    location

CROSS-REFERENCE
See **URL**, **URI**, and **server**.

posHeight

Property

DHTML

Scripts use this property either to set or to retrieve the height of the object as specified by its Cascading Style Sheets `height` attribute.

The syntax of this command is

```
object.posHeight [ = Height ]
```

Parameters

Height

This floating-point number represents the height of the object.

Objects

    style

CROSS-REFERENCE
See **pixel**, **height**, **pixelLeft**, **pixelTop**, **pixelWidth**, **posLeft**, **posTop**, **posWidth**, and **position**.

position

Attribute

CSS

This attribute is used to define how an object is positioned on the page. Objects can be fixed, absolute, relative, static, or floating. A floating object—one placed using the `float` attribute—is interpreted differently, using a different positioning algorithm, than objects positioned using the `position` attribute.

The syntax of this command is

```
position: static | relative | absolute | fixed | inherit
```

JAVASCRIPT

```
[ sPosition = ] object.style.position
```

Values

absolute

The object's position has to be specified by the `left`, `right`, `top`, and `bottom` properties or by the `left` and `top` properties in conjunction with the `width` and `height` properties.

fixed

The object is positioned in the same manner as the `absolute` box, but it is positioned in relation to a stable object that is not moved. In general, this position is relative to the viewable area of the computer monitor. For instance, an object that has been placed in a fixed position might stay in one location on your computer monitor as you scroll the remainder of the document past the object.

relative

This places an object according to the normal flow of the document but offsets it relative to its normal position.

static

A static box is laid out according to the normal flow of the document. Statically positioned boxes do not use the `left` and `top` attributes to position the element.

Example

The following example code is used to position two distinct objects at different positions on the HTML page.

```
<STYLE TYPE="text/css">
  <!-
    #layer1 {position:absolute; top: 60px; left:140px; height:
350; width:650px; overflow: auto;}
    #layer2 {position:fixed; top: 160px; left:35px; height:
50; width:650px; overflow: auto;}
  ->
  </STYLE>
```

CROSS-REFERENCE
See **float**, **<DIV>**, **<LAYER>**, and **<SPAN>**.

posLeft

Property

DHTML

Document objects use this property either to set or to retrieve the left edge of the object as specified by its Cascading Style Sheets `left` attribute.

The syntax of this command is

```
object.posLeft [ = Position ]
```

Parameters

Position

This floating-point number represents the left edge of the object.

Objects

style

CROSS-REFERENCE

See **pixel**, **height**, **pixelLeft**, **pixelTop**, **pixelWidth**, **posHeight**, **posTop**, **posWidth**, and **position**.

POST

Concept

When you have created a form and placed it on the Internet, that form has to be sent to or collected by the form processing engine. The `method` attribute of the `FORM` element specifies the HTTP method used to send the form to the processing agent. `POST` is one of the values that this attribute can accept.

When you use the HTTP `POST` method, the form data is blocked together and then sent to the address specified with the `action` attribute. This enables you to use more than just ASCII characters in your form collections.

CROSS-REFERENCE

See **<FORM>** and **<GET>**.

posTop

Property

DHTML

Scripted objects use this property either to set or to retrieve the top edge of the object as specified by its Cascading Style Sheets `top` attribute.

The syntax of this command is

```
object.posTop [ = Position ]
```

Parameters

Position

This floating-point number represents the top edge of the object.

Objects

style

CROSS-REFERENCE
See pixel, height, pixelLeft, pixelTop, pixelWidth, posHeight, posLeft, posWidth, and position.

posWidth

Property

DHTML

Objects use this property either to set or to retrieve the width of the object as specified by its Cascading Style Sheets `width` attribute.

The syntax of this command is

```
object.posWidth [ = Width ]
```

Parameters

Width

This floating-point number represents the width of the object.

Objects

style

CROSS-REFERENCE
See **pixel**, **height**, **pixelLeft**, **pixelTop**, **pixelWidth**, **width**, **posLeft**, **posTop**,
posHeight, and **position**.

<PRE>

Element

HTML

Start Tag: Required
End Tag: Required

This element is used to create monospace-formatted text, by default, that is
laid out exactly as it appears in the HTML source code. If the font face has
been specified in a style sheet, with the FONT element, or throughout the user
agent, the text used in the PRE object may not be monospaced.

Attributes

class

```
class="cdata-list"
```

This attribute is used to assign a class name to an element. User agents employ
classes to group specific types of information for later use.

id

```
id="name"
```

This attribute is used to assign a name to an element.

lang

```
lang="language code"
```

This attribute specifies the language in which an element and its values should be
rendered.

onclick

```
onclick=script
```

This attribute takes effect when a user clicks the button on a pointing device with
the pointer over an element.

ondblclick

```
ondblclick=script
```

This attribute takes effect when a user double-clicks the button on a pointing device with the pointer over an element.

onkeydown

```
onkeydown=script
```

This attribute takes effect when a user presses a key and the pointer is over an element.

onkeypress

```
onkeypress=script
```

This attribute takes effect when a key is pressed and released while the pointer is over an element.

onkeyup

```
onkeyup=script
```

This attribute takes effect when a user releases a key with the pointer over an element.

onmousedown

```
onmousedown=script
```

This attribute takes effect when a user presses the button on a pointing device while the pointer is over an element.

onmousemove

```
onmousemove=script
```

This attribute is activated when the mouse pointer is moved while it is over an element.

onmouseout

```
onmouseout=script
```

This attribute is activated when the mouse pointer is moved away from an element.

onmouseover

```
onmouseover=script
```

This attribute is activated when the mouse pointer is moved over an element.

o
p
q

onmouseup

```
onmouseup=script
```

This attribute takes effect when the button on a pointing device is released while the pointer is over an element.

style

```
style=style descriptors
```

This attribute applies specific style-sheet information to one particular element.

title

```
title=text
```

This attribute provides annotation information to the element.

width

```
width = length
```

This attribute is used to specify the width of the applet's display area.

Example

This example code uses the PRE element and the DIV element to display two paragraphs side by side.

ON THE CD-ROM

Look for **pre.htm** on the accompanying CD-ROM.

```
<BODY>
<H1> The American Broadcasting System - Take 3 </H1>
<PRE>
This is a test. This is a test of the American Broadcasting
System. If this were not a test this message would be followed
immediately by an important viewer announcement.
</PRE>
<DIV>
This is a test. This is a test of the American Broadcasting
System. If this were not a test this message would be followed
immediately by an important viewer announcement.
</DIV>
</BODY>
```

CROSS-REFERENCE

See **<PLAINTEXT>** and **<DIV>**.

previousPage

Method

DHTML

This JavaScript method is used to display the previous page of records in the table's data set. To use this method, you must use the `dataPageSize` property to set the number of records that should be displayed in the table.

The syntax needed to use this method is

```
object.previousPage()
```

Elements

TABLE

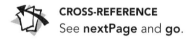 **CROSS-REFERENCE**
See **nextPage** and **go**.

Printing

Concept

With the development and implementation of the Cascading Style Sheets, level 2, specification in the most popular browsers, the birth of true document dispersal through Web pages begins. This latest implementation of Cascading Style Sheets incorporates controls for widows and orphans, page breaks, line breaks, and floating objects.

Each of these features enables you to control how your page appears and how it prints on most printers. With the incorporation of these properties, you can now place full newsletters on the Internet and have members or readers view these newsletters as they were meant to look, not as a string of relatively unformatted text.

 CROSS-REFERENCE
See **page-break-before**, **page-break-after**, **page-break-inside**, **orphan**, and **widow**.

Privacy

Concept

Personal privacy on the Internet is important to everyone. Everything you do on the Internet, whether with Web browser or e-mail, leaves an electronic trail behind you. Hackers or crackers can follow this trail and collect personal information about you—including credit card, bank account, and social security numbers—as well as your name, phone number, and address. You can safely assume that nothing you send unencrypted across the Internet is private information. Let's look at the situation closely.

Heather sends Michael the following e-mail message:

```
To: Mikey (smtp: michaelw@houstonnet.net)
From: Heather (smtp: raven@oregonnet.net)
Hey Mikey,
What are you doing today? How has class been? Did Houston get
hit by ol' Hurricane George as it went through the Gulf? What
about your folks? Did they get hit? I didn't think that the
storm went south of Houston at all, but I wanted to ask you.

I have my plane reservations for November. I'll be flying
United, and will be there for two weeks. I'll get there the
2nd, and leave around the 16th. Were you still gonna be able to
pick me up at the airport? I hope so, cause otherwise I'll
have an expensive taxi ride to your apartment. You know, it
was kind of neat. I made the plane reservations over the net,
and it took less time than it does to call them. But I didn't
save any more money. I was hoping to though.

I'll be making the trip to Western Oregon sometime after the
15th of October. But I'll still be able to send email. We will
probably have snow on the mountains around the house by then,
but with the 4x4 I'll have no problems getting through Minam.

Ahh, I'm getting a new phone line added into the office. The
number will be 555-6060. So you can call me there also,
although my computer and fax machine will be hooked up to it
most of the time. At least that leaves the 6099 and the 4050
number free most of the time.

Well I need to get back to work. This book still needs to get
finished for the publisher.

Ciao,
Heather
```

Now let's look at what sort of information we have gotten about these two people from this one e-mail message.

We know the following about Michael:

- Michael's last name most likely starts with a W.
- He lives in Houston, TX.
- He uses the Houston Net ISP. From this information, a good hacker can find out Mike's full name, phone number, and address from the billing system in Mike's ISP. The hacker can even find Mike's credit card number if Mike made automatic payments from a credit card.
- He lives in an apartment.
- His parents live south of him, most likely outside of Houston somewhere.
- He is expecting a visit from Heather in November.
- He is going to school.

We know the following about Heather:

- Her nickname and login name with her ISP is raven.
- She lives in Eastern Oregon. You can discover this from the name of the ISP, by checking out its service area, and from her reference to Minam, which can be found on a map.
- She uses the Oregon Net ISP. From this information, hackers can find Heather's full name, phone number, and address from the billing system in her ISP. They can even find her credit card number if she made automatic payments from a credit card.
- She has an office with at least three phone lines, and we know all of their numbers.
- She uses a credit card to make reservations over the Internet, and she travels frequently.

 NOTE

In case you're wondering, the information I've used in this example is fictional.

This information can be used by hackers or other interested parties to discover almost everything that they would like to about a person. In the case of e-mail, anyone with access to a server that the e-mail message is transferred through can read your letters. Private investigation agencies can be hired to trace down every piece of information on the Internet about you, including phone book listings, copies of e-mail that you have sent or received, Usenet News messages that you have sent, mailing lists that you are involved with, and Web sites that you have visited. This type of information can be used hundreds of ways by lawyers, stalkers, or anyone else interested in discovering information about you and your actions for their own purposes.

CROSS-REFERENCE
See **security**.

Processing Instructions

Concept

Processing instructions provide the user agent with information about how a rule, object, element, attribute, or script instruction should be used and acted upon. The DOM is used by HTML user agents and XML user agents as a means of controlling how those languages are interpreted and implemented.

CROSS-REFERENCE
See **Document Object Model**.

<PROCESSOR>

Element

OSD

This element, a child of IMPLEMENTATION, is used to identify the processor that this software requires for installation.

Attributes
value

This is the name of the type of processor required for the software being installed.

Example
The following example shows how the PROCESSOR element is used to define the type of system processor required for the software being installed.

```
<SOFTPKG>
<IMPLEMENTATION>
   <IMPLTYPE value="java" />
   <PROCESSOR value="x86" />
   <OS value="WinNT" />
   <MEMSIZE value="1024Kb" />
</IMPLEMENTATION>
</SOFTPKG>
```

Elements
This element is a child of IMPLEMENTATION.

CROSS-REFERENCE
See **OSD — Open Software Description**, **<SOFTPKG>**, and **<MEMSIZE>**.

profile

Attribute

HTML

This attribute is used to specify the location of a meta-data profile or of multiple profiles if the URLs are separated by white spaces. A *meta-data profile* is one that can be accessed by a variety of pages that contain a series of information about the documents. This information can be accessed by all the pages on a Web site or on a series of sites.

The syntax of this command is

```
profile=uri
```

Example
The following HEAD object uses the profile attribute to grab a copy of a profile that will be used in addition to the existing META tags.

```
<HEAD profile="http://www.catsback.com/profiles/cbc">
  <TITLE>How to complete Letter of Agreement with
Clients</TITLE>
  <META name="author" content="Heather Williamson">
<META name="copyright" content="&copy; 1999 Cat's Back Corp.">
  <META name="keywords" content="legal,guidelines,agreement">
</HEAD>
```

Elements

HEAD

CROSS-REFERENCE
See **<META>** and **meta data**.

Prolog

Concept

XML

In XML, the Prolog is used to identify the specification conformance level of the document being read by a user agent. This statement enables document authors and future versions of user agents to take advantage of automatic version recognition. The prolog for a document that conforms to the XML 1.0 specification is as follows:

```
<?xml version="1.0"?>
```

The prolog is developed by using the following pieces.

```
prolog ::=XMLDecl? Misc* (doctypedecl Misc*)?
XMLDecl ::= '<?xml' VersionInfo EncodingDecl? SDDecl? S? '?>'
```

The preceding statement lays out the main structure of the declaration and the order in which each of its individual parts must be implemented.

```
VersionInfo ::= S 'version' Eq (' VersionNum' | " VersionNum")
```

This specifies the version information with the string word version followed by the version number either in or out of quotation marks.

```
Eq ::=S? '='S?
```

This inserts the equivalency sign into the version information. It can be either enclosed in quotes or not and should be followed by a string value.

```
VersionNum ::= ([a-zA-Z0-9_.:] | '-')+
```

The version number is a string value containing any letters or numbers, a space, a period, a column, or a hyphen.

```
Misc ::= Comment | PI | S
```

This field contains a comment that can be used to provide extra information to the user agent.

CROSS-REFERENCE

See **<!DOCTYPE>** and **Document Type Definition**.

prompt

Method

DHTML

This document object method is used to display a prompting dialog box that enables the reader to insert an answer to the prompt in a string form.

The syntax needed to use this method is

```
TextData = object.prompt([Message] [,DefaultValue] )
```

Parameters

DefaultValue

This optional string provides a default value for the string to be entered at the prompt.

Message

This optional string provides the default message to be displayed in the dialog window.

TextData

This is the string or integer value entered by the user.

Objects

window

CROSS-REFERENCE
See **alert**.

Properties

Concept

CSS

Documents using Cascading Style Sheets properties or attributes enable you to identify the specific way you wish your objects to be displayed. Cascading Style Sheets has properties for controlling fonts, size, position, color, borders, and practically every type of formatting question that arises in the design and layout of multimedia information.

The document object model, on which Cascading Style Sheets is implemented, enables these attributes and properties to be altered through the use of scripts or other user-agent-implemented devices. This gives you greater flexibility when you develop documents for dispersal to a variety of systems and media types.

CROSS-REFERENCE
See **attributes**, **block**, and **elements**.

protocol

Property

DHTML

This property is used either to set or to retrieve the URL's initial access method.

The syntax of this property is

```
object.protocol [ = sProtocol ]
```

Parameters
sProtocol

This string contains the protocol used to access a URL. Valid values for this string are HTTP, FTP, mailto, file, gopher, Telnet, and news.

Example
The following code creates an alert dialog that identifies the type of protocol used within that link.

```
<body>
<a href="http://www.idgbooks.com"
onClick="alert(this.protocol)">What protocol?</a>
<a href="ftp://ftp.microsoft.com"
onClick="alert(this.protocol)"> What protocol?</a>
<a href="mailto:okohke@hotmail.com"
onClick="alert(this.protocol)"> What protocol?</a>
<a href="#" onClick="alert(this.protocol)"> What protocol?</a>
</body>
```

Elements

A   AREA   IMG

Objects

document   location

 **CROSS-REFERENCE**
See **URI** and **URL**.

Pseudo-Class

Class

CSS

A *pseudo-class* is similar to a normal class, but it is not included within the document tree of a document. Because some documents require formatting that cannot be based on a complete object, these types of pseudo-classes are allowed. Pseudo-classes are used to classify elements based solely on their names, not their characteristics, attributes, or content.

You can use scripts to create dynamic pseudo-classes that change as a reader interacts with your document. The exception to this rule is the `:first-child` pseudo-class, which can be discovered by going through the document tree. Some of these classes can be mutually exclusive, but most can be applied simultaneously to the same element and can be placed anywhere within that element selector. When classes do conflict, the cascading order will determine which classes are rendered.

:active

```
A:active {color: lime}
```

The `:active` Anchor pseudo-class is applied only when the link is being selected by the user. This class enables you to control the color of your anchors while they are active.

:first

This pseudo-class is applied only to the `@page` rule. Using this pseudo-class, you can apply information directly to the page layout of your document's first printed page.

:focus

This pseudo-class applies when an element has the focus of the reader's cursor.

:hover

```
A:hover {color: red}
```

This Anchor pseudo-class is applied to all links that have the mouse hovering over them. A link with the :hover class applied becomes the specified color automatically when the mouse is dragged over it.

:left

This pseudo-class is applied only to the @page rule. Using this pseudo-class, you can apply information directly to the page layout of the left-hand printed pages of your document.

:link

```
A:link {color: blue}
```

This Anchor pseudo-class is applied to all links that have not been selected. A link with the :link class applied is automatically displayed with the specified color.

:right

This pseudo-class is only applied to the @page rule. Using this pseudo-class, you can apply information directly to the page layout of the right-hand printed pages of your document.

:visited

```
A:visited {color: fuchsia}
```

This Anchor pseudo-class is applied to all links that have been selected. A link with the :visited class applied changes automatically to the specified color after it has been visited.

CROSS-REFERENCE
See **Pseudo-Element**.

Pseudo-Element

Element

CSS

Pseudo-elements are not included in the document source or the document tree, outside of the style sheet specification. These types of elements create abstractions within the document tree that cannot be specified any other way. For example, there is no other way within the HTML language to identify the first letter or line of a paragraph. Using pseudo-elements, you can now identify these specific pieces of content and assign a style to them. Pseudo-elements are not case-sensitive and may only appear directly after the subject of a style sheet selector.

:after

The `:after` pseudo-element is used to insert the information specified in the `content` parameter after every instance of the tag, or tags, that it is applied to.

:before

The `:before` pseudo-element is used to insert the information specified in the `content` parameter before every instance of the tag, or tags, that it is applied to.

:first-child

This element is used to alter the first child of an element as it is mapped within the document tree.

:first-letter

This element is used to create graphical effects such as "drop-caps" and "initial-caps." These elements can be either inline or floating, depending upon the status of their `float` attribute.

:first-line

This pseudo-element applies special style properties to the first line of a block-level element. It cannot be used with any other style of element. This pseudo-element is similar to inline elements, but it has some specific restrictions.

:lang

This pseudo-class specifies the language in which an element should be rendered.

CROSS-REFERENCE
See **Pseudo-Class**.

Pull Technology

Concept

CROSS-REFERENCE
See **Client Pull**.

<PURGETIME>

Element

CDF

This element is used to identify the number of days old for which log-file entries will be reported when the log file is uploaded.

Values
hour

```
hour="number"
```

This is how old, in hours, a log entry can be before it is automatically purged.

Example
The following example code posts the log entries to the logbook directory on the Cat's Back server if those entries are less than 24 hours old.

```
<LOGTARGET HREF="http://www.catsback.com/logbook"
Method="POST" SCOPE="OFFLINE">
    <PURGETIME HOUR="24"/>
</LOGTARGET>
```

CROSS-REFERENCE
See **<LOGTARGET>**.

Push Button

Concept

There are three types of buttons within the constructs of an HTML document. Submit buttons enable you to submit a form. A reset button enables you to return a form to its initial values. The third type of button is a push button.

Push buttons have no default value and can be created using either the INPUT element or the BUTTON element. Each push button has a client-side script that is activated through one of the element's associated events. When the user activates the button, the associated script is triggered. Push buttons can appear as a standard text-block button or as an image.

CROSS-REFERENCE
See **<FORM>**, **<INPUT>**, **radio button**, **menus**, **text input**, **buttons**, **file select**, **hidden controls**, and **object controls**.

Push Technology

Concept

CROSS-REFERENCE
See **Server Push**.

o
p
q

<Q>

Element

HTML

This element is used to identify inline blocks of quoted text. In some user agents the Q element automatically places quotation marks around the text that it marks; the BLOCKQUOTE element does not. If you want quotation marks around your quoted text all the time, use the :before and :after pseudo-classes in a style sheet.

Attributes

cite

    cite="*url*"

This attribute is used to identify the URL of the original material quoted in this document.

class

    class="*cdata-list*"

This attribute is used to assign a class name to an element. User agents employ classes to group specific types of information for later use.

id

    id="*name*"

This attribute is used to assign a name to an element.

lang

    lang="*language code*"

This attribute specifies the language in which an element and its values should be rendered.

onclick

`onclick=script`

This attribute takes effect when a user clicks the button on a pointing device with the pointer over an element.

ondblclick

`ondblclick=script`

This attribute takes effect when a user double-clicks the button on a pointing device with the pointer over an element.

onkeydown

`onkeydown=script`

This attribute takes effect when a user presses a key while the pointer is over an element.

onkeypress

`onkeypress=script`

This attribute takes effect when a key is pressed and released with the pointer over an element.

onkeyup

`onkeyup=script`

This attribute takes effect when a key is released with the pointer over an element.

onmousedown

`onmousedown=script`

This attribute takes effect when the button on a pointing device is pressed with the pointer over an element.

onmousemove

`onmousemove=script`

This attribute is activated when the mouse is moved while the pointer is over an element.

onmouseout

`onmouseout=script`

This attribute is activated when the mouse pointer is moved away from an element.

onmouseover

```
onmouseover=script
```

This attribute is activated when the mouse pointer is moved over an element.

onmouseup

```
onmouseup=script
```

This attribute takes effect when the button on a pointing device is released with the pointer over an element.

style

```
style=style descriptors
```

This attribute is used to apply specific style-sheet information to one particular element.

title

```
title=text
```

This attribute serves to provide annotation information to the element to which it is applied.

Example

ON THE CD-ROM

Look for **q.htm** on the accompanying CD-ROM.

```
<HTML>
<HEAD>
   <TITLE>Quotes Everywhere</TITLE>
   <META name="generator" content="Macromedia Dreamweaver">
   <style type="text/css">
   <!-
   hr {  color: #33FF00}
   ->
   </style>
</HEAD>

<BODY bgcolor="#FFFFCC">
<H1><font color="#33FF00">S</font>ome of my <font
color="#33FF00">F</font>avorite
  <font color="#33FF00">Q</font>uotes</H1>
   <Q cite="http://rbhatnagar.ececs.uc.edu:8080/vivekananda/
   quotes/quotes_intro" title="Swami Vivekananda Quotes">
```

p

q

r

```
      BE FREE ; hope for nothing from any one. I am sure if you
      look back upon your    lives, you will find that you were
      always vainly trying to get help from others
      which never came. All the help that has come was from
      within YOURSELVES.
  </Q>
  <HR>
      <Q cite="http://rbhatnagar.ececs.uc.edu:8080/vivekananda/
      quotes/quotes_intro" title="Swami Vivekananda Quotes">
      Whatever you THINK, that you WILL BE. If you think
      yourselves weak, weak you will be; if you think yourselves
      strong, strong you will be.
      </Q>
  <HR>
      <Q    cite="http://rbhatnagar.ececs.uc.edu:8080/
      vivekananda/quotes/quotes_intro" title="Swami Vivekananda
      Quotes">
      The remedy for weakness is not brooding over weakness, but
      thinking of strength. Teach men of the STRENGTH that is
      already WITHIN them.
      </Q>
  </BODY>
  </HTML>
```

CROSS-REFERENCE
See **inline**, **Block-Level Element**, and **<BLOCKQUOTE>**.

queryCommandEnabled

Method

DHTML

This document object method is used to return a permission of sorts to the
script so that it knows if a particular command can be used given the current
state of the document.

The syntax for activating this method is

Enabled = object.queryCommandEnabled(CmdID)

Parameters
CmdID

This string is used to specify the command identifier that needs to be checked.
Enabled
This Boolean variable is used to tell if the command is enabled (**true**) or disabled
(**false**).

Objects

document   textrange

CROSS-REFERENCE
See **execCommand**, **queryCommandIndeterm**, **queryCommandState**,
queryCommandSupported, and **queryCommandValue**.

queryCommandIndeterm

Method

DHTML

This document method is used to return a notice to the script so that it knows
if a particular command is in an indeterminate state.
The syntax for activating this method is

```
Indeterminate = object.queryCommandIndeterm(CmdID)
```

Parameters
CmdID

This string is used to specify the command identifier that needs to be checked.

Indeterminate

This Boolean variable is used to tell if the command is in an indeterminate state
(**true**) or not (**false**).

Objects

document   textrange

CROSS-REFERENCE
See **execCommand**, **queryCommandEnabled**, **queryCommandState**,
queryCommandSupported, and **queryCommandValue**.

queryCommandState

Method

DHTML

This document object method is used to return the command state of the identified command.

The syntax for activating this method is

```
Done = object.queryCommandState(CmdID)
```

Parameters
CmdID

This string is used to specify the command identifier that needs to be checked.

Done

This Boolean variable is used to tell if the command has completed its task (**true**) or not (**false**). If the script is unable to tell, then the state will be **null**.

Objects

document   textrange

CROSS-REFERENCE
See **execCommand**, **queryCommandExecute**, **queryCommandIndeterm**, **queryCommandSupported**, and **queryCommandValue**.

queryCommandSupported

Method

DHTML

This document object method is used to determine whether the current command is supported over the identified range.

The syntax for activating this method is

```
Supported = object.queryCommandSupported(CmdID)
```

Parameters
CmdID

This string is used to specify the command identifier that needs to be checked.

Supported

This Boolean variable is used to tell if the command is supported (**true**) or not (**false**).

Objects

    document   textrange

CROSS-REFERENCE

See **execCommand**, **queryCommandExecute**, **queryCommandIndeterm**, **queryCommandState**, and **queryCommandValue**.

queryCommandValue

Method

DHTML

This document object method is used to return the current value of the identified command.

    The syntax for activating this method is

```
CmdValue = object.queryCommandValue(CmdID)
```

Parameters

CmdID

This string is used to specify the command identifier that needs to be checked.

CmdValue

This variable is used to return the value of the command, whether it is a Boolean value, a string, or an integer.

Objects

    document   textrange

CROSS-REFERENCE

See **execCommand**, **queryCommandExecute**, **queryCommandIndeterm**, **queryCommandState**, and **queryCommandSupported**.

p

q

r

Radio Buttons

Concept

Radio buttons are used in forms to enable a reader to make one choice from a selection. (By contrast, a checkbox enables readers to select multiple options from a single list.) Radio buttons generally have a default selection and are always used in control groups. Each group works as a single control on an HTML document because each button uses the same name.

For instance, the following code creates a group of radio buttons that enables you to select a range of ages on a questionnaire.

```
Your Age:
    <input type="radio" name="yourage" value="under21" checked>
    under 21
    <input type="radio" name="yourage" value="21to30">
    21-30
    <input type="radio" name="yourage" value="31to40">
    31-40
    <input type="radio" name="yourage" value="41to50">
    41-50
    <input type="radio" name="yourage" value="51to60">
    51-60
    <input type="radio" name="yourage" value="61to70">
    61-70
    <input type="radio" name="radiobutton" value="radiobutton">
    Over 70
```

You can select only one of these age ranges. If you select one option and then select another, your original selection is automatically replaced with the second.

CROSS-REFERENCE
See **<FORM>**, **<INPUT>**, **Checkboxes**, **Menus**, **Text Input**, **Buttons**, **file select**, **Hidden Controls**, and **Object Controls**.

RDF — Resource Description Framework

Concept

The *Resource Description Framework (RDF)* is used to provide a series of algorithms for directing applications that are attempting to provide services to Internet users and developers. RDF documents are used for identifying valid resources and contents for Web specifications, providing bibliographic descriptions of Web resources, identifying digital signature schematics, managing rights and privacy issues, and so on. RDF documents are also used for identifying content rating schemas and for evaluating and classifying Web sites.

The descriptions provided by RDF documents are, at their most basic, models of the variety of resources available on the Internet that draw relationships between the resources. The basic RDF document represents the information needed by applications but does not provide instructions on how to build them, nor does it provide any rules identifying whether the current description is sufficient to meet the applications' needs.

CROSS-REFERENCE
See **World Wide Web**.

readonly

Attribute

HTML

This attribute is used to force FORM controls to be read-only. This means that you can set the focus to them, but you cannot change their values.

The syntax of this attribute is

```
readonly
```

JAVASCRIPT
```
bRead = object.readOnly
```

This property is **false** when the object is readable, and **true** when it is not.

Elements
INPUT   TEXTAREA

CROSS-REFERENCE
See **disabled**.

readOnly

Property

DHTML

This scripted property is used to identify whether a style sheet or rule is defined on a page or has been linked.

The syntax of this property is

```
[ bReadOnly = ] object.readOnly
```

Parameters
bReadOnly

This Boolean value is set to true when the style sheet or rule is a part of the current document. It is set to false when the style sheet or rule has been attached through the `<LINK>` element or an `@import` rule.

Objects
stylesheet   rule

CROSS-REFERENCE
See **<LINK>**, **@Import**, and **styleSheets**.

Read-Only Controls

Concept

CROSS-REFERENCE
See **readonly**.

readyState

Property

DHTML

This document object property is used to find out whether the current object being downloaded is initialized, currently loading, interacting with the reader, or completed with its tasks.

The syntax for using readyState is

```
state=object.readyState
```

Parameters
state

This option can contain four valid strings: uninitialized means the object has no data loaded; loading shows that it is currently loading data; interactive shows that the object can be worked with even though it has not completely loaded; and completed shows that it has completely loaded.

Example

The following example uses the readyState property to identify the current state of an image.

```
<html>
<head>
<title>readyState example</title>
</head>
<body onload="myform.myinput.value=myimg.readyState">
<p>This is the readyState of the image:<br>
</p>
<form name="myform">
  <p><input name="myinput" type="text" size="20"> </p>
</form>
<p><img name="myimg" src="myimg.gif"> </p>
</body>
</html>
```

Elements

FIELDSET   IMG   LINK   OBJECT
SCRIPT   STYLE

Objects

document

CROSS-REFERENCE
See **onreadystatechange**.

reason

Property

DHTML

This document object property is used to identify the reason for the current data transfers state.

The syntax of this command is

```
[ Reason = ] object.reason
```

Parameters
Reason

This integer variable has three options. If it is set to 0, the transfer completed successfully. A 1 indicates that the data transfer was aborted, and a 2 indicates that the transfer failed.

Objects
event

 CROSS-REFERENCE
See **events** and **object**.

recordNumber

Property

DHTML

This object property is used to retrieve a record from a bound table or from a collection of objects.

The syntax of this command is

```
[ Number = ] object.recordNumber
```

Parameters
Number

This is an integer variable specifying the record to retrieve.

q
r
s

Elements

<!— —>	A	ACRONYM	ADDRESS
APPLET	AREA	B	BGSOUND
BIG	BLOCKQUOTE	BR	BUTTON
CAPTION	CENTER	CITE	CODE
COL	COLGROUP	DD	DEL
DFN	DIR	DIV	DL
DT	EM	EMBED	FIELDSET
FONT	FORM	H1–H6	HEAD
HR	I	IFRAME	IMG
INPUT	INS	KBD	LABEL
LI	LISTING	MAP	MARQUEE
MENU	NEXTID	OBJECT	OL
OPTION	P	PLAINTEXT	PRE
Q	S	SAMP	SCRIPT
SELECT	SMALL	SPAN	STRIKE
STRONG	SUB	SUP	TABLE
TBODY	TD	TEXTAREA	TFOOT
TH	THEAD	TR	TT
U	UL	VAR	XMP

CROSS-REFERENCE
See **Collections** and **recordset**.

recordset

Property

DHTML

This document object property is used to retrieve a recordset if the object is the data provider.

The syntax of this command is

```
[ Recordset = ] object.recordset
```

Parameters

Recordset

> This is the string specifying the recordset.

Elements

> OBJECT

Objects

> event

CROSS-REFERENCE
See **recordNumber**.

Reference Pixel

Concept

CSS

In the world of rescalable screen sizes and multiple Web viewing devices, document authors have difficulty telling exactly how their pages will look on all screens for all readers. To assist in this matter, many user agents use a reference pixel, which has been defined to be the visual angle of one pixel on a 90 dpi screen viewed at the distance of the reader's arm. This provides user agents enough information to calculate roughly the angle and size of each pixel. This enables them to adjust for various printing types and mechanisms also.

For example, if we assume an average arm length of 28 inches, the visual angle of your pixels would be approximately .0227 degrees. This corresponds to each pixel being roughly .28 mm in size. On a laser printer, a single pixel is roughly .21 mm. In the same document on a 300-dpi-resolution dot-matrix printer, the pixels are roughly .25 mm.

CROSS-REFERENCE
See **Cartesian Positioning Points** and **Pixel**.

referrer

Property

DHTML

This property is used to retrieve the URL of the location that led your readers to the current document. This can be used for creating a Back or Previous button within the HTML page that is capable of moving a reader about a site, rather than through a predetermined path. This property works only when the current page has been reached through a link from another page.

The syntax of this property is

```
[sUrl = ] object.referrer
```

Parameters
sURL

This is a string containing the URL of the referring page. This string is empty if the document was reached through a secure site or from a direct URL input.

Objects
document

CROSS-REFERENCE
See **go**, **back**, and **forward**.

refresh

Method

DHTML

This method is used to refresh the contents of a table using a script.
The syntax for this command is

```
object.refresh()
```

Elements
TABLE

CROSS-REFERENCE
See **recordset**, **rows**, and **cols**.

rel

Attribute

HTML

This attribute is used to describe the relationship between the current document and the document identified by the href attribute of an object.

The syntax of this attribute is

```
rel= alternate | stylesheet | start | next | prev | contents |
index | glossary | copyright | chapter | section | subsection
| appendix | help | bookmark
```

JAVASCRIPT

object.rel [= sStylesheet]

This property is used to set the rel attribute from a script.

Values

alternate

This value identifies an alternate document to load. This is often done for document translations or different mediums.

stylesheet

This identifies the URL as an external style sheet.

start

This identifies the first document in a collection of documents. This is used for the first chapter of a book or a large segmented report.

next

This identifies the next document in the series.

prev

This identifies the previous document in the series.

contents

This refers to a table of contents for a series of documents.

index

This identifies the index for the current series of documents.

q
r
s

glossary

This identifies the glossary of terms pertaining to the current document.

copyright

This identifies the copyright for the current document.

chapter

This identifies a document that is a chapter of the collection but that is not necessarily located next to the current document.

section

This refers to a document that is serving as a section of the collection but that is not necessarily located next to the current document.

subsection

This identifies a document that serves as a subsection of the current document.

appendix

This identifies the link pointing to a document serving as an appendix for the current collection.

help

This identifies a document serving as additional help for the collection being viewed.

bookmark

This is a bookmark.

Elements
A   LINK

CROSS-REFERENCE
See **rev**.

Relative Positioning

Concept

CSS

As a document is originally being laid out, it is set up according to the normal flow of the objects and text. After this has been completed, the objects may be shifted relative to their current position. This adjustment in an object's position, known as *relative positioning,* can happen without affecting the objects that follow the repositioned object. This means that using relative positioning may cause boxes to overlap; relatively positioned boxes retain all their normal flow sizes and spacings.

You can generate a relatively positioned object by using the `position=relative` property. Its offset is controlled by the `left`, `right`, `top`, and `bottom` properties. By scripting these properties, you can create movable objects and layers on your documents. You can make images or text move, appear and disappear, or change in midstream.

CROSS-REFERENCE
See **position**, **<DIV>**, **<LAYER>**, and **<SPAN>**.

Relative Size

Concept

When a dimension is sized based upon its relationship to another similar object, this value is used with the `font-size` attribute.

If a relative-size value (`larger | smaller`) is specified, it is always in relation to the parent element's font size. So, if the parent element's font is `medium`, `larger` changes the size of the current element to `large`. In addition, when the parent element's size isn't similar to a table entry, the user agent can adjust either the table entries to match or the font to fit the table.

CROSS-REFERENCE
See **Absolute Size** and **Font-Size**.

reload

Method

DHTML

This scripting method is used to reload the current document.
The syntax for this command is

```
object.reload([ReloadSource])
```

Parameters

ReloadSource

This Boolean variable is set to true if the page should be reloaded from the server.
By default, it is set to false, which causes the page to load from the local user's cache.

Objects

location

CROSS-REFERENCE
See **history**, **go**, **back**, and **forward**.

Relative Units

Concept

Relative units are measurements that are based upon their association to something else that is either within a document or associated with a document.

- **em** This unit is defined by the height of the font's *m* character. This is a unit that is equivalent to the computed value of the font-size property of the element with which it is currently being used. If the relative value em appears in the font-size setting of an element, the size is defined in relation to that element's parent. This may also be used for vertical and horizontal measurements.

- **ex** This unit is defined by the font's *x*-height. This is the height of the font's lowercase *x*.

- **px**   A *pixel* is a viewable unit that is relative to the resolution of the viewing hardware. This could be a computer screen, a handheld PDA, or a digital display. If the pixel density of an output display is widely different from that of the computer screen, the user agent rescales the pixel values.

CROSS-REFERENCE
See **number (Value)**, **Reference Pixel**, and **<FONT>**.

remove

Method

DHTML

This method is used to remove an element from any collection within a scripted document.

The syntax of this method is

```
collection.remove(Index)
```

Parameters
Index

This required integer is used to identify the element within a collection that you wish to have removed from the collection. All collections use a zero-based index.

Collections

All	Anchors	Applets	Areas
Cells	Children	Elements	Embeds
Filters	Forms	Frames	Images
Imports	Links	Options	Plugins
Rows	Rules	Scripts	StyleSheets
tbodies			

CROSS-REFERENCE
See **Collections**, **add**, and **zIndex**.

removeAttribute

Method

DHTML

This document object method is used to remove an attribute from an element to which it has been applied. If two attributes have the same name, only the last is removed unless they use different cases and case sensitivity has been enabled.

```
bSuccess = object.removeAttribute("sName" [,iCaseSensitive ])
```

Parameters
iCaseSensitive

This optional parameter is used to define whether the script is case-sensitive (1) or not (0) in reference to the name of the attribute.

sName

This required parameter is used to identify the specific attribute that must be removed.

bSuccess

This Boolean variable is set to true if the attribute has been successfully removed and to false otherwise.

Elements

<!— —>	A	ADDRESS	APPLET
AREA	B	BASE	BASEFONT
BGSOUND	BIG	BLOCKQUOTE	BODY
BR	BUTTON	CAPTION	CENTER
CITE	CODE	COL	COLGROUP
DD	DFN	DIR	DIV
DL	DT	EM	EMBED
FIELDSET	FONT	FORM	FRAME
FRAMESET	H1–H6	HEAD	HR
HTML	I	IFRAME	IMG
INPUT	KBD	LABEL	LI
LINK	LISTING	MAP	MARQUEE
MENU	META	NEXTID	OBJECT
OL	OPTION	P	PLAINTEXT

PRE	S	SAMP	SCRIPT
SELECT	SMALL	SPAN	STRIKE
STRONG	STYLE	SUB	SUP
TABLE	TBODY	TD	TEXTAREA
TFOOT	TH	THEAD	TITLE
TR	TT	U	UL
VAR	WBR	XMP	

Objects

style

CROSS-REFERENCE
See **remove**.

Rendered Content

Concept

At times, the content of an element is drawn in accordance to a style sheet that is being applied. This is *rendered content,* essentially the content that has been designated as a replacement for contents originally designated in the source HTML document. This content includes the use of `alt` text in place of an `IMG`, designated bullets and numbers, or any content that has been designated from an outside source such as a JavaScript scriptlet.

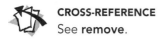

CROSS-REFERENCE
See **Inline Element**, **Block-Level Element**, **alt**, and **longdesc**.

replace

Method

DHTML

This document object method is used to replace the document currently being viewed with a document identified by location.

The syntax used to implement this method is

```
location.replace("URL")
```

Parameters
URL

> This is the address of the document to load.

Objects

> location

 CROSS-REFERENCE
See **history**, **go**, **back**, **forward**, and **refresh**.

Replaced Element

Concept

> *Replaced elements* are those for which the intrinsic dimensions of the element, designated by the start and end tags, are already known to the style sheet formatter. These elements are replaced by the contents specified by one of their attributes. For example, the IMG object is replaced by the contents of its src attribute.

Elements

> APPLET   IMG   INPUT   OBJECT
> SELECT   TEXTAREA

 CROSS-REFERENCE
See **Inline Element**, **Block-Level Element**, **alt**, and **longdesc**.

reset

Method

DHTML

> This script method is used to reset a form through a script. It performs the same function as pressing the Reset button on a form.
>
> The syntax used to implement this method is

```
object.reset()
```

Elements

> FORM

CROSS-REFERENCE
See **<INPUT>**, **<FORM>**, **type**, and **submit**.

resizeBy

Method

DHTML

This script method is used to adjust the size of the current window by the specified offsets.

The syntax used to implement this method is

```
object.resizeBy(x,y)
```

Parameters

x

This integer is used to identify the horizontal offset for the window.

y

This integer is used to identify the vertical offset for the window.

Objects

window

CROSS-REFERENCE
See **resizeTo, offsetX,** and **offsetY.**

resizeTo

Method

DHTML

This script method is used to adjust the size of the current window to the specified dimensions.

The syntax used to implement this method is

```
object.resizeTo(width,height)
```

Parameters
height

> This integer is used to identify the vertical height for the window.

width

> This integer is used to identify the horizontal width for the window.

Objects
window

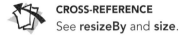

CROSS-REFERENCE
See **resizeBy** and **size**.

Resolution

Concept

The *resolution* of a computer monitor or image is the total number of pixels that can be displayed on the viewable area of a monitor. The resolution of a monitor is measured by the total number of pixels displayed horizontally and vertically. The standard ratio of a computer monitor is 4:3, which is the same as a conventional television set.

The resolution of your monitor is dependent on a couple of things. One of these is your video card (in particular, its memory and other capabilities). The other is the capability of your monitor. There really is not a general way to define what resolution and color count the average Web viewer is going to be using. Table R-1 lists standard monitor resolutions.

Table R-1 Standard Monitor Resolutions Based on Card Memory

Video Memory	Resolutions	Colors
4MB	640×480 800×600 1024×768 1152×864	256 64,000 16.7MB
4MB	1280×1024	256 64,000
4MB	1600×1200	256

Video Memory	Resolutions	Colors
8MB	640×480	256
	800×600	64,000
	1024×768	16,700,000
	1152×864	
	1280×1024	
1600×1200	1600×1200	256
		64,000

CROSS-REFERENCE
See **Pixel**.

Resource Description Format

Concept

CROSS-REFERENCE
See **RDF**.

returnValue

Property

DHTML

This property is used in a script to set or retrieve the value that is returned from the identified event.

The syntax of this property is

```
object.returnValue [ = Value ]
```

Parameters
Value

This Boolean value is set to true if the event return value has been returned and to false otherwise.

Objects
> event

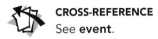

CROSS-REFERENCE
See **event**.

rev

Property

DHTML

This attribute is used to describe the relationship of the current document to the document identified by the `href` attribute of a linking object.

The syntax of this attribute is

```
rev= alternate | stylesheet | start | next | prev | contents |
index | glossary | copyright | chapter | section | subsection
| appendix | help | bookmark
```

JAVASCRIPT
> `object.rev [ = sStylesheet ]`

This property is used to set the `rev` attribute from a script.

Values
alternate

> This value identifies the current document as the alternate document to the one being loaded. This is often done for document translations or different mediums.

stylesheet

> This identifies the current document as an external style sheet for the linked document.

start

> This identifies the current document as the first document in a collection of documents. This is used for the first chapter of a book or a large segmented report.

next

> This identifies the current document as the next document in the series in relation to the one being linked to.

prev

This identifies the current document as the previous document in the series in relation to the one being linked to.

contents

This refers to the current document as a table of contents for a series of documents.

index

This identifies the current document as the index for the current series of documents.

glossary

This identifies the current document as the glossary of terms pertaining to the document identified by the link.

copyright

This identifies the current document as the copyright for the linked document.

chapter

This identifies the current document as a chapter of the collection. The current document is not necessarily located next to the linked document.

section

This refers to the current document as a section of the collection. The current document is not necessarily located next to the linked document.

subsection

This identifies the current document as a subsection of the linked document.

appendix

This identifies the current document as an appendix for the linked document collection.

help

This identifies the current document as additional help for the linked collection.

bookmark

The current document is a bookmark.

Elements

A   LINK

CROSS-REFERENCE
See **rel**.

RFC

Concept

Internet Requests For Comments (RFCs) are the written definitions of protocols and policies in effect on the Internet. The RFCs have all been created and submitted by committees of individuals that have an interest in the growth and develop of the Internet as a community for educators, students, businessmen, and consumers.

A good resource for checking out the many available RFCs is located at `http://www.cis.ohio-state.edu/hypertext/information/rfc.html`.

CROSS-REFERENCE
See **ISO**.

RGB

Concept

RGB stands for *Red-Green-Blue*, the three colors used to create all the millions of colors you see on your computer screen. When attempting to identify a specific RGB color, you use hexadecimal notation. This notation is a pound sign (#) immediately followed by either three (rgb) or six (rrggbb) hexadecimal characters. This enables you to identify white as #FFF or #FFFFFF without worrying about the color depth of the display. A light shade of green could be identified as #66ff00 or #6f0 and still be displayed properly.

RGB colors can also be displayed by using the notation rgb(x,x,x), where x represents either a percentage or a decimal integer value. In this notation, rgb(100%,100%,100%) and rgb(255,255,255) are equal to each other and also equal to #FFF and #FFFFFF.

CROSS-REFERENCE
See **Gamma Correction** and **color**.

richness

Attribute

CSS

This attribute is used with Aural Style Sheets to specify the richness or brightness of the speaking voice used by the speech synthesizer. The richer the voice, the better its carrying capacity because of its wave shape. Smooth voices don't carry because their wave forms are not as deeply pitched as rich voices.

```
richness: number | inherit
```

Values

number

This is a numerical value between 1 and 100; the default is 50. Higher values produce voices that carry better, whereas lower values produce softer, easier voices.

Elements

This attribute applies to all HTML elements.

CROSS-REFERENCE
See **pitch**, **frequency**, and **stress**.

ridge

Value

CSS

This value is used to identify the style of the border encasing an element. A border identified as a ridge appears to rise out of your documents.

CROSS-REFERENCE
See **Border**.

right

Attribute

CSS

The `right` Cascading Style Sheets attribute specifies the distance between the right edge of the object box and the right edge of the containing block.

`right: length | percentage | auto | inherit`

Values

length

This is the amount of the offset in pixels. This value is any whole signed or unsigned integer.

percentage

This is the percentage of offset from the edge of the reference side of the containing block. The percentage is based upon the visible area of the page in your user agent.

auto

This is the default setting. It automatically calculates the offset based upon the width and height of the object box.

inherit

The value for this distance is inherited from its parent elements.

Elements

This attribute is available for all HTML elements.

 CROSS-REFERENCE
See **@page**, **margin**, **padding**, and **Containing Block**.

rightMargin

Property

DHTML

This document object property is used to set or retrieve the right page margin for the entire document.

The syntax for this property is

```
object.rightMargin [ = Margin ]
```

Parameters
Margin

This string is used to specify the margin in pixels. The default value is 10. If this value is an empty string, the right margin is against the right of the viewable area of the document.

Elements
BODY

CROSS-REFERENCE
See **leftMargin** and **margin**.

Robots

Concept

A variety of search engines use *robots* — also called *spiders* and *crawlers* — to search through all the computers connected to the Internet in an attempt to index all the pages found there so they can be added to their searchable indexes.

The names of the most common search engines and their robots are listed in Table R-2.

Table R-2 Search Engine Robots Scouring the Internet

Search Engine	Robot Name	Address
Alta Vista (normal)	Scooter/2.0 scooter@pa.dec.com	`scooter3.av.pa-x.dec.com` `scooter.pa-x.dec.com`
Alta Vista (instant)	Scooter 1.0	`add-url.altavista.digital.com`
Excite	ArchitextSpider	`craw*.atext.com`
Inkotomi	Slurp/2.0	`*.inkotomi.com`
Infoseek	Infoseek Sidewinder/0.9	`*-bbn.infoseek.com`
Lycos	Lycos_Spider_(T-Rex)	`lycosidae.lycos.com`
Northern Light	Gulliver/1.2	`taz.northernlight.com`
PlanetSearch	Fido/1.0 Harvest/1.4	`fido.planetsearch.com`
Webcrawler	ArchitextSpider	`crawl*.atext.com`

q
r
s

CROSS-REFERENCE
See **<META>** and **Robots.txt**.

Robots.txt

Concept

The robots.txt file is used to identify documents, or directories, that you do not want indexed by search engine robots. The robots.txt file really has only two statements in it. The first line of each segment of the file identifies a user agent, and the second identifies a directory or file to ignore when searching. A typical robots.txt file looks like this:

```
User-agent: *
Disallow: /directoryname/
```

Depending on your goal for the robots.txt file, you can write it with a variety of segments to control how much of your server is indexed and how much is ignored.

To exclude all robots from the entire server, write

```
User-agent: *
Disallow: /
```

To allow all robots complete access, create an empty robots.txt file, or write

```
User-agent: *
Disallow:
```

To exclude all robots from part of the server, write

```
User-agent: *
Disallow: /cgi-bin/
Disallow: /membersonly/
Disallow: /~raven/
Disallow: /private/
```

To exclude a single robot, write

```
User-agent: SpiderBot
Disallow: /
```

To allow a single robot access, write

```
User-agent: WebCrawler
Disallow:
```

```
User-agent: *
Disallow: /
```

To exclude all files except one, you have two options, since there is currently no "Allow" field. The first—and possibly easiest—is to set all the files to be disallowed into a separate directory, leaving the one acceptable file in the directory above it:

```
User-agent: *
Disallow: /~raven/docs/
```

The other alternative is explicitly to disallow all disallowed pages:

```
User-agent: *
Disallow: /~raven/diary.html
Disallow: /~raven/addybook.html
Disallow: /~raven/blackbook.html
```

CROSS-REFERENCE
See **Robots** and **<META>**.

Root Node

Concept

The root node of a document is generally the HTML element in an HTML document. This is the first node of the document, based on the specifications of the Document Object Model, that serves as the foundation, or trunk, for all other objects and nodes to branch off from.

CROSS-REFERENCE
See **Document Object Model**, **Node**, and **Document Tree**.

rowIndex

Property

DHTML

This property is used to retrieve a specified object's position from within the rows collection associated with the specified table.

The syntax for this property is

```
[ Index = ] object.rowIndex
```

Parameters
Index

This is the identifying number of the object in the row.

Elements
TR

CROSS-REFERENCE
See **cellIndex**, **sectionRowIndex**, and **sourceIndex**.

rows

Collection

DHTML

This document object collection creates a list of all the TR elements (rows) found within the current TABLE object.

This collection can be used in the following ways:

```
[ collRows = ] object.rows
[ oObject = ] object.rows (vIndex [, iSubIndex] )
```

Parameters
collRows

This variable refers to the array of rows contained by the object.

oObject

This variable refers to an individual item in the array.

vIndex

This parameter is required and contains the number or string identifying the element or collection to retrieve. When a number is specified, the method returns the element in the zero-based collection at the identified position. When a string identifier is used and multiple elements with the same name or id attributes match the string, this method returns a collection of those matched elements.

iSubIndex

This optional parameter is used to identify the position of the element being retrieved when vIndex is a string. ISubIndex becomes the index of the specific item in the collection of matching elements identified by the vIndex string contents.

Elements

TABLE	TBODY	TFOOT	THEAD

CROSS-REFERENCE
See **rows** and **rowIndex**.

rows

Attribute

HTML

This attribute is used by two elements in relatively different ways. The TEXTAREA and the FRAMESET elements both use this attribute to control the visible area of rows on your screen.

For the TEXTAREA element, this attribute is used to set the visible height of the text range. Because users can enter more lines than the visible height can display, user agents should provide a means of scrolling through the contents of the control.

When this attribute is used with the TEXTAREA element, the syntax is

```
rows= number
```

When the attribute is used with the FRAMESET element, the cols attribute is used to identify the height of each row that defines the frames. This is a comma-separated list of absolute dimensions or percentages used as guides for rendering the borders of the frames.

When this attribute is used with the FRAMESET element, the syntax is

```
rows= length list
```

JAVASCRIPT

```
object.rows [ = iRows ]
```

This command is used to identify the number of rows an object should contain.

```
object.rows [ = "iHeight [ ,iHeight...]" ]
```

This command is used to identify the height of a series of rows within a frameset.

Values
length list

This is the absolute or percentage value representing the width of the columns used in the FRAMESET.

number

This is the width in pixels of the visible area of the text range.

Example

The following code shows you how to use the cols attribute to set up absolute values for the size of frames drawn by the FRAMSET element.

ON THE CD-ROM

Look for **rows.htm** on the accompanying CD-ROM.

```
<frameset cols="*" rows="75,*,75" bordercolor="#9900CC"
border="3" framespacing="3">
  <frame src="topdocument.html">
  <frame src="middledocument.html">
  <frame src="bottomdocument.html">
</frameset>
```

CROSS-REFERENCE

See **colspan**, **cols**, and **rowspan**.

rowspan

Attribute

HTML

This HTML attribute is used to specify the number of rows TD or TH cells should span.

The syntax for this attribute is

```
rowspan= number
```

JAVASCRIPT

```
object.rowSpan [ = Count ]
```

This script property is used to set or retrieve the number of rows in the TABLE that a single object should span. It can be changed only after the document has been loaded.

Values

number

This is the total number of columns that this particular cell should encompass. The default value of this attribute is 1. If this value is 0, the cell encompasses all the cells from the current cell to the end of the row.

Example

The six-by-six table created by the following sample code displays a variety of values for the rowspan attribute.

ON THE CD-ROM

Look for **rowspan.htm** on the accompanying CD-ROM.

```
<html>
<head>
<title>Rowspan and Mondrian</title>
<meta http-equiv="Generator" content="Macromedia Dreamweaver">
</head>

<body bgcolor="#FFFFFF">
<table border="1" width="75%">
  <tr>
    <td rowspan="1" bgcolor="#000000"> </td>
    <td rowspan="2" bgcolor="#3366FF"> </td>
    <td rowspan="1" bgcolor="#009900"> </td>
    <td rowspan="2" bgcolor="#999966"> </td>
    <td rowspan="1" bgcolor="#FF0066"> </td>
    <td rowspan="2" bgcolor="#99FF00"> </td>
  </tr>
  <tr>
    <td bgcolor="#33FF00"> </td>
    <td bgcolor="#FF00FF"> </td>
    <td bgcolor="#CC99CC"> </td>
  </tr>
  <tr>
    <td rowspan="2" colspan="2" bgcolor="#00FFFF"> </td>
    <td rowspan="2" bgcolor="#0000FF"> </td>
    <td colspan="2" bgcolor="#FFFF00"> </td>
    <td bgcolor="#003333"> </td>
  </tr>
  <tr>
    <td rowspan="2" bgcolor="#CCCCCC"> </td>
    <td bgcolor="#00CCFF"> </td>
    <td rowspan="2" bgcolor="#CC0033"> </td>
  </tr>
  <tr>
    <td rowspan="2" bgcolor="#FF9900"> </td>
    <td bgcolor="#FFCC99"> </td>
    <td rowspan="2" bgcolor="#996600"> </td>
    <td rowspan="2" bgcolor="#FFCCCC"> </td>
  </tr>
```

```
    <tr>
      <td bgcolor="#9966FF"> </td>
      <td bgcolor="#9933CC"> </td>
      <td bgcolor="#3399CC"> </td>
    </tr>
  </table>
  </body>
  </html>
```

Elements
  TD   TH

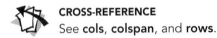

CROSS-REFERENCE
See **cols**, **colspan**, and **rows**.

Rule Set

Concept

A *rule set* — also referred to as a *rule* — is a two-part statement consisting of a selector followed by a declaration block. The selector is the name of the object, or the identifier of an object, for which you are setting the rules. Selectors can list multiple objects or identifiers and can contain punctuation that aids in the identification of the objects or items being identified. A declaration block starts with an opening curly brace ({) and ends with a closing curly brace (}). This block contains all the declarations that are being set for the selector. Each declaration must be separated by a semicolon.

Every selector must be matched with a declaration block. If the selector is invalid, the declaration block is also ignored. Any characters that are invalid in a selector, such as ampersands, cause the entire rule set to be ignored.

Example
The following statements are rule sets. In the first rule set, the selector is H1 and the descriptor sets the `font-color` to blue, the `padding` to 1 cm, and the `font-face` to Arial.

```
H1 { font-color: blue;
    padding: 1cm;
    font-face: Arial;}
```

This second rule set uses the selector to `IMG`, `TABLE`, and `#layer1`, which making the contents of the descriptor valid for all `IMG` and `TABLE` objects and for the object named `#layer1`.

```
IMG, TABLE, #layer1 { border-style: ridge;
                      border-color: green;
                      border-width: 3px }
```

CROSS-REFERENCE
See **Block**, **@rules**, **Declaration**, and **Style Sheet**.

rules

Attribute

HTML

This attribute is used with the `frame` and `border` attributes to set up how the vertical and horizontal rules between the cells within a table appear.

```
rules = none | groups | rows | cols | all
```

JAVASCRIPT
```
object.rules [=rule]
```

Values

none

No rules are displayed.

groups

Rules appear between row groups such as `<THEAD>`, `<TFOOT>`, and `<TBODY>` and column groups such as `<COL>` and `<COLGROUP>` only.

rows

Rules appear only between rows.

cols

Rules appear only between columns.

all

Rules appear between all rows and columns. This is the default value.

Example

All values of border imply `rules="all"` as shown in figure R-1.

```
<TABLE border="1" rules="all">
```

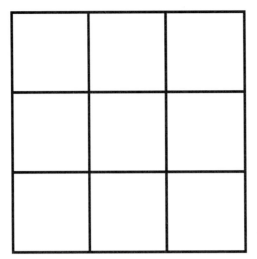

Figure R-1 The default table shows all rules and frames
when the border attribute is set.

If you wish to create a different-looking table, you need to set your frame
and rules attributes to different values. The following two code examples and
Figures R-2 and R-3 show you how you can change the rules on a table to
create a specific effect.

```
<TABLE border="2" frame="vsides" rules="cols">
```

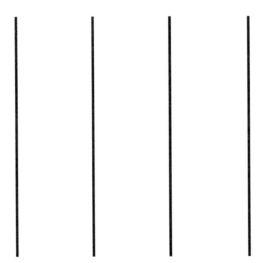

Figure R-2 Rules=cols shows only the vertical
lines between the columns of data.

```
<TABLE border="2" frame="hsides" rules="rows">
```

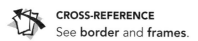

Figure R-3 Rules=rows shows only the horizontal lines between the rows of data.

Elements
> TABLE

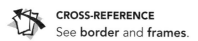

CROSS-REFERENCE
See **border** and **frames**.

q
r
s

S

<S>

Element

HTML

Start Tag: Required
End Tag: Required

This element is used to render text that is marked with a strike through character. This element has been deprecated in HTML 4.0.

Attributes
class

```
class="cdata-list"
```

This attribute is used to assign a class name to an element. User agents employ classes to group specific types of information for later use.

dir

```
dir = LTR | RTL
```

This attribute defines the direction of the text flow in a document so a user agent can display it correctly.

id

```
id="name"
```

This attribute is used to assign a name to an element.

lang

```
lang="language code"
```

This attribute specifies the language in which an element and its values should be rendered.

onclick

> onclick=*script*

This attribute takes effect when a user clicks the button on a pointing device with the pointer over an element.

ondblclick

> ondblclick=*script*

This attribute takes effect when the button on a pointing device is double-clicked with the pointer over an element.

onkeydown

> onkeydown=*script*

This attribute takes effect when a key is pressed while the pointer is over an element.

onkeypress

> onkeypress=*script*

This attribute takes effect when a key is pressed and released with the pointer over an element.

onkeyup

> onkeyup=*script*

This attribute takes effect when a key is released with the pointer over an element.

onmousedown

> onmousedown=*script*

This attribute takes effect when the button on a pointing device is pressed with the pointer over an element.

onmousemove

> onmousemove=*script*

This attribute is activated when the mouse is moved while the pointer is over an element.

onmouseout

> onmouseout=*script*

This attributed is activated when the mouse pointer is moved away from an element.

onmouseover

```
onmouseover=script
```

This attribute is activated when the mouse pointer is moved over an element.

onmouseup

```
onmouseup=script
```

This attribute takes effect when the button on a pointing device is released with the pointer over an element.

style

```
style=style descriptors
```

This attribute is used to apply specific style-sheet information to one particular element.

title

```
title=text
```

This attribute serves to provide annotation information for the element.

Example

The following example code uses the S attribute to strike through missing children's names on an attendance sheet for an individual teacher.

ON THE CD-ROM

Look for **s.htm** on the accompanying CD-ROM.

```
<html>
<head>
<title>Checking Attendance</title>
<meta http-equiv="Generator" content="Macromedia Dreamweaver">
</head>

<body bgcolor="#FFFFFF">
<h1>Mr. Meyer's 4th Grade Class</h1>
<h3>Attendance sheet for 10/13/99</h3>
<p><s>Stanley Coggins</s><br>
  George Gabrial<br>
  <s>Harold Harley</s><br>
  Wilma Hawkins<br>
  <s>Lois Frei</s><br>
  <s>Wylie French</s><br>
  <s>Mike Fuchs</s><br>
  <s>Ted Gates</s><br>
```

r
s
t

```
        Clifford Towne<br>
        Rocky VanArsdale<br>
        Bob VanCleave<br>
        Don Nuss<br>
        Debra O'Kelley<br>
        Earl Purvis<br>
        <s>Reed Walters</s><br>
        Debbie Reser</p>
<i>***Children with marked out names were not in attendance at
roll call. </i>
</body>
</html>
```

CROSS-REFERENCE
See **<STRIKE>**.

<SAMP>

Element

HTML

Start Tag: Required
End Tag: Required

This element is used to render text in a monospaced font and is meant to represent sample output from programs and scripts.

Attributes
class

```
class="cdata-list"
```

This attribute is used to assign a class name to an element. User agents employ classes to group specific types of information for later use.

dir

```
dir = LTR | RTL
```

This attribute defines the direction of the text flow in a document so a user agent can display it correctly.

id

```
id="name"
```

This attribute is used to assign a name to an element.

lang

```
lang="language code"
```

This attribute specifies the language in which an element and its values should be rendered.

onclick

```
onclick=script
```

This attribute takes effect when a user clicks the button on a pointing device with the pointer over an element.

ondblclick

```
ondblclick=script
```

This attribute takes effect when the button on a pointing device is double-clicked with the pointer over an element.

onkeydown

```
onkeydown=script
```

This attribute takes effect when a key is pressed while the pointer is over an element.

onkeypress

```
onkeypress=script
```

This attribute takes effect when a key is pressed and released with the pointer over an element.

onkeyup

```
onkeyup=script
```

This attribute takes effect when a key is released with the pointer over an element.

onmousedown

```
onmousedown=script
```

This attribute takes effect when the button on a pointing device is pressed with the pointer over an element.

r
s
t

onmousemove

```
onmousemove=script
```

This attribute is activated when the mouse is moved while the pointer is over an element.

onmouseout

```
onmouseout=script
```

This attribute is activated when the mouse pointer is moved away from an element.

onmouseover

```
onmouseover=script
```

This attribute is activated when the mouse pointer is moved over an element.

onmouseup

```
onmouseup=script
```

This attribute takes effect when the button on a pointing device is released with the pointer over an element.

style

```
style=style descriptors
```

This attribute is used to apply specific style-sheet information to one particular element.

title

```
title=text
```

This attribute serves to provide annotation information for the element.

Example
The following example uses the CODE and SAMP objects to show the code and the results of a small "hello world" program.

ON THE CD-ROM
Look for **samp.htm** on the accompanying CD-ROM.

```
<html>
<head>
<title>Hello World - NOT!!!</title>
<meta http-equiv="Content-Type" content="text/html;
charset=iso-8859-1">
</head>
```

```
<body bgcolor="#FFFFFF">
<h1><font color="#FF0000">HELLO WORLD - NOT!!</font></h1>
<p><font color="#0000FF">Create a file named
MyHelloWorldApp.java with the following
  Java code:</font></p>
<p><code> /** * The MyHelloWorldApp class implements an
application <br>
   * simply displays a message to the standard
output.<br>
   */</code></p>
<p><code> class HelloWorldApp { <br>
       public static void main(String[] args) {
<br>
             
System.out.println("Hello World! I'm
  out to dominate you!"); <br>
              //Display the
string. <br>
         } <br>
  } </code></p>
<p> <font color="#0000FF">You will see the string:</font></p>
<p><samp>Hello World! I'm out to dominate you!</samp></p>
<p><font color="#0000FF">Displayed for your
pleasure.</font></p>
</body>
</html>
```

CROSS-REFERENCE
See **<CODE>** and **<XMP>**.

<SCHEDULE>

Element

CDF

Start Tag: Required
End Tag: Required

This element is used to schedule the specific interval of time during which the channel will be shared with its subscribers.

Example

This example channel—located at `http://mychannels.com/channels.cdf`—must be delivered between midnight and noon on the first of each month.

```
<CHANNEL HREF="http://mychannels.com/channels.cdf">
    <SCHEDULE>
        <INTERVALTIME Day=30 />
        <EARLIESTTIME Hour=0 />
        <LATESTTIME Hour=12 />
    </SCHEDULE>
</CHANNEL>
```

Child Elements

EarliestTime	IntervalTime	LatestTime
StartDate	EndDate	

CROSS-REFERENCE
See **<CHANNEL>** and **<USERSCHEDULE>**.

scheme

Attribute

HTML

This attribute identifies a specific set of rules to use when interpreting the value of an object.

The syntax of this attribute is

```
scheme= cdata
```

Values

cdata

This is strict character data used to identify a specific string.

Elements

META

CROSS-REFERENCE
See **profile**.

scope

Attribute

HTML

This attribute is used to specify the specific set, or range of data cells for which the current headers cell is providing information. You can use this attribute in place of the `headers` attribute on simple tables.

The syntax of this attribute is

```
scope= col | colgroup | row | rowgroup
```

Values

col

The current cell is the heading for all the cells in its column.

colgroup

The header cell is the heading for all of the cells in its column group.

row

The current cell is the heading for all the cells in its row.

rowgroup

The header cell is the heading for all of the cells in its row group.

Example

The following HTML code uses the scope attribute to control the area covered by the existing headers.

ON THE CD-ROM

Look for **scope.htm** on the accompanying CD-ROM.

```
<table border="1" width="75%">
  <tr>
    <th> </th>
    <th scope= col>1st Half</th>
    <th scope= col>2nd Half</th>
  </tr>
  <tr>
    <th scope= row>Income</th>
    <td>$10K</td>
    <td>$15K</td>
  </tr>
  <tr>
```

```
        <th scope= row>Expenses</th>
        <td>$8K</td>
        <td>$8K</td>
      </tr>
    </table>
```

Elements
      TD   TH

CROSS-REFERENCE
See **headers**, **colspan**, **<COLGROUP>**, and **rowspan**.

screenX

Property

DHTML

This property is used to retrieve the horizontal position of the mouse in pixels. You can use the screenX and the screenY properties to find the current location of the reader's pointer.

The syntax for this property is

```
[ Size = ] object.screenX
```

Parameters
Size

This integer receives the position of the mouse, in pixels.

Example
This script uses the screenX and the screenY properties to track the current position of the mouse, and display it in text fields.

```
<html>
<head>
  <title>screenX and screenY Example</title>
</head>
<body
onmousemove="document.forms[0].textx.value=event.screenX;docum
ent.forms[0].texty.value=event.screenY">
```

```
<form name="myform">
  <p>Check your position.</p>
  <p>X position: <input type="text" name="textx" size="20">
<br>
  Y position: <input type="text" name="texty" size="20"> </p>
</form>
</body>
</html>
```

Objects

event

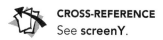

CROSS-REFERENCE
See **screenY**.

screenY

Property

DHTML

This property is used to retrieve the vertical position of the mouse in pixels. You can use the screenX and the screenY properties to find the current position of the reader's pointer.

The syntax for this property is

```
[ Size = ] object.screenY
```

Parameters
Size

This integer receives the position of the mouse in pixels.

Objects

Event

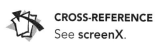

CROSS-REFERENCE
See **screenX**.

<SCRIPT>

Element

HTML

Start Tag: Required
End Tag: Required

This element is used to insert a script into a document. You can have as many SCRIPT elements appearing within the HEAD or BODY of an HTML document as you wish. You have the option of defining the script within the contents of the SCRIPT element, or in an external file linked to the SCRIPT object through the src attribute. If the src attribute is not set, the user agent will automatically interpret the contents of the element as the script.

NOTE
A user agent must have a compatible script engine to read the scripts on your pages. The Internet Information Server, by Microsoft, allows you to specify a server-side script by adding the "runat=server" attribute to this element's start tag.

Attributes

charset

```
charset=character-encoding
```

This HTML attribute is used to identify the character set that will be used by the resource pointed to in the link or in the script.

defer

```
defer
```

The presence of this attribute indicates to the user agent that the script will not generate any document content, and the page can continue to load freely.

language

```
language=cdata
```

This deprecated attribute can be used to identify the name of the scripting language in which the script has been written.

src

```
src=url
```

This attribute identifies the location of an external script.

type

```
type=content-type
```

This attribute identifies the MIME content type of the object. The scripting language can be specified as part of the content type — for example, "text/JavaScript."

Example

The following script example moves an animated GIF in a circle around a poem in the center. A wav is played at the beginning of the loop, which is then followed by a couple of popup dialog boxes.

ON THE CD-ROM

Look for **script.htm** on the accompanying CD-ROM.

```html
<html>
<head>
<title>Friends</title>
<meta http-equiv="Generator" content="Macromedia Dreamweaver">

  <script language="JavaScript">
<!--
function MM_initTimelines() {
    //MM_initTimelines() Copyright 1997 Macromedia, Inc. All
    rights reserved.
    var ns = navigator.appName == "Netscape";
    document.MM_Time = new Array(1);
    document.MM_Time[0] = new Array(4);
    document.MM_Time["Timeline1"] = document.MM_Time[0];
    document.MM_Time[0].MM_Name = "Timeline1";
    document.MM_Time[0].fps = 15;
    document.MM_Time[0][0] = new String("sprite");
    document.MM_Time[0][0].slot = 1;
    if (ns)
        document.MM_Time[0][0].obj = document.Layer1;
    else
        document.MM_Time[0][0].obj = document.all ? document.
        all["Layer1"] : null;
    document.MM_Time[0][0].keyFrames = new Array(1, 15, 30,
    45, 60);
    document.MM_Time[0][0].values = new Array(2);
    document.MM_Time[0][0].values[0] = new Array(8,31,54,77,
    100,123,146,169,191,214,237,259,281,302,321,333,342,348,35
    3,356,358,359,359,358,356,353,348,342,333,319,299,278,256,
    234,211,188,166,143,121,100,79,59,40,22,6,-5,-11,-15,-16,-
    15,-14,-12,-10,-7,-4,0,3,6,9,11);
    document.MM_Time[0][0].values[0].prop = "left";
```

```
            document.MM_Time[0][0].values[1] = new Array(23,22,19,17,
        14,11,9,7,6,5,5,6,9,14,24,38,55,72,90,108,126,143,161,179,
        197,215,233,250,267,280,288,292,293,292,291,288,285,280,27
        5,270,264,257,250,241,230,217,202,187,172,157,143,129,116,
        103,89,76,63,50,36,23);
            document.MM_Time[0][0].values[1].prop = "top";
            if (!ns) {
                document.MM_Time[0][0].values[0].prop2 = "style";
                document.MM_Time[0][0].values[1].prop2 = "style";
            }
            document.MM_Time[0][1] = new String("behavior");
            document.MM_Time[0][1].frame = 5;
            document.MM_Time[0][1].value = "MM_controlSound('play',
        'document.MM_controlSound1')";
            document.MM_Time[0][2] = new String("behavior");
            document.MM_Time[0][2].frame = 20;
            document.MM_Time[0][2].value = "MM_popupMsg('Sooo
        Romantic.. Thought you would love this.')";
            document.MM_Time[0][3] = new String("behavior");
            document.MM_Time[0][3].frame = 40;
            document.MM_Time[0][3].value = "MM_popupMsg('Dont you
        think this is cool!')";
            document.MM_Time[0].lastFrame = 60;
            for (i=0; i<document.MM_Time.length; i++) {
                document.MM_Time[i].ID = null;
                document.MM_Time[i].curFrame = 0;
                document.MM_Time[i].delay = 1000/document.MM_Time[i].
                fps;
            }
        }
        //-->
        </script>
          <script language="JavaScript">
        <!-
        function MM_popupMsg(theMsg) { //v1.2
          alert(theMsg);
        }
        //-->
        </script>
          <script language="JavaScript">
        <!-
        function MM_controlSound(sndAction,sndObj) { //v1.2
          if (eval(sndObj) != null) {
            if (navigator.appName=='Netscape') eval(sndObj+((sndAction
            ='stop')?'.stop()':'.play(false)'));
```

```
      else if (eval(sndObj+".FileName")) eval(sndObj+((sndAction
      =='stop')?'.stop()':'.run()'));
  }
}
//-->
</script>
  <script language="JavaScript">
<!-
function MM_timelinePlay(tmLnName, myID) { //v1.2
  //Copyright 1997 Macromedia, Inc. All rights reserved.
  var
i,j,tmLn,props,keyFrm,sprite,numKeyFr,firstKeyFr,propNum,theOb
j,firstTime=false;
  if (document.MM_Time == null) MM_initTimelines(); //if
  *very* 1st time
  tmLn = document.MM_Time[tmLnName];
  if (myID == null) { myID = ++tmLn.ID; firstTime=true;}//if
  new call, incr ID
  if (myID == tmLn.ID) { //if Im newest
    setTimeout('MM_timelinePlay("'+tmLnName+'",'+myID+')',
    tmLn.delay);
    fNew = ++tmLn.curFrame;
    for (i=0; i<tmLn.length; i++) {
      sprite = tmLn[i];
      if (sprite.charAt(0) == 's') {
        if (sprite.obj) {
          numKeyFr = sprite.keyFrames.length; firstKeyFr =
          sprite.keyFrames[0];
          if (fNew >= firstKeyFr && fNew <=
          sprite.keyFrames[numKeyFr-1]) {//in range
            keyFrm=1;
            for (j=0; j<sprite.values.length; j++) {
              props = sprite.values[j];
              if (numKeyFr != props.length) {
                if (props.prop2 == null) sprite.obj[props.
                prop] = props[fNew-firstKeyFr];
                else        sprite.obj[props.prop2][props.
                prop] = props[fNew-firstKeyFr];
              } else {
                while (keyFrm<numKeyFr && fNew>=sprite.
                keyFrames[keyFrm]) keyFrm++;
                if (firstTime || fNew==sprite.keyFrames
                [keyFrm-1]) {
```

```
                              if (props.prop2 == null) sprite.obj[props.
                              prop] = props[keyFrm-1];
                              else        sprite.obj[props.prop2]
                              [props.prop] = props[keyFrm-1];
                  } } } } }
              } else if (sprite.charAt(0)=='b' && fNew == sprite.
              frame) eval(sprite.value);
              if (fNew > tmLn.lastFrame) tmLn.ID = 0;
        } }
    }
    //-->
    </script>
    </head>

    <body bgcolor="#FFFFFF" onLoad="MM_timelinePlay('Timeline1')">
    <!- #BeginBehavior MM_controlSound1 -->
    <embed name='MM_controlSound1' src='Titanic.wav'
    loop=false autostart=false mastersound hidden=true width=0
    height=0></embed>
    <!- #EndBehavior MM_controlSound1 -->
    <div id="Layer1" style="position:absolute; left:8px; top:23px;
    width:104px; height:102px; z-index:1"><img src="kids.gif"
    width="150" height="150" name="Image1"></div>
    <div id="Layer2" style="position:absolute; left:159px;
    top:175px; width:160px; height:103px; z-index:2">
      <div align="center">Friends are like knots. <br>
        Sometimes they pull us. <br>
        Sometimes they push us. <br>
        But they are always together.</div>
    </div>
    </body>
    </html>
```

CROSS-REFERENCE
See **scripting**, **scripts**, **JavaScript**, **JScript**, **ECMAScript**, and **VBScript**.

Scripting

Concept

All scripting languages rely on their environments—your HTML document and Web browser, for example—to provide them with external data needed to process information. Most scripting languages were designed for performing computations and manipulating objects within their environments. Both programmers and non-programmers use scripting languages. This has a tendency to make them less powerful than their full programming language brothers, but still perfectly capable of functioning within their environment.

Scripting code is contained within the HTML documents processed by the Web browser. Due to the amount of document manipulation done by a Web browser, your script is able to interact with your browser each time a document is opened or closed; each time an item receives focus, or the focus is changed; each time a form is submitted, a mouse is moved, or an error is encountered. Since the script is responsive to all user interactions, there is no need to have a main program.

The Web server provides and additional environment for working with information requests, clients, and files. The servers provide you with a mechanism for sharing data. The combination of client-side and server-side scripting allows you to distribute the workload, and provide a completely customized interface for your Web applications.

CROSS-REFERENCE

See <SCRIPT>, **JavaScript**, **ECMAScript**, **VBScript**, **script**, and **scriptlets**.

scripts

Collection

DHTML

This collection of document objects creates a list of all the SCRIPT elements found within the current document.

This collection can be used in the following ways:

```
[ collScripts = ] object.scripts
[ oObject = ] object.scripts (vIndex [, iSubIndex] )
```

Parameters

collScripts

This variable refers to the array of elements contained by the object.

oObject

This variable refers to an individual item in the array.

vIndex

This parameter is required, and contains the number or string identifying the element or collection to retrieve. When a number is specified, the method returns the element in the zero-based collection at the identified position. When a string identifier is used, and there are multiple elements with the same name or id attributes matching the string, this method returns a collection of those matched elements.

iSubIndex

This optional parameter is used to identify the position of the element being retrieved, when vIndex is a string. ISubIndex becomes the index of the specific item in the collection of matching elements identified by the vIndex string contents.

Examples

The following example code uses the scripts collection to identify a specific script entry, and write it to the document.

```
<html>
<head>
<title>The scripts collections</title>
</head>
<body onload="alert(document.scripts[0].name)">
<script name="Script one">
</script>
<script name="Script two">
document.write(document.scripts[1].name)
</script>
</body>
</html>
```

Objects

document

CROSS-REFERENCE
See **script**, **<SCRIPT>**, **JScript**, **VBScript**, **JavaScript**, and **ECMAScript**.

scroll

Method

DHTML

This object method is used to force the window to scroll until a set of specified x and y offset values are visible in the upper left hand corner.

The syntax of this method is

```
object.scroll (x,y)
```

Parameters

x

This required integer represents the horizontal offset of the window in pixels.

y

This required integer represents the vertical offset of the window in pixels.

Objects

window

CROSS-REFERENCE

See **scrollTo, scroll, scrollBy, scrollIntoView, scrollAmount, scrollDelay, scrollHeight, scrolling, scrollLeft, scrollTop,** and **scrollWidth.**

scroll

Property

DHTML

This property is used to turn on or off the scroll bars associated with the user windows.

The syntax for this property is

```
object.scroll [ = yes | no]
```

Parameters

Yes

This allows scroll bars to be provided for the document if needed. This is the default value.

No

This prohibits any scrolling mechanisms from displaying.

Examples

The following example code uses the scroll property to control whether there are scrolling mechanisms available with the document.

```
<html>
<head>
  <title>Scroll</title>
</head>

<body>
<p onmouseover="document.body.scroll='no'">Mouse here for
scroll off</p>
<p onmouseover="document.body.scroll='yes'">Mouse here for
scroll on</p>
</body>
</html>
```

Elements
> BODY

CROSS-REFERENCE
See **scrollTo**, **scroll**, **scrollBy**, **scrollIntoView**, **scrollAmount**, **scrollDelay**, **scrollHeight**, **scrolling**, **scrollLeft**, **scrollTop**, and **scrollWidth**.

scrollAmount

Property

DHTML

This property is used to set the number of pixels the MARQUEE will move between times it is redrawn on a user's screen.

The syntax for this property is

```
object.scrollAmount [ = Amount ]
```

Parameters
Amount

This integer represents the number of pixels the object has moved.

Elements
MARQUEE

CROSS-REFERENCE
See **scrollTo**, **scroll**, **scrollBy**, **scrollIntoView**, **scrollDelay**, **scrollHeight**, **scrolling**, **scrollLeft**, **scrollTop**, and **scrollWidth**.

scrollBy

Method

DHTML

This object method is used to force the window to scroll in reference to the current visual area by the offset values supplied.

The syntax of this method is

```
object.scrollBy (x,y)
```

Parameters
x

This required integer represents the horizontal offset of the window in pixels. Positive values scroll the window to the left, and negative values scroll the window to the right.

y

This required integer represents the vertical offset of the window in pixels. Positive values scroll the window down, and negative values scroll the window up.

Example
The following example script scrolls a document using buttons on your screen.

```
<html>
<head>
  <title>scrollBy example</title>
</head>

<body>
<script>
  var myloop = 1;
  while (myloop <=15) {
```

```
        document.writeln(myloop + "<BR>");
        myloop++;
    }
</script>
<button onclick="window.scrollBy(10,10)">
<p>Click for up</button>   
<button onclick="window.scrollBy(-10,-10)">Click for down
</button><br>
<script>
  var myloop = 1;
  while (myloop <=150) {
    document.writeln(myloop + "<br>");
    myloop++;
  }
</script>
</p>
</body>
</html>
```

Objects
window

CROSS-REFERENCE
See **scrollTo**, **scroll**, **scrollIntoView**, **scrollAmount**, **scrollDelay**, **scrollHeight**, **scrolling**, **scrollLeft**, **scrollTop**, and **scrollWidth**.

scrollDelay

Property

DHTML

This property is used to set the speed of the MARQUEE movement.
The syntax for this property is

```
object.scrollDelay [ = Speed ]
```

Parameters
Speed

This integer represents the speed of the object in milliseconds.

Elements
MARQUEE

CROSS-REFERENCE
See **scrollTo**, **scroll**, **scrollBy**, **scrollIntoView**, **scrollAmount**, **scrollHeight**, **scrolling**, **scrollLeft**, **scrollTop**, and **scrollWidth**.

scrollHeight

Property

DHTML

This property retrieves the height of the objects scrolling space in pixels. The syntax for using this property is

```
[ Height = ] object.scrollHeight
```

Parameters
Height

This integer holds the number of pixels between the top and bottom edge of an object's content.

Elements

A	ADDRESS	APPLET	B
BIG	BLOCKQUOTE	BODY	BUTTON
CAPTION	CENTER	CITE	CODE
COL	COLGROUP	DD	DFN
DIR	DIV	DL	DT
EM	EMBED	FIELDSET	FORM
HEAD	H1–H6	HTML	I
IMG	INPUT	ISINDEX	KBD
LABEL	LEGEND	LI	
MARQUEE	MENU	META	OBJECT
OL	OPTION	P	PLAINTEXT
PRE	S	SAMP	SCRIPT
SELECT	SMALL	SPAN	STRIKE
STRONG	STYLE	SUB	SUP
TABLE	TBODY	TD	TEXTAREA
TFOOT	TH	THEAD	TR
TT	U	UL	VAR
XMP			

CROSS-REFERENCE
See **scrollTo**, **scroll**, **scrollBy**, **scrollIntoView**, **scrollAmount**, **scrollDelay**, **scrolling**, **scrollLeft**, **scrollTop**, and **scrollWidth**.

scrolling

Attribute

HTML

This attribute identifies how the contents of a FRAME window will scroll. The syntax of this attribute is

```
scrolling = auto | yes | no
```

JAVASCRIPT

```
object.scrolling [ = sScrolling ]
```

This property is used to retrieve information on whether scrolling is allowed.

Values
auto

If the contents of the frame are larger than its visible area, scroll bar will be provided.

no

No matter the size of the FRAME contents, the window will not scroll.

yes

A scrolling mechanism is always provided for the frame.

Example
The following example code uses the scrolling attribute to control the readers ability to navigate through the non-visible information contained within two frames.

ON THE CD-ROM
Look for **scrolling.htm** on the accompanying CD-ROM.

```
<frameset rows="194,195" bordercolor="#3333FF" border="2"
framespacing="2" frameborder="YES">
  <frame src="headerinfo.htm" scrolling=no>
  <frame src="bodyinfo.htm" scrolling=yes>
</frameset>
```

Elements
    FRAME   IFRAME

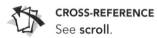

CROSS-REFERENCE
See **scroll**.

scrollIntoView

Method

DHTML

This document object method is used to scroll a specific object into the viewable area of your user agent.

The syntax used to implement this method is

```
object.scrollIntoView( [AlignToTop] )
```

Parameters
AlignToTop

This optional Boolean value is used to specify whether the object will be placed at the top of the window, or the bottom. If set to **true**, the top of the object will be aligned to the top of the window. If set to **false**, the bottom of the object will be aligned to the bottom of the window.

Elements

<!— —>	A	ADDRESS	APPLET
AREA	B	BIG	BLOCKQUOTE
BR	BUTTON	CAPTION	CENTER
CITE	CODE	COL	COLGROUP
DD	DFN	DIR	DIV
DL	DT	EM	EMBED
FIELDSET	FONT	FORM	H1–H6
HR		I	IFRAME
IMG	INPUT	KBD	LABEL
LEGEND	LI		MAP
MARQUEE	MENU	OBJECT	OL
P	PLAINTEXT	PRE	S
SAMP	SELECT	SMALL	SPAN
STRIKE	STRONG	SUB	SUP

TABLE	TBODY	TD	TEXTAREA
TFOOT	TH	THEAD	TR
TT	U	UL	VAR
WBR	XMP		

Objects

TextRange

CROSS-REFERENCE

See **scrollTo**, **scroll**, **scrollBy**, **scrollAmount**, **scrollDelay**, **scrollHeight**, **scrolling**, **scrollLeft**, **scrollTop**, and **scrollWidth**.

scrollLeft

Property

DHTML

This property is used to identify the space between the left edge of the selected object, and the leftmost corner of the visible area of the document content.

The syntax for this property is

```
object.scrollLeft [ = Distance ]
```

Parameters

Distance

This integer represents the distance in pixels between the object and the visible area of the content.

Elements

A	ADDRESS	APPLET	B
BIG	BLOCKQUOTE	BODY	BUTTON
CAPTION	CENTER	CITE	CODE
COL	COLGROUP	DD	DFN
DIR	DIV	DL	DT
EM	EMBED	FIELDSET	FORM
HEAD	H1–H6	HTML	I
IMG	INPUT	ISINDEX	KBD
LABEL	LEGEND	LI	
MARQUEE	MENU	META	OBJECT

OL	OPTION	P	PLAINTEXT
PRE	S	SAMP	SCRIPT
SELECT	SMALL	SPAN	STRIKE
STRONG	STYLE	SUB	SUP
TABLE	TBODY	TD	TEXTAREA
TFOOT	TH	THEAD	TR
TT	U	UL	VAR
XMP			

CROSS-REFERENCE

See **scrollTo**, **scroll**, **scrollBy**, **scrollIntoView**, **scrollAmount**, **scrollDelay**, **scrollHeight**, **scrolling**, **scrollTop**, and **scrollWidth**.

scrollTo

Method

DHTML

This object method is used to force the window to scroll until a set of specified *x* and *y* offset values are visible in the upper left-hand corner.

The syntax of this method is

```
object.scrollTo(x,y)
```

Parameters

x

This required integer represents the horizontal offset of the window in pixels.

y

This required integer represents the vertical offset of the window in pixels.

Objects

window

CROSS-REFERENCE

See **scroll**, **scrollBy**, **scrollIntoView**, **scrollAmount**, **scrollDelay**, **scrollHeight**, **scrolling**, **scrollLeft**, **scrollTop**, and **scrollWidth**.

scrollTop

Property

DHTML

This property is used to identify the space between the top edge of the selected object, and the topmost corner of the visible area of the document content.

The syntax for this property is

```
object.scrollTop [ = Distance ]
```

Parameters

Distance

This integer represents the distance in pixels between the object and the visible area of the content.

Elements

A	ADDRESS	APPLET	B
BIG	BLOCKQUOTE	BODY	BUTTON
CAPTION	CENTER	CITE	CODE
COL	COLGROUP	DD	DFN
DIR	DIV	DL	DT
EM	EMBED	FIELDSET	FORM
HEAD	H1–H6	HTML	I
IMG	INPUT	ISINDEX	KBD
LABEL	LEGEND	LI	
MARQUEE	MENU	META	OBJECT
OL	OPTION	P	PLAINTEXT
PRE	S	SAMP	SCRIPT
SELECT	SMALL	SPAN	STRIKE
STRONG	STYLE	SUB	SUP
TABLE	TBODY	TD	TEXTAREA
TFOOT	TH	THEAD	TR
TT	U	UL	VAR
XMP			

CROSS-REFERENCE

See **scrollTo**, **scroll**, **scrollBy**, **scrollIntoView**, **scrollAmount**, **scrollDelay**, **scrollHeight**, **scrolling**, **scrollLeft**, and **scrollWidth**.

scrollwidth

Property

DHTML

This property retrieves the width of the objects scrolling space in pixels. The syntax for using this property is

```
[ Width = ] object.scrollWidth
```

Parameters
Width

This integer holds the number of pixels between the left and right edge of an object's content.

Elements

A	ADDRESS	APPLET	B
BIG	BLOCKQUOTE	BODY	BUTTON
CAPTION	CENTER	CITE	CODE
COL	COLGROUP	DD	DFN
DIR	DIV	DL	DT
EM	EMBED	FIELDSET	FORM
HEAD	H1–H6	HTML	I
IMG	INPUT	ISINDEX	KBD
LABEL	LEGEND	LI	
MARQUEE	MENU	META	OBJECT
OL	OPTION	P	PLAINTEXT
PRE	S	SAMP	SCRIPT
SELECT	SMALL	SPAN	STRIKE
STRONG	STYLE	SUB	SUP
TABLE	TBODY	TD	TEXTAREA
TFOOT	TH	THEAD	TR
TT	U	UL	VAR
XMP			

CROSS-REFERENCE
See **scrollTo**, **scroll**, **scrollBy**, **scrollIntoView**, **scrollAmount**, **scrollDelay**, **scrollHeight**, **scrolling**, **scrollLeft**, and **scrollTop**.

Search

Property

DHTML

This property is used to select the portion of the `href` attribute that from the '?' to the end of the string.

The syntax for using this property is

```
object.search [ = sSearch ]
```

Parameters

sSearch

This string contains the portion of the address that follows the '?' within the contents of the `href` attribute.

Elements

A   AREA

Objects

location

CROSS-REFERENCE
See **href**, **URL**, **URI**, and **URN**.

Search Engines

Concept

Search engines are like large card catalogs on the Internet. They sort through the millions of sites on the Web, index them, and then provide Internet users a means of sorting for just the sites that they are interested in. All of the documents provided on the Internet are not listed with every single search engine. It takes a lot of work to get the information on the engines where people can find it, and then keep it close enough to the top of a search results list, that people will actually click on your name.

There are a lot of places that you can get information about specific search engines, and how to use them for the best results for your pages.

- www.submit-it.com/subopt.htm
- www.searchenginewatch.com/resources/

- www.bruceclay.com/
- www.webpromote.com/

There are a few main areas of your pages to watch when you are developing pages that you wish to be found on a search engine results list. These areas include META tag keywords and descriptions, the document TITLE, alt attribute text, comment text, frequency of main terms and phrases, and HTML body copy.

META Tags

Although not all search engines use META tags, most do use them for indexing purposes.

- Use phrases of two or more words separated by a colon or a comma.
- Don't use a single term more than 5 times.
- Make sure your description uses all of your main keywords.
- Always use lowercase for the keywords in your list.

Table S-1 Text Cases Used by Search Engines

Type	AltaVista	InfoSeek	Northern Lights	HotBot	Excite	Lycos	Web-Crawler
case-sensitive?	yes	yes	mixed/title	mixed	no	no	no
lowercase	all	all	all	all	all	all	all
uppercase	exact	exact	all	all	all	all	all
mixed case	exact	exact	exact	exact	all	all	all
title case	exact	exact	exact	all	all	all	all
Sentence case	exact	Exact	exact	all	all	all	all

Title

The document TITLE is the most important element of your search engine placement on the majority of search engines.

- Include all of your main key word phrases in their most popular order.
- Altering the TITLE with each document update will encourage many spiders to reindex site.

Alt Text

Alt text is included as a description for IMG and other elements. Use this text to both describe the image, and push your main indexing phrases.

Comment Text

Use this text to both describe the section of upcoming code, and push your main indexing phrases. You can switch around your paragraphs so the phrases are not appearing identical each time. By adding multiple comment blocks to the top of your page, you can help counteract the use of a table or frames on your site.

HTML Body Copy

There are lots of ways that you can use your HTML body copy to your advantage.

- Move your scripts further down your document.
- Place paragraphs with keywords HIGH on the page.
- Don't spam words. This causes some search engines to ignore you.
- Don't use small or invisible text. Some search engines will not index your site if you have large portions of text that are the same color as your background.
- Use text instead of graphics if at all possible.
- Link to lots of other sites, and build lots of reciprocal links. You can get reciprocal links from friends, clients, general information groups, and even competitor sites if possible.
- Create a complete map of the site and submit it along with the main site URL to the search engines.
- Use descriptive NOFRAMES tags on Frames pages. It is even best to incorporate a site map within this object, and some paragraphical text about your pages.
- Use BODY tags with the NOFRAMES tags.
- Add links to the home page from within the NOFRAMES page.
- Use Database to update pages, rather than build on the fly.

In addition to these ideas, you should submit multiple pages to the search engines each time your site is changed. Some of the best pages to submit are those that discuss your organization, your main page, and your site index. Once you have submitted your pages you will need to check on your URL's every week or 2. You should check in all the search engines that you have the time to, but the top 10 are a necessity.

Search Engine Specific Info

Each search engine uses a different set of rules and works on a different schedule than the others. The following information may help you when designing your pages, and submitting them to the following search engines.

Excite
- Takes 2–4 weeks to be indexed
- Uses META Tags
- Needs HTML Text
- Uses Proper Grammar

HotBot/Inktomi
- Takes 2–4 weeks to be indexed
- Uses META Tags

Lycos
- Takes 2–4 weeks to be indexed
- Titles and description from document content.
- META Tags are not used.
- Use more text than images since keywords are chosen from this text.

Yahoo
- Takes 6–8 weeks to be indexed
- All indexing is done manually.

InfoSeek
- Takes 1–2 weeks to be indexed.
- Uses META Tags
- Don't repeat keywords more than 5 times; if so, list will be ignored.
- Use META Description
- Lower JavaScript down page
- Uses ALT attributes for Images

WebCrawler
- Takes 2–4 weeks to be indexed.
- Uses the TITLE Tag for page name.
- Uses META Tags
- Uses summary from BODY Text.

AltaVista
- Takes 1–2 weeks to be indexed.
- Uses META Tags

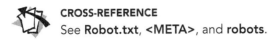

CROSS-REFERENCE
See **Robot.txt**, **<META>**, and **robots**.

sectionRowIndex

Property

DHTML

This property retrieves the position of the selected object from within the TBODY, THEAD, or TFOOT rows collection.

The syntax of this command is

    [Index =] object.sectionRowIndex

Parameters
Index

This integer identifies the index position of the selected object.

Elements
TR

CROSS-REFERENCE
See **rows**, **<TBODY>**, **<THEAD>**, and **<TFOOT>**.

Security

Concept

Security has been a concern since the inception of the Internet. You have over 70 million people accessing the same networks every day, so you know there are a few "bad apples" in the lot.

In order to deal with the incursions of hackers/crackers/phreaks who might like to play a little bit on your network (maybe replacing your Web site, downloading your internal company address book, or maybe grabbing all the credit card sales numbers from your accounting system), software and hardware have been developed to provide a wall of protection around you.

Proxy servers create a gateway between a corporate intranet and the Internet. They typically authenticate users before allowing them access to the internal information. Some of them allow no outside access at all, simply letting traffic out of the company. Proxy servers can use anything from passwords, to highly complicated digital keys, as a means of authenticating a user.

Firewalls build a compound around your network with one gate. They can be configured to only let email traffic out and in, or they can let a whole range of information be distributed. It is possible to set firewalls within firewalls. The outmost wall might let all Web, email, and ftp traffic through, while the internal wall only allows authenticated email messages.

Cryptography is also used to ensure security and privacy. By using complex data encryption keys around your information you can "ensure" that only another individual with the correct decoding key will be able to read it.

CROSS-REFERENCE
See **Passwords** and **Robot.txt**.

select

Method

DHTML

This method is used to highlight the input area of a specified form element. The syntax used to implement this method is

```
object.select()
```

Examples

The following example code uses the select attribute to collect the information that is displayed in the textarea window.

```
<html>
<head>
  <title>select example</title>
</head>

<body>
<form>
  <p><textarea name="mytext" rows="5" cols="20">This is the
  text in the textrange</textarea></p>
  <p><input type="button"
  onclick="document.all.mytext.select()" value="Select "> </p>
</form>
</body>
</html>
```

Elements

INPUT   TEXTAREA

Objects
> TextRange

 CROSS-REFERENCE
See **<SELECT>**, **read-only**, **onselect**, and **disabled**.

<SELECT>

Element

HTML

Start Tag: Required
End Tag: Required

This element creates a menu of options that allows either one or multiple selections to be made. A `SELECT` object must have at least one `OBJECT` element in its contents.

Attributes
disabled

> `disabled`

This is a Boolean attribute, that when set, will disable the option or option group, disallowing any user input.

multiple

> `multiple`

This attribute allows multiple selections to be made from the available options. Without this setting, the reader can only select one option.

name

> `name=cdata`

This attribute is used to give the object a name that will be used as an identifier when automating your data with a script.

onblur

> `onblur=script`

This attribute activates when an element loses the focus either through the actions of a mouse or other pointing device, or by tabbing navigation.

onchange

```
onchange=script
```

This attribute is in effect when an element receives focus from either a mouse or another pointing device, or through tabbed navigation.

onfocus

```
onfocus=script
```

This attribute is in effect when an element receives focus from either a mouse or another pointing device, or through tabbed navigation. It is also activated when an object receives the focus through a scripted focus method.

size

```
size=cdata
```

This attribute is used to specify the initial width of the control for the user agent. The width is given in pixels for all control types except **text** or **password**, for which the width is considered to be the number of characters to display.

tabindex

```
tabindex=number
```

This attribute provides the position of the current element within the overall tabbing order of the document.

Example

The following form uses the SELECT and OPTION objects to create a menu of selectable options for a software installation form.

ON THE CD-ROM

Look for **select.htm** on the accompanying CD-ROM.

```
<FORM action="" method="POST">
<SELECT name="Software" multiple size="4">
    <OPTION selected value="W95">Windows 95</OPTION>
    <OPTION value="W31">Windows 3.1</OPTION>
    <OPTION value="WNT">Windows NT</OPTION>
    <OPTION value="WFWG">Windows for Work Groups</OPTION>
    <OPTION value="UNIX">UNIX</OPTION>
    <OPTION value="LINX">LINUX</OPTION>
    <OPTION value="OS2">OS/2 WARP</OPTION>
    <OPTION value="APPL">Apple</OPTION>
    <OPTION value="MAC">MacIntosh</OPTION>
    <OPTION value="SUN">Sun Unix</OPTION>
    <OPTION value="SOL">Solaris</OPTION>
```

r
s
t

```
</SELECT>
<INPUT type=submit name=Submit>
</FORM>
```

CROSS-REFERENCE
See **<OPTION>**, **<INPUT>**, and **<OPTGROUP>**.

selected

Attribute

HTML

This attribute is used to identify the default selection for a group of radio buttons or other OPTIONs.

The syntax for this Boolean value is

```
selected
```

JAVASCRIPT
```
[ Selected = ] select.options[iIndex].selected
```

This Boolean property is used to set a specific item as the default selection.

Example

The following code uses a SELECT element within an HTML FORM with the selected attribute to select the ZIP drive as the most popular backup storage devices for home users.

ON THE CD-ROM
Look for **selected.htm** on the accompanying CD-ROM.

```
<form method="post" action="">
Select the device that you use to perform backups at your
home:<br>
  <select name="select" size="9" multiple>
    <option value="zip" selected>Zip</option>
    <option value="ditto">Ditto</option>
    <option value="jaz">Jaz</option>
    <option value="syquest">SyQuest</option>
    <option value="floppy">3.5 Floppy</option>
    <option value="cdrw">CDRW</option>
    <option value="cdr">CDR</option>
  </select>
</form>
```

Elements
OPTION

CROSS-REFERENCE
See **<SELECT>**, **<INPUT>**, **Radio Button**, and **<OPTGROUP>**.

selectedIndex

Property

DHTML

This property is used to collect the index of the selected option within a
SELECT object.

The syntax for this parameter is

```
object.selectedIndex [ = Index ]
```

Parameters

Index

This integer identifies the index position of the selected object.

Example

The following example code uses the selectedIndex property to place the
index of the readers selection in a text field.

```
<html>
<head>
<title>selectedIndex example</title>
</head>

<body>
<p>Make a selection:<br>
</p>
<form action method="post">
  <p><select name="Software"

onchange="document.all.mytext.value=document.all.Software.sele
ctedIndex" size="1">
    <option selected value="W95">Windows 95</option>
    <option value="W31">Windows 3.1</option>
    <option value="WNT">Windows NT</option>
    <option value="WFWG">Windows for Work Groups</option>
    <option value="UNIX">UNIX</option>
```

```
            <option value="LINX">LINUX</option>
            <option value="OS2">OS/2 WARP</option>
            <option value="APPL">Apple</option>
            <option value="MAC">MacIntosh</option>
            <option value="SUN">Sun Unix</option>
            <option value="SOL">Solaris</option>
         </select> <input name="mytext" value size="20"> </p>
      </form>
      </body>
      </html>
```

Elements
> SELECT

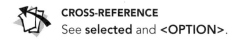

CROSS-REFERENCE
See **selected** and **<OPTION>**.

selectorText

Property

DHTML

This property is used to identify the element to which a specific style sheet rule has been applied.

The syntax for this parameter is

```
[ Selector = ] object.selectorText
```

Parameters
Selector

This string identifies the elements being affected by the selected rule.

Objects
rule

CROSS-REFERENCE
See **rule** and **rules**.

self

Property

DHTML

This property is used to retrieve the current window or frame. The syntax used to implement this property is

```
[ Self = ] object.self
```

Parameters
Self

This object contains the entire window or frame that has been selected.

Objects

window

CROSS-REFERENCE
See **window**, **<FRAME>**, and **<IFRAME>**.

<SERVER>

Element

HTML – Netscape Browsers Only

Start Tag: Required
End Tag: Required

This element is used to identify server-side script statements that rest within an application on the server. When using Netscape, the SERVER tag allows you to run a script on the server before a page is ever loaded into a browser.

Example
The following line of code uses a server-side JavaScript to collect the IP address of the document reader, and paste it into the current document.

```
<P>Your IP address is <SERVER>write(request.ip);</SERVER>
```

CROSS-REFERENCE
See **Server Push**, **<SCRIPT>**, **Scripts**, and **Scripting**.

Server Push

Concept

Both server push and client pull were developed to provide dynamic document mechanisms for HTTP information exchanges. In the case of client pull, the server sends information to the client when the client requests it. In the case of server push, the server holds open the connection to the browser so the server can send it information any time it wishes. One advantage of this is that a server can be more efficient, and not waste time re-establishing a connection with a client when the client wishes to have another piece of information. The major disadvantage of this method is that the server uses extra resources to maintain the open connection. This can mean less clients served over time.

Server push uses a variation of MIME to incorporate multiple instructions within a single message, instead of using the HTTP response header to collect information, as is done with client pull. They typical server push scenario will use the MIME type "multipart/mixed" as a means of sending information.

In the following example MIME message, you identify the content type as "multipart/mime" and then set the boundary string for marking the beginning and end of each part of the message.

```
Content-type: multipart/mixed;boundary=ThisRandomString
—ThisRandomString
Content-type: text/plain
Data for the first object.
—ThisRandomString
Content-type: text/plain
Data for the second and last object.
—ThisRandomString—
```

The code just given creates a message containing two data blocks. Each block is composed of "text/plain" information, and the end of the block is noted by the "—ThisRandomString" boundary marker. The end of the message is marked by the "—ThisRandomString—" marker. The final double dashes identifying this boundary as the close of the message block.

Server-Side Image Maps

Concept

CROSS-REFERENCE
See **Image Maps**.

setAttribute

Method

DHTML

This method is used with document objects to set the value of a specified attribute. If the attribute is currently present, this method will change its value. If the attribute is not present, it will be created, and its value set.

The syntax used to implement this method is

```
object.setAttribute ("Name" , Value [, Flags])
```

Parameters
Flags

This optional parameter is used to control how the setAttribute method interacts with the preexisting attributes of an object. If it is set to **1**, then any attributes with the same name, regardless of case, will be overwritten. If set to **0**, the default, only attributes using the same case will be overwritten.

Name

This required string parameter contains the name of the attribute you are setting.

Value

This required string parameter contains the value of the attribute you are setting.

Examples

The following example code uses the setAttribute method to alter the appearance of objects when a button is clicked.

```
<html>
<head>
  <title>setAttribute example</title>
</head>
```

```
<body bgcolor="white">
<p>This example shows how to change the attributes of the
image and the buttons using the onClick event.</p>

<p><img name="mycircle" src="red.gif" width="75" height="75">
</p>

<form name="myform">
  <p><input type="button" name="large" value="Larger"
onclick="document.all.mycircle.setAttribute('width','150',1);d
ocument.all.small.setAttribute('disabled',false,1);document.al
l.large.setAttribute('disabled','true',1);">
  <input type="button" name="small" value="Smaller" disabled
onclick="document.all.mycircle.setAttribute('width','75',1);do
cument.all.small.setAttribute('disabled',true,1);document.all.
large.setAttribute('disabled',false,1);">
  </p>
</form>
</body>
</html>
```

Elements

<!— —>	A	ADDRESS	APPLET
AREA	B	BASE	BASEFONT
BGSOUND	BIG	BLOCKQUOTE	BODY
BR	BUTTON	CAPTION	CENTER
CITE	CODE	COL	COLGROUP
DD	DFN	DIR	DIV
DL	DT	EM	EMBED
FIELDSET	FONT	FORM	FRAME
FRAMESET	HEAD	H1–H6	HR
HTML	I	IFRAME	IMG
INPUT	KBD	LABEL	LEGEND
LI	LINK		MAP
MARQUEE	MENU	META	NEXTID
OBJECT	OL	OPTION	P
PLAINTEXT	PRE	S	SAMP
SCRIPT	SELECT	SMALL	SPAN
STRIKE	STRONG	STYLE	
SUB	SUP	TABLE	TBODY

TD	TEXTAREA	TFOOT	TH
THEAD	TITLE	TR	TT
U	UL	VAR	WBR
XMP			

CROSS-REFERENCE
See **Attribute**, **Object**, **Element**, and **Style Sheets**.

setEndPoint

Method

DHTML

This method is used to set the end point of a TextRange based upon the end point of another.

The syntax used to implement this method is

```
object.setEndPoint(Type, oTextRange)
```

Parameters
oTextRange

This is the object that is used as a reference point for moving the end of the existing TextRange.

Type

This required string is used to describe the end point to transfer to the current TextRange. If set to **StartToEnd,** the start of the current TextRange object will be moved to the end of the specified oTextRange parameter. When set to **StartToStart**, the start of the current TextRange object will be moved to the start of the specified oTextRange parameter. A type of **EndToStart** moves the end of the current TextRange object to the start of the specified oTextRange parameter. A value of **EndToEnd** moves the end of the current TextRange object to the end of the specified oTextRange parameter.

Example
The following example moves the selected textrange's end points to the identified position.

```
<html>
<head>
  <title> setEndPoint Example</title>
</head>
```

```
<body>
<script language="Javascript">
 function changeEPts() {
  var p = document.all.tags("input");
  if (p!=null) {
    var r1 = p[0].createTextRange();
    var r2 = p[2].createTextRange();
    if (r2 != null) {
      r1.setEndPoint("StartToStart", r2);
      alert(r1.EndPoint);
      r1.text = "Selected";
    }
  }
}
</script>
<input type="text" value="This is a test">
<input type="text" value="This is a test">
<input type="text" value="This is a test">
<input type="button" name="b1" value="Click Me"
onclick="changeEPts()">

</body>
</html>
```

Objects

textrange

CROSS-REFERENCE
See **createRange**, **createTextRange**, **inRange**, **moveEnd**, **moveStart**, and **moveTo**.

setInterval

Method

DHTML

This method is used to set the interval on which a specific expression will be evaluated.

The syntax for this command is

```
TimerID = object.setInterval(Code, MilliSeconds [, Language])
```

Parameters
Code

This required string contains the code to be executed on the specified intervals.

Language

This optional string contains one of the possible values for the language attribute.

MilliSeconds

This integer identifies the number of milliseconds that should occur between executions of the code. This parameter is required.

TimerID

This integer contains the information necessary to cancel the timing interval with the clearInterval method.

Objects
window

CROSS-REFERENCE
See **clearInterval** and **setTimeout**.

setTimeout

Method

DHTML

This method is used to force the evaluation of an expression after a specific number of milliseconds has elapsed.

The syntax for this command is

```
TimerID = object.setTimeout(Code, MilliSeconds [, Language])
```

Parameters
Code

This required string contains the code to be executed on the specified intervals.

Language

This optional string contains one of the possible values for the language attribute.

MilliSeconds

This integer identifies the number of milliseconds that should occur between executions of the code. This parameter is required.

TimerID

This integer contains the information necessary to cancel the timing interval with the `clearTimeout` method.

Objects

window

CROSS-REFERENCE
See **setInterval** and **clearTimeout**.

SGML

Concept

SGML (Standard Generalized Markup Language) is used for defining markup languages that assist in dispersing and encoding information electronically. HTML and XML are SGML based markup languages that are used daily in the Internet. SGML can be used to develop other markup languages that may be either hardware or software dependent, as well as cross platform languages. In 1986 SGML became an ISO standard (ISO 8879). One of the key commitments of SGML is to separate the structure of information in a document from the content of that document while it is being processed. Each object identified within an SGML-based language is named and described, using attributes and child elements, in term of what they are, not how they are supposed to be displayed.

CROSS-REFERENCE
See **HTML** and **XML**.

shape

Attribute

HTML

This attribute is used to define the shape of a region within a `MAP` element. This attribute is required to set the clickable area on an image map. Each shape attribute must have an associated `coords` attribute to set the dimensions of the specified hot spot.

The syntax used to implement this attribute is

```
shape = default | rect | circle | poly
```

JAVASCRIPT

```
object.shape [ = sShape ]
```

This property is used to set the shape of an A or AREA element on a MAP.

Values
default

This sets the entire region as the shape.

rect

This identifies a rectangular region for the hot spot.

circle

This identifies a circular region for the clickable area.

poly

This identifies a polygonal region for the hot spot.

Example

The following example code shows the three most used options for the shape attribute with its associated coords designations.

ON THE CD-ROM

Look for **shape.htm** on the accompanying CD-ROM.

```
<img src="addylabel.gif" width="200" height="200"
usemap="#addybook">
<map name="addybook">
  <area shape="circle" coords="179,73,43">
  <area shape="rect" coords="14,122,199,188">
  <area shape="poly" coords="25,31,2,85,45,98,119,58,129,12,
  84,0,25,32">
</map>
```

Elements
A   AREA

CROSS-REFERENCE
See **coords**, **Image Map**, **<IMG>**, and **<MAP>**.

shiftKey

Property

DHTML

This property is used to discover the current state of the Shift key.
The syntax for using this property is

```
[ true | false = ] object.shiftKey
```

Parameters
false

The Shift key is not pressed.

true

The Shift key is pressed.

Examples
The following example shows how you can use the shiftKey property to check
the state of the shft and perform specific functions or place text into fields.

```
<html>
<head>
<title>shiftKey example</title>
</head>

<body>
<p>Click the button while depressing and releasing the Shift
key</p>
<form>
  <p><input type="button" value="Check"
  onclick="document.all.shftstate.value=event.shiftKey">
<input type="text" name="shftstate"
  size="20"> </p>
</form>
</body>
</html>
```

Objects
    event

CROSS-REFERENCE
See **onkeyup**, **onkeydown**, and **onkeypress**.

showHelp

Method

DHTML

This method is used to display an HTML Help file.
    The syntax to implement this method is

```
window.showHelp(URL [,ContextID | Title], Features])
```

Parameters
ContextID

This optional value is either a string or an integer specifying the context identifier
of the Help file.

Features

This optional string identifies how the help file will be open. If the string is empty,
it will open in the current window. If the strIng is "popup," a new window will be
opened.

Title

This optional string provides you with the contents of the Title Bar for the HTML.

URL

This required string is used to specify the address of the help file which needs to
be displayed.

Objects
    window

CROSS-REFERENCE
See **Help**.

showModalDialog

Method

DHTML

This method is used to display a modal dialog box that displays an HTML document. A modal dialog box must retain the focus until the user closes it.

```
ReturnValue = object.showModalDialog(sURL [, vArguments] [,
Features])
```

Parameters
vArguments

This optional string contains the specific arguments to use when displaying the document. You can use this string to share values of any type including arrays.

Features

This optional string specifies the window ornaments to use on the dialog box. A combination of values can be used to create just the type of box that you need. When **dialogWidth:iWidth** is used, you can set the width of the dialog window. **dialogHeightiHeight** sets the height of the dialog window in pixels. **DialogTop:iYPos** sets the top position of the dialog window to the top edge of the user's desktop. **dialogLeft:iXPos** sets the left position of the dialog window to the upper left corner of the user's desktop. The '**center: {yes | no | 1 | 0}**' option allows you to specify the location of the dialog window when it appears on the users desktop. The default value is **yes** placing the dialog box in the center of the desktop.

ReturnValue

This is a variant, either string, integer, float, or some other value, that has been set to be returned by the document identified in the URL.

sURL

This required string is used to specify the address of the document which needs to be displayed.

Objects
window

CROSS-REFERENCE
See **Dialog Box**.

sibling

Concept

Within the structure of a well-formed document you have a series of objects. Within an HTML document each object is an element that may have children, siblings, and a variety of descendants. A sibling in the world of an HTML document is the same as the siblings in our families. Any child of your parent is a sibling.

For example, if you look at the following HTML document, you see a series of relationships that are created. Table S-2 identifies each relationship found within the document.

```
<html>
<head>
<title>A Look At Color</title>
</head>

<body bgcolor="#FFFF99" text="#000000" link="#FF0000"
vlink="#00FF00" alink="#FFCC00">
<p>Lets look at all the places color can be added to table
cells:</p>
<table border="1" width="75%">
  <tr id="row1">
    <td id="r1c1" bgcolor="Red">Red</td>
    <td id="r1c2" bgcolor="white">White</td>
    <td id="r1c3" bgcolor="Green">Green</td>
  </tr>
  <tr id="row2">
    <td id="r2c1" bgcolor="#0000FF">Blue</td>
    <td id="r2c2" bgcolor="#9900CC">Purple</td>
    <td id="r2c3" bgcolor="#FFCC00">Orange</td>
  </tr>
  <tr id="row3">
    <td id="r3c1" bgcolor="#FFFF00">Yellow</td>
    <td id="r3c2" bgcolor="#FF00FF">Pink</td>
    <td id="r3c3" bgcolor="#00FFFF">Light Blue</td>
  </tr>
</table>
</body>
</html>
```

Table S-2 Siblings, Parents, and Children Relationships

Element	Parent	Siblings	Children
HTML	-	-	HEAD BODY
HEAD	HTML	BODY	TITLE
BODY	HTML	HEAD	P TABLE
TITLE	HEAD	-	-
P	BODY	TABLE	-
TABLE	BODY	P	TR (row 1) TR (row 2) TR (row 3)
TR (row 1)	TABLE	TR (row 2) TR (row 3)	TD (r1c1) TD (r1c2) TD (r1c3)
TR (row 2)	TABLE	TR (row 1) TR (row 3)	TD (r2c1) TD (r2c2) TD (r2c3)
TR (row 3)	TABLE	TR (row 1) TR (row 2)	TD (r3c1) TD (r3c2) TD (r3c3)
TD (r1c1)	TR (row 1)	TD (r1c2) TD (r1c3)	-
TD (r1c2)	TR (row 1)	TD (r1c1) TD (r1c3)	-
TD (r1c3)	TR (row 1)	TD (r1c1) TD (r1c2)	-
TD (r2c1)	TR (row 2)	TD (r2c2) TD (r2c3)	-
TD (r2c2)	TR (row 2)	TD (r2c1) TD (r2c3)	-
TD (r2c3)	TR (row 2)	TD (r2c1) TD (r2c2)	-
TD (r3c1)	TR (row 3)	TD (r3c2) TD (r3c3)	-
TD (r3c2)	TR (row 3)	TD (r3c1) TD (r3c3)	-
TD (r3c3)	TR (row 3)	TD (r3c1) TD (r1c2)	-

CROSS-REFERENCE

See **Parent**, **Child**, **Ancestor**, **Descendant**, and **Document Tree**.

Simple Selector

Concept

CSS

CROSS-REFERENCE
See **rules**.

size

Attribute

CSS

This attribute is used to set the size and the orientation of the page box. The syntax for this command is

```
size:  <length>{1,2} | auto | portrait | landscape | inherit
```

Values
<length>

This sets the absolute dimensions of the page, overriding the target page size.

auto

The page will automatically size to the target screen or sheet.

landscape

The page will automatically be formatted to fit the target page, but in a landscape fashion (long sides horizontal).

portrait

The page will be automatically formatted to fit the target, but in a portrait fashion (long sides vertical).

Elements
@Page

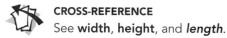

CROSS-REFERENCE
See **width**, **height**, and *length*.

size

Attribute

HTML

This attribute is used in HTML to set the size of an object. When used with the HR element this sets the thickness of the rule in pixels. When used with the FONT and BASEFONT elements it identifies the size of the font to be displayed. The INPUT element uses the size to control the number of characters that can be displayed within a text or multiline field. When the size attribute is used with the SELECT element, it identifies the number of lines to be displayed simultaneously in the multiline select box.

The syntax of this attribute is

```
size=<number>
```

JAVASCRIPT
```
object.size [ = Size ]
```
This property allows you to retrieve the current size of an object.

Values
number

This is an integer value that represents the size of the specified dimension of the object.

Example
The following example shows the use of the size attribute with the HR and the FONT elements. Within the HR element the size attribute is thickening the height of the line to 4 pixels. Within the FONT element the size attribute is enlarging the font to a size 6 font.

ON THE CD-ROM
Look for **size.htm** on the accompanying CD-ROM.

```
<p><font size="6">This is a test, </font></p>
<p><font size="6">This is only a test. </font></p>
<hr size="4">
<p>This is a test of the American Broadcasting System. <br>
   If this were not a test it would be followed by and
   informative but useless announcement. </p>
```

Elements
BASEFONT   FONT   HR   INPUT
SELECT

CROSS-REFERENCE
See **width**, **height**, and **font-size**.

slope

Descriptor

CSS

This descriptor is used in font matching to identify the vertical slope of the font being matched.

The syntax for this command is

```
slope= <number>
```

Values
number

This integer is the angle of the slope.

CROSS-REFERENCE
See font **matching** and **@fontface**.

<SMALL>

Element

HTML

Start Tag: Required
End Tag: Required

This attribute is used to render text in a small font, without explicitly changing it through the FONT size attribute.

Attributes
class

```
class="cdata-list"
```

This attribute is used to assign a class name to an element. User agents employ classes to group specific types of information for later use.

dir

```
dir = LTR | RTL
```

This attribute defines the direction of the text flow in a document so a user agent can display it correctly.

id

```
id="name"
```

This attribute is used to assign a name to an element.

lang

```
lang="language code"
```

This attribute specifies the language in which an element and its values should be rendered.

onclick

```
onclick=script
```

This attribute takes effect when a user clicks the button on a pointing device with the pointer over an element.

ondblclick

```
ondblclick=script
```

This attribute takes effect when the button on a pointing device is double-clicked with the pointer over an element.

onkeydown

```
onkeydown=script
```

This attribute takes effect when a key is pressed while the pointer is over an element.

onkeypress

```
onkeypress=script
```

This attribute takes effect when a key is pressed and released with the pointer over an element.

onkeyup

```
onkeyup=script
```

This attribute takes effect when a key is released with the pointer over an element.

onmousedown

```
onmousedown=script
```

This attribute takes effect when the button on a pointing device is pressed with the pointer over an element.

onmousemove

```
onmousemove=script
```

This attribute is activated when the mouse is moved while the pointer is over an element.

onmouseout

```
onmouseout=script
```

This attribute is activated when the mouse pointer is moved away from an element.

onmouseover

```
onmouseover=script
```

This attribute is activated when the mouse pointer is moved over an element.

onmouseup

```
onmouseup=script
```

This attribute takes effect when the button on a pointing device is released with the pointer over an element.

style

```
style=style descriptors
```

This attribute is used to apply specific style-sheet information to one particular element.

title

```
title=text
```

This attribute serves to provide annotation information for the element.

Example

The following example code uses the SMALL element to provide changes to specific words in a sales paragraph.

ON THE CD-ROM

Look for **small.htm** on the accompanying CD-ROM.

```
<HTML>
<HEAD>
   <TITLE>Various forms of Emphasis being Used    </TITLE>
</HEAD>
<BODY bgcolor="#FFFFFF">
```

```
<H1><FONT color="#FF9933">Looking for Computer Help</font>
</H1>
<SMALL>HTML, VB, DHTML, JAVA, ODBC, OLE, XMP, MathML
</SMALL>,<BR>
Not up to speed on the latest technological innovations?
<P align="left"><b>We are. </b>
<P>Whether its <SMALL>Web</SMALL> pages, <SMALL>brochures
</SMALL>,
<SMALL>business cards</SMALL>, or <SMALL>databases</SMALL>,
Cat's Back <BR>
Consulting can get your company up and running in the
technological age.
<P>Give us a call.
<H3><FONT color="#FF9933">Cat's Back Consulting</FONT></H3>
555-CATS or <FONT color="#FF9933">www.catsback.com</FONT>
on the Internet.<BR>
We're the answer to your information needs.
</BODY>
</HTML>
```

CROSS-REFERENCE
See **\<FONT\>**, **\<BIG\>**, **\<SUB\>**, and **\<SUP\>**.

SMIL

Concept

SMIL (Synchronized Multimedia Integration Language) is a new language, based on XML that allows you to incorporate audio, video, images, and text into streaming multimedia applications on your Web pages. All you will need is a compatible browser and you can forget about downloading a dozen plug-ins for every type of potential video or audio clip you want to watch.

SMIL support is being incorporated into many different multimedia viewers, although Microsoft at one point stated they would not provide support for SMIL in their Internet Explorer 5.0 browser software.

For an example of using SMIL and some software currently supporting it, check out the RealPlayer G2 site at `http://www.realnetworks.com`.

CROSS-REFERENCE
See **XML**.

<SOFTPKG>

Element

OSD

Start Tag: Required
End Tag: Required

This element is used to identify a software package that has been placed on the Internet

Attributes
href

```
href=url
```

This attribute identifies the Web page associated with the software being distributed.

name

```
name= <string>
```

This is the name of the software being distributed. This should be a unique identifier for the software.

version

```
version = <string>
```

This is the version information for the software being distributed.

Example
The following example code identifies a cat screen saver program for distribute to Windows NT machines.

```
<SOFTPKG name="Victorian Cat Screen Saver" version=" 2.0">
<IMPLEMENTATION>
   <IMPLTYPE value="java" />
   <CODEBASE href="http://www.mysoftware.com/soft.cab" />
   <OS value="WinNT" />
   <MEMSIZE value="1024Kb" />
</IMPLEMENTATION>
</SOFTPKG>
```

CROSS-REFERENCE
See **<IMPLEMENTATION>**.

sourceIndex

Property

DHTML

This property retrieves the ordinal position of the current object from within the all collection.

The syntax used for this property is

```
[ Index = ] object.sourceIndex
```

Parameters

Index

This integer identifies the position of the object in the collection.

Elements

<!— —>	A	ACRONYM	ADDRESS
APPLET	AREA	B	BASE
BASEFONT	BGSOUND	BIG	BLOCKQUOTE
BODY	BR	BUTTON	CAPTION
CENTER	CITE	CODE	COL
COLGROUP	DD	DEL	DFN
DIR	DIV	DL	DT
EM	EMBED	FIELDSET	FONT
FORM	FRAME	FRAMESET	HEAD
H1–H6	HR	HTML	
I	IFRAME	IMG	INPUT
INS	KBD	LABEL	LI
LINK		MAP	MARQUEE
MENU	META	NEXTID	OBJECT
OL	P	PLAINTEXT	PRE
Q	S	SAMP	SCRIPT
SELECT	SMALL	SPAN	STRIKE
STRONG	STYLE	SUB	SUP
TABLE	TBODY	TD	TEXTAREA
TFOOT	TH	THEAD	TITLE
TR	TT	U	UL
VAR	XMP		

CROSS-REFERENCE
See **all** and **collection**.

<SPACER>

Element

HTML — Netscape Navigator Only

Start Tag: Required
End Tag: Required

This element is only available with Netscape Navigator. It was created as a means of providing horizontal spacing control to your document without the use of empty table cells or transparent GIF images.

Attributes

type

```
type= horizontal | vertical | block
```

This identifies the type of space to be inserted. If the value is **horizontal**, the space is the height of one line, and placed between the specified characters. **Vertical** places white space between lines of text as identified by the `size` attribute. **Block** inserts a rectangular block spreading both horizontally and verti-cally as specified by the `align`, `height` and `width` attributes.

align

```
align= left | right | top | absmiddle | absbottom | texttop |
middle | baseline | bottom
```

This controls how the space shall be aligned against the current line of text or object. The default setting is bottom.

height

```
height=height
```

When the type attribute is block, this attribute is used to specify the height of the space in pixels.

width

```
width = width
```

When the type attribute is block, this attribute is used to specify the width of the space in pixels.

size

```
size=size
```

When the `type` is not **block**, this size is used to specify the absolute width or height of the space.

Example

The following code uses the SPACER element to insert horizontal and vertical space between a series of paragraphs.

ON THE CD-ROM

Look for **spacer.htm** on the accompanying CD-ROM.

```
<p>
  <font size="+2" face="Verdana, Arial, Helvetica, sans-serif">
  The Story:
  </font>
</p>
<SPACER type="verticle" size="10">
<p>
  <SPACER type="horizontal" size="10">
  <font face="Verdana, Arial, Helvetica, sans-serif" size="+1">
Decature is the creation of <a href="drdec.html">Dr. Decmented.
</a> He was once a great geneticist working for the Decathlon
Federal Government. One day, a huge explosion shook his laboratory
while he was working with the genetic material of a Giant Red
Octopus, and a blow up Happy Face doll. The explosion merged their
materials, and the evil creature known as Dectoid was
born.</font></p>
<spacer type=block width=100 height=80 align=middle>
<p><font face="Verdana, Arial, Helvetica, sans-serif" size="+1">
The world has never been the same...and never will be
again.</font></p>
```

CROSS-REFERENCE

See **<TABLE>**, **GIF**, and **white-space**.

span

Attribute

HTML

This attribute is used to identify the number of columns that can be spanned by a single COL or COLGROUP element.

The syntax of this attribute is

```
span = <number>
```

JAVASCRIPT

```
object.span [ = iSpan ]
```

This property retrieves the number of columns that the object spans.

Values

number

This is a positive integer representing the total number of table columns included in the group.

Example

This attribute is used to set the total number of columns that the COLGROUP and COL attributes shall include.

ON THE CD-ROM

Look for **spana.htm** on the accompanying CD-ROM.

```
<table border="1" width="75%">
<COL span="1"></COL>
<COLGROUP span="2" style="color: red; font:verdana;"
align="center" valign="top"></COLGROUP>
  <tr>
    <th> </th>
    <th scope= col>1st Half</th>
    <th scope= col>2nd Half</th>
  </tr>
  <tr>
    <th scope= row>Income</th>
    <td>$10K</td>
    <td>$15K</td>
  </tr>
  <tr>
    <th scope= row>Expenses</th>
```

r
s
t

```
      <td>$8K</td>
      <td>$8K</td>
    </tr>
  </table>
```

Elements

COL   COLGROUP

CROSS-REFERENCE
See **colspan** and **rowspan**.

<SPAN>

Element

HTML

Start Tag: Required
End Tag: Required

The SPAN element works with the id and class attributes to provide a generic mechanism for providing structure within a document. SPAN is an inline element that places no other visual structure on the screen. Authors can then use this element with a style sheet to tailor that object to their needs.

Attributes
align

```
align=center | justify | left | right
```

This attribute controls the horizontal and vertical alignment of text and objects within the bounds of the document margins.

class

```
class="cdata-list"
```

This attribute is used to assign a class name to an element. User agents employ classes to group specific types of information for later use.

dir

```
dir = LTR | RTL
```

This attribute defines the direction of the text flow in a document so a user agent can display it correctly.

id

> `id="`*name*`"`

This attribute is used to assign a name to an element.

lang

> `lang="`*language code*`"`

This attribute specifies the language in which an element and its values should be rendered.

onclick

> `onclick=`*script*

This attribute takes effect when a user clicks the button on a pointing device with the pointer over an element.

ondblclick

> `ondblclick=`*script*

This attribute takes effect when the button on a pointing device is double-clicked with the pointer over an element.

onkeydown

> `onkeydown=`*script*

This attribute takes effect when a key is pressed while the pointer is over an element.

onkeypress

> `onkeypress=`*script*

This attribute takes effect when a key is pressed and released with the pointer over an element.

onkeyup

> `onkeyup=`*script*

This attribute takes effect when a key is released with the pointer over an element.

onmousedown

> `onmousedown=`*script*

This attribute takes effect when the button on a pointing device is pressed with the pointer over an element.

onmousemove

> onmousemove=*script*

This attribute is activated when the mouse is moved while the pointer is over an element.

onmouseout

> onmouseout=*script*

This attributed is activated when the mouse pointer is moved away from an element.

onmouseover

> onmouseover=*script*

This attribute is activated when the mouse pointer is moved over an element.

onmouseup

> onmouseup=*script*

This attribute takes effect when the button on a pointing device is released with the pointer over an element.

style

> style=*style descriptors*

This attribute is used to apply specific style-sheet information to one particular element.

title

> title=*text*

This attribute serves to provide annotation information for the element.

Example

The following script shows how the inline SPAN element differs from the block-level DIV element. As you can see from the example, the two span elements run together; by contrast, the DIV element is set aside as a block.

ON THE CD-ROM

Look for **span.htm** on the accompanying CD-ROM.

```
<HTML>
<HEAD>
  <META NAME="GENERATOR" Content="NetObjects ScriptBuilder
2.0">
  <TITLE>Using Span</TITLE>
```

```
</HEAD>
<BODY>
<SPAN id="span1">
This is the time that all good men must come to the aid of
their country.
The quick brown fox jumped over the lazy dog.
This is the time that all good men must come to the aid of
their country.
The quick brown fox jumped over the lazy dog.
</SPAN>
<SPAN id="span2">
This is the time that all good men must come to the aid of
their country.
The quick brown fox jumped over the lazy dog.
This is the time that all good men must come to the aid of
their country.
The quick brown fox jumped over the lazy dog.
</SPAN>
<DIV id="div1">
This is the time that all good men must come to the aid of
their country.
The quick brown fox jumped over the lazy dog.
This is the time that all good men must come to the aid of
their country.
The quick brown fox jumped over the lazy dog.
</DIV>
</BODY>
</HTML>
```

CROSS-REFERENCE
See **<DIV>** and **<LAYER>**.

speak

Attribute

CSS

This attribute is used to control how the speech synthesizer used with Aural
style sheets is going to display the text.

The syntax of this command is

```
speak: normal | none | spell-out | inherit
```

Values

none

This value prohibits the speech synthesizer from displaying these words or phrases.

normal

The synthesizer will attempt to function normally, speaking full words that are found in its dictionary, and spelling those that it does not recognize.

spell-out

This value forces all words to be spelled, rather than stated.

Elements

This attribute is available for all HTML elements.

 CROSS-REFERENCE

See **display**, **speak-header**, **speak-numeral**, **speak-punctuation**, and **speech-rate**.

speak-header

Attribute

CSS

This attribute is used to specify how the headers of a table will be spoken through the speech synthesizer most often used with Aural style sheets.

The syntax for this command is

```
speak-header: once | always | inherit
```

Values

always

This forces the contents of the header to be read for each data cell that header is related to.

once

The header is read one time before a series of cells.

Elements

TD   TH

CROSS-REFERENCE
See **display**, **header**, **<TH>**, **<TD>**, **speak**, **speak-numeral**, **speak-punctuation**, and **speech-rate**.

speak-numeral

Attribute

CSS

This attribute is used to identify how the individual digits found within a number are to be read through the speech synthesizer used with an Aural style sheet.

The syntax used with this attribute is

```
speak-numeral: continuous | digits | inherited
```

Values

continuous

The numbers are spoken as a full string. For example, the number 102 would be read "one hundred and two".

digits

The numbers are spoken individually. For example the number 102 would be read "one zero two."

Elements

This attribute applies to all HTML elements.

CROSS-REFERENCE
See **display**, **speak**, **speak-header**, **speak-punctuation**, and **speech-rate**.

speak-punctuation

Attribute

CSS

This property is used to specify how a speech synthesizer will read punctuation associated with narrative text and numbers.

The syntax used to implement this attribute is

```
speak-punctuation: code | none | inherit
```

Values
code

All punctuation will be spoken literally, so a statement such as "The cat, Tom, ate all of his food" would be read "The cat comma Tom comma ate all of his food period."

none

None of the punctuation will be spoken, but will be paused for, as in a natural speaking voice. For example, the statement "The cat, Tom, ate all of his food." would be rendered "The cat pause Tom pause ate all of his food silence."

Elements
This attribute is available for all HTML elements.

CROSS-REFERENCE
See **display**, **speak**, **speak-header**, **speak-numeral**, and **speech-rate**.

specific-voice

Descriptor

CSS

This descriptor is used to identify the specific voice used when a speech synthesizer is rendering text.

The syntax for this descriptor is

```
specific-voice = voice-name
```

Values
voice-name

This is the name of a specific voice such as Harry, Sally, Ilan, Mike, Genie, Comedian, clown, or Phyllis.

CROSS-REFERENCE
See **generic-voice**, **font-family**, **generic-font**, and **family-name**.

speech-rate

Attribute

CSS

This attribute is used to identify the speed at which the speech synthesize will read the text contained within the document.

The syntax for this command is

```
speech-rate: <number> | x-slow | slow | medium | fast | x-fast
| faster | slower | inherit
```

Values
<number>

This integers specifies the number of words per minute spoken by the synthesizer.

x-slow

This is the same as 80 wpm.

slow

This is the same as 120 wpm.

medium

This is a speaker between 180 and 200 wpm.

fast

This is approximately 300 wpm.

x-fast

This is approximately 500 wpm.

faster

This adds 40 wpm to the inherited speech rate.

slower

This subtracts 40 wpm from the inherited speech rate.

Elements
This attribute is available with all HTML elements.

CROSS-REFERENCE
See **speak**, **display**, and **font-size**.

src

Attribute

HTML

This attribute is used to identify the address of the resource that should be displayed, or otherwise used, by the object that is identifying it.

The syntax used to implement this attribute is

```
src=url
```

JAVASCRIPT
```
[ sURL = ] object.src
```

This property is used to retrieve the address (URL) of the src attribute.

Values
url

This is the address of a document or other resource requested by the object.

Example
In the following code segment, the FRAME and the IMG tags use the src attribute to identify the resources that need to be loaded for those elements.

ON THE CD-ROM
Look for **src.htm** on the accompanying CD-ROM.

```
<frameset rows="194,195" bordercolor="#3333FF" border="2"
framespacing="2" frameborder="YES">
  <frame src="FrameContents1.htm" scrolling=no>
  <frame src="FrameContents2.htm" scrolling=yes>
</frameset>
<noframes>
<body bgcolor="#FFFFFF">
<img src="addylabel.gif" width="200" height="200">
</body>
</noframes>
```

Elements
FRAME   IFRAME   INPUT   IMG   SCRIPT

CROSS-REFERENCE
See **href**, **code**, **codebase**, **nohref**, **URN**, **URL**, and **URI**.

src

Descriptor

CSS

This descriptor is used to provide a reference to the font, or its associated data during font matching. This can be either a local or Internet address.

The syntax for this descriptor is

```
src=url
```

Values
url

This is the address of the font resource being requested.

CROSS-REFERENCE
See **font matching**, **units-per-em**, and **@fontface**.

srcElement

Property

DHTML

This property is used to retrieve the object that fired the event containing the `src` attribute.

The syntax for this command is

```
[ oObject = ] object.srcElement
```

Parameters
object

This is the object that fired the event.

Examples
The following example code pops up an alert box identifying the button that was clicked on the HTML document.

```
<html>
<head>
<title>srcElement example</title>
</head>

<body>
<form>
  <p><input type="button" name="thefirstbutton" value="Click
to find out what was clicked."
  onclick="alert(event.srcElement.name)"></p>
  <p><input type="button" name="thesecondbutton" value="Click
to find out what was clicked."
  onclick="alert(event.srcElement.name)"> </p>
</form>
</body>
</html>
```

Objects

event

CROSS-REFERENCE
See **src**, **URL**, **object**, and **srcFilter**.

srcFilter

Property

DHTML

This property is used to retrieve the filter object that fired the `onfilterchange` event to fire.

The syntax for this command is

```
[Object = ] event.srcFilter
```

Parameters
Object

This is the object that fired the event.

Objects

event

CROSS-REFERENCE
See **onfilterchange** and **srcElement**.

specified value

Concept

CROSS-REFERENCE
See **Actual Value** and **Computed Value**.

standby

Attribute

HTML

This attribute is used to specify the message that a reader will see while an object is waiting to load.

The syntax for this command is

```
standby = text
```

Values

text

This is a string of characters containing the message displayed in the object box while it is loading.

Elements

OBJECT

CROSS-REFERENCE
See **queryCommandState**.

start

Method

DHTML

This method is used to start a marquee scrolling.
The syntax used to implement this method is

```
object.start()
```

Elements
MARQUEE

 CROSS-REFERENCE
See **loop**, **behavior**, and **stop**.

start

Attribute

HTML

This deprecated attribute is used to set the starting number of a list of items. Even though the values specified here are integers, if the type attribute specified for the list is non-numeric the numbers will correlate. For example, if **start = 6** and **type =“A”** then the first item in the list will be lettered “**F**.”
The syntax for this attribute is

```
start = <number>
```

 JAVASCRIPT
```
object.start [ = Start ]
```
This property retrieves the starting number for an ordered list.

Values
number

This is an integer value greater than 0.

Example
This segment of HTML code shows you how the start and value attributes can work together. The line items with Horses, Dogs, and Cats will be numbered 13, 14, and 15 respectively. The Cows line item will be numbered 20, and the Pigs and Chickens will be number 21 and 22 respectively.

```
<BODY>
    <H1>Farm Animals</H1>
    <OL type="i" start="13" >
        <LI>Horses
        <LI>Dogs
        <LI>Cats
        <LI value="20">Cows
        <LI>Pigs
        <LI>Chickens
    </OL>
</BODY>
```

Elements
    OL

CROSS-REFERENCE
See **type** and **value**.

<StartDate>

Element

CDF

    Start Tag: Required
    End Tag: Forbidden

This element is used to identify when the delivery of a channel should commence.

Attributes

value

This is the date that the channel should be distributed starting. The default is immediately.

Example

This example channel, located at http://mychannels.com/channels.cdf must be delivered between midnight and noon on the first of each month.

```
<CHANNEL HREF="http://mychannels.com/channels.cdf ">
    <SCHEDULE>
        <STARTDATE value="1999.01.09T00:00-0000" />
        <INTERVALTIME Day=30 />
        <EARLIESTTIME Hour=0 />
```

r
s
t

```
        <LATESTTIME Hour=12 />
      </SCHEDULE>
    </CHANNEL>
```

CROSS-REFERENCE
See **EndDate**.

Start-Tags

Concept

HTML, XML

All elements have `start tags`, but they don't all have `end tags`. The `start tag` is the opening declaration for an object. It identifies the placement of the element within the document hierarchy, and identifies any attribute that a user agent needs to use when it is rendering the object.

CROSS-REFERENCE
See **Empty Elements**, **Elements**, **Objects**, **End Tags**, and **DTD**.

Statements

Concept

CROSS-REFERENCE
See **At-Rules**, **Rule Sets**, and **Declaration-Block**.

Static

Media group

Cascading Style Sheet 2 has defined the following media groups, which are all referred to with `all`:

- Visual/Aural/Tactile
- Continuous/Paged
- Grid/Bitmapped
- Interactive/Static

Each media group is used to describe a specific type of media. There are many media types that are identified as part of these groups. Most of the media types fall into multiple categories. For example, Static media contains such media types as printed materials and projected materials. These are types of media that can not be changed or altered after their creation.

CROSS-REFERENCE
See **Media Groups** and **Media Types**.

Static Positioning

Concept

CROSS-REFERENCE
See **Absolute Positioning**, **Positioning**, **Float**, and **Relative Positioning**.

status

Property

DHTML

This property is used to set or retrieve the message in the status bar of the current window, or to tell whether a radio button or check box has been selected.

The syntax used to implement this property can be one of the following options:

```
object.status [ = Status ]
object.status [ = false | true ]
```

Parameters

Status

This is the string contents of the window's status-bar message.

False

This value means that the form control is not selected.

True

This value implies that the form control is selected.

Elements
> INPUT

Objects
> window

stemh

Descriptor

CSS

This descriptor is used in font matching to identify the horizontal stem width of the characters of the font. If this descriptor is used, the `units-per-em` descriptor must also be used.

The syntax for this descriptor is

```
stemh=<number>
```

Values
number

> The width of the character stem in reference to the value of the `unit-per-em` descriptor.

 CROSS-REFERENCE
See **stemv**, **units-per-em**, **font matching**, and **@fontface**.

stemv

Descriptor

CSS

This descriptor is used in font matching to identify the vertical stem height of the characters of the font. If this descriptor is used, the `units-per-em` descriptor must also be used.

The syntax for this descriptor is

```
stemv=<number>
```

Values

number

The height of the character stem in reference to the value of the `unit-per-em` descriptor.

 CROSS-REFERENCE
See **stemh**, **units-per-em**, **font matching**, and **@fontface**.

stop

Method

DHTML

This method is used to stop a marquee from scrolling.
The syntax used to implement this method is

```
object.stop()
```

Elements

MARQUEE

 CROSS-REFERENCE
See **loop**, **behavior**, and **start**.

stress

Attribute

CSS

This attribute is used to identify the amount of stress to apply to the language being spoken. For example, in English, many words have "stress" placed upon a specific syllable in a word. The word "cat" places the stress on the 't'. In the word "picture" the stress is placed on the strong 'c' sound.
The syntax of this attribute is

```
stress: <number>
```

Values
number

This number between 1 and 100, the default is 50, that identifies the strength of the stress to place on specific sounds and syllables. The value and effect of this attribute has a different effect in each language being spoken.

Elements
This attribute applies to all HTML elements.

 CROSS-REFERENCE
See **pitch, richness,** and **range.**

<STRIKE>

Element

HTML

Start Tag: Required
End Tag: Required

This element is used to render text that is marked with a strike through character. This element has been deprecated in HTML 4.0.

Attributes
class

```
class="cdata-list"
```

This attribute is used to assign a class name to an element. User agents employ classes to group specific types of information for later use.

dir

```
dir = LTR | RTL
```

This attribute defines the direction of the text flow in a document so a user agent can display it correctly.

id

```
id="name"
```

This attribute is used to assign a name to an element.

lang

```
lang="language code"
```

This attribute specifies the language in which an element and its values should be rendered.

onclick

```
onclick=script
```

This attribute takes effect when a user clicks the button on a pointing device with the pointer over an element.

ondblclick

```
ondblclick=script
```

This attribute takes effect when the button on a pointing device is double-clicked with the pointer over an element.

onkeydown

```
onkeydown=script
```

This attribute takes effect when a key is pressed while the pointer is over an element.

onkeypress

```
onkeypress=script
```

This attribute takes effect when a key is pressed and released with the pointer over an element.

onkeyup

```
onkeyup=script
```

This attribute takes effect when a key is released with the pointer over an element.

onmousedown

```
onmousedown=script
```

This attribute takes effect when the button on a pointing device is pressed with the pointer over an element.

onmousemove

```
onmousemove=script
```

This attribute is activated when the mouse is moved while the pointer is over an element.

onmouseout

```
onmouseout=script
```

This attribute is activated when the mouse pointer is moved away from an element.

onmouseover

```
onmouseover=script
```

This attribute is activated when the mouse pointer is moved over an element.

onmouseup

```
onmouseup=script
```

This attribute takes effect when the button on a pointing device is released with the pointer over an element.

style

```
style=style descriptors
```

This attribute is used to apply specific style-sheet information to one particular element.

title

```
title=text
```

This attribute serves to provide annotation information for the element.

Example

The following example code uses the STRIKE attribute to strike through missing children's names on an attendance sheet for an individual teacher.

ON THE CD-ROM

Look for **strike.htm** on the accompanying CD-ROM.

```
<html>
<head>
<title>Checking Attendance</title>
<meta http-equiv="Generator" content="NetObjects ScriptBuilder
2.0">
</head>

<body bgcolor="#FFFFFF">
<h1>Mr. Meyer's 4th Grade Class</h1>
<h3>Attendance sheet for 10/13/99</h3>
<p><strike>Stanley Coggins</strike><br>
```

```
        George Gabrial<br>
        <strike>Harold Harley</strike><br>
        Wilma Hawkins<br>
        <strike>Lois Frei</strike><br>
        <strike>Wylie French</strike><br>
        <strike>Mike Fuchs</strike><br>
        <strike>Ted Gates</strike><br>
        Clifford Towne<br>
        Rocky VanArsdale<br>
        Bob VanCleave<br>
        Don Nuss<br>
        Debra O'Kelley<br>
        Earl Purvis<br>
        <strike>Reed Walters</strike><br>
        Debbie Reser</p>
<i>***Children with marked out names were not in attendance at
roll call. </i>
</body>
</html>
```

CROSS-REFERENCE
See **<S>**.

<STRONG>

Element

HTML

Start Tag: Required
End Tag: Required

This element is used to provide additional emphasis to text. It works very similar to the B element.

Attributes
class

```
class="cdata-list"
```

This attribute is used to assign a class name to an element. User agents employ classes to group specific types of information for later use.

id

    id="name"

This attribute is used to assign a name to an element.

lang

    lang="language code"

This attribute specifies the language in which an element and its values should be rendered.

onclick

    onclick=script

This attribute takes effect when a user clicks the button on a pointing device with the pointer over an element.

ondblclick

    ondblclick=script

This attribute takes effect when the button on a pointing device is double-clicked with the pointer over an element.

onkeydown

    onkeydown=script

This attribute takes effect when a key is pressed while the pointer is over an element.

onkeypress

    onkeypress=script

This attribute takes effect when a key is pressed and released with the pointer over an element.

onkeyup

    onkeyup=script

This attribute takes effect when a key is released with the pointer over an element.

onmousedown

    onmousedown=script

This attribute takes effect when the button on a pointing device is pressed with the pointer over an element.

onmousemove

`onmousemove=script`

This attribute is activated when the mouse is moved while the pointer is over an element.

onmouseout

`onmouseout=script`

This attribute is activated when the mouse pointer is moved away from an element.

onmouseover

`onmouseover=script`

This attribute is activated when the mouse pointer is moved over an element.

onmouseup

`onmouseup=script`

This attribute takes effect when the button on a pointing device is released with the pointer over an element.

style

`style=style descriptors`

This attribute is used to apply specific style-sheet information to one particular element.

title

`title=text`

This attribute serves to provide annotation information for the element.

Example
The following example uses the STRONG element to highlight measurements in a cookie recipe.

 NOTE
This is really a great recipe . . . if you like making eight dozen cookies.

ON THE CD-ROM

Look for **strong.htm** on the accompanying CD-ROM.

```
<HTML>
<HEAD>
<TITLE> Cooking with Strength</TITLE>
</HEAD>
<BODY>
    <H1> Cooking with Cleo</H1>
    <H2> Cleo's Fabulouse Dish Pan Cookies </H2>
    <P> <IMG src="chocchip.gif" alt="Dish Pan Cookies">
    First collect the following ingredients:
    <UL>
        <LI> <STRONG>2 Cups</STRONG> Sugar
        <LI> <STRONG>2 Cups</STRONG> Brown Sugar
        <LI> <STRONG>1 Cup</STRONG> Butter
        <LI> <STRONG>2 Tsp</STRONG> Vanilla<BR>

        <LI> <STRONG>2 Cups</STRONG> Oats
        <LI> <STRONG>4 Cups</STRONG> Flour
        <LI> <STRONG>4</STRONG> Eggs
        <LI> <STRONG>1 lb.</STRONG> Chocolate Chips
        <LI> <STRONG>2 Cups</STRONG> Coconut
        <LI> <STRONG>2 Cups</STRONG> Corn Flakes
        <LI> <STRONG>1.5 Cups</STRONG> Nuts
        <LI> <STRONG>1 Cup</STRONG> Raisins
        <LI> <STRONG>2 Tsp</STRONG> Salt
</UL>
    <P>Now follow all the remaining directions to mix and bake
your cookies:
    <UL>
        <LI>Mix the brown sugar, sugar, butter, and
vanilla.</LI>
        <LI>Mix the remaining ingredients thoroughly.</LI>
        <LI>Bake <STRONG>9 - 10</STRONG> minutes at 350deg.
</UL>
    <H2> Don't Over Bake!!!</H2>
</BODY>
</HTML>
```

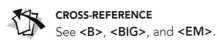

CROSS-REFERENCE

See **<B>**, **<BIG>**, and **<EM>**.

style

Attribute

HTML

This attribute is used to incorporate style sheet elements directly into the HTML object designator. When you use the `style` attribute, rather than the `STYLE` element, you can set rules for individual objects, rather than all of the objects of one type.

The syntax for implementing this attribute is

```
style="rule; rule ; . . ."
```

JAVASCRIPT

```
object.style [ = sStyle ]
```

This property is used to retrieve the rules associated with a particular object.

Values

rule

A *rule set*, also referred to as a *rule*, is a two-part statement consisting of a selector followed by a declaration block. The selector is the name of the object, or the identifier of an object, for which you are setting the rules. The declaration block is the set of properties or attributes you are setting for the selector.

Example

The following example code uses the style attribute to set the text decoration for the header, and an italic font for the second level header.

ON THE CD-ROM

Look for **styleinline.htm** on the accompanying CD-ROM.

```
<html>
<head>
<title>Dectiod - Uses style commands</title>
<meta http-equiv="Content-Type" content="text/html;
charset=iso-8859-1">
<style type="text/css">
<!--
font {  font-family: "Comic Sans MS"}
-->
</style></head>
```

r
s
t

```
<body bgcolor="#FFFFFF">
<p align="center"><img src="cartoon.jpg" width="400"
height="210">
</p>
<h1 align="center" style="text-decoration:underline"><font
face="Verdana, Arial, Helvetica, sans-serif"
color="#FF3300">DECTOID </font></h1>
  <br>

<h1 style="font-style:italic" align="center"><font
face="Verdana, Arial, Helvetica, sans-serif" color="#FF3300">-
  The Scurge of the Universe -</font></h1>
<table border="1" width="75%" align="center">
  <tr>
    <td colspan="2">
      <div align="center"><font size="+1" face="Verdana,
Arial, Helvetica, sans-serif" color="#CC3300">WATCH
        OUT!</font><font size="+1" face="Verdana, Arial,
Helvetica, sans-serif">
        Dectiod is after YOU. <br>
        If you haven't deduced the despoiling destruction that
Dectiod delivers on the desolate Universe, hold onto your
derriere, your about to be devastated.<br>
        <br>
        <a href="#contactinfo">Contact us for more
information.</a></font></div>
    </td>
  </tr>
  </table>
<p align="center"><font size="+2" color="#CC3300">DECATURE
Creation Staff<a name="contactinfo"></a></font><br>
  101010 Decaway Ave.<br>
  Dectune, DE 00011</p>
<p align="center">(555) 111 - 2222<br>
  email: <a
href="mailto:dectoid@decature.com">dectoid@decature.com</a></p
>
<p align="center"> </p>
</body>
</html>
```

Elements

`<!— —>`	A	ADDRESS	APPLET
AREA	B	BGSOUND	BIG
BLOCKQUOTE	BODY	BR	BUTTON
CAPTION	CENTER	CITE	CODE
COL	COLGROUP	DD	DFN
DIR	DIV	DL	DT
EM	EMBED	FIELDSET	FONT
FORM	FRAME	FRAMESET	H1–H6
HR	I	IFRAME	IMG
INPUT	KBD	LABEL	LEGEND
LI	LINK		MAP
MARQUEE	MENU	NEXTID	OBJECT
OL	OPTION	P	PLAINTEXT
PRE	S	SAMP	SELECT
SMALL	SPAN	STRIKE	STRONG
SUB	SUP	TABLE	TBODY
TD	TEXTAREA	TFOOT	TH
THEAD	TR	TT	U
UL	VAR	WBR	XMP

 CROSS-REFERENCE
See **rule set**, **`<STYLE>`**, **Cascading Style Sheets**, **SMIL**, and **DSSL**.

`<STYLE>`

Element

HTML

Start Tag: Required
End Tag: Required

This element is used to create a style sheet, or multiple style sheets, which has been embedded in the HEAD section of a document.

Not all user agents support style sheets, or if they do, might not support the style sheet language included in the document by the STYLE element. If the user agent does not support it, then the user agent needs to make the style sheet invisible to the readers.

Some types of style sheets that you can implement on HTML documents will allow you to use more rules with the STYLE element than with the style attribute. For example, when you are using Cascading Style Sheets you can control the appearance of all instances of a specific HTML element, rather than just the element itself.

 NOTE
The algorithm used for style rule precedence and inheritance depends on the style sheet language.

 JAVASCRIPT
`[booleanVar = ] stylesheet.disabled`

This JavaScript property can be used to disable a style sheet that has been either imported, or included within the document.

Attributes
lang
`lang=langcode`

This is the language that the style sheet will implement on your document.

media
`media=media-descriptor`

This attribute identifies the type of media that this style sheet has been designed for. There are many types of media groups that you can use to associate your style sheet with.

title
`title=text`

This is a short description or title for the style sheet being loaded into the document.

type
`type=content-type`

This identifies the type of content that is being provided within the style sheet. Most of the time for style sheets used with HTML documents, the type will be "text/css." This attribute is required.

Example

The following example code uses style sheets to control the headings and paragraphs contained within this document. Each object used within the document has an associated style sheet element that sets its font, font color, borders, backgrounds, spacing, and so on.

ON THE CD-ROM

Look for **style.htm** on the accompanying CD-ROM.

```html
<html>
<head>
<title> Getting a CyberEducation</title>
<style type="text/css">
<!--
h4 {  font-family: "Comic Sans MS";
      font-style: italic;
      font-variant: small-caps;
      color: #3300FF}
h1 {  font-family: Georgia, "Times New Roman", Times, serif;
      font-style: oblique;
      font-weight: 700;
      font-variant: normal;
      text-transform: uppercase;
      color: #FF0000;
      letter-spacing: 2em}
p {   background-color: #FFFFCC;
      border-style: inset;
      border-top-width: medium;
      border-right-width: medium;
      border-bottom-width: medium;
      border-left-width: medium}
h2 {  border: #FF0000;
      border-style: outset;
      border-top-width: thin;
      border-right-width: thick;
      border-bottom-width: thin;
      border-left-width: thick;
      list-style-position: inside;
      list-style-type: circle;
      clip:  rect(   )}
-->
</style>
</head>

<body>
```

```
<h1> Giving your Kids a CyberEducation </h1>
<h4>Pages: 300 </h4>
<h4>Images: Yes </h4>
<h4>Disk/CD: Yes </h4>
<h2>Description:</h2>
<p> This book would look at educational games for kids,
specifically looking at how boys and girls edutainment needs
differ. It would cover what systems are out there on the net
to protect your kids, while letting them still access the vast
numbers of kids safe sites. We would look at the other game
and edutainment software for your children. In the process
breaking it down into learning age groups to help parents
evaluate what will help their kids best as they grow, and
looking at games and educational software differently. Look at
how to help your kids make learning fun on the computer, both
on and off the net. A just for the parents section would
contain information about kids information resources on the
Internet, and where you can get all that free stuff that your
kids will love. </p>
<h2>About the Author:</h2>
<p>Heather Williamson is both the manager and owner of Cat's
Back Consulting in the Wallowa Valley of Oregon. She
specializes in technical writing and training for all ranges
of computer users and topics including the Internet, Fax
technology, data communications, operating systems, and
Microsoft Office applications. She is the author of Internet
Explorer 6 in 1, and contributed on a variety of other books
including some of the Special Edition Using series by QUE.
<br>
  <br>
  In her free time, between writing and raising her family,
  Heather raises American Quarter Horses, barrel races in
  local rodeo circuits, spoils her Cocker Spaniel, and gets
  shot while robbing a bank every Wednesday during the summer.
  She is in an old west reenactment group, for those with
  legal concerns. </p>
<h2> What's Unique about Your Book? </h2>
<p>It is the only book of its kind that actually talks you
through the step by step process of picking out, purchasing,
and installing the latest and greatest software for your
kids.</p>
<h2>How does this project compare with the competition? </h2>
<p>There is none!!!</p>
<h2>Who is your audience? </h2>
```

```
<p>This book is focused on the parent with the young 3-12 year
old child who wants to find the best software available on the
market, for the specific needs of their children. </p>
</body>
</html>
```

CROSS-REFERENCE

See **Style Sheet**, **stylesheets**, **styles**, **DSSSL**, **SMIL**, and **Cascading Style Sheets**.

Style Sheet

Concept

A *style sheet* is a separate document that allows you to globally alter the appearance of every item on a document or a series of documents by editing a single document. You can control the size of fonts, their color, backgrounds, borders, speech synthesizer controls, etc. You name it, there is a style sheet rule that will allow you to control its rendering within a document.

CROSS-REFERENCE

See **Cascading Style Sheets**, **DSSSL**, **Styles**, **stylesheets**, **Rule Sets**, and **XSL**.

styleFloat

Property

DHTML

This property sets or retrieves how the float attribute is implemented on an object.

The syntax of this command is

```
object.style.styleFloat [ = Float ]
```

Parameters
Float

This string is one of three values depending on the state of the object. When set to none, the object does not float. Left places the object on the left edge of the screen. Right places the object on the right edge of the screen.

Elements

A	ADDRESS	APPLET	B
BIG	BLOCKQUOTE	BUTTON	CENTER
CITE	CODE	DD	DFN
DIR	DIV	DL	DT
EM	EMBED	FIELDSET	FORM
Hn	HR		I
IFRAME	IMG	INPUT	
KBD	LABEL	LEGEND	LI
	MARQUEE	MENU	OBJECT
OL	P	PRE	S
SAMP	SELECT	SMALL	SPAN
STRIKE	STRONG	SUB	SUP
TABLE	TEXTAREA	TT	U
UL	VAR	XMP	

Objects

style

CROSS-REFERENCE
See **Float**, **Relative Positioning**, and **Absolute Positioning**.

styleSheets

Collection

DHTML

This collection creates a list of all the STYLE and LINK elements containing style sheet information in the current document.

This collection can be used in the following ways:

```
[ collStylesheets = ] object.stylesheets
```

```
[ oObject = ] object.stylesheets (vIndex [, iSubIndex] )
```

Parameters
collStylesheets

This variable refers to the array of elements contained by the object.

oObject

This variable refers to an individual item in the array.

vIndex

This parameter is required, and contains the number or string identifying the element or collection to retrieve. When a number is specified, the method returns the element in the zero-based collection at the identified position. When a string identifier is used, and there are multiple elements with the same name or id attributes matching the string, this method returns a collection of those matched elements.

iSubIndex

This optional parameter is used to identify the position of the element being retrieved, when vIndex is a string. ISubIndex becomes the index of the specific item in the collection of matching elements identified by the vIndex string contents.

Objects

document

CROSS-REFERENCE
See **Style Sheets**, **Cascading Style Sheets**, **\<STYLE\>**, **\<LINK\>**, **DSSSL**, and **SMIL**.

\<SUB\>

Element

HTML

Start Tag: Required
End Tag: Required

This element is used to mark up subscripts on your documents. These subscripts can show footnote numbers, or serve as any other sort of subscript in either mathematical or text content.

Attributes
class

```
class="cdata-list"
```

This attribute is used to assign a class name to an element. User agents employ classes to group specific types of information for later use.

id

> id="*name*"

This attribute is used to assign a name to an element.

lang

> lang="*language code*"

This attribute specifies the language in which an element and its values should be rendered.

onclick

> onclick=*script*

This attribute takes effect when a user clicks the button on a pointing device with the pointer over an element.

ondblclick

> ondblclick=*script*

This attribute takes effect when the button on a pointing device is double-clicked with the pointer over an element.

onkeydown

> onkeydown=*script*

This attribute takes effect when a key is pressed while the pointer is over an element.

onkeypress

> onkeypress=*script*

This attribute takes effect when a key is pressed and released with the pointer over an element.

onkeyup

> onkeyup=*script*

This attribute takes effect when a key is released with the pointer over an element.

onmousedown

> onmousedown=*script*

This attribute takes effect when the button on a pointing device is pressed with the pointer over an element.

onmousemove

```
onmousemove=script
```

This attribute is activated when the mouse is moved while the pointer is over an element.

onmouseout

```
onmouseout=script
```

This attribute is activated when the mouse pointer is moved away from an element.

onmouseover

```
onmouseover=script
```

This attribute is activated when the mouse pointer is moved over an element.

onmouseup

```
onmouseup=script
```

This attribute takes effect when the button on a pointing device is released with the pointer over an element.

style

```
style=style descriptors
```

This attribute is used to apply specific style-sheet information to one particular element.

title

```
title=text
```

This attribute serves to provide annotation information for the element.

Example

The following sample code uses the SUB and SUP objects to mark links to footnotes and cross-reference information within text.

ON THE CD-ROM

Look for **subsup.htm** on the accompanying CD-ROM.

```
<html>
<head>
<title>SubScripts and SuperScripts</title>
<meta http-equiv="Content-Type" content="text/html;
charset=iso-8859-1">
</head>
```

```
<body bgcolor="#FFFFFF">
<h1>Cat's Back Consulting</h1>
<h2>Income and Expenses for 1998 <sub>1</sub></h2>
<table border="1" width="75%" summary="The quarterly income
and expense comparison for CBC leaves us with a total profit
of $1150 in 1998.">
  <caption> The quarterly income and expense comparison for
CBC shows a varying,
  but profitable year for CBC. With a yearly<sub>2</sub>
income of $4400 <sup>1</sup> and expenses of $3250
<sup>2</sup>,
  an overall profitable year was achieved.</caption>
  <tr>
    <td bgcolor="#FFFF99"> </td>
    <td bgcolor="#FFCCFF">Q1</td>
    <td bgcolor="#FFCCFF">Q2</td>
    <td bgcolor="#FFCCFF">Q3</td>
    <td bgcolor="#FFCCFF">Q4</td>
  </tr>
  <tr>
    <td bgcolor="#FFFF99">Income</td>
    <td bgcolor="#CCFFFF">1200</td>
    <td bgcolor="#CCFFFF">1000</td>
    <td bgcolor="#CCFFFF">1000</td>
    <td bgcolor="#CCFFFF">1200</td>
  </tr>
  <tr>
    <td bgcolor="#FFFF99">Expense</td>
    <td bgcolor="#CCFFFF">700</td>
    <td bgcolor="#CCFFFF">750</td>
    <td bgcolor="#CCFFFF">900</td>
    <td bgcolor="#CCFFFF">900</td>
  </tr>
  <tr>
    <td bgcolor="#66FF99">Profit</td>
    <td bgcolor="#66CCCC">500</td>
    <td bgcolor="#66CCCC">250</td>
    <td bgcolor="#66CCCC">100</td>
    <td bgcolor="#66CCCC">300</td>
  </tr>
</table>
<p> </p>
</body>
</html>
```

CROSS-REFERENCE
See **<SUP>**.

<SUBCHANNEL>

Element

CDF

Start Tag: Required
End Tag: Forbidden

This identifies another channel, often containing more specific information that can be delivered as part of the main channel being identified.

Attributes
href

This attribute is used to specify the location of the next updated version of this channel.

isclonable

This attribute is used to specify whether a channel can be copied or moved within the channel-changer hierarchy.

Example
The following example code identifies a channel document, and its subchannel, to be accessed by a CDF compatible software package.

```
<CHANNEL href="http://mychannels.com/mychannel.cdf" isclonable=yes>
  <SUBCHANNEL>
  <INTROURL value="http://mychannels.com/setup.htm" />
  <LASTMOD value="1999.01.01T12:10-0300" />
  <TITLE value="My Favorite Hobbies Channel" />
  <ABSTRACT value="The latest information in sports hobby gear."
  />
  </SUBCHANNEL>
  <AUTHOR value="Webner Masterson" />
</CHANNEL>
```

CROSS-REFERENCE
See **<ITEM>**, **<CHANNEL>**, and **Channels**.

submit

Method

DHTML

This method is used to submit a form to the process or in the same fashion as it would be if the reader clicked the **Submit** button.

Elements
FORM

CROSS-REFERENCE
See **<INPUT>**, **<BUTTON>**, and **type**.

Subscriptions

Concept

If a reader likes your channel information they can subscribe to your channel. This means they get added to a list allowing your channel to be automatically sent to them whenever the channel is updated.

CROSS-REFERENCE
See **Channel Definition Format** and **<SCHEDULE>**.

summary

Attribute

HTML

This attribute is used to provide a summary of the information contained within a table. This is provided for the use of user agents that do not support tables or are not visual in nature.

The syntax of this attribute is

```
summary=text
```

Values
text

This is the string containing the table description information.

Elements
TABLE

CROSS-REFERENCE
See **alt**, **<CAPTION>**, **longdesc**, and **title**.

<SUP>

Element

HTML

Start Tag: Required
End Tag: Required

This element is used to mark up superscripts on your documents. These superscripts can show cross-reference numbers, or serve as any other sort of superscript in either mathematical or text content.

Attributes
class

```
class="cdata-list"
```

This attribute is used to assign a class name to an element. User agents employ classes to group specific types of information for later use.

id

```
id="name"
```

This attribute is used to assign a name to an element.

lang

```
lang="language code"
```

This attribute specifies the language in which an element and its values should be rendered.

onclick

`onclick=script`

This attribute takes effect when a user clicks the button on a pointing device with the pointer over an element.

ondblclick

`ondblclick=script`

This attribute takes effect when the button on a pointing device is double-clicked with the pointer over an element.

onkeydown

`onkeydown=script`

This attribute takes effect when a key is pressed while the pointer is over an element.

onkeypress

`onkeypress=script`

This attribute takes effect when a key is pressed and released with the pointer over an element.

onkeyup

`onkeyup=script`

This attribute takes effect when a key is released with the pointer over an element.

onmousedown

`onmousedown=script`

This attribute takes effect when the button on a pointing device is pressed with the pointer over an element.

onmousemove

`onmousemove=script`

This attribute is activated when the mouse is moved while the pointer is over an element.

onmouseout

`onmouseout=script`

This attribute is activated when the mouse pointer is moved away from an element.

onmouseover

```
onmouseover=script
```

This attribute is activated when the mouse pointer is moved over an element.

onmouseup

```
onmouseup=script
```

This attribute takes effect when the button on a pointing device is released with the pointer over an element.

style

```
style=style descriptors
```

This attribute is used to apply specific style-sheet information to one particular element.

title

```
title=text
```

This attribute serves to provide annotation information for the element.

Example

The following sample code uses the SUB and SUP objects to mark linking to footnotes and cross-reference information within text.

ON THE CD-ROM

Look for **subsup.htm** on the accompanying CD-ROM.

```
<html>
<head>
<title>SubScripts and SuperScripts</title>
<meta http-equiv="Content-Type" content="text/html; charset=iso-
8859-1">
</head>

<body bgcolor="#FFFFFF">
<h1>Cat's Back Consulting</h1>
<h2>Income and Expenses for 1998 <sub>1</sub></h2>
<table border="1" width="75%" summary="The quarterly income and
expence comparison for CBC leaves us with a total profit of
$1150 in 1998.">
```

r
s
t

```
<caption> The quarterly income and expense comparison for
CBC shows a varying, but profitable year for CBC. With a
yearly<sub>2</sub> income of $4400 <sup>1</sup> and expenses
of $3250 <sup>2</sup>, an overall profitable year was
achieved.</caption>
<tr>
  <td bgcolor="#FFFF99"> </td>
  <td bgcolor="#FFCCFF">Q1</td>
  <td bgcolor="#FFCCFF">Q2</td>
  <td bgcolor="#FFCCFF">Q3</td>
  <td bgcolor="#FFCCFF">Q4</td>
</tr>
<tr>
  <td bgcolor="#FFFF99">Income</td>
  <td bgcolor="#CCFFFF">1200</td>
  <td bgcolor="#CCFFFF">1000</td>
  <td bgcolor="#CCFFFF">1000</td>
  <td bgcolor="#CCFFFF">1200</td>
</tr>
<tr>
  <td bgcolor="#FFFF99">Expense</td>
  <td bgcolor="#CCFFFF">700</td>
  <td bgcolor="#CCFFFF">750</td>
  <td bgcolor="#CCFFFF">900</td>
  <td bgcolor="#CCFFFF">900</td>
</tr>
<tr>
  <td bgcolor="#66FF99">Profit</td>
  <td bgcolor="#66CCCC">500</td>
  <td bgcolor="#66CCCC">250</td>
  <td bgcolor="#66CCCC">100</td>
  <td bgcolor="#66CCCC">300</td>
</tr>
</table>
<p> </p>
</body>
</html>
```

CROSS-REFERENCE
See **<SUB>**.

systemLanguage

Property

DHTML

This property is used to identify the default language that the current reader's system is using.

The syntax for implementing this property is

```
[ Language = ] object.systemLanguage
```

Parameters

Language

This string contains the valid language code used with the user agent.

Object

Navigator

CROSS-REFERENCE

See **lang** and **language**.

r
s
t

Tab Order

Concept

The *tab order* (or *tabbing order*) of a document defines the path that a user takes through the links or fields on a document when using the Tab key or other keyboard keys as a navigational tool. To be included in the tabbing order, an object must have a `tabindex` attribute or have that as a valid optional attribute.

CROSS-REFERENCE
See **Tabbing Navigation** and **tabindex**.

Tabbing Navigation

Concept

You must be able to navigate all elements that can receive the focus of the user, such as links and form fields, with the keyboard. The following rules apply to the tabbable elements within a document.

- All elements that support the `tabindex` attribute and have been assigned a positive value for this attribute should be navigated first. Objects with a `tabindex` value are navigated from lowest to highest value, although those values do not need to be sequential or to start at any predefined point. When elements with matching `tabindex` values are encountered, they are navigated in the order in which they appear on the source document.

- All elements that don't support the `tabindex` attribute or that have a `tabindex` value of 0 are navigated next. All of these objects are navigated in their source-document order.

- Any element that is disabled is not included in the tabbing order.

CROSS-REFERENCE
See **tab order** and **tabindex**.

tabindex

Attribute

HTML

This attribute is used to identify the position of the current element within the tabbing order of a document.

The syntax of this command is

```
tabindex=number
```

 JAVASCRIPT

```
object.tabindex [=index]
```

This allows you to set the tab order for a document on the fly.

Values
number

This value must be an integer between 0 and 32767. All user agents should ignore leading zeros found within the number.

Example
The following example code uses JavaScript to manipulate the document objects. First you will see two list items that, when clicked, drop down to provide you with sublists of information. Each of these entries has a tab order. Press the Tab key to see what gets selected first.

```
<STYLE TYPE='text/css'>
<!-
/*Define elements with children with the
class='outlineParentItem', and all elements without children
with class='outlineItem'*/
li.oItem { color: #000000; cursor: text; } ;
li.oParent { color: #0000FF; cursor: hand; } ;
ul ul { display: none; } ;
// ->
</STYLE>

<SCRIPT LANGUAGE='Javascript'>
<!-
  // Returns the closest parent tag with tagName containing
  // the src tag. If no such tag is found - null is returned.
  function checkParent( src, tagName ) {
    while ( src != null ) {
      if (src.tagName == tagName)
```

```
        return src;
      src = src.parentElement;
    }
    return null;
  }


  // Returns the first tag with tagName contained by
  // the src tag. If no such tag is found - null is returned.
  function checkContent( src, tagName ) {
    var pos = src.sourceIndex ;
    while ( src.contains( document.all[++pos] ) )
      if ( document.all[pos].tagName == tagName )
        return document.all[pos] ;
    return null ;
  }


  // Handle onClick event in the outline box
  function outlineAction() {
    var src = event.srcElement ;
    var item = checkParent( src, "LI" ) ;

    if ( parent != null ) {
      var content = checkContent( item, "UL" ) ;

    if ( content != null )
      if ( content.style.display == "" )
        content.style.display = "block" ;
      else
        content.style.display = "" ;
    }
    event.cancelBubble = true;
  }

// -->
</SCRIPT>

<DIV onClick="JavaScript: outlineAction();">
  <UL>
  <LI class='oParent'>Java and JavaScript
    <UL>
    <a href="http://www.hotwired.com/webmonkey/" tabindex=2>
    <LI class='oItem'>WebMonkey</LI></a>
    a href="http://javascript.internet.com" tabindex=1>
    <LI class='oItem'>JavaScript Resource</LI></a>
    <a href="http://javascript.internet.com" tabindex=3>
```

s
t
u

```
        <LI class='oItem'>Java Resource</LI></a>
        </UL>
    </LI>
    <LI class='oParent'>HTML
      <UL>
      <a href="http://www.webreview.com/guides/style/"
tabindex=4>
      <LI class='oItem'>WebResources</LI></a>
      <a href="http://www.developer.com/" tabindex=9>
      <LI class='oItem'>Developers.com</LI></a>
      <a href="http://www.hotwired.com/webmonkey/" tabindex=6>
      <LI class='oItem'>WebMonkey</LI></a>
      <a href="http://www.webreference.com/" tabindex=7>
      <LI class='oItem'>WebReference.com</LI></a>
      <a href="http://builder.com/" tabindex=5>
      <LI class='oItem'>Builder.com</LI></a>
      </UL>
    </LI>
    </UL>
</DIV>
```

Elements

A	AREA	BUTTON	INPUT
OBJECT	SELECT	TEXTAREA	

CROSS-REFERENCE
See **Tab Order** and **Tabbing Navigation**.

<TABLE>

Element

HTML

Start Tag: Required
End Tag: Required

This element is used to display formatted objects and text within an HTML document. Tables are block elements that can be aligned horizontally on your document. This element contains a variety of other elements that add meaning to or control the formatting of the table itself. These elements include CAPTION, COL, COLGROUP, TD, TFOOT, TH, THEAD, and TR.

User agents should make any summary information available to all users. This helps individuals using older browsers without table support or individuals with nonvisual user agents gain a better understanding of the table. The use of the CAPTION element also assists in this manner by providing additional information about the contents and intended use of the table. User agents need to display all information associated with the table, including headers and footers, although the user agent generally defines how those headers and footers are implemented.

Attributes

align

```
align= left | center | right
```

This controls the alignment of the table within the margins of the document.

bgcolor

```
bgcolor= colorname | RGBvalue
```

This attribute is used to control the overall background color of the entire table.

border

```
border= width
```

This identifies the overall width of the borders surrounding and used inside of the table.

bordercolor

```
bordercolor=colorname | RGBvalue
```

This attribute identifies the color in which the border should be displayed.

cellpadding

```
cellpadding=length | percentage
```

This attribute is used to force a specific amount of space between the cell's border and its contents.

cellspacing

```
cellspacing=length | percentage
```

This attribute is used to force a specific amount of space between the individual cells within a table.

class

```
class="cdata-list"
```

This attribute assigns a class name to an element. User agents use classes to group specific types of information for later use.

dir

```
dir = LTR | RTL
```

This attribute defines the direction of the text flow in a document so a user agent can correctly display it to the reader.

frame

```
frame= "void" | "above" | "below" | "border" | "box" |
"hsides" | "lhs" | "rhs" | "vsides"
```

This attribute controls how the border around the outside edge of a table is displayed. **Void** removes all borders; **above** shows the top border; **below** shows the bottom border; **border** and **box** show all borders; **hsides** displays borders on the horizontal edges; **vsides** displays borders on the vertical edges; **lhs** displays borders on the left side of the table; and **rhs** displays the border on the right side of the table.

id

```
id="name"
```

This attribute is used to assign a name to an element.

lang

```
lang="language code"
```

This attribute specifies the language in which an element and its values should be rendered.

onclick

```
onclick=script
```

This attribute takes effect when the button on a pointing device is clicked while the pointer is over an on-screen element.

ondblclick

```
ondblclick=script
```

This attribute takes effect when the button on a pointing device is double-clicked while the pointer is over an on-screen element.

onkeydown

```
onkeydown=script
```

This attribute takes effect when a key is pressed while the pointer is over an on-screen element.

onkeypress

```
onkeypress=script
```

This attribute takes effect when a key is pressed and released while the pointer is over an on-screen element.

onkeyup

```
onkeyup=script
```

This attribute takes effect when a key is released while the pointer is over an on-screen element.

onmousedown

```
onmousedown=script
```

This attribute takes effect when the button on a pointing device is pressed while the pointer is over an on-screen element.

onmousemove

```
onmousemove=script
```

This attribute is activated when the mouse pointer is moved while it is over an on-screen element.

onmouseout

```
onmouseout=script
```

This attribute is activated when the mouse pointer is moved away from an on-screen element.

onmouseover

```
onmouseover=script
```

This attribute is activated when the mouse pointer is moved over an on-screen element.

onmouseup

```
onmouseup=script
```

This attribute takes effect when the button on a pointing device is released while the pointer is over an on-screen element.

rules

```
rules=rows | cols | none | all
```

This attribute controls the vertical and horizontal rules displayed within the table grid.

style

```
style=style descriptors
```

This attribute is used to apply specific style-sheet information to one particular element.

summary

```
summary=string
```

This text string is used to define the contents of the table to help users understand the table's contents.

title

```
title=text
```

This attribute provides annotation information for the element.

width

```
width=length
```

This is the width of the table in either pixels or percentage of the viewable area of the document or screen.

Example

The following example code creates a three-by-three table that sets the table borders, alignment, width, cell spacing, background color, and border colors.

 ON THE CD-ROM

Look for **table.htm** on the accompanying CD-ROM.

```
<html>
<head>
<title>Checking Tables</title>
<meta http-equiv="Generator" content="Macromedia Dreamweaver">
</head>

<body bgcolor="#FFFFFF">
<table border="3" width="557" align="right" cellspacing="3"
cellpadding="4" bgcolor="#CC3399" bordercolor="#006600"
bordercolorlight="#00FF66" bordercolordark="#006600"
hspace="10" vspace="15" name="payscale">
```

```
<tr>
    <td width="176"><font color="#FFFFFF"
size="+2">BA</font></td>
    <td width="176"><font color="#99FFFF" size="+2"
face="Comic Sans MS">40K</font></td>
    <td width="176"><font face="monospace" color="#FFFF00"
size="+2">4 yrs</font></td>
  </tr>
  <tr>
    <td width="176"><font size="+2" color="#FFFFFF"><b><font
size="+3">MS</font></b></font></td>
    <td width="176"><font color="#33FFFF" size="+3"
face="Comic Sans MS">75K</font></td>
    <td width="176"><font size="+3" face="monospace"
color="#FFFF00">6 yrs</font></td>
  </tr>
  <tr>
    <td width="176"><font color="#FFFFFF"
size="+4">PhD</font></td>
    <td width="176"><font color="#00FFFF" size="+4"
face="Comic Sans MS">100K</font></td>
    <td width="176"><font color="#FFFF00" size="+4"
face="monospace">8 yrs</font></td>
  </tr>
</table>
</body>
</html>
```

CROSS-REFERENCE
See **<CAPTION>**, **<COL>**, **<COLGROUP>**, **<TBODY>**, **<TD>**, **<TFOOT>**,
<TH>, **<THEAD>,** and **<TR>**.

table-caption

Value

CSS

This property value is used with the display attribute to force an object to
function as a table caption, rather than in its normal fashion. For example, the
CAPTION element is the only object that normally is displayed as the caption of
a table. Although the exact appearance of this object can change between user
agents, it is defined as an identifiable display type within the user agent. If you

define the P element to be displayed like a table-caption, a user agent automatically assigns the text styles that it normally reserves for the CAPTION element to the P element.

Example

The following style sheet forces all P elements to act like table captions, rather than as normal block P elements. It also forces the element labeled cap1 to be treated as a table caption.

```
<STYLE type="text/css">
<!—
P { display: table-caption }
#cap1 { display: table-caption }
—>
</STYLE>
```

CROSS-REFERENCE

See **display**, **<CAPTION>**, **<TABLE>**, **inline-table**, **table-row-group**, **table-caption**, **table-column-group**, **table-header-group**, **table-footer-group**, **table-row**, and **table-cell**.

table-cell

Value

CSS

This property value is used with the display attribute to force an object to function as a table cell, rather than in its normal fashion.

Example

The following style sheet forces all Q and BLOCKQUOTE elements to act like table captions, rather than as normal Q and BLOCKQUOTE elements.

```
<STYLE type="text/css">
<!—
Q           { display: table-cell }
BLOCKQUOTE { display: table-cell }
—>
</STYLE>
```

CROSS-REFERENCE

See **display**, **<CAPTION>**, **<TABLE>**, **inline-table**, **table-row-group**, **table-caption**, **table-column-group**, **table-header-group**, **table-footer-group**, **table-row**, and **table-cell**.

table-column-group

Value

CSS

This property value is used with the `display` attribute to force an object to function as a table column group, rather than in its normal fashion.

 CROSS-REFERENCE
See **display**, **<CAPTION>**, **<TABLE>**, **inline-table**, **table-row-group**, **table-caption**, **table-column group**, **table-header-group**, **table-footer-group**, **table-row,** and **table-cell**.

table-footer-group

Value

CSS

This property value is used with the `display` attribute to force an object to function as a table footer group, rather than in its normal fashion.

 CROSS-REFERENCE
See **display**, **<CAPTION>**, **<TABLE>**, **inline-table**, **table-row-group**, **table-caption**, **table-header-group**, **table-column-group**, **table-row,** and **table-cell**.

table-header-group

Value

CSS

This property value is used with the `display` attribute to force an object to function as a table header group, rather than in its normal fashion.

 CROSS-REFERENCE
See **display**, **<CAPTION>**, **<TABLE>**, **inline-table**, **table-row-group**, **table-caption**, **table-footer-group**, **table-column-group**, **table-row,** and **table-cell**.

s
t
u

table-layout

Attribute

CSS

This Cascading Style Sheets attribute is used to provide constraints on the layout of a table. It provides the user agent with a set of rules that can be used when displaying a table. User agents are free to use their own algorithms unless this value is set to **fixed.**

The syntax of this attribute is

```
table-layout: auto | fixed | inherit
```

 JAVASCRIPT

```
table.style.tableLayout [ = Layout ]
```

This property can be used to determine whether the layout of the table is fixed.

Values

auto

This is the default value and uses whatever algorithm is automatically selected by the user agent.

fixed

This forces the user agent to use the algorithm provided with the Cascading Style Sheets specification to render tables.

Elements

TABLE

 CROSS-REFERENCE
See **<TABLE>** and **display**.

table-row

Value

CSS

This property value is used with the `display` attribute to force an object to function as a table row, rather than in its normal fashion.

Example

The following style sheet forces all HR elements to act like table rows, rather than as normal block elements. It also forces the element labeled "Line1" to be treated as a table row.

```
<STYLE type="text/css">
<!-
HR { display: table-row }
#Line1 { display: table-row }
->
</STYLE>
```

 CROSS-REFERENCE
See **display**, **<CAPTION>**, **<TABLE>**, **inline-table**, **table-row-group**, **table-caption**, **table-header-group**, **table-footer-group**, **table-column-group**, and **table-cell**.

table-row-group

Descriptor

CSS

This property value is used with the display attribute to force an object to function as a table row group, rather than in its normal fashion.

 CROSS-REFERENCE
See **display**, **<CAPTION>**, **<TABLE>**, **inline-table**, **table-row**, **table-caption**, **table-header-group**, **table-footer-group**, **table-column-group,** and **table-cell**.

Tactile

Media Group

The Cascading Style Sheets, level 2, specification defines the following media groups:

- Visual/Aural/Tactile
- Continuous/Paged
- Grid/Bitmap
- Interactive/Static

Each media group is used to describe a specific type of medium. Many media types are identified as part of these groups. The tactile media group is used to identify specific types of media that are touchable and have a texture of some sort. Braille and embossed documents are considered tactile media.

CROSS-REFERENCE
See **media group** and **media types**.

tagName

Property

DHTML

This document property is used to identify the specific tag used to create the object.

The syntax for this property is

```
[ name= ] object.tagName
```

JAVASCRIPT
```
[ sName = ] object.tagName
```

This property is used to retrieve the tag name creating the object.

Parameters
name

This is the string name of the tag that is used to display the object.

Example
The following example retrieves the tag name for an object that has the identifier that a user has specified in the prompt window.

```
<SCRIPT language="JavaScript">
var idValue = window.prompt("Get the tag with this ID:");
if (idValue != null) {
    alert(document.all[idValue].tagName)
}
</SCRIPT>
```

Elements

A	ACRONYM	ADDRESS	APPLET
AREA	B	BASE	BASEFONT

BGSOUND	BIG	BLOCKQUOTE	BODY
BR	BUTTON	CAPTION	CENTER
CITE	CODE	COL	COLGROUP
COMMENT	DD	DEL	DFN
DIR	DIV	DL	DT
EM	EMBED	FIELDSET	FONT
FORM	FRAME	FRAMESET	HEAD
H1–H6	HR	HTML	I
IFRAME	IMG	INPUT	INS
KBD	LABEL	LEGEND	LI
LINK	LISTING	MAP	MARQUEE
MENU	META	NEXTID	OBJECT
OL	OPTION	P	PLAINTEXT
PRE	Q	S	SAMP
SCRIPT	SELECT	SMALL	SPAN
STRIKE	STRONG	STYLE	SUB
SUP	TABLE	TBODY	TD
TEXTAREA	TFOOT	TH	THEAD
TITLE	TR	TT	U
UL	VAR	XMP	

CROSS-REFERENCE
See **elements**, **id**, **name**, **objects**, and **tags**.

tags

Method

DHTML

This document object method retrieves a collection of tags that have been created with the same HTML tag.

The syntax to invoke this method is

```
Elements = object.tags("Tag")
```

Parameters
Elements

This is the collection of elements that have been created using the specified tag.

Tag

This required string contains the tag name that you are attempting to collect.

Example

In this script example, all of the LI elements are collected, counted (using the *length* parameter), and then accessed in order and made to blink.

```
<html>
<head>
<title>textDecoration example</title>
<script language="JavaScript">
function dotreatment(decor) {
  var coll = document.all.tags("LI");
  if (coll!=null)
  {
    for (i=0; i<coll.length; i++)
      coll[i].style.textDecoration=decor;
  }
}
</script>
</head>

<body name="mybody" bgcolor="#FFFFFF">

<ol onmouseover="dotreatment('underline');"
onmouseout="dotreatment('none');">
  <li>Pass your mouse over! </li>
  <li>Then pass it out. </li>
</ol>
</body>
</html>
```

Objects

all	anchors	applets	areas
boundElements	cells	children	eelements
rmbeds	filters	forms	frames
images	imports	links	options
plugins	rows	rules	scripts
styleSheets	tbodies		

CROSS-REFERENCE
See **collections**, **elements**, **id**, **name**, **objects**, and **tags**.

target

Attribute

HTML

This attribute points to the specific frame into which a link opens a document. If you wish to use a specific frame name as your target, you must specify it in the `name` attribute of the `FRAME` element.

The syntax of this command is

```
target= _blank | _self | _parent | _top | name
```

JAVASCRIPT
```
object.target [ = sTarget ]
```

This property is used to collect or set the target of a link.

Values
_blank

The user agent loads the designated document in a new, unnamed window.

_parent

The user agent loads the document into the immediate `FRAMESET` parent of the current frame. This value is equivalent to `_self` if the current frame has no parent.

_self

The user agent loads the document into the frame from which the element was called.

_top

The user agent loads the document into the full original window thereby deleting all other frames. This value is equivalent to `_self` if the current frame has no parent.

name

This string represents the name given to a particular `FRAME` object.

Example

The following example code creates a FRAMESET with all of its files. The FRAME-SET uses a variety of targets for the links on its pages.

ON THE CD-ROM

Look for **target.htm**, **targframe.htm**, and **targright.htm** on the accompanying CD-ROM.

target.htm

```
<html>
<head>
<title>Framesets and Targets</title>
</head>

<frameset cols="173,575" rows="*" bordercolor="#0000FF"
border="3" framespacing="3">
  <frame src="targframe.htm" >
  <frame src="targright.htm" name="rightframe">
</frameset>
<noframes><body bgcolor="#FFFFFF">

</body></noframes>
</html>
```

targframe.htm

```
<html>
<head>
<title>Left Page</title>
</head>

<body bgcolor="#FFFF00">
<p><b>TARGFRAME.HTM </b></p>
<p><a href="bgcolor.htm" target="_top">Link to Full
Window</a></p>
<p><a href="a.htm" target="_blank">Load a New Window</a></p>
<a href="acronym.html" target="rightframe">Load To Right
Window</a>
<p><a href="caption.htm" target="_self">Load in this
Frame</a></p>
</body>
</html>
```

targright.htm

```
<html>
<head>
<title>Right Page</title>
</head>

<body bgcolor="#99FFFF">
<b>TARGRIGHT.HTM</b>
</body>
</html>
```

Elements

A   AREA   BASE   FORM
LINK

CROSS-REFERENCE
See **target**, **<FRAME>**, **<FRAMESET>**, and **%Frameset**.

Target Frame

Concept

CROSS-REFERENCE
See **target**, **<FRAME>**, **<FRAMESET>**, and **%Frameset**.

tbodies

Collection

DHTML

This script collection creates a list of all the TBODY elements found within the current TABLE object. All of the objects in this collection occur in source order.
This collection can be used in the following ways:

```
[ collTBodies = ] object.tbodies
[ oObject = ] object.tbodies (vIndex [, iSubIndex] )
```

Parameters
collTBodies

This variable refers to the array of elements contained by the object.

oObject

This variable refers to an individual item in the array.

vIndex

This parameter is required and contains the number or string identifying the element or collection to retrieve. When a number is specified, the method returns the element in the zero-based collection at the identified position. When a string identifier is used and multiple elements with the same name or id attributes match the string, this method returns a collection of those matched elements.

iSubIndex

This optional parameter is used to identify the position of the element being retrieved when vIndex is a string. ISubIndex becomes the index of the specific item in the collection of matching elements identified by the vIndex string contents.

Elements

TABLE

 **CROSS-REFERENCE**
See **rows** and **cols**.

<TBODY>

Element

HTML

Start Tag: Optional
End Tag: Optional

This element is used to identify the specific body section of a table. You do not need to place it in a document because it will be inferred if there are no THEAD or TFOOT sections. If you wish to break a table into multiple segments, you need to use the TBODY element tags to separate each segment.

Attributes

align

```
cellhalign=  left | right | center
```

This attribute enables the document author to specify the position of the object within the individual cells of the table. A value of **left** aligns the object against the cell's left border; a value of **right** places the object against the cell's right. A value of **center** horizontally centers the object within the cell.

class

```
class="cdata-list"
```

This attribute assigns a class name to an element. User agents use classes to group specific types of information for later use.

dir

```
dir = LTR | RTL
```

This attribute defines the direction of the text flow in a document so that a user agent can correctly display it to the reader.

id

```
id="name"
```

This attribute is used to assign a name to an element.

lang

```
lang="language code"
```

This attribute specifies the language in which an element and its values should be rendered.

onclick

```
onclick=script
```

This attribute takes effect when the button on a pointing device is clicked while the pointer is over an on-screen element.

ondblclick

```
ondblclick=script
```

This attribute takes effect when the button on a pointing device is double-clicked while the pointer is over an on-screen element.

onkeydown

> `onkeydown=script`

This attribute takes effect when a key is pressed while the pointer is over an on-screen element.

onkeypress

> `onkeypress=script`

This attribute takes effect when a key is pressed and released while the pointer is over an on-screen element.

onkeyup

> `onkeyup=script`

This attribute takes effect when a key is released while the pointer is over an on-screen element.

onmousedown

> `onmousedown=script`

This attribute takes effect when the button on a pointing device is pressed while the pointer is over an on-screen element.

onmousemove

> `onmousemove=script`

This attribute is activated when the mouse pointer is moved while it is over an on-screen element.

onmouseout

> `onmouseout=script`

This attribute is activated when the mouse pointer is moved away from an on-screen element.

onmouseover

> `onmouseover=script`

This attribute is activated when the mouse pointer is moved over an on-screen element.

onmouseup

> `onmouseup=script`

This attribute takes effect when the button on a pointing device is released while the pointer is over an on-screen element.

style

```
style=style descriptors
```

This attribute is used to apply specific style-sheet information to one particular element.

title

```
title=text
```

This attribute provides annotation information for the element.

valign

```
valign= top | bottom | middle | baseline
```

This attribute enables the document author to specify the position of the object within the individual cells of the table. A value of **top** aligns the object against the cell's top border; a value of **bottom** places the object against the cell's bottom. A value of **middle** vertically centers the object within the cell. **Baseline** aligns the contents of the table with the baseline of the text contained in the table cells.

Example
The following table uses the TBODY element to provide sections for separate Income and Expense portions of this company's year-end statement.
CD ROM
Look for **tbody.htm** on the accompanying CD-ROM.

```
<html>
<head>
<title>Using Tbody</title>
<meta http-equiv="Content-Type" content="text/html;
charset=iso-8859-1">
</head>

<body bgcolor="#FFFFFF">
<TABLE border="1" width="75%">
  <THEAD>
  <TR>
    <td>
      <h1>..YTD Income and Expense Chart...</h1>
    </td>
  </TR>
  </THEAD>

<TBODY>
<TR>
    <td bordercolor="#0000FF">
```

```
      <h2>Income</h2>
    </td>
  </TR>
<TR>
    <td>Profit - <font color="#FF0000">Less than
Astronomical</font></td>
  </TR>
</TBODY>
<TBODY>
<TR>
    <td bordercolor="#FF0000">
      <h2>Expenses:</h2>
    </td>
  </TR>
<TR>
    <td bordercolor="#FFFFFF">Operating Costs -<font
color="#FF0000"> Astronomical</font></td>
  </TR>
<TR>
    <td bordercolor="#FFFFFF">Salaries - <font
color="#FF0000">Got off Cheap!</font></td>
  </TR>
</TBODY>
<TFOOT>
  <TR>
    <td>
      <div align="center"><font size="-1">...See the Annual
Report for More Information...</font></div>
    </td>
  </TR>
</TFOOT>
</TABLE>
</body>
</html>
```

CROSS-REFERENCE
See <**TABLE**>, tbodies, <**TD**>, <**TFOOT**>, <**TH**>, <**THEAD**>, and <**TR**>.

<TD>

Element

HTML

Start Tag: Required
End Tag: Optional

This element is used to create table cells that are designed to hold data. These cells are generally used to make up the body of the table. Because you can specify header cells and data cells separately, user agents can display information contained within these cells differently, even without the use of a style sheet.

Attributes

abbr

```
abbr= text
```

This attribute is used to provide an abbreviated form of the cell's contents. Some user agents that don't support tables use this to provide information to the reader.

align

```
align= left | right | center
```

This attribute enables the document author to specify the position of the object within the individual cells of the table. A value of **left** aligns the object against the cell's left border; a value of **right** places the object against the cell's right. A value of **center** horizontally centers the object within the cell.

axis

```
axis=cdata
```

This attribute enables document authors to organize the information in tables by creating categories that form an axis in the table.

bgcolor

```
bgcolor=color
```

This attribute sets the default background color of the cell.

s
t
u

char

```
char = "character"
```

This attribute enables you to specify a particular character to serve as an alignment point within a table and its subdivisions.

charoff

```
charoff=length
```

This attribute is used to offset the first occurrence of the alignment character specified by the char attribute.

class

```
class="cdata-list"
```

This attribute assigns a class name to an element. User agents use classes to group specific types of information for later use.

colspan

```
colspan=number
```

This HTML attribute specifies the number of columns TD or TH cells should span.

dir

```
dir = LTR | RTL
```

This attribute defines the direction of the text flow in a document so that a user agent can correctly display it to the reader.

headers

```
headers=idrefs
```

This attribute identifies a list of header cells that are related to the contents of the current data cell.

id

```
id="name"
```

This attribute is used to assign a name to an element.

lang

```
lang="language code"
```

This attribute specifies the language in which an element and its values should be rendered.

onclick

```
onclick=script
```

This attribute takes effect when the button on a pointing device is clicked while the pointer is over an on-screen element.

ondblclick

```
ondblclick=script
```

This attribute takes effect when the button on a pointing device is double-clicked while the pointer is over an on-screen element.

onkeydown

```
onkeydown=script
```

This attribute takes effect when a key is pressed while the pointer is over an on-screen element.

onkeypress

```
onkeypress=script
```

This attribute takes effect when a key is pressed and released while the pointer is over an on-screen element.

onkeyup

```
onkeyup=script
```

This attribute takes effect when a key is released while the pointer is over an on-screen element.

onmousedown

```
onmousedown=script
```

This attribute takes effect when the button on a pointing device is pressed while the pointer is over an on-screen element.

onmousemove

```
onmousemove=script
```

This attribute is activated when the mouse pointer is moved while it is over an on-screen element.

onmouseout

```
onmouseout=script
```

This attribute is activated when the mouse pointer is moved away from an on-screen element.

onmouseover

onmouseover=*script*

This attribute is activated when the mouse pointer is moved over an on-screen element.

onmouseup

onmouseup=*script*

This attribute takes effect when the button on a pointing device is released while the pointer is over an on-screen element.

rowspan

rowspan=*number*

This HTML attribute specifies the number of rows a TD or TH cell should span.

scope

scope= row | col | rowgroup | colgroup

This identifies the range that the header cell is applied to.

style

style=*style descriptors*

This attribute is used to apply specific style-sheet information to one particular element.

title

title=*text*

This attribute provides annotation information for the element.

valign

valign= top | bottom | middle

This attribute enables the document author to specify the position of the object within the individual cells of the table. A value of **top** aligns the object against the cell's top border; a value of **bottom** places the object against the cell's bottom. A value of **middle** vertically centers the object within the cell.

Example
The following example uses the TD elements within a table to format information on a page. Using the table to format enables you to ensure that most of your viewers will see the information in a similar fashion.

```
<html>
<head>
<title>Table Cells adding to Formatting</title>
<meta http-equiv="generator" content="Macromedia Dreamweaver">

  <script language="JavaScript">
<!—
function MM_initTimelines() {
    //MM_initTimelines() Copyright 1997 Macromedia, Inc. All
rights reserved.
    var ns = navigator.appName == "Netscape";
    document.MM_Time = new Array(1);
    document.MM_Time[0] = new Array(6);
    document.MM_Time["Timeline1"] = document.MM_Time[0];
    document.MM_Time[0].MM_Name = "Timeline1";
    document.MM_Time[0].fps = 15;
    document.MM_Time[0][0] = new String("sprite");
    document.MM_Time[0][0].slot = 2;
    if (ns)
        document.MM_Time[0][0].obj = document.Image2;
    else
        document.MM_Time[0][0].obj = document.Image2;
    document.MM_Time[0][0].keyFrames = new Array(1, 11, 25,
50);
    document.MM_Time[0][0].values = new Array(1);
    document.MM_Time[0][0].values[0] = new
Array("td1.gif","td9.gif","td1.gif","td1.gif");
    document.MM_Time[0][0].values[0].prop = "src";
    document.MM_Time[0][1] = new String("sprite");
    document.MM_Time[0][1].slot = 4;
    if (ns)
        document.MM_Time[0][1].obj = document.Image4;
    else
        document.MM_Time[0][1].obj = document.Image4;
    document.MM_Time[0][1].keyFrames = new Array(1, 11, 25,
36, 50);
    document.MM_Time[0][1].values = new Array(1);
    document.MM_Time[0][1].values[0] = new
Array("td3.gif","td3.gif","td9.gif","td3.gif","td3.gif");
    document.MM_Time[0][1].values[0].prop = "src";
    document.MM_Time[0][2] = new String("sprite");
    document.MM_Time[0][2].slot = 1;
```

s

t

u

```
    if (ns)
        document.MM_Time[0][2].obj = document.Image5;
    else
        document.MM_Time[0][2].obj = document.Image5;
    document.MM_Time[0][2].keyFrames = new Array(1, 25, 50);
    document.MM_Time[0][2].values = new Array(1);
    document.MM_Time[0][2].values[0] = new
Array("td5.gif","td5.gif","td9.gif");
    document.MM_Time[0][2].values[0].prop = "src";
    document.MM_Time[0][3] = new String("sprite");
    document.MM_Time[0][3].slot = 3;
    if (ns)
        document.MM_Time[0][3].obj = document.Image6;
    else
        document.MM_Time[0][3].obj = document.Image6;
    document.MM_Time[0][3].keyFrames = new Array(1, 36, 50);
    document.MM_Time[0][3].values = new Array(1);
    document.MM_Time[0][3].values[0] = new
Array("td7.gif","td9.gif","td7.gif");
    document.MM_Time[0][3].values[0].prop = "src";
    document.MM_Time[0][4] = new String("sprite");
    document.MM_Time[0][4].slot = 5;
    if (ns)
        document.MM_Time[0][4].obj = document.Image7;
    else
        document.MM_Time[0][4].obj = document.Image7;
    document.MM_Time[0][4].keyFrames = new Array(1, 11, 25,
36, 50);
    document.MM_Time[0][4].values = new Array(1);
    document.MM_Time[0][4].values[0] = new
Array("td4.gif","td9.gif","td4.gif","td9.gif","td4.gif");
    document.MM_Time[0][4].values[0].prop = "src";
    document.MM_Time[0][5] = new String("behavior");
    document.MM_Time[0][5].frame = 21;
    document.MM_Time[0][5].value =
"MM_timelineGoto('Timeline1','1')";
    document.MM_Time[0].lastFrame = 50;
    for (i=0; i<document.MM_Time.length; i++) {
        document.MM_Time[i].ID = null;
        document.MM_Time[i].curFrame = 0;
        document.MM_Time[i].delay =
1000/document.MM_Time[i].fps;
    }
}
```

```
//->
</script>
  <script language="JavaScript">
<!-
function MM_timelinePlay(tmLnName, myID) { //v1.2
  //Copyright 1997 Macromedia, Inc. All rights reserved.
  var
i,j,tmLn,props,keyFrm,sprite,numKeyFr,firstKeyFr,propNum,theOb
j,firstTime=false;
  if (document.MM_Time == null) MM_initTimelines(); //if
*very* 1st time
  tmLn = document.MM_Time[tmLnName];
  if (myID == null) { myID = ++tmLn.ID; firstTime=true;}//if
new call, incr ID
  if (myID == tmLn.ID) { //if Im newest

setTimeout('MM_timelinePlay("'+tmLnName+'",'+myID+')',tmLn.del
ay);
    fNew = ++tmLn.curFrame;
    for (i=0; i<tmLn.length; i++) {
      sprite = tmLn[i];
      if (sprite.charAt(0) == 's') {
        if (sprite.obj) {
          numKeyFr = sprite.keyFrames.length; firstKeyFr =
sprite.keyFrames[0];
          if (fNew >= firstKeyFr && fNew <=
sprite.keyFrames[numKeyFr-1]) { //in range
            keyFrm=1;
            for (j=0; j<sprite.values.length; j++) {
              props = sprite.values[j];
              if (numKeyFr != props.length) {
                if (props.prop2 == null)
sprite.obj[props.prop] = props[fNew-firstKeyFr];
                else
sprite.obj[props.prop2][props.prop] = props[fNew-firstKeyFr];
              } else {
                while (keyFrm<numKeyFr &&
fNew>=sprite.keyFrames[keyFrm]) keyFrm++;
                if (firstTime ||
fNew==sprite.keyFrames[keyFrm-1]) {
                  if (props.prop2 == null)
sprite.obj[props.prop] = props[keyFrm-1];
                  else
sprite.obj[props.prop2][props.prop] = props[keyFrm-1];
```

\

```
        } } } } }
      } else if (sprite.charAt(0)=='b' && fNew ==
sprite.frame) eval(sprite.value);
      if (fNew > tmLn.lastFrame) tmLn.ID = 0;
  } }
}
//-->
</script>
  <script language="JavaScript">
<!--
function MM_timelineGoto(tmLnName, fNew, numGotos) { //v1.2
  //Copyright 1997 Macromedia, Inc. All rights reserved.
  var
i,j,tmLn,props,keyFrm,sprite,numKeyFr,firstKeyFr,lastKeyFr,pro
pNum,theObj;
  if (document.MM_Time == null) MM_initTimelines(); //if
*very* 1st time
  tmLn = document.MM_Time[tmLnName];
  if (numGotos != null)
    if (tmLn.gotoCount == null) tmLn.gotoCount = 1;
    else if (tmLn.gotoCount++ >= numGotos) {tmLn.gotoCount=0;
return}
  jmpFwd = (fNew > tmLn.curFrame);
  for (i = 0; i < tmLn.length; i++) {
    sprite = (jmpFwd)? tmLn[i] : tmLn[(tmLn.length-1)-i];
//count bkwds if jumping back
    if (sprite.charAt(0) == "s") {
      numKeyFr = sprite.keyFrames.length;
      firstKeyFr = sprite.keyFrames[0];
      lastKeyFr = sprite.keyFrames[numKeyFr - 1];
      if ((jmpFwd && fNew<firstKeyFr) || (!jmpFwd &&
lastKeyFr<fNew)) continue; //skip if untouchd
      for (keyFrm=1; keyFrm<numKeyFr &&
fNew>=sprite.keyFrames[keyFrm]; keyFrm++);
      for (j=0; j<sprite.values.length; j++) {
        props = sprite.values[j];
        if (numKeyFr == props.length) propNum = keyFrm-1
//keyframes only
        else propNum = Math.min(Math.max(0,fNew-
firstKeyFr),props.length-1); //or keep in legal range
        if (sprite.obj != null) {
          if (props.prop2 == null) sprite.obj[props.prop] =
props[propNum];
```

```
          else          sprite.obj[props.prop2][props.prop] =
props[propNum];
  } } } }
  tmLn.curFrame = fNew;
  if (tmLn.ID == 0) eval('MM_timelinePlay(tmLnName)');
}
//-->
</script>
</head>

<body bgcolor="#FFFFFF" onLoad="MM_timelinePlay('Timeline1')">
<table border="1" width="75%">
  <tr>
    <td align="center" valign="middle"><img src="td.gif"
width="92" height="92" name="Image1"></td>
    <td align="center" valign="middle"><img src="td1.gif"
width="92" height="92" name="Image2"></td>
    <td align="center" valign="middle"><img src="td2.gif"
width="92" height="92" name="Image3"></td>
  </tr>
  <tr>
    <td align="center" valign="middle"><img src="td9.gif"
width="92" height="92" name="Image4"></td>
    <td align="center" valign="middle"><img src="td4.gif"
width="92" height="92" name="Image7"></td>
    <td align="center" valign="middle"><img src="td5.gif"
width="92" height="92" name="Image5"></td>
  </tr>
  <tr>
    <td align="center" valign="middle"><img src="td6.gif"
width="92" height="92"></td>
    <td align="center" valign="middle"><img src="td7.gif"
width="92" height="92" name="Image6"></td>
    <td align="center" valign="middle"><img src="td8.gif"
width="92" height="92"></td>
  </tr>
</table>
</body>
</html>
```

CROSS-REFERENCE

See **<TABLE>**, **<TBODY>**, **<TFOOT>**, **<TH>**, **<THEAD>,** and **<TR>**.

text

Attribute

HTML

This attribute is used to set the color of the text contained within the body of the document.

The syntax of this attribute is

```
text=colorname | RGBvalue
```

JAVASCRIPT

```
object.text [ = string ]
```

This property sets the text value for the object. Its use varies depending upon the object that it is applied to. For example, when used with the BODY object, it sets the color of the text; when used with the textrange object, it sets or collects the text content of the range.

Values

colorname

This is one of the valid color names specified by the HTML 4.0 standard or, if viewed with Internet Explorer 4.0, one of Microsoft's identified color names.

RGBvalue

The name of the color is returned in hexadecimal format representing the RGB value of the color.

Example

The following code creates a document with red text on a white background.

ON THE CD-ROM

Look for **text.htm** on the accompanying CD-ROM.

```
<BODY text=red bgcolor=white>
...Add some paragraph text here ...
</BODY>
```

Elements

BODY

CROSS-REFERENCE

See **color** and **bgcolor**.

Text Input

Concept

Within a form, a text input field can contain a single string of characters. You can control the field's visual size and the total number of characters that it can contain. The following code creates a form that uses text fields to collect an individual's name, address, e-mail address, and phone number.

```
<form method="post" action="">
  <p align="left">Name:
    <input type="text" name="name" size="75">
    <br>
    Address:
    <input type="text" name="address" size="75">
    <br>
    City, State, Zip:
    <input type="text" name="cstz" size="75">
  </p>
  <p align="left">Email:
    <input type="text" name="email" size="75">
    <br>
    Daytime Phone:
    <input type="text" name="phone" size="25">
</form>
```

CROSS-REFERENCE
See **<FORM>**, **<INPUT>**, **<TEXTAREA>**, **checkboxes**, **menus**, **radio buttons**, **buttons**, **file select**, **hidden controls**, and **object controls**.

text-align

Attribute

CSS

This attribute is used to align the inline-text contents of the block element to which the attribute is applied.

The syntax of this command is

```
text-align: left | right | center | justify | <string> |
inherit
```

JAVASCRIPT

```
object.style.textAlign [ = sAlign ]
```

This property is used to set the alignment of text within an object's contents.

Values

center

> This centers the text horizontally within the block.

justify

> This double-justifies the text within the block.

left

> This aligns the text to the left edge of the block.

right

> This aligns the text to the right edge of the block.

string

> This is the character content that the cells should align themselves against. You may want to use a comma or a period for cells containing numbers or a space for cells containing a series of two-word phrases.

Example

The following style sheet sets the alignment for all TD cells to **center** and all TH cells to **justify.**

```
<STYLE type="text/css">
<!—
TD    { text-align: center }
TH    { text-align: justify }
—>
</SCRIPT>
```

Elements

BLOCKQUOTE	BODY	BUTTON	CAPTION
CENTER	COL	COLGROUP	DIV
FIELDSET	FORM	FRAME	FRAMESET
H1–H6	HEAD	HR	IFRAME
INPUT	LABEL	LAYER	LEGEND
LI	MAP	MARQUEE	OBJECT
OL	P	PRE	Q

SCRIPT	SELECT	SPAN	TABLE
TD	TEXTAREA	TFOOT	TH
THEAD	TR	UL	

CROSS-REFERENCE
See **align**, **halign**, and **valign**.

<TEXTAREA>

Element

HTML

Start Tag: Required
End Tag: Required

This element is used to create a multiline text input box that can be used within a form to gather information.

Attributes

accesskey

```
accesskey="character"
```

You can assign an access key to an element. This key enables you to put the focus on an element quickly. In the case of a form element, the user is immediately able to input information. In the case of a link, the link is activated and followed.

class

```
class="cdata-list"
```

This attribute assigns a class name to an element. User agents use classes to group specific types of information for later use.

cols

```
cols=number
```

This assigns the number of characters that can be displayed on a single line of a text field.

dir

```
dir = LTR | RTL
```

This attribute defines the direction of the text flow in a document so that a user agent can correctly display it to the reader.

s
t
u

disabled

   disabled

This is a Boolean attribute that, when set, will disable the object, preventing any user input.

id

   id="*name*"

This attribute is used to assign a name to an element.

lang

   lang="*language code*"

This attribute specifies the language in which an element and its values should be rendered.

name

   name=*cdata*

This attribute is used to give the <TEXTAREA> element a name that is used as an identifier when the element is identified for the FORM.

onblur

   onblur=*script*

This attribute becomes active when an element loses the focus either through the actions of a mouse or another pointing device or through tabbing navigation.

onchange

   onchange = *script*

If a control's value is changed while the control has input focus, this event occurs when the control loses the focus.

onclick

   onclick=*script*

This attribute takes effect when the button on a pointing device is clicked while the pointer is over an on-screen element.

ondblclick

   ondblclick=*script*

This attribute takes effect when the button on a pointing device is double-clicked while the pointer is over an on-screen element.

onfocus

```
onfocus=script
```

This attribute takes effect when an element receives focus from either a mouse or another pointing device or through tabbed navigation.

onkeydown

```
onkeydown=script
```

This attribute takes effect when a key is pressed while the pointer is over an on-screen element.

onkeypress

```
onkeypress=script
```

This attribute takes effect when a key is pressed and released while the pointer is over an on-screen element.

onkeyup

```
onkeyup=script
```

This attribute takes effect when a key is released while the pointer is over an on-screen element.

onmousedown

```
onmousedown=script
```

This attribute takes effect when the button on a pointing device is pressed while the pointer is over an on-screen element.

onmousemove

```
onmousemove=script
```

This attribute is activated when the mouse pointer is moved while it is over an on-screen element.

onmouseout

```
onmouseout=script
```

This attribute is activated when the mouse pointer is moved away from an on-screen element.

onmouseover

```
onmouseover=script
```

This attribute is activated when the mouse pointer is moved over an on-screen element.

onmouseup

```
onmouseup=script
```

This attribute takes effect when the button on a pointing device is released while the pointer is over an on-screen element.

onselect

```
onselect=script
```

This event occurs when a user selects text within a text field.

readonly

```
readonly
```

This is a Boolean attribute that prohibits change in a control. A reader cannot modify the contents of the control in any way, although the control can still receive the focus and is included in the tabbing order.

rows

```
rows=number
```

This is the number of lines of text that can be displayed in the text box.

style

```
style=style descriptors
```

This attribute is used to apply specific style-sheet information to one particular element.

tabindex

```
tabindex=number
```

This attribute provides the position of the current element within the overall tabbing order of the document.

title

```
title=text
```

This attribute provides annotation information for the element.

Example

The following script code creates a form using a singular TEXTAREA field.

 ON THE CD-ROM
Look for **textarea.htm** on the accompanying CD-ROM.

```
<html>
```

```
<head>
<title>Textarea in Forms</title>
<meta http-equiv="Generator" content="Macromedia Dreamweaver">
</head>

<body bgcolor="#FFFFFF" background="cartbkg.gif">
<p align="center"><img src="cartoon.jpg" width="400"
height="210"></p>
<p align="center"><b><font color="#FF0000" size="7">- Dectoid
-<br>
  Scourge of the Universe</font></b></p>
<p>Let us know what you think of our site:</p>
<form method="post" action="">
  <p align="left">Name:
    <input type="text" name="name" size="75">
    <br>
    Email:
    <input type="text" name="email" size="75">
    <br>
    Web:
    <input type="text" name="web" size="75">
  </p>
Comments or questions:<br>
    <textarea name="commentbox" cols="75" rows="3"></textarea>
</form>

</body>
</html>
```

CROSS-REFERENCE
See **<FORM>**, **<INPUT>**, **text, checkboxes, menus, radio buttons, buttons, file select, hidden controls,** and **object controls.**

text-decoration

Attribute

CSS

This Cascading Style Sheets attribute is used to add decorative properties to an element. For example, it can cause an element to be underlined or to blink.

The syntax of this command is

```
text-decoration: none | underline | blink | overline | line-
through
```

JAVASCRIPT

The following scripting elements can be used to set the value of these text-decoration options:

```
object.style.textAlign [=Decoration]
object.style.textDecorationBlink [=bVar]
object.style.textDecorationLineThrough [=bVar]
object.style.textDecorationNone [=bVar]
object.style.textDecorationOverLine [=bVar]
object.style.textDecorationUnderLine [=bVar]
```

Values
blink

All of the text will blink.

none

No decoration is applied.

overline

A line is placed above every line of text.

underline

All text is underlined.

Example
The following style sheet underlines all text appearing as part of a P element and makes all text appearing as part of a DIV element blink.

```
<STYLE type="text/css">
<–
P   { text-decoration: underline }
DIV { text-decoration: blink }
–>
</STYLE>
```

Elements
This attribute can be applied to all elements.

CROSS-REFERENCE
See **text**, **<BLINK>**, and **<B>**.

text-indent

Attribute

CSS

This Cascading Style Sheets text attribute is used to indent the first line of a paragraph. If the text in the block is a left-to-right flowing paragraph, the indent is on the left edge of the first line. If the text in the block is a right-to-left flowing paragraph, the indent is on the right edge of the first line.

The syntax used to implement this attribute is

```
text-indent: length | percentage
```

JAVASCRIPT

```
object.style.textIndent [ = sIndent ]
```

This property is used to set or retrieve the indentation length of a block object.

Values
length

This is the distance the line should be indented. This is a number and unit identifier.

percentage

This forces the indentation to be a percentage of the entire block width.

Example
The following style sheet forces the first line of all P elements to be indented 3 cm.

```
<STYLE type="text/css">
<-
P    { text-indent: 3cm }
->
</STYLE>
```

Elements

BLOCKQUOTE	BODY	BUTTON	CAPTION
CENTER	COL	COLGROUP	DIV
FIELDSET	FORM	FRAME	FRAMESET
H1–H6	HEAD	HR	IFRAME
INPUT	LABEL	LAYER	LEGEND
LI	MAP	MARQUEE	OBJECT

s
t
u

OL	P	PRE	Q
SCRIPT	SELECT	SPAN	TABLE
TD	TEXTAREA	TFOOT	TH
THEAD	TR	UL	

 CROSS-REFERENCE
See **:first-line** and **:first-letter**.

text-shadow

Attribute

CSS

This attribute is used to apply shadows to text contents of an element. This comma-separated list of shadow effects enables you to control the order, color, and dimensions of the shadows that are overlaid on your text. Shadows do not extend the size of the block containing the text, but they may extend over the boundaries of the block. The stacking level of the shadows is the same as the element itself.

Each shadow effect must specify the offset of the shadow. You can also specify a blur radius and a shadow color. The shadow offset is specified with two *length* variables that identify how far out from the text the shadow extends. The first *length* specifies the horizontal distance from the text, and the second *length* specifies the vertical depth of the shadow. If you apply a negative value to the shadow offsets, the shadow appears to the left and top of the text, rather than to the lower right.

The blur radius is specified as a third *length* property. This value is used to identify the boundary of the blur effect. The other optional value is color, which can be used to control the specific shade and tone of the rendered shadow effect.

The syntax used to implement this attribute is

```
text-shadow: none | [color || length length length? ,]* [color
|| length length length?] | inherit
```

Values

none

No shadow effects are applied to the text.

color

This is either the name or the RGB value of the color used to display the text.

length

This is the offset value of the horizontal, vertical, or blur dimensions of the shadow.

Example

The following example text applies a series of shadows to the H1 and H2 elements rendered with the document.

ON THE CD-ROM

Look for **textshadow.htm** on the accompanying CD-ROM.

```
<html>
<head>
<title>Text-Shadows... what way to look at information</title>
<meta http-equiv="generator" content="Macromedia Dreamweaver">
<style type="text/css">
<!-
h1 {  text-shadow: "red 5px 5px 3px" }
h2 {  text-shadow: "green 3px 3px 2px" }
->
</style></head>

<body bgcolor="#FFFFFF">
<h1>Heading 1</h1>
<h1> Heading 1</h1>
<h1>Heading 1</h1>
<h2>heading 2</h2>
<h2>heading 2</h2>
<h2>heading 2</h2>
</body>
</html>
```

Elements

This attribute applies to all elements.

NOTE

You can apply the text-shadow attribute to the :first-letter and :first-line pseudo-elements.

CROSS-REFERENCE

See **text-transform** and **text-decoration**.

s
t
u

text-transform

Attribute

CSS

This attribute is used to apply a specified capitalization style to your text. The syntax of this attribute is

```
text-transform: capitalize | uppercase | lowercase | none
```

JAVASCRIPT

```
object.style.textTransform [ = sTransform ]
```

This property is used to set or retrieve the transformation applied to a block object.

Values
capitalize

This places the sentence or phrase in Title case, in which the first letter of each word is capitalized.

lowercase

This forces all characters of the words to be lowercase.

uppercase

This forces all characters of the words to be uppercase.

Example
The following code uses the `textTransform` property to alter the text of a paragraph when it is coordinated with movements or clicks of the mouse.

```
<html>
<head>
<title>textTransform Example</title>
</head>

<body bgcolor="#FFFFFF">

<h1 onclick="this.style.textTransform='lowercase'"
onmouseover="this.style.textTransform='uppercase'"
onmouseout="this.style.textTransform='capitalize'">roll over
me and click me!</h1>
</body>
</html>
```

Elements

This applies to all elements.

CROSS-REFERENCE
See **text-decoration** and **text-shadow**.

\<TFOOT\>

Element

HTML

Start Tag: Required
End Tag: Optional

This element is used to separate out a specific group of cells to serve as footer material for the table. User agents can use this to control how information is rendered on tables with distinct headers, footers, and bodies.

Attributes

align

```
align= left | right | center
```

This attribute enables the document author to specify the position of the object within the individual cells of the table. A value of **left** aligns the object against the cell's left border; a value of **right** places the object against the cell's right. A value of **center** horizontally centers the object within the cell.

class

```
class="cdata-list"
```

This attribute assigns a class name to an element. User agents use classes to group specific types of information for later use.

dir

```
dir = LTR | RTL
```

This attribute defines the direction of the text flow in a document so that a user agent can correctly display it to the reader.

id

```
id="name"
```

This attribute is used to assign a name to an element.

lang

    lang="*language code*"

This attribute specifies the language in which an element and its values should be rendered.

onclick

    onclick=*script*

This attribute takes effect when the button on a pointing device is clicked while the pointer is over an on-screen element.

ondblclick

    ondblclick=*script*

This attribute takes effect when the button on a pointing device is double-clicked while the pointer is over an on-screen element.

onkeydown

    onkeydown=*script*

This attribute takes effect when a key is pressed while the pointer is over an on-screen element.

onkeypress

    onkeypress=*script*

This attribute takes effect when a key is pressed and released while the pointer is over an on-screen element.

onkeyup

    onkeyup=*script*

This attribute takes effect when a key is released while the pointer is over an on-screen element.

onmousedown

    onmousedown=*script*

This attribute takes effect when the button on a pointing device is pressed while the pointer is over an on-screen element.

onmousemove

    onmousemove=*script*

This attribute is activated when the mouse pointer is moved while it is over an on-screen element.

onmouseout

```
onmouseout=script
```

This attribute is activated when the mouse pointer is moved away from an on-screen element.

onmouseover

```
onmouseover=script
```

This attribute is activated when the mouse pointer is moved over an on-screen element.

onmouseup

```
onmouseup=script
```

This attribute takes effect when the button on a pointing device is released while the pointer is over an on-screen element.

style

```
style=style descriptors
```

This attribute is used to apply specific style-sheet information to one particular element.

title

```
title=text
```

This attribute provides annotation information for the element.

valign

```
valign=  top | bottom | middle
```

This attribute enables the document author to specify the position of the object within the individual cells of the table. A value of **top** aligns the object against the cell's top border; a value of **bottom** places the object against the cell's bottom. A value of **middle** vertically centers the object within the cell.

Example

The following example code creates a table with a distinct header, footer, and body section. The footer is used to provide information that will take the reader to an alternate source of information.

```
<TABLE border="1" width="75%">
  <THEAD>
  <TR>
    <td>
      <h1>..YTD Income and Expense Chart...</h1>
```

```
        </td>
    </TR>
    </THEAD>

    <TBODY>
    <TR>
        <td bordercolor="#0000FF">
            <h2>Income</h2>
        </td>
    </TR>
    <TR>
        <td>Profit - <font color="#FF0000">Less than
Astronomical</font></td>
    </TR>
    </TBODY>
    <TBODY>
    <TR>
        <td bordercolor="#FF0000">
            <h2>Expenses:</h2>
        </td>
    </TR>
    <TR>
        <td bordercolor="#FFFFFF">Operating Costs -<font
color="#FF0000"> Astronomical</font></td>
    </TR>
    <TR>
        <td bordercolor="#FFFFFF">Salaries - <font
color="#FF0000">Got off Cheap!</font></td>
    </TR>
    </TBODY>
    <TFOOT>
    <TR>
        <td>
            <div align="center"><font size="-1"><a
href="98rept.htm">...See the Annual Report for More
Information...</A></font></div>
        </td>
    </TR>
    </TFOOT>
    </TABLE>
```

 CROSS-REFERENCE
See **<TABLE>**, **<TBODY>**, **<TD>**, **<TH>**, **<THEAD>,** and **<TR>**.

tFoot

Property

DHTML

This document object property is used to select the TFOOT section of a table. The syntax used to implement this property is

```
[ sVar = ] object.tFoot
```

Parameters
sVar

This string variable holds the value of the footer.

Elements

TABLE

CROSS-REFERENCE
See **<TFOOT>**, **<THEAD>**, and **tHead**.

<TH>

Element

HTML

Start Tag: Required
End Tag: Optional

This element is used to create table cells that are designed to hold header information. These cells are generally used to make up the THEAD of the table. Because you can specify header cells and data cells separately, user agents can display information contained within these cells differently, even without the use of a style sheet.

Attributes
abbr

```
abbr=text
```

This attribute is used to provide an abbreviated form of the cell's contents. Some user agents that don't support tables use this to provide information to the reader.

align

```
align=  left | right | center
```

This attribute enables the document author to specify the position of the object within the individual cells of the table. A value of **left** aligns the object against the cell's left border; a value of **right** places the object to the cell's right. A value of **center** horizontally centers the object within the cell.

axis

```
axis=cdata
```

This attribute enables document authors to organize the information in tables by creating categories that form an axis in the table.

bgcolor

```
bgcolor=color
```

This attribute sets the default background color of the cell.

char

```
char="character"
```

This attribute enables you to specify a particular character to serve as an alignment point within a table and its subdivisions.

charoff

```
charoff=length
```

This attribute is used to offset the first occurrence of the alignment character specified by the char attribute.

class

```
class="cdata-list"
```

This attribute assigns a class name to an element. User agents use classes to group specific types of information for later use.

colspan

```
colspan=number
```

This HTML attribute specifies the number of columns TD or TH cells should span.

dir

```
dir = LTR | RTL
```

This attribute defines the direction of the text flow in a document so that a user agent can correctly display it to the reader.

headers

> headers=*idrefs*

This attribute identifies a list of header cells that are related to the current cell.

id

> id="*name*"

This attribute is used to assign a name to an element.

lang

> lang="*language code*"

This attribute specifies the language in which an element and its values should be rendered.

onclick

> onclick=*script*

This attribute takes effect when the button on a pointing device is clicked while the pointer is over an on-screen element.

ondblclick

> ondblclick=*script*

This attribute takes effect when the button on a pointing device is double-clicked while the pointer is over an on-screen element.

onkeydown

> onkeydown=*script*

This attribute takes effect when a key is pressed while the pointer is over an on-screen element.

onkeypress

> onkeypress=*script*

This attribute takes effect when a key is pressed and released while the pointer is over an on-screen element.

onkeyup

> onkeyup=*script*

This attribute takes effect when a key is released while the pointer is over an on-screen element.

s
t
u

onmousedown

onmousedown=*script*

This attribute takes effect when the button on a pointing device is pressed while the pointer is over an on-screen element.

onmousemove

onmousemove=*script*

This attribute is activated when the mouse pointer is moved while it is over an on-screen element.

onmouseout

onmouseout=*script*

This attribute is activated when the mouse pointer is moved away from an on-screen element.

onmouseover

onmouseover=*script*

This attribute is activated when the mouse pointer is moved over an on-screen element.

onmouseup

onmouseup=*script*

This attribute takes effect when the button on a pointing device is released while the pointer is over an on-screen element.

rowspan

rowspan=*number*

This HTML attribute specifies the number of rows a TD or TH cell should span.

scope

scope= row | col | rowgroup | colgroup

This identifies the range that the header cell is applied to.

style

style=*style descriptors*

This attribute is used to apply specific style-sheet information to one particular element.

title

```
title=text
```

This attribute provides annotation information for the element.

valign

```
valign=  top | bottom | middle
```

This attribute enables the document author to specify the position of the object within the individual cells of the table. A value of **top** aligns the object against the cell's top border; a value of **bottom** places the object against the cell's bottom. A value of **middle** vertically centers the object within the cell.

Example

The following code creates a short roll sheet for tracking the name, attendance, and GPA of four students. The TH elements are used to differentiate header information from the accompanying data.

ON THE CD-ROM

Look for **th.htm** on the accompanying CD-ROM.

```
<html>
<head>
<title>Table Header Cells</title>
<meta http-equiv="Generator" content="NetObjects
ScriptBuilder">
</head>

<body bgcolor="#FFFFFF">
<table border="1" width="75%">
  <tr align="center" valign="middle" bgcolor="#FFFF00">
    <th>Name</th>
    <th>Attendance</th>
    <th>GPA</th>
  </tr>
  <tr>
    <td>George</td>
    <td>80%</td>
    <td>3.74</td>
  </tr>
  <tr>
    <td>Harold</td>
    <td>90%</td>
    <td>
      <p>3.65</p>
    </td>
```

```
      </tr>
      <tr>
        <td>Amy</td>
        <td>75%</td>
        <td>3.54</td>
      </tr>
      <tr>
        <td>Katie</td>
        <td>100%</td>
        <td>2.7</td>
      </tr>
    </table>
  </body>
</html>
```

CROSS-REFERENCE
See **<TABLE>**, **<TD>**, **<TBODY>**, **<THEAD>**, **<TFOOT>**, and **<TR>**.

<THEAD>

Element

HTML

Start Tag: Required
End Tag: Optional

This element is used to separate out a specific group of cells to serve as header material for the table. User agents can use this to control how information is rendered on tables with distinct headers, footers, and bodies.

Attributes
align

```
align= left | right | center | justify  | char
```

This attribute enables the document author to specify the position of the object within the individual cells of the table. A value of **left** aligns the object against the cell's left border; a value of **right** places the object against the cell's right. A value of **center** horizontally centers the object within the cell. **Justify** aligns the text to both the left and right edges of a cell. **Char** aligns all of the information within a column against a specific character, such as a comma or a period for numerical data.

class

```
class="cdata-list"
```

This attribute assigns a class name to an element. User agents use classes to group specific types of information for later use.

dir

```
dir = LTR | RTL
```

This attribute defines the direction of the text flow in a document so that a user agent can correctly display it to the reader.

id

```
id="name"
```

This attribute is used to assign a name to an element.

lang

```
lang="language code"
```

This attribute specifies the language in which an element and its values should be rendered.

onclick

```
onclick=script
```

This attribute takes effect when the button on a pointing device is clicked while the pointer is over an on-screen element.

ondblclick

```
ondblclick=script
```

This attribute takes effect when the button on a pointing device is double-clicked while the pointer is over an on-screen element.

onkeydown

```
onkeydown=script
```

This attribute takes effect when a key is pressed while the pointer is over an on-screen element.

onkeypress

```
onkeypress=script
```

This attribute takes effect when a key is pressed and released while the pointer is over an on-screen element.

onkeyup

> `onkeyup=script`

This attribute takes effect when a key is released while the pointer is over an on-screen element.

onmousedown

> `onmousedown=script`

This attribute takes effect when the button on a pointing device is pressed while the pointer is over an on-screen element.

onmousemove

> `onmousemove=script`

This attribute is activated when the mouse pointer is moved while it is over an on-screen element.

onmouseout

> `onmouseout=script`

This attribute is activated when the mouse pointer is moved away from an on-screen element.

onmouseover

> `onmouseover=script`

This attribute is activated when the mouse pointer is moved over an on-screen element.

onmouseup

> `onmouseup=script`

This attribute takes effect when the button on a pointing device is released while the pointer is over an on-screen element.

style

> `style=style descriptors`

This attribute is used to apply specific style-sheet information to one particular element.

title

> `title=text`

This attribute provides annotation information for the element.

valign

```
valign=  top | bottom | middle | baseline
```

This attribute enables the document author to specify the position of the object within the individual cells of the table. A value of **top** aligns the object against the cell's top border; a value of **bottom** places the object against the cell's bottom. A value of **middle** vertically centers the object within the cell. **Baseline** aligns the contents of the table with the baseline of the text contained in the table cells.

Example

The following example code creates a table with a distinct header, footer, and body section. The header is used to provide information that makes the information displayed in the table easier to understand.

ON THE CD-ROM

Look for **th.htm** on the accompanying CD-ROM.

```
<TABLE border="1" width="75%">
  <THEAD>
  <TR>
    <td>
      <h1>..YTD Income and Expense Chart...</h1>
    </td>
  </TR>
  </THEAD>

  <TBODY>
  <TR>
    <td bordercolor="#0000FF">
      <h2>Income</h2>
    </td>
  </TR>
  <TR>
    <td>Profit - <font color="#FF0000">Less than
Astronomical</font></td>
  </TR>
  </TBODY>
  <TBODY>
  <TR>
    <td bordercolor="#FF0000">
      <h2>Expenses:</h2>
    </td>
  </TR>
  <TR>
```

```
    <td bordercolor="#FFFFFF">Operating Costs -<font
color="#FF0000"> Astronomical</font></td>
  </TR>
<TR>
    <td bordercolor="#FFFFFF">Salaries - <font
color="#FF0000">Got off Cheap!</font></td>
  </TR>
</TBODY>
<TFOOT>
  <TR>
    <td>
      <div align="center"><font size="-1">...See the Annual
Report for More Information...</font></div>
    </td>
  </TR>
</TFOOT>
</TABLE>
```

CROSS-REFERENCE
See **<TABLE>, <TBODY>, <TD>, <TH>, <TFOOT>,** and **<TR>.**

tHead

Property

DHTML

This document object property is used to select the THEAD section of a table. The syntax used to implement this property is

```
[ sVar = ] object.tHead
```

Parameters
sVar

This string variable holds the value of the header.

Elements

TABLE

CROSS-REFERENCE
See **<TFOOT>, <THEAD>,** and **tFoot.**

time

Value

CSS

Times are used in Aural style sheets to set the length of pauses and to set timing on cues. Times cannot be negative. They are composed of a *number* followed by either a millisecond (ms) or second (s) identifier.

 CROSS-REFERENCE
See **%datetime**, **length**, **number**, and *percentage*.

<TITLE>

Element

HTML – OSD – CDF

Start Tag: Required (HTML, OSD, CDF)
End Tag: Required (HTML, OSD); Optional (CDF)

This element is used to provide a title for a document. To comply with the HTML 4.0 specification, an HTML document must have a TITLE element within its HEAD block. The title is used to identify the overall contents of a document. This object should provide enough information to help users who read it out-of-context understand what they are reading. Titles that add sufficient context to their page will read like "Norton's Toastmasters Club — October Meeting Minutes" rather than "Meeting Minutes."

User agents must also always make the contents of the TITLE element available to users. Most Web browsers do this by displaying the document title in the application's title bar. Other agents may place the contents of the title in a caption or on the status bar, or they may make it audible to the user.

Attributes
dir

```
dir = LTR | RTL
```

This attribute defines the direction of the text flow in a document so that a user agent can correctly display it to the reader.

lang

```
lang="language code"
```

This attribute specifies the language in which an element and its values should be rendered.

Example

The title element shown below appears on the title bar of the user agent window in Web browsers.

```
<TITLE dir="ltr" lang="en">Zebra's Venetian Blinds</TITLE>
```

CROSS-REFERENCE
See **<BODY>**, **<HEAD>,** and **<HTML>.**

title

Attribute

HTML

This attribute is used to set the value for additional advisory information for an object. This can be the name of a LINKed style sheet or simply additional information about an object.

The syntax for this attribute is

```
title = string
```

JAVASCRIPT

```
object.title [ = string ]
```

This document object can be used either to set or retrieve additional information on the specified object.

Values
string

This is the text content to apply to the `title`.

Elements

A	ACRONYM	ADDRESS	APPLET
AREA	B	BASE	BASEFONT
BGSOUND	BIG	BLOCKQUOTE	BODY
BR	BUTTON	CAPTION	CENTER

CITE	CODE	COL	COLGROUP
COMMENT	DD	DEL	DFN
DIR	DIV	DL	DT
EM	EMBED	FIELDSET	FONT
FORM	FRAME	FRAMESET	HEAD
HN	HR	HTMLAREA	I
IFRAME	IMG	INPUT	INS
KBD	LABEL	LEGEND	LI
LISTING	MAP	MARQUEE	MENU
META	NEXTID	OBJECT	OL
OPTION	P	PLAINTEXT	PRE
Q	S	SAMP	SCRIPT
SELECT	SMALL	SPAN	STRIKE
STRONG	SUB	SUP	TABLE
TBODY	TD	TEXTAREA	TFOOT
TH	THEAD	TR	TT
U	UL	VAR	XMP

CROSS-REFERENCE
See **<TITLE>**.

toElement

Property

DHTML

This document property retrieves the name of the object being moved as a result of the `onmouseover` and `onmouseout` events.

The syntax used to implement this property is

```
[ Object = ] event.toElement
```

Parameters
Object

This is the object that is being moved.

Example

The following example code uses the toElement to identify the object currently being affected by the onmouseover event.

```
<html>
<head>
<title>toElement Example</title>
</head>

<body bgcolor="#FFFFFF">

<p name="Paragraph1"
onmouseover="document.forms[0].thetext.value=event.toElement.
name">Rollthe mouse here and watch below. This is
&quot;Paragraph1&quot;.</p>

<p name="Paragraph2"
onmouseover="document.forms[0].thetext.value=event.toElement.
name">This is &quot;Paragraph2&quot;</p>

<form>
  <p>The name of the &quot;mouseovered&quot; object is: <input
  type="text" name="thetext"
  size="20"> </p>
</form>
</body>
</html>
```

Objects

event

CROSS-REFERENCE
See **onmouseover**, **onmouseout**, and **event**.

Tokenizer

Concept

The *tokenizer* is the engine that reads all of the variables, constants, and object names and creates identifiable segments of code from them.

CROSS-REFERENCE
See **tokens**.

Tokens
Concept

A token is the basic unit of a program or markup on a document. It is a unit of language that cannot be separated. All tags and element names serve as tokens within HTML documents.

CROSS-REFERENCE
See **element**, **object**, **property**, **attribute**, **collection**, **variable,** and **identifier**.

top
Attribute

CSS

The top Cascading Style Sheets attribute specifies the distance between the top edge of the object box and the left edge of the containing block.

```
top=length | percentage | auto | inherit
```

JAVASCRIPT
```
object.style.top [ = Top ]
```

This JavaScript property is used to set the location of the top edge of an object.

Values
length

This is the amount of the offset in pixels. This value is any whole signed or unsigned integer.

percentage

This is the percentage of offset from the edge of the reference side of the containing block. The percentage is based upon the visible area of the page in your user agent.

auto

This is the default setting and automatically calculates the offset based upon the width and height of the object box.

s
t
u

inherit

The value for this distance is inherited from its parent elements.

Elements

This attribute is available for all elements.

 CROSS-REFERENCE
See **@page**, **margin**, **padding**, **left**, **bottom**, **right**, and **Containing Block**.

top

Property

DHTML

This property is used to find the location of the top ancestor (or parent) of the current window.

```
[window =] object.top
```

Parameters

window

This is the window that is the parent (or highest-level ancestor) of the identified object.

Objects

window

 CROSS-REFERENCE
See **top**, **ancestor**, **window**, **parentWindow**, and **parent**.

topline

Descriptor

CSS

This descriptor is used to identify the top baseline for a font. It is often used to attempt to align a variety of text on a document. If this value is used, you must also specify a units-per-em descriptor.

```
topline= number
```

Values

number

This value must be an integer between 0 and 32767. All user agents should ignore leading zeros found within the number.

CROSS-REFERENCE
See **units-per-em**, **baseline**, **centerline**, and **mathline**.

topMargin

Property

DHTML

This object property is used to set the top margin of the document.

```
object.topMargin [ = Margin ]
```

Parameters

Margin

This is an integer value with a unit identifier that identifies the size of the margin.

Elements

BODY

CROSS-REFERENCE
See **margin** and **padding**.

<TR>

Element

HTML

Start Tag: Required
End Tag: Optional

This element is used to identify the individual rows of a table. TD or TH cells can be instructed to take up multiple rows, but a TR element must exist for each row, even if it does not have any data cells within it.

Attributes

align

```
align=  left | right | center
```

This attribute enables the document author to specify the position of the object within the individual cells of the table. A value of **left** aligns the object against the cell's left border; a value of **right** places the object to the cell's right. A value of **center** horizontally centers the object within the cell.

char

```
char = "character"
```

This attribute enables you to specify a particular character to serve as an alignment point within a table and its subdivisions.

charoff

```
charoff=length
```

This attribute is used to offset the first occurrence of the alignment character specified by the char attribute.

class

```
class="cdata-list"
```

This attribute assigns a class name to an element. User agents use classes to group specific types of information for later use.

dir

```
dir = LTR | RTL
```

This attribute defines the direction of the text flow in a document so that a user agent can correctly display it to the reader.

id

```
id="name"
```

This attribute is used to assign a name to an element.

lang

```
lang="language code"
```

This attribute specifies the language in which an element and its values should be rendered.

onclick

> onclick=*script*

This attribute takes effect when the button on a pointing device is clicked while the pointer is over an on-screen element.

ondblclick

> ondblclick=*script*

This attribute takes effect when the button on a pointing device is double-clicked while the pointer is over an on-screen element.

onkeydown

> onkeydown=*script*

This attribute takes effect when a key is pressed while the pointer is over an on-screen element.

onkeypress

> onkeypress=*script*

This attribute takes effect when a key is pressed and released while the pointer is over an on-screen element.

onkeyup

> onkeyup=*script*

This attribute takes effect when a key is released while the pointer is over an on-screen element.

onmousedown

> onmousedown=*script*

This attribute takes effect when the button on a pointing device is pressed while the pointer is over an on-screen element.

onmousemove

> onmousemove=*script*

This attribute is activated when the mouse pointer is moved while it is over an on-screen element.

onmouseout

```
onmouseout=script
```

This attribute is activated when the mouse pointer is moved away from an on-screen element.

onmouseover

```
onmouseover=script
```

This attribute is activated when the mouse pointer is moved over an on-screen element.

onmouseup

```
onmouseup=script
```

This attribute takes effect when the button on a pointing device is released while the pointer is over an on-screen element.

style

```
style=style descriptors
```

This attribute is used to apply specific style-sheet information to one particular element.

title

```
title=text
```

This attribute provides annotation information for the element.

valign

```
valign= top | bottom | middle
```

This attribute enables the document author to specify the position of the object within the individual cells of the table. A value of **top** aligns the object against the cell's top border; a value of **bottom** places the object against the cell's bottom. A value of **middle** vertically centers the object within the cell.

Example

The following example code creates a "li'l black book" of ranked names, using a table.

ON THE CD-ROM
Look for **tr.htm** on the accompanying CD-ROM.

```
<html>
<head>
```

```
<title>Table Rows organizing information</title>
</head>

<body bgcolor="#FFFFFF">
<h1>My Little Black Book</h1>
<p>The more little coins they get...the hotter they are. Of
course...</p>
<table border="1" width="75%" bgcolor="#FFFFFF"
bordercolor="#0066FF">
  <tr>
    <td align="center" valign="middle" bgcolor="#CCFFFF"
bordercolor="#0066FF">Mike</td>
    <td bordercolor="#3366FF">
    <img src="coin.jpg" width="51" height="49">
    <img src="coin.jpg" width="51" height="49">
    <img src="coin.jpg" width="51" height="49">
    <img src="coin.jpg" width="51" height="49">
    </td>
  </tr>
  <tr>
    <td align="center" valign="middle" bgcolor="#CCFFFF"
bordercolor="#0066FF">Jack</td>
    <td bordercolor="#3366FF">
    <img src="coin.jpg" width="51" height="49">
    </td>
  </tr>
  <tr>
    <td align="center" valign="middle" bgcolor="#CCFFFF"
bordercolor="#0066FF">Kilroy</td>
    <td bordercolor="#3366FF">
    <img src="coin.jpg" width="51" height="49">
    <img src="coin.jpg" width="51" height="49">
    </td>
  </tr>
  <tr>
    <td align="center" valign="middle" bgcolor="#CCFFFF"
bordercolor="#0066FF">Eddie</td>
    <td bordercolor="#3366FF">
    <img src="coin.jpg" width="51" height="49">
    <img src="coin.jpg" width="51" height="49">
    <img src="coin.jpg" width="51" height="49">
    <img src="coin.jpg" width="51" height="49">
    <img src="coin.jpg" width="51" height="49">
    </td>
```

s
t
u

```
     </tr>
     <tr>
       <td align="center" valign="middle" bgcolor="#CCFFFF"
bordercolor="#0066FF">Ramon</td>
       <td bordercolor="#3366FF">
       <img src="coin.jpg" width="51" height="49">
       <img src="coin.jpg" width="51" height="49">
       <img src="coin.jpg" width="51" height="49">
       </td>
     </tr>
     <tr>
       <td align="center" valign="middle" bgcolor="#CCFFFF"
bordercolor="#0066FF">George</td>
       <td bordercolor="#3366FF">
       <img src="coin.jpg" width="51" height="49">
       <img src="coin.jpg" width="51" height="49">
       <img src="coin.jpg" width="51" height="49">
       <img src="coin.jpg" width="51" height="49"></td>
     </tr>
     <tr>
       <td align="center" valign="middle" bgcolor="#CCFFFF"
bordercolor="#0066FF">Luis</td>
       <td bordercolor="#3366FF">
       <img src="coin.jpg" width="51" height="49">
       <img src="coin.jpg" width="51" height="49">
       <img src="coin.jpg" width="51" height="49">
       <img src="coin.jpg" width="51" height="49">
       <img src="coin.jpg" width="51" height="49">
       </td>
     </tr>
     <tr>
       <td align="center" valign="middle" bgcolor="#CCFFFF"
bordercolor="#0066FF">Frank</td>
       <td bordercolor="#3366FF">
       <img src="coin.jpg" width="51" height="49">
       <img src="coin.jpg" width="51" height="49">
       <img src="coin.jpg" width="51" height="49">
       </td>
     </tr>
     <tr>
       <td align="center" valign="middle" bgcolor="#CCFFFF"
bordercolor="#0066FF">Randy</td>
       <td bordercolor="#3366FF">
```

```
        <img src="coin.jpg" width="51" height="49">
        </td>
      </tr>
      <tr>
        <td align="center" valign="middle" bgcolor="#CCFFFF"
bordercolor="#0066FF">John</td>
        <td bordercolor="#3366FF">
        <img src="coin.jpg" width="51" height="49">
        <img src="coin.jpg" width="51" height="49">
        <img src="coin.jpg" width="51" height="49">
        <img src="coin.jpg" width="51" height="49">
        </td>
      </tr>
      <tr>
        <td align="center" valign="middle" bgcolor="#CCFFFF"
bordercolor="#0066FF">Lew</td>
        <td bordercolor="#3366FF">
        <img src="coin.jpg" width="51" height="49">
        <img src="coin.jpg" width="51" height="49">
        </td>
      </tr>
    </table>
    </body>
    </html>
```

CROSS-REFERENCE

See **<TABLE>**, **<TD>**, **<TBODY>**, **<TFOOT>**, **<TH>,** and **<THEAD>**.

trueSpeed

Property

DHTML

This property is used to identify whether the position of the marquee is being calculated using the scrollDelay and the scrollAmount properties along with the actual time that has elapsed since the last clock tick.

The syntax of this property is

```
object.trueSpeed [ = Speed ]
```

Parameters
Speed

This is a Boolean value that identifies whether TrueSpeed is being used. If this value is **false** (the default), the marquee is moving based upon the 60-second clock tick of the computer, and the `scrollDelay` property is being ignored. If this value is **true,** the speed of the marquee is being calculated based upon the true-speed algorithm.

Elements

MARQUEE

CROSS-REFERENCE
See **scrollAmount** and **scrollDelay**.

<TT>

Element

HTML

Start Tag: Required
End Tag: Required

Use this element when displaying teletype-styled text. This type of text is also referred to as Monospaced. Fonts that can be used to display Monospaced text include such fonts as Courier, Fixedsys, and Lucida Console.

Attributes
class

```
class="cdata-list"
```

This attribute assigns a class name to an element. User agents use classes to group specific types of information for later use.

dir

```
dir = LTR | RTL
```

This attribute defines the direction of the text flow in a document so that a user agent can correctly display it to the reader.

id

```
id="name"
```

This attribute is used to assign a name to an element.

lang

> lang="*language code*"

This attribute specifies the language in which an element and its values should be rendered.

onclick

> onclick=*script*

This attribute takes effect when the button on a pointing device is clicked while the pointer is over an on-screen element.

ondblclick

> ondblclick=*script*

This attribute takes effect when the button on a pointing device is double-clicked while the pointer is over an on-screen element.

onkeydown

> onkeydown=*script*

This attribute takes effect when a key is pressed while the pointer is over an on-screen element.

onkeypress

> onkeypress=*script*

This attribute takes effect when a key is pressed and released while the pointer is over an on-screen element.

onkeyup

> onkeyup=*script*

This attribute takes effect when a key is released while the pointer is over an on-screen element.

onmousedown

> onmousedown=*script*

This attribute takes effect when the button on a pointing device is pressed while the pointer is over an on-screen element.

onmousemove

> onmousemove=*script*

This attribute is activated when the mouse pointer is moved while it is over an on-screen element.

onmouseout

```
onmouseout=script
```

This attribute is activated when the mouse pointer is moved away from an on-screen element.

onmouseover

```
onmouseover=script
```

This attribute is activated when the mouse pointer is moved over an on-screen element.

onmouseup

```
onmouseup=script
```

This attribute takes effect when the button on a pointing device is released while the pointer is over an on-screen element.

style

```
style=style descriptors
```

This attribute is used to apply specific style-sheet information to one particular element.

title

```
title=text
```

This attribute provides annotation information for the element.

Example

The following example code uses the TT element to display the text of a tele-type report received at a 911 office.

 ON THE CD-ROM

Look for **tt.htm** on the accompanying CD-ROM.

```
<P> The following transcript was taken from a 911 call in
Tillamook, Oregon.
<TT> Operator: 911. Where is your emergency?<br>
Caller: There is a man down. <br>
Operator: Where are you? <br>
Caller: The corner of Oak and Vine. The kids are everywhere!
<br>
Operator: OK. It's all right. <br>
Caller: You have to hurry. The driver is being brutalized.
<br>
```

```
Operator: Ok hold on, what is wrong with the children? <br>
Caller: They are attacking him. We need an ambulance. <br>
Operator: The children are attacking the driver? <br>
Caller: Yes. He ran out of ice-cream. <br>
Operator: The driver ran out of ice-cream? <br>
Caller: Yes, the driver of the ice-cream truck ran out. They
came from everywhere. He is in the street now. <br>
Operator: Who came from everywhere? <br>
Caller: The kids. They pulled him from the truck. There is
blood all over. <br>
Operator: OK. We have an ambulance en-route. <br>
Caller: The parents are there, but the kids are attacking them
too. <br>
Operator: The ambulance and the police are en-route. They
should be there shortly. <br>
```

CROSS-REFERENCE
See **<PRE>**, **<CODE>**, **<VAR>**, and **<XMP>**.

type

Attribute

HTML

This attribute represents many different things for different elements. For the A, LINK, OBJECT, PARAM, SCRIPT, and STYLE objects, this attribute identifies the type of content being referenced by the link. These are all MIME Types that are being identified.

The syntax for the type command for A, LINK, OBJECT, PARAM, SCRIPT, and STYLE is

```
type = content-type
```

When this command is used with the INPUT element, it identifies the type of INPUT control to be created.

The syntax for the type command for the INPUT object is

```
type = text | password | checkbox | radio | submit | reset |
file | hidden | image | button
```

When type is used with the LI, OL, and UL objects, it identifies the type of list item that is created.

When used with the LI, OL, and UL objects, the syntax of this attribute is

```
type = style
```

Values

content-type

This identifies a MIME Type that is used to identify the source type of the object's resource.

input-types

```
(text | password | checkbox | radio | submit | reset | file |
hidden | image | button )
```

This identifies the various types of controls that can be used with FORMs.

style

This identifies the type of input that is allowed for the list types or items.

Elements

A	INPUT	LI	LINK
OBJECT	OL	PARAM	SCRIPT
STYLE	UL		

CROSS-REFERENCE
See **MIME Types**.

<U>

Element

HTML

Start Tag: Required
EndTag: Required

This element is used to underline the text content of an object.

Attributes
class

```
class="cdata-list"
```

Use this attribute to assign a class name to an element. User agents employ classes to group specific types of information for later use.

dir

```
dir = LTR | RTL
```

This attribute defines the direction of the text flow in a document so that a user agent can display it correctly.

id

```
id="name"
```

Use this attribute to assign a name to an element.

lang

```
lang="language code"
```

This attribute specifies the language in which an element and its values should be rendered.

onclick

`onclick=script`

This attribute takes effect when a user clicks the button on a pointing device with the pointer over an element.

ondblclick

`ondblclick=script`

This attribute takes effect when a user double-clicks the button on a pointing device with the pointer over an element.

onkeydown

`onkeydown=script`

This attribute takes effect when a user presses a key and the pointer is over an element.

onkeypress

`onkeypress=script`

This attribute takes effect when a key is pressed and released while the pointer is over an element.

onkeyup

`onkeyup=script`

This attribute takes effect when a user releases a key with the pointer over an element.

onmousedown

`onmousedown=script`

This attribute takes effect when a user presses the button on a pointing device while the pointer is over an element.

onmousemove

`onmousemove=script`

This attribute is activated when the mouse pointer is moved while it is over an element.

onmouseout

`onmouseout=script`

This attribute is activated when the mouse pointer is moved away from an element.

onmouseover

```
onmouseover=script
```

This attribute is activated when the mouse pointer is moved over an element.

onmouseup

```
onmouseup=script
```

This attribute takes effect when the button on a pointing device is released while the pointer is over an element.

style

```
style=style descriptors
```

This attribute applies specific style-sheet information to one particular element.

title

```
title=text
```

This attribute provides annotation information for the element.

Example

The following example uses the <U> element to underline specific words in a bibliography.

ON THE CD-ROM

Look for **u.htm** on the accompanying CD-ROM.

```
<html>
<head>
<title>Underlines, Underlines, where have you gone?</title>
<meta http-equiv="generator" content="Macromedia Dreamweaver">
</head>

<body bgcolor="#FFFFFF">
<h1>Bibliography</h1>
<p>Arthur Griffith, <u>JAVA Master Reference,</u> IDG Books
Worldwide, 1998.</p>
<p>Brian Underdahl, Edward Willett, <u>Internet Bible</u>, IDG
Books Worldwide, 1998</p>
<p>Danny Goodman, <u> JavaScript Bible</u>, IDG Books
Worldwide, 3 ed., 1998.</p>
<p>Ed Tittel, James Michael Stewart, Natanya Pits, <u>Hip
Pocket Guide to HTML 4</u>,
  IDG Books Worldwide, 1998</p>
</body>
</html>
```

CROSS-REFERENCE
See **<B>**, **<I>**, **<BIG>**, **<TT>**, **<SMALL>**, and **<STRIKE>**.

UA

Concept

CROSS-REFERENCE
See **user agent**.

<UL>

Element

HTML

Start Tag: Required
EndTag: Required

This element is used to identify an unordered list. Unordered lists use symbols or characters to identify the various items within the list. As the document author, you can control not only the object that identifies a list entry, but also its text direction.

Attributes

class

```
class="cdata-list"
```

Use this attribute to assign a class name to an element. User agents employ classes to group specific types of information for later use.

compact

```
compact
```

This attribute is freely interpreted by the user agent, but it should instruct the user agent to display the list in a compact manner.

dir

```
dir = LTR | RTL
```

This attribute defines the direction of the text flow in a document so that a user agent can display it correctly.

id

```
id="name"
```

Use this attribute to assign a name to an element.

lang

```
lang="language code"
```

This attribute specifies the language in which an element and its values should be rendered.

onclick

```
onclick=script
```

This attribute takes effect when a user clicks the button on a pointing device with the pointer over an element.

ondblclick

```
ondblclick=script
```

This attribute takes effect when a user double-clicks the button on a pointing device with the pointer over an element.

onkeydown

```
onkeydown=script
```

This attribute takes effect when a user presses a key and the pointer is over an element.

onkeypress

```
onkeypress=script
```

This attribute takes effect when a key is pressed and released while the pointer is over an element.

onkeyup

```
onkeyup=script
```

This attribute takes effect when a user releases a key with the pointer over an element.

onmousedown

```
onmousedown=script
```

This attribute takes effect when a user presses the button on a pointing device while the pointer is over an element.

onmousemove

```
onmousemove=script
```

This attribute is activated when the mouse pointer is moved while it is over an element.

onmouseout

```
onmouseout=script
```

This attribute is activated when the mouse pointer is moved away from an element.

onmouseover

```
onmouseover=script
```

This attribute is activated when the mouse pointer is moved over an element.

onmouseup

```
onmouseup=script
```

This attribute takes effect when the button on a pointing device is released while the pointer is over an element.

start

```
start=number
```

This number identifies the initial item in the list.

style

```
style=style descriptors
```

This attribute applies specific style-sheet information to one particular element.

title

```
title=text
```

This attribute provides annotation information for the element.

type

```
type= disc | circle | square | 1 | a | A | i | I
```

This deprecated attribute is used to designate the type of bullet or number to be used when displaying the list. This attribute is only used by visual user agents.

Type	Example	Description
disc	●	Solid black dot — default
circle	○	Outlined circle
square	□	Outlined square
1	1, 2, 3, . . .	Arabic numbers
a	a, b, c, . . .	Lowercase roman letters
A	A, B, C, . . .	Uppercase roman letters
i	i, ii, iii, . . .	Lowercase Roman numerals
I	I, II, III, . . .	Uppercase Roman numerals

value

```
value=number
```

This attribute is used to set the value of the element. Although you always specify this element in an integer form, it may be displayed in another format.

Example

The following unordered list identifies many of the women in history, some well known and others almost completely unknown, that have had a great effect on the world that we live in. You might want to look some of them up.

ON THE CD-ROM

Look for **ul.htm** on the accompanying CD-ROM.

```
<html>
<head>
<title>Unordered list.. but not Women</title>
</head>

<body bgcolor="#FFFFFF">
<h1>Influential Women in History <font size="-1">(in no
particular order)</font></h1>
<ul>
  <li type="CIRCLE">Eleanor of Aquitaine</li>
  <li>Joan of Arc</li>
  <li>Helen of Troy</li>
  <li>Isabel la Catolica</li>
  <li>Heloise</li>
  <li>Jimena de El Cid</li>
  <li>Margaurite de la Roque</li>
  <li>Catherine de Medici</li>
  <li>Nzinga Mhande</li>
  <li>Phillipa of Hainult</li>
```

```
        <li>Juliana Berners</li>
        <li>Kuang Tao-sheng</li>
        <li>Alesandra Giliani</li>
    </ul>
    </body>
    </html>
```

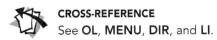

CROSS-REFERENCE
See **OL**, **MENU**, **DIR**, and **LI**.

Unicode

Language

Unicode is a character encoding system similar to ISO-10646 that identifies all of the characters used in the majority of languages in the world. Because each character is encoded at a single code point, all of the world's computers can exchange information without ambiguity. Unicode is not a sorting sequence, a definition for glyph characters, or a language definition. It is strictly a 16-bit universal character encoding system.

CROSS-REFERENCE
See **unicode-range**, **urange**, and **<ISO>**.

unicode-range

Descriptor

CSS

This descriptor is used to ensure that a user agent will not download a font that does not have sufficient glyph characters to cover the requirements of the document.

They syntax for this descriptor is

```
unicode-range: urange, urange,...
```

Values
urange

This is the individual Unicode character in U+ hex number notation.

CROSS-REFERENCE
See **Unicode**, **urange**, and **ISO**.

units

Property

DHTML

This document object property is used either to collect or set the units of measure for the EMBED object.

```
object.units [ = Unit ]
```

Parameters
Unit

This string contains the unit identifier for the measurement used with the EMBED object.

Elements

EMBED

CROSS-REFERENCE
See **pixel**, **em**, and **ex**.

units-per-em

Descriptor

CSS

This Cascading Style Sheets descriptor identifies the specific size of the design grid used for laying out font character glyphs.

Values
number

This is the total number of units specified within a single character grid. There is no default value.

NOTE
If you are using another descriptor that depends on the size of this descriptor, you must specify it within your style sheet; otherwise, errors occur and your grid sizes are not specified.

CROSS-REFERENCE
See **font matching** and **font size**.

Universal Character Set

Concept

CROSS-REFERENCE
See **Unicode**.

updateInterval

Property

DHTML

This property is used to control the time interval, in seconds, that occurs between screen updates. If this value is set too slow or too fast, it will have a negative impact on the rendering speed of your information.

```
object.updateInterval [ = Interval ]
```

Parameters

Interval

This is the time, in seconds, that elapses before the screen is again automatically refreshed.

Objects

screen

CROSS-REFERENCE
See **clearInterval**.

urange

Value

CSS

This value is used to identify the specific range of Unicode characters that can be displayed by this object. All of these values are prefaced with 'U+' and then contain the hexadecimal number representing the Unicode character to be displayed.

 CROSS-REFERENCE
See **Unicode**.

URI

Concept

The Uniform Resource Identifier—URI—is the combination of the Uniform Resource Name and the Uniform Resource Locator. This provides a specific way of accessing a particular item on a particular document in any location on the Internet.

 CROSS-REFERENCE
See **URN** and **URL—Uniform Resource Locator**.

URL

Property

DHTML

This document property is used to set the URL, or address, of a document to load when the contents of the existing document have expired.
    The syntax of this command is

```
object.URL [=URL]
```

Parameters

URL

This is the address of the new document to load.

Elements

META

Objects

document

CROSS-REFERENCE
See **URL — Uniform Resource Locator**, **URN**, **URI**, **content**, **name**, and **http-equiv**.

URL — Uniform Resource Locator

Concept

The Uniform Resource Locator of a document is simply its address. By using an address, you can go directly to the page you wish to view without the frustrating experience of searching through the long results of a search-engine list or of trying to navigate links on a hundred other documents.

Consider the following URL:

```
http://www.catsback.com/raven/index.html
```

The URL is composed of three main sections. The first, `http://`, identifies what sort of server you are looking for and the protocol to use. Other options for this section of the URL include `ftp://`, `mailto:`, `news://`, `telnet://`, and `gopher://`. The second section of the address, `www.catsback.com`, identifies the computer or DNS identity of the site for which you are looking. The computer can also be identified by its IP address, for example, `201.29.264.33`. The third portion of the address is the directory and optional filename of the page to load. In the preceding example, `/raven/index.html` forces the visiting user agent to load the document named `index.html` that is located in the `raven` directory on this server.

There are also some specific rules as to how a computer can be named. Organizations such as InterNIC (`http://rs.internic.net`) provide you with a means of reserving a specific address for your Web site. There are restrictions on the first-level domain name that you can have, although the second- and third-level names are completely up to the individual reserving the address. First-level domain names include the following:

- **.com** Commercial Organizations
- **.edu** Educational Organizations
- **.gov** Government Organizations
- **.mil** Military Organizations
- **.net** Network Companies
- **.org** Nonprofit Organizations

Some domain names contain country codes as a means of identifying a site location. In many countries, it is necessary to implement the country code because many of the other URLs are reserved for U.S.-only organizations. Table U-1 lists all country codes available for use with URLs, as well as the country each code represents.

Table U-1 Standard Country Codes Used Within URLs

Code	Country	Code	Country
AD	Andorra	BM	Bermuda
AE	United Arab Emirates	BN	Brunel Darussalam
AF	Afghanistan	BO	Bolivia
AG	Antigua and Barbuda	BR	Brazil
AI	Anguilla	BS	Bahamas
AL	Albania	BT	Bhutan
MM	Armenia	BV	Bouvet Island
AN	Netherlands, Antilles	BW	Botswana
AO	Angola	BY	Belarus
AQ	Antarctica	BZ	Belize
AR	Argentina	CA	Canada
AS	American Samoa	CC	Cocos (Keeling) Islands
AT	Austria	CF	Central African Republic
AU	Australia	CG	Congo
AW	Aruba	CH	Switzerland
AZ	Azerbaijan	CI	Côte d'Ivoire (Ivory Coast)
BA	Bosnia and Herzegovina	CK	Cook Island
BB	Barbados	CL	Chile
BD	Bangladesh	CM	Cameroon
BE	Belgium	CN	China
BF	Burkina Faso	CO	Colombia
BG	Bulgaria	CR	Costa Rica
BH	Bahrain	CS	Czechoslovakia (former)
BI	Burundi	CU	Cuba
BJ	Benin		

Continued

Table U-1 *Continued*

Code	Country	Code	Country
CV	Cape Verde	GT	Guatemala
CX	Christmas Island	GU	Guam
CY	Cyprus	GW	Guinea-Bissau
CZ	Czech Republic	GY	Guyana
DE	Germany	HK	Hong Kong
DJ	Djibouti	HM	Heard and McDonald Islands
DK	Denmark	HN	Honduras
DM	Dominica	HR	Croatia (Hrvatska)
DO	Dominican Republic	HT	Haiti
DZ	Algeria	HU	Hungary
EC	Ecuador	ID	Indonesia
EE	Estonia	IE	Ireland
EG	Egypt	IL	Israel
EH	Western Sahara	IN	India
ER	Eritrea	IO	British Indian Ocean Territory
ES	Spain	IQ	Iraq
ET	Ethiopia	IR	Iran
FI	Finland	IS	Iceland
FJ	Fiji	IT	Italy
FK	Falkland Islands (Malvinas)	JM	Jamaica
FM	Micronesia	JO	Jordan
FO	Faroe Islands	JP	Japan
FR	France	KE	Kenya
FX	France, Metropolitan	KG	Kyrgyzstan
GA	Gabon	KH	Cambodia
GB	Great Britain (UK)	KI	Kiribati
GD	Grenada	KM	Comoros
GE	Georgia	KN	Saint Kitts and Nevis
GF	French Guiana	KP	North Korea
GH	Ghana	KR	South Korea
GI	Gibraltar	KW	Kuwait
GL	Greenland	KY	Cayman Islands
GM	Gambia	KZ	Kazakhstan
GN	Guinea	LA	Laos
GP	Guadeloupe	LB	Lebanon
GQ	Equatorial Guinea	LC	Saint Lucia
GR	Greece	LI	Liechtenstein
GS	South Georgia and South Sandwich Islands	LK	Sri Lanka

Code	Country	Code	Country
LR	Liberia	OM	Oman
LS	Lesotho	PA	Panama
LT	Lithuania	PE	Peru
LU	Luxembourg	PF	French Polynesia
LV	Latvia	PG	Papua New Guinea
LY	Libya	PH	Philippines
MA	Morocco	PK	Pakistan
MC	Monaco	PL	Poland
MD	Moldova	PM	St. Pierre and Miquelon
MG	Madagascar	PN	Pitcairn Island
MH	Marshall Islands	PR	Puerto Rico
MK	Macedonia	PT	Portugal
ML	Mali	PW	Palau
MM	Myanmar	PY	Paraguay
MN	Mongolia	QA	Qatar
MO	Macao	RE	Reunion
MP	Northern Mariana Islands	RO	Romania
MQ	Martinique	RU	Russian Federation
MR	Mauritania	RW	Rwanda
MS	Montserrat	SA	Saudi Arabia
MT	Malta	SB	Solomon Islands
MU	Mauritius	SC	Seychelles
MV	Maldives	SD	Sudan
MW	Malawi	SE	Sweden
MX	Mexico	SG	Singapore
MY	Malaysia	SH	St. Helena
MZ	Mozambique	SI	Slovenia
NA	Namibia	SJ	Svalbard and Jan Mayen Islands
NC	New Caledonia	SK	Slovak Republic
NE	Niger	SL	Sierra Leone
NF	Norfolk Island	SM	San Marino
NG	Nigeria	SN	Senegal
NI	Nicaragua	SO	Somalia
NL	Netherlands	SR	Suriname
NO	Norway	ST	Sao Tome and Principe
NP	Nepal	SU	USSR (former)
NR	Nauru	SV	El Salvador
NT	Neutral Zone	SY	Syria
NU	Niue	SZ	Swaziland
NZ	New Zealand (Aotearoa)		

Continued

Table U-1 *Continued*

Code	Country	Code	Country
TC	Turks and Caicos Islands	US	United States
TD	Chad	UY	Uruguay
TF	French Southern Territories	UZ	Uzbekistan
TG	Togo	VA	Vatican City State (Holy See)
TH	Thailand	VC	Saint Vincent and the Grenadines
TJ	Tajikistan	VE	Venezuela
TK	Tokelau Islands	VG	Virgin Islands (British)
TM	Turkmenistan	VI	Virgin Islands (US)
TN	Tunisia	VN	Vietnam
TO	Tonga	VU	Vanuatu
TP	East Timor	WF	Wallis and Futuna Islands
TR	Turkey	WS	Samoa
TT	Trinidad and Tobago	YE	Yemen
TV	Tuvalu	YT	Mayotte
TW	Taiwan	YU	Yugoslavia
TZ	Tanzania	ZA	South Africa
UA	Ukraine	ZM	Zambia
UG	Uganda	ZR	Zaire
UK	United Kingdom	ZW	Zimbabwe
UM	US Minor Outlying Islands		

CROSS-REFERENCE
See **URN** and **URI**.

URN

Concept

A Uniform Resource Name — URN — is not used to specify the location or address of an item or document; it is used to specify the name of the object or document. When used with the URL of a page, a URN creates a URI.

Example
A URN would link the name of an Image map's `MAP` object to the image itself. For example

```
<MAP name="WorldMap">
    ...
```

```
</MAP>
<IMG src="worldmap.gif" usemap="#WorldMap">
```

CROSS-REFERENCE
See **URL** and **URI**.

urn

Property

DHTML

This document object is used to retrieve the Uniform Resource Name for the target of an object link.

```
object.urn [ = URN ]
```

Parameters
URN

This string parameter is the name of a resource, not its address.

Elements

A

CROSS-REFERENCE
See **URL** and **URI**.

<USAGE>

Element

CDF

Start Tag:	Required
EndTag:	Required

This element is used to control the use of the channel item.

Attributes

value

> This string attribute identifies how the item is used. For example, the item could be used as a **screensaver** or **desktop**.

CROSS-REFERENCE
See <ITEM>.

usemap

Attribute

HTML

This attribute is used to associate a map with an image. This allows you to create a client-side image map that is referenced by multiple images.

The syntax for this command is

```
usemap=uri
```

JAVASCRIPT

```
object.useMap [=uri]
```

This property is used to set the name of a linked map file from within a script. This enables you to use the same image on multiple screens with only a few mappings being applied to it.

Values

uri

> This is the address of the map code used to create the hyperlinks on a specified image. This address needs to match the name attribute of the associated MAP designation.

Example

The following code creates a MAP, named animap, that is then used in conjunction with the tswheelani.gif file. These two objects are linked together through the MAP name attribute and the IMG usemap attribute.

ON THE CD-ROM
Look for **usemap.htm** on the accompanying CD-ROM.

```
<MAP name="animap">
```

```
     <AREA href="email.html" shape="poly"
coords="40,40,146,146,0,146,40,40">
     <AREA href="fax.html" shape="poly"
coords="40,40,146,146,146,0,40,40">
     <AREA href="faq.html" shape="poly"
coords="146,0,146,146,256,40,146,0">
     <AREA href="online.html" shape="poly"
coords="256,40,146,146,299,146,256,40">
     <AREA href="news.html" shape="poly"
coords="299,146,146,146,260,260,299,146">
     <AREA href="dbase.html" shape="poly"
coords="260,260,146,146,146,299,260,260">
     <AREA href="write.html" shape="poly"
coords="146,299,146,146,40,260,146,299">
     <AREA href="call.html" shape="poly"
coords="40,260,146,146,0,146,40,260">
     </MAP>
     <IMG src="tswheelani.gif" type="image/gif"
usemap="#animap">
```

Elements

IMG   INPUT   OBJECT

CROSS-REFERENCE
See **<MAP>**, **<A>**, and **<AREA>**.

User Agent

Concept

A *user agent* is basically the software, the hardware, or a combination of such that is used to look at the documents you are placing on the Internet. Some of the most popular clients are Web browsers such as Internet Explorer and Netscape Navigator. Other user agents might be Braille readers, TTY machines, or Web TVs. Some type of user agent exists for practically every type of medium that is used or implemented with technology. Other user agents may be robots that crawl the Web, looking for information.

CROSS-REFERENCE
See **Web Browser**, **Media Groups**, and **Media Types**.

userAgent

Property

DHTML

This property retrieves the string that is sent for an HTTP user agent request. The syntax used for this property is

```
[ uaName = ] object.userAgent
```

Parameters
uaName

This string variable is used to hold the name of the user agent that is currently viewing the document. Table U-2 shows the various results of running this command with the variety of user agents available.

Table U-2 userAgent Return Values for Popular Web Browsers

userAgent Results	Web Browser	Operating System
Mozilla/3.x (compatible; MSIE 3.x; Win95)	Internet Explorer 3.x	Windows 95
Mozilla/3.x (compatible; MSIE 3.x Win98)	Internet Explorer 3.x	Windows 98
Mozilla/3.x (compatible; MSIE 3.x; Windows NT)	Internet Explorer 3.x	Windows NT
Mozilla/3.x (compatible; MSIE 3.x; Macintosh; PPC)	Internet Explorer 3.x	Mac PowerPC
Mozilla/4.x (compatible; MSIE 4.x; Win95)	Internet Explorer 4.x	Windows 95
Mozilla/4.x (compatible; MSIE 4.x; Win98)	Internet Explorer 4.x	Windows 98
Mozilla/4.x (compatible; MSIE 4.x; Windows NT)	Internet Explorer 4.x	Windows NT
Mozilla/4.x (compatible; MSIE 4.x; Macintosh; PPC)	Internet Explorer 4.x	Mac PowerPC
Mozilla/3.x (Win16; I)	Navigator 3.x	Windows 3.x
Mozilla/3.x Gold (Win95; I)	Navigator 3.x Gold	Windows 95
Mozilla/3.x (Win98; I)	Navigator 3.x	Windows 98
Mozilla/3.x Gold (WinNT; U)	Navigator 3.x Gold (U.S. only)	Windows NT

userAgent Results	Web Browser	Operating System
Mozilla/3.x (Macintosh; I; 68K)	Navigator 3.x	Mac 68xxx Processor
Mozilla/4.x [fr] (Win95; I)	Navigator 4.x (French only)	Windows 95
Mozilla/4.x (Win95; I)	Navigator 4.x	Windows 98
Mozilla/4.x (Win95; I)	Navigator 4.x	Windows NT
Mozilla/4.x (Macintosh; U; PPC)	Navigator 4.x (U.S. only)	Mac PowerPC
Mozilla/4.x (X11; I; HP-UX)	Navigator 4.x	HP-UX
Mozilla/4.x (X11; I; IRIX)	Navigator 4.x	IRIX
Mozilla/4.x (X11; I; SunOS 5.0)	Navigator 4.x	SunOS 5.0

Example

The following example writes the name and language of the user currently browsing software onto an HTML document.

```
<html>
<head>
  <title>User Agent</title>
</head>
<body>
<script>
  document.write(navigator.userAgent);
  document.write("<p>");
  document.write(navigator.userLanguage);
</script>
</body>
</html>
```

Objects

navigator

CROSS-REFERENCE
See **userLanguage**.

userLanguage

Property

DHTML

This parameter is used to identify the current language being supported by the user agent.

The syntax for this command is

```
[ Language = ] object.userLanguage
```

Parameters

Language

This string can contain any of the possible language code values used with the lang HTML attribute.

Objects

navigator

CROSS-REFERENCE
See **userAgent**, **lang**, and **language**.

valign

Attribute

HTML

This attribute is used with a variety of table-related elements to control the positioning of data within a cell.

The syntax of this command is

```
valign = top | middle | bottom | baseline
```

Values

top

The cell data is rendered flush with the top of the cell.

middle

The cell data is centered vertically within the cell. This is the default value.

bottom

The cell data is rendered flush with the bottom of the cell.

baseline

The cell data is aligned vertically in relation to the baseline set for other objects.

Example

The following example code uses the `valign` attribute to align three images within three data cells in a table row. The alignment chosen—top, middle, and bottom, respectively—provides a staggered appearance for the images.

```
<TABLE>
  <TR>
    <TD valign="top">
      <IMG src="janmagcvr.jpg" height="150" alt="The Journals
cover for January">
    </TD>
```

```
    <TD valign="middle">
      <IMG src="febmagcvr.jpg" height="150" alt="The Journals
cover for February">
    </TD>
    <TD valign="bottom">
      <IMG src="marmagcvr.jpg" height="150" alt="The Journals
cover for March">
    </TD>
  </TR>
</TABLE>
```

Elements

COL	COLGROUP	TBODY	TD
TFOOT	TH	THEAD	TR

CROSS-REFERENCE
See **halign** and **align**.

value

Attribute

HTML

This attribute is used to identify the initial value of a variety of controls or objects. When this attribute is used with the APPLET element, it identifies the value of the run-time parameter identified by the name attribute. When used with the BUTTON element, it assigns an initial value to the button.

The syntax for specifying this value is

```
value = cdata
```

NOTE
When you use this attribute with the LI element, the syntax will be treated as follows:

```
value = number
```

This attribute is then used to set the number shown in front of the current list item. The value is always a number, but the label may be nonnumeric. For example, in a list designated to use lowercase roman characters, a "value=7" entry would show a lowercase g as the line-item label.

Elements

APPLET   BUTTON   LI   OBJECT   OPTION

 CROSS-REFERENCE
See **valuetype**, **name**, **type**, **code**, and **codebase**.

valuetype

Attribute

HTML

This attribute is used to identify the type of information contained within the `value` attribute.

The syntax for this attribute is

```
valuetype = data | ref | object
```

Values

data

This setting forces the content of the `value` attribute to be treated as a string and passed on to the object's implementor as a string. This is the default value for this attribute.

ref

When this value is used, the constants of `value` is a URI designating a resource containing run-time values for the object's implementation. The URI is transferred to the object unresolved.

object

This setting identifies the `value` attribute as a reference to an `OBJECT` declaration within that document. In this instance, the contents of the `value` attribute must match the contents of the `id` attribute for the referenced object.

Elements

APPLET   BUTTON   OBJECT   OPTION

 CROSS-REFERENCE
See **value**, **id**, **href**, **code**, and **codebase**.

<VAR>

Element

HTML

Start Tag: Required
End Tag: Required

This element is used to identify a singular variable program argument that has been included within a series of textual paragraphs. This is an inline element, which user agents generally display using monospaced characters.

Attributes

class

```
class="cdata-list"
```

Use this attribute to assign a class name to an element. User agents employ classes to group specific types of information for later use.

id

```
id="name"
```

Use this attribute to assign a name to an element.

lang

```
lang="language code"
```

This attribute specifies the language in which an element and its values should be rendered.

onclick

```
onclick=script
```

This attribute takes effect when a user clicks the button on a pointing device with the pointer over an element.

ondblclick

```
ondblclick=script
```

This attribute takes effect when a user double-clicks the button on a pointing device with the pointer over an element.

onkeydown

```
onkeydown=script
```

This attribute takes effect when a user presses a key and the pointer is over an element.

onkeypress

```
onkeypress=script
```

This attribute takes effect when a key is pressed and released while the pointer is over an element.

onkeyup

```
onkeyup=script
```

This attribute takes effect when a user releases a key with the pointer over an element.

onmousedown

```
onmousedown=script
```

This attribute takes effect when a user presses the button on a pointing device while the pointer is over an element.

onmousemove

```
onmousemove=script
```

This attribute is activated when the mouse pointer is moved while it is over an element.

onmouseout

```
onmouseout=script
```

This attributed is activated when the mouse pointer is moved away from an element.

onmouseover

```
onmouseover=script
```

This attribute is activated when the mouse pointer is moved over an element.

onmouseup

```
onmouseup=script
```

This attribute takes effect when the button on a pointing device is released while the pointer is over an element.

style

```
style=style descriptors
```

This attribute applies specific style-sheet information to one particular element.

title

```
title=text
```

This attribute provides annotation information to the element.

Example

The following example uses the VAR element to identify the names of variables used in a document showing a small "hello world" program.

ON THE CD-ROM

Look for **var.htm** on the accompanying CD-ROM.

```
<BODY>
<P>In the following code example, the variable
<VAR>hloWrld</VAR>
is used to hold the string which will be displayed by the
<VAR>document.writeln
</VAR> statement.
<P>
<SAMP>
var hloWrld=string;<BR>
hloWrld="Hal'oooo my trouncy bouncy world";<BR>
document.writeln("!!!"+hloWorld+"!!!")<BR>
</SAMP>
</BODY>
```

CROSS-REFERENCE

See **<CITE>**, **<KEY>**, **<SAMP>**, and **<XMP>**.

Variable

Concept

A variable is a programming structure that is used by a programmer to hold information that has been given a unique name. Variables hold the data assigned to them until a new value is assigned or the program is reset or completed. They can also be used to hold data while it is being processed within the program.

Variables can be global or local. A global variable is available to be used throughout the entire program. A local variable is only accessible within the procedure or function in which it is defined.

Variables are generally assigned a value with an equal sign. This creates statements such as `income=10000`, `expense=7000`, and `total=income-expense`. When the data is numeric, it is not enclosed in quotes, but string information such as `title="HTML Master Reference"` is enclosed in quotation marks.

JAVASCRIPT

In JavaScript scripts, variables are assigned in the following manner:

```
var varname=string | integer | float
```

CROSS-REFERENCE

See **Constants**, **Functions**, and **Expressions**.

VBScript

Language

Visual Basic, Scripting Edition — referred to as VBScript — was developed by Microsoft for use with the Internet Explorer Web browser. VBScript is based on Visual Basic but is much simpler. It provides a short, succinct way for Web developers to add interactive controls and objects, such as buttons and automated multimedia devices, on their Web pages. The problem with using VBScript for Internet page automation is that it is only supported by Microsoft products. This makes it a nice tool for intranets but limiting on the open Internet.

CROSS-REFERENCE

See **JavaScript**, **Visual Basic**, **Java**, and **ECMAScript**.

u

▶ v

w

version

Attribute

HTML

This deprecated element identifies which HTML DTD version is used with a document. This attribute has been replaced with the `!DOCTYPEDTD` declaration statement.

```
version = cdata
```

 CROSS-REFERENCE
See **!DOCUMENT** and **Document Type Definition**.

verticalAlign

Property

DHTML

This JavaScript property is used to set or retrieve the vertical positioning of an object.

The syntax required to use this command is

```
Object.style.verticalAlign [ = sAlign ]
```

Parameters

sAlign

This parameter sets aside the types of alignments that are allowed, including **baseline, sub, super, top, middle, bottom, text-top,** and **text-bottom. Baseline** aligns the contents to the baseline of the text of the object. **Sub** aligns the text to a subscript, whereas **super** aligns the text to a superscript. **Top** aligns the contents of the object to the top of the object's containment block. **Middle** aligns the object's contents to the vertical middle of the object's containment block. **Bottom** aligns the contents to the bottom of the block. **Text-top** aligns the text contents of an object to the top of the object's block, whereas **text-bottom** aligns the text to the bottom edge of the object.

Elements

CAPTION	COL	IMG	SPAN
TABLE	TBODY	TD	TFOOT
TH THEAD	TR		

CROSS-REFERENCE
See **vertical-align**, **horizontalAlign**, and **horizontal-align**.

vertical-align

Attribute

CSS

This property is used to control the vertical alignment of text within an inline box that is found within a block element.

The syntax of this attribute is

```
vertical-align:   baseline | sub | super | top | text-top |
middle | bottom | text-bottom | percentage | length | inherit
```

Values

baseline

This aligns the baseline of the inline box with the baseline of the block box. If the inline box does not have a baseline, its bottom is aligned with the block box.

middle

This aligns the midpoint of the inline box with the baseline of the block box plus half of the x-height of the block box.

sub

This aligns the baseline of the inline box to the position for subscripts inside the parent block box.

super

This raises the baseline of the box to the proper position for superscripts of the parent's box. (This value has no effect on the font size of the element's text.)

text-top

This aligns the top of the box with the top of the parent element's font.

text-bottom

This aligns the bottom of the box with the bottom of the parent element's font.

u
v
w

percentage

This raises (positive value) or lowers (negative value) the box by the specified distance (a percentage of the line-height value). The value 0% produces the same effect as **baseline**.

length

This raises (positive value) or lowers (negative value) the box by the specified distance. The value 0cm produces the same effect as **baseline**. The remaining values refer to the line box in which the generated box appears:

top

This aligns the top of the box with the top of the line box.

bottom

This aligns the bottom of the box with the bottom of the line box.

Example
The following example sets the vertical alignment of a series of table cells.

```
<SCRIPT type="text/css">
   TD      { vertical-align: top }
   TR      { vertical-align: middle }
   TFOOT   { vertical-align: bottom }
</SCRIPT>
```

Elements

A	ACRONYM	ADDRESS	AREA
B	BGSOUND	BIG	BR
BUTTON	CENTER	CITE	CODE
COL	COLGROUP	DD	DEL
DFN	DIR	DIV	DL
DT	EM	EMBED	FIELDSET
FONT	I	INPUT	INS
KBD	MAP	OPTION	PLAINTEXT
Q	S	SAMP	SELECT
SMALL	STRIKE	STRONG	SUB
SUP	TD	TFOOT	THEAD
TR	VAR	XMP	

CROSS-REFERENCE
See **valign**, **halign**, **verticalAlign**, **horizontal-align**, **horizontal-Align**, and **align**.

visibility

Attribute

CSS

This property is used to control how the generated content of a box is rendered. Even invisible or fully transparent boxes still affect the layout of the document.

The syntax of this attribute is

```
visibility:    visible | hidden | collapse | inherit
```

JAVA SCRIPT

```
object.style.visibility= [visible | hidden | collapse]
```

This parameter is used to adjust the visibility of your objects on the fly.

Values
visible

This forces the generated box to be visible.

hidden

This forces the generated box to be invisible, but the box still affects the layout.

collapse

If this is used on an element other than a row or column for a table, it will have the same effect as hidden.

Example
In the following example, a reader can press a form button to activate a user-defined script function that makes its corresponding DIV box visible while hiding the other. Because each box is the same size and is located in the same position, the selected box replaces the other.

ON THE CD-ROM
Look for **visibility.htm** on the accompanying CD-ROM.

```
<HTML>
<HEAD>
```

```
<STYLE type="text/css">
  <!--
  #box1 { position: absolute;
          top: 2in;
          left: 2in;
          width: 2in;
          visibility: hidden; }
  #box2 { position: absolute;
          top: 2in;
          left: 2in;
          width: 2in;
          visibility: hidden; }
  -->
</STYLE>
</HEAD>
<BODY onload="box1.style.visility='hidden'">
   <P>Who Killed Professor Plum:</P>
   <DIV id="box1">
      <IMG alt="Mrs. White" width="100" height="100"
src="mrswhite.jpg">
      <P>Name: Mrs. White</P>
      <P>Room: Library</P>
      <P>Weapon: Pipe </P>
   </DIV>
   <DIV id="box2">
      <IMG alt="Ms. Scarlet" width="100" height="100"
src="msscarlet.jpg">
      <P>Name: Ms. Scarlet</P>
      <P>Room: Kitchen</P>
      <P>Weapon: Rope<P>
   </DIV>
   <BUTTON name="Mrs. White"
onclick="box1.style.visiblity='visible';
box2.style.visiblity='hidden'">
   <BUTTON name="Ms. Scarlet"
onclick="box1.style.visiblity='hidden';
box2.style.visiblity='visible'">
</BODY>
</HTML>
```

Elements

This attribute applies to all HTML elements.

CROSS-REFERENCE
See **position**, **<LAYER>**, **<SPAN>**, and **<DIV>**.

Visited

Concept

CROSS-REFERENCE
See **:visited** and **pseudo-class**.

Visual Basic

Language

This is a full programming language and environment developed by Microsoft but based on the age-old BASIC language. Visual Basic provides a graphical environment for object-oriented programming. This language serves as the foundation for VBScript and Visual Basic for Applications. Each of these programming languages is proprietary to Microsoft products. Netscape Web browsers cannot be used to view documents VBScripted effects on HTML documents.

Visual Basic was the first language to be provided with a visual interface. This graphical programming environment enables programmers to create large chunks of code simply by dragging and placing objects on their programming screens or by clicking a button to insert a common type of functionality in their software. All that is left for programmers to do is to define the appearance and specific behavior of the objects.

Although Visual Basic is not truly an object-oriented programming language, unlike Visual C or Visual Java, it uses the majority of the object-oriented philosophy. Visual Basic is more truly an event-driven language since each object reacts differently to different events within the application's environment.

CROSS-REFERENCE
See **VBScript**, **JavaScript**, **Java**, **Jscript**, and **ECMAScript**.

u

v

w

Visual

Media Group

CSS

Cascading Style Sheets, level 2, has defined the following media groups:

- Visual/Aural/Tactile
- Continuous/Paged
- Grid/Bitmap
- Interactive/Static

Each media group is used to describe a specific type of medium. Many media types are identified as part of these groups. The visual media group is composed of a variety of information that can be viewed with your eyes. It can be continuous or paged, bitmapped or on a grid, interactive or static. Most visual media include the information you see in this book, if you are not reading a Braille version, of course. Your computer screen is visual, although you might have a speech synthesizer that allows you both to see and hear the contents of the documents that you are viewing. Other types of communication devices that are visual include newspapers, TV, TTY, books, pictures, and billboards.

 CROSS-REFERENCE
See **Media Groups** and **Media Types**.

vLink

Attribute

HTML

This attribute sets the color for a visited link. Although this attribute has been deprecated in favor of the `visited` pseudo-class, it is still safe to use with all current browsers. It may be removed from use at a later date.

The syntax for vLink is

```
vLink=color
```

Values
color

The color can be either a valid HTML color name or a Hex value representing the RGB value of the color.

Example

In the following example code, the vLink attribute is used to turn all links in a document green when they are active.

ON THE CD-ROM

Look for **vlink.htm** on the accompanying CD-ROM.

```
<HTML>
<HEAD>
<TITLE> Use vLink to change link colors </TITLE>
<BODY vlink="green">
<H1> My Favorite Web Sites </H1>
    <A href="http://www.catsback.com/sbothum"> Shirly Bothum -
World Class Artist in Bronze </A><BR>
    <A href="http://www.bluemountain.com"> Blue Mountain
Greeting Cards </A><BR>
    <A href="http://www.homearts.com">HomeArts - Horoscopes
</A><BR>
    <A href="http://www.cnn.com">CNN</A>
 </BODY>
</HTML>
```

Elements

BODY

CROSS-REFERENCE

See **color**, **Appendix A**, **vlinkColor**, **:active**, **:hover**, and **:visited**.

vlinkColor

Property

DHTML

This readable and writable scripted object statement is used to set the color for a visited link.

The syntax of this command is

```
object.vlinkColor[ = color]
```

u
v
w

Values

color

> The color can be either a valid HTML color name or a Hex value representing the RGB value of the color.

Objects

document

CROSS-REFERENCE
See **linkColor**, **color**, **Appendix A**, **alinkcolor**, **:active**, **:hover**, and **:visited**.

<VM>

Element

OSD

This element is a child of the IMPLEMENTATION element and is used to identify the location of the virtual machine that is required to complete the installation.

Attributes

Value

```
Value=string
```

This is the URI of the virtual machine used for this software.

CROSS-REFERENCE
See **<IMPLEMENTATION>** and **Open Software Definition**.

voice-family

Attribute

CSS

This attribute contains a prioritized list of voice family names and generic voice names that are used by the speech synthesizer for aural style sheets.

The syntax of this attribute is

```
voice-family: [[specific-voice | generic-voice ],]* [specific-
voice | generic-voice ] | inherit
```

Values
generic-voice

Valid values for this setting are voice families. Possible values are male, female, and child.

specific-voice

These values describe specific instances or voices such as comedian, talkshow, Mike, and Jose. These names must be enclosed in quotation marks if they do not conform to syntax rules for identifiers or if they consist of more than one word.

Example
The following statements show how you can select either a generic or specific voice for reading of parts of a document.

```
H1 { voice-family: announcer, male }
P.part.fred { voice-family: fred, male }
P.part.ginger { voice-family: ginger, female }
```

Elements
This attribute is available for all elements.

CROSS-REFERENCE
See **family-name**, **font-family**, and **generic-name**.

volume

Attribute

CSS

The volume attribute allows you to control the average volume of the speaking voice of your speech synthesizer. This is the median value of the analog wave of the voice. In other words, a highly inflected voice at a volume of 50 might peak at 75. This property is used to adjust the dynamic range of the voice's volume within the expected range of human comfort.

```
volume: number | percentage | silent | x-soft | soft | medium
 | loud | x-loud | inherit
```

Values
number

This value can be any number between 0 and 100, with 0 representing the minimum audible volume level and 100 the maximum comfortable level.

percentage

Percentages are calculated relative to the inherited value and then clipped to the 0–100 range.

silent

This value produces no sound at all; 0 is not equivalent to silent.

x-soft

This value is equivalent to 0.

soft

This value is equivalent to 25.

medium

This value is equivalent to 50.

loud

This value is equivalent to 75.

x-loud

This value is equivalent to 100.

Elements

This attribute applies to all HTML elements.

CROSS-REFERENCE
See **pitch** and **frequency**.

vspace

Attribute

HTML

This attribute is used to specify the amount of white space to insert above and below an object created by an IMG, APPLET, or OBJECT tag.

The syntax for using this attribute is

```
vspace=length
```

Values
length

This is any floating-point integer with a designated unit identifier that can be used to define either an absolute or a relative amount of white space around the designated object.

Elements

APPLET   IMG   OBJECT

CROSS-REFERENCE
See **hspace**, **margins**, **padding**, and **white-space**.

<WBR>

Element

HTML

Start Tag: Required
End Tag: Optional

This element inserts a soft line break within a NOBR delimited section of text. This element has been deprecated, and should not be used. Escape sequences, along with the page- and line-break attributes used with Cascading Style Sheets, have replaced its functionality.

Attributes
class

    class="cdata-list"

This attribute is used to assign a class name to an element. User agents employ classes to group specific types of information for later use.

id

    id="name"

This attribute is used to assign a name to an element.

lang

    lang="language code"

This attribute specifies the language in which an element and its values should be rendered.

onclick

`onclick=`*script*

This attribute takes effect when a user double-clicks the button on a pointing device with the pointer over an element.

ondblclick

`ondblclick=`*script*

This attribute takes effect when a user double-clicks the button on a pointing device with the pointer over an element.

onkeydown

`onkeydown=`*script*

This attribute takes effect when a user presses a key and the pointer is over an element.

onkeypress

`onkeypress=`*script*

This attribute takes effect when a key is pressed and released with the pointer over an element.

onkeyup

`onkeyup=`*script*

This attribute takes effect when a user releases a key with the pointer over an element.

onmousedown

`onmousedown=`*script*

This attribute takes effect when a user double-clicks the button on a pointing device with the pointer over an element.

onmousemove

`onmousemove=`*script*

This attribute is activated when the mouse pointer is moved while it is over an element.

onmouseout

`onmouseout=`*script*

This attributed is activated when the mouse pointer is moved away from an element.

onmouseover

```
onmouseover=script
```

This attribute is activated when the mouse pointer is moved over an element.

onmouseup

```
onmouseup=script
```

This attribute takes effect when the button on a pointing device is released while the pointer is over an element.

style

```
style=style descriptors
```

This attribute applies specific style-sheet information to one particular element.

title

```
title=text
```

This attribute provides annotation information to the element.

Example

In the following example, the WBR element is inserted to provide a soft line break between lines in a poem, depending on how narrow the window gets. Without the WBR, the contents of a NOBR do not break.

ON THE CD-ROM

Look for **wbr.htm** on the accompanying CD-ROM.

```
<NOBR>Peter Piper Picked a Peck of Pickled Peppers <WBR> If
Peter Piper Picked a Peck of Pickled Peppers, <WBR> How Many
Pecks of Pickled Peppers did Peter Piper Pick? <WBR> Peter
Piper Picked a Peck of Pickled Peppers <WBR> If Peter Piper
Picked a Peck of Pickled Peppers, <WBR> How Many Pecks of
Pickled Peppers did Peter Piper Pick? <WBR> Peter Piper Picked
a Peck of Pickled Peppers <WBR> If Peter Piper Picked a Peck
of Pickled Peppers, <WBR> How Many Pecks of Pickled Peppers
did Peter Piper Pick?</NOBR>
```

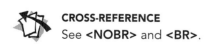

CROSS-REFERENCE
See **<NOBR>** and **
**.

Web Fonts

Concept

With the advent of font matching with Cascading Style Sheets, the world of electronic publishing is reaching beyond its infancy. Your viewers can now see your document the way you intended. You provide your readers with fonts to download, or simply match the font you're using to other, similar fonts that might reside on readers' systems. This means document developers no longer must rely on images to provide text logos for their pages.

 CROSS-REFERENCE
See **font matching**.

WebCasting

Concept

WebCasting is a relatively intricate Web technology that allows multimedia content to broadcast live across the Internet or an intranet. This allows clients to view events as they happen, whether it is the unveiling of new memorial, a presidential speech, or simply the guy in the corner eating his lunch.

There are five main steps to producing WebCasting content:

1. Capture the event to be dispersed across the Internet.
2. Create an HTML document to include the video.
3. Convert the video into a compressed stream, and then send the stream to a live-video-capable server available to your clients.
4. Configure the bandwidth on the server to optimize viewing performance.
5. Let your potential audience know that the video is available, and encourage them to view it.

 CROSS-REFERENCE
See **Channels** and **Channel Definition Format**.

Weight

Concept

CSS

Weight in reference to a Cascading Style Sheet entry refers to the amount of emphasis placed on one style-sheet rule over another. As all style sheets load into a user agent, they are weighted based on their origin, their loading order, and the presence or lack of the `!important` descriptor. This weight is then used to determine whether a rule is from one particular style sheet or another.

 CROSS-REFERENCE
See **Cascade** and **Cascading Style Sheets**.

Well-Formed Document

Concept

XML

Each XML document has logical and physical structures. If both structures meet XML specifications and interact appropriately with each other, the document is *well formed*. Physically, a document is made up of a series of entities. Each entity provides a piece of the document, sort of like building blocks. Some of these entities refer to other documents for inclusion in the current document. All documents have a root document entity that serves as the foundation for building blocks. Logically, a document is composed of elements, declarations, comments, processing instructions, and character references. Each of these logical structures is identified in the document using markup text.

For the document to meet the specification and restrictions of XML it must meet all of the following requirements:

- Contains one or more elements.
- Has one root- or document-level element that does not appear in the content of any other element.
- All elements that are part of the content of other elements are nested appropriately.
- All entities used in the document meet the restrictions of the XML specification.

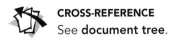

CROSS-REFERENCE
See **document tree**.

white-space

Attribute

CSS

This attribute is used to identify how to treat white-space found within elements.

```
white-space: normal | pre | nowrap | inherit
```

Values

normal

The white-space will collapse and line breaks will be inserted as necessary to fill the boxes appropriately.

pre

This prevents a user agent from collapsing a series of white-space characters within an element. It also prevents text wrapping.

nowrap

This value collapses white-space, as does normal; it also suppresses line breaks within the text.

Example

This example style sheet shows the use of white-space characters as they normally appear for the following elements.

```
PRE { white-space: pre }
P { white-space: normal }
DIV { white-space: normal }
NOBR{ white-space: nowrap }
```

Elements

BODY	BLOCKQUOTE	BUTTON	CAPTION
CENTER	COL	COLGROUP	DIV
FIELDSET	FORM	FRAME	FRAMESET
H1–H6	HEAD	HR	IFRAME
INPUT	LABEL	LAYER	LEGEND
LI	MAP	MARQUEE	OBJECT
OL	P	PRE	Q
SCRIPT	SELECT	SPAN	TABLE
TD	TEXTAREA	TFOOT	TH
THEAD	TR	UL	

CROSS-REFERENCE
See **margins**, **borders**, and **padding**.

Widows

Attribute

CSS

This attribute is used to specify the minimum number of lines in a paragraph that must remain at the top of a page when a paragraph is broken between two pages.

The syntax for this element is

```
widow: integer | inherit
```

Values

integer

This is a positive integer identifying the number of lines that must occur after a page break that splits a paragraph.

V
►W
X

Elements

BODY	BLOCKQUOTE	BUTTON	CAPTION
CENTER	COL	COLGROUP	DIV
FIELDSET	FORM	FRAME	FRAMESET
H1–H6	HEAD	HR	IFRAME
INPUT	LABEL	LAYER	LEGEND
LI	MAP	MARQUEE	OBJECT
OL	P	PRE	Q
SCRIPT	SELECT	SPAN	TABLE
TD	TEXTAREA	TFOOT	TH
THEAD	TR	UL	

CROSS-REFERENCE
See **<WBR>**, **<NOBR>**, **
, and **<P>.

Width

Attribute

CSS

This attribute is used to identify the content width of boxes created by block level and replaced elements.

```
width: length  | percentage | auto | inherit
```

Values

length

A positive integer and unit specifier identify a fixed width.

percentage

This is calculated with respect to the width of the boxes containing a block.

auto

This forces the width of the object to depend on the values of other properties associated with the object.

Example

The following style-sheet rule fixes images' content width to 200 pixels.

```
IMG { width: 200px }
```

Elements

BODY	BLOCKQUOTE	BUTTON	CAPTION
CENTER	COL	COLGROUP	DIV
FIELDSET	FORM	FRAME	FRAMESET
H1–H6	HEAD	HR	IFRAME
INPUT	LABEL	LAYER	LEGEND
LI	MAP	MARQUEE	OBJECT
OL	P	PRE	Q
SCRIPT	SELECT	SPAN	TABLE
TD	TEXTAREA	TFOOT	TH
THEAD	UL		

CROSS-REFERENCE
See **width**, **widths**, and **height**.

width

Attribute

HTML

This attribute is used to identify an object's width. When used with the COL or COLGROUP elements it identifies the width of the individual columns in the group, not the group itself.

```
width=<length>
```

Values
<length>

This is a positive integer value and its associated unit identifier that specifies the total width of the object.

Example
The following code is used to set the width of an individual image.

```
<IMG  width=100 height=100 src="http://images.com/
bookback.gif" alt="Good looking books.">
```

Elements

APPLET	COL	COLGROUP	HR
IFRAME	IMG	OBJECT	PRE
TABLE	TD	TH	

CROSS-REFERENCE
See **height**, **widths**, and **width**.

widths

Descriptor

CSS

This descriptor defines the width of individual characters. This is a comma-separated list of ⟨urange⟩ values followed by a number representing a character glyph width. When this descriptor is used the units-per-em descriptor must also be used.

```
widths:[urange ]? [number ]+ [,[urange ]? number ]+]
```

Values

urange

This is a range of values, associated with the Unicode values for international characters, used to represent the character for which you are specifying the width.

number

This is a number representing the width of the character you have identified.

CROSS-REFERENCE
See **glyph**, **character**, and **height**.

Word-Spacing

Attribute

CSS

This attribute is used to control the spaces found between words.

The syntax of this attribute is

```
word-spacing: normal | length | inherit
```

Values
length

A positive integer and unit specifier identify a fixed width.

normal

This setting leaves the spacing between the words to the control of the font or user agent.

CROSS-REFERENCE
See **letter-spacing**.

World Wide Web (WWW)

Concept

The World Wide Web is a source of information and entertainment for about 70 million individuals every day. But underneath its glossy commercial and educational shell, the Web is a conglomeration of text files, image files, applets, and programming code. All of these elements work together to provide you with the information that you need — generally in an attractive form.

Information on the Web is located on a variety of computers, or servers, connected to form a huge spiderweb network of corporations, schools, services businesses, online services, and individuals. This network, using HTTP, can transmit information found on one computer to another in just a few seconds. This allows developers to work with partners across the world, sharing and developing information in record time. It allows individuals in educational systems to learn about the latest happenings at NASA, or how their university's battery-powered car development is going.

There are many things that help the Web transmit information. User agents, more often called Web browsers, are designed to talk to Web servers and request information for a user. Search engines — like big, library card catalogs — exist to help a user find his or her way to information on a particular subject. Corporations give users free access to information that can help them create their own top-of-the-line presence on the Internet. All the services and information on the Web may feel claustrophobic to some, but to others it provides a challenge that can't be matched.

CROSS-REFERENCE
See **HTML**, **HTTP**, **User Agent**, and **browser**.

wrap

Property

DHTML

This scripting property is used to control word wrapping within a TEXTAREA object.

The syntax for using this expression is

```
object.wrap (=sVar)
```

Values

sVar

This is a string variable that can contain the values **soft**, **hard**, or **off**. If the value of this variable is **soft**, then the text shows carriage returns and line feeds but those characters are not submitted to the HTTP server when the TEXTAREA is. If **hard** is the value, then the text wraps and those characters are submitted to the HTTP server with TEXTAREA. If the value is off, then word wrapping is disabled and text is displayed exactly as the user typed it.

Elements

TEXTAREA

CROSS-REFERENCE
See **nowrap**.

Wrapping Text

Concept

Text can be displayed in your document in one of two ways. You can allow the user agent to automatically wrap your text where it best fits the size of the viewable area of the agent, or you can force each part of your document to be a specific size. When text wraps through an inline box, a soft carriage return and line feed is added at the appropriate point within the text box.

CROSS-REFERENCE
See **wrap**, **nowrap**, **<WBR>**, **<NOBR>**, **
, and **<P>.

write

Method

DHTML

This method is used to write a full line of information to a document through an HTML script. The cursor is left at the end of the entered string.
The syntax for using this method is

```
document.write(string || stringVar)
```

Parameters
string

This is the actual quoted text string placed within the document.

stringVar

This is the name of a string-formatted variable that needs to be placed in the document.

Objects
document

CROSS-REFERENCE
See **alert** and **writeln**.

writeln

Method

DHTML

This method is used to write a full line of information to a document through an HTML script. A carriage return automatically appears once the contents of the string are placed in the document.
The syntax for using this method is

```
document.writeln(string || stringVar)
```

Parameters
string

This is the actual quoted text string that is placed within the document.

stringVar

This is the name of a string-formatted variable that needs to be placed in the document.

Objects
document

 CROSS-REFERENCE
See **alert** and **write**.

X

Property

DHTML

This property is used to return the horizontal position of the mouse click in relation to the next parent object positioned via one of the Cascading Style Sheet positioning attributes.

The syntax of this property is

```
[iX = ] event.x
```

Parameters
iX

This integer specifies the horizontal coordinate of the mouse, in pixels. When the mouse pointer is outside the window, the value of this parameter is −1. If no object in the document hierarchy was positioned using a Cascading Style Sheet, the BODY element is the default object.

Objects

event

CROSS-REFERENCE
See **y**.

x-height

Descriptor

CSS

This descriptor is used to identify the height of a font's lowercase characters. When this value is defined, it is used in conjunction with the "units-per-em" descriptor for font matching by the user agent. When undefined, it is not used. Font matching is best served by using this descriptor in conjunction with the `font-size-adjust` property to enable proper computation of the heights and sizes of candidate fonts.

```
x-height: <number>
```

CROSS-REFERENCE
See **font-height**, **@fontface**, and **font-family**.

XML — eXtensible Markup Language

Language

The eXtensible Markup Language is a subset of SGML. It was designed to enable the standard SGML markup to be distributed and processed on the Internet in the manner of HTML. In order to meet this goal, it was designed to be easily used and implemented, as well as highly interoperable with both HTML and SGML.

XML describes a series of data objects referred to as XML documents and outlines the required behavior of programs that process those documents. Each XML document is composed of a series of entities, or information storage units, which contain either parsed or unparsed data. Parsed data is a mix of characters forming both markup text and character-based information. The markup text provides the information for the layout and logical structure of the document. XML enables document authors to impose constraints upon the layout and logical structure of documents in a fashion not available with HTML. The XML processor, generally running within the user agent, is used to read the XML documents, providing access to content and structure.

CROSS-REFERENCE
See **Channel Definition Format**, **Open Software Description**, and **XSL**.

<XMP>

Element

HTML

Start Tag: Required
End Tag: Required

This element should no longer be used, although it is still valid (the PRE and SAMP elements should be used instead). This element renders text in a monospaced font and is generally used for example code.

Attributes
class

```
class="cdata-list"
```

This attribute is used to assign a class name to an element. User agents employ classes to group specific types of information for later use.

id

```
id="name"
```

This attribute is used to assign a name to an element.

lang

```
lang="language code"
```

This attribute specifies the language in which an element and its values should be rendered.

onclick

```
onclick=script
```

This attribute takes effect when a user double-clicks the button on a pointing device with the pointer over an element.

ondblclick

```
ondblclick=script
```

This attribute takes effect when a user double-clicks the button on a pointing device with the pointer over an element.

onkeydown

```
onkeydown=script
```

This attribute takes effect when a user presses a key and the pointer is over an element.

onkeypress

```
onkeypress=script
```

This attribute takes effect when a key is pressed and released over an element.

w
x
y

onkeyup

> onkeyup=*script*

This attribute takes effect when a user releases a key with the pointer over an element.

onmousedown

> onmousedown=*script*

This attribute takes effect when a user presses the button on a pointing device while the pointer is over an element.

onmousemove

> onmousemove=*script*

This attribute is activated when the mouse pointer is moved while it is over an element.

onmouseout

> onmouseout=*script*

This attributed is activated when the mouse pointer is moved away from an element.

onmouseover

> onmouseover=*script*

This attribute is activated when the mouse pointer is moved over an element.

onmouseup

> onmouseup=*script*

This attribute takes effect when the button on a pointing device is released while the pointer is over an element.

style

> style=*style descriptors*

This attribute applies specific style-sheet information to one particular element.

title

> title=*text*

This attribute provides annotation information to the element.

Example

The following example uses the XMP element to display the code used in the following cookie recipe, which, by the way, is quite tasty.

ON THE CD-ROM

Look for **xmp.htm** on the accompanying CD-ROM.

```
<H2> Cleo's Fabulous Dish Pan Cookies </H2>
    <P> <IMG src="chocchip.gif" alt="Dish Pan Cookies">
    First collect the following ingredients:
    <XMP>
    <UL>
        <LI> 2 Cups <B> Sugar</B>
        <LI> 2 Cups <B>Brown Sugar</B>
        <LI> 1Cup <B>Butter</B>
        <LI> 2 tsp. <B> Vanilla</B><BR>
        _____

        <LI> 2 Cups <B>Oats</B>
        <LI> 4 Cups <B>Flour</B>
        <LI> 4 <B>Eggs</B>
        <LI> 1 lb. <B>Chocolate Chips</B>
        <LI> 2 Cups <B>Coconut</B>
        <LI> 2 Cups <B>Corn Flakes</B>
        <LI> 1.5 Cups <B>Nuts</B>
        <LI> 1 Cup <B>Raisins</B>
        <LI> 2 Tsp. <B>Coconut</B>
    </UL>
    </XMP>
```

CROSS-REFERENCE

See **<EM>**, **<BIG>**, **<CODE>**, **<SAMP>**, **<ABBR>**, and **<ACRONYM>**.

XSL — eXtensible Style Language

Language

XSL is a proposed style-sheet language for the XML implementation of SGML. The XSL language is a subset of DSSSL and is being designed with an eye toward satisfying the widest cross-section of the Web-developing community.

XSL is available to document authors, providing a variety of defined solutions to many of the data description and rendering problems encountered on the Web today. When developers diverge into uncommon tasks, XSL enables them to escape to scriptlike environments with more flexibility and control.

XSL enables document creators to format elements based on ancestry, descendancy, position, and uniqueness. It enables the creation of generated text and graphics through the use of formatting constructs. With XSL, it is possible to create reusable formatting macros and write direction-independent style sheets.

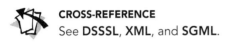

CROSS-REFERENCE
See **DSSSL**, **XML**, and **SGML**.

y

Property

DHTML

This property is used to return the vertical position of the mouse click in relation to the next parent object positioned via one of the Cascading Style Sheet positioning attributes.

The syntax of this property is

```
[iY = ] object.y
```

Parameters
iY

This integer specifies the vertical coordinate of the mouse, in pixels. When the mouse pointer is outside the window, the value of this parameter is –1. If no object in the document hierarchy was positioned using a Cascading Style Sheet, the BODY element is the default object.

Object

event

CROSS-REFERENCE
See **x**.

Z

z-index

Attribute

CSS

This attribute is used for boxes with positioning attributes. The z-index attribute has two jobs. The first is to control the stacking order of positioned boxes. The second is to identify whether the box can be used to establish a local stacking context.

The syntax of this command is

```
z-index= auto | integer | inherit
```

Values

auto

In this case the box inherits the same stacking value as its parent. This is this attribute's default value.

integer

The integer specified is a positive or negative whole number that identifies the stacking order of the box used with this element.

inherit

This value simply implies that this next layer should follow the same positioning scheme as its parent elements.

Example

The following code shows how the z-index attribute can be used to create a multipart graphical overlay.

ON THE CD-ROM

Look for **zindex.htm** on the accompanying CD-ROM.

```
<HTML>
<HEAD>
```

```
<TITLE>zindex animations</TITLE>
  <SCRIPT language="JavaScript">
<!—
function MM_initTimelines() {
    //MM_initTimelines() Copyright 1997 Macromedia, Inc. All
rights reserved.
    var ns = navigator.appName == "Netscape";
    document.MM_Time = new Array(1);
    document.MM_Time[0] = new Array(1);
    document.MM_Time["Timeline1"] = document.MM_Time[0];
    document.MM_Time[0].MM_Name = "Timeline1";
    document.MM_Time[0].fps = 15;
    document.MM_Time[0][0] = new String("sprite");
    document.MM_Time[0][0].slot = 1;
    if (ns)
        document.MM_Time[0][0].obj = document.Layer2;
    else
        document.MM_Time[0][0].obj = document.all ?
document.all["Layer2"] : null;
    document.MM_Time[0][0].keyFrames = new Array(1, 15);
    document.MM_Time[0][0].values = new Array(2);
    document.MM_Time[0][0].values[0] = new
Array(316,316,316,316,316,316,316,316,316,316,316,316,316,316,
316);
    document.MM_Time[0][0].values[0].prop = "left";
    document.MM_Time[0][0].values[1] = new
Array(17,35,52,70,87,105,122,140,157,175,192,210,227,245,262);
    document.MM_Time[0][0].values[1].prop = "top";
    if (!ns) {
        document.MM_Time[0][0].values[0].prop2 = "style";
        document.MM_Time[0][0].values[1].prop2 = "style";
    }
    document.MM_Time[0].lastFrame = 15;
    for (i=0; i<document.MM_Time.length; i++) {
        document.MM_Time[i].ID = null;
        document.MM_Time[i].curFrame = 0;
        document.MM_Time[i].delay =
1000/document.MM_Time[i].fps;
    }
}
//—>
</SCRIPT>
</HEAD>
<BODY bgcolor="#FFFFFF">
```

```
<IMG src="blocks.jpg" width="300" height="300">
<DIV id="Layer1" style="position:absolute; left:11px;
top:16px; width:300px; height:300px; z-index:1">
  <IMG src="spideranim.gif" width="300" height="300">
</DIV>
<DIV id="Layer2" style="position:absolute; left:316px;
top:17px; width:150px; height:53px; z-index:2">
  <P align="center"><FONT size="+2"
color="#6600FF"><B>SPIDER<BR>
    ATTACK</B></FONT> </P>
</DIV>
</BODY>
</HTML>
```

Elements

This attribute can be applied to all positioned elements through the use of the HTML style attribute.

CROSS-REFERENCE
See **<LAYER>**, **<SPAN>**, **<DIV>**, **style**, **integer**, **Zindex**, and **zOrder**.

zIndex

Property

DHTML

This document object property is used to set or retrieve the stacking order of positioned elements. By default all positioned elements are stacked from bottom to top, but that order can be adjusted using the z-index Cascading Style Sheet attribute or the zIndex scripting property. Because the z-index value can be either positive or negative, the layers are ordered from most negative to most positive. If multiple layers have the same index value, then they are ordered by source documentation order.

The syntax of this command is

```
object.style.zIndex[=integer]
```

Parameters

integer

The integer specified is a positive or negative whole number used to place the layer in the proper position in the stack of layers.

x
y
z

Elements

A	ADDRESS	APPLET	B
BIG	BLOCKQUOTE	BODY	CAPTION
CENTER	CITE	CODE	COL
COLGROUP	DD	DFN	DIR
DIV	DL	DT	EM
FIELDSET	FORM	H1–H6	HTML
I	INPUT	KBD	LABEL
LEGEND	LI	LISTING	MARQUEE
MENU	OL	P	PLAINTEXT
PRE	SAMP	SMALL	SPAN
STRIKE	STRONG	SUB	SUP
TABLE	TBODY	TD	TEXTAREA
TFOOT	TH	THEAD	TR
TT	U	UL	VAR
XMP			

zOrder

Method

DHTML

This scripting method is used to set the z-index for positions. The syntax of this command is

```
object.zOrder([position])
```

Parameters
position

This is a variable parameter. It can consist of an integer, or it can be one of two fixed values: **front** or **back**. If the parameter's value is **front**, the element is placed at the beginning of the z-order. If the parameter's value is **back**, the element is placed at the end of the z-order.

Elements

APPLET	BUTTON	CAPTION	DIV
EMBED	HR	IMG	INPUT
MARQUEE	OBJECT	SPAN	TD
TEXTAREA			

CROSS-REFERENCE
See **z-index** and **zIndex**.

appendix

A

What's on the CD-ROM?

Organization of the CD-ROM

The CD-ROM contains many, though not all, examples from the book. If an example is included on the disc, it is marked with a CD icon followed by a note that directs you to the name of the appropriate HTML document. To access the HTML examples located on the disc, open the `index.htm` file on the CD-ROM's root directory.

Table AA-1 shows the structure of the information on the CD-ROM.

Table AA-1 Structure of the HTML Master Reference CD-ROM

Root Directory	Subdirectories	Description
`index.htm`		Main file that provides access to all other examples and documentation on the CD-ROM
Adobe/	Win	Windows version of Adobe Acrobat Reader
	Mac	Mac version of Adobe Acrobat Reader
Aladdin/		Main directory for the StuffIt products
	ExpanderWin/	PC version of the StuffIt Expander
	StuffIT/	Demo version of the StuffIt compression and expansion software
	StuffITExpander/	Mac version of StuffIt Expander
Allaire/		Executable for the HomeSite HTML Editor
Chapters/		PDF versions of the alphabetized reference text of the book
HTML/		Source code for the examples
	Images/	All of the images associated with the example pages
Macromedia/		Main directory for all Macromedia products
	Windows/	Windows versions of the included Macromedia products

Continued

1263

Table AA-1 *Continued*

Root Directory	Subdirectories	Description
	Mac/	Mac versions of the included Macromedia products
Marketwave/		Executable installation program for Hit List Pro
Microsoft/		Main directory for the Internet Explorer versions included on the CD-ROM
	Windows/	Setup program for Internet Explorer 4.01 for Windows
	Mac/	Setup program for Internet Explorer for Macintosh
NetObjects/		Setup program for NetObjects ScriptBuilder 2.0 demo
Netscape/		Main directory for the Netscape Navigator versions included on the CD-ROM
	Windows/	Setup program for Netscape Navigator for Windows
	Mac/	Setup program for Netscape Navigator for Macintosh
NikoMak/		Main directory for the versions of WinZip installed on the CD-ROM
	Win31/	Setup program for the Windows 3.1 version of WinZip
	Win95.98.NT/	Setup program for the Windows 95, 98, and NT version of WinZip

---

Using the Examples in the Book

The CD-ROM contains about 200 example HTML documents and images, reachable through the `index.htm` file located in the root directory of the CD-ROM. (This page has links to all examples included in the book.) Across the top of the index is a link to the examples sorted by Cascading Style Sheets, HTML, MathML, and All. The examples are linked on these pages in alphabetical order, just as you find them in the book.

If you do not wish to hunt for your example through the indexes provided, you can open examples from of the CD-ROM. By each CD icon in the book is a filename. In this file, located in the HTML directory on the CD, you will find the example in its complete and active form.

You can also link to descriptions of the various programs on the CD-ROM, and you can access the documentation associated with these programs through a link on the software page.

Adobe Acrobat Reader

Acrobat Reader by Adobe is one of the most popular document-format readers used on the Internet for help files and software documentation. The Portable Document Format (PDF) files read by Acrobat can be viewed through a browser window with the addition of the Adobe Acrobat plug-in. You can use this reader to view the chapters included in the disc.

Installation

To install the Acrobat Reader, follow these instructions:

1. Open the **Adobe** directory on the CD-ROM.
2. Open the **Win** folder (for Windows 95 or NT users) or the **Mac** folder (for Macintosh users).
3. Double-click the **setup.exe** file, and follow the directions included in the installation program.

Contact Information

Adobe Systems, Inc.
345 Park Avenue
San Jose, CA 95110-2704
Tel: (408) 536-6000
Fax: (408) 537-7000
www.adobe.com

Aladdin Systems StuffIt (Mac)

StuffIt by Aladdin Systems is the most popular encoding and compression software available for the Macintosh. This software can be used to encode and decode information in BinHex, the industry standard StuffIt, and all other compression formats commonly encountered on the Internet, including files that have been compressed on PCs and UNIX systems.

Installation

To install the StuffIt demonstration software, follow these instructions:

1. Open the **Aladdin** directory on the CD-ROM.
2. Open the **StuffIT** folder.
3. Double-click the installation file, and follow the remaining directions included in the CD-ROM.

Contact Information

Aladdin Systems, Inc.
165 Westridge Dr.
Watsonville, CA 95076
Tel: (831) 761-6200
Fax: (831) 761-6206
www.aladdinsys.com

Aladdin Systems StuffIt Expander (PC and Mac)

StuffIt Expander by Aladdin Systems is designed to expand all common Macintosh compressed files, such as StuffIt, CompactPro, BinHex, and MacBinary files. The Windows version also expands ZIP compressed files.

Installation

To install the StuffIt Expander freeware software, follow these instructions:

1. Open the **Aladdin** directory on the CD-ROM.
2. Open the **ExpanderWin** folder (for Windows 95 or NT users) or the **StuffITExpander** folder (for Macintosh users).
3. In Windows, double-click the **Aladdin_Expander.exe** file, and use a **binhex** expander to decompress the **stuffit_exp_45_installer** file.

Contact Information

Aladdin Systems, Inc.
165 Westridge Dr.
Watsonville, CA 95076
Tel: (831) 761-6200
Fax: (831) 761-6206
www.aladdinsys.com

Allaire HomeSite

Allaire HomeSite is a text-based HTML editor that can be used in conjunction with Macromedia Dreamweaver or on its own. HomeSite has a variety of prebuilt templates that help you build pages faster. You can edit pages taken directly from the Internet (or from your intranet) and upload them again when you are done.

Windows System Requirements

- Intel 486 or later processor
- Windows 95, 98, or NT 4.0
- 8MB RAM (16MB recommended)
- 5MB of available hard disk space
- CD-ROM drive (packaged version)

Installation

To install the Allaire HomeSite demonstration software, follow these instructions:

1. Open the **Allaire** directory on the CD-ROM.
2. Double-click the **homesite.exe** file.

Contact Information

Allaire
One Alewife Center
Cambridge, MA 02140
Tel: (888) 939-2545
www.allaire.com

Macromedia Dreamweaver 2.1

Macromedia Dreamweaver enables you to create cross-platform DHTML pages with advanced JavaScript animations and behaviors that play without the use of a plug-in. When using Dreamweaver, you can have direct access to both the visual implementation of your page and its HTML code.

Windows System Requirements

- Intel Pentium 90MHz or equivalent processor
- Windows 95 or NT 4.0
- 16MB RAM
- 20MB of available hard disk space
- Color monitor
- CD-ROM drive

Macintosh System Requirements

- Power Macintosh or later equivalent model
- Mac OS 7.5.5 or later
- 24MB RAM
- 20MB of available hard disk space
- Color monitor
- CD-ROM drive

Installation

To install the Macromedia Dreamweaver demonstration software, follow these instructions:

1. Open the **Macromedia** directory on the CD-ROM.
2. Open the **Windows** folder (for Windows 95 or NT users) or the **Mac** folder (for Macintosh PowerPC users).
3. Double-click the **setup.exe** file.

Contact Information

Macromedia
600 Townsend
San Francisco, CA 94103
Tel: (415) 252-2000
Fax: (451) 626-0554
www.macromedia.com

Marketwave Hit List Pro

Hit List Pro is a log analyzer for both Internet servers and intranets. It includes 40 comprehensive ready-to-run reports, organized into logical report folders. You can create and edit reports with the built-in report wizard and toolbox. Other features include support for analyzing virtual domains, advertising effectiveness, broken links, and the keywords used in search engines to find your site.

Windows System Requirements

- Intel Pentium 166MHz or equivalent processor
- Windows 95, 98, or NT 3.51/4.0

- 24MB RAM
- 2GB hard disk for the software and developed reports

Installation

To install the Marketwave Hit List Pro demonstration software, follow these instructions:

1. Open the **Marketwave** directory on the CD-ROM.
2. Double-click the **hl40p.exe** file.

Contact Information

Marketwave Inc.
601 Union Street
Suite 4601
Seattle, WA 98101
Tel: (206) 682-6801
Fax: (206) 682-6805
www.marketwave.com

Microsoft Internet Explorer 4

Microsoft is the maker of one of the more popular Web browsers, Internet Explorer. This browser supports most HTML 4.0 commands, JScript, Java, CGI, most Cascading Style Sheets, level 2, attributes, and XML.

Windows System Requirements

- Intel 486 processor or faster
- Windows 3.1, 95, 98, or NT 4.0 with Service Pack 3
- 8MB RAM (base; up to 16MB for max installs); 24MB for Windows NT
- 56–98MB of available hard disk space, depending on installation options

Installation

To install the Internet Explorer Web browser, follow these instructions:

1. Open the **Microsoft** directory on the CD-ROM.
2. Double-click the **setup.exe** file.

Contact Information

Microsoft Inc.
One Microsoft Way
Redmond, WA 98052-6399
Tel: (425) 882-8080
www.microsoft.com

NetObjects ScriptBuilder 2.0

This software is used not only to create HTML 3.2-compatible HTML documents, but also to create Netscape JavaScript, Microsoft JScript, Active Server pages, and VBScript pages. You no longer have to switch software constantly when developing your site.

Windows System Requirements

- Intel 486/66 or faster processor (Pentium recommended)
- Windows 95 or NT 3.51 or later
- 10MB RAM (Windows 95) or 12MB RAM (Windows NT)
- 5MB of available hard disk space
- VGA or higher resolution
- Internet connection for Web-based language references

Installation

To install the NetObjects ScriptBuilder software, follow these instructions:

1. Open the **NetObjects** directory on the CD-ROM.
2. Double-click the **setup.exe** file.

Contact Information

NetObjects, Inc.
602 Galveston Dr
Redwood City, CA 94063
Tel: 1-888-449-6400
www.netobjects.com

Netscape Navigator 4

This is one of the most popular Web browsers available. It shares a high market percentage with Microsoft Internet Explorer in both the private and corporate markets. Navigator provides you support for JavaScript, Java, CGI, HTML 3.2 (some 4.0), and some Cascading Style Sheets attributes.

Windows System Requirements

- Intel 486 processor or faster
- Windows 3.1, 95, 98, or NT 3.51 or later
- 8MB RAM

Macintosh System Requirements

- Power Macintosh or Mac64K
- Mac OS 7.5 or later
- 16MB RAM

Installation

To install the Netscape Navigator Web browser, follow these instructions:

1. Open the **Netscape** directory on the CD-ROM.
2. Open the **Windows** folder (for Windows 95 or NT users) or the **Mac** folder (for Macintosh PowerPC users).
3. Double-click the **n32e407.exe** file in the Windows directory. Macintosh users need to extract the **Nav4_07_EX_PPC.bin** file and run the setup program that is created.

Contact Information

Netscape World Headquarters
501 E. Middlefield Road
Mountain View, CA 94043
Tel: (650) 254-1900
Fax: (650) 528-4124
www.netscape.com

Nico Mak WinZip (PC)

Nico Mak is the creator of one of the most popular compression and expansion programs available for the PC. WinZip provides built-in support for popular Internet file formats, including ZIP, TAR, gzip, UNIX compress, UUencode, BinHex, and MIME. ARJ, LZH, and ARC files are supported through links to external programs. You can also have WinZip interfaces to your virus scanner, giving you constant protection while you are working with files you find online.

Windows 95, 98, and NT System Requirements

- Windows 95, 98, or NT 4.0
- 4MB of available hard disk space

Windows 3.1 System Requirements

- 4MB of available hard disk space

Installation

To install the WinZip shareware software, follow these instructions:

1. Open the **NikoMak** directory on the CD-ROM.
2. Open the **Win95.98.NT** folder (for Windows 95, 98, or NT users) or the **Win31** folder (for Windows 3.1 or Windows for WorkGroups users).
3. Double-click the **winzip70.exe** (in Win95.98.NT) or the **winzip31.exe** (in Win31) self-extracting executable.
4. Click the **Setup** button, and follow the instructions in the program.

Contact Information

Nico Mak Computing, Inc.
P.O. Box 540
Mansfield, CT 06268-0540
www.winzip.com

Color Reference for HTML 4.0

Tables AB-1 and AB-2 list colors for HTML 4.0, arranged by name and by hexadecimal value respectively.

Table AB-1 Color Reference for HTML 4.0 (Arranged by Name)

Name	Hex Value
Aqua	00FFFF
Black	000000
Blue	0000FF
Fuchsia	FF00FF
Gray	808080
Green	008000
Lime	00FF00
Maroon	800000
Navy	000080
Olive	808000
Purple	800080
Red	FF0000
Silver	C0C0C0
Teal	008080
White	FFFFFF
Yellow	FFFF00

Table AB-2 Color Reference for HTML 4.0 (Arranged by Hex Value)

Hex Value	Name
000000	Black
000080	Navy

Continued

Table AB-2 *Continued*

Hex Value	Name
0000FF	Blue
008000	Green
008080	Teal
00FF00	Lime
00FFFF	Aqua
800000	Maroon
800080	Purple
808000	Olive
808080	Gray
C0C0C0	Silver
FF0000	Red
FF00FF	Fuchsia
FFFF00	Yellow
FFFFFF	White

Tables AB-3 and AB-4 list colors for Microsoft Internet Explorer 4.0, arranged by name and by hexadecimal value respectively.

Table AB-3 Color Reference for Internet Explorer 4.0 (Arranged by Name)

Name	Hex Value
AliceBlue	F0F8FF
AntiqueWhite	FAEBD7
Aqua	00FFFF
Aquamarine	7FFFD4
Azure	F0FFFF
Beige	F5F5DC
Bisque	FFE4C4
Black	000000
BlancheDalmond	FFEBCD
Blue	0000FF
BlueViolet	8A2BE2
Brown	A52A2A
Burlywood	DEB887
CadetBlue	5F9EA0
Chartreuse	7FFF00
Chocolate	D2691E

Name	Hex Value
Coral	FF7F50
Cornflower	6495ED
Cornsilk	FFF8DC
Crimson	CD143C
Cyan	00FFFF
DarkBlue	00008B
DarkCyan	008B8B
DarkGoldenrod	B8860B
Darkgray	A9A9A9
DarkGreen	006400
DarkKhaki	BDB76B
DarkMagenta	8B008B
DarkOliveGreen	556B2F
DarkOrange	FF8C00
DarkOrchid	9932CC
DarkRed	8B0000
DarkSalmon	E9967A
DarkSeaGreen	8FBC8B
DarkSlateBlue	483D8B
DarkSlateGray	2F4F4F
DarkTurquoise	00CED1
DarkViolet	9400D3
DeepPink	FF1493
DeepSkyBlue	00BFFF
DimGray	696969
DodgerBlue	1E90FF
FireBrick	B22222
FloralWhite	FFFAF0
ForestGreen	228B22
Fuchsia	FF00FF
Gainsboro	DCDCDC
GhostWhite	F8F8FF
Gold	FFD700
GoldenRod	DAA520
Gray	808080
Green	008000
GreenYellow	ADFF2F
HoneyDew	F0FFF0
HotPink	FF69B4

Continued

Table AB-3 *Continued*

Name	Hex Value
IndianRed	CD5C5C
Indigo	4b0082
Ivory	FFFFF0
Khaki	F0E68C
Lavender	E6E6FA
LavenderBlush	FFF0F5
LawnGreen	7CFC00
LemonChiffon	FFFACD
LightBlue	ADD8E6
LightCoral	F08080
LightCyan	E0FFFF
LightGoldenrodYellow	FAFAD2
LightGreen	90EE90
LightSkyBlue	87CEFA
LightSlateGray	778899
LightSteelBlue	B0C4DE
LightYellow	FFFFE0
Lime	00FF00
LimeGreen	32CD32
Linen	FAF0E6
Magenta	FF00FF
Maroon	800000
MediumAquamarine	66CDAA
MediumBlue	0000CD
MediumOrchid	BA55D3
MediumPurple	9370DB
MediumSeaGreen	3CB371
MediumSlateBlue	7B68EE
MediumSpringGreen	00FA9A
MediumTurquoise	48D1CC
MediumVioletRed	C71585
MidnightBlue	191970
MintCream	F5FFFA
MistyRose	FFE4E1
Moccasin	FFE4B5
NavajoWhite	FFDEAD
Navy	000080
OldLace	FDF5E6

Name	Hex Value
Olive	808000
OliveDrab	6B8E23
Orange	FFA500
OrangeRed	FF4500
Orchid	DA70D6
PaleGoldenrod	EEE8AA
PaleGreen	98FB98
PaleTurquoise	AFEEEE
PaleVioletRed	DB7093
PapayaWhip	FFEFD5
PeachPuff	FFDAB9
Peru	CD853F
Pink	FFC0CB
Plum	DDA0DD
PowderBlue	B0E0E6
Purple	800080
Red	FF0000
RosyBrown	BC8F8F
RoyalBlue	4169E1
SaddleBrown	8B4513
Salmon	FA8072
SandyBrown	F4A460
SeaGreen	2E8B57
SeaShell	FFF5EE
Sienna	A0522D
Silver	C0C0C0
SkyBlue	87CEEB
SlateBlue	6A5ACD
SlateGray	708090
Snow	FFFAFA
SpringGreen	00FF7F
SteelBlue	4682B4
Tan	D2B48C
Teal	008080
Thistle	D8BFD8
Tomato	FF6347
Turquoise	40E0D0
Violet	EE82EE
Wheat	F5DEB3

Continued

Table AB-3 *Continued*

Name	Hex Value
White	FFFFFF
WhiteSmoke	F5F5F5
Yellow	FFFF00
YellowGreen	9ACD32

Table AB-4 Color Reference for Internet Explorer 4.0
(Arranged by Hex Value)

Hex Value	Name
000000	Black
000080	Navy
00008B	DarkBlue
0000CD	MediumBlue
0000FF	Blue
006400	DarkGreen
008000	Green
008080	Teal
008B8B	DarkCyan
00BFFF	DeepSkyBlue
00CED1	DarkTurquoise
00FA9A	MediumSpringGreen
00FF00	Lime
00FF7F	SpringGreen
00FFFF	Aqua
00FFFF	Cyan
191970	MidnightBlue
1E90FF	DodgerBlue
228B22	ForestGreen
2E8B57	SeaGreen
2F4F4F	DarkSlateGray
32CD32	LimeGreen
3CB371	MediumSeaGreen
40E0D0	Turquoise
4169E1	RoyalBlue
4682B4	SteelBlue
483D8B	DarkSlateBlue
48D1CC	MediumTurquoise
4B0082	Indigo

Hex Value	Name
556B2F	DarkOliveGreen
5F9EA0	CadetBlue
6495ED	Cornflower
66CDAA	MediumAquamarine
696969	DimGray
6A5ACD	SlateBlue
6B8E23	OliveDrab
708090	SlateGray
778899	LightSlateGray
7B68EE	MediumSlateBlue
7CFC00	LawnGreen
7FFF00	Chartreuse
7FFFD4	Aquamarine
800000	Maroon
800080	Purple
808000	Olive
808080	Gray
87CEEB	SkyBlue
87CEFA	LightSkyBlue
8A2BE2	BlueViolet
8B0000	DarkRed
8B008B	DarkMagenta
8B4513	SaddleBrown
8FBC8B	DarkSeaGreen
90EE90	LightGreen
9370DB	MediumPurple
9400D3	DarkViolet
98FB98	PaleGreen
9932CC	DarkOrchid
9ACD32	YellowGreen
A0522D	Sienna
A52A2A	Brown
A9A9A9	Darkgray
ADD8E6	LightBlue
ADFF2F	GreenYellow
AFEEEE	PaleTurquoise
B0C4DE	LightSteelBlue
B0E0E6	PowderBlue
B22222	FireBrick

Continued

Table AB-4 *Continued*

Hex Value	Name
B8860B	DarkGoldenrod
BA55D3	MediumOrchid
BC8F8F	RosyBrown
BDB76B	DarkKhaki
C0C0C0	Silver
C71585	MediumVioletRed
CD143C	Crimson
CD5C5C	IndianRed
CD853F	Peru
D2691E	Chocolate
D2B48C	Tan
D8BFD8	Thistle
DA70D6	Orchid
DAA520	GoldenRod
DB7093	PaleVioletRed
DCDCDC	Gainsboro
DDA0DD	Plum
DEB887	Burlywood
E0FFFF	LightCyan
E6E6FA	Lavender
E9967A	DarkSalmon
EE82EE	Violet
EEE8AA	PaleGoldenrod
F08080	LightCoral
F0E68C	Khaki
F0F8FF	AliceBlue
F0FFF0	HoneyDew
F0FFFF	Azure
F4A460	SandyBrown
F5DEB3	Wheat
F5F5DC	Beige
F5F5F5	WhiteSmoke
F5FFFA	MintCream
F8F8FF	GhostWhite
FA8072	Salmon
FAEBD7	AntiqueWhite
FAF0E6	Linen
FAFAD2	LightGoldenrodYellow

Hex Value	Name
FDF5E6	OldLace
FF0000	Red
FF00FF	Fuchsia
FF00FF	Magenta
FF1493	DeepPink
FF4500	OrangeRed
FF6347	Tomato
FF69B4	HotPink
FF7F50	Coral
FF8C00	DarkOrange
FFA500	Orange
FFC0CB	Pink
FFD700	Gold
FFDAB9	PeachPuff
FFDEAD	NavajoWhite
FFE4B5	Moccasin
FFE4C4	Bisque
FFE4E1	MistyRose
FFEBCD	BlancheDalmond
FFEFD5	PapayaWhip
FFF0F5	LavenderBlush
FFF5EE	SeaShell
FFF8DC	Cornsilk
FFFACD	LemonChiffon
FFFAF0	FloralWhite
FFFAFA	Snow
FFFF00	Yellow
FFFFE0	LightYellow
FFFFF0	Ivory
FFFFFF	White

appendix

C

Character Charts

General Printing Characters

Table AC-1 lists printing characters that include special punctuation, bullet points, and foreign-language characters. Many of these will be familiar from other applications.

Table AC-1 General Printing Characters

Character	Name	Description
"	&quot;	Quotation mark
&	&amp;	Ampersand
<	&lt;	Less than
>	&gt;	Greater than
		Nonbreaking space
¡	&iexcl;	Inverted exclamation point
¢	&cent;	Cent sign
£	&pound;	Pound sign
¤	&curren;	General currency sign
¥	&yen;	Yen sign
¦	¦ or &brkbar;	Broken vertical bar
§	&sect;	Section sign
¨	¨ or ¨	Diæresis/Umlaut
©	&copy;	Copyright
ª	&ordf;	Feminine ordinal
«	&laquo;	Left angle quote/Guillemet left
¬	&not;	Not sign
	&shy;	Soft hyphen
®	&reg;	Registered trademark
¯	¯ or &hibar;	Macron accent

Continued

Table AC-1 *Continued*

Character	Name	Description
°	&deg;	Degree sign
±	&plusmn;	Plus or minus
2	&sup2;	Superscript 2
3	&sup3;	Superscript 3
´	&acute;	Acute accent
µ	&micro;	Micro sign
¶	&para;	Paragraph sign
·	&middot;	Middle dot
¸	&cedil;	Cedilla
1	&sup1;	Superscript 1
º	&ordm;	Masculine ordinal
»	&raquo;	Right angle quote/Guillemet right
¼	&frac14;	Fraction one-fourth
½	&frac12;	Fraction one-half
¾	&frac34;	Fraction three-fourths
¿	&iquest;	Inverted question mark
À	&Agrave;	Capital *A*, grave accent
Á	&Aacute;	Capital *A*, acute accent
Â	&Acirc;	Capital *A*, circumflex
Ã	&Atilde;	Capital *A*, tilde
Ä	&Auml;	Capital *A*, diæresis/umlaut
Å	&Aring;	Capital *A*, ring
Æ	&Aelig;	Capital *AE*, ligature
Ç	&Ccedil;	Capital *C*, cedilla
È	&Egrave;	Capital *E*, grave accent
É	&Eacute;	Capital *E*, acute accent
Ê	&Ecirc;	Capital *E*, circumflex
Ë	&Euml;	Capital *E*, diæresis/umlaut
Ì	&Igrave;	Capital *I*, grave accent
Í	&Iacute;	Capital *I*, acute accent
Î	&Icirc;	Capital *I*, circumflex
Ï	&Iuml;	Capital *I*, diæresis/umlaut
Ð	&ETH;	Capital Eth, Icelandic
Ñ	&Ntilde;	Capital *N*, tilde
Ò	&Ograve;	Capital *O*, grave accent
Ó	&Oacute;	Capital *O*, acute accent
Ô	&Ocirc;	Capital *O*, circumflex
Õ	&Otilde;	Capital *O*, tilde

Character	Name	Description
Ö	&Ouml;	Capital *O*, diæresis/umlaut
x	&times;	Multiplication sign
Ø	&Oslash;	Capital *O*, slash
Ù	&Ugrave;	Capital *U*, grave accent
Ú	&Uacute;	Capital *U*, acute accent
Û	&Ucirc;	Capital *U*, circumflex
Ü	&Uuml;	Capital *U*, diæresis/umlaut
Y	&Yacute;	Capital *Y*, acute accent
_	&THORN;	Capital Thorn, Icelandic
ß	&szlig;	Lowercase sharp *s*, German *sz*
à	&agrave;	Lowercase *a*, grave accent
á	&aacute;	Lowercase *a*, acute accent
â	&acirc;	Lowercase *a*, circumflex
ã	&atilde;	Lowercase *a*, tilde
ä	&auml;	Lowercase *a*, diæresis/umlaut
å	&aring;	Lowercase *a*, ring
æ	&aelig;	Lowercase *ae*, ligature
ç	&ccedil;	Lowercase *c*, cedilla
è	&cgrave;	Lowercase *e*, grave accent
é	&cacute;	Lowercase *e*, acute accent
ê	&ccirc;	Lowercase *e*, circumflex
ë	&cuml;	Lowercase *e*, diæresis/umlaut
ì	&igrave;	Lowercase *i*, grave accent
í	&iacute;	Lowercase *i*, acute accent
î	&icirc;	Lowercase *i*, circumflex
ï	&iuml;	Lowercase *i*, diæresis/umlaut
∂	&eth;	Lowercase eth, Icelandic
ñ	&ntilde;	Lowercase *n*, tilde
ò	&ograve;	Lowercase *o*, grave accent
ó	&oacute;	Lowercase *o*, acute accent
ô	&ocirc;	Lowercase *o*, circumflex
õ	&otilde;	Lowercase *o*, tilde
ö	&ouml;	Lowercase *o*, diæresis/umlaut
÷	&divide	Division sign
ø	&oslash;	Lowercase *o*, slash
ù	&ugrave;	Lowercase *u*, grave accent
ú	&uacute;	Lowercase *u*, acute accent
û	&ucirc;	Lowercase *u*, circumflex
ü	&uuml;	Lowercase *u*, diæresis/umlaut

Continued

Table AC-1 *Continued*

Character	Name	Description
ý	&yacute;	Lowercase y, acute accent
_	&thorn;	Lowercase thorn, Icelandic
ÿ	&yuml;	Lowercase y, diæresis/umlaut
	&fnof;	Latin lowercase f with hook, = function, =florin
Α	&Alpha;	Greek capital letter alpha
Β	&Beta;	Greek capital letter beta
Γ	&Gamma;	Greek capital letter gamma
Δ	&Delta;	Greek capital letter delta
Ε	&Epsilon;	Greek capital letter epsilon
Ζ	&Zeta;	Greek capital letter zeta
Η	&Eta;	Greek capital letter eta
Θ	&Theta;	Greek capital letter theta
Ι	&Iota;	Greek capital letter iota
Κ	&Kappa;	Greek capital letter kappa
Λ	&Lambda;	Greek capital letter lambda
Μ	&Mu;	Greek capital letter mu
Ν	&Nu;	Greek capital letter nu
Ξ	&Xi;	Greek capital letter xi
Ο	&Omicron;	Greek capital letter omicron
Π	&Pi;	Greek capital letter pi
Ρ	&Rho;	Greek capital letter rho
Σ	&Sigma;	Greek capital letter sigma
Τ	&Tau;	Greek capital letter tau
Υ	&Upsilon;	Greek capital letter upsilon
Φ	&Phi;	Greek capital letter phi
Χ	&Chi;	Greek capital letter chi
Ψ	&Psi;	Greek capital letter psi
Ω	&Omega;	Greek capital letter omega
α	&alpha;	Greek lowercase letter alpha
β	&beta;	Greek lowercase letter beta
γ	&gamma;	Greek lowercase letter gamma
δ	&delta;	Greek lowercase letter delta
ε	&epsilon;	Greek lowercase letter epsilon
ζ	&zeta;	Greek lowercase letter zeta
η	&eta;	Greek lowercase letter eta
τ	&theta;	Greek lowercase letter theta
ι	&iota	Greek lowercase letter iota
κ	&kappa;	Greek lowercase letter kappa

Character	Name	Description
λ	&lambda;	Greek lowercase letter lambda
μ	&mu;	Greek lowercase letter mu
ν	&nu;	Greek lowercase letter nu
ξ	&xi;	Greek lowercase letter xi
ο	&omicron;	Greek lowercase letter omicron
π	&pi;	Greek lowercase letter pi
ρ	&rho;	Greek lowercase letter rho
	&sigmaf;	Greek lowercase letter final sigma
σ	&sigma;	Greek lowercase letter sigma
τ	&tau;	Greek lowercase letter tau
υ	&upsilon;	Greek lowercase letter upsilon
φ	&phi;	Greek lowercase letter phi
χ	&chi;	Greek lowercase letter chi
ψ	&psi;	Greek lowercase letter psi
ω	&omega;	Greek lowercase letter omega
π	&thetasym;	Greek lowercase letter theta symbol
θ	&upsih;	Greek upsilon with hook symbol
π	&piv;	Greek pi symbol
•	&bull;	Bullet
…	&hellip;	Horizontal ellipse
′	&prime;	Prime, =minutes, =feet
″	&Prime;	Double prime, =seconds, = inches
[Not Shown]	&oline;	Overline, = spacing overscore
/	&frasl;	Fraction slash
[Not Shown]	&weierp;	Script capital *P*, power set, =Weierstrass
[Not Shown]	&image;	Blackletter capital *I*, = imaginary part
[Not Shown]	&real;	Blackletter capital *R*, = real part symbol
™	&trade;	Trademark sign
[Not Shown]	&alefsym;	Alef symbol, = first transfinite cardinal
←	&larr;	Leftward arrow
↑	&uarr;	Upward arrow
→	&rarr;	Rightward arrow
↓	&darr;	Downward arrow
↵	&crarr;	Downward arrow with corner leftward, =carriage return
⇐	&lArr;	Leftward double arrow
⇑	&uArr;	Upward double arrow
⇒	&rArr;	Rightward double arrow
⇓	&dArr;	Downward double arrow
⇔	&hArr;	Left-right double arrow

Continued

Table AC-1 *Continued*

Character	Name	Description
[Not Shown]	&lceil;	Left ceiling
[Not Shown]	&rceil;	Right ceiling
[Not Shown]	&lfloor;	Left floor
[Not Shown]	&rfloor;	Right floor
[Not Shown]	&lang;	Left-pointing angle bracket = bra
[Not Shown]	&rang;	Right-pointing angle bracket =ket
[Not Shown]	&loz;	Lozenge
♠	&spades;	Black spade suit
♣	&clubs;	Black club suit
♥	&hearts;	Black heart suit
♦	&diams;	Black diamond suit
Œ	&OElig;	Latin capital ligature *OE*
œ	&oelig;	Latin lowercase ligature *oe*
—	&Scaron;	Latin capital letter *s* with caron
—	&scaron;	Latin lowercase letter *s* with caron
Ÿ	&Yuml;	Latin capital letter *y* with diæresis
ˆ	&circ;	Modifier letter circumflex accent
˜	&tilde;	Small tilde
(not visible)		En space
(not visible)	ace;	Em space
(not visible)		Thin space
(not visible)	&zwnj;	Zero-width nonjoiner
(not visible)	&zwj;	Zero-width joiner
(not visible)	&lrm;	Left-to-right mark
(not visible)	&rlm;	Right-to-left mark
–	&ndash;	En dash
—	&mdash;	Em dash
'	&lsquo;	Left single quotation mark
'	&rsquo;	Right single quotation mark
‚	&sbquo;	Single low-9 quotation mark
"	&ldquo;	Left double quotation mark
"	&rdquo;	Right double quotation mark
„	&bdquo;	Double low-9 quotation mark
†	&dagger;	Dagger
‡	&Dagger;	Double dagger
‰	&permil;	Per mill sign
‹	&lsaquo;	Single left-pointing angle quotation mark
›	&rsaquo;	Single right-pointing angle quotation mark

Available Mathematical Characters

Tables AC-2 through AC-27 list all MathML printing character entities alphabetically, according to ISO 9573-13 (extended with aliases).

Table AC-2 MathML Printing Characters, A Names

Name	Group	Code	Description
ac	ISOAMSB	E207	most positive
acd	ISOTECH	E3A6	AC current
acE	ISOAMSB	E290	most positive, two lines below
acute	ISODIA	0301	acute accent
Afr	ISOMFRK	E47C	Fraktur letter *A*
afr	ISOMFRK	E495	Fraktur letter *a*
aleph	ISOTECH	2135	/aleph aleph, Hebrew
alpha	ISOGRK3	03B1	lowercase alpha, Greek
amalg	ISOAMSB	E251	amalgamation or coproduct
amp	ISONUM	0026	ampersand
And	MMALIAS	2227	logical AND
and	ISOTECH	2227	logical AND
andand	ISOTECH	E36E	two logical ANDs
andd	ISOTECH	E394	AND, horizontal dash
andslope	ISOTECH	E50A	sloping large AND
andv	ISOTECH	E391	AND with middle stem
ang	ISOAMSO	2220	angle
ange	ISOAMSO	E2D6	angle, equal
angle	MMALIAS	2220	angle
angmsd	ISOAMSO	2221	angle (measured)
angmsdaa	ISOAMSO	E2D9	angle (measured), arrow, up, right
angmsdab	ISOAMSO	E2DA	angle (measured), arrow, up, left
angmsdac	ISOAMSO	E2DC	angle (measured), arrow, down, left
angmsdae	ISOAMSO	E2DD	angle (measured), arrow, right, up
angmsdaf	ISOAMSO	E2DE	angle (measured), arrow, left, up
angmsdag	ISOAMSO	E2DF	angle (measured), arrow, right, down
angmsdah	ISOAMSO	E2E0	angle (measured), arrow, left, down
angrt	ISOTECH	221F	right (90-degree) angle
angrtvb	ISOAMSO	E418	right angle (measured)
angrtvbd	ISOAMSO	E2E1	right angle (measured), dot
angsph	ISOTECH	2222	/sphericalangle angle (spherical)

Continued

Table AC-2 *Continued*

Name	Group	Code	Description
angst	ISOTECH	212B	Angstrom capital *A*, ring
angzarr	ISOAMSA	E248	angle with down zigzag arrow
Aopf	ISOMOPF	E4AF	open-face letter *A*
ap	ISOTECH	2248	approximate
apacir	ISOTECH	E38C	approximate, circumflex accent
apE	ISOAMSR	E315	approximately equal or equal to
ape	ISOAMSR	224A	approximate, equals
apid	ISOAMSR	224B	approximately identical to
apos	ISONUM	0027	apostrophe
approx	MMALIAS	2248	approximate
approxeq	MMALIAS	224A	approximate, equals
Ascr	ISOMSCR	E4C5	script letter *A*
ascr	ISOMSCR	E4DF	script letter *a*
ast	MMALIAS	2217	centered asterisk
asymp	ISOAMSR	224D	asymptotically equal to
awconint	ISOTECH	2233	contour integral, anticlockwise
awint	ISOTECH	E39B	anticlockwise integration

Table AC-3 MathML Printing Characters, B Names

Name	Group	Code	Description
backcong	MMALIAS	224C	reverse congruent
backepsilon	MMALIAS	E420	such that
backprime	MMALIAS	2035	reverse prime
backsim	MMALIAS	223D	reverse similar
backsimeq	MMALIAS	22CD	reverse similar, equals
Backslash	MMALIAS	2216	reverse solidus
Barv	ISOAMSR	E311	vert, double bar (over)
barvee	ISOAMSB	22BD	bar, vee
Barwed	ISOAMSB	2306	logical AND, double bar above
barwed	ISOAMSB	22BC	logical AND, bar above
barwedge	MMALIAS	22BC	logical AND, bar above
bbrk	ISOAMSO	E2EE	bottom square bracket
bbrktbrk	ISOAMSO	E419	bottom above top square bracket
bcong	ISOAMSR	2235	because
Because	MMALIAS	2235	because
because	MMALIAS	2235	because

Name	Group	Code	Description
bemptyv	ISOAMSO	E41A	reversed circle, slash
benzen	ISOCHEM	E43C	benzene ring
benzena	ISOCHEM	E42A	benzene ring, one double binding
benzenb	ISOCHEM	E42B	benzene ring, one double binding
benzenc	ISOCHEM	E42C	benzene ring, one double binding
benzend	ISOCHEM	E42D	benzene ring, one double binding
benzene	ISOCHEM	E42E	benzene ring, one double binding
benzenf	ISOCHEM	E42F	benzene ring, one double binding
benzeng	ISOCHEM	E430	benzene ring, two double bindings
benzenh	ISOCHEM	E431	benzene ring, two double bindings
benzeni	ISOCHEM	E432	benzene ring, two double bindings
benzenj	ISOCHEM	E433	benzene ring, two double bindings
benzenk	ISOCHEM	E434	benzene ring, two double bindings
benzenl	ISOCHEM	E435	benzene ring, two double bindings
benzenm	ISOCHEM	E436	benzene ring, two double bindings
benzenn	ISOCHEM	E437	benzene ring, two double bindings
benzeno	ISOCHEM	E438	benzene ring, two double bindings
benzenp	ISOCHEM	E439	benzene ring, three double bindings
benzenq	ISOCHEM	E43A	benzene ring, three double bindings
benzenr	ISOCHEM	E43B	benzene ring, circle
bepsi	ISOAMSR	E420	such that
bernou	ISOTECH	212C	Bernoulli function (script capital *B*)
beta	ISOGRK3	03B2	lowercase beta, Greek
beth	ISOAMSO	2136	beth, Hebrew
between	MMALIAS	226C	between
Bfr	ISOMFRK	E47D	Fraktur letter *B*
bfr	ISOMFRK	E496	Fraktur letter *b*
bigcap	MMALIAS	22C2	intersection operator
bigcirc	MMALIAS	25CB	large circle
bigcup	MMALIAS	22C3	union operator
bigodot	MMALIAS	2299	circle dot operator
bigoplus	MMALIAS	2295	circle plus operator
bigotimes	MMALIAS	2297	circle times operator
bigsqcup	MMALIAS	2294	square union operator
bigstar	MMALIAS	2605	star, filled
bigtriangle	MMALIAS	25BD	big down triangle, opendown
bigtriangle up	MMALIAS	25B3	big up triangle, open
biguplus	MMALIAS	228E	big up plus

Continued

Table AC-3 *Continued*

Name	Group	Code	Description
bigvee	MMALIAS	22C1	logical AND operator
bigwedge	MMALIAS	22C0	logical OR operator
bkarow	MMALIAS	E405	right broken arrow
blacklozenge	MMALIAS	E501	lozenge, filled
blacksquare	MMALIAS	25A0	square, filled
blacktriangle	MMALIAS	25B4	up triangle, filled
blacktriangle down	MMALIAS	25BE	down triangle, filled
blacktriangle left	MMALIAS	25C2	left triangle, filled
blacktriangle right	MMALIAS	25B8	right triangle, filled
blank	ISOPUB	E4F9	significant blank symbol
blk12	ISOPUB	2592	50%-shaded block
blk14	ISOPUB	2591	25%-shaded block
blk34	ISOPUB	2593	75%-shaded block
block	ISOPUB	2588	full block
bne	ISOTECH	E388	reverse not equals
bnequiv	ISOTECH	E387	reverse not equivalent
bNot	ISOTECH	E3AD	reverse not with two horizontal strokes
bnot	ISOTECH	2310	reverse not
Bopf	ISOMOPF	E4B0	open-face letter *B*
bot	MMALIAS	22A5	bottom
bottom	ISOTECH	22A5	bottom
bowtie	ISOAMSR	22C8	bow tie
boxbox	ISOAMSO	E2E6	two joined squares
boxminus	MMALIAS	229F	minus sign in box
boxplus	MMALIAS	229E	plus sign in box
boxtimes	MMALIAS	22A0	multiplication sign in box
bprime	ISOAMSO	2035	reverse prime
Breve	MMALIAS	0305	breve
breve	ISODIA	0305	breve
brvbar	ISONUM	00A6	broken (vertical) bar
Bscr	ISOMSCR	E4C6	script letter *B*
bscr	ISOMSCR	E4E0	script letter *b*
bsemi	ISOAMSO	E2ED	reverse semicolon
bsim	ISOAMSR	223D	reverse similar
bsime	ISOAMSR	22CD	reverse similar, equals

Name	Group	Code	Description
bsol	ISONUM	005C	/backslash reverse solidus
bsolb	ISOAMSB	E280	reverse solidus in square
bsolhsub	ISOAMSR	E34D	reverse solidus, subset
bull	ISOPUB	2022	round bullet, filled
bullet	MMALIAS	2022	round bullet, filled
bump	ISOAMSR	224E	bumpy equals
bumpe	ISOAMSR	224F	bumpy equals, equals
Bumpeq	MMALIAS	224E	bumpy equals
bumpeq	MMALIAS	224F	bumpy equals, equals

Table AC-4 MathML Printing Characters, C Names

Name	Group	Code	Description
Cap	MMALIAS	2322	down curve
cap	ISOTECH	2229	intersection
capand	ISOAMSB	E281	intersection, and
capbrcup	ISOAMSB	E271	intersection, bar, union
capcap	ISOAMSB	E273	intersection, intersection, joined
capcup	ISOAMSB	E26F	intersection above union
capdot	ISOAMSB	E261	intersection, with dot
caps	ISOAMSB	E275	intersection, serifs
caret	ISOPUB	2038	caret (insertion mark)
caron	ISODIA	030C	caron
ccaps	ISOAMSB	E279	closed intersection, serifs
Cconint	ISOTECH	2230	triple contour integral operator
ccups	ISOAMSB	E278	closed union, serifs
ccupssm	ISOAMSB	E27A	closed union, serifs, smash product
cdot	MMALIAS	22C5	small middle dot
cedil	ISODIA	0327	cedilla
Cedilla	MMALIAS	0327	cedilla
cemptyv	ISOAMSO	E2E8	circle, slash, small circle above
cent	ISONUM	00A2	cent sign
CenterDot	MMALIAS	00B7	middle dot
centerdot	MMALIAS	00B7	middle dot
Cfr	ISOMFRK	E47E	Fraktur letter C
cfr	ISOMFRK	E497	Fraktur letter c
check	ISOPUB	2713	tick, check mark
checkmark	MMALIAS	2713	tick, check mark

Continued

Table AC-4 *Continued*

Name	Group	Code	Description
chi	ISOGRK3	03C7	lowercase chi, Greek
cir	ISOPUB	2218	circle, open
circ	MMALIAS	2218	composite function (small circle)
circeq	MMALIAS	2257	circle, equals
circle	ISOPUB	E4FA	circle, open
circlearrow left	MMALIAS	21BA	left arrow in circle
circlearrow right	MMALIAS	21BB	right arrow in circle
circledast	MMALIAS	229B	asterisk in circle
circledcirc	MMALIAS	229A	small circle in circle
circleddash	MMALIAS	229D	hyphen in circle
CircleDot	MMALIAS	2299	middle dot in circle
circledR	MMALIAS	00AF	registered sign
circledS	MMALIAS	E41D	capital S in circle
circlef	ISOPUB	25CF	circle, filled
circlefb	ISOPUB	25D2	circle, filled bottom half
circlefl	ISOPUB	25D0	circle, filled left half (Harvey ball)
circlefr	ISOPUB	25D1	circle, filled right half
circleft	ISOPUB	25D3	circle, filled top half
CircleMinus	MMALIAS	2296	minus sign in circle
CirclePlus	MMALIAS	2295	plus sign in circle
CircleTimes	MMALIAS	2297	multiplication sign in circle
cirE	ISOAMSO	E41B	circle, two horizontal stroked to the right
cire	ISOAMSR	2257	circle, equals
cirfnint	ISOTECH	E395	circulation function
cirmid	ISOAMSA	E250	circle, mid below
cirscir	ISOAMSO	E41C	circle, small circle to the right
Clockwise Contour Integral	MMALIAS	2232	contour integral, clockwise
CloseCurly DoubleQuote	MMALIAS	201D	double quotation mark, right
CloseCurly Quote	MMALIAS	2019	single quotation mark, right
clubs	ISOPUB	2663	club suit symbol
clubsuit	MMALIAS	2663	club suit symbol
Colon	MMALIAS	2236	ratio
colon	ISONUM	003A	colon

Name	Group	Code	Description
Colone	ISOAMSR	E30E	double colon, equals
colone	ISOAMSR	2254	colon, equals
coloneq	MMALIAS	2254	colon, equals
comma	ISONUM	002C	comma
commat	ISONUM	0040	commercial at
comp	ISOAMSO	2201	complement sign
compfn	ISOTECH	2218	composite function (small circle)
complement	MMALIAS	2201	complement sign
cong	ISOTECH	2245	congruent with
congdot	ISOAMSR	E314	congruent, dot
Congruent	MMALIAS	2261	identical with
Conint	ISOTECH	222F	double contour integral operator
conint	ISOTECH	222E	contour integral operator
Contour Integral	MMALIAS	222E	contour integral operator
Copf	ISOMOPF	2102	open-face letter *C*
coprod	ISOAMSB	2210	coproduct operator
Coproduct	MMALIAS	2210	coproduct operator
copy	ISONUM	00A9	copyright sign
copysr	ISOPUB	2117	sound recording copyright sign
Counter Clockwise Contour Integral	MMALIAS	2233	contour integral, anticlockwise
cross	ISOPUB	2612	ballot cross
Cscr	ISOMSCR	E4C7	script letter *C*
cscr	ISOMSCR	E4E1	script letter *c*
csub	ISOAMSR	E351	subset, closed
csube	ISOAMSR	E353	subset, closed, equals
csup	ISOAMSR	E352	superset, closed
csupe	ISOAMSR	E354	superset, closed, equals
ctdot	ISOTECH	22EF	/cdots, three dots, centered
cudarrl	ISOAMSA	E23E	left curved down arrow
cudarrr	ISOAMSA	E219	right curved down arrow
cuepr	ISOAMSR	22DE	curly equals, precedes
cuesc	ISOAMSR	22DF	curly equals, succeeds
cularr	ISOAMSA	21B6	left curved arrow
cularrp	ISOAMSA	E24A	curved left arrow with plus
Cup	MMALIAS	2323	up curve
cup	ISOTECH	222A	union or logical sum

Continued

Table AC-4 *Continued*

Name	Group	Code	Description
cupbrcap	ISOAMSB	E270	union, bar, intersection
CupCap	MMALIAS	224D	asymptotically equal to
cupcap	ISOAMSB	E26E	union above intersection
cupcup	ISOAMSB	E272	union, union, joined
cupdot	ISOAMSB	228D	union, with dot
cupor	ISOAMSB	E282	union, or
cups	ISOAMSB	E274	union, serifs
curarr	ISOAMSA	21B7	right curved arrow
curarrm	ISOAMSA	E249	curved right arrow with minus
curlyeqprec	MMALIAS	22DE	curly equals, precedes
curlyeqsucc	MMALIAS	22DF	curly equals, succeeds
curlyvee	MMALIAS	22CE	curly logical OR
curlywedge	MMALIAS	22CF	curly logical AND
curren	ISONUM	00A4	general currency sign
curvearrow left	MMALIAS	21B6	left curved arrow
curvearrow right	MMALIAS	21B7	right curved arrow
cuvee	ISOAMSB	22CE	curly logical OR
cuwed	ISOAMSB	22CF	curly logical AND
cwconint	ISOTECH	2232	contour integral, clockwise
cwint	ISOTECH	2231	clockwise integral
cylcty	ISOTECH	232D	cylindricity

Table AC-5 MathML Printing Characters, D Names

Name	Group	Code	Description
Dagger	ISOPUB	2021	double dagger
dagger	ISOPUB	2020	dagger
daleth	ISOAMSO	2138	daleth, Hebrew
Darr	ISOAMSA	21A1	down two-headed arrow
dArr	ISOAMSA	21D3	down double arrow
darr	ISONUM	2193	downward arrow
dash	ISOPUB	2010	hyphen (true graphic)
Dashv	ISOAMSR	E30F	double dash, vertical
dashv	ISOAMSR	22A3	dash, vertical
dbkarow	MMALIAS	E207	right doubly broken arrow

Name	Group	Code	Description
dblac	ISODIA	030B	double acute accent
ddagger	MMALIAS	2021	double dagger
ddarr	ISOAMSA	21CA	two down arrows
DDotrahd	ISOAMSA	E238	right arrow with dotted stem
ddotseq	MMALIAS	E309	equal with four dots
deg	ISONUM	00B0	degree sign
Del	MMALIAS	2207	del, Hamilton operator
Delta	ISOGRK3	0394	capital Delta, Greek
delta	ISOGRK3	03B4	lowercase delta, Greek
demptyv	ISOAMSO	E2E7	circle, slash, bar above
dfisht	ISOAMSA	E24C	down fish tail
Dfr	ISOMFRK	E47F	Fraktur letter *D*
dfr	ISOMFRK	E498	Fraktur letter *d*
dHar	ISOAMSA	E227	down harpoon-left, down harpoon-right
dharl	ISOAMSA	21C3	down harpoon-left
dharr	ISOAMSA	21C2	down harpoon-right
diam	ISOAMSB	22C4	open diamond
diamond	MMALIAS	22C4	open diamond
diamondf	ISOPUB	E4FB	diamond, filled
diamondsuit	MMALIAS	2662	diamond suit symbol
diamonfb	ISOPUB	E4FC	diamond, filled bottom half
diamonfl	ISOPUB	E4FD	diamond, filled left half
diamonfr	ISOPUB	E4FE	diamond, filled right half
diamonft	ISOPUB	E4FF	diamond, filled top half
diams	ISOPUB	2662	diamond suit symbol
die	ISODIA	0308	diæresis
digamma	MMALIAS	03DC	digamma, old Greek
disin	ISOTECH	E3A0	set membership, long horizontal stroke
div	MMALIAS	00F7	division sign
divide	ISONUM	00F7	division sign
divideontimes	MMALIAS	22C7	division on times
divonx	ISOAMSB	22C7	division on times
dlcorn	ISOAMSC	231E	lower-left corner
dlcrop	ISOPUB	230D	downward left crop mark
dollar	ISONUM	0024	dollar sign
Dopf	ISOMOPF	E4B1	open-face letter *D*
Dot	ISOTECH	0308	diæresis or umlaut mark
dot	ISODIA	0306	dot above

Continued

Table AC-5 *Continued*

Name	Group	Code	Description
DotDot	ISOTECH	20DC	four dots above
doteq	MMALIAS	2250	equals, single dot above
doteqdot	MMALIAS	2251	equals, even dots
DotEqual	MMALIAS	2250	equals, single dot above
dotminus	MMALIAS	2238	minus sign, dot above
dotplus	MMALIAS	2214	plus sign, dot above
dotsquare	MMALIAS	22A1	small dot in box
doublebar wedge	MMALIAS	2306	logical AND, double bar above
Double Contour Integral	MMALIAS	222F	double contour integral operator
DoubleDot	MMALIAS	0308	diæresis
DoubleDown Arrow	MMALIAS	21D3	down double arrow
DoubleLeft Arrow	MMALIAS	21D0	is implied by
DoubleLeft RightArrow	MMALIAS	21D4	left-and-right double arrow
DoubleLong LeftArrow	MMALIAS	E200	long left double arrow
DoubleLong LeftRightArrow	MMALIAS	E202	long left-and-right double arrow
DoubleLong RightArrow	MMALIAS	E204	long right double arrow
DoubleRight Arrow	MMALIAS	21D2	implies
DoubleRight Tee	MMALIAS	22A8	vertical, double dash
DoubleUp Arrow	MMALIAS	21D1	up double arrow
DoubleUp DownArrow	MMALIAS	21D5	up-and-down double arrow
Double VerticalBar	MMALIAS	2225	parallel
DownArrow	MMALIAS	2193	downward arrow
Downarrow	MMALIAS	21D3	down double arrow
downarrow	MMALIAS	2193	downward arrow
DownArrow UpArrow	MMALIAS	E216	down arrow, up arrow
downdown arrows	MMALIAS	21CA	two down arrows

Name	Group	Code	Description
downharpoon left	MMALIAS	21C3	down harpoon-left
downharpoon right	MMALIAS	21C2	down harpoon-right
DownLeft Vector	MMALIAS	21BD	left harpoon-down
DownRight Vector	MMALIAS	21C1	right harpoon-down
DownTee	MMALIAS	22A4	top
drbkarow	MMALIAS	E209	two-headed right broken arrow
drcorn	ISOAMSC	231F	lower-right corner
drcrop	ISOPUB	230C	downward right crop mark
Dscr	ISOMSCR	E4C8	script letter D
dscr	ISOMSCR	E4E2	script letter d
dsol	ISOTECH	E3A9	solidus, bar above
dtdot	ISOTECH	22F1	/ddots, three dots, descending
dtri	ISOPUB	25BF	down triangle, open
dtrif	ISOPUB	25BE	down triangle, filled
duarr	ISOAMSA	E216	down arrow, up arrow
duhar	ISOAMSA	E217	down harp, up harp
dwangle	ISOTECH	E3AA	large downward-pointing angle
dzigrarr	ISOAMSA	21DD	right long zig-zag arrow

Table AC-6 MathML Printing Characters, E Names

Name	Group	Code	Description
easter	ISOAMSR	225B	equals, asterisk above
ecir	ISOAMSR	2256	circle on equals sign
ecolon	ISOAMSR	2255	equals, colon
eDDot	ISOAMSR	E309	equals with four dots
eDot	ISOAMSR	2251	equals, even dots
efDot	ISOAMSR	2252	equals, falling dots
Efr	ISOMFRK	E480	Fraktur letter E
efr	ISOMFRK	E499	Fraktur letter e
eg	ISOAMSR	E328	equal-or-greater
egs	ISOAMSR	22DD	equal-or-greater, slanted
egsdot	ISOAMSR	E324	equal-or-greater, slanted, dot inside
el	ISOAMSR	E327	equal-or-less

Continued

Table AC-6 *Continued*

Name	Group	Code	Description
Element	MMALIAS	2208	set membership, variant
elinters	ISOTECH	E3A7	electrical intersection
ell	ISOAMSO	2113	cursive lowercase *l*
els	ISOAMSR	22DC	equal-or-less, slanted
elsdot	ISOAMSR	E323	equal-or-less, slanted, dot inside
empty	ISOAMSO	E2D3	letter *O* slashed
emptyset	MMALIAS	E2D3	letter *O* slashed
emptyv	ISOAMSO	2205	circle, slash
emsp	ISOPUB	2003	em space
emsp13	ISOPUB	2004	third-of-an-em-space
emsp14	ISOPUB	2005	quarter-of-an-em space
ensp	ISOPUB	2002	en space (half an em)
Eopf	ISOMOPF	E4B2	open-face letter *E*
epar	ISOTECH	22D5	parallel, equal; equal or parallel
eparsl	ISOTECH	E384	parallel, slanted, equal; homothetically congruent to
eplus	ISOAMSB	E268	equals, plus
epsi	ISOGRK3	220A	lowercase epsilon, Greek
epsiv	ISOGRK3	03B5	rounded lowercase epsilon, Greek
eqcirc	MMALIAS	2256	circle on equals sign
eqcolon	MMALIAS	2255	equals, colon
eqsim	MMALIAS	2242	equals, similar
eqslantgtr	MMALIAS	22DD	equal-or-greater, slanted
eqslantless	MMALIAS	22DC	equal-or-less, slanted
equals	ISONUM	003D	equals sign
EqualTilde	MMALIAS	2242	equals, similar
equest	ISOAMSR	225F	equals with question mark
Equilibrium	MMALIAS	21CC	right harp over *l*
equiv	ISOTECH	2261	identical with
equivDD	ISOAMSR	E318	equivalent, four dots above
eqvparsl	ISOTECH	E386	equivalent, equal; congruent and parallel
erarr	ISOAMSA	E236	equals, right arrow below
erDot	ISOAMSR	2253	equals, rising dots
Escr	ISOMSCR	E4C9	script letter *E*
escr	ISOMSCR	E4E3	script letter *e*
esdot	ISOAMSR	2250	equals, single dot above
Esim	ISOAMSR	E317	equals, similar
esim	ISOAMSR	2242	equals, similar

Name	Group	Code	Description
eta	ISOGRK3	03B7	lowercase eta, Greek
excl	ISONUM	0021	exclamation point
exist	ISOTECH	2203	/exists at least one exists
Exists	MMALIAS	2203	/exists at least one exists

Table AC-7 MathML Printing Characters, F Names

Name	Group	Code	Description
fallingdotseq	MMALIAS	2252	equals, falling dots
female	ISOPUB	2640	Venus, female
ffilig	ISOPUB	FB03	lowercase ffi ligature
fflig	ISOPUB	FB00	lowercase ff ligature
ffllig	ISOPUB	FB04	lowercase ffl ligature
Ffr	ISOMFRK	E481	Fraktur letter F
ffr	ISOMFRK	E49A	Fraktur letter f
filig	ISOPUB	FB01	lowercase fi ligature
fjlig	ISOPUB	E500	lowercase fj ligature
flat	ISOPUB	266D	musical flat
fllig	ISOPUB	FB02	lowercase fl ligature
fltns	ISOTECH	E381	flatness
fnof	ISOTECH	E364	function of (italic lowercase f)
Fopf	ISOMOPF	E4B3	open-face letter F
ForAll	MMALIAS	2200	/forall for all
forall	ISOTECH	2200	/forall for all
fork	ISOAMSR	22D4	pitchfork
forkv	ISOAMSR	E31B	fork, variant
fpartint	ISOTECH	E396	finite part integral
frac12	ISONUM	00BD	fraction one-half
frac13	ISOPUB	2153	fraction one-third
frac14	ISONUM	00BC	fraction one-quarter
frac15	ISOPUB	2155	fraction one-fifth
frac16	ISOPUB	2159	fraction one-sixth
frac18	ISONUM	215B	fraction one-eighth
frac23	ISOPUB	2254	fraction two-thirds
frac25	ISOPUB	2156	fraction two-fifths
frac34	ISONUM	00BE	fraction three-quarters
frac35	ISOPUB	2157	fraction three-fifths
frac38	ISONUM	215C	fraction three-eighths

Continued

Table AC-7 *Continued*

Name	Group	Code	Description
frac45	ISOPUB	2158	fraction four-fifths
frac56	ISOPUB	215A	fraction five-sixths
frac58	ISONUM	215D	fraction five-eighths
frac78	ISONUM	215E	fraction seven-eighths
frown	ISOAMSR	2322	down curve
Fscr	ISOMSCR	E4CA	script letter *F*
fscr	ISOMSCR	E4E4	script letter *f*

Table AC-8 MathML Printing Characters, G Names

Name	Group	Code	Description
Gamma	ISOGRK3	0393	capital Gamma, Greek
gamma	ISOGRK3	03B3	lowercase gamma, Greek
Gammad	ISOGRK3	03DC	capital digamma
gammad	ISOGRK3	03DC	digamma, old Greek
gap	ISOAMSR	2273	greater, approximate
gE	ISOAMSR	2267	greater, double equals
ge	ISOTECH	2265	greater-than-or-equal
gEl	ISOAMSR	22DB	greater, double equals, less
gel	ISOAMSR	22DB	greater, equals, less
geq	MMALIAS	2265	greater-than-or-equal
geqq	MMALIAS	2267	greater, double equals
geqslant	MMALIAS	E421	greater-or-equal, slanted
ges	ISOAMSR	E421	greater-or-equal, slanted
gescc	ISOAMSR	E358	greater-than, closed by curve, equals, slanted
gesdot	ISOAMSR	E31E	greater-than-or-equal, slanted, dot inside
gesdoto	ISOAMSR	E320	greater-than-or-equal, slanted, dot above
gesdotol	ISOAMSR	E322	greater-than-or-equal, slanted, dot above left
gesl	ISOAMSR	E32C	greater, equals, slanted, less
gesles	ISOAMSR	E332	greater, equals, slanted, less, equals, slanted
Gfr	ISOMFRK	E482	Fraktur letter *G*
gfr	ISOMFRK	E49B	Fraktur letter *g*
Gg	ISOAMSR	22D9	triple greater-than sign
gg	MMALIAS	226B	double greater-than sign
ggg	MMALIAS	22D9	triple greater-than sign
gimel	ISOAMSO	2137	gimel, Hebrew
gl	ISOAMSR	2277	greater, less
gla	ISOAMSR	E330	greater, less, apart

Name	Group	Code	Description
glE	ISOAMSR	E32E	greater, less, equals
glj	ISOAMSR	E32F	greater, less, overlapping
gnap	ISOAMSN	E411	greater, not approximate
gnapprox	MMALIAS	E411	greater, not approximate
gnE	ISOAMSN	2269	greater, not double equals
gne	ISOAMSN	2269	greater, not equals
gneq	MMALIAS	2269	greater, not equals
gneqq	MMALIAS	2269	greater, not double equals
gnsim	ISOAMSN	22E7	greater, not similar
Gopf	ISOMOPF	E4B4	open-face letter G
grave	ISODIA	0300	grave accent
GreaterEqual	MMALIAS	2265	greater-than-or-equal
GreaterEqualLess	MMALIAS	22DB	greater, equals, less
GreaterFullEqual	MMALIAS	2267	greater, double equals
GreaterLess	MMALIAS	2277	greater, less
GreaterSlantEqual	MMALIAS	E421	greater-or-equal, slanted
GreaterTilde	MMALIAS	2273	greater, similar
Gscr	ISOMSCR	E4CB	script letter G
gscr	ISOMSCR	E4E5	script letter g
gsim	ISOAMSR	2273	greater, similar
gsime	ISOAMSR	E334	greater, similar, equal
gsiml	ISOAMSR	E336	greater, similar, less
Gt	ISOAMSR	226B	double greater-than sign
gt	ISONUM	003E	greater-than sign
gtcc	ISOAMSR	E356	greater-than, closed by curve
gtcir	ISOAMSR	E326	greater-than, circle inside
gtdot	ISOAMSR	22D7	greater-than, with dot
gtlPar	ISOAMSC	E296	double left parenthesis, greater
gtquest	ISOAMSR	E32A	greater-than, question mark above
gtrapprox	MMALIAS	2273	greater, approximate
gtrarr	ISOAMSR	E35F	greater-than, right arrow
gtrdot	MMALIAS	22D7	greater-than, with dot
gtreqless	MMALIAS	22DB	greater, equals, less
gtreqqless	MMALIAS	22DB	greater, double equals, less
gtrless	MMALIAS	2277	greater, less
gtrsim	MMALIAS	2273	greater, similar
gvertneqq	MMALIAS	E2A1	greater, vertical, not double equals
gvnE	ISOAMSN	E2A1	greater, vertical, not double equals

Table AC-9 MathML Printing Characters, H Names

Name	Group	Code	Description
Hacek	MMALIAS	030C	caron
hairsp	ISOPUB	200A	hair space
half	ISONUM	00BD	fraction one-half
hamilt	ISOTECH	210B	Hamiltonian (script capital *H*)
hArr	ISOAMSA	21D4	left-and-right double arrow
harr	ISOAMSA	2194	left-and-right arrow
harrcir	ISOAMSA	E240	left-and-right arrow with a circle
harrw	ISOAMSA	21AD	left-and-right arrow, wavy
hbar	MMALIAS	E2D5	Planck's over 2pi
hbenzen	ISOCHEM	E44F	horizontal benzene ring
hbenzena	ISOCHEM	E43D	horizontal benzene ring, one double binding
hbenzenb	ISOCHEM	E43E	horizontal benzene ring, one double binding
hbenzenc	ISOCHEM	E43F	horizontal benzene ring, one double binding
hbenzend	ISOCHEM	E440	horizontal benzene ring, one double binding
hbenzene	ISOCHEM	E441	horizontal benzene ring, one double binding
hbenzenf	ISOCHEM	E442	horizontal benzene ring, one double binding
hbenzeng	ISOCHEM	E443	horizontal benzene ring, two double bindings
hbenzenh	ISOCHEM	E444	horizontal benzene ring, two double bindings
hbenzeni	ISOCHEM	E445	horizontal benzene ring, two double bindings
hbenzenj	ISOCHEM	E446	horizontal benzene ring, two double bindings
hbenzenk	ISOCHEM	E447	horizontal benzene ring, two double bindings
hbenzenl	ISOCHEM	E448	horizontal benzene ring, two double bindings
hbenzenm	ISOCHEM	E449	horizontal benzene ring, two double bindings
hbenzenn	ISOCHEM	E44A	horizontal benzene ring, two double bindings
hbenzeno	ISOCHEM	E44B	horizontal benzene ring, two double bindings
hbenzenp	ISOCHEM	E44C	horizontal benzene ring,three double bindings
hbenzenq	ISOCHEM	E44D	horizontal benzene ring, three double bindings
hbenzenr	ISOCHEM	E44E	horizontal benzene ring, circle
hearts	ISOPUB	2661	heart suit symbol
heartsuit	MMALIAS	2661	heart suit symbol
hellip	ISOPUB	2026	ellipsis (horizontal)
hercon	ISOAMSB	22B9	Hermitian conjugate matrix
Hfr	ISOMFRK	E483	Fraktur letter *H*
hfr	ISOMFRK	E49C	Fraktur letter *h*
hksearow	MMALIAS	E20B	SE arrow, hooked
hkswarow	MMALIAS	E20A	SW arrow, hooked
hoarr	ISOAMSA	E243	horizontal open arrow
homtht	ISOAMSR	223B	homothetic

Name	Group	Code	Description
hookleft arrow	MMALIAS	21A9	left arrow, hooked
hookright arrow	MMALIAS	21AA	right arrow, hooked
Hopf	ISOMOPF	E4B5	open-face letter *H*
horbar	ISONUM	2015	horizontal bar
Hscr	ISOMSCR	E4CC	script letter *H*
hscr	ISOMSCR	E4E6	script letter *h*
hslash	MMALIAS	210F	variant Planck's over 2pi
HumpDown Hump	MMALIAS	224E	bumpy equalsHump
HumpEqual	MMALIAS	224F	bumpy equals, equals
hybull	ISOPUB	2043	rectangle, filled (hyphen bullet)
hyphen	ISONUM	E4F8	hyphen

Table AC-10 MathML Printing Characters, I Names

Name	Group	Code	Description
iexcl	ISONUM	00A1	inverted exclamation mark
iff	ISOTECH	E365	/iff if and only if
Ifr	ISOMFRK	E484	Fraktur letter *I*
ifr	ISOMFRK	E49D	Fraktur letter *i*
iiiint	MMALIAS	E378	quadruple integral operator
iiint	MMALIAS	222D	triple integral operator
iinfin	ISOTECH	E372	infinity sign, incomplete
iiota	ISOAMSO	2129	inverted iota
Im	MMALIAS	2111	imaginary
image	ISOAMSO	2111	imaginary
imath	ISOAMSO	0131	lowercase *i*, no dot
imof	ISOAMSA	22B7	image of
imped	ISOTECH	E50B	impedance
in	MMALIAS	220A	set membership
incare	ISOPUB	2105	in-care-of symbol
infin	ISOTECH	221E	/infty infinity
infintie	ISOTECH	E50C	tie, infinity
Int	ISOTECH	222C	double integral operator
int	ISOTECH	222B	integral operator
intcal	ISOAMSB	22BA	intercal
Integral	MMALIAS	222B	integral operator

Continued

Table AC-10 *Continued*

Name	Group	Code	Description
intercal	MMALIAS	22BA	intercal
Intersection	MMALIAS	22C2	intersection operator
intlarhk	ISOTECH	E39A	integral, left arrow with hook
intprod	MMALIAS	E259	interior product
Iopf	ISOMOPF	E4B6	open-face letter *I*
iota	ISOGRK3	03B9	lowercase iota, Greek
iprod	ISOAMSB	E259	interior product
iquest	ISONUM	00BF	inverted question mark
Iscr	ISOMSCR	E4CD	script letter *I*
iscr	ISOMSCR	E4E7	script letter *i*
isin	ISOTECH	220A	set membership
isindot	ISOTECH	E39C	set membership, dot above
isinE	ISOTECH	E39E	set membership, two horizontal strokes
isins	ISOTECH	E3A4	set membership, vertical bar on horizontal stroke
isinsv	ISOTECH	E3A2	large set membership, vertical bar on horizontal stroke
isinv	ISOTECH	2208	set membership, variant

Table AC-11 MathML Printing Characters, J Names

Name	Group	Code	Description
Jfr	ISOMFRK	E485	Fraktur letter *J*
jfr	ISOMFRK	E49E	Fraktur letter *j*
jmath	ISOAMSO	E2D4	lowercase *j*, no dot
Jopf	ISOMOPF	E4B7	open-face letter *J*
Jscr	ISOMSCR	E4CE	script letter *J*
jscr	ISOMSCR	E4E8	script letter *j*

Table AC-12 MathML Printing Characters, K Names

Name	Group	Code	Description
kappa	ISOGRK3	03BA	lowercase kappa, Greek
kappav	ISOGRK3	03F0	rounded lowercase kappa, Greek
Kfr	ISOMFRK	E486	Fraktur letter *K*
kfr	ISOMFRK	E49F	Fraktur letter *k*
Kopf	ISOMOPF	E4B8	open-face letter *K*
Kscr	ISOMSCR	E4CF	script letter *K*
kscr	ISOMSCR	E4E9	script letter *k*

Table AC-13 MathML Printing Characters, L Names

Name	Group	Code	Description
lAarr	ISOAMSA	21DA	left triple arrow
laemptyv	ISOAMSO	E2EA	circle, slash, left arrow above
lagran	ISOTECH	2112	Lagrangian (script capital *L*)
Lambda	ISOGRK3	039B	capital Lambda, Greek
lambda	ISOGRK3	03BB	lowercase lambda, Greek
Lang	ISOTECH	300A	left angle bracket, double
lang	ISOTECH	3008	left angle bracket
langd	ISOAMSC	E297	left angle, dot
langle	MMALIAS	3008	left angle bracket
lap	ISOAMSR	2272	less, approximate
laquo	ISONUM	00AB	angle quotation mark, left
Larr	ISOAMSA	219E	two-headed left arrow
lArr	ISOTECH	21D0	is implied by
larr	ISONUM	2190	leftward arrow
larrbfs	ISOAMSA	E220	left arrow-bar, filled square
larrfs	ISOAMSA	E222	left arrow, filled square
larrhk	ISOAMSA	21A9	left arrow, hooked
larrlp	ISOAMSA	21AB	left arrow, looped
larrpl	ISOAMSA	E23F	left arrow, plus
larrsim	ISOAMSA	E24E	left arrow, similar
larrtl	ISOAMSA	21A2	left arrow, tailed
lat	ISOAMSR	E33A	larger than
lAtail	ISOAMSA	E23D	left double arrow, tailed
latail	ISOAMSA	E23C	left arrow, tailed
late	ISOAMSR	E33C	larger-than or equal
lates	ISOAMSR	E33E	larger-than or equal, slanted
lBarr	ISOAMSA	E206	left doubly broken arrow
lbarr	ISOAMSA	E402	left broken arrow
lbbrk	ISOTECH	3014	left broken bracket
lbrace	MMALIAS	007B	left curly bracket
lbrack	MMALIAS	005B	left square bracket
lbrke	ISOAMSC	E299	left bracket, equals
lbrksld	ISOAMSC	E29D	left bracket, solidus bottom corner
lbrkslu	ISOAMSC	E29B	left bracket, solidus top corner
lceil	ISOAMSC	2308	left ceiling
lcub	ISONUM	007B	left curly bracket
ldca	ISOAMSA	E21A	left down curved arrow

Continued

Table AC-13 *Continued*

Name	Group	Code	Description
ldquo	ISONUM	201C	double quotation mark, left
ldquor	ISOPUB	201E	rising double quote, left (low)
ldrdhar	ISOAMSA	E22C	left harpoon-down over right harpoon-down
ldrushar	ISOAMSA	E228	left-down-right-up harpoon
ldsh	ISOAMSA	21B2	left down angled arrow
lE	ISOAMSR	2266	less, double equals
le	ISOTECH	2264	less-than-or-equal
LeftAngleBracket	MMALIAS	3008	left angle bracket
LeftArrow	MMALIAS	2190	leftward arrow
Leftarrow	MMALIAS	21D0	is implied by
leftarrow	MMALIAS	2190	leftward arrow
LeftArrowRightArrow	MMALIAS	21C6	left arrow over right arrow
leftarrowtail	MMALIAS	21A2	left arrow, tailed
LeftCeiling	MMALIAS	2308	left ceiling
LeftDownVector	MMALIAS	21C3	down harpoon-left
LeftFloor	MMALIAS	230A	left floor
leftharpoondown	MMALIAS	21BD	left harpoon-down
leftharpoonup	MMALIAS	21BC	left harpoon-up
leftleftarrows	MMALIAS	21C7	two left arrows
LeftRightArrow	MMALIAS	2194	left-and-right arrow
Leftrightarrow	MMALIAS	21D4	left-and-right double arrow
leftrightarrow	MMALIAS	2194	left-and-right arrow
leftrightarrows	MMALIAS	21C6	left arrow over right arrow
leftrightharpoons	MMALIAS	21CB	left harp over
leftrightsquigarrow	MMALIAS	21AD	left and right arrow, wavy
LeftTee	MMALIAS	22A3	dash, vertical
leftthreetimes	MMALIAS	22CB	left three times
LeftTriangle	MMALIAS	22B2	left triangle, open, variant
LeftTriangleEqual	MMALIAS	22B4	left triangle, equals

Character	Name	Group	Code	Description
LeftUpVector	MMALIAS	21BF	up harpoon-left	
LeftVector	MMALIAS	21BC	left harpoon-up	
lEg	ISOAMSR	22DA	less, double equals, greater	
leg	ISOAMSR	22DA	less, equals, greater	
leq	MMALIAS	2264	less-than-or-equal	
leqq	MMALIAS	2266	less, double equals	
leqslant	MMALIAS	E425	less-than-or-equal, slant	
les	ISOAMSR	E425	less-than-or-equal, slant	
lescc	ISOAMSR	E357	less than, closed by curve, equals, slanted	
lesdot	ISOAMSR	E31D	less-than-or-equal, slanted, dot inside	
lesdoto	ISOAMSR	E31F	less-than-or-equal, slanted, dot above	
lesdotor	ISOAMSR	E321	less-than-or-equal, slanted, dot above right	
lesg	ISOAMSR	E32B	less, equals, slanted, greater	
lesges	ISOAMSR	E331	less, equals, slanted, greater, equals, slanted	
lessapprox	MMALIAS	2272	less, approximate	
lessdot	MMALIAS	22D6	less than, with dot	
lesseqgtr	MMALIAS	22DA	less, equals, greater	
lesseqqgtr	MMALIAS	22DA	less, double equals, greater	
LessEqualGreater	MMALIAS	22DA	less, equals, greater	
LessFullEqual	MMALIAS	2266	less, double equals	
LessGreater	MMALIAS	2276	less, greater	
lessgtr	MMALIAS	2276	less, greater	
lesssim	MMALIAS	2272	less, similar	
LessSlantEqual	MMALIAS	E425	less-than-or-equal, slant	
LessTilde	MMALIAS	2272	less, similar	
lfisht	ISOAMSA	E214	left fish tail	
lfloor	ISOAMSC	230A	left floor	
Lfr	ISOMFRK	E487	Fraktur letter *L*	
lfr	ISOMFRK	E4A0	Fraktur letter *l*	
lg	ISOAMSR	2276	less, greater	
lgE	ISOAMSR	E32D	less, greater, equals	
lHar	ISOAMSA	E225	left harpoon-up over left harpoon-down	
lhard	ISOAMSA	21BD	left harpoon-down	
lharu	ISOAMSA	21BC	left harpoon-up	

Continued

Table AC-13 *Continued*

Name	Group	Code	Description
lharul	ISOAMSA	E22E	left harpoon-up over long dash
lhblk	ISOPUB	2584	lower half block
Ll	ISOAMSR	22D8	triple less-than sign
ll	MMALIAS	226A	double less-than sign
llarr	ISOAMSA	21C7	two left arrows
llcorner	MMALIAS	231E	lower-left corner
Lleftarrow	MMALIAS	21DA	left triple arrow
llhard	ISOAMSA	E231	left harpoon-down below long dash
lltri	ISOAMSO	E2E5	lower left triangle
lmoust	ISOAMSC	E294	left moustache
lmoustache	MMALIAS	E294	left moustache
lnap	ISOAMSN	E2A2	less, not approximate
lnapprox	MMALIAS	E2A2	less, not approximate
lnE	ISOAMSN	2268	less, not double equals
lne	ISOAMSN	2268	less, not equals
lneq	MMALIAS	2268	less, not equals
lneqq	MMALIAS	2268	less, not double equals
lnsim	ISOAMSN	22E6	less, not similar
loang	ISOTECH	3018	left open angular bracket
loarr	ISOAMSA	E242	left open arrow
lobrk	ISOTECH	301A	left open bracket
LongLeftArrow	MMALIAS	E201	long left arrow
Longleftarrow	MMALIAS	E200	long left double arrow
longleftarrow	MMALIAS	E201	long left arrow
LongLeftRightArrow	MMALIAS	E203	long left-and-right arrow
Longleftrightarrow	MMALIAS	E202	long left-and-right double arrow
longleftrightarrow	MMALIAS	E203	long left-and-right arrow
longmapsto	MMALIAS	E208	long maps-to
LongRightArrow	MMALIAS	E205	long right arrow
Longrightarrow	MMALIAS	E204	long right double arrow
longrightarrow	MMALIAS	E205	long right arrow
looparrow	MMALIAS	21AB	left arrow, loopedleft

Name	Group	Code	Description
looparrow right	MMALIAS	21AC	right arrow, looped
lopar	ISOTECH	E379	left open parenthesis
Lopf	ISOMOPF	E4B9	open-face letter *L*
loplus	ISOAMSB	E25C	plus sign in left half circle
lotimes	ISOAMSB	E25E	multiplication sign in left half circle
lowast	ISOTECH	E36A	low asterisk
lowbar	ISONUM	005F	low line
LowerLeft Arrow	MMALIAS	2199	SW-pointing arrow
LowerRight Arrow	MMALIAS	2198	SE-pointing arrow
loz	ISOPUB	25CA	lozenge or total mark
lozenge	MMALIAS	25CA	lozenge or total mark
lozf	ISOPUB	E501	lozenge, filled
lpar	ISONUM	0028	left parenthesis
lparlt	ISOAMSC	E292	left parenthesis, lt
lrarr	ISOAMSA	21C6	left arrow over right arrow
lrcorner	MMALIAS	231F	lower-right corner
lrhar	ISOAMSA	21CB	left harp over r
lrhard	ISOAMSA	E22F	right harpoon-down below long dash
lrtri	ISOAMSO	E2E3	lower right triangle
Lscr	ISOMSCR	E4D0	script letter *L*
lscr	ISOMSCR	E4EA	script letter *l*
Lsh	MMALIAS	21B0	Lsh
lsh	ISOAMSA	21B0	Lsh
lsim	ISOAMSR	2272	less, similar
lsime	ISOAMSR	E333	less, similar, equals
lsimg	ISOAMSR	E335	less, similar, greater
lsqb	ISONUM	005B	left square bracket
lsquo	ISONUM	2018	single quotation mark, left
lsquor	ISOPUB	201A	rising single quote, left (low)
Lt	ISOAMSR	226A	double less-than sign
lt	ISONUM	003C	less-than sign
ltcc	ISOAMSR	E355	less-than, closed by curve
ltcir	ISOAMSR	E325	less-than, circle inside
ltdot	ISOAMSR	22D6	less-than, with dot
lthree	ISOAMSB	22CB	left three times
ltimes	ISOAMSB	22C9	times sign, left closed
ltlarr	ISOAMSR	E35E	less-than, left arrow

Continued

Table AC-13 *Continued*

Name	Group	Code	Description
ltquest	ISOAMSR	E329	less-than, question mark above
ltri	ISOPUB	25C3	left triangle, open
ltrie	ISOAMSR	22B4	left triangle, equals
ltrif	ISOPUB	25C2	left triangle, filled
ltrPar	ISOAMSC	E295	double right parenthesis, less
lurdshar	ISOAMSA	E229	left-up-right-down harpoon
luruhar	ISOAMSA	E22B	left harpoon-up over right harpoon-up
lvertneqq	MMALIAS	E2A4	less, vertical, not double equals
lvnE	ISOAMSN	E2A4	less, vertical, not double equals

Table AC-14 MathML Printing Characters, M Names

Name	Group	Code	Description
macr	ISODIA	0304	macron
male	ISOPUB	2642	Mars, male
malt	ISOPUB	2720	Maltese cross
maltese	MMALIAS	2720	Maltese cross
Map	ISOAMSA	E212	two-headed maps-to
map	ISOAMSA	21A6	maps-to
mapsto	MMALIAS	21A6	maps-to
marker	ISOPUB	E502	histogram marker
mcomma	ISOAMSR	E31A	minus, comma above
mdash	ISOPUB	2014	em dash
mDDot	ISOAMSR	223A	minus with four dots, geometric properties
measured angle	MMALIAS	2221	angle (measured)
Mfr	ISOMFRK	E488	Fraktur letter *M*
mfr	ISOMFRK	E4A1	Fraktur letter *m*
mho	ISOAMSO	2127	conductance
micro	ISONUM	00B5	micro sign
mid	ISOAMSR	2223	mid
midast	ISOAMSB	2217	centered asterisk
midcir	ISOAMSA	E20F	mid, circle below
middot	ISONUM	00B7	middle dot
minus	ISOTECH	2212	minus sign
minusb	ISOAMSB	229F	minus sign in box
minusd	ISOAMSB	2238	minus sign, dot above

Name	Group	Code	Description
minusdu	ISOAMSB	E25B	minus sign, dot below
MinusPlus	MMALIAS	2213	minus-or-plus sign
mlcp	ISOAMSR	E30A	transversal intersection
mldr	ISOPUB	E503	em leader
mnplus	ISOTECH	2213	minus-or-plus sign
models	ISOAMSR	22A7	models
Mopf	ISOMOPF	E4BA	open-face letter *M*
mp	MMALIAS	2213	minus-or-plus sign
Mscr	ISOMSCR	E4D1	script letter *M*
mscr	ISOMSCR	E4EB	script letter *m*
mstpos	ISOAMSR	223E	most positive
mu	ISOGRK3	03BC	lowercase mu, Greek
multimap	MMALIAS	22B8	multimap
mumap	ISOAMSA	22B8	multimap

Table AC-15 MathML Printing Characters, N Names

Name	Group	Code	Description
nabla	ISOTECH	2207	del, Hamilton operator
nang	ISOAMSO	E2D8	not, vertical, angle
nap	ISOAMSN	2249	not approximate
napE	ISOAMSN	E2C7	not approximately equal or equal to
napid	ISOAMSN	E2BC	not approximately identical to
napprox	MMALIAS	2249	not approximate
natur	ISOPUB	266E	music natural
natural	MMALIAS	266E	music natural
nbsp	ISONUM	00A0	no break (required) space
ncap	ISOAMSB	E284	bar, intersection
ncong	ISOAMSN	2247	not congruent with
ncongdot	ISOAMSN	E2C5	not congruent, dot
ncup	ISOAMSB	E283	bar, union
ndash	ISOPUB	2013	en dash
ne	ISOTECH	2260	not equals
nearhk	ISOAMSA	E20D	NE arrow, hooked
neArr	ISOAMSA	21D7	NE-pointing double arrow
nearr	ISOAMSA	2197	NE-pointing arrow
nearrow	MMALIAS	2197	NE-pointing arrow
nedot	ISOTECH	E38A	not equals, dot

Continued

Table AC-15 *Continued*

Name	Group	Code	Description
nequiv	ISOAMSN	2262	not identical with
nesear	ISOAMSA	E20E	NE & SE arrows
Nested Greater Greater	MMALIAS	226B	double greater-than sign
NestedLess Less	MMALIAS	226A	double less-than sign
nexist	ISOAMSO	2204	negated exists
nexists	MMALIAS	2204	negated exists
Nfr	ISOMFRK	E489	Fraktur letter N
nfr	ISOMFRK	E4A2	Fraktur letter n
ngE	ISOAMSN	2271	not greater, double equals
nge	ISOAMSN	E2A6	not greater-than-or-equal
ngeq	MMALIAS	E2A6	not greater-than-or-equal
ngeqq	MMALIAS	2271	not greater, double equals
ngeqslant	MMALIAS	2271	not greater-or-equals, slanted
nges	ISOAMSN	2271	not greater-or-equals, slanted
nGg	ISOAMSN	E2CE	not triple greater-than
ngsim	ISOAMSN	2275	not greater, similar
nGt	ISOAMSN	E2CA	not, vertical, much-greater-than
ngt	ISOAMSN	226F	not greater-than
ngtr	MMALIAS	226F	not greater-than
nGtv	ISOAMSN	E2CC	not much-greater-than, variant
nhArr	ISOAMSA	21CE	not left and right double arrow
nharr	ISOAMSA	21AE	not left-and-right arrow
nhpar	ISOTECH	E38D	not, horizontal, parallel
ni	ISOTECH	220D	contains
nis	ISOTECH	E3A5	contains, vertical bar on horizontal stroke
nisd	ISOTECH	E3A1	contains, long horizontal stroke
niv	ISOTECH	220B	contains, variant
nlArr	ISOAMSA	21CD	not implied by
nlarr	ISOAMSA	219A	not left arrow
nldr	ISOPUB	2025	double baseline dot (en leader)
nlE	ISOAMSN	2270	not less, double equals
nle	ISOAMSN	E2A7	not less-than-or-equal
nLeftarrow	MMALIAS	21CD	not implied by
nleftarrow	MMALIAS	219A	not left arrow
nLeftright arrow	MMALIAS	21CE	not left-and-right double arrow

Name	Group	Code	Description
nleftright arrow	MMALIAS	21AE	not left-and-right arrow
nleq	MMALIAS	E2A7	not less-than-or-equal
nleqq	MMALIAS	2270	not less, double equals
nleqslant	MMALIAS	2270	not less-or-equal, slant
nles	ISOAMSN	2270	not less-or-equal, slant
nless	MMALIAS	226E	not less-than
nLl	ISOAMSN	E2CD	not triple less-than
nlsim	ISOAMSN	2274	not less, similar
nLt	ISOAMSN	E2C9	not, vertical, much-less-than
nlt	ISOAMSN	226E	not less-than
nltri	ISOAMSN	22EA	not left triangle
nltrie	ISOAMSN	22EC	not left triangle, equals
nLtv	ISOAMSN	E2CB	not much less than, variant
nmid	ISOAMSN	2224	negated mid
Nopf	ISOMOPF	E4BB	open-face letter *N*
Not	MMALIAS	00AC	/neg /lnot not sign
not	ISONUM	00AC	/neg /lnot not sign
Not Congruent	MMALIAS	2262	not identical with
NotDouble VerticalBar	MMALIAS	2226	not parallel
NotElement	MMALIAS	2209	negated set membership
NotEqual	MMALIAS	2260	not equals
NotExists	MMALIAS	2204	negated exists
NotGreater	MMALIAS	226F	not greater-than
NotGreater Equal	MMALIAS	E2A6	not greater-than-or-equal
NotGreater FullEqual	MMALIAS	2270	not less, double equals
NotGreater Greater	MMALIAS	E2CC	not much-greater-than, variant
NotGreater Less	MMALIAS	2279	not, vertical, greater, less
NotGreater SlantEqual	MMALIAS	2271	not greater-or-equal, slanted
NotGreater Tilde	MMALIAS	2275	not greater, similar
notin	ISOTECH	2209	negated set membership
notindot	ISOTECH	E39D	negated set membership, dot above
notinE	ISOTECH	E50D	negated set membership, two horizontal strokes

Continued

Table AC-15 *Continued*

Name	Group	Code	Description
notinva	ISOTECH	E370	negated set membership, variant
notinvb	ISOTECH	E37B	negated set membership, variant
notinvc	ISOTECH	E37C	negated set membership, variant
NotLeft Triangle	MMALIAS	22EA	not left triangle
NotLeft Triangle Equal	MMALIAS	22EC	not left triangle, equals
NotLess	MMALIAS	226E	not less-than
NotLess Equal	MMALIAS	E2A7	not less-than-or-equal
NotLess Greater	MMALIAS	2278	not vertical, less, greater
NotLessLess	MMALIAS	E2CB	not much-less-than, variant
NotLessSlant Equal	MMALIAS	2270	not less-or-equal, slant
NotLessTilde	MMALIAS	2274	not less, similar
notni	ISOTECH	220C	negated contains
notniva	ISOTECH	220C	negated contains, variant
notnivb	ISOTECH	E37D	contains, variant
notnivc	ISOTECH	E37E	contains, variant
NotPrecedes	MMALIAS	2280	not precedes
NotPrecedes Equal	MMALIAS	E412	not precedes, equals
NotPrecedes SlantEqual	MMALIAS	22E0	not curly precedes, equals
NotReverse Element	MMALIAS	220C	negated contains, variant
NotRight Triangle	MMALIAS	22EB	not right triangle
NotRight TriangleEqual	MMALIAS	22ED	not right triangle, equals
NotSquare SubsetEqual	MMALIAS	22E2	not, square subset, equals
NotSquare Superset Equal	MMALIAS	22E3	not, square superset, equals
NotSubset	MMALIAS	2284	not subset, variant
NotSucceeds	MMALIAS	2281	not succeeds
NotSucceeds Equal	MMALIAS	E413	not succeeds, equals

NotSucceeds SlantEqual	MMALIAS	22E1	not succeeds, curly equals
NotSuperset	MMALIAS	2285	not superset, variant
NotTilde	MMALIAS	2241	not similar
NotTilde Equal	MMALIAS	2244	not similar, equals
NotTildeFull Equal	MMALIAS	2247	not congruent with
NotTilde Tilde	MMALIAS	2249	not approximate
NotVertical Bar	MMALIAS	2224	negated mid
npar	ISOAMSN	2226	not parallel
nparallel	MMALIAS	2226	not parallel
nparsl	ISOTECH	E389	not parallel, slanted
npart	ISOTECH	E390	not partial differential
npolint	ISOTECH	E399	line integration, not including the pole
npr	ISOAMSN	2280	not precedes
nprcue	ISOAMSN	22E0	not curly precedes, equals
npre	ISOAMSN	E412	not precedes, equals
nprec	MMALIAS	2280	not precedes
npreceq	MMALIAS	E412	not precedes, equals
nrArr	ISOAMSA	21CF	not implies
nrarr	ISOAMSA	219B	not right arrow
nrarrc	ISOAMSA	E21D	not right arrow, curved
nrarrw	ISOAMSA	E21B	not right arrow, wavy
nRightarrow	MMALIAS	21CF	not implies
nrightarrow	MMALIAS	219B	not right arrow
nrtri	ISOAMSN	22EB	not right triangle
nrtrie	ISOAMSN	22ED	not right triangle, equals
nsc	ISOAMSN	2281	not succeeds
nsccue	ISOAMSN	22E1	not succeeds, curly equals
nsce	ISOAMSN	E413	not succeeds, equals
Nscr	ISOMSCR	E4D2	script letter *N*
nscr	ISOMSCR	E4EC	script letter *n*
nshortmid	MMALIAS	E2AA	negated short mid
nshortparallel	MMALIAS	E2AB	not short parallel
nsim	ISOAMSN	2241	not similar
nsime	ISOAMSN	2244	not similar, equals
nsimeq	MMALIAS	2244	not similar, equals
nsmid	ISOAMSN	E2AA	negated short mid

Continued

Table AC-15 *Continued*

Name	Group	Code	Description
nspar	ISOAMSN	E2AB	not short parallel
nsqsube	ISOAMSN	22E2	not, square subset, equals
nsqsupe	ISOAMSN	22E3	not, square superset, equals
nsub	ISOAMSN	2284	not subset
nsubE	ISOAMSN	2288	not subset, double equals
nsube	ISOAMSN	2288	not subset, equals
nsubset	MMALIAS	2284	not subset, variant
nsubseteq	MMALIAS	2288	not subset, equals
nsubseteqq	MMALIAS	2288	not subset, double equals
nsucc	MMALIAS	2281	not succeeds
nsucceq	MMALIAS	E413	not succeeds, equals
nsup	ISOAMSN	2285	not superset
nsupE	ISOAMSN	2289	not superset, double equals
nsupe	ISOAMSN	2289	not superset, equals
nsupset	MMALIAS	2285	not superset, variant
nsupseteq	MMALIAS	2289	not superset, equals
nsupseteqq	MMALIAS	2289	not superset, double equals
ntgl	ISOAMSN	2279	not greater, less
ntlg	ISOAMSN	2278	not less, greater
ntriangleleft	MMALIAS	22EA	not left triangle
ntriangle lefteq	MMALIAS	22EC	not left triangle, equals
ntriangleright	MMALIAS	22EB	not right triangle
ntriangle righteq	MMALIAS	22ED	not right triangle, equals
ntvgl	ISOAMSN	2279	not, vertical, greater, less
ntvlg	ISOAMSN	2278	not, vertical, less, greater
nu	ISOGRK3	03BD	lowercase nu, Greek
num	ISONUM	0023	number sign
numsp	ISOPUB	2007	digit space (width of a number)
nvap	ISOAMSN	E2C6	not, vertical, approximate
nVDash	ISOAMSN	22AF	not double vertical, double dash
nVdash	ISOAMSN	22AE	not double vertical, dash
nvDash	ISOAMSN	22AD	not vertical, double dash
nvdash	ISOAMSN	22AC	not vertical, dash
nvge	ISOAMSN	2271	not, vertical, greater-than-or-equal
nvgt	ISOAMSN	226F	not, vertical, greater-than
nvhArr*	ISOAMSA	21CE	not, vertical, left and right double arrow
nvinfin	ISOTECH	E38E	not, vertical, infinity

Name	Group	Code	Description
nvlArr	ISOAMSA	21CD	not, vertical, left double arrow
nvle	ISOAMSN	2270	not, vertical, less-than-or-equal
nvlt	ISOAMSN	226E	not, vertical, less-than
nvltrie	ISOAMSN	E2D0	not, vertical, left triangle, equals
nvrArr	ISOAMSA	21CF	not, vertical, right double arrow
nvrtrie	ISOAMSN	E2CF	not, vertical, right triangle, equals
nvsim	ISOAMSN	E415	not, vertical, similar
nwarhk	ISOAMSA	E20C	NW arrow, hooked
nwArr	ISOAMSA	21D6	NW-pointing double arrow
nwarr	ISOAMSA	2196	NW-pointing arrow
nwarrow	MMALIAS	2196	NW-pointing arrow
nwnear	ISOAMSA	E211	NW & NE arrows

Table AC-16 MathML Printing Characters, O Names

Name	Group	Code	Description
oast	ISOAMSB	229B	asterisk in circle
ocir	ISOAMSB	229A	small circle in circle
odash	ISOAMSB	229D	hyphen in circle
odiv	ISOAMSB	E285	divide in circle
odot	ISOAMSB	2299	middle dot in circle
odsold	ISOAMSB	E286	dot, solidus, dot in circle
ofcir	ISOAMSB	E287	filled circle in circle
Ofr	ISOMFRK	E48A	Fraktur letter O
ofr	ISOMFRK	E4A3	Fraktur letter o
ogon	ISODIA	0328	ogonek
ogt	ISOAMSB	E289	greater-than in circle
ohbar	ISOAMSB	E260	circle with horizontal bar
ohm	ISONUM	2126	ohm sign
oint	MMALIAS	222E	contour integral operator
olarr	ISOAMSA	21BA	left arrow in circle
olcir	ISOAMSB	E409	large circle in circle
olcross	ISOTECH	E3A8	circle, cross
olt	ISOAMSB	E288	less-than in circle
Omega	ISOGRK3	03A9	capital Omega, Greek
omega	ISOGRK3	03C9	lowercase omega, Greek
omicron	ISOGRK3	03BE	lowercase omicron, Greek
omid	ISOAMSB	E40A	vertical bar in circle

Continued

Table AC-16 *Continued*

Name	Group	Code	Description
ominus	ISOAMSB	2296	minus sign in circle
Oopf	ISOMOPF	E4BC	open-face letter *O*
opar	ISOAMSB	E28A	parallel in circle
OpenCurlyDoubleQuote	MMALIAS	201C	double quotation mark, left
OpenCurlyQuote	MMALIAS	2018	single quotation mark, left
operp	ISOAMSB	E28B	perpendicular in circle
oplus	ISOAMSB	2295	plus sign in circle
Or	MMALIAS	2228	logical OR
or	ISOTECH	2228	logical OR
orarr	ISOAMSA	21BB	right arrow in circle
ord	ISOTECH	E393	or, horizontal dash
order	ISOTECH	2134	order of (script lowercase *o*)
ordf	ISONUM	00AA	ordinal indicator, feminine
ordm	ISONUM	00BA	ordinal indicator, masculine
origof	ISOAMSA	22B6	original of
oror	ISOTECH	E50E	two logical ORs
orslope	ISOTECH	E3AE	sloping large OR
orv	ISOTECH	E392	OR with middle stem
oS	ISOAMSO	E41D	capital *S* in circle
Oscr	ISOMSCR	E4D3	script letter *O*
oscr	ISOMSCR	E4ED	script letter *o*
oslash	MMALIAS	2298	solidus in circle
osol	ISOAMSB	2298	solidus in circle
Otimes	ISOAMSB	E28C	multiplication sign in double circle
otimes	ISOAMSB	2297	multiplication sign in circle
otimesas	ISOAMSB	E28D	multiplication sign in circle, circumflex accent
ovbar	ISOAMSB	E40B	circle with vertical bar

Table AC-17 MathML Printing Characters, P Names

Name	Group	Code	Description
par	ISOTECH	2225	parallel
para	ISONUM	00B6	pilcrow (paragraph sign)
parallel	MMALIAS	2225	parallel
parsim	ISOAMSN	E2C8	parallel, similar
parsl	ISOTECH	E382	parallel, slanted

Name	Group	Code	Description
part	ISOTECH	2202	/partial partial differential
PartialD	MMALIAS	2202	/partial partial differential
percnt	ISONUM	0025	percent sign
period	ISONUM	002E	full stop, period
permil	ISOTECH	2030	per thousand
perp	ISOTECH	22A5	perpendicular
pertenk	ISOTECH	2031	per ten thousand
Pfr	ISOMFRK	E48B	Fraktur letter *P*
pfr	ISOMFRK	E4A4	Fraktur letter *p*
Phi	ISOGRK3	03A6	capital Phi, Greek
phi	ISOGRK3	03C6	lowercase phi, Greek
phiv	ISOGRK3	03D5	curly or open lowercase phi, Greek
phmmat	ISOTECH	2133	physics M-matrix (script capital *M*)
phone	ISOPUB	260E	telephone symbol
Pi	ISOGRK3	03A0	capital Pi, Greek
pi	ISOGRK3	03C0	lowercase pi, Greek
pitchfork	MMALIAS	22D4	pitchfork
piv	ISOGRK3	03D6	rounded lowercase pi (pomega), Greek
plank	ISOAMSO	E2D5	Planck's over 2pi
plankv	ISOAMSO	210F	variant Planck's over 2pi
plus	ISONUM	002B	plus sign
plusacir	ISOAMSB	E26A	plus, circumflex accent above
plusb	ISOAMSB	229E	plus sign in box
pluscir	ISOAMSB	E266	plus sign, small circle above
plusdo	ISOAMSB	2214	plus sign, dot above
plusdu	ISOAMSB	E25A	plus sign, dot below
pluse	ISOAMSB	E267	plus sign, equals
PlusMinus	MMALIAS	00B1	plus-or-minus sign
plusmn	ISONUM	00B1	plus-or-minus sign
plussim	ISOAMSB	E26C	plus sign, similar below
plustwo	ISOAMSB	E269	plus sign, two; Nim-addition
pm	MMALIAS	00B1	plus-or-minus sign
pointint	ISOTECH	E376	integral around a point operator
Popf	ISOMOPF	2119	open-face letter *P*
pound	ISONUM	00A3	pound sign
Pr	ISOAMSR	E35C	double precedes
pr	ISOAMSR	227A	precedes
prap	ISOAMSR	227E	precedes, approximate
prcue	ISOAMSR	227C	precedes, curly equals

Continued

Table AC-17 *Continued*

Name	Group	Code	Description
prE	ISOAMSR	227C	precedes, double equals
pre	ISOAMSR	227C	precedes, equals
prec	MMALIAS	227A	precedes
precapprox	MMALIAS	227E	precedes, approximate
preccurlyeq	MMALIAS	227C	precedes, curly equals
Precedes	MMALIAS	227A	precedes
Precedes Equal	MMALIAS	227C	precedes, equals
Precedes SlantEqual	MMALIAS	227C	precedes, curly equals
Precedes Tilde	MMALIAS	227E	precedes, similar
preceq	MMALIAS	227C	precedes, equals
precnapprox	MMALIAS	22E8	precedes, not approximate
precneqq	MMALIAS	E2B3	precedes, not double equals
precnsim	MMALIAS	22E8	precedes, not similar
precsim	MMALIAS	227E	precedes, similar
Prime	ISOTECH	2033	double prime or second
prime	ISOTECH	2032	/prime prime or minute
prnap	ISOAMSN	22E8	precedes, not approximate
prnE	ISOAMSN	E2B3	precedes, not double equals
prnsim	ISOAMSN	22E8	precedes, not similar
profalar	ISOTECH	232E	all-around profile
profline	ISOTECH	2312	profile of a line
profsurf	ISOTECH	2313	profile of a surface
prop	ISOTECH	221D	is proportional to
Proportion	MMALIAS	2237	/Colon, two colons
Proportional	MMALIAS	221D	is proportional to
propto	MMALIAS	221D	is proportional to
prsim	ISOAMSR	227E	precedes, similar
prurel	ISOAMSR	22B0	element precedes under relation
Pscr	ISOMSCR	E4D4	script letter *P*
pscr	ISOMSCR	E4EE	script letter *p*
Psi	ISOGRK3	03A8	capital Psi, Greek
psi	ISOGRK3	03C8	lowercase psi, Greek
puncsp	ISOPUB	2008	punctuation space (width of comma)

Table AC-18 MathML Printing Characters, Q Names

Name	Group	Code	Description
Qfr	ISOMFRK	E48C	Fraktur letter Q
qfr	ISOMFRK	E4A5	Fraktur letter q
qint	ISOTECH	E378	quadruple integral operator
Qopf	ISOMOPF	211A	open-face letter Q
qprime	ISOTECH	E371	quadruple prime
Qscr	ISOMSCR	E4D5	script letter Q
qscr	ISOMSCR	E4EF	script letter q
quatint	ISOTECH	E377	quaternion integral operator
quest	ISONUM	003F	question mark
questeq	MMALIAS	225F	equal with question mark
quot	ISONUM	0022	quotation mark

Table AC-19 MathML Printing Characters, R Names

Name	Group	Code	Description
rAarr	ISOAMSA	21DB	right triple arrow
race	ISOAMSB	E28F	reverse most positive, line below
radic	ISOTECH	221A	/surd radical
raemptyv	ISOAMSO	E2E9	circle, slash, right arrow above
Rang	ISOTECH	300B	right angle bracket, double
rang	ISOTECH	3009	right angle bracket
rangd	ISOAMSC	E298	right angle, dot
range	ISOAMSO	E2D7	reverse angle, equal
rangle	MMALIAS	3009	right angle bracket
raquo	ISONUM	00BB	angle quotation mark, right
Rarr	ISOAMSA	21A0	two-headed right arrow
rArr	ISOTECH	21D2	implies
rarr	ISONUM	2192	rightward arrow
rarrap	ISOAMSA	E235	approximate, right arrow above
rarrbfs	ISOAMSA	E221	right arrow-bar, filled square
rarrc	ISOAMSA	E21C	right arrow-curved
rarrfs	ISOAMSA	E223	right arrow, filled square
rarrhk	ISOAMSA	21AA	right arrow, hooked
rarrlp	ISOAMSA	21AC	right arrow, looped
rarrpl	ISOAMSA	E21E	right arrow, plus
rarrsim	ISOAMSA	E24D	right arrow, similar

Continued

Table AC-19 *Continued*

Name	Group	Code	Description
Rarrtl	ISOAMSA	E239	right two-headed arrow with tail
rarrtl	ISOAMSA	21A3	right arrow, tailed
rarrw	ISOAMSA	219D	right arrow, wavy
rAtail	ISOAMSA	E23B	right double arrow, tailed
ratail	ISOAMSA	21A3	right arrow, tailed
ratio	ISOAMSR	2236	ratio
RBarr	ISOAMSA	E209	two-headed right broken arrow
rBarr	ISOAMSA	E207	right doubly broken arrow
rbarr	ISOAMSA	E405	right broken arrow
rbbrk	ISOTECH	3015	right broken bracket
rbrace	MMALIAS	007D	right curly bracket
rbrack	MMALIAS	005D	right square bracket
rbrke	ISOAMSC	E29A	right bracket, equal
rbrksld	ISOAMSC	E29C	right bracket, solidus bottom corner
rbrkslu	ISOAMSC	E29E	right bracket, solidus top corner
rceil	ISOAMSC	2309	right ceiling
rcub	ISONUM	007D	right curly bracket
rdca	ISOAMSA	E219	right down curved arrow
rdldhar	ISOAMSA	E22D	right harpoon-down over left harpoon-down
rdquo	ISONUM	201D	double quotation mark, right
rdquor	ISOPUB	201B	rising double quote, right (high)
rdsh	ISOAMSA	21B3	right down angled arrow
Re	MMALIAS	211C	real
real	ISOAMSO	211C	real
rect	ISOPUB	E504	rectangle, open
reg	ISONUM	00AF	registered sign
Reverse Element	MMALIAS	220B	contains, variant
Reverse Equilibrium	MMALIAS	21CBl	left harp over r
ReverseUp Equilibrium	MMALIAS	E217	down harp, up harp
rfisht	ISOAMSA	E215	right fish tail
rfloor	ISOAMSC	230B	right floor
Rfr	ISOMFRK	E48D	Fraktur letter *R*
rfr	ISOMFRK	E4A6	Fraktur letter *r*
rHar	ISOAMSA	E224	right harpoon-up over right harpoon-down
rhard	ISOAMSA	21C1	right harpoon-down
rharu	ISOAMSA	21C0	right harpoon-up

Name	Group	Code	Description
rharul	ISOAMSA	E230	right harpoon-up over long dash
rho	ISOGRK3	03C1	lowercase rho, Greek
rhov	ISOGRK3	03F1	rounded lowercase rho, Greek
RightAngle Bracket	MMALIAS	3009	right angle bracket
RightArrow	MMALIAS	2192	rightward arrow
Rightarrow	MMALIAS	21D2	implies
rightarrow	MMALIAS	2192	rightward arrow
RightArrow LeftArrow	MMALIAS	21C4	right arrow over left arrow
rightarrowtail	MMALIAS	21A3	right arrow, tailed
RightCeiling	MMALIAS	2309	right ceiling
RightDown Vector	MMALIAS	21C2	down harpoon-right
RightFloor	MMALIAS	230B	right floor
rightharpoon down	MMALIAS	21C1	right harpoon-down
rightharpoon up	MMALIAS	21C0	right harpoon-up
rightleft arrows	MMALIAS	21C4	right arrow over left arrow
rightleft harpoons	MMALIAS	21CC	right harp over l
rightright arrows	MMALIAS	21C9	two right arrows
rightsquig arrow	MMALIAS	219D	right arrow, wavy
RightTee	MMALIAS	22A2	vertical, dash
RightTee Arrow	MMALIAS	21A6	maps-to
rightthree times	MMALIAS	22CC	right three times
RightTriangle	MMALIAS	22B3	right triangle, open, variant
RightTriangle Equal	MMALIAS	22B5	right triangle, equals
RightUp Vector	MMALIAS	21BE	up harp-right
RightVector	MMALIAS	21C0	right harpoon-up
ring	ISODIA	030A	ring
risingdotseq	MMALIAS	2253	equals, rising dots
rlarr	ISOAMSA	21C4	right arrow over left arrow
rlhar	ISOAMSA	21CC	right harp over l

Continued

Table AC-19 *Continued*

Name	Group	Code	Description
rmoust	ISOAMSC	E293	right moustache
rmoustache	MMALIAS	E293	right moustache
rnmid	ISOAMSN	E2D1	reverse nmid
roang	ISOTECH	3019	right open angular bracket
roarr	ISOAMSA	E241	right open arrow
robrk	ISOTECH	301B	right open bracket
ropar	ISOTECH	E37A	right open parenthesis
Ropf	ISOMOPF	211D	open-face letter *R*
roplus	ISOAMSB	E25D	plus sign in right half circle
rotimes	ISOAMSB	E40D	multiplication sign in right half circle
rpar	ISONUM	0029	right parenthesis
rpargt	ISOAMSC	E291	right parenthesis, gt
rppolint	ISOTECH	E397	line integration, rectangular path around pole
rrarr	ISOAMSA	21C9	two right arrows
Rrightarrow	MMALIAS	21DB	right triple arrow
Rscr	ISOMSCR	E4D6	script letter *R*
rscr	ISOMSCR	211B	script letter *r*
Rsh	MMALIAS	21B1	Rsh
rsh	ISOAMSA	21B1	Rsh
rsqb	ISONUM	005D	right square bracket
rsquo	ISONUM	2019	single quotation mark, right
rsquor	ISOPUB	201F	rising single quote, right (high)
rthree	ISOAMSB	22CC	right three times
rtimes	ISOAMSB	22CA	times sign, right closed
rtri	ISOPUB	25B9	right triangle, open
rtrie	ISOAMSR	22B5	right triangle, equals
rtrif	ISOPUB	25B8	right triangle, filled
rtriltri	ISOAMSR	E359	right triangle above left triangle
ruluhar	ISOAMSA	E22A	right harpoon-up over left harpoon-up
rx	ISOPUB	211E	pharmaceutical prescription (Rx)

Table AC-20 MathML Printing Characters, S Names

Name	Group	Code	Description
Sc	ISOAMSR	E35D	double succeeds
sc	ISOAMSR	227B	succeeds
scap	ISOAMSR	227F	succeeds, approximate
sccue	ISOAMSR	227D	succeeds, curly equals

Name	Group	Code	Description
scE	ISOAMSR	227E	succeeds, double equals
sce	ISOAMSR	227D	succeeds, equals
scnap	ISOAMSN	22E9	succeeds, not approximate
scnE	ISOAMSN	E2B5	succeeds, not double equals
scnsim	ISOAMSN	22E9	succeeds, not similar
scpolint	ISOTECH	E398	line integration, semicircular path around pole
scsim	ISOAMSR	227F	succeeds, similar
sdot	ISOAMSB	22C5	small middle dot
sdotb	ISOAMSB	22A1	small dot in box
sdote	ISOAMSR	E319	equals, dot below
searhk	ISOAMSA	E20B	SE arrow, hooked
seArr	ISOAMSA	21D8	SE-pointing double arrow
searr	ISOAMSA	2198	SE-pointing arrow
searrow	MMALIAS	2198	SE-pointing arrow
sect	ISONUM	00A7	section sign
semi	ISONUM	003B	semicolon
seswar	ISOAMSA	E20F	SE & SW arrows
setminus	MMALIAS	2216	reverse solidus
setmn	ISOAMSB	2216	reverse solidus
sext	ISOPUB	E505	sextile (6-pointed star)
Sfr	ISOMFRK	E48E	Fraktur letter *S*
sfr	ISOMFRK	E4A7	Fraktur letter *s*
sfrown	ISOAMSR	E426	small down curve
sharp	ISOPUB	266F	musical sharp
ShortLeftArrow	MMALIAS	E233	short left arrow
shortmid	MMALIAS	E301	shortmid
shortparallel	MMALIAS	E302	short parallel
ShortRightArrow	MMALIAS	E232	short right arrow
shy	ISONUM	00AD	soft hyphen
Sigma	ISOGRK3	03A3	capital Sigma, Greek
sigma	ISOGRK3	03C3	lowercase sigma, Greek
sigmav	ISOGRK3	03C2	terminal sigma, Greek
sim	ISOTECH	223C	similar
simdot	ISOTECH	E38B	similar, dot
sime	ISOTECH	2243	similar, equals
simeq	MMALIAS	2243	similar, equals
simg	ISOAMSR	E30C	similar, greater

Continued

Table AC-20 *Continued*

Name	Group	Code	Description
simgE	ISOAMSR	E338	similar, greater, equals
siml	ISOAMSR	E30B	similar, less
simlE	ISOAMSR	E337	similar, less, equals
simne	ISOAMSN	2246	similar, not equals
simplus	ISOAMSB	E26B	plus, similar above
simrarr	ISOAMSA	E234	similar, right arrow below
slarr	ISOAMSA	E233	short left arrow
SmallCircle	MMALIAS	2218	composite function (small circle)
smallfrown	MMALIAS	E426	small down curve
smallsetminus	MMALIAS	E844	small reverse solidus
smallsmile	MMALIAS	E303	small up curve
smashp	ISOAMSB	E264	smash product
smeparsl	ISOTECH	E385	similar, parallel, slanted, equals
smid	ISOAMSR	E301	shortmid
smile	ISOAMSR	2323	up curve
smt	ISOAMSR	E339	smaller-than
smte	ISOAMSR	E33B	smaller-than or equal
smtes	ISOAMSR	E33D	smaller-than or equal, slanted
sol	ISONUM	002F	solidus
solb	ISOAMSB	E27F	solidus in square
solbar	ISOAMSN	E416	solidus, bar through
Sopf	ISOMOPF	E4BD	open-face letter *S*
spades	ISOPUB	2660	spades suit symbol
spadesuit	MMALIAS	2660	spades suit symbol
spar	ISOAMSR	E302	short parallel
sqcap	ISOAMSB	2293	square intersection
sqcaps	ISOAMSB	E277	square intersection, serifs
sqcup	ISOAMSB	2294	square union
sqcups	ISOAMSB	E276	square union, serifs
Sqrt	MMALIAS	221A	/surd radical
sqsub	ISOAMSR	228F	square subset
sqsube	ISOAMSR	2291	square subset, equals
sqsubset	MMALIAS	228F	square subset
sqsubseteq	MMALIAS	2291	square subset, equals
sqsup	ISOAMSR	2290	square superset
sqsupe	ISOAMSR	2292	square superset, equals
sqsupset	MMALIAS	2290	square superset

Name	Group	Code	Description
sqsupseteq	MMALIAS	2292	square superset, equals
squ	ISOPUB	*25A1	square, open
square	ISOTECH	25A1	square
Square Intersection	MMALIAS	2293	square intersection
Square Subset	MMALIAS	228F	square subset
Square SubsetEqual	MMALIAS	2291	square subset, equals
Square Superset	MMALIAS	2290	square superset
Square Superset Equal	MMALIAS	2292	square superset, equals
SquareUnion	MMALIAS	2294	square union
squarf	ISOTECH	25A0	square, filled
squarfb	ISOPUB	E507	square, filled bottom half
squarfbl	ISOPUB	E506	square, filled bottom-left corner
squarfbr	ISOPUB	25EA	square, filled bottom-right corner
squarfl	ISOPUB	25E7	square, filled left half
squarfr	ISOPUB	25E8	square, filled right half
squarft	ISOPUB	E509	square, filled top half
squarftl	ISOPUB	25E9	square, filled top-left corner
squarftr	ISOPUB	E508	square, filled top-right corner
squf	ISOPUB	*25AA	blacksquare (square bullet, filled)
srarr	ISOAMSA	E232	short right arrow
Sscr	ISOMSCR	E4D7	script letter *S*
sscr	ISOMSCR	E4F0	script letter *s*
ssetmn	ISOAMSB	E844	small reverse solidus
ssmile	ISOAMSR	E303	small up curve
sstarf	ISOAMSB	22C6	small star, filled, low
Star	MMALIAS	22C6	small star, filled, low
star	MMALIAS	22C6	small star, filled, low
starf	ISOPUB	2605	star, filled
straight epsilon	MMALIAS	220A	lowercase epsilon, Greek
straightphi	MMALIAS	03C6	lowercase phi, Greek
strns	ISOTECH	E380	straightness
Sub	ISOAMSR	22D0	double subset
sub	ISOTECH	2282	subset or is implied by

Continued

Table AC-20 *Continued*

Name	Group	Code	Description
subdot	ISOAMSB	E262	subset, with dot
subE	ISOAMSR	2286	subset, double equals
sube	ISOTECH	2286	subset, equals
subedot	ISOAMSR	E34F	subset, equals, dot
submult	ISOAMSR	E343	subset, multiplication sign
subnE	ISOAMSN	228A	subset, not double equals
subne	ISOAMSN	228A	subset, not equals
subplus	ISOAMSR	E341	subset, plus
subrarr	ISOAMSR	E33F	subset, right arrow
Subset	MMALIAS	22D0	double subset
subset	MMALIAS	2282	subset or is implied by
subseteq	MMALIAS	2286	subset, equals
subseteqq	MMALIAS	2286	subset, double equals
SubsetEqual	MMALIAS	2286	subset, equals
subsetneq	MMALIAS	228A	subset, not equals
subsetneqq	MMALIAS	228A	subset, not double equals
subsim	ISOAMSR	E345	subset, similar
subsub	ISOAMSR	E349	subset above subset
subsup	ISOAMSR	E347	subset above superset
succ	MMALIAS	227B	succeeds
succapprox	MMALIAS	227F	succeeds, approximate
succcurlyeq	MMALIAS	227D	succeeds, curly equals
Succeeds	MMALIAS	227B	succeeds
Succeeds Equal	MMALIAS	227D	succeeds, equals
Succeeds SlantEqual	MMALIAS	227D	succeeds, curly equals
Succeeds Tilde	MMALIAS	227F	succeeds, similar
succeq	MMALIAS	227D	succeeds, equals
succnapprox	MMALIAS	22E9	succeeds, not approximate
succneqq	MMALIAS	E2B5	succeeds, not double equals
succnsim	MMALIAS	22E9	succeeds, not similar
succsim	MMALIAS	227F	succeeds, similar
SuchThat	MMALIAS	220D	contains
Sum	MMALIAS	2211	summation operator
sum	ISOAMSB	2211	summation operator
sung	ISONUM	2669	musical note (sung text sign)
Sup	ISOAMSR	22D1	double superset

Name	Group	Code	Description
sup	ISOTECH	2283	superset or implies
sup1	ISONUM	00B9	superscript 1
sup2	ISONUM	00B2	superscript 2
sup3	ISONUM	00B3	superscript 3
supdot	ISOAMSB	E263	superset, with dot
supdsub	ISOAMSR	E34C	superset, subset, dash joining them
supE	ISOAMSR	2287	superset, double equals
supe	ISOTECH	2287	superset, equals
supedot	ISOAMSR	E350	superset, equals, dot
Superset	MMALIAS	2283	superset or implies
SupersetEqual	MMALIAS	2287	superset, equals
suphsol	ISOAMSR	E34E	superset, solidus
suphsub	ISOAMSR	E34B	superset, subset
suplarr	ISOAMSR	E340	superset, left arrow
supmult	ISOAMSR	E344	superset, multiplication sign
supnE	ISOAMSN	228B	superset, not double equals
supne	ISOAMSN	228B	superset, not equals
supplus	ISOAMSR	E342	superset, plus
Supset	MMALIAS	22D1	double superset
supset	MMALIAS	2283	superset or implies
supseteq	MMALIAS	2287	superset, equals
supseteqq	MMALIAS	2287	superset, double equals
supsetneq	MMALIAS	228B	superset, not equals
supsetneqq	MMALIAS	228B	superset, not double equals
supsim	ISOAMSR	E346	superset, similar
supsub	ISOAMSR	E348	superset above subset
supsup	ISOAMSR	E34A	superset above superset
swarhk	ISOAMSA	E20A	SW arrow, hooked
swArr	ISOAMSA	21D9	SW-pointing double arrow
swarr	ISOAMSA	2199	SW-pointing arrow
swarrow	MMALIAS	2199	SW-pointing arrow
swnwar	ISOAMSA	E210	SW & NW arrows

Table AC-21 MathML Printing Characters, T Names

Name	Group	Code	Description
target	ISOPUB	2316	register mark or target
tau	ISOGRK3	03C4	lowercase tau, Greek

Continued

Table AC-21 *Continued*

Name	Group	Code	Description
tbrk	ISOAMSO	E2EF	top square bracket
tdot	ISOTECH	20DB	three dots above
telrec	ISOPUB	2315	telephone recorder symbol
Tfr	ISOMFRK	E48F	Fraktur letter *T*
tfr	ISOMFRK	E4A8	Fraktur letter *t*
there4	ISOTECH	2234	therefore
Therefore	MMALIAS	2234	therefore
therefore	MMALIAS	2234	therefore
Theta	ISOGRK3	0398	capital Theta, Greek
theta	ISOGRK3	03B8	straight theta, lowercase theta, Greek
thetav	ISOGRK3	03D1	curly or open theta
thickapprox	MMALIAS	E306	thick approximate
thicksim	MMALIAS	E429	thick similar
thinsp	ISOPUB	2009	thin space (sixth of an em)
thkap	ISOAMSR	E306	thick approximate
thksim	ISOAMSR	E429	thick similar
Tilde	MMALIAS	223C	similar
tilde	ISODIA	0303	tilde
TildeEqual	MMALIAS	2243	similar, equals
TildeFull Equal	MMALIAS	2245	congruent with
TildeTilde	MMALIAS	2248	approximate
times	ISONUM	00D7	multiplication sign
timesb	ISOAMSB	22A0	multiplication sign in box
timesbar	ISOAMSB	E28E	multiplication sign, bar below
timesd	ISOAMSB	E26D	times, dot
tint	ISOTECH	222D	triple integral operator
toea	MMALIAS	E20E	NE & SE arrows
top	ISOTECH	22A4	top
topbot	ISOTECH	2336	top and bottom
topcir	ISOTECH	E383	top, circle below
Topf	ISOMOPF	E4BE	open-face letter *T*
topfork	ISOAMSR	E31C	fork with top
tosa	MMALIAS	E20F	SE & SW arrows
tprime	ISOTECH	2034	triple prime
trade	ISONUM	2122	trademark sign
triangle	MMALIAS	25B5	up triangle, open
triangledown	MMALIAS	25BF	down triangle, open
triangleleft	MMALIAS	25C3	left triangle, open

Name	Group	Code	Description
triangleleft eq	MMALIAS	22B4	left triangle, equals
triangleq	MMALIAS	225C	triangle, equals
triangleright	MMALIAS	25B9	right triangle, open
triangleright eq	MMALIAS	22B5	right triangle, equals
tridot	ISOAMSB	25EC	dot in triangle
trie	ISOAMSR	225C	triangle, equals
triminus	ISOAMSB	E27C	minus in triangle
TripleDot	MMALIAS	20DB	three dots above
triplus	ISOAMSB	E27B	plus in triangle
trisb	ISOAMSB	E27E	triangle, serifs at bottom
tritime	ISOAMSB	E27D	multiplication sign in triangle
trpezium	ISOAMSO	E2EC	trapezium
Tscr	ISOMSCR	E4D8	script letter *T*
tscr	ISOMSCR	E4F1	script letter *t*
twixt	ISOAMSR	226C	between
twoheadleft arrow	MMALIAS	219E	two-headed left arrow
twoheadright arrow	MMALIAS	21A0	two-headed right arrow

Table AC-22 MathML Printing Characters, U Names

Name	Group	Code	Description
Uarr	ISOAMSA	219F	up two-headed arrow
uArr	ISOAMSA	21D1	up double arrow
uarr	ISONUM	2191	upward arrow
Uarrocir	ISOAMSA	E237	up two-headed arrow above circle
udarr	ISOAMSA	21C5	up arrow, down arrow
udhar	ISOAMSA	E218	up harp, down harp
ufisht	ISOAMSA	E24B	up fish tail
Ufr	ISOMFRK	E490	Fraktur letter *U*
ufr	ISOMFRK	E4A9	Fraktur letter *u*
uHar	ISOAMSA	E226	up harpoon-left, up harpoon-right
uharl	ISOAMSA	21BF	up harpoon-left
uharr	ISOAMSA	21BE	up harp-right
uhblk	ISOPUB	2580	upper half block
ulcorn	ISOAMSC	231C	upper-left corner

Continued

Table AC-22 *Continued*

Name	Group	Code	Description
ulcorner	MMALIAS	231C	upper-left corner
ulcrop	ISOPUB	230F	upward left crop mark
ultri	ISOAMSO	E2E4	upper left triangle
uml	ISODIA	E450	umlaut mark
Union	MMALIAS	22C3	union operator
UnionPlus	MMALIAS	228E	open-face letter *U*
UpArrow	MMALIAS	2191	upward arrow
Uparrow	MMALIAS	21D1	up double arrow
uparrow	MMALIAS	2191	upward arrow
UpArrow DownArrow	MMALIAS	21C5	up arrow, down arrow
UpDown Arrow	MMALIAS	2195	up-and-down arrow
Updown arrow	MMALIAS	21D5	up-and-down double arrow
updown arrow	MMALIAS	2195	up-and-down arrow
Up Equilibrium	MMALIAS	E218	up harp, down harp
upharpoon left	MMALIAS	21BF	up harpoon-left
upharpoon right	MMALIAS	21BE	up harp-right
uplus	ISOAMSB	228E	plus sign in union
UpperLeft Arrow	MMALIAS	2196	NW-pointing arrow
UpperRight Arrow	MMALIAS	2197	NE-pointing arrow
Upsi	ISOGRK3	03D2	capital Upsilon, Greek
upsi	ISOGRK3	03C5	lowercase upsilon, Greek
Upsilon	MMALIAS	03D2	capital Upsilon, Greek
upsilon	MMALIAS	03C5	lowercase upsilon, Greek
UpTee	MMALIAS	22A5	perpendicular
upuparrows	MMALIAS	21C8	two up arrows
urcorn	ISOAMSC	231D	upper-right corner
urcorner	MMALIAS	231D	upper-right corner
urcrop	ISOPUB	230E	upward right crop mark
urtri	ISOAMSO	E2E2	upper right triangle
Uscr	ISOMSCR	E4D9	script letter *U*
uscr	ISOMSCR	E4F2	script letter *u*

Name	Group	Code	Description
utdot	ISOTECH	22F0	three dots, ascending
utri	ISOPUB	25B5	up triangle, open
utrif	ISOPUB	25B4	up triangle, filled
uuarr	ISOAMSA	21C8	two up arrows
uwangle	ISOTECH	E3AB	large upward pointing angle

Table AC-23 MathML Printing Characters, V Names

Name	Group	Code	Description
vangrt	ISOTECH	22BE	right angle, variant (with arc)
varepsilon	MMALIAS	03B5	rounded lowercase epsilon, Greek
varkappa	MMALIAS	03F0	rounded lowercase kappa , Greek
varnothing	MMALIAS	2205	circle, slash
varphi	MMALIAS	03D5	curly or open lowercase phi, Greek
varpi	MMALIAS	03D6	rounded lowercase pi (pomega), Greek
varpropto	MMALIAS	221D	proportional, variant
vArr	ISOAMSA	21D5	up-and-down double arrow
varr	ISOAMSA	2195	up-and-down arrow
varrho	MMALIAS	03F1	rounded lowercase rho, Greek
varsigma	MMALIAS	03C2	terminal sigma, Greek
varsubset neq	MMALIAS	E2B9	subset, not equals, variant
varsubset neqq	MMALIAS	E2B8	subset, not double equals, variant
varsupset neq	MMALIAS	E2BA	superset, not equals, variant
varsupset neqq	MMALIAS	E2BB	superset, not double equals, variant
vartheta	MMALIAS	03D1	curly or open theta
vartriangle left	MMALIAS	22B2	left triangle, open, variant
vartriangle right	MMALIAS	22B3	right triangle, open, variant
Vbar	ISOAMSR	E30D	double vertical, bar (under)
vBar	ISOAMSR	E310	vertical, double bar (under)
vBarv	ISOAMSR	E312	double bar, vertical over and under
VDash	ISOAMSR	22AB	double vertical, double dash
Vdash	ISOAMSR	22A9	double vertical, dash
vDash	ISOAMSR	22A8	vertical, double dash

Continued

Table AC-23 *Continued*

Character	Name	Group	Code	Description
vdash	ISOAMSR	22A2		vertical, dash
Vdashl	ISOAMSR	E313		vertical, dash (long)
Vee	MMALIAS	22C1		logical AND operator
vee	MMALIAS	2228		logical OR
veebar	ISOAMSB	225A		logical OR, equals
vellip	ISOPUB	22EE		vertical ellipsis
Verbar	ISOTECH	2016		double vertical bar
verbar	ISONUM	007C		vertical bar
Vert	MMALIAS	2016		double vertical bar
vert	MMALIAS	007C		vertical bar
Vertical Bar	MMALIAS	2223		mid
Vertical Tilde	MMALIAS	2240		Fraktur letter V
vfr	ISOMFRK	E4AA		Fraktur letter v
vltri	ISOAMSR	22B2		left triangle, open, variant
vnsub	ISOAMSN	2285		not superset, variant
Vopf	ISOMOPF	E4C0		open-face letter V
vprop	ISOAMSR	221D		proportional, variant
vrtri	ISOAMSR	22B3		right triangle, open, variant
Vscr	ISOMSCR	E4DA		script letter V
vscr	ISOMSCR	E4F3		script letter v
vsubnE	ISOAMSN	E2B8		subset, not double equals, variant
vsubne	ISOAMSN	E2B9		subset, not equals, variant
vsupnE	ISOAMSN	E2BB		superset, not double equals, variant
vsupne	ISOAMSN	E2BA		superset, not equals, variant
Vvdash	ISOAMSR	22AA		triple vertical, dash
vzigzag	ISOAMSO	E2EB		vertical zigzag line

Table AC-24 MathML Printing Characters, W Names

Name	Group	Code	Description
wedbar	ISOAMSB	E265	wedge, bar below
Wedge	MMALIAS	22C0	logical OR operator
wedge	MMALIAS	2227	logical AND operator
wedgeq	ISOTECH	2259	corresponds to (wedge, equals)
weierp	ISOAMSO	2118	Weierstrass p
Wfr	ISOMFRK	E492	Fraktur letter W

Name	Group	Code	Description
wfr	ISOMFRK	E4AB	Fraktur letter *w*
Wopf	ISOMOPF	E4C1	Weierstrass *p*
wr	MMALIAS	2240	wreath product
wreath	ISOAMSB	2240	wreath product
Wscr	ISOMSCR	E4DB	script letter *W*
wscr	ISOMSCR	E4F4	script letter *w*

Table AC-25 MathML Printing Characters, X Names

CharacterName	Group	Code	Description
xcap	ISOAMSB	22C2	intersection operator
xcirc	ISOAMSB	25CB	large circle
xcup	ISOAMSB	22C3	union operator
xdtri	ISOAMSB	25BD	big down triangle, open
Xfr	ISOMFRK	E493	Fraktur letter *X*
xfr	ISOMFRK	E4AC	Fraktur letter *x*
xhArr	ISOAMSA	E202	long left-and-right double arrow
xharr	ISOAMSA	E203	long left-and-right arrow
Xi	ISOGRK3	039E	capital Xi, Greek
xi	ISOGRK3	03BE	lowercase xi, Greek
xlArr	ISOAMSA	E200	long left double arrow
xlarr	ISOAMSA	E201	long left arrow
xmap	ISOAMSA	E208	long maps-to
xnis	ISOTECH	E3A3	large contains, vertical bar on horizontal stroke
xodot	ISOAMSB	2299	circle dot operator
Xopf	ISOMOPF	E4C2	open-face letter *X*
xoplus	ISOAMSB	2295	circle plus operator
xotime	ISOAMSB	2297	circle times operator
xrArr	ISOAMSA	E204	long right double arrow
xrarr	ISOAMSA	E205	long right arrow
Xscr	ISOMSCR	E4DC	script letter *X*
xscr	ISOMSCR	E4F5	script letter *x*
xsqcup	ISOAMSB	2294	square union operator
xuplus	ISOAMSB	228E	big up plus
xutri	ISOAMSB	25B3	big up triangle, open
xvee	ISOAMSB	22C1	logical AND operator
xwedge	ISOAMSB	22C0	logical OR operator

Table AC-26 MathML Printing Characters, Y Names

Name	Group	Code	Description
yen	ISONUM	00A5	yen sign
Yfr	ISOMFRK	E494	Fraktur letter Y
yfr	ISOMFRK	E4AD	Fraktur letter y
Yopf	ISOMOPF	E4C3	open-face letter Y
Yscr	ISOMSCR	E4DD	script letter Y
yscr	ISOMSCR	E4F6	script letter y

Table AC-27 MathML Printing Characters, Z Names

Name	Group	Code	Description
zeta	ISOGRK3	03B6	lowercase zeta, Greek
Zfr	ISOMFRK	2124	Fraktur letter Z
zfr	ISOMFRK	E4AE	Fraktur letter z
zigrarr	ISOAMSA	E244	right zigzag arrow
Zopf	ISOMOPF	E4C4	open-face letter Z
Zscr	ISOMSCR	E4DE	script letter Z
zscr	ISOMSCR	E4F7	script letter z

List of Example DHTML Web Sites

Royal Airways Newsletter Demo

http://developer.netscape.com/docs/example/dynhtml/html

HexWeb Type Gallery

http://www.hexmac.com/hexmac/engl/webtools/typograph/gallery/
gallery.html

NET Investor

http://www.net-investor.com/

Hackers.com

http://www.hackers.com

Disney

http://www/disney.com

ZDNet Demo

http://www.zdnet.com/products/internetuser.html

Microsoft Samples

http://www.microsoft.com/sitebuilder/

O2 Music Party Ltd.

http://www.o2music.com/homeno.html

CK Arts

http://users.qual.net/~ckawalek

Jeff Rule's Dynamic HTML Demos

```
http://www.erols.com/jrule/dhtml/
```

Web Masters DHTML Demos

```
http://www.wmcentral.com/dhtml/demos.html
```

WWW. BRATTA.COM

```
http://www.bratta.com/
```

HTML Guru

```
http://www.htmlguru.com
```

Inter-Web Data Corporation

```
http://www.iwdc.net/dhtml.asp
```

Quantum Marketing Systems

```
http://valuecom.com/dhtmldemo.htm
```

Club IE

```
http://www.supernet.net/~edtiley/win95/
```

appendix

E

Web-Based Resources

Web-Based Resources

These three tables summarize three different types of useful resources to be found on the World Wide Web.

Each site in Table AE-1 is maintained by a consortium that has an important impact on the development of HTML and related techologies.

Table AE-1 Official Web Consortium Sites

Specification	Consortium Web Site
HTML 4.0	`http://www.w3.org/MarkUp/`
XML 1.0	`http://www.w3.org/XML/`
CSS 1.0	`http://www.w3.org/Style/css/`
CSS 2.0	`http://www.w3.org/Style/css/`
DOM	`http://www.w3.org/DOM/`
CDF	`http://www.w3.org/TR/NOTE-CDFsubmit.html`
OSD	`http://www.w3.org/TR/NOTE-OSD.html`
MathML	`http://www.w3.org/TR/REC-MathML/`

Table AE-2 lists relevant sites maintained by major corporations.

Table AE-2 Corporate Sites

Company	URL
Microsoft	`http://www.microsoft.com/workshop/default.asp`
Netscape	`http://developer.netscape.com/`

Continued

Table AE-2 *Continued*

Company	URL
Macromedia	`http://www.macromedia.com`
BitStream	`http://www.bitstream.com/`
IBM	`http://www.ibm.com`
NCSA Guide to HTML	`http://www.ncsa.uiuc.edu/General/Internet/WWW/HTMLPrimer.html`

Table AE-3 lists general-reference sites that provide further useful information for users of HTML.

Table AE-3 General-Reference Sites

Provider	Web Site
Developer.com	`http://www.developer.com/`
WebReference	`http://www.webreference.com/`
DHTML Zone	`http://www.dhtmlzone.com/`
Project Cool	`http://www.projectcool.com/`
HTML Guru	`http://www.htmlguru.com/`
WebMonkey	`http://www.hotwired.com/webmonkey/`
HTML Writer's Guild	`http://www.hwg.org/`
ZDNet	`http://www.zdnet.com/products/internetuser.html`
ClNet Builder.com	`http://www.builder.com`
Association for Computing Machinery	`http://www.acm.org`
FOLDOC	`http://wombat.doc.ic.ac.uk/foldoc/`
NetLingo	`http://www.netlingo.com`
HTML Form Tests	`http://www.research.digital.com/nsl/formtest`
Advanced HTML	`http://www.markradcliffe.co.uk/html/index.html0`
Wacky HTML	`http://www.nctweb.com/wacky/wacky.html`
WDVL	`http://www.charm.net/~web/Style/`
HotSource HTML Help	`http://www.sbrady.com/hotsource/`
DJ Quad's HTML Site	`http://www.quadzilla.com`
Provider	**Web Site**
WebTech's HTML Validation Site	`http://valsvc.webtechs.com`
Doctor HTML	`http://www2.imagiware.com/RxHTML`
Yale Web Style Guide	`http://info.med.yale.edu/caim/manual/`

The Web Diner	`http://www.webdiner.com`
Web Coder	`http://www.webcoder.com`
WebDeveloper.com	`http://www.webdeveloper.com`
Web Week	`http://www.webweek.com`
Web Techniques	`http://www.webtechniques.com`
NerdHeaven	`http://www.riv.be`
Seer Media	`http://www.seer-media.com`

appendix

F

HTML Elements and Their Properties

Table AF-1 lists HTML elements, along with their start tags and end tags, their attributes, and brief descriptions.

Table AF-1 HTML Elements and Their Properties

Element	Start Tag	End Tag	Attributes	Description
A	R	R	accesskey, class, coords, dir, href, hreflang, id, lang, name, onblur, onclick, ondblclick, onfocus, onkey down, onkeypress, onkeyup, on mousedown, onmousemove, on mouseout, onmouseover, onmouse up, rel, rev, shape, style, tabindex, target, title, type	anchor
ABBR	R	R	class, dir, id, lang, onclick, ondbl click, onkeydown, onkeypress, on keyup, onmousedown, onmouse move, onmouseout, onmouseover, onmouseup, style, title	abbreviation
ACRONYM	R	R	class, dir, id, lang, onclick, ondbl click, onkeydown, onkeypress, on keyup, onmousedown, onmouse move, onmouseout, onmouseover, onmouseup, style, title	acronyms
ADDRESS	R	R	class, dir, id, lang, onclick, ondblclick, onkeydown, onkeypress, onkeyup, onmousedown, onmouse move, onmouseout, onmouseover, onmouseup, style, title	author information
APPLET	R	R	align, alt, archive, class, code, codebase, height, hspace, id, name, object, style, title, vspace, width	Java applet

Continued

Table AF-1 *Continued*

Element	Start Tag	End Tag	Attributes	Description
AREA	R	F	accesskey, alt, class, coords, dir, href, id, lang, name, nohref, onblur, onclick, ondblclick, onfocus, onkey down, onkeypress, onkeyup, on mousedown, onmousemove, on mouseout, onmouseover, onmouse up, shape, style, tabindex, target, title	client-side image map partition
B	R	R	class, dir, id, lang, onclick, ondbl click, onkeydown, onkeypress, on keyup, onmousedown, onmouse move, onmouseout, onmouseover, onmouseup, style, title	bold text style
BASE	R	F	href, target	base document URL
BASEFONT	R	F	color, face, id, lang, title, size, style	base font size
BDO	R	R	class, dir, id, lang, style, title	BiDi over-ride
BIG	R	R	class, dir, id, lang, onclick, ondbl click, onkeydown, onkeypress, on keyup, onmousedown, onmouse move, onmouseout, onmouseover, onmouseup, style, title	use a large text style
BLINK	R	R	class, dir, id, lang, onclick, ondbl click, onkeydown, onkeypress, on keyup, onmousedown, onmouse move, onmouseout, onmouseover, onmouseup, style, title	Netscape only – blink text
BLOCKQUOTE	R	R	cite, class, dir, id, lang, onclick, on dblclick, onkeydown, onkeypress, onkeyup, onmousedown, onmouse move, onmouseout, onmouseover, onmouseup, style, title	long quotation block
BODY	O	O	align, alink background, bgcolor, class, dir, id, lang, link, onclick, ondblclick, onkeydown, onkeypress, onkeyup, onload, onmousedown, onmousemove, onmouseout, on mouseover, onmouseup, onunload, style, text, title, vlink	notes body of document
BR	R	F	class, clear, id, style, title	forces a line break
BUTTON	R	R	accesskey, class, dir, disabled, id, lang, name, onblur, onclick, ondbl click, onfocus, onkeydown, onkey press, onkeyup, onmousedown, on mousemove, onmouseout, on mouseover, onmouseup, style, tab index, title, type, value	push button

Element	Start Tag	End Tag	Attributes	Description
CAPTION	R	R	align, class, dir, id, lang, onclick, on dblclick, onkeydown, onkeypress, onkeyup, onmousedown, onmouse move, onmouseout, onmouseover, onmouseup, style, title	caption for a table
CENTER	R	R	class, dir, id, lang, onclick, ondbl click, onkeydown, onkeypress, onkeyup, onmousedown, on mousemove, onmouseout, on mouseover, onmouseup, style, title	centers text and images
CITE	R	R	class, dir, id, lang, onclick, ondbl click, onkeydown, onkeypress, onkeyup, onmousedown, on mousemove, onmouseout, on mouseover, onmouseup, style, title	citation
CODE	R	R	class, dir, id, lang, onclick, ondbl click, onkeydown, onkeypress, on keyup, onmousedown, onmouse move, onmouseout, onmouse over, onmouseup, style, title	code sample text
COL	R	F	align, char, charoff, class, dir, id, lang, onclick, ondblclick, onkey down, onkeypress, onkeyup, on mousedown, onmousemove, on mouseout, onmouseover, on mouseup, span, style, title, valign width	column in a table
COLGROUP	R	O	align, char, charoff, class, dir, id, lang, onclick, ondblclick, onkey down, onkeypress, onkeyup, on mousedown, onmousemove, on mouseout, onmouseover, on mouseup, span, style, title, valign, width	group of table columns
DD	R	O	class, dir, id, lang, onclick, ondbl click, onkeydown, onkeypress, onkeyup, onmousedown, on mousemove, onmouseout, on mouseover, onmouseup, style, title	definition description
DEL	R	R	cite, class, datetime, dir, id, lang, onclick, ondblclick, onkeydown, onkeypress, onkeyup, onmouse down, onmousemove, onmouse out, onmouseover, onmouseup, style, title	deleted text

Continued

Table AF-1 *Continued*

Element	Start Tag	End Tag	Attributes	Description
DFN	R	R	class, dir, id, lang, onclick, ondbl click, onkeydown, onkeypress, on keyup, onmousedown, onmouse move, onmouseout, onmouseover, onmouseup, style, title	definition
DIR	R	R	class, compact, dir, id, lang, onclick, ondblclick, onkeydown, onkey press, onkeyup, onmousedown, onmousemove, onmouseout, on mouseover, onmouseup, style, title	directory link
DIV	R	R	align, class, dir, id, lang, onclick, ondblclick, onkeydown, onkey press, onkeyup, onmousedown, onmousemove, onmouseout, onmouseover, onmouseup, style, title	generic style container
DL	R	R	class, compact, dir, id, lang, onclick, ondblclick, onkeydown, onkeypress, onkeyup, onmousedown, onmousemove, onmouseout, onmouseover, onmouseup, style, title	definition list
DT	R	O	class, dir, id, lang, onclick, ondbl click, onkeydown, onkeypress, onkeyup, onmousedown, onmousemove, onmouseout, onmouseover, onmouseup, style, title	definition term
EM	R	R	class, dir, id, lang, onclick, ondbl click, onkeydown, onkeypress, onkeyup, onmousedown, onmousemove, onmouseout, onmouseover, onmouseup, style, title	emphasis
FIELDSET	R	R	class, dir, id, lang, onclick, ondbl click, onkeydown, onkeypress, onkeyup, onmousedown, onmousemove, onmouseout, onmouseover, onmouseup, style, title	form control grouping
FONT	R	R	class, color, dir, face, id, lang, size, style, title	local font change

Element	Start Tag	End Tag	Attributes	Description
FORM	R	R	accept-charset, action, class, dir, enctype, id, lang, method, onclick, ondblclick, onkeydown, onkeypress, onkeyup, onmousedown, onmousemove, onmouseout, onmouseover, onmouseup, onreset, onsubmit, style, target, title	interactive form
FRAME	R	F	class, frameborder, id, longdesc, marginheight, marginwidth, name, noresize, scrolling, src, style, title	subwindow of user agent
FRAMESET	R	R	class, cols, id, onload, onunload, rows, style, title	window subdivision
H1 – H6	R	R	align, class, dir, id, lang, onclick, ondblclick, onkeydown, onkeypress, onkeyup, onmousedown, onmousemove, onmouseout, onmouseover, onmouseup, style, title	heading
HEAD	O	O	dir, lang, profile	document header block
HR	R	F	align, class, dir, id, noshade, onclick, ondblclick, onkeydown, onkeypress, onkeyup, onmouse down, onmousemove, onmouseout, onmouseover, onmouseup, size, style, title, width	horizontal rule
HTML	O	O	dir, lang, version	document root element
I	R	R	class, dir, id, lang, onclick, ondblclick, onkeydown, onkeypress, onkeyup, onmousedown, onmousemove, onmouseout, onmouseover, onmouseup, style, title	italic text
IFRAME	R	R	align, class, frameborder, height, id, longdesc, marginheight, marginwidth, name, scrolling, src, style, title, width	inline subwindow
IMG	R	F	align, alt, border, class, dir, height, hspace, id, ismap, lang, longdesc, onclick, ondblclick, onkeydown, onkeypress, onkeyup, onmouse down, onmousemove, onmouse out, onmouseover, onmouseup, src, style, title, usemap, vspace, width	image

Continued

Table AF-1 *Continued*

Element	Start Tag	End Tag	Attributes	Description
INPUT	R	F	accept, accesskey, align, alt, checked, class, dir, disabled, id, lang, maxlength, name, onblur, onchange, onclick, ondblclick, onfocus, onkeydown, onkeypress, onkeyup, onmousedown, onmouse move, onmouseout, onmouseover, onmouseup, onselect, prompt, readonly, size, src, style, tabindex, title, type usemap, value	form control
INS	R	R	cite, class, datetime, dir, id, lang, onclick, ondblclick, onkeydown, onkeypress, onkeyup, onmouse down, onmousemove, onmouse out, onmouseover, onmouseup, style, title	inserted text
ISINDEX	R	F	class, dir, id, lang, prompt, readonly, style, title	Single-line prompt
KBD	R	R	class, dir, id, lang, onclick, ondbl click, onkeydown, onkeypress, onkeyup, onmousedown, onmousemove, onmouseout, onmouseover, onmouseup, style, title	Keyboard text
LABEL	R	R	accesskey, class, dir, for, id, lang, onblur, onclick, ondblclick, onfocus, onkeydown, onkeypress, onkeyup, onmousedown, onmousemove, onmouseout, onmouseover, onmouseup, style, title	Label text for form field
LAYER	R	R	above, background, below, bgcolor, clip, height, left, name, src, top, visibility, width, z-index	Netscape only – layered objects
LEGEND	R	R	accesskey, align, class, dir, id, lang, onclick, ondblclick, onkeydown, onkeypress, onkeyup, onmouse down, onmousemove, onmouse out, onmouseover, onmouseup, style, title	Label for a form fieldset
LI	R	O	class, dir, id, lang, onclick, ondbl click, onkeydown, onkeypress, onkeyup, onmousedown, onmousemove, onmouseout, onmouseover, onmouseup, style, title, type, value	List items

Element	Start Tag	End Tag	Attributes	Description
LINK	R	F	class, charset, dir, href, hreflang, id, lang, media, onclick, ondblclick, onkeydown, onkeypress, onkeyup, onmousedown, onmousemove, onmouseout, onmouseover, onmouseup, rev, rel, style, target, title, type	Media-independent link
MAP	R	R	alt, accesskey, class, dir, href, id, lang, name, onclick, ondblclick, onkeydown, onkeypress, onkeyup, onmousedown, onmousemove, onmouseout, onmouseover, onmouseup, shape, style, tabindex, title	client-side image map
MARQUEE	R	R	behavior, bgcolor, class, datafld, dataformatas, datasrc, direction, height, hspace, id, lang, language, loop, onafterupdate, onblur, onbounce, onclick, ondblclick, ondragstart, onfinish, onfocus, onhelp, onkeydown, onkeypress, onkeyup, onmousedown, onmousemove, onmouseout, onmouseover, onmouseup, onresize, onrowenter, onrowexit, onselectstart, onstart, scrollamount, scrolldelay, style, title, truespeed, vspace, width	(Internet Explorer only) scrolling text
MENU	R	R	class, dir, id, lang, onclick, ondbl click, onkeydown, onkeypress, onkeyup, onmousedown, onmousemove, onmouseout, onmouseover, onmouseup, style, title	display menu type list
META	R	F	content, dir, http-equiv, lang, name, scheme	meta information
NOFRAMES	R	R	class, dir, id, lang, onclick, ondbl click, onkeydown, onkeypress, onkeyup, onmousedown, onmousemove, onmouseout, onmouseover, onmouseup, style, title	content container for non-frame-based information
NOSCRIPT	R	R	class, dir, id, lang, onclick, ondbl click, onkeydown, onkeypress, onkeyup, onmousedown, onmousemove, onmouseout, onmouseover, onmouseup, style, title	content container for non-script-based information

Continued

Table AF-1 *Continued*

Element	Start Tag	End Tag	Attributes	Description
OBJECT	R	R	accesskey, align, archive, border, class, classid, code, codebase, codetype, data, declare, dir, height, hspace, id, lang, name, onclick, ondblclick, onkeydown, onkeypress, onkeyup, onmouse down, onmousemove, onmouse out, onmouseover, onmouseup, standby, style, tabindex, title, type, usemap, vspace, width	embedded objects
OL	R	R	class, compact, dir, id, lang, onclick, ondblclick, onkeydown, onkeypress, onkeyup, onmousedown, onmousemove, onmouseout, onmouseover, onmouseup, start, style, title, type	ordered list
OPTGROUP	R	R	class, dir, disabled, id, label, lang, onclick, ondblclick, onkeydown, onkeypress, onkeyup, onmouse down, onmousemove, onmouse out, onmouseover, onmouseup, style, title	option group
OPTION	R	O	class, dir, disabled, id, label, lang, onclick, ondblclick, onkeydown, onkeypress, onkeyup, onmouse down, onmousemove, onmouse out, onmouseover, onmouseup, selected, style, title, value	selectable choices
P	R	O	align, class, dir, id, lang, onclick, ondblclick, onkeydown, onkey press, onkeyup, onmousedown, onmousemove, onmouseout, onmouseover, onmouseup, style, title	paragraph
PARAM	R	F	id, name, type, value, valuetype	named property value
PRE	R	R	class, dir, id, lang, onclick, ondbl click, onkeydown, onkeypress, onkeyup, onmousedown, onmousemove, onmouseout, onmouseover, onmouseup, style, title, width	preformatted text
Q	R	R	cite, class, dir, id, lang, onclick, ondblclick, onkeydown, onkeypress, onkeyup, onmousedown, onmouse move, onmouseout, onmouseover, onmouseup, style, title	short quotation

Element	Start Tag	End Tag	Attributes	Description
S	R	R	class, dir, id, lang, onclick, ondbl click, onkeydown, onkeypress, onkeyup, onmousedown, onmousemove, onmouseout, onmouseover, onmouseup, style, title	strike-through text
SAMP	R	R	class, dir, id, lang, onclick, ondbl click, onkeydown, onkeypress, onkeyup, onmousedown, onmousemove, onmouseout, onmouseover, onmouseup, style, title	sample program output
SCRIPT	R	R	charset, defer, language, src, type	included script
SELECT	R	R	class, dir, disabled, id, lang, multiple, name, onblur, onchange, onclick, ondblclick, onfocus, onkey down, onkeypress, onkeyup, onmousedown, onmousemove, onmouseout, onmouseover, onmouseup, size, style, tabindex, title	option selector
SMALL	R	R	class, dir, id, lang, onclick, ondbl click, onkeydown, onkeypress, onkeyup, onmousedown, onmouse move, onmouseout, onmouseover, onmouseup, style, title	small text
SPAN	R	R	align, class, dir, id, lang, onclick, ondblclick, onkeydown, onkey press, onkeyup, onmousedown, onmousemove, onmouseout, onmouseover, onmouseup, style, title	generic style container
STRIKE	R	R	class, dir, id, lang, onclick, ondbl click, onkeydown, onkeypress, onkeyup, onmousedown, onmouse move, onmouseout, onmouseover, onmouseup, style, title	strike-through text
STRONG	R	R	class, dir, id, lang, onclick, ondbl click, onkeydown, onkeypress, onkeyup, onmousedown, onmouse move, onmouseout, onmouseover, onmouseup, style, title	emphasized text
STYLE	R	R	dir, lang, media, title, type	style sheet informa-tion

Continued

Table AF-1 *Continued*

Element	Start Tag	End Tag	Attributes	Description
SUB	R	R	class, dir, id, lang, onclick, ondbl click, onkeydown, onkeypress, onkeyup, onmousedown, onmouse move, onmouseout, onmouseover, onmouseup, style, title	subscript
SUP	R	R	class, dir, id, lang, onclick, ondbl click, onkeydown, onkeypress, onkeyup, onmousedown, onmousemove, onmouseout, onmouseover, onmouseup, style, title	superscript
TABLE	R	R	align, bgcolor, border, cellpadding, cellspacing, class, dir, frame, id, lang, onclick, ondblclick, onkey down, onkeypress, onkeyup, onmousedown, onmousemove, onmouseout, onmouseover, onmouseup, rules, style, summary, title, width	table
TBODY	O	O	align, char, charoff, class, dir, id, lang, onclick, ondblclick, onkey down, onkeypress, onkeyup, onmousedown, onmousemove, onmouseout, onmouseover, onmouseup, style, title, valign	table body
TD	R	O	abbr, align, axis, bgcolor, char, charoff, class, colspan, dir, headers, height, id, lang, nowrap, onclick, ondblclick, onkeydown, onkey press, onkeyup, onmousedown, onmousemove, onmouseout, onmouseover, onmouseup, rowspan, scope, style, title, valign, width	table data cell
TEXTAREA	R	R	accesskey, class, cols, dir, disabled, id, lang, name, onblur, onchange, onclick, ondblclick, onfocus, onkeydown, onkeypress, onkeyup, onmousedown, onmousemove, onmouseout, onmouseover, onmouseup, onselect, readonly, rows, style, tabindex, title	multi-line text area
TFOOT	R	O	align, char, charoff, class, dir, id, lang, onclick, ondblclick, onkey down, onkeypress, onkeyup, onmousedown, onmousemove, onmouseout, onmouseover, onmouseup, style, title, valign	table footer

Element	Start Tag	End Tag	Attributes	Description
TH	R	O	abbr, align, axis, bgcolor, char, charoff, class, colspan, dir, headers, height, id, lang, nowrap, onclick, ondblclick, onkeydown, onkeypress, onkeyup, onmousedown, onmousemove, onmouseout, onmouseover, onmouseup, rowspan, scope, style, title, valign, width	table header cell
THEAD	R	O	align, char, charoff, class, dir, id, lang, onclick, ondblclick, onkey down, onkeypress, onkeyup, onmousedown, onmousemove, onmouseout, onmouseover, onmouseup, style, title, valign	table header
TITLE	R	R	dir, lang	document title
TR	R	O	align, bgcolor, char, charoff, class, dir, id, lang, onclick, ondblclick, onkeydown, onkeypress, onkeyup, onmousedown, onmousemove, onmouseout, onmouseover, onmouseup, style, title, valign	table row
TT	R	R	class, dir, id, lang, onclick, ondbl click, onkeydown, onkeypress, onkeyup, onmousedown, onmousemove, onmouseout, onmouseover, onmouseup, style, title	teletype or monospaced text
U	R	R	class, dir, id, lang, onclick, ondbl click, onkeydown, onkeypress, onkeyup, onmousedown, onmousemove, onmouseout, onmouseover, onmouseup, style, title	underlined text
UL	R	R	class, compact, dir, id, lang, listonclick, ondblclick, onkeydown, onkeypress, onkeyup, onmouse down, onmousemove, onmouse out, onmouseover, onmouseup, style, title, type	unordered
VAR	R	R	class, dir, id, lang, onclick, ondbl click, onkeydown, onkeypress, onkeyup, onmousedown, onmousemove, onmouseout, onmouseover, onmouseup, style, title	program variable or argument

IDG Books Worldwide, Inc. End-User License Agreement

READ THIS. You should carefully read these terms and conditions before opening the software packet(s) included with this book ("Book"). This is a license agreement ("Agreement") between you and IDG Books Worldwide, Inc. ("IDGB"). By opening the accompanying software packet(s), you acknowledge that you have read and accept the following terms and conditions. If you do not agree and do not want to be bound by such terms and conditions, promptly return the Book and the unopened software packet(s) to the place you obtained them for a full refund.

1. **License Grant.** IDGB grants to you (either an individual or entity) a nonexclusive license to use one copy of the enclosed software program(s) (collectively, the "Software") solely for your own personal or business purposes on a single computer (whether a standard computer or a workstation component of a multiuser network). The Software is in use on a computer when it is loaded into temporary memory (RAM) or installed into permanent memory (hard disk, CD-ROM, or other storage device). IDGB reserves all rights not expressly granted herein.

2. **Ownership.** IDGB is the owner of all right, title, and interest, including copyright, in and to the compilation of the Software recorded on the disk(s) or CD-ROM ("Software Media"). Copyright to the individual programs recorded on the Software Media is owned by the author or other authorized copyright owner of each program. Ownership of the Software and all proprietary rights relating thereto remain with IDGB and its licensers.

3. **Restrictions on Use and Transfer.**

   (a) You may only (i) make one copy of the Software for backup or archival purposes, or (ii) transfer the Software to a single hard disk, provided that you keep the original for backup or archival purposes. You may not (i) rent or lease the Software, (ii) copy or reproduce the Software through a LAN or other network system or through any computer subscriber system or bulletin-board system, or (iii) modify, adapt, or create derivative works based on the Software.

(b) You may not reverse engineer, decompile, or disassemble the Software. You may transfer the Software and user documentation on a permanent basis, provided that the transferee agrees to accept the terms and conditions of this Agreement and you retain no copies. If the Software is an update or has been updated, any transfer must include the most recent update and all prior versions.

4. **Restrictions on Use of Individual Programs.** You must follow the individual requirements and restrictions detailed for each individual program in the "What's on the CD-ROM?" section of this Book. These limitations are also contained in the individual license agreements recorded on the Software Media. These limitations may include a requirement that after using the program for a specified period of time, the user must pay a registration fee or discontinue use. By opening the Software packet(s), you will be agreeing to abide by the licenses and restrictions for these individual programs that are detailed in the "What's on the CD?" section and on the Software Media. None of the material on this Software Media or listed in this Book may ever be redistributed, in original or modified form, for commercial purposes.

5. **Limited Warranty.**

(a) IDGB warrants that the Software and Software Media are free from defects in materials and workmanship under normal use for a period of sixty (60) days from the date of purchase of this Book. If IDGB receives notification within the warranty period of defects in materials or workmanship, IDGB will replace the defective Software Media.

(b) **IDGB AND THE AUTHOR OF THE BOOK DISCLAIM ALL OTHER WARRANTIES, EXPRESS OR IMPLIED, INCLUDING WITHOUT LIMITATION IMPLIED WARRANTIES OF MERCHANTABILITY AND FITNESS FOR A PARTICULAR PURPOSE, WITH RESPECT TO THE SOFTWARE, THE PROGRAMS, THE SOURCE CODE CONTAINED THEREIN, AND/OR THE TECHNIQUES DESCRIBED IN THIS BOOK. IDGB DOES NOT WARRANT THAT THE FUNCTIONS CONTAINED IN THE SOFTWARE WILL MEET YOUR REQUIREMENTS OR THAT THE OPERATION OF THE SOFTWARE WILL BE ERROR-FREE.**

(c) This limited warranty gives you specific legal rights, and you may have other rights that vary from jurisdiction to jurisdiction.

6. **<u>Remedies</u>.**

   (a) IDGB's entire liability and your exclusive remedy for defects in materials and workmanship shall be limited to replacement of the Software Media, which may be returned to IDGB with a copy of your receipt at the following address: Software Media Fulfillment Department, Attn.: *HTML Master Reference*, IDG Books Worldwide, Inc., 7260 Shadeland Station, Ste. 100, Indianapolis, IN 46256, or call 1-800-762-2974. Please allow three to four weeks for delivery. This Limited Warranty is void if failure of the Software Media has resulted from accident, abuse, or misapplication. Any replacement Software Media will be warranted for the remainder of the original warranty period or thirty (30) days, whichever is longer.

   (b) In no event shall IDGB or the author be liable for any damages whatsoever (including without limitation damages for loss of business profits, business interruption, loss of business information, or any other pecuniary loss) arising from the use of or inability to use the Book or the Software, even if IDGB has been advised of the possibility of such damages.

   (c) Because some jurisdictions do not allow the exclusion or limitation of liability for consequential or incidental damages, the above limitation or exclusion may not apply to you.

7. **<u>U.S. Government Restricted Rights</u>.** Use, duplication, or disclosure of the Software by the U.S. Government is subject to restrictions stated in paragraph (c)(1)(ii) of the Rights in Technical Data and Computer Software clause of DFARS 252.227-7013, and in subparagraphs (a) through (d) of the Commercial Computer — Restricted Rights clause at FAR 52.227-19, and in similar clauses in the NASA FAR supplement, when applicable.

8. **<u>General</u>.** This Agreement constitutes the entire understanding of the parties and revokes and supersedes all prior agreements, oral or written, between them and may not be modified or amended except in a writing signed by both parties hereto that specifically refers to this Agreement. This Agreement shall take precedence over any other documents that may be in conflict herewith. If any one or more provisions contained in this Agreement are held by any court or tribunal to be invalid, illegal, or otherwise unenforceable, each and every other provision shall remain in full force and effect.

my2cents.idgbooks.com

Installing the CD-ROM

The CD-ROM that accompanies this book contains many of the examples provided in the text, as well as a variety of other software. Appendix A provides detailed instructions for installing the editing software, browsers, and other utilities.

To begin installation, follow these steps:

1. Remove the disc from the CD-ROM pocket and insert it into your CD-ROM drive.

2. Double-click the appropriate folder to open and view files.

3. Double-click the .exe file to begin installation and copy example files to your hard drive.